NURSE'S LEGAL HANDBOOK

Fifth Edition

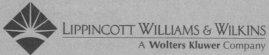

LIPPINCOTT WILLIAMS & WILKINS
A **Wolters Kluwer** Company

Philadelphia • Baltimore • New York • London
Buenos Aires • Hong Kong • Sydney • Tokyo

STAFF

Executive Publisher
Judith A. Schilling McCann, RN, MSN

Editorial Director
H. Nancy Holmes

Clinical Director
Joan M. Robinson, RN, MSN

Senior Art Director
Arlene Putterman

Art Director
Mary Ludwicki

Editorial Project Manager
William Welsh

Clinical Project Manager
Minh N. Luu, RN, BSN, JD

Editor
Stacey A. Follin

Clinical Editors
Joanne Bartelmo, RN, MSN, CCRN;
Louise Melchor, MSE, JD(c)

Copy Editors
Kim Bilotta (supervisor), Tom DeZego,
Heather Ditch, Carolyn Peterson,
Lisa Stockslager, Bill Wine, Pamela Wingrod

Designer
Marsha Biderman (project manager)

Digital Composition Services
Diane Paluba (manager),
Joyce Rossi Biletz, Donna S. Morris

Manufacturing
Patricia K. Dorshaw (director), Beth Janae Orr

Editorial Assistants
Megan L. Aldinger, Tara L. Carter-Bell,
Arlene Claffee, Linda K. Ruhf

Librarian
Wani Z. Larsen

Indexer
Karen C. Comerford

FOCUS CHARTING is a registered trademark of Creative Healthcare Management, Inc.

**Library of Congress
Cataloging-in-Publication Data**

Nurse's legal handbook. — 5th ed.
    p. ; cm.
Includes bibliographical references and indexes.
    1. Nursing — Practice — United States. 2. Nursing ethics. 3. Nursing — Law and legislation — United States. I. Springhouse Corporation.
    [DNLM: 1. Legislation, Nursing — United States. 2. Ethics, Nursing — United States. 3. Malpractice — United States — Nurses' Instruction. 4. Patient Rights — United States--Nurses' Instruction. WY 33 AA1 N79 2004]
RT86.73.N855 2004
344.7304'14 — dc22
ISBN 1-58255-280-0 (alk. paper)   2003022628

CONTENTS

Contributors

Sally Austin, ADN, BGS, JD
Compliance Officer
Cognesa
Atlanta

Penny Simpson Brooke, APRN, MS, JD
Professor/Director of Outreach
University of Utah
Salt Lake City

Linda MacDonald Glenn, JD, LLM
Senior Fellow
Institute for Ethics
American Medical Association
Chicago

Ginny Wacker Guido, RN, MSN, JD, FAAN
Associate Dean and Director,
    Graduate Studies
University of North Dakota,
    College of Nursing
Grand Forks

David M. Keepnews, RN, PhD, JD, FAAN
Assistant Professor, School of Nursing
Adjunct Assistant Professor,
    School of Law
University of Washington
Seattle

Janet E. Michael, RN, MS, JD
Nurse Attorney
Law Office of Janet E. Michael
Portland, Maine

Susan Salladay, RN, PhD
Director – The Center for Bioethics
BryanLGH College of Health Sciences
Lincoln, Nebr.

Beverly A. Snyder, RN, MHA
Administrator/Nurse Executive
Good Shepherd Specialty Hospital
Allentown, Pa.

Jacqueline Walus-Wigle, RN, JD, CPAQ
Compliance, Regulatory,
    External Affairs Director
UCSD Healthcare
San Diego

LaTonia Denise Wright, RN, BSN, JD
Attorney
Law Office of LaTonia Denise Wright,
    RN, LLC
Cincinnati

FOREWORD

As a nurse, you're in a constant state of flux. You constantly strive to keep up with technological advances in equipment and procedures — even as new innovations are introduced seemingly on a daily basis. You accept the challenge of acquiring knowledge on emerging diseases, and you've either introduced yourself to or refreshed your memory of the dangers posed by bioterrorism.

Yes, you may have graduated from nursing school years ago, but your nursing education never really ends.

If the demands of continuing professional education aren't enough, the new specter of cost containment has forced you to work faster and more efficiently than ever before. You must often make immediate, crucial choices during high-pressure patient care situations. Because of this, you have little time to reflect on the legal and ethical consequences of your actions before you must perform them.

Nurse's Legal Handbook, now in its fifth edition, offers concise and easy-to-understand advice on numerous contemporary legal issues that will help you to choose the most appropriate actions to protect your patients and avoid the myraid risks of legal liability. You'll be able to easily access important laws and regulations (with examples from actual court cases) affecting your practice. Throughout the text, Canadian law is compared and contrasted with U.S. law, so that nurses in both countries will find this reference useful.

Chapter 1 provides fundamental information on the laws that govern nursing. It outlines the various levels of nursing practice and provides a detailed look at nurse practice acts. The chapter also looks at standards of nursing care, their evolution, and their legal significance, plus an in-depth look at nursing licensure and what to expect if you're being investigated for violating your license's provisions.

Chapter 2 discusses the differences between nursing practice and medical practice and the changes that are starting to blur the line between the two. It also covers the pros and cons that come with working in diverse clinical settings, such as agency nursing and home care. This information is important to have, because each setting has nuances the others don't.

Chapter 3 discusses your legal obligation to uphold your patient's rights. It outlines your responsibilities in obtaining informed consent, protecting your patient's right to refuse treatment, and upholding privacy rights. This chapter also summarizes major U.S. Supreme Court rulings on reproductive rights issues.

Chapter 4 presents straightforward facts about the greatest legal worry of the nursing profession — malpractice liability. The chapter provides common causes of nursing liability and special tips on how you can avoid a lawsuit. It outlines the role of the health care facility's legal counsel and includes a helpful section on how to shop for professional liability insurance.

Chapter 5 continues the discussion of malpractice liability by providing a description of the medical malpractice lawsuit, including the four elements that must be shown before a nurse can be held liable for malpractice. There's also a step-by-step outline of the litigation process, including pretrial maneuvers and common legal arguments used to defend a malpractice claim. In addition, the chapter provides advice on what to do if you're served with a malpractice lawsuit.

Chapter 6 covers on-the-job risks. You'll learn how to change your facility's policies and "legally safe" steps to help you cope with understaffing. You'll read about your legal obligation to assure patient safety by preventing falls, medication errors, and disease transmission. You'll learn what to do if you must restrain a patient or care for a minor or a mentally disabled patient. New sections on telephone triage and quality management highlight what you need to know when performing in either of these vital capacities.

Chapter 7 covers the all-important topic of documentation. It discusses the implications of signing, countersigning, and witnessing legal documents and provides advice on how to handle verbal orders and avoid documentation errors.

Legal risks and responsibilities in nursing practice extend beyond the workplace. Chapter 8 discusses your liability when providing off-duty nursing services. It describes the legal protections provided by Good Samaritan laws as well as steps you can take to protect yourself from risk when providing free health care advice to friends and neighbors.

Chapter 9 covers your rights as an employee by focusing on employer-employee relations, unions, and collective bargaining—issues that can be difficult to discuss in the workplace. You'll learn about the role of the National Labor Relations Board in regulating collective bargaining, what may or may not be considered unfair labor practices, and under what circumstances nurses can go out on strike. The chapter also discusses strategies for reading an employment contract and the arguments for and against joining a union.

Chapter 10 compares and contrasts the fields of law and ethics and provides a framework to help apply the nursing process to ethical decision making. It includes discussions on the ethical theories that have helped to shape today's ethical codes and the importance of clarifying your own values.

Chapter 11 takes the discussion of ethics further by providing the opportunity for practical application of the principles of ethical decision making to a number of controversial issues in health care: the right to die and euthanasia, organ transplantation, perinatal ethics, human immunodeficiency virus and acquired immunodeficiency syndrome, abortion and reproductive technology, and genetic screening and engineering. The chapter also details your rights for safety in the workplace. It provides you with a course of action if you're confronted with sexual harassment, violence in the workplace, or a colleague's professional misconduct or substance abuse, and provides new information on your employer's responsibility to provide safer needle delivery devices.

After chapter 11, you'll find a glossary of legal terms, a chart to help you understand the judicial process, a special section that breaks down the types of managed-care organizations, a cheat-sheet to help you interpret legal citations, and a listing of court cases mentioned in the text. You'll refer to these valuable additions many times.

Nurse's Legal Handbook, Fifth Edition, doesn't stop there. Graphic symbols highlight important sidebar information. *Legal tip* provides legally sound advice for legally perilous sitations, *Law Q&A* answers many of nursing law's most frequently asked questions, and *Court case* illustrates important legal points by providing examples of how nurses just like you fared in their court proceedings.

Nurse's Legal Handbook, Fifth Edition, is a comprehensive resource that no practicing nurse should be without. The topics presented encompass a wide variety of legal issues that arise daily in practice — issues for which you, as a nurse, must have sound legal advice. Whether you're an experienced nurse or a new graduate, *Nurse's Legal Handbook,* Fifth Edition, is the perfect legal resource, no matter your specialty.

> **Ann B. Mech,** RN, MS, JD
> Assistant Professor and
> Coordinator, Legal Affairs
> University of Maryland School
> of Nursing
> Baltimore

Chapter 1

Nursing practice and the law

As with other professionals, nurses want opportunities for personal advancement, increased economic benefits, and a sense that their profession will keep pace with the latest technological advances. To help realize these goals, each nurse must keep pace with current nursing trends, provide proper patient care, and understand, accept, and follow the legal and ethical responsibilities of her practice. By performing these actions, the nurse not only puts herself in a good position for advancement, she also sidesteps many legal and professional pitfalls that may otherwise present themselves.

This chapter provides fundamental information on the laws that directly govern nursing. It includes detailed discussions of the *nurse practice act* — the state law that regulates nursing. You'll also find out about the role of your state's board of nursing, and you'll examine how nursing law is applied in court. You'll learn about standards of care, including how these standards are applied and how they may be used as evidence during malpractice litigation.

This chapter also explains the legal significance of your nursing license and what to expect if you're disciplined for violating any of its provisions. Throughout the chapter, you'll find practical advice that reflects legal precedents or expected standards of care.

Levels of nursing practice

Three levels of nursing practice exist — the advanced practice nurse (APN), the registered nurse (RN), and the licensed practical or licensed vocational nurse (LPN or LVN.) All three levels are designed with special, unique functions in mind. APNs, such as nurse practitioners (NPs), clinical nurse specialists, nurse midwives, and nurse anesthetists, are RNs who have national certification or a master's degree in a clinical specialty. RNs may graduate from diploma (decreasing in numbers), two-year associate of science in nursing (ASN), or four-year bachelor of science in nursing (BSN) programs. LPNs, who complete a shorter and less intensive educational program for entry into practice than RNs, graduate from a one-year program. When licensed, the RN is responsible for developing and managing patient care. She must also make professional nursing judgments based on the nursing process: patient assessment, planning, nursing diagnosis, implementation, and evaluation.

According to the American Nurses Association (ANA), the *professional RN* is a graduate of a BSN or higher degree program, and the *technical RN* is a graduate of an ASN program. The function of the professional RN is to develop procedures and protocols and to set standards for practice; the technical RN implements policies, procedures, and protocols developed by the professional RN. The ANA published its latest *Standards of Nursing Practice* in the fall of 2003.

In state law, definitions of the RN's role vary, but basic responsibilities include observing patients' signs and symptoms, recording these observations, notifying the physician of any changes in a patient's health status, carrying out physicians' orders for treatments, and appropriately delegating responsibilities for patient care.

The LPN is commonly referred to as the "bedside nurse" because her role has traditionally centered on the patient's basic physical needs for hygiene and comfort. Many state nurse practice acts define LPN practice as the performance of duties that assist the professional nurse in a team relationship. In some states, the duties of LPNs are more clearly defined in terms of *scope of practice*; for example, states may prohibit LPNs from inserting I.V. lines.

Because of changes in the workplace, including an emphasis on cutting labor costs, the role of the LPN has expanded over the years. For example, in Pennsylvania, LPNs can now "perform venipuncture and administer and withdraw I.V. fluids" and "administer immunizing agents and do skin testing" if the right requirements are met. Through pressure from long-term care facilities, the Pennsylvania State

Board of Nursing is considering expanding the LPN's role in regard to verbal orders from prescribers. Currently, the Board allows LPNs to take verbal orders only in an emergency or for a written prescription that she doesn't understand. 49 Pa. Code § 21.145(b) (*amended*, 1983).

Many states are undertaking measures to deal with unlicensed assistive personnel (UAP). In 1999, several states passed legislation that defines either the scope of practice or level of accountability of UAPs. The Arizona State Board of Nursing now has the authority to certify nurse assistants and to impose disciplinary measures upon them. In Montana, UAPs are subject to criminal prosecution. North Dakota permits licensed nurses to delegate drug administration to UAPs in specific settings. Virginia allows UAPs to handle insulin administration in the school setting.

NURSING PRACTICE IN CANADA

All Canadian jurisdictions support licensure (commonly known as *registration*) of RNs and nursing auxiliaries (commonly known as LPNs). However, in some jurisdictions, registration isn't mandatory. Some Canadian nursing associations recognize clinical nurse specialists (who usually have master's degrees or doctoral degrees in a specific specialty) and NPs — nurses in expanded roles oriented to primary health care.

In most of Canada's 10 jurisdictions, professional nurses' associations set requirements for graduation from an approved school of nursing, licensing, nurses' professional behavior, and registration fees.

The Canadian RN may receive her education in a diploma school (such as a hospital school of nursing), in a community college, or in a BSN program. One jurisdiction requires a BSN for entry into private practice, and several others may soon have the same requirement. All nurses wishing to practice in Canada must pass the Canadian Nurses Association Test. A nurse also needs to be licensed in the province where she would like to work. Individual provinces issue their own license to practice. A nurse should contact her province board of nursing to confirm the requirement.

Laws, rules, and regulations

Each state has a nurse practice act and board of nursing rules and regulations that are designed to protect the public by broadly defining the legal scope of nursing practice. The state legislature enacts the nurse practice act and any amendments. The board of nursing, in accordance with the nurse practice act, publishes its rules and regulations. These rules and regulations, which are generally more specific than what's found in the nurse practice act, establish procedure and carry the same weight as the nurse practice act.

Every nurse is expected to care for patients within these defined practice limits — the most important ones affecting nursing care; if she gives care beyond these limits, she becomes vulnerable to charges of violating the law and losing her licensure. These laws, rules, and regulations also serve to exclude untrained or unlicensed people from practicing nursing. For a copy of your state's nurse practice act or board of nursing rules and regulations, contact your state nurses' association or the state board of nursing. (See *U.S. and Canadian nurses' associations,* pages 4 to 8.)

NURSING PRACTICE ACTS

Most nurse practice acts begin by defining important terms, including "the practice of registered nursing" and "the practice of licensed practical nursing." These definitions differentiate between RNs and LPNs, according to their specific scopes of practice and their educational requirements. Some states have separate nurse practice acts for RNs and LPNs.

Scope of practice

Early nurse practice acts contained statements prohibiting nurses from performing tasks considered to be within the scope of medical practice. Nurses couldn't diagnose any patient problem or treat a patient without instructions from a physician. Later, interdisciplinary committees (consisting of nurses, physicians, pharmacists, dentists, and hospital representatives) have helped to ease this restriction on nursing practice. After reviewing some medical procedures that nurses commonly perform, these committees issued joint statements recommending that nurses be legally permitted to perform these procedures in specified circumstances. Some joint statements specifically recommend allowing nurses to perform venipunctures, cardiopulmonary resuscitation, and cardiac defibrillation. Still other joint statements (as well as interpretive statements issued by state boards of nursing and nursing organizations) specifically recommend permitting nurses to perform such functions as nursing assessment and nursing diagnosis. Such joint statements don't have the force of the law — unless state legislatures amend their nurse practice acts to include them. Many state legislatures have incorporated such statements into nurse

(Text continues on page 9.)

U.S. and Canadian nurses' associations

This chart lists the name, address, and telephone number, plus the Web site addresses (when available), of nurses' associations in the United States, its territories, and Canada. The American Nurses Association has a Web site (*www.nursingworld.org*) with links to each state's nurses' association Web site.

National associations

American Nurses Association
600 Maryland Ave., SW
Suite 100 West
Washington, DC 20024
(202) 651-7000
1-800-274-4ANA
Web site: *www.nursingworld.org*

Federal Nurses Association
600 Maryland Ave., SW
Suite 100 West
Washington, DC 20024
(202) 651-7333
Web site: *www.nursingworld.org/fedna*

State associations

Alabama Nurses' Association
360 N. Hull St.
Montgomery, AL 36104-3658
(334) 262-8321
Web site: *www.alabamanurses.org*

Alaska Nurses Association
2207 East Tudor Rd., Suite 34
Anchorage, AK 99507-1069
(907) 274-0827
Web site: *www.aknurse.org*

Arizona Nurses Association
1850 E. Southern Ave., Suite 1
Tempe, AZ 85282-5832
(480) 831-0404
Web site: *www.aznurse.org*

Arkansas Nurses Association
1401 W. Capitol Ave., Suite 155
Little Rock, AR 72201
(501) 664-5853
Web site: *www.arna.org*

American Nurses Association/California
1121 L St., Suite 409
Sacramento, CA 95814
(916) 447-0225
Web site: *www.anacalifornia.org*

Colorado Nurses Association
5453 E. Evans Pl.
Denver, CO 80222
(303) 757-7483
Web site: *www.nurses-co.org*

Connecticut Nurses' Association
377 Research Pkwy., Suite 2D
Meriden, CT 06450-7160
(203) 238-1207
Web site: *www.ctnurses.org*

Delaware Nurses Association
2644 Capitol Tr., Suite 330
Newark, DE 19711
(302) 368-2333
Web site: *www.nursingworld.org/snas/de*

Dist. Of Columbia Nurses Association
5100 Wisconsin Ave., N.W. Suite 306
Washington, DC 20016
(202) 244-2705
Web site: *www.dcna.org*

Florida Nurses Association
P.O. Box 536985
Orlando, FL 32853-6985
(407) 896-3261
Web site: *www.floridanurse.org*

Georgia Nurses Association
3032 Briarcliff Rd.
Atlanta, GA 30329-2655
(404) 325-5536
Web site: *www.georgianurses.org*

U.S. and Canadian nurses' associations *(continued)*

Guam Nurses Association
P.O. Box CG
Hagatna, Guam 96933
011 (671) 477-6877

Hawaii Nurses Association
677 Ala Moana Blvd., Suite 301
Honolulu, HI 96813
(808) 531-1628
Web site: *www.hawaiinurses.org*

Idaho Nurses Association
200 N. Fourth St., Suite 20
Boise, ID 83702-6001
(208) 345-0500
Web site: *nursingworld.org/snas/id*

Ilinois Nurses Association
105 West Adams St., Suite 2101
Chicago, IL 60603
(312) 419-2900
Web site: *www.illinoisnurses.com*

Indiana State Nurses Association
2915 N. High School Rd.
Indianapolis, IN 46224
(317) 299-4575
Web site: *www.indiananurses.org*

Iowa Nurses' Association
1501 42nd St., Suite 471
West Des Moines, IA 50266
(515) 255-0495
Web site: *www.iowanurses.org*

Kansas State Nurses Association
1208 S.W. Tyler
Topeka, KS 66612-1735
(785) 233-8638
Web site: *www.nursingworld.org/snas/ks*

Kentucky Nurses Association
1400 S. First St.
P.O. Box 2616
Louisville, KY 40201-2616
(502) 637-2546
1-800-348-5411
Web site: *www.kentucky-nurses.org*

Louisiana State Nurses Association
5700 Florida Blvd., Suite 720
Baton Rouge, LA 70806
(225) 201-0993
Web site: *www.lsna.org*

American Nurses Association of Maine
P.O. Box 254
Auburn, ME 04212-0254
(207) 667-0260
Web site: *www.anamaine.org*

Maryland Nurses Association
21 Governor's Ct., Suite 195
Baltimore, MD 21244
(410) 944-5800
Web site: *www.nursingworld.org/snas.md*

Massachusetts Association of Registered Nurses
P.O. Box 70668
Worcester, MA 01607-0668
(886) 627-6262
Web site: *www.marnonline.org*

Michigan Nurses Association
2310 Jolly Oak Rd.
Okemos, MI 48864
(517) 349-5640
1-800-832-2051
Web site: *www.minurses.org*

Minnesota Nurses Association
1625 Energy Path Dr.
St Paul, MN 55108
(651) 646-4807
1-800-536-4662
Web site: *www.mnnurses.org*

Mississippi Nurses Association
31 Woodgreen Pl.
Madison, MS 39110
(601) 898-0670
Web site: *www.msnurses.org*

(continued)

U.S. and Canadian nurses' associations *(continued)*

Missouri Nurses Association
1904 Bubba La., P.O. Box 105228
Jefferson City, MO 65110
(573) 636-4623
Web site: *www.missourinurses.org*

Montana Nurses' Association
104 Broadway, Suite G2
Helena, MT 59601
(406) 442-6710
Web site: *www.mtnurses.org*

Nebraska Nurses Association
715 S. 14th St.
Lincoln, NE 68508
(402) 475-3859
1-800-201-3625
Web site: *www.nursingworld.org./snas/ne*

Nevada Nurses Association
P.O. Box 34660
Reno, NV 89533
(775) 747-2333
Web site: *www.nvnurses.org*

New Hampshire Nurses' Association
48 West St.
Concord, NH 03301-3595
(603) 225-3783
Web site: *www.nhnurses.org*

New Jersey State Nurses Association
1479 Pennington Rd.
Trenton, NJ 08618-2661
(609) 883-5335
1-888-876-5762
Web site: *www.njsna.org*

New Mexico Nurses Association
P.O. Box 29658
Santa Fe, NM 87592-9658
(505) 471-3324
Web site: *www.nmna.org*

New York State Nurses Association
11 Cornell Rd.
Latham, NY 12110
(518) 782-9400
Web site: *www.nysna.org*

North Carolina Nurses Association
103 Enterprise St.
P.O. Box 12025
Raleigh, NC 27605-2025
(919) 821-4250
1-800-626-2153
Web site: *www.ncnurses.org*

North Dakota Nurses Association
531 Airport Rd.
Bismarck, ND 58504-6107
(701) 223-1385
Web site: *www.ndna.org*

Ohio Nurses Association
4000 E. Main St.
Columbus, OH 43213-2983
(614) 237-5414
Web site: *www.ohnurses.org*

Oklahoma Nurses' Association
6414 N. Santa Fe, Suite A
Oklahoma City, OK 73116
(405) 840-3476
Web site: *www.oknurses.com*

Oregon Nurses Association
18765 S.W. Boones Ferry Rd., Suite 200
Tualatin, OR 97062
(503) 293-0011
Web site: *www.oregonrn.org*

Pennsylvania Nurses Association
2578 Interstate Dr., Suite 101
Harrisburg, PA 17110
(717) 657-1222
1-888-707-7762
Web site: *www.psna.org*

U.S. and Canadian nurses' associations (continued)

**Rhode Island State
Nurses Association**
550 S. Water St.
Providence, RI 02903-4344
(401) 421-9703
Web site: www.risnarn.org

**South Carolina Nurses
Association**
1821 Gadsden St.
Columbia, SC 29201
(803) 252-4781
Web site: www.scnurses.org

**South Dakota Nurses
Association**
P.O. Box 1015
Pierre, SD 57501-1015
(605) 945-4265
Web site: www.nursingworld.org/snas/sd

Tennessee Nurses' Association
545 Mainstream Dr., Suite 405
Nashville, TN 37228-1296
(615) 254-0350
Web site: www.traonline.org

Texas Nurses Association
7600 Burnet Rd., Suite 440
Austin, TX 78757-1292
(512) 452-0645
Web site: www.texasnurses.org

Utah Nurses Association
4505 South Wasatach Blvd. #290
Salt Lake City, UT 84124
(801) 272-4510
Web site: www.utahnurses.org

**Vermont State Nurses'
Association**
100 Dorset St., Suite 13
South Burlington, VT 05403
(802) 651-8886
Web site: www.uvm.edu/~vsna

Virgin Islands Nurses' Association
P.O. Box 583
Christiansted, St. Croix
U.S. Virgin Islands 00821-0583
(809) 773-1261

Virginia's Nurses Association
7113 Three Chopt Rd., Suite 204
Richmond, VA 23226
(804) 282-1808
Web site: www.virginianurses.com

**Washington State Nurses
Association**
575 Andover Park West, Suite 101
Seattle, WA 98188
(206) 575-7979
Web site: www.wsna.org

West Virginia Nurses Association
P.O. Box 1946
Charleston, WV 25327
(304) 342-1169
Web site: www.wvnurses.org

Wisconsin Nurses Association
6117 Monona Dr.
Madison, WI 53716
(608) 221-0383
Web site: www.wisconsinnurses.org

Wyoming Nurses Association
1603 Capitol Ave.
Majestic Bldg., Room 305
Cheyenne, WI 82001
(307) 635-3955

Canadian associations
Canadian Nurses Association
50 Driveway, Ottawa ON
Canada K2P 1E2
(613) 237-2133
1-800-361-8404
Web site: www.can-nurses.ca

(continued)

U.S. and Canadian nurses' associations (continued)

Alberta Association of Registered Nurses
11620-168 St.
Edmonton AB T5M 4A6
(780) 451-0043
Web site: www@nurses.ab.ca

Registered Nurses Association of British Columbia
2855 Arbutus St.
Vancouver, BC V6J 3Y8
(604) 736-7331
1-800-565-6505
Web site: www.rnabc.bc.ca

College of Registered Nurses of Manitoba
647 Broadway Ave.
Winnipeg, MB R3C 0X2
(204) 774-3477
Web site: www.crnm.mb.ca

Nurses Association of New Brunswick
165 Regent St.
Fredericton, NB E3B 7B4
(506) 458-8731
1-800-442-4417
Web site: www.nanb.nb.ca

Association of Registered Nurses of Newfoundland and Labrador
55 Military Rd.
Box 6116
St. Johns, NF A1C 5X8
(709) 753-6040
1-800-563-3200
Web site: www.arnn.nf.ca

Northwest Territory Registered Nurses' Association
Box 2757
Yellowknife, NT X1A 2R1
(867) 873-2745
Web site: www.nwtrna.com

College of Registered Nurses Association of Nova Scotia
1894 Barrington St., Barrington Tower, Suite 600
Halifax, NS B3J 2A8
(902) 491-9744
Web site: www.crnns.ca

College of Nurses of Ontario
101 Davenport Rd.
Toronto, ON M5R 3P1
(416) 928-0900
1-800-387-5526
Web site: www.cno.org

Registered Nurses Association of Ontario
438 University Ave., Suite 1600
Toronto, ON M5G 2K8
(416) 599-1925
1-800-268-7199
Web site: www.rnao.org

Association of Nurses of Prince Edward Island
137 Queen St., Suite 303
Charlottetown, PEI C1A 4B3
(902) 368-3764
Web site: www.iwpei.com/nurses

L'Ordre des Infirmières et Infirmiers du Québec
4200 Dorchester Blvd. W.
Montreal, Quebec H3Z 1V4
(514) 935-1501
1-800-363-6048
Web site: www.oiiq.org

Saskatchewan Registered Nurses' Association
2066 Retallack St.
Regina, SK S4T 7X5
(306) 359-4200
Web site: www.srna.org

Yukon Registered Nurses Association
204-4133 4th Ave.
Whitehorse, YT Y1A 1H8
(867) 667-4062

Defining the boundaries of nursing practice

You may characterize your state's nurse practice act as traditional, transitional, or modern, depending on how it defines the boundaries of nursing practice.

Traditional
These nurse practice acts allow only conventional nursing activities. They limit the nurse's responsibilities to traditional patient care, disease prevention, and health maintenance. Traditional nurse practice acts don't allow registered nurses (RNs) to participate in such expanded nursing activities as diagnosis, prescription, and treatment. Only a few states continue to have such limited practice acts.

Transitional
These nurse practice acts have broader boundaries, and may include a "laundry list" of permitted nursing functions. For example, Maine's act lists six specific RN activities:
• traditional patient care
• collaboration with other health professionals in planning care

• diagnosis and prescription delegated by physicians
• delegation of tasks to licensed practical nurses, licensed vocational nurses, and nurses' aides
• supervision and teaching
• carrying out physicians' orders.

Because it allows expanded duties such as diagnosis and prescription, Maine is edging toward a modern type of nurse practice act.

Other states with transitional acts, such as Massachusetts, broaden the nurses' role by including a separate definition of nurse practitioners. This wording allows nurse practitioners to diagnose and treat patients.

Modern
States with modern nurse practice acts – New York, for example – allow RNs to diagnose and treat health problems as well as to provide traditional nursing care. New York's definition of registered nursing is so broad that it encompasses not only current nursing activities, but also much of what nurses are likely to do in the future.

---

practice acts. (See *Defining the boundaries of nursing practice*.)

Conditions for licensure
Your state's nurse practice act sets down the requirements for obtaining a license to practice nursing. To become licensed as an RN or LPN, you must pass the NCLEX and meet certain other qualifications. All states require completion of the basic professional nursing education program. Your state may have additional requirements; examples include good moral character, good physical and mental health, a minimum age, fluency in English, and no drug or alcohol addiction.

In addition to specifying the conditions for RN and LPN licensure, your state's nurse practice act may specify the rules and regulations for licensure in special areas of nursing practice (usually termed *certification*).

State boards of nursing
In every state and Canadian jurisdiction, a nurse practice act creates a state or provincial board of nursing, sometimes called the state board of nurse examiners. The nurse practice act authorizes this board to administer and enforce rules and regulations concerning the nursing profession and specifies the makeup of the board — the num-

ber of members as well as their educational and professional requirements. In some states, the nurse practice act requires two nursing boards — one for RNs and one for LPNs. (See *State boards of nursing,* pages 11 to 15.)

The board of nursing is bound by the provisions of the nurse practice act that created it. The nurse practice act is the law; the board of nursing can't grant exemptions to it or waive any of its provisions. Only the state or provincial legislature can change the law. For example, if the nurse practice act specifies that, to be licensed, a nurse must have graduated from an approved school of nursing, then the board of nursing must deny a license to anyone who hasn't done so. This provision applies even to applicants who can provide evidence of equivalency and competency. *Richardson v. Brunelle* (1979).

In many states and jurisdictions, the board of nursing may grant exemptions and waivers to its own rules and regulations. For example, if a regulation states that all nursing faculty must have master's degrees, the board might be able to waive this requirement temporarily for a faculty member who's in the process of obtaining one.

In most states, the board of nursing consists of practicing RNs. Many boards also include LPNs, health care facility administrators, and *consumers* — members of the community at large. The state legislature decides on the board's mix; in almost every state, the governor appoints members from a list of nominees submitted by the state nursing association. One state, North Carolina, replaced this appointment process with an elective one, allowing licensed nurses to elect their own board members.

In recent years, there has been some erosion in the concept of the free-standing nursing board. For example, a bill was introduced into the Pennsylvania legislature to eliminate the nursing board and to consolidate all licensing boards and commissions under one bureau, but it wasn't passed into law.

Violations

The nurse practice act also lists violations that can result in disciplinary action against a nurse. Depending on the nature of the violation, a nurse may face not only state board disciplinary action, but also civil liability for her actions.

Interpreting your nurse practice act

Nurse practice acts are broadly worded, and the wording varies from state to state. Understanding your nurse practice act's general provisions will help you stay within the legal limits of nursing practice.

Interpreting the nurse practice act isn't always easy. One problem stems from the fact that nurse practice acts are statutory laws. Any amendment to a nurse practice act, then, must be accomplished by means of the inevitably slow legislative process. Because of the time involved in pondering, drafting, and enacting laws, amendments to nurse practice acts lag well behind the progress of changes in nursing.

NURSING DIAGNOSIS DILEMMA

You may be expected to perform tasks that seem to be within the accepted scope of nursing but in fact violate your state's nurse practice act. Consider this common example: Most nurses regularly make nursing diagnoses, although in many cases, their state nurse

(Text continues on page 15.)

State boards of nursing

Alabama Board of Nursing
RSA Plaza, Suite 250
770 Washington Ave.
Montgomery, AL 36130-3900
Phone: (334) 242-4060
Web site: *www.abn.state.al.us*

Alaska Board of Nursing
Division of Occupational Licensing
Department of Community & Economic
Development
3601 C St., Suite 722
Anchorage, AK 99503
Phone: (907) 269-8161
Web site: *www.dced.state.ak.us/occ/
pnur.htm*

American Samoa Health Services
Regulatory Board
LBJ Tropical Medical Center
Pago Pago, AS 96799
Phone: (684) 633-1222

Arizona State Board of Nursing
1651 E. Morten Ave., Suite 150
Phoenix, AZ 85020
Phone: (602) 331-8111
Web site: *www.azboardofnursing.org*

Arkansas State Board of Nursing
University Tower Bldg.
1123 S. University, Suite 800
Little Rock, AR 72204
Phone: (501) 686-2700
Web site: *www.state.ar.us/nurse*

**California Board of
Registered Nursing**
400 R St., Suite 4030
P.O. Box 944210
Sacramento, CA 95814
Phone: (916) 322-3350
Web site: *www.rn.ca.gov*

**California Board of
Vocational Nursing and
Psychiatric Technicians**
2535 Capitol Oaks Dr., Suite 205
Sacramento, CA 95833
Phone: (916) 263-7800
Web site: *www.bvnpt.ca.gov*

Colorado Board of Nursing
1560 Broadway, Suite 880
Denver, CO 80202
Phone: (303) 894-2430
Web site: *www.dora.state.co.us/nursing/*

**Connecticut Board of
Examiners for Nursing**
Division of Health Systems Regulation
410 Capitol Ave., MS #13PHO
P.O. Box 340308
Hartford, CT 06134-0328
Phone: (860) 509-7624
Web site: *www.state.ct.us/dph*

Delaware Board of Nursing
861 Silver Lake Blvd.
Cannon Bldg., Suite 203
Dover, DE 19904
Phone: (302) 739-4522
Web site: *www.professionallicensing.state.
de.us/boards/nursing/index.shtml*

**District of Columbia
Board of Nursing**
Department of Health
825 N. Capitol St., N.E.
2nd Floor, Room 2224
Washington, DC 20002
Phone: (202) 442-4778
Web site: *www.dchealth.dc.gov*

Florida Board of Nursing
4080 Woodcock Dr., Suite 202
Jacksonville, FL 32207
Phone: (904) 858-6940
Web site: *www.doh.state.fl.us/mqa*

(continued)

State boards of nursing *(continued)*

Georgia Board of Nursing
237 Coliseum Dr.
Macon, GA 31217-3858
Phone: (478) 207-1640
Web site: *www.sos.state.ga.us/plb/rn*

Guam Board of Nurse Examiners
P.O. Box 2816
Agana, GU 96910
Phone: (671) 475-0251

Hawaii Board of Nursing
Professional and Vocational
Licensing Division
P.O. Box 3469
Honolulu, HI 96801
Phone: (808) 586-3000
Web site: *www.state.hi.us/dcca/pvl/
areas_nurse.html*

Idaho Board of Nursing
280 N. 8th St., Suite 210
P.O. Box 83720
Boise, ID 83720
Phone: (208) 334-3110
Web site: *www.state.id.us/ibn/
ibnhome.htm*

**Illinois Department of
Professional Regulation**
James R. Thompson Center
100 W. Randolph, Suite 9-300
Chicago, IL 60601
Phone: (312) 814-2715
Web site: *www.dpr.state.il.us*

Indiana State Board of Nursing
Health Professions Bureau
402 W. Washington St., Room W041
Indianapolis, IN 46204
Phone: (317) 232-2960
Web site: *www.state.in.us/hpb/boards/
isbn*

Iowa Board of Nursing
River Point Business Park
400 S.W. 8th St., Suite B
Des Moines, IA 50309-4685
Phone: (515) 281-3255
Web site: *www.state.ia.us/government/
nursing*

Kansas State Board of Nursing
Landon State Office Bldg.
900 S.W. Jackson, Suite 551 S.
Topeka, KS 66612-1230
Phone: (785) 296-4929
Web site: *www.ksbn.org*

Kentucky Board of Nursing
312 Whittington Pkwy., Suite 300
Louisville, KY 40222
Phone: (502) 329-7000
Web site: *www.kbn.ky.gov*

Louisiana State Board of Nursing
3510 N. Causeway Blvd., Suite 501
Metairie, LA 70003
Phone: (504) 838-5332
Web site: *www.lsbn.state.la.us*

Maine State Board of Nursing
158 State House Station
Augusta, ME 04333
Phone: (207) 287-1133
Web site: *www.state.me.us/
boardofnursing*

Maryland Board of Nursing
4140 Patterson Ave.
Baltimore, MD 21215
Phone: (410) 585-1900
Web site: *www.mbon.org*

**Massachusetts Board of
Registration in Nursing**
Commonwealth of Massachusetts
239 Causeway St.
Boston, MA 02114
Phone: (617) 727-9961
Web site: *www.state.ma.us/reg/boards/rn*

State boards of nursing (continued)

Michigan CIS/Office of Health Services
Ottawa Towers N.
611 W. Ottawa, 4th Floor
Lansing, MI 48933
Phone: (517) 373-9102
Web site: *www.michigan.gov/cis*

Minnesota Board of Nursing
2829 University Ave. S.E., Suite 500
Minneapolis, MN 55414
Phone: (612) 617-2270
Web site: *www.nursingboard.state.mn.us*

Mississippi Board of Nursing
1935 Lakeland Dr., Suite B
Jackson, MS 39216
Phone: (601) 987-4188
Web site: *www.msbn.state.ms.us*

Missouri State Board of Nursing
3605 Missouri Blvd.
P.O. Box 656
Jefferson City, MO 65102-0656
Phone: (573) 751-0681
Web site: *www.ecodev.state.mo.us/pr/nursing*

Montana State Board of Nursing
301 South Park
Helena, MT 59620-0513
Phone: (406) 444-2071
Web site: *www.discoveringmontana.com/dli/bsd/license/bsd_boards/nur_board/board_page.htm*

Nebraska Health and Human Services Department of Regulation and Licensure
Dept. of Regulation and Licensure
Nursing Section
301 Centennial Mall S.
P.O. Box 94986
Lincoln, NE 68509-4986
Phone: (402) 471-4376
Web site: *www.hhs.state.ne.us/crl/nursing/nursingindex.htm*

Nevada State Board of Nursing
License Certification and Education
4330 S. Valley View Blvd., Suite 106
Las Vegas, NV 89103
Phone: (702) 486-5800
Web site: *www.nursingboard.state.nv.us*

New Hampshire Board of Nursing
78 Regional Dr., Bldg. B
P.O. Box 3898
Concord, NH 03302
Phone: (603) 271-2323
Web site: *www.state.nh.us/nursing*

New Jersey Board of Nursing
124 Halsey St., 6th Floor
P.O. Box 45010
Newark, NJ 07101
Phone: (973) 504-6586
Web site: *www.state.nj.us/lps/ca/medical.htm*

New Mexico Board of Nursing
4206 Louisiana Blvd., N.E., Suite A
Albuquerque, NM 87109
Phone: (505) 841-8340
Web site: *www.state.nm.us/clients/nursing*

New York State Board of Nursing
Education Bldg.
80 Washington Ave.
2nd Floor West Wing
Albany, NY 12234
Phone: (518) 474-3817, ext. 120
Web site: *www.nysed.gov/prof/nurse.htm*

North Carolina Board of Nursing
3724 National Dr., Suite 201
Raleigh, NC 27602
Phone: (919) 782-3211
Web site: *www.ncbon.com*

North Dakota Board of Nursing
919 S. 7th St., Suite 504
Bismarck, ND 58504
Phone: (701) 328-9777
Web site: *www.ndbon.org*

(continued)

State boards of nursing (continued)

Commonwealth Board of Nurse Examiners (Northern Mariana Islands)
Public Health Center
P.O. Box 1458
Saipan, MP 96950
Phone: (670) 234-8950

Ohio Board of Nursing
77 South High St., Suite 400
Columbus, OH 43215-3413
Phone: (614) 466-3947
Web site: www.state.oh.us/nur

Oklahoma Board of Nursing
2915 N. Classen Blvd., Suite 524
Oklahoma City, OK 73106
Phone: (405) 962-1800
Web site: www.youroklahoma.com/nursing

Oregon State Board of Nursing
800 N.E. Oregon St., Box 25
Suite 465
Portland, OR 97232
Phone: (503) 731-4745
Web site: www.osbn.state.or.us

Pennsylvania State Board of Nursing
124 Pine St.
Harrisburg, PA 17101
Phone: (717) 783-7142
Web site: www.dos.state.pa.us/bpoa/cwp/view.asp?a=1004&q=432869

Commonwealth of Puerto Rico
Board of Nurse Examiners
800 Roberto H. Todd Ave.
Room 202, Stop 18
Santurce, PR 00908
Phone: (787) 725-8161

Rhode Island Board of Nurse Registration and Nursing Education
105 Cannon Bldg.
Three Capitol Hill
Providence, RI 02908
Phone: (401) 222-5700
Web site: www.healthri.org/hsr/professions/nurses.htm

South Carolina State Board of Nursing
110 Centerview Dr., Suite 202
Columbia, SC 29210
Phone: (803) 896-4550
Web site: www.llr.state.sc.us/pol/nursing

South Dakota Board of Nursing
4300 S. Louise Ave., Suite C-1
Sioux Falls, SD 57106-3124
Phone: (605) 362-2760
Web site: www.state.sd.us/dcr/nursing

Tennessee State Board of Nursing
426 Fifth Ave. N.
1st Floor, Cordell Hull Bldg.
Nashville, TN 37247
Phone: (615) 532-5166
Web site: www.state.tn.us/health

Texas Board of Nurse Examiners
333 Guadalupe St., Suite 3-460
Austin, TX 78701
Phone: (512) 305-7400
Web site: www.bne.state.tx.us

Texas Board of Vocational Nurse Examiners
William P. Hobby Bldg.
Tower 3
333 Guadalupe St., Suite 3400
Austin, TX 78701
Phone: (512) 305-8100
Web site: www.bvne.state.tx.us

State boards of nursing *(continued)*

Utah State Board of Nursing
Heber M. Wells Bldg.
4th Floor
160 East 300 S.
Salt Lake City, UT 84111
Phone: (801) 530-6628
Web site: *www.commerce.state.ut.us*

Vermont State Board of Nursing
109 State St.
Montpelier, VT 05609-1106
Phone: (802) 828-2396
Web site: *www.vtprofessionals.org/opr1/
nurses*

**Virgin Islands Board of
Nurse Licensure**
Veterans Drive Station
St. Thomas, VI 00803
Phone: (340) 776-7397

Virginia Board of Nursing
6606 W. Broad St., 4th Floor
Richmond, VA 23230
Phone: (804) 662-9909
Web site: *www.dhp.state.va.us*

**Washington State Nursing Care
Quality Assurance Commission**
Department of Health
1300 Quince St. S.E.
Olympia, WA 98504-7864
Phone: (360) 236-4740
Web site: *https://fortress.wa.gov/doh/
hpqa1/HPS6/Nursing/default.htm*

**West Virginia State Board of
Examiners for Licensed
Practical Nurses**
101 Dee Dr.
Charleston, WV 25311
Phone: (304) 558-3572
Web site: *www.lpnboard.state.wv.us*

**West Virginia Board of
Examiners for Registered
Professional Nurses**
101 Dee Dr.
Charleston, WV 25311
Phone: (304) 558-3596
Web site: *www.state.wv.us/nurses/rn*

**Wisconsin Department of
Regulation and Licensing**
1400 E. Washington Ave.
P.O. Box 8935
Madison, WI 53708
Phone: (608) 266-0145
Web site: *www.drl.state.wi.us*

Wyoming State Board of Nursing
2020 Carey Ave., Suite 110
Cheyenne, WY 82002
Phone: (307) 777-7601
Web site: *http://nursing.state.wy.us*

practice acts don't spell out whether they legally may do so.

Even some nurse practice acts that do permit nursing diagnosis fail to define what the term means. For instance, the Pennsylvania Nurse Practice Act defines the practice of professional nursing as "*diagnosing and treating* human responses to actual or potential health problems through such services as casefinding, health teaching, health counseling, and provision care supportive to or restorative of life and well-being, and executing medical regimens as prescribed by a licensed physician or dentist. The foregoing shall not be deemed to include acts of medical diagnosis or prescription of medical therapeutic or corrective measures." This definition and others like it don't distinguish clearly between medical and nursing diagnoses.

Your state's nurse practice act isn't a word-for-word checklist on how you should do your work. You must rely on your own education and knowledge of your hospital's policies and procedures. For example, you know that a nursing diagnosis is part of your nursing assessment. It's your professional evaluation of the patient's progress, his responses to treatment, and his nursing care needs. You perform this evaluation so that you can develop and carry out your nursing care plan. It isn't a judgment about a patient's medical disorder. So, if your state's nurse practice act permits you to make nursing diagnoses, your sound judgment in applying its provisions should help you avoid legal consequences. If your employer's practice and procedures conflict with the nurse practice act, you may be assisted in working out this conflict by going to your state nursing organization to lobby the nursing board for resolution of the conflict.

LIMITS OF PRACTICE

Make sure you're familiar with the legally permissible scope of your nursing practice, as defined in your state's nurse practice act and board of nursing rules and regulations, and never exceed those limits. Otherwise, you're inviting legal problems.

Here's an example. The Pennsylvania Nurse Practice Act forbids a nurse to give an anesthetic unless the patient's physician is present. The case of *McCarl v. State Board of Nurse Examiners* (1979) involved a hospital nurse who violated this provision. The Pennsylvania Board of Nursing received a complaint about the incident and conducted a hearing. The nurse admitted to knowing about the law's requirement but argued that

the requirement was satisfied by the presence of another physician, although this physician didn't supervise her actions. The board ruled that the nurse had willfully violated a section of the Pennsylvania Nurse Practice Act and issued a reprimand. The nurse appealed, but the court upheld the reprimand.

WHEN TO ACT INDEPENDENTLY

Most nurse practice acts pose another problem: They state that you have a legal duty to carry out a physician's or a dentist's orders. Yet, as a licensed professional, you also have an ethical and legal duty to use your own judgment when providing patient care.

In an effort to deal with this issue, some nurse practice acts give guidance on how to obey orders and still act independently. For example, the Delaware Nurse Practice Act states that the RN practices the profession of nursing by performing certain activities; among these are "executing regimens, as prescribed by a licensed physician, dentist, podiatrist, or advanced practice nurse, including the dispensing and/or administration of medications and treatments." Having said this, the Delaware statute defines the practice of professional nursing as "the performance of professional services by a person who holds a valid license" and "who bears primary responsibility and accountability for nursing practices based on specialized knowledge, judgment, and skill derived from the principles of biological, physical, and behavioral sciences." This wording may be interpreted to mean that a nurse practicing in Delaware is required to follow a physician's or a dentist's orders, unless those orders are clearly wrong or the physician or dentist is unqualified to give them.

When you think an order is wrong, tell the physician. If you're confused about an order, ask the physician to clarify it. If he fails to correct the error or answer your questions, inform your head nurse or supervisor of your doubts.

A similar problem may arise when you deal with physician assistants (PAs) or APNs. Nurse practice acts in some states specify that you may only follow orders given by physicians or dentists — but medical practice acts in those states may allow PAs or APNs to give orders to nurses. Washington and Florida, for example, have decided that PAs and NPs are physicians' agents and may legally transmit the supervising physician's orders to nurses *(Washington State Nurses Ass'n. v. Board of Medical Examiners,* [1980]; Fla. Op. Atty. Gen. [077-96, September 1977]). The State of Delaware permits nurses with advanced credentials to prescribe regimens executed by RNs. Find out if your health care facility's policy allows PAs or APNs to give you orders. If it doesn't, don't follow such orders. If facility policy does permit PAs or APNs to give you orders, check if such orders must have verification or countersignature of the physician. For further clarification, check with your state board of nursing.

CONFLICTS WITH HOSPITAL POLICY

Nurse practice acts and hospital policies don't always agree. Hospital licensing laws require each hospital to establish policies and procedures for its operation. The nursing service department develops detailed policies and procedures for staff nurses. These policies and procedures usually specify the allowable scope of nursing practice within the hospital. The scope may be narrower than the scope described in your nurse practice act, but it shouldn't be broader.

A nurse filed suit in federal court after she was fired for not accepting an assignment outside the scope of her nursing practice. She had 9 years' experience in nursing care of adolescents and no training, orientation, or experience in pediatric intensive care, so she refused to accept an assignment floating in the hospital's pediatric intensive care unit. The hospital maintains that the Board's Standards of Nursing Conduct and Administrative Code are intended as guidelines to assist nurses in making day-to-day judgments required by nurses and don't constitute an affirmative duty to refuse an assignment. *Hudock v. Children's Hospital of Philadelphia* (filed and pending in federal court).

Keep in mind that your employer can't legally expand the scope of your nursing practice to include tasks prohibited by your state's nurse practice act. For example, nurses who measured, weighed, compounded, and mixed ingredients in preparation of parenteral hyperalimentation solutions and I.V. solutions (a longtime hospital practice and procedure) were censured and reprimanded by the New York State Board of Nursing even though their hospital allowed them to do so. They were placed on an 18-month probation and charged with the unlicensed practice of pharmacy in violation of the State of New York's Nurse Practice Act.

You have a legal obligation to practice within your nurse practice act's limits. Except in a life-threatening emergency, you can't exceed those limits without risking disciplinary action. To protect yourself, compare your facility's policies with your nurse practice act and board of nursing rules and regulations.

READING BETWEEN THE LINES

Most nurse practice acts don't specify a nurse's day-to-day legal responsibilities with respect to specific procedures and functions. For instance, along with omitting any reference to nursing diagnosis, many nurse practice acts don't address a nurse's responsibility for patient teaching or the legal limitations on nurse-patient discussions about treatment. However, board of nursing rules and regulations — depending on the state — may provide more guidance.

In an Idaho case, *Tuma v. Board of Nursing* (1979), a state board of nursing took disciplinary action against a nurse who discussed, at a patient's request, the possibility of using laetrile as alternative therapy. The board suspended her license on the grounds of unprofessional conduct. The Idaho Supreme Court revoked the suspension and ordered the board to reinstate the nurse's license. Why? Because the Idaho Nurse Practice Act contained no provision stating that such a nurse-patient discussion constitutes a violation of the nurse practice act.

Keeping nurse practice acts up to date

To align nurse practice acts with current nursing practice, professional nursing organizations and state boards of nursing generally propose revisions to regulations. Also, the nurse practice act can be changed by amendments or redefinition.

An *amendment* adds or repeals portions of a nurse practice act or its regulations, thereby giving nurses legal permission to perform certain procedures or functions that have become part of accepted nursing practice. Amendments have the same legal force as the original act. They do, however, have a disadvantage: They represent a piecemeal approach that may allow an outdated nurse practice act to remain in effect.

Redefinition is a rewriting of the fundamental provision of a nurse practice act — the definition of nursing practice. This approach changes the basic premise of the entire act without amending or repealing it. Redefinition might be used, for example, to reverse a definition of nursing practice that prohibits diagnosis. How? By clarifying the term diagnosis to allow nurses to make nursing diagnoses. This type of change helps nurses understand exactly what is and isn't prohibited.

When a state legislature changes or expands the state's nurse practice act, it must also repeal sections that conflict with its changes. For example, if a state legislature decides to adopt the nursing board's recommendation for a newly broadened definition of nursing, it must repeal the old definition in the state nurse practice act before it can enact the new definition into law.

Be aware that nurse practice acts are constantly being changed. To help protect yourself legally, you need to thoroughly understand your state's nurse practice act and board of nursing rules and regulations and keep up with any changes. You can do this easily by periodically checking your board of nursing's Web site. (See *State boards of nursing,* pages 11 to 15.)

Standards of nursing care

Standards of care set minimum criteria for your proficiency on the job, enabling you and others to judge the quality of care you and your nursing colleagues provide. States may refer to standards in their nurse practice acts. Unless included in a nurse practice act, professional standards aren't laws — they're guidelines for sound nursing practice.

Some nurses regard standards of nursing care as pie-in-the-sky ideals that have little bearing on the reality of working life. This is a dangerous misconception. You're expected to meet standards of nursing care for every nursing task you perform.

For example, if you're a medical-surgical nurse, minimal standards require that you develop a nursing care plan for your patient based on the nursing process, including nursing diagnoses, goals, and interventions for implementing the care plan. Standards also call for documentation, in the patient's record, of your completion and evaluation of the plan. When you document patient care, you're really writing a record of how well you've met these standards. A court may interpret an absence of documentation as an absence of patient care. *Pommier v. ABC Insurance Company et al.*, 715 So.2d 1270 (La.App.3d Cir. 1998).

EVOLUTION OF NURSING STANDARDS

Before 1950, nurses had only Florence Nightingale's early treatments, plus reports of court cases, to use as standards. As nursing gradually became recognized as an independent profession, nursing organizations stressed the importance of having recognized standards for all nurses. Then, in 1950, the ANA published the "Code of Ethics for Nursing," a general mandate stating that nurses should offer nursing care without prejudice and in a confidential and safe manner. Although not specific, this code marked the beginning of written nursing standards.

In 1973, the ANA Congress for Nursing Practice established the first generic standards for the profession — standards that could be applied to all nurses in all settings. (See *ANA standards of nursing practice,* pages 20 to 24.) The Canadian Nurses Association (CNA) has established similar nursing standards. Some states and jurisdictions have incorporated ANA and CNA standards into their nurse practice acts.

By 1974, each of the ANA divisions of nursing practice (such as community health, geriatrics, maternal-child, mental health, and medical-surgical) had established distinct standards for its specialty. The ANA Congress called these specialty standards. State nursing associations also helped develop specialty standards. (See *ANA standards for nursing administration*, pages 25 to 29.)

Other organizations have contributed to the development of nursing standards. The Joint Commission on Accreditation of Healthcare Organizations (JCAHO), a private, nongovernmental agency that is responsible for evaluating and accrediting more than 17,000 health care organizations in the United States, such as hospitals, nursing homes, health care networks, health care providers, and long-term care facilities, has also developed nursing standards to be used in hospital audit systems. In some states, JCAHO standards have been incorporated into law, resulting in broadly applicable stan-

(Text continues on page 24.)

ANA standards of nursing practice

The standards below are adapted from standards of nursing practice published by the American Nurses Association (ANA). They developed the standards (last revised in 2003) to provide registered nurses with guidelines for determining quality nursing care. The courts, hospitals, nurses, and patients may refer to these standards. The standards of nursing practice are divided into the "standards of practice," which identify the care that is provided to recipients of nursing services, and the "standards of professional performance," which explain the level of behavior expected in professional role activities. Each standard is followed by measurement criteria that give key indicators of competent practice for that standard. This adaptation of the standards doesn't present the standards that are specific to only advanced practice nurses.

Standards of Practice
Standard 1: Assessment
The nurse collects patient health data.

Measurement criteria
1. Data collection is systematic and ongoing.
2. Data collection involves the patient, partners, and health care providers when appropriate.
3. Priority of data collection activities is determined by the patient's immediate condition or needs.
4. Pertinent data are collected using appropriate evidence-based assessment techniques and instruments.
5. Analytical models and problem-solving tools are used.
6. Patterns and variances are identified by synthesizing relevant data and knowledge.
7. Relevant data are documented in a retrievable form.

Standard 2: Diagnosis
The nurse analyzes the assessment data in determining diagnosis.

Measurement criteria
1. Diagnoses are derived from the assessment data.
2. Diagnoses are validated with the patient, partners, and health care providers when possible.
3. Diagnoses are documented in a manner that facilitates the determination of expected outcomes and plan of care.

Standard 3: Outcomes identification
The nurse identifies expected outcomes individualized to the patient.

Measurement criteria
1. Identification of outcomes involves the patient, family, and health care providers when possible and appropriate.
2. Outcomes are culturally appropriate and are derived from the diagnoses.
3. Outcomes are formulated taking into account any associated risks, benefits, costs, current scientific evidence, and clinical expertise.
4. Outcomes are defined in terms of the patient, the patient's values, ethical considerations, environment, or situation along with any associated risks, benefits, costs, and current scientific evidence.
5. Outcomes include a time estimate for attainment.
6. Outcomes provide direction for continuity of care.
7. Outcomes are modified based on patient's status.
8. Outcomes are documented as measurable goals.

Standard 4: Planning
The nurse develops a plan of care that prescribes interventions to attain expected outcomes.

ANA standards of nursing practice *(continued)*

Measurement criteria

1. The plan is individualized to the patient's condition or needs.
2. The plan is developed with the patient, partners, and health care providers.
3. The plan includes strategies that address each of the diagnoses.
4. The plan provides for continuity of care.
5. The plan includes a pathway or timeline.
6. Priorities for care are established with the patient, family, and others when appropriate.
7. The plan provides directions to other health care providers.
8. The plan reflects current statutes, rules and regulations, and standards.
9. The plan integrates current trends and research.
10. The economic impact of the plan is considered.
11. The plan is documented using standardized language and terminology.

Standard 5: Implementation
The nurse implements the plan.

Measurement criteria

1. Interventions are implemented in a safe and timely manner.
2. Interventions and any modifications to the plan are documented.
3. Interventions are evidence-based and specific to the diagnosis.
4. Interventions include community resources and systems.
5. Implementation includes collaboration with other health care providers.

Standard 5a: Coordination of care
The nurse coordinates care delivery.

Measurement criteria

1. The nurse coordinates implementation of the plan.
2. The coordination of care is documented.

Standard 5b: Health teaching and health promotion
The nurse promotes health and a safe environment.

Measurement criteria

1. Health teaching includes healthy lifestyles, risk-reducing behaviors, developmental needs, activities of daily living, and preventative self-care.
2. Health promotion and teaching are appropriate to the patient's needs.
3. Feedback is received on the effectiveness of health promotion and teachings.

Standard 6: Evaluation
The nurse evaluates the patient's progress toward attainment of outcomes.

Measurement criteria

1. Evaluation is systematic, ongoing, and criteria-based.
2. The patient, partners, and health care providers are involved in the evaluation process.
3. The effectiveness of the plan is evaluated in relation to the patient's responses and outcomes.
4. The results of the evaluation are documented.
5. Ongoing assessment data are used to revise diagnoses, outcomes, and the plan of care as needed.
6. Results of the evaluation are disseminated to the patient and other health care providers involved with the patient's care in accordance with all laws and regulations.

Standards of professional performance

Standard 7: Quality of practice
The nurse systematically enhances the quality and effectiveness of nursing practice.

(continued)

ANA standards of nursing practice *(continued)*

Measurement criteria

1. Quality is demonstrated by documenting the application of nursing process in a responsible, accountable, and ethical manner.

2. The nurse uses the results of quality-of-care activities to initiate changes in nursing practice and throughout the health care delivery system.

3. The nurse uses creativity and innovation to improve care delivery.

4. The nurse participates in quality improvement activities. Such activities may include:
- identifying aspects of care important for quality monitoring
- identifying indicators used to monitor quality and effectiveness of nursing care
- collecting data to monitor quality and effectiveness of nursing care
- analyzing quality data to identify opportunities for improving care
- formulating recommendations to improve nursing practice or patient outcomes
- implementing activities to enhance the quality of nursing practice
- developing policies, procedures, and practice guidelines to improve quality of care
- participating on interdisciplinary teams that evaluate clinical practice or health services
- participating in efforts to minimize cost and unnecessary duplication
- analyzing factors related to safety, satisfaction, effectiveness, and cost/benefit options.
- analyzing organizational barriers
- implementing processes to remove or decrease organizational barriers
- incorporates new knowledge to initiate change in nursing practice if outcomes aren't achieved.

Standard 8: Education
The nurse acquires current knowledge and competency in nursing practice.

Measurement criteria

1. The nurse participates in ongoing educational activities related to knowledge bases and professional issues.

2. The nurse is committed to lifelong learning through self-reflection and inquiry to identify learning needs.

3. The nurse seeks experiences that reflect current practice to maintain current clinical practice and competency.

4. The nurse seeks knowledge and skills appropriate to the practice setting.

5. The nurse maintains professional records that evidence competency and life-long learning.

6. The nurse seeks experiences and formal and independent learning activities to maintain and develop clinical and professional skills and knowledge.

Standard 9: Professional practice evaluation
The nurse evaluates her own nursing practice in relation to professional practice standards and relevant statutes and regulations.

Measurement criteria

1. The nurse provides culturally, ethnically sensitive, and age-appropriate care.

2. The nurse engages in self-evaluation of practice on a regular basis, identifying areas of strength as well as areas where professional development would be beneficial.

3. The nurse seeks constructive feedback regarding his or her own practice.

4. The nurse participates in systematic peer review as appropriate.

5. The nurse takes action to achieve goals identified during the evaluation process.

6. The nurse provides rationales for practice beliefs, decisions, and actions as part of the evaluation process.

ANA standards of nursing practice *(continued)*

Standard 10: Collegiality
The nurse interacts with and contributes to the professional development of peers and colleagues.

Measurement criteria
1. The nurse shares knowledge and skills with colleagues and others through such activities as patient care conferences and presentations.

2. The nurse provides peers with constructive feedback regarding their practice.

3. The nurse interacts with colleagues to enhance her own professional practice.

4. The nurse maintains compassionate and caring relationships with peers and colleagues.

5. The nurse contributes to an environment that is conducive to education of health care professionals.

6. The nurse contributes to a supportive and healthy work environment.

Standard 11: Collaboration
The nurse collaborates with the patient, family, and others in providing patient care.

Measurement criteria
1. The nurse communicates with the patient, family, and health care providers regarding patient care and nurse's role in providing that care.

2. The nurse involves the patient, family, and others in creating a documented plan focused on outcomes and decisions related to care and the delivery of services.

3. The nurse collaborates with others to effect change and get positive outcomes for patient care.

4. The nurse makes and documents referrals, including provisions for continuity of care.

5. The nurse documents plans, communications or collaborative discussions, and rationales for plan changes.

Standard 12: Ethics
The nurse's integrates ethics in all areas of practice.

Measurement criteria
1. The nurse's practice is guided by the *Code for Ethics for Nurses with Interpretive Statements* (ANA, 2001).

2. The nurse preserves and protects patient autonomy, dignity, and rights.

3. The nurse maintains patient confidentiality.

4. The nurse acts as a patient advocate and assists patients in developing skills so they can advocate for themselves.

5. The nurse maintains a therapeutic and professional patient-nurse relationship within professional role boundaries.

6. The nurse is committed to practicing self-care, managing stress, and connecting with self and others.

7. The nurse helps resolve ethical issues, including participating in ethics committees.

8. The nurse reports illegal, incompetent, or impaired practices.

Standard 13: Research
The nurse uses research findings in practice.

Measurement criteria
1. The nurse uses best available evidence, including research findings to guide practice decisions.

2. The nurse participates in research activities as appropriate to her position and education. Such activities may include:
- identifying clinical problems suitable for nursing research
- participating in data collection
- participating in a formal committee or program
- sharing research findings with others
- conducting research

(continued)

ANA standards of nursing practice *(continued)*

◆ critiquing research for application to practice

◆ using research findings in the development of policies, procedures, and standards for patient care

◆ incorporating research as a basis for learning.

Standard 14: Resource utilization

The nurse considers factors related to safety, effectiveness, cost, and impact in planning and delivering patient care.

Measurement criteria

1. The nurse evaluates factors related to safety, effectiveness, availability, cost and benefits, efficiencies, and impact when choosing practice options that would result in the same expected patient outcome.
2. The nurse assists the patient and family in securing appropriate health-related services.
3. The nurse delegates tasks as appropriate.
4. The nurse assists the patient and family in becoming informed consumers about health care treatment.

Standard 15: Leadership

The nurse shows leadership in the practice setting and in the profession.

Measurement criteria

1. The nurse is a team player and a team builder.
2. The nurse creates and maintains healthy work environments.
3. The nurse is able to define clear visions, associated goals, and plan to implement and measure progress.
4. The nurse is committed to continuous, lifelong learning for self and others.
5. The nurse teaches others to succeed by mentoring and other strategies.
6. The nurse is creative and flexible through changing times.
7. The nurse exhibits energy, excitement, and passion for quality work.
8. The nurse takes accountability of self and others.
9. The nurse inspires loyalty through valuing people as the most precious asset in an organization.
10. The nurse directs the coordination of care across settings and among caregivers, including licensed and unlicensed personnel.
11. The nurse serves on committees, councils, and administrative teams.
12. The nurse promotes the advancement of the profession by participating in professional organizations.

dards of patient care. (See *JCAHO standards*, pages 30 to 33.) In addition, state nursing associations and the specialty nursing organizations actively work with hospital nursing administrators for adoption of standards.

JCAHO continuously creates and publishes new standards to improve patient safety. Hospitals and other health care organizations must comply with these standards to receive JCAHO accreditation. JCAHO has implemented the new "Patient Safety Standards" for hospitals, which became effective in July 2001, requiring hospitals to create an environment of safety. It also issued National Patient Safety Goals for 2003,

(Text continues on page 33.)

ANA standards for nursing administration

The standards below are adapted from standards for nursing administration published by the American Nurses Association (ANA). They were last revised in 2003. In the original document, the ANA referred to nursing administration as "organized nursing services."

Standards of practice
Standard 1: Assessment
The nurse administrator develops, maintains, and evaluates patients and data collection systems to support the nursing practice and the delivery of patient care.

Measurement criteria
  1. Identifies assessment elements, including nursing-sensitive indicators appropriate to a given organizational context.
  2. Utilizes current research findings and current practice guidelines and standards to modify data collection elements.
  3. Monitors and evaluates assessment processes that are sensitive to the unique and diverse needs of individuals and target populations.
  4. Identifies and documents the necessary resources to support data collection, and advocates for appropriate resources.
  5. Analyzes the workflow related to effectiveness and efficiency of assessment processes in the target environment.
  6. Develops, maintains, and evaluates systems for efficient data collection as part of the overall institutional data collection system.
  7. Promotes, maintains, and evaluates a data collection system in an accessible and retrievable format.
  8. Initiates processes to modify information systems as needed to meet changing data requirements and needs.
  9. Develops criteria and establishes procedures to assure confidentiality of data.
  10. Facilitates integration of unified assessment processes developed in collaboration with other health care disciplines and across the continuum of care.
  11. Evaluates assessment practices to assure timely, reliable, valid, and comprehensive data collection.
  12. Collaborates with appropriate departments.

Standard 2: Diagnosis and problem identification
The nurse administrator supports the professional nurse in analysis of assessment data and in making decisions based on that information.

Measurement criteria
  1. Identifies and advocates for adequate resources for decision analysis in conjunction with appropriate departments.
  2. Assists and supports staff in developing and maintaining competency in the diagnostic process.
  3. Facilitates interdisciplinary collaboration in data analysis and decision-making processes.
  4. Promotes an organizational climate that supports validation of diagnoses.
  5. Assures a system for documentation of diagnoses that facilitates development of a patient-centered plan of care and determination of desired outcomes.
  6. Conducts and formulates a diagnosis of the organization's context of care.

Standard 3: Identification of outcomes
The nurse administrator develops, maintains, and evaluates information processes that promote desired, client-centered, and organizational outcomes.

Measurement criteria
  1. Participates in the design and development of multidisciplinary processes to establish and maintain standards consistent with the identified outcomes.

(continued)

ANA standards for nursing administration *(continued)*

2. Facilitates nurse, client, and other staff member participation in interdisciplinary identification of desired outcomes.

3. Assists in identification, development, and utilization of databases that include nursing measures and desired outcomes.

4. Facilitates nurse participation in the monitoring and evaluating of nursing care in accordance with established professional, regulatory, and organizational standards of practice.

5. Fosters establishment and continuous improvement of clinical guidelines linked to client outcomes that provide direction for continuity of care, and are attainable with available resources.

6. Collaborates with appropriate departments.

7. Integrates clinical, human resource, and financial data to support decision-making.

Standard 4: Planning
The nurse administrator develops, maintains, and evaluates organizational planning systems to facilitate the delivery of nursing care.

Measurement criteria
1. Contributes to the development and continuous improvement of organizational systems in which plans related to the delivery of nursing services can be developed, modified, documented, and evaluated.

2. Contributes to the development and continuous improvement of organizational systems that support prioritization of activities within plans related to the delivery of nursing services and patient care.

3. Contributes to the development and continuous improvement of mechanisms for plans to be recorded, retrieved, and updated across the continuum of care.

4. Advocates organizational processes that allow for creativity in the development of alternative plans for achieving desired, client-centered, cost-effective outcomes.

5. Fosters interdisciplinary planning and collaboration that focuses on the individuals and populations served.

6. Promotes the integration of applicable contemporary management and organizational theories, nursing and related research findings, and practice standards and guidelines into the planning process.

7. Assists and supports staff in developing and maintaining competency in the planning and change process.

8. Advocates integration of policies into action plans for achieving desired client-centered outcomes.

9. Participates in the development, implementation, and use of a system for preventing and reporting abuse of client's rights, and incompetent, unethical, or illegal practices by health care providers.

10. Reviews and evaluates plans for appropriate utilization of staff at all levels of practice in accordance with the provision of the state's nurse practice act and the professional standards of practice.

11. Integrates clinical, human resource, and financial data to appropriately plan standards of nursing and patient care, facilitating continuity across a continuum.

12. Collaborates with appropriate departments.

Standard 5: Implementation
The nurse administrator develops, maintains, and evaluates organizational systems that support implementation of plans and delivery of care.

Measurement criteria
1. Participates in the development, evaluation, and maintenance of organizational systems that integrate policies and procedures with regulations, practice standards, and clinical guidelines.

ANA standards for nursing administration *(continued)*

2. Designs and improves systems and identifies resources that support interventions that are consistent with the established plans.

3. Facilitates staff participation in decision-making regarding the development and implementation of organizational systems, and the specification of resources necessary for implementation of the plan.

4. Collaborates with appropriate departments.

5. Collaborates in the design and improvement of systems and the identification of resources that ensure that interventions are safe, effective, efficient, and culturally sensitive.

6. Collaborates in the design and improvement of systems and processes, which ensures that the most appropriate personnel implement interventions.

7. Collaborates in the design and improvement of systems to ensure appropriate and efficient documentation of interventions.

Standard 6: Evaluation

The nurse administrator evaluates the plan and its progress in relation to the attainment of outcomes.

Measurement criteria

1. Promotes implementation of processes and resources that deliver data and information to empower staff to participate meaningfully in clinical decision-making.

2. Ensures educational opportunities for staff specific to current interventions, available technologies, or other skills to enhance ability to promote quality in health care delivery.

3. Utilizes appropriate research methods and findings to improve care processes, structures, and measurement of desired outcomes.

4. Facilitates staff participation in the systematic, interdisciplinary, and ongoing evaluation of programs, processes, and desired client-centered outcomes.

5. Sets priorities for allocation of resources.

6. Advocates for resources sufficient to provide time for critical assessment and evaluation of desired outcomes.

7. Fosters participation and recognition of staff in formal and informal organizational committees, teams, and task forces.

8. Advocates for and supports a process of governance that includes participation of nurses.

9. Participates in the peer review, credentialing, certification, and privileging process for all appropriate health care providers.

10. Supports effective information handling processes and technologies that facilitate evaluation of effectiveness and efficiency of decisions, plans, and activities in relation to desired outcomes.

11. Promotes the development of policies, procedures, and guidelines based on research findings and institutional measurement of quality outcomes.

12. Utilizes data generated from outcome research to develop innovative changes in patient care delivery.

Standards of professional performance

Standard 1: Quality of care and administrative practice

The nurse administrator systematically evaluates the quality and effectiveness of nursing practice and nursing services administration.

Measurement criteria

1. Leads the development, implementation, and performance improvement of care delivery models and services that meet or exceed customer expectation.

2. Identifies key indicators including measures of quality of nursing practice and customer needs and expectations.

3. Advocates for and participates in the development of clinical, operational, and finan-

(continued)

ANA standards for nursing administration *(continued)*

cial databases upon which nurse-sensitive outcomes can be derived, reported, and used for improvement.

4. Leads in creating and evaluating systems, processes, and programs that support institutional and nursing core values and objectives.

5. Evaluates and ensures safe care delivery.

Standard 2: Performance appraisal

The nurse administrator evaluates personal performance based on professional practice standards, relevant statutes, regulations, and organizational criteria.

Measurement criteria

1. Systematically identifies industry trends and competencies in nursing administration and nursing practice.

2. Engages in self-assessment of role accountabilities on a regular basis, identifying areas of strength as well as areas for professional development.

3. Evaluates efficacy of the plan and the vision for professional nursing.

4. Seeks constructive feedback regarding own practice.

5. Takes action to achieve plans for performance improvement.

6. Participates in peer review as appropriate.

Standard 3: Education

The nurse administrator maintains and demonstrates current knowledge in the administration of health care organizations to advance clinical practice.

Measurement criteria

1. Seeks experiences to advance skills and knowledge base in areas of responsibilities.

2. Seeks formal education and certification for career path.

3. Networks with peers to share ideas and conduct mutual problem solving.

Standard 4: Professional environment

The nurse administrator must provide a professional environment.

Measurement criteria

1. Creates a professional practice environment that fosters excellence in nursing services.

2. Creates a climate of effective communication.

3. Fosters professional nurse empowered decision-making, accountability, and autonomy in nursing practice.

4. Leads through a well-established nursing leadership structure and as a formal authority participant in organizational senior leadership.

5. Establishes and promotes a framework for professional nursing practice built on core ideology which includes vision, mission, philosophy, core values, evidence-based practice, and standards of practice.

6. Assures mutual respect for individuals and the profession at work.

7. Develops strategies to recruit and retain, mentor, assure quality education and training, and ensure meaningful work to maximize job satisfaction of nursing staff.

8. Promotes understanding and effective use of organization, management, and nursing theories and research.

9. Contributes to nursing management education and professional development of staff, students, and colleagues.

10. Adheres to the *Bill of Rights for Registered Nurses* (ANA, 2001).

11. Shares knowledge and skills with students, colleagues, and others, and acts as a role model and mentor.

Standard 5: Ethics

The nurse administrator's decisions and actions are ethical.

ANA standards for nursing administration *(continued)*

Measurement criteria

1. Advocates for recipients of services and personnel.
2. Maintains privacy, confidentiality, and security of patient, client, staff, and organization data.
3. Adheres to the *Code of Ethics for Nurses with Interpretive Statements* (ANA, 2001).
4. Assures compliance with regulatory and professional standards, as well as integrity in business practices.
5. Assures that nursing care is given in a nondiscriminatory and socioculturally sensitive manner.
6. Assures a system to identify and address ethical issues within nursing and the organization.

Standard 6: Collaboration

The nurse administrator collaborates with all nursing staff, interdisciplinary teams, executive leaders, and other stakeholders.

Measurement criteria

1. Facilitates and models collaboration within nursing services and the organization.
2. Collaborates with nursing staff and other disciplines at all levels in the development, implementation, and evaluation of programs and services.
3. Collaborates with administrative peers in determining the acquisition, allocation, and utilization of fiscal and human resources.
4. Fosters relationships that support the continuous enhancement of care delivery and patient, client, and employee satisfaction.

Standard 7: Research

The nurse administrator supports research and integrates it into nursing administration and the delivery of nursing care.

Measurement criteria

1. Creates the environment and advocates for resources supportive of nursing research and scholarly inquiry.
2. Assures nursing research priorities align with plan and objectives.
3. Supports research that promotes evidence-based, clinically effective and efficient, nurse-sensitive patient outcomes.
4. Facilitates the dissemination of research findings and the integration of evidence-based guidelines and practices into health care.
5. Supports procedures for review of proposed research studies, including protection of the rights of human subjects.
6. Identifies areas of clinical and administrative inquiry suitable for nurse researchers.

Standard 8: Resource utilization

The nurse administrator evaluates and administers the resources of nursing services.

Measurement criteria

1. Assures nursing workload is measured and resources are allocated based upon patient or client need.
2. Develops systems to continuously monitor and measure the quality, safety, and outcomes of nursing services.
3. Develops, values, and expands the intellectual capital of the organization.
4. Assures and optimizes fiscal resource allocation to support current and potential nursing objectives and initiatives.
5. Provides fiscal oversight of allocated resources to optimize the provision of quality, cost-effective care.
6. Guides the delegation of responsibilities appropriate to the licensure, education, and experience of staff.
7. Designs and negotiates organizational acceptance of appropriate roles for the utilization of all staff.
8. Monitors and evaluates appropriate utilization of staff.

(continued)

JCAHO standards

The standards listed below are based on the *Comprehensive Accreditation Manual for Hospitals* published by the Joint Commission on Accreditation of Healthcare Organizations (JCAHO). These standards are used by JCAHO to evaluate and monitor the clinical and organizational performance of health care facilities.

Standards for patient assessment
◆ Patients should receive nursing care based on a documented assessment of their needs.

Structure supporting the assessment of patients
◆ The activities that comprise the patient assessment function should be defined in writing.
◆ A registered nurse (RN) should assess the patient's need for nursing care in all settings in which nursing care is to be provided.

Standards for planning and providing care
◆ The care, treatment, and rehabilitation planning process should ensure that care is appropriate to the patient's specific needs and the severity level of his disease, condition, impairment, or disability.
◆ Qualified individuals must plan and provide care, treatment, and rehabilitation in a collaborative and disciplined manner, as appropriate to the patient.

Care decisions
◆ The information generated through the analysis of assessment data should be used to identify and prioritize the patient's needs for care.
◆ Care decisions should be based on the identified patient needs and on care priorities.

Patient's rights
◆ The organization should have a functioning process to address ethical issues.
◆ The process should be based on a framework that recognizes the interdependence of patient care and organizational ethical issues.
◆ The process should include mechanisms that address the patient's involvement in all aspects of care.

Standards for human resources planning
◆ The organization's leaders should define for their respective areas the qualifications and job expectations of the staff and develop a system to evaluate how well the expectations are met.
◆ The organization should provide an adequate number of staff members whose qualifications are commensurate with defined job responsibilities and applicable licensure, law, and regulation and certification.
◆ Processes should be designed to ensure that the competence of all staff members is assessed, maintained, demonstrated, and improved on an ongoing basis.
◆ The organization should assess each individual's ability to achieve job expectations as stated in her job description.

Initial assessment
◆ An initial screening or assessment of each patient's physical, psychological, and social status should be performed to determine the need for care, the type of care to be provided, and the need for any further assessment.
◆ The need for an assessment of the patient's nutritional status should be determined.
◆ The need for a discharge planning assessment of the patient should be determined.
◆ The initial assessment of each patient admitted should be conducted within a certain

JCAHO standards (continued)

time frame preceding or following admission, as specified by policy.

◆ The patient's history and physical examination, nursing care assessment, and other screening assessments should be completed within the first 24 hours of admission as an inpatient.

Reassessment

◆ Each patient should be reassessed periodically.

◆ The patient should be reassessed when a significant change occurs in his condition.

Standards for organizational planning

◆ The leadership should provide for organizational planning.

◆ Planning should include setting a mission, a vision, and values for the organization and providing strategic, operational, programmatic, and other plans and policies to achieve the mission and vision.

◆ When the larger organization is composed of many subunits, there should be a mechanism for leaders of individual units to participate in policy decisions affecting their organization.

Patient care services

◆ The plan for the provision of patient care should respond to identified patient needs and be consistent with the organization's mission.

◆ The organization's leaders and, as appropriate, community leaders and heads of other organizations should collaborate to design services.

◆ The design of patient care services to be provided throughout the organization should be appropriate to the scope and level of care required by the patients served.

◆ The leaders should collaborate with representatives from the appropriate disciplines and

services to develop an annual operating budget and, at least as required by applicable law and regulation, a long-term capital expenditure plan, including a strategy to monitor the plan's implementation.

◆ The budget review process should include consideration of the appropriateness of the organization's plan for providing care to meet patient needs.

◆ The leaders and other representatives of the organization should participate, as appropriate, in the organization's decision-making structure and processes.

◆ The organization's leaders should develop programs to promote the recruitment, retention, development, and continuing education of all staff members. These programs should include mechanisms for promoting the job-related educational and advancement goals of staff members.

Directing departments

◆ Each department of the organization should have effective leadership. Department directors are responsible, either personally or through delegation, for:

– developing and implementing policies and procedures that guide and support the provision of services

– recommending a sufficient number of qualified and competent persons to provide care, including treatment

– continuously assessing and improving the performance of care and services provided

– maintaining quality control programs, as appropriate

– orienting and providing inservice training and continuing education of all persons in the department.

Integrating services

◆ Patient care services must be appropriately integrated throughout the organization. The

(continued)

JCAHO standards *(continued)*

leaders should individually and jointly develop and participate in systematic and effective mechanisms for:
- – fostering communication among individuals and components of the organization and coordinating internal activities
- – communicating with the leaders of any health care delivery organization that is corporately or functionally related to the organization seeking accreditation.

Improving performance
◆ The organization's leaders should set expectations, develop plans, and manage processes to assess, improve, and maintain the quality of the organization's governance, management, clinical, and support activities.

Standards for information management planning
◆ Information management processes should be planned and designed to meet the health care organization's internal and external information needs.
◆ The information management processes within and among departments, the medical staff, the administration, and the governing body, and with outside services and agencies, should be appropriate for the organization's size and complexity.
◆ Based on the organization's information needs, appropriate staff members should participate in assessing, selecting, and integrating health care information technology and, as appropriate, using efficient interactive information management systems for clinical and organizational information.
◆ The information management function must provide for information confidentiality, security, and integrity.
◆ The organization should determine how data and information could be retrieved easily

and on a timely basis without compromising its security and confidentiality.

Patient information
◆ The information management function should provide for the definition, capture, analysis, transformation, transmission, and reporting of individual patient information related to the process and outcome of the patient's care.
◆ The medical record must contain sufficient information to identify the patient, support the diagnosis, justify the treatment, document the course and results accurately, and facilitate continuity of care among health care providers. Each medical record should contain at least the following:
- – the diagnosis or diagnostic impression
- – diagnostic and therapeutic orders, if any
- – all diagnostic and therapeutic procedures and tests performed and the results
- – goals of treatment and treatment plan
- – progress notes made by the medical staff and other authorized individuals
- – all reassessments, when necessary
- – the response to the care provided.
◆ At discharge, a concise clinical résumé should summarize the reason for hospitalization, any significant findings, the procedures performed and treatment rendered, the patient's condition on discharge, and any specific instructions given to the patient and family, as pertinent.

Standards for nursing
◆ A nurse-executive who is an RN, qualified by advanced education and management experience, should direct nursing services.

The nurse-executive
◆ If the organization's structure is decentralized, an identified nurse leader at the executive level should provide authority and ac-

JCAHO standards *(continued)*

countability for, and coordination of, the nurse-executive functions.

◆ The nurse-executive has the authority and responsibility for establishing standards of nursing practice.

◆ The nurse-executive and other nursing leaders should participate with leaders from the governing body, management, medical staff, and clinical areas in planning, promoting, and conducting organization-wide performance improvement activities.

Policies and procedures

◆ Nursing policies and procedures, nursing standards of patient care, and standards of nursing practice must be created in a set sequence.

◆ Policies, procedures, and standards should be developed by the nurse-executive, RNs, and other designated nursing staff members. These documents must be in writing.

◆ Policies, procedures, and standards should be approved by the nurse-executive or a designee.

---

which focuses on the prevention of health care errors. (See *JCAHO's National Patient Safety Goals*, page 34.)

Federal regulations for staffing Medicare and Medicaid services have influenced the development of standards, especially nursing home standards. By suggesting ethical approaches to nursing practice, ethics codes written by the ANA, the CNA, and the International Council of Nurses also influence how nursing care standards are developed.

Local or national standards

The courts use local standards — reflecting a community's accepted, common nursing practices — to judge the quality of nursing care. This practice has been eroded in recognition of national standards applied by accreditation agencies. More often, nurses are held to a national standard.

Local standards are established in two ways: by individual health care facilities, through their policies and procedures, and by expert witnesses who testify in court cases that involve nurses. Every facility establishes standards

to fit its own community's needs. An expert witness interprets local standards by testifying about how nursing is commonly practiced in the community.

Legal significance

Even though they aren't law, nursing standards have important legal significance. The allegation that a nurse failed to meet appropriate standards of care, and that breach of these standards caused the harm (proximate cause) to the patient, is the basic premise of every nursing malpractice lawsuit.

During a malpractice trial, the court will measure the defendant-nurse's action against the answer it obtains to the following question: *What would a reasonably prudent nurse, with like training and experience, do under these circumstances?*

To answer this question, the plaintiff-patient, through his attorney, has the burden to prove that certain standards of care exist and that the defendant-nurse failed to meet those

JCAHO's National Patient Safety Goals

The goals listed below are based on the 2004 National Patient Safety Goals published by the Joint Commission on Accreditation of Healthcare Organizations (JCAHO). JCAHO's Board of Commissioners approved goals to help accredited organizations address specific areas of concern in regard to patient safety.

◆ Improve the accuracy of patient identification by:
- using at least two patient identifiers whenever taking blood samples or administering medications or blood products
- conducting a final patient verification using active communication techniques prior to the start of any invasive procedure.

◆ Improve the effectiveness of communication among caregivers by:
- implementing a process for taking verbal or telephone orders that requires verification of the entire order
- standardizing abbreviations, acronyms, and symbols used throughout the facility.

◆ Improve the safety of using high-alert medications by:
- removing concentrated electrolytes from patient care units
- standardizing and limiting the number of drug concentrations available.

◆ Eliminate wrong-site, wrong-patient, wrong-procedure surgery by:
- using a preoperative verification process to confirm appropriate documentation
- implementing a process to mark the surgical site that involves the patient in the marking process.

◆ Improve the safety of using infusion pumps by ensuring free-flow protection on all general-use and patient-controlled analgesia I.V. infusion pumps.

◆ Improve the effectiveness of clinical alarm systems by:
- implementing regular preventive maintenance (including testing) of alarm systems
- assuring that alarms are activated with appropriate settings and are sufficiently audible.

◆ Reduce the risk of health care-acquired infections by:
- complying with current Centers for Disease Control and Prevention hand hygiene guidelines
- managing as sentinel events all identified cases of unanticipated death or major permanent loss of function associated with a health care-acquired infection

---

standards in her treatment of him. He must also prove the appropriateness of those standards, show how the nurse failed to meet them, and show how that failure caused him injury.

When the standard of care is at issue, the plaintiff–patient must present expert witness testimony to support his claims. The defendant–nurse and her attorney will also produce expert witness testimony to support her claim that her actions didn't fall below ac-

cepted standards of care and that she acted in a reasonable and prudent manner.

The court may consider written standards when considering the standards of care involved in a nursing malpractice lawsuit. The court seeks information about all the national and state standards applicable to the defendant–nurse's actions. The court may also seek applicable information about the policies of the defendant-nurse's employer.

Because of two trends — uniform nursing educational requirements and standardized medical treatment regimens — national standards are gaining increasing favor with the courts. These trends have made the ANA's standards more influential than local standards or the standards of other organizations. For example, in the case of *Planned Parenthood of Northwest Indiana v. Vines* (1980), an NP who inserted an intra-uterine device was held to the minimum standard of care that was uniform throughout the country.

As the role of nurses is expanding across the country, so is the standard of care. Nurses who perform the same medical services are subject to the same standard of care and liability as physicians. *Pommier v. ABC Insurance Company*, 715 So.2d 1270, 1297-1342 (La. App. 3d Cir. 1998).

HOW NURSING STANDARDS ARE APPLIED IN COURT

In *Story v. St. Mary Parish Service District* (1987), a 66-year-old man was admitted to the hospital complaining of abdominal distention, pain, nausea, and vomiting. During the next 2 days, he complained several times to the nurses and attendants about shortness of breath and severe pain in his elbows and chest.

One evening, the staff nurse (a new graduate who had only recently taken her nursing boards) wrote in her nurses' notes, "Complains of both elbows hurting severely, denied pain anywhere else. Slightly irritable and confused. Assisted back to bed. Admits to arthritis. Slight shortness of breath noted. Abdominal distention in moderation noted; soft to touch. Blood pressure 150/98; pulse 88. Will have

medicated." She didn't indicate any consultation with the charge nurse. The patient died; autopsy revealed a myocardial infarction.

Pretrial testimony revealed that the patient had stated that the nurses didn't listen to his reports of pain. In the pretrial memorandum, the plaintiff's attorney cited a variety of nursing practice standards, including the following:
◆ the Louisiana Nurse Practice Act, which describes the nurse's responsibility for performing patient assessment and intervening as appropriate
◆ a board of nursing rule stating that graduate nurses must have RN supervision when they provide care
◆ nursing care standards established by JCAHO.

Although this case was settled out of court, it provides a good example of the extensive use of nursing practice standards as evidence in a lawsuit.

In *Hodges v. Effingham County Hospital* (1987), a woman entered the emergency department (ED) and complained to the nurses of chest pains. No physician was present. After conferring with the nurses by telephone, the physician on call decided to discharge the patient. The nurses didn't tell the physician that the patient had a history of heart disease and had recently taken a nitroglycerin tablet. The patient later died.

The plaintiff alleged that the nurses in the ED demonstrated negligence because they failed to obtain an accurate medical history and to "fully report known and observable symptoms to the physician on call." The physician wasn't sued: The plaintiff thought that the physician had treated the patient appropriately based on the information given to him.

Although the nurses won the trial court decision; on appeal, the higher court found the nurses liable. The higher court stated that because the nursing action in question involved nursing judgment rather than the adequacy of services or facility, the question was whether the nurses followed general standards of nursing care.

ALL PHYSICIANS AREN'T CREATED EQUAL

Consider the case of a nurse found negligent for not recognizing and reporting inconsistent intentions of the attending physician and the first-year resident.

In *St. Germain v. Pfeifer*, 637 N.E.2d 848 (Mass. 1994), a first-year orthopedic resident ordered the plaintiff-patient, who underwent a midlumbar osteotomy, out of bed on the 2nd postoperative day, whereas the attending orthopedic surgeon's postoperative plan was for the patient to be confined to bed for 4 or 5 days after surgery. The charge nurse noted the resident's order without question and without considering the patient's care plan, of which she should have been aware. Therefore, she should have known and reported the inconsistent intentions of both physicians regarding the movement of the patient. The nurse got the patient out of bed and, as he moved, he heard a loud snapping sound in the back of his neck and fell backward, screaming in pain. The hooks and rods in his back snapped out of position, and he was severely injured. The nurse's motion to dismiss the case against her was granted, but later the grant was overturned because there was expert opinion that her acts fell below the standard of care.

NONNURSING PROFESSIONALS

During a malpractice trial, nonnursing professionals who are trained and educated in medicine, are familiar with standards of nursing care, and delegate nursing orders may provide expert witness testimony with regard to standards of nursing care. For example, in *Hiatt v. Groce* (1974), a patient sued an obstetric nurse for failing to notify a physician when the patient was about to deliver a baby. The court permitted a physician to testify about the adequacy of the nurse's care. In *Gugino v. Harvard Community Health Plan* (1980), the court allowed a physician to testify about the standards for a nurse practitioner.

In cases in which the act of negligence is within the common knowledge and experience of a lay person, it may not be necessary to produce expert testimony. In *Jones v. Hawkes Hospital* (1964), the court instructed jurors to rely on their own common sense to judge whether a nurse met standards of practice instead of relying on expert testimony. In this case, a nurse left a sedated patient in labor to assist a physician with another patient in labor. She did this because the hospital had a rule that no physician could attend a woman in labor unless a nurse was present. Left alone, the plaintiff-patient got out of bed, fell, and suffered serious injuries. The nurse wanted the court to allow expert testimony to establish what standard of care should have been applied. However, the court ruled that any reasonably prudent person could determine this case on the basis of ordinary experience and knowledge and that the jurors could decide on their own whether the defendant-nurse's nontechnical nursing tasks met reasonable standards of care. The jury found the nurse negligent.

In a similar case, *Larrimore v. Homeopathic Hospital Association*, a nurse was found liable for failing to read a new order or for reading it negligently. The court stated that the jury could apply ordinary common sense, without an expert witness, to establish the applicable standard of care because the standard of care applied depends upon the given circumstances. (176 A.2d 362, 367-68 [Del. Supr. 1961], *off'd* 181 A.2d 573, 576-77 [Del. Supr. 1962].)

Nursing licensure

Your nursing license entitles you to practice as a professionally qualified nurse. However, like most privileges, your nursing license imposes certain responsibilities. As a licensed RN or LPN, you're responsible for providing quality care to your patients. To meet this responsibility and to protect your right to practice, you need to understand the professional and legal significance of your nursing license.

LICENSING LAWS

Each nurse practice act contains licensing laws. They establish qualifications for obtaining and maintaining a nursing license. They also broadly define the legally permissible scope of nursing practice.

Although they vary from state to state, most licensing laws specify:
◆ the qualifications a nurse needs to be granted a license
◆ license application procedures for new licenses and reciprocal (state-to-state) licensing arrangements
◆ application fees
◆ authorization to grant use of the title registered nurse or licensed practical or vocational nurse to applicants who receive their licenses

◆ grounds for license denial, revocation, or suspension
◆ license renewal procedures.

Most state licensing laws don't prohibit nursing students, a patient's friends, or members of his family from caring for him on a routine basis, provided that no fee is involved. They also permit a newly graduated nurse to practice for a specified period while her license application is being processed, and they allow unlicensed people to give care (such as administering cardiopulmonary resuscitation) in an emergency. According to state and federal constitutional requirements, state laws must exempt the following types of nurses from state licensure requirements:
◆ nurses working in federal institutions
◆ nurses practicing in accordance with their religious beliefs
◆ nurses traveling with patients from one state to another.

LEGAL SIGNIFICANCE OF THE LICENSE

Licensing laws help you to avoid civil and criminal liabilities by defining the scope of your professional nursing practice. If you're named in a malpractice lawsuit, your state licensing laws will be used as partial evidence to determine whether you acted within the legal limits of your profession.

In *Barber v. Reinking* (1966), the court used the licensing laws in the Washington State Nurse Practice Act to rule against the defendant-nurse. In this case, a 2-year-old boy was taken to a physician's office for a polio booster shot. The physician (also named in the suit) delegated this task to the LPN who worked in his office. While the nurse was administering the shot, the child moved suddenly and the needle broke off in his buttock. Despite attempts to remove it surgically and with a magnet, the needle remained lodged in the child's buttock for 9 months.

During the trial, the licensing law for practical nurses became the crucial factor in the court's decision. The court declared that the nurse had violated the nurse practice act by performing services beyond the legal limit of her practice. (Until the 1970s, the Washington State Nurse Practice Act didn't allow a practical nurse to legally give an injection.) The nurse's attorney attempted to introduce as evidence the fact that LPNs in the local community commonly gave injections. This evidence wasn't allowed. Instead, the judge instructed the jury to consider the violation of the nurse practice act along with other evidence in the case, including the physician's liability under the *respondeat superior* doctrine, to determine if the nurse was negligent.

Canadian licensing laws

Because each jurisdiction in Canada has its own nurse practice act, the laws vary somewhat from one to the next. Licensing laws in all jurisdictions except Ontario require nurses to join jurisdictional nursing associations to obtain their licenses.

Canadian jurisdictions require licensure to practice nursing. Licensing laws establish:
◆ qualifications for membership in the provincial nurses' association
◆ examination requirements
◆ applicable fees
◆ conditions for reciprocal licensure
◆ penalties for practicing without a license
◆ grounds for denial, suspension, or revocation of a nurse's license.

Within those jurisdictions that license practical nurses, licensing laws for LPNs are similar to those for RNs.

KEEPING THE LICENSE CURRENT

When you begin a new job, your employer is responsible for checking your credentials and confirming that you're properly licensed. Make sure your nursing license is current, and be prepared to furnish proof that you've renewed your license, if necessary.

If you fail to renew your license, you can no longer legally practice nursing. In the United States, you can be prosecuted and fined for practicing without a license; fines usually range from as little as $5 to $2,000. The same is true in Canadian jurisdictions that have mandatory registration; in those that don't, you can be fined only for using the initials "RN" after your name.

Fines vary from state to state. For example, section 223 of the Professional Nursing Law of Pennsylvania states that practicing nursing without a license is a *misdemeanor*, a crime punishable by a jail sentence of 12 months or less. For a first violation, the nurse must pay a fine of up to $1,000 or face a 6-month prison term. For a second violation, the penalty may be a fine of up to $2,000 or 6 months to 1 year in prison, or both. In addition to the criminal penalty, the nurse may be required to pay a civil penalty of up to $1,000.

States are beginning to mandate active practice in nursing to maintain a license. Maryland requires 1,000 hours of active nursing practice within a five-year period immediately preceding the date of anticipated renewal. *(Title 8 Annotated Code of Maryland, Section 309.)*

License renewal and the law

The courts have addressed questions concerning license renewal, usually during an appeal of disciplinary action taken by a state board of nursing. The courts don't always agree with the boards' decisions. In *Kansas State Board of Nursing v. Burkman* (1975), an RN failed to renew her license and continued to practice nursing. No evidence existed to suggest that she had intentionally not renewed her license or knowingly practiced without it. The state board of nursing ruled that her action constituted a violation of state licensing laws and suspended her license for six months. After several appeals, a high court ruled that the board had erred, and instructed the board to renew the license.

In *Oliff v. Florida State Board of Nursing* (1979), the court also ruled in a nurse's favor. In this case, the board of nursing refused to renew an LPN's certificate because her application hadn't arrived on time. Evidence indicated that the nurse had mailed her application before the board's specified date. The court ruled that the board's date was a deadline for applications to be mailed, not received.

Failure to renew

If you find that you've forgotten to renew your license, simple measures can help you avoid legal repercussions:
◆ Notify your employer.
◆ Find your original license application and immediately notify the state board of nursing of your oversight. Ask them for a temporary license or for authorization to continue nursing until you receive your license.
◆ If you can't find your license application, write to the state board of nursing for a renewal application and instructions on how to proceed. Then follow the board's instructions exactly.

WORKING IN A DIFFERENT STATE

Until the National League for Nursing established the first standardized examination for nursing licensure, each state had its own qualifications for entry into nursing practice. As a result, arranging to obtain a license in a different state than your own was usually difficult.

All candidates for licensure currently are required to pass the NCLEX, administered under the auspices of the National Council of State Boards of Nursing. Due to national standards, nurses are now able to move more freely to new jobs in different states.

When you move to another state to practice nursing, you must obtain a license or temporary practice permit from that state before you may legally practice. Most state boards of nursing will license you if you're currently licensed to practice nursing in another state or territory. If you're licensed to practice in Canada, most boards will license you if your education fulfills the issuing state's requirements; however, some may require you to take the written licensing examination. The policy of accepting out-of-state licensure is called *endorsement*. Many state boards waive reexamination if you're licensed in Canada and want to practice in the United States. The same usually applies if you hold a U.S. license and want to practice in Canada.

If you move to another state, you may be granted a temporary license before its board of nursing has had time to approve your application. Check both the time limit of the temporary license and the specific nursing functions it authorizes.

If you travel with a patient from one state to another, your license is valid for the duration of the trip in most states and Canadian jurisdictions.

Failure to qualify

If the state board finds that you don't have the necessary qualifications to practice nursing in that state, it may reject your application or require that you complete a written examination — regardless of your education or the laws of the state in which you live.

In *Richardson v. Brunelle* (1979), an LPN who had practiced in Massachusetts for 15 years brought suit after being refused a license to practice in New Hampshire. In her New Hampshire application, she requested a decree of educational equivalency. Although she had originally taken and passed a Massachusetts State licensing examination, she had never graduated from an approved school of practical nursing. At that time, only nursing school graduates were permitted to practice in New Hampshire, so her request was denied. Her lawsuit was unsuccessful in reversing the New Hampshire decision, and subsequent appeals upheld the original ruling.

A similar case, *Snelson v. Culton* (1949), involved Maine's licensing requirements, which also require a graduation for licensing.

FEDERAL LAW AND LICENSURE

Even though no federal law has jurisdiction over state boards of nursing, federal laws may affect nursing licensure. For example, if you're a nurse in the armed forces who is often subject to transfer, you're required by federal law to hold a current state license but not necessarily in the state to which you're assigned.

A federal public health code requires all state boards that license health care professionals to develop systems for verifying those professionals' continued competence. (42 U.S.C. § 13965-2) (2000)

FOREIGN LICENSURE

If you move to a foreign country, your U.S. nursing license will be reviewed by the appropriate authority, which will either reject or accept it (possibly with conditions). If you're a nurse in the American armed forces working in an American installation, you're exempt from this review.

In a non-English-speaking country, the licensing authority may require you to complete a language-proficiency examination.

If you're an RN or LPN licensed in a foreign country, you can't practice nursing in any state, territory, or province until the appropriate licensing authority has approved your application and issued your nursing license. When you're granted licensure in the United States or Canada, you function at the same legal status as a U.S.- or Canadian-educated RN or LPN. You're also equally accountable for your professional actions.

All states and the federal government require that foreign nurses pass the examination prepared by the Commission on Graduates of Foreign Nursing Schools (the CGFNS examination). If a foreign nurse successfully completes this examination — which includes an English-proficiency segment — she may then take the NCLEX. If she passes, she qualifies for licensure and a work visa.

DISCIPLINARY ACTION

The state board of nursing can take disciplinary action against a nurse for any violation of the state's nurse practice act. In all states and in Canadian jurisdictions, a nurse faces discipline if she endangers a patient's health, safety, or welfare. Depending on the severity of the violation, a state board may formally reprimand the nurse, place her on probation, suspend or refuse to renew her license, or even revoke her license. Other types of disciplinary action include imposing a probationary period, imposing a fine, and restricting the nurse's scope of practice. Some boards may require a nurse to take courses in the legal aspects of nursing.

The list of punishable violations varies from state to state. The most common are:

◆ conviction of a crime involving moral turpitude, if the offense bears directly on whether the person is fit to be licensed

◆ use of fraud or deceit in obtaining or attempting to obtain a nursing license

◆ incompetence because of negligence or because of physical or psychological impairments

◆ habitual use of or addiction to drugs or alcohol

◆ unprofessional conduct, including (but not limited to) falsifying, inaccurately recording, or improperly altering patient records; negligently administering medications or treatments; performing tasks beyond the limits of the state's nurse practice act; failing to take appropriate action to safeguard the patient from incompetent health care; violating the patient's confidentiality; taking on nursing duties that require skills and education beyond one's competence; violating the patient's dignity and human rights by basing nursing care on prejudice; abandoning a patient; and abusing a patient verbally or physically. The Pennsylvania Board of Nursing also has sexual misconduct regulations.

Administrative review process

When a nurse is accused of professional misconduct, the state board of nursing usually conducts an investigation, followed by an administrative review if the investigation warrants it.

Usually, the board's actions are "complaint driven," meaning that the board investigates complaints about licensees rather than actively looking for infractions of the nurse practice act to prosecute.

As an administrative body, the state board of nursing wields broad discretionary powers and can issue a decision or ruling. As a result, court proceedings, and possibly legal penalties, may result from the board's administrative review findings. You have the right to appeal through the court system for reversal of the nursing board's decision. (See *Disciplinary proceedings for nurse misconduct,* page 42.) It's important to remember that administrative proceedings are civil proceedings that are intended to be remedial in nature; they have no criminal bearing.

Steps in administrative review

In most states and jurisdictions, the nurse practice act and board of nursing rules and regulations specify the steps that the board of nursing must follow during an administrative review. In some states, a general administrative procedure act (separate from the nurse practice act) specifies the steps; in still other states, the board of nursing determines protocol.

An administrative review begins when a person, a health care facility (the nurse's employer), or a professional organization files a signed complaint against a nurse with the state board of nursing, or when the board itself initiates such action.

The board then reviews the complaint to decide if the nurse's action appears to violate the state's nurse practice act. It may begin the process by requesting a meeting with the nurse to discuss the allegations or ask the

Disciplinary proceedings for nurse misconduct

The flow chart below shows what happens when the state board of nursing takes disciplinary action against a nurse for violation of the state's nurse practice act.

Sworn complaint filed

A sworn complaint is brought before a state board by:
◆ a health care agency
◆ a professional organization
◆ an individual.
If the board finds sufficient evidence, it will conduct a formal review.

State board of nursing review

The board:
◆ reviews the evidence
◆ calls witnesses
◆ determines if the nurse is guilty of misconduct.
If the board finds the nurse guilty of misconduct, it can take disciplinary action.

Disciplinary action

The board can:
◆ issue a reprimand
◆ place the nurse on probation
◆ refuse to renew her license
◆ suspend her license
◆ revoke her license.
If the nurse wants to challenge the board's decision or disciplinary action, she can file an appeal in court.

Court review

The court will do one of two things, depending on the jurisdiction:
◆ rexamine the board's decision and decide if the board conducted the hearing properly
◆ conduct a trial.
If the nurse wants to challenge the court's ruling, she can appeal to a higher court.
If the board wants to appeal the court's ruling, it, too, can appeal to a higher court.

Appellate review

The nurse or the board can appeal for a reversal of the lower court's ruling.

nurse to submit a statement about the specific incident that led to the complaint. (The nurse should consult with a nurse-attorney, who has experience in disciplinary matters, before submitting any information to the board of nursing.) If the board decides that the nurse's actions were in violation of the state's nurse practice act, it prepares for a formal hearing, including subpoenaing witnesses. When these preparations begin, the accused nurse's due process rights include the right to receive timely notice of both the charge against her and the hearing date.

At the hearing, the nurse has the following due process rights:
◆ to have an attorney represent her
◆ to present evidence and cross-examine witnesses
◆ to appeal the board's decision to a court.

At the formal hearing, an impartial attorney may act as a hearing officer (in lieu of a judge), or the board itself may hear the case. A court reporter documents the entire proceeding, or it may be taped. Members of the board act as the plaintiffs bringing the claim against the defendant-nurse. Witnesses — including coworkers — testify for the board and the nurse.

It's possible to buy a medical insurance liability policy to cover legal expenses to defend against a complaint filed against you. Although nurses are usually protected by their health care employer's insurance liability policy, these employer policies only protect the nurse in the event of a civil nursing negligence or medical malpractice action. They don't protect the nurse in the event of an administrative board of nursing disciplinary investigation or hearing. Buying your own professional liability insurance policy provides you with protection against civil and administrative actions. Check with your malpractice carrier and expand your insurance coverage, if necessary.

Canadian administrative review
In Canada, the process for administrative review of complaints against nurses is similar to that in the United States. In some jurisdictions, a complaints committee of the jurisdictional nursing board hears the complaint first and either dismisses or endorses it. If the complaints committee endorses it, the complaint is sent along to a discipline committee for a full hearing. In other jurisdictions, only a discipline committee hears the complaint.

Note that, in many jurisdictions, an employer who terminates a nurse's employment for incompetence, misconduct, or incapacity must report the termination to the board of nursing in writing (this rule doesn't apply if the nurse's employer is a patient). If the employer fails to do this, the board may impose a fine.

Judicial review process
In every state, nurses have the right to challenge the board's disciplinary decisions by the process of appeal through the courts. This basic right can't be revoked by any means; in many states, this right is spelled out in the nurse practice act.

Each state and court jurisdiction sets its own rules on how to file this type of appeal. In some jurisdictions, the nurse, through her attorney, must appeal to a special court that handles only cases from state agencies. In other states, she must appeal to the lowest level court.

In an appeal, the court reviews the legality of the state board's original decision against the nurse — not the nurse's allegedly improper conduct. The court attempts only to determine whether the board of nursing exceeded its legal powers or conducted the hearing improperly. It decides if the state board's decision is unlawful, arbitrary, or unreasonable according to law, or whether it constitutes "abuse of discretion" (meaning the board didn't have enough evidence to determine unprofessional conduct, and so made a decision without proper foundation). The court may also review the original evidence before deciding whether to sustain or reverse the board's decision.

The court also may allow a *trial de novo*, in which the court hears the board's complete case against the nurse as though the administrative review had never happened. New evidence, if it exists, may be introduced by the plaintiff (the board) or by the defendant-nurse, through her attorney. The court hears the case and then either sustains or reverses the board's original decision.

If the defendant-nurse loses this appeal, she may — depending on the jurisdiction — appeal to a higher court. (If the nurse wins, the board of nursing can appeal to a higher court.) To begin the new appeal, the nurse's attorney must file it with the lower court that ruled against the nurse; this court will send the trial transcript and the appeal to the higher court. All states have rules and regulations governing appeals, and abiding by them is an attorney's legal responsibility.

The higher court decides whether to hear the appeal, based on its merits. The appeal usually must establish that the lower court made an error of law. The higher court won't hear the case a second time or reconsider facts, but the defendant-nurse and her attorney may continue to appeal through all higher courts up to the state's highest court. Exceptional cases may reach the U.S. Supreme Court.

Canadian nurses may also challenge disciplinary action through the court system. An appeal involves a written application to a superior court. The application states that the disciplinary tribunal made an error and requests that the superior court correct or modify the decision of the tribunal.

Court cases

Consider the following two cases, which describe the experience of two nurses during the administrative and judicial review.

In a Connecticut case, *Leib v. Board of Examiners for Nursing* (1979), a nurse was accused of improper conduct: charting the administration of meperidine to her patient but using the drug herself. After voluntarily admitting to this action, she testified on her own behalf at the board hearing. The board issued an order revoking her nursing license. The nurse appealed the revocation order to the court of common pleas. When this court dismissed her appeal, she appealed to the Supreme Court of Connecticut. This higher court also ruled that the evidence supported the board's findings of unprofessional conduct. The nurse's license was revoked. Other cases in which courts have upheld boards' decisions include *Tighe v. State Board of Nurse Examiners* (1979) and *Ullo v. State Board of Nurse Examiners* (1979).

In *Colorado State Board of Nurse Examiners v. Hohu* (1954), a physician filed a complaint of incompetence against a nurse, claiming that her failure to admit a patient quickly and to contact the physician caused the patient's injury. The board of nursing ordered the nurse's license revoked. However, when the nurse appealed, the court reversed the board's revocation order. This court ruled that the board of nursing had abused its discretionary powers because the evidence didn't support the physician's charges.

License reinstatement

License revocation, if sustained despite all appeal efforts, is usually permanent. Check to see whether your state's nurse practice act provides for revoked-license reinstatement.

If your license is suspended, you may petition for reinstatement. Every nurse practice act contains a provision allowing reinstatement of a suspended license, and some license-suspension orders specify a date when the nurse may apply. In most states, after a suspension has been in effect for more than a year, the board of nursing will consider reinstatement.

Your first step would probably be to petition the board for reinstatement. Then the board would have to decide whether you're qualified to practice nursing again. In some states, you have the right to another hearing before the board makes this decision.

The board usually bases its decision on current evidence of the nurse's fitness to practice. For example, in a drug violation case, the board may consider whether a nurse has successfully completed a drug rehabilitation program.

Selected references

American Nurses Association. *Standards of Clinical Nursing Practice*, 3rd ed. Washington, D.C.: American Nurses Publishing, 2004.

Buppert, C. "Choosing Among the Options of Malpractice Insurance," *The Gold Sheet* 4(8), 2002.

Carson, W.Y. "Nursing Malpractice: Protect Yourself," *AJN* 101(12):81, December 2001.

Clarke, S.P., and Patrician, P.A. "Entry into Practice in Ontario: A New Initiative May Have Implications for American Nursing," *AJN* 101(2):73-76, February 2001.

Wacker Guido, G. *Legal and Ethical Issues in Nursing*, 3rd ed. Upper Saddle River, N.J.: Prentice Hall, Inc., 2001.

Joint Commission of Accreditation of Healthcare Organizations. 2004 National Patient Safety Goals. Online: *www.jcaho.org.*

Michel, L.G. "Leveling the Playing Field: Nurses' Rights in State Board Disciplinary Actions," *Kansas Nurse* 78(1):1-2, January 2003.

Pohlman, K.J. "Nursing Discipline: Demystifying the Process," *Journal of School Nurses* 19(1):52-57, February 2003.

Rodgers, S.J. "The Role of Nursing Theory in Standards of Practice: A Canadian Perspective," *Nursing Sciences Quarterly* 13(3):260-62, July 2000.

Thomas, S.A., et al. "State and Territorial Boards of Nursing Approaches to the Use of Unlicensed Assistive Personnel," *JONA'S Healthcare Law, Ethics, and Regulation* 2(1):13-21, March 2000.

Chapter 2

Working in diverse clinical settings

Although each state's and each province's nurse practice act and medical practice act are intended to distinguish between the two professions, social, professional, and judicial forces have blurred the distinction. In an era of managed care, nurses are now expected and legally able to perform many of the tasks formerly reserved for physicians. Therefore, nurses are required to take on more responsibility.

Nursing practice vs. medical practice

Knowing precisely where nurse and medical practice acts differ and where they overlap can be difficult; relevant statutes may lack specific detail. Be aware that not knowing exactly where nursing practice begins and ends can create some legal risks.

When state legislatures began writing medical and nurse practice acts, a physician could legally perform any task a nurse performed. That remains true, although many physicians today are unfamiliar with certain nursing practices. Legislatures also reserved certain tasks exclusively for physicians, and a nurse who performs such tasks does so at her own legal peril. To help

limit liability, learn as much as you can about your state's nurse practice act. Doing so will help you better determine where your practice stops and where medical practice begins.

FORCES CAUSING CHANGE

In part, the law is responding to patients' increasing expectations of nurses. Patients are filing (and winning) more lawsuits that express their expectation that nurses provide expanded patient care, including some forms of medical diagnosis, treatment, and referral. In addition, hospitals and physicians have delegated more authority to nurses. For example, nursing responsibilities in intensive care units (ICUs) and critical care units (CCUs) include diagnosis (reading electrocardiograms) and treatment (performing cardiopulmonary resuscitation).

Reductions in health care funding have also led to increased responsibilities for nurses, whose lower salaries make them less costly than physicians.

DEFINING MEDICAL PRACTICE

Medical practice acts may be divided into two types: those that define medical practice and those that don't. Both types forbid non-physicians from practicing medicine. (No Canadian law related to medical practice defines it.)

When a state's medical practice act includes a definition, it usually defines *medicine* as any act of diagnosis, prescription, surgery, or treatment. However, not every definition includes all four elements, and some states' definitions include additional elements while excluding others.

LEGISLATIVE RESPONSE

Some states have solved the problem of overlap between the nursing and medical professions by passing laws making some functions common to both. New York's law, for example, allows both registered nurses (RNs) and physicians to diagnose and treat patients, with the proviso that a nursing diagnosis shouldn't alter a patient's medical regimen. Almost all states permit a nurse to perform patient care that a physician requests, as long as a written or an oral order exists and the requested action is reasonable and safe.

Some state medical practice acts limit physicians' rights to delegate tasks. For example, the Texas Medical Practice Act permits physicians to delegate tasks only to "any qualified and properly trained person or persons," and then only if doing so is "reasonable and prudent," and if the delegating doesn't violate any other state laws. Most state courts would probably interpret their state medical practice acts similarly, even if this restriction isn't written explicitly into their acts.

In most jurisdictions, the boards of nursing and medicine jointly determine which medical tasks may be delegated to nurses and specify the requirements for appropriate delegation.

COURT RULINGS

The courts are called on regularly to decide if a specific action constitutes medical practice. One area of considerable overlap between nursing and medicine is midwifery. In the past, the courts often decided that delivering babies was a medical rather than a nursing function. In the early case of *Commonwealth v. Porn* (1907), a Massachusetts court upheld the conviction of a nurse-midwife for practicing medicine without a license. More recently, however, in *Leigh v. Board of Registration in Nursing* (1985), the same court said that the basis for conviction in the *Porn* case wasn't the practice of midwifery *per se,* but the nurse's use of obstetric instruments and prescription formulas. The court went so far as to hold that the practice of midwifery, in ordinary circumstances, isn't to be considered the practice of medicine.

Some court decisions have concluded that a physician need not be present during patient care once he has delegated a task to a nurse. These decisions have been interpreted to mean that a nurse may perform some medical tasks on the basis of standing orders and nursing protocols as well as on the basis of a physician's written and oral orders. Consequently, a nurse's scope of actions, when working under standing orders or nursing protocols, can be broad in certain practice settings, no matter how restrictive her state nurse practice act.

Standing orders and nursing protocols allow the nurse to perform tasks that involve overlap of nursing and medical practices—such as ICU, CCU, and I.V. team practice—in states where the nurse practice acts don't typically grant nurses clear-cut independent authority to treat patients.

Argument over anesthesia

Many court cases that test principles involving the overlap of nursing and medical practice concern anesthesia treatment and emergency department diagnosis. Interestingly, courts seldom give more than a passing reference to their state practice acts when dealing with these problems.

In *Mohr v. Jenkins* (1980), the patient sued a nurse anesthetist, claiming that she incorrectly injected diazepam into his arm and caused phlebitis. The court dismissed the suit, saying that the nurse "performed the procedure correctly and conformed to accepted medical practice." The patient appealed, but the appellate court affirmed that the standard for "specialists in similar circumstances" is "accepted medical practice" and that the defendant-nurse had met the appropriate standards.

A similar result occurred in *Whitney v. Day* (1980). In this case, a Michigan court said—without reference to the practice acts—that nurse anesthetists are professionals with expertise in an area akin to medical practice. As such, the court said they could be held to the same practice standards as those of the "similar specialist."

AVOIDING MEDICAL DECISIONS MAY BE ILLEGAL

In some situations, you have no alternative to practicing medicine without a license, and the courts expect you to do so when a patient requires treatment. In *Cooper v. National Motor Bearing Co.* (1955), a California nurse was accused of failing to make a medical diagnosis of cancer in one of her patients. The nurse defended herself by arguing that state law at that time prohibited her from making diagnoses of any sort. The court ruled against her, finding that nurses were supposed to

have sufficient education to tell whether a patient had signs or symptoms of a disease that would require a physician's attention. In *Stahlin v. Hilton Hotels Corp.* (1973), a federal court in Illinois reached a similar conclusion when a nurse failed to recognize that her patient's complaint resulted from a subdural hematoma rather than from drunkenness.

Don't assume, however, that courts always ignore the difference between medical practice and expanded nursing roles. A case in point is *Hernicz v. Florida Department of Professional Regulation* (1980). It involved a nurse practitioner who examined and treated two patients without a physician's orders. The state board of nursing suspended his license, and the court's decision upheld the suspension.

In general, the courts interpret the law in ways most likely to protect patients. If protecting patients means not strictly interpreting nursing and medical practice acts, the courts usually follow that course.

Of course, in all situations in which you've called a physician about the care and treatment of a patient, document that communication in the medical record. Such documentation will support an argument that it wasn't acceptable for a nurse to make the final decision.

DEFINING NURSING PRACTICE

Although nurse practice acts vary from state to state, they set the minimum standards for safe and competent nursing practice. These acts define the legal boundaries of the scope of nursing. However, the scope of nursing is more than about legal boundaries and minimum standards.

According to the Social Policy Statement of the American Nurses Association (ANA), *nursing* is the diagnosis and treatment of human responses to health and illness. This is essentially the scope of nursing practice. However, the way each nurse functions and performs her duties within the scope of nursing practice is defined by the education and experience of that particular nurse, her current role or position, the nature of the patient population she cares for, and the clinical setting in which the nurse practices nursing.

Nursing practice and unlicensed assistive personnel

Besides defining the scope of nursing practice with respect to the medical profession, nurses must also define their responsibilities with respect to supervising unlicensed assistive personnel (UAPs).

Pressures to limit health care costs are causing employers to use more UAPs to assist in patient care. UAPs aren't new to the health care system. In fact, many nurse practice acts allow a nurse to delegate to UAPs. For example, the Maryland Nurse Practice Act states that the nurse may delegate the responsibility to perform a nursing task to an unlicensed individual.

For years, hospitals and extended-care facilities have employed nurses' aides and assistants; both of these groups fall into the category of UAP. However, educational requirements and on-the-job responsibilities for UAPs aren't uniformly defined by statutes. Thus, RNs may not have a clear understanding of what UAPs are capable of doing or how to utilize them.

To avoid liability, the nurse must understand the state's position regarding delegation. If the nurse practice act doesn't address the topic, the nurse must rely on the employer's policy. At a minimum, the employer should have a policy dictating criteria for such delegation. Typically, the criteria mandate that the nurse understand the UAP's level of skill. The nurse should delegate only when the UAP is competent to perform the task. Even then, the nurse must evaluate the outcome and assure that the task and outcome are accurately performed and documented in the medical record. The nurse must understand that the responsibility for the task can be delegated but not the accountability.

The ANA has defined UAPs as individuals trained to function in an assistive role to the professional registered nurse in the provision of patient care activities, as delegated by and under the supervision of that nurse. Therefore, nurses are responsible for the education, training, and supervision of UAPs who participate in direct patient care. However, many questions remain unanswered, including questions about the educational requirements for UAPs and to what extent UAPs can participate in direct patient care. (See *Supervising unlicensed assistive personnel*, page 50.)

Legal risks in diverse clinical settings

Nurses work in a wide range of clinical settings. Although most nurses work in the hospital setting, many others work as private-duty nurses or in long-term care facilities, home health care, schools, or free-standing clinics. The law affects these nurses in different ways, which is why it's important to know the subtleties of your particular field.

LEGAL TIP
Supervising unlicensed assistive personnel

If you supervise unlicensed assistive personnel (UAPs), you're responsible and liable for their performance. Limit your liability by educating yourself and advocating that your employer establish policies that clearly delineate the responsibilities of registered nurses, licensed practical nurses, and UAPs.

◆ Attend all educational programs your employer sponsors with respect to supervising UAPs.

◆ Encourage your supervisors to establish a written policy that defines the actions UAPs may take.

◆ Work cooperatively with UAPs. It's in your patients' best interest for you to establish a solid working relationship with them.

◆ Educate your patients about what UAPs can and can't do for them during your assigned work time. This will help them ask the appropriate individuals to assist them with their needs.

◆ If problems or disagreements arise over the appropriate functions for UAPs, report to your nurse-manager for immediate resolution.

◆ Review your state nurse practice act for provisions about delegation to UAPs. Follow all criteria for proper delegation set forth in the act.

◆ Stay current with your state nursing board's recommendations about working with UAPs.

WORKING AS A PRIVATE-DUTY NURSE

A private-duty nurse is any authorized RN or licensed practical nurse (LPN) that a patient or his family hires for total nursing care. (Some states, such as Maine, don't allow LPNs to become private-duty nurses.) Working as a private-duty nurse allows you to devote all your nursing skills to the care of one patient. Other advantages of working as a private-duty nurse include choosing where you work, when you work, and what type of patient you care for as well as setting your own fee.

Employment status is the major factor that distinguishes a private-duty nurse from an agency nurse. A private-duty nurse is an independent contractor. She bills her patient or a third-party insurer directly. (See *Should you practice as an independent contractor?*) An agency may indirectly provide authorized private-duty nursing services, but in that instance the nurse works for the agency. (For more information, see "Working as an agency nurse," page 65.)

A hospital or other health care facility may also hire a private-duty nurse. If that's the case, the private-duty nurse will bill the hospital for reimbursement directly. (See the discussion of *Emory University v. Shadburn* [1933] under "Hospital Care," page 52.)

Patients are referred to a private-duty nurse through nurse registries and referrals from other nurses and physicians who are familiar with the nurse's practice. Many hospitals maintain referral lists of private-duty nurses. If you work as a private-duty nurse long enough, you'll build up a clientele of hospitals, other health care facilities, nurses, physicians, and families.

LEGAL
TIP

Should you practice as an independent contractor?

Thousands of nurses in the United States have chosen to become independent contractors. They work directly for patients (or patients' families) and bill their patients (or third-party insurers) on a fee-for-service basis. If you're considering practicing on an independent contractor basis, first weigh the pros and cons.

Pros

◆ You can schedule your work hours to suit your lifestyle.

◆ You can put your nursing philosophy into practice by independently planning each patient's nursing care.

◆ You'll be relatively free from institutional politics and bureaucracy.

◆ You can negotiate your own contract with each patient and set your own fee.

◆ You'll assume a more prestigious role in the health care community, and your working relations with other professionals may improve.

◆ You'll keep more of your earnings because tax laws favor self-employment.

◆ You can tailor your benefits package to your own personal needs.

◆ You can become more involved in the total care of your patient.

Cons

◆ You'll lose the security that continuous employment provides.

◆ You may experience strained working relations with professionals who feel threatened by your autonomy.

◆ You'll have to compete for work with other nurses who also are independent contractors.

◆ Your patients may be admitted to hospitals or other health care facilities where you don't have privileges.

◆ You'll have to educate yourself about the financial and legal aspects of running a business.

◆ You'll have to deal with getting patients to pay their bills.

◆ You'll carry the full responsibility for your liability and, if named in a lawsuit, be obligated to pay the entire cost of any damages awarded to a plaintiff.

Scope and limits of private-duty nursing

A private-duty nurse performs most tasks a hospital staff nurse performs, and she's expected to have the same degree of knowledge and skill. She plans a patient's care, observes and evaluates his condition, reports signs and symptoms, carries out treatments under a physician's direction, and keeps accurate records so that the patient's physician has the data he needs to diagnose and prescribe. It's a private-duty nurse's obligation to perform her job within the scope of her state nurse practice act—the same as a staff nurse. A private-duty nurse working in a hospital setting can expect the hospital to provide her with adequate equipment and support services for proper patient care.

Private-duty nurses should be aware of the various states' laws on reimbursement, because they vary from state-to-state. Depending on the state, certain services may not be reimbursable under a state's Medicaid Administrative Code because they may not fall under the category of "skilled nursing."

Legal risks

A private-duty nurse faces legal risks not encountered by the hospital staff nurse. For example, a private-duty nurse doesn't retain professional liability insurance through an employer. As an independent contractor, she's solely liable for any damages assessed as the result of a lawsuit—although a court may decide that a hospital shares liability for her actions if the malpractice or injury occurred within the hospital. So, if you work as a private-duty nurse, you must purchase professional liability insurance.

Home health care

As an independent contractor, your legal risks are highest when you care for a patient in his home. You're responsible not only for providing proper care but also for obtaining and correctly using any equipment the patient requires, and for recognizing and acting on the need for appropriate referral. These added responsibilities naturally increase your chances of making a mistake. What's more, because you're self-employed, legally you're solely responsible for paying court-ordered damages if you're sued and found negligent.

Making written contracts with your patient can help to reduce your legal risks. Although a contract spells out the conditions of your employment, having a contract doesn't prevent a lawsuit, nor can it provide evidence that will exonerate you if you're sued.

Hospital care

The case of *Emory University v. Shadburn* (1933) set a precedent for a hospital's liability for a private-duty nurse's wrongful conduct. A patient jumped out a window after the assigned private-duty nurse—who had reason to know that his condition warranted continuous watching—left him unattended. The court ruled that the hospital was liable for the nurse's negligence because the hospital had hired and paid the nurse on a private-duty basis.

A hospital usually insists on tight control of a private-duty nurse's practice, both to protect patients and to demonstrate "reasonable supervision" in case of a lawsuit. Because of the trend to make hospitals share liability, you'll probably face liability alone only if you commit a negligent act despite the hospital's reasonable supervision.

Hospital controls include checking every private-duty nurse's credentials and approving her nursing qualifications. The case of *Ashley v. Nyack Hospital* (1979) ruled that a hospital has the right to refuse practice privileges to a nurse if the hospital doesn't approve her qualifications. Most hospitals also establish policies to govern how private-duty nursing relates to hospital nursing practice. Hospitals are obligated to inform all health care team members about private-duty nurses' responsibilities and rights in the hospital.

Financial burdens

If you work as an independent contractor, you must manage certain financial burdens. For example, you're responsible for making social security payments and paying federal, state, and local taxes on schedule. If you're injured on the job, you aren't eligible for workers' compensation benefits. The courts have repeatedly rejected private-duty nurses' claims for workers' compensation. For example, in a Maryland case, *Edith Anderson Nursing Homes, Inc. v. Bettie Walker* (1963), a private-duty nurse was hurt caring for a nursing home patient who was in a wheelchair. The nurse attempted to collect workers' compensation benefits from the nursing home because her injury occurred there. At that time, however, the nurse was an independent contractor who was paid by the patient's family, didn't work for the nursing home, and took her orders only from the patient's physician. As an independent contractor, the court ruled, she wasn't entitled to the benefits available to the nursing home's employees. A subsequent appellate court decision upheld the denial of the nurse's claim. Therefore, the private-duty nurse should obtain her own insurance for such situations.

Professional challenges

Working *as* a private-duty nurse and working *with* a private-duty nurse each present their own unique challenges.

Working as a private-duty nurse requires you to conform to your state's laws. Many states impose a laundry list of regulations on private-duty nurses (such as the minimum number of hours they must work for each patient), and it's important to follow them and keep up with any changes. You must also know how your patient is paying. If the patient is insured by a health maintenance organization, Medicare, or Medicaid, you must meet the requirements listed in order to obtain reimbursement.

Other professional challenges include building a clientele; collaborating with physicians, health care prescribers, and patients and their families; and keeping up on medical research and clinical techniques.

If you're working on a unit on which a private-duty nurse is working, you're responsible for seeing that the private-duty nurse receives the help she needs. However, your responsibility doesn't end there — you're still responsible for the patient.

Monitor the private-duty nurse's care. If you're a staff nurse and you see the private-duty nurse negligently performing care, inform your charge nurse. If you're the charge nurse, intervene immediately. Regardless of your staff position, if you see the private-duty nurse negligently performing emergency care when the patient's life is in danger, intervene immediately. If you ignore the private-duty nurse's negligence, you and the hospital could be liable if the patient or his family files a malpractice lawsuit.

If you're a charge nurse, remember that the private-duty nurse's contract outlines her responsibilities. Read over the contract and keep its provisions in mind when you make assignments. Never assign a private-duty nurse a job that involves responsibilities not included in her contract.

WORKING IN A LONG-TERM CARE FACILITY

The United States Census Bureau estimates that by 2010, Americans age 65 and older will make up more than 13% of the population. This trend means that more patients will be cared for in long-term care facilities such as nursing homes.

The rapid growth in the number of nursing homes and nursing home patients began in 1965, when Congress passed the Medicare and Medicaid amendments to the Social Security Act. These amendments provided government reimbursement for long-term care of elderly and disabled patients.

The Medicare and Medicaid amendments also provided reimbursement for skilled nursing care in extended-care facilities. These facilities were initially planned to deliver short-term nursing care to elderly patients who no longer needed intensive medical and nursing

Helping your patient select a long-term care facility

Your elderly or disabled patient may need the care provided at a long-term care facility. Help the patient and his family choose a facility by explaining the three types of long-term care facilities available and what type of care each offers.

Residential-care facility
Best for a patient who needs minimal medical attention, a residential-care facility provides meals, modest medical care, and assistance with housekeeping responsibilities. Some offer recreational and social programs as well.

Intermediate-care facility
Best for a patient who can't manage independently, an intermediate-care facility provides room, board, and daily nursing care. The cost may be covered by government subsidy programs. Some offer rehabilitation programs as well as recreational programs.

Skilled nursing facility
Best for a patient who needs constant medical attention, a skilled nursing facility provides 24-hour nursing care, medical care when needed, and such rehabilitation services as physical and occupational therapies. Depending on the patient's eligibility, Medicare or Medicaid may subsidize the cost.

Scope and limits of long-term care nursing

Nurses in long-term care facilities provide skilled nursing, such as administering medications and patient teaching. They must be familiar with geriatric and rehabilitative medicine. The majority of the long-term care workforce includes nursing assistants, home health care aides, personal care workers, and personal care attendants. It's important for the nurse to work with these health care workers effectively and delegate responsibilities efficiently.

Liability
Although the focus of long-term care nursing is on caring for those who are recovering from an illness (short-term) and providing supervision and medical care for those who have chronic medical problems (long-term), all patients in such facilities must be under the care of a physician. However, the fact that a patient is under a physican's care doesn't absolve you from sharing in the responsibility for his care. If a patient's medical condition becomes emergent and goes unnoticed or if a patient's care doesn't meet reasonable standards, you may be held liable.

Substandard care
Many long-term care facilities come under attack by state licensing and certification agencies for providing substandard care. (See *Helping your patient select a long-term care facility.*) One major problem is that long-term care facilities employ only a small number of registered nurses. In 1996, the Institute of Medicine, which was chartered in 1970 by the National Academy of Sciences, released the results of a study that found that, although sickness and disability have increased among nursing home patients, employers' demands for nursing services haven't kept pace.

care in a hospital. Today, most patients admitted to long-term care facilities come directly from hospitals or other health care facilities.

Medicare and Medicaid payments aren't sufficient to pay for adequate nursing staff. Ironically, Medicare and Medicaid payments, intended by Congress to help elderly and disabled patients, have inadvertently resulted in substandard care by subsidizing unsafe and understaffed facilities.

Aware of these trying circumstances, many RNs and LPNs working in long-term care facilities are greatly concerned about their legal rights and responsibilities. Areas of concern include staffing patterns, quality of care, and patients' rights.

Staffing patterns

In most long-term care facilities, RNs hold administrative positions, shouldering supervisory responsibility for the quality of care. LPNs in many facilities work as charge nurses, performing most nursing procedures and supervising nursing assistants. Patients may depend on nurses' aides for a substantial amount of care. This arrangement, created by minimal licensed-personnel staffing, may lead to legal problems concerning both supervision and the scope of nursing practice. (See *Minimal licensed-personnel staffing*.)

Legally, a supervisor is responsible for her supervisory acts and decisions. Suppose a supervisor knows — or should know — that a subordinate is inexperienced, untrained, or unable to perform a task safely. A court may indeed find that supervisor liable in a malpractice lawsuit for delegating such a task to the subordinate. To limit liability, a supervisor must determine that the individual to whom tasks are delegated is competent to perform the tasks. Even then, the supervisor must evaluate the outcomes of the performance of the tasks.

If the subordinate performs a task negligently, she'll also be liable. Fur-

Minimal licensed-personnel staffing

Health care professionals use the term minimal licensed-personnel staffing to describe the staffing situation in many long-term care facilities. Consider the following statistics:

◆ Only about 1 of every 20 nursing home employees is an registered nurse.

◆ Only about 1 licensed health care professional is employed for every 100 nursing home patients.

◆ Physicians spend only about 2 hours per month with their nursing home patients.

◆ In some extended-care facilities, about 6 of 10 charge nurses on the 3 p.m. to 11 p.m. shift and about 7 of 10 charge nurses on the 11 p.m. to 7 a.m. shift are licensed practical nurses.

thermore, if the court finds that the supervisor and the subordinate were working within the scope of their employment, the nursing home may share liability under the doctrine of *respondeat superior*.

In determining whether the defendant-nurse's actions met professional standards for her position, the courts may review details of the staffing situation. For example, a New York court found that nurses were negligent when an unsupervised patient jumped from a balcony (*Horton v. Niagara Falls Memorial Medical Center* [1976]). The court reached this conclusion after reviewing evidence detailing how many patients were on the unit, how many staff members were there, and what each staff member was doing. During this review, the court discovered that a charge nurse had permitted the only available nurses' aide to go to supper when she had the authority to prevent it, leaving the disoriented patient unsupervised.

As an RN or LPN working in a long-term care facility, you must practice within the legal limits set by your state's nurse practice act, meet professional standards for your position, and be familiar with state regulations for the type of facility in which you work.

If you're an RN, make sure you possess the management and supervisory skills required by your job. Keep in mind that if you're sued for malpractice, you'll be judged according to how a reasonably prudent nursing supervisor would act in similar circumstances. You can't defend yourself by claiming that you weren't trained to supervise.

If you're an LPN working in a long-term care facility, remember that no person or facility can force you to practice beyond the limits outlined in your state's nurse practice act. If you exceed the legally permissible scope of nursing practice in your state, your state board of nursing can suspend or revoke your license. You won't be able to use your employer's expectations to excuse your actions.

Under the law, an LPN who performs a nursing function legally restricted to RNs will be held to the RN standard if she's sued for malpractice. *Barber v. Reinking* (1966) involved an LPN who had performed an RN function. The court stated, "In accordance with public policy of this state, one who undertakes to perform the services of a trained or graduate nurse must have the knowledge and skill possessed by the registered nurse."

Quality of care

Many nurses working in long-term care facilities are particularly concerned about the fragmentation of the nursing process. Although an RN remains responsible for overall patient assessment and evaluation, an LPN decides on the daily assessments, planning, and evaluation, and a nurses' aide implements the assessment plan.

Fragmenting the nursing process can greatly reduce the quality of patient care. It can also have legal consequences if nursing actions are performed improperly — or not performed at all. This list describes poor nursing practices that plague long-term care facilities:

◆ Failing to make a nursing diagnosis
◆ Being careless in the observation of a patient's condition
◆ Failing to document
◆ Writing illegibly when documenting
◆ Failing to keep up with current nursing knowledge required to care for elderly and disabled patients
◆ Failing to use nursing consultants
◆ Delegating improperly
◆ Failing to insist on clear facility policies
◆ Failing to question an order
◆ Taking a dangerous patient care shortcut
◆ Excluding the patient's family from patient care
◆ Failing to call the physician whenever nursing judgment indicates that a patient needs medical attention.

Consider the case of an RN named Adams who reported unsafe staffing levels at his facility in Massachusetts. He was harassed by management and then fired in 1996. Mr. Adams filed a lawsuit and a complaint with the National Labor Relations Board (NLRB), and both a judge and the NLRB ruled that he was wrongfully terminated (NLRB case 1-CA-34663[1-2] and 1-CA-34699). Mr. Adams filed a complaint with the Massachusetts Board of Nursing against his former nursing supervisor alleging unprofessional and unethical conduct. The complaint stated that, based on her actions, she condoned the unsafe staffing levels that may have contributed to a patient's death. Massachusetts Board of Nursing members said the allegations were either lacking in sufficient evidence or had been resolved.

Patients' rights
Many states have enacted patients' rights legislation patterned after the Patient's Bill of Rights published by the American Hospital Association. Most of these states have passed laws that make reporting maltreatment of patients a legal responsibility. Some states have even established an ombudsman's office that has the authority to investigate complaints of abuse and the obligation to post complaint procedures in all geriatric facilities.

On the federal level, the Omnibus Budget Reconciliation Act of 1987 dramatically strengthens the rights of nursing home residents. The law says that nursing home residents have the right to choose a personal attending physician, to participate in planning their own care and treatment, and to be free from physical or mental abuse, corporal punishment, and physical or chemical restraints imposed for purposes of discipline or convenience. The law also imposes new requirements for additional nursing staff. In 1989, the Department of Health and Human Services, in an effort to carry out the 1987 law, issued new rules governing Medicare and Medicaid reimbursement for nursing homes.

Steps you can take
If you work in a long-term care facility, you should request that your facility:
◆ require a patient's signature for any release of information

◆ clearly specify who has access to medical records and impose penalties for unauthorized disclosure of patient information
◆ foster a patient's right to know about his condition and provide for informed consent for his treatment
◆ help combat drug abuse and misuse by requiring nurses who administer drugs to know the effects of the drugs and know how to assess each patient's changing needs
◆ ensure prompt, effective communication between physicians and nurses
◆ acknowledge and respect a patient's right to refuse treatment
◆ encourage nurses to evaluate the quality of nursing services
◆ encourage nurses to work cooperatively with patient representatives and accreditation agencies
◆ restrict the use of chemical and physical restraints; restraints should be used only when the patient's physical or mental status gives evidence that they're necessary (and even then only with a physician's order) and solely for the patient's safety.

Protecting your job
Most health care professionals are patients' rights advocates, but advocating your patient's rights may lead to conflicts with your coworkers and employers. This is one paradox of nursing practice: You have a professional obligation to protect your patient's rights — but doing so could cost you your job. Unfortunately, your legal protection in this situation is limited. If you're an employee working without a contract, also known as *employee-at-will,* you can be dismissed for any reason your employer wants to give. You do have legal grounds to protest your dismissal if:
◆ your contract clearly states that you can't be fired on these grounds

◆ your facility guarantees you the right to notice and a hearing before dismissal

◆ your state's laws prevent your employer from retaliating if you report violations to the appropriate agency

◆ you're a government employee and can claim the First Amendment right to free speech.

Financial burdens

Because many long-term care patients are Medicare or Medicaid recipients, the nurse must be familiar with the strict federal medical coding for billing. She should ensure that the long-term care facility follows strict billing procedures.

Professional challenges

You'll encounter many challenges working in a long-term care facility, including those related to time management, a patient's quality of life, declining functional and cognitive status, chronic health conditions, interactions with a patient and his family over an extended period, and end-of-life issues. It's important to handle these challenges with care that's based on your nursing practice act and your board of nursing rules and regulations; doing so ensures you solid legal standing.

Opportunities

In a long-term care facility, in which physicians' involvement with patients is limited, RNs and LPNs have an opportunity to grow professionally and to influence the quality of patient care. If you're an RN, you'll learn not only geriatric nursing but also good management. If you're an LPN, you may have the chance to fill a charge nurse position and to expand your nursing skills. Depending on your nurse practice act, you may also learn how to

perform nursing assessment and patient teaching. However, keep in mind that along with opportunity comes responsibility — for practicing within legal limits and for continuing your education to meet professional standards.

WORKING IN AN ALTERNATIVE PRACTICE SETTING

Practicing nursing outside of traditional settings — such as hospitals, clinics, and nursing homes — dates back to the 19th century. Back then, most nurses worked outside hospitals: in physicians' offices, in patients' homes, and on battlefields. Today, many nurses practice in alternative settings. Their employers include factories, schools, the military, insurance companies, and claims review agencies. (See *Providing nursing care in alternative settings,* pages 59 and 60, and *Legal considerations in hospice care,* page 61.)

When working in an alternative setting, you may not have the legal services of a hospital's administration to provide assistance during a dispute. You must take on the special challenge of knowing your legal responsibilities.

Scope and limits of alternative practice nursing

Most states' nurse practice acts don't discuss professional standards for nurses working in alternative settings. However, you still must meet the same practice standards as a hospital nurse. If you violate those standards, your state board of nursing may suspend or revoke your license, just as it would if you were a hospital nurse, and your patient may sue you for malpractice.

Historically, courts have held nurses who work in alternative settings to state standards for nursing practice. A California malpractice case, *Cooper v. National Motor Bearing Co.* (1955), con-

Providing nursing care in alternative settings

Nurses choose to practice in alternative settings for many reasons: to take on greater challenges and achieve more responsibility, for a change of pace, to increase their earning power, or to make an impact on public health policy.

The list below describes some of the important options for nurses today: school nursing, occupational health nursing, air rescue nursing, and hospice nursing. You'll also find descriptions of nursing opportunities in the business world: working as a case coordinator for an insurance company, making it on your own as an entrepreneur, or working in the legal arena.

School nurse

As a school nurse, your responsibilities include providing nursing care for sick or injured students and giving first aid in emergencies. When authorized, you also administer medications to students. Other tasks include:
◆ assisting in examinations
◆ giving annual screening tests – for example, vision, audiometry, and scoliosis tests – and referring students for further testing or treatment when appropriate
◆ counseling parents and students
◆ meeting with teachers and other staff members about health problems and health education programs
◆ enforcing state immunization policies for school-age children
◆ visiting sick or injured students at home when necessary
◆ helping identify and meet special needs of disabled students.

Occupational health nurse

As an occupational health nurse, your primary responsibility is to provide nursing care for sick or injured employees. Other responsibilities include:
◆ giving first aid in emergencies

◆ performing medical screening tests or helping the physician perform them
◆ referring sick or injured employees for appropriate treatment
◆ counseling employees on health matters
◆ meeting with management regarding health-related issues
◆ developing and maintaining employee medical records
◆ maintaining records for government agencies such as workers' compensation agencies, the Occupational Safety and Health Administration, and state or federal labor and health departments
◆ alerting management to potential health and safety hazards.

Air rescue nurse

As an air rescue nurse, you have a job that's glamorous, challenging, and hazardous. Many of the dilemmas that you and your fellow air rescue nurses face are unique and, as a small group, you don't have much power to exact change. Dilemmas include:
◆ scheduled 24-hour shifts for nurses and pilots, which cause concerns for quality work and safety for everyone on board the helicopter
◆ right to refuse an assigned flight because of personal safety concerns
◆ applying patient restraints unnecessarily or risking patients with borderline behavior becoming violent during flight and jeopardizing all on board
◆ safety concerns related to loading and unloading while rotor blades are in motion
◆ protective equipment for the helicopter and protective gear for crew members, which is lacking in most helicopters
◆ air rescue nurse familiarity with aircraft-specific emergency procedures and equipment.

(continued)

Providing nursing care in alternative settings *(continued)*

Hospice nurse

As a hospice nurse, your most important responsibility is to provide skilled nursing care to the terminally ill patient. Expect to focus on providing pain relief and symptom control. Patients and their families rely heavily on you for emotional and psychosocial support. Professional satisfaction typically comes from knowing that you've helped the dying patient maintain dignity and make the most of the time he has left. The most significant means of limiting your liability is to review advance directives and living wills that have been prepared on behalf of the patients. If these documents haven't been drafted, you need to consider reviewing these issues with the patient to prepare for the ultimate care and treatment. Before your patient becomes unconscious, review options with him so his wishes are carried out.

Nursing case coordinator for an insurance company

When working for an insurance company, your responsibilities may include reviewing records and assessing insurance claims by talking with the patient, his physician, his family, and his employer. You may be asked to help design patient care plans. These care plans typically include medical, nursing, social service, and payment goals. You may also monitor the patient's progress and prognosis by talking with the patient and his physicians. Other tasks include:

◆ helping to coordinate medical, rehabilitation, and other services

◆ supervising other nursing case reviewers

◆ developing and maintaining insurance company records.

Nurse entrepreneur

As an entrepreneur, you must organize and manage your own business undertaking. You take on the risk of failure for the sake of potential profit. Your opportunity to apply nursing skills as an entrepreneur is limited only by your own imagination. For example, nurses have established successful businesses providing such services as reviewing medical records and performing research for insurance companies and personal injury lawyers; finding medical experts for testimony in medical malpractice actions, personal injury litigation, and workers' compensation matters; and developing educational programs for use inside hospitals.

In Canada, self-employed nurses are permitted to offer any service that falls within the practice of nursing and doesn't infringe upon the exclusive practice of another health discipline. The service requires applying professional nursing knowledge. Services offered include direct patient care such as patient teaching about breast-feeding for new mothers; family counseling; health promotion services, such as stress management or occupational health nursing services; and administrative services such as quality assurance monitoring in health care facilities and agencies.

Nursing in the legal arena

As a legal nurse consultant, you provide valuable support during the investigation and litigation of claims, serve as expert witnesses, and review medical records. Many nurses work as independent contractors to provide these services to law firms.

Nurse expert witnesses provide advice during litigation and testify in court about nursing issues. Although there's no special training for the witness role, an attorney will consider nursing experience and credentials when choosing an expert witness.

Nurses who pursue additional education may become attorneys or paralegals. Nurse paralegals primarily research law and write as well as organize and examine medical records in a medical negligence case.

cerned an occupational health nurse who failed to diagnose suspected cancer and didn't refer the patient for further evaluation and treatment. At the trial, the court ruled that the only point of law to be considered in deciding the case was whether the nurse met the standards of nursing practice in her area. When expert testimony showed that she had breached those standards, the court found her negligent. Her occupational setting was irrelevant to the court's decision. Similar court cases illustrating this principle include *Planned Parenthood of Northwest Ind. v. Vines* (1989), *Barber v. Reinking* (1966), and *Stahlin v. Hilton Hotels Corp.* (1973).

The Canadian approach to such cases is similar to the American approach. In *Dowey v. Rothwell* (1974), a nurse who worked in a physician's office knew that an epileptic patient was about to have a seizure, yet she failed to stay with the patient. This patient did have a seizure, fell, and fractured an arm. The court found that the nurse failed "to provide that minimum standard of care which a patient has a right to expect in an office setting." The court based its findings on testimony about the expected performance standards of experienced RNs in many settings.

Liability

In certain cases, if you work in an alternative setting, you may be protected from a liability suit. For example, if you work for a government agency, you may be protected from lawsuits because of the doctrine of sovereign immunity. Depending on the state in which you're working, this immunity may be complete or partial. To determine the extent of the immunity, check with your personnel office or

LEGAL TIP

Legal considerations in hospice care

If you work in a hospice, be aware of these special legal responsibilities.

Standing orders

A hospital staff nurse can follow standing orders for pain medication. When working in a hospice, however, never rely on standing orders as authorization to administer pain medication. Always obtain specific orders signed by the patient's physician.

Advice on making a will

In a hospice, never give the patient advice concerning his will. If he asks for advice, tell him you aren't allowed to provide such advice. Suggest that he discuss the matter with his attorney or his family.

Living wills

Unlike the hospital nurse, whose duty with respect to living wills varies from state to state, the nurse who works in a hospice must respect the patient's living will. Don't violate it in any way, unless a court order instructs you to do so.

agency attorney. (See *Understanding sovereign immunity,* page 62.)

If you work for a privately owned business, such as an insurance company or a small medical practice group, you're still vulnerable to malpractice suits. In some states, however, you can't be sued by a fellow employee you've treated for a job-related injury. State workers' compensation laws, which protect the employer from excessive business costs, also protect you.

Understanding sovereign immunity

The doctrine of sovereign immunity goes back to the days when a person couldn't sue a sovereign or his agents unless the sovereign consented. In the United States, the courts transferred this privilege, applicable in most circumstances, to the elected government and its appointed agents – government employees. So government employees ordinarily can't be sued for their on-the-job mistakes.

Unfair results

In the past, this immunity has had some unfair results. A patient harmed in a private hospital could sue the hospital and its employees, but a patient harmed in a municipal or state hospital couldn't.

Perhaps because of this immunity, public hospitals gained a reputation for substandard practice; the public suspected that because public hospitals couldn't be sued for malpractice, their standards of care were lax.

Legislative action

In recent decades, most state legislatures have recognized the unfairness of this system. Many have passed laws that allow patients to sue public hospitals and other government agencies on a full or limited basis. In some states, legislatures have created special courts – usually called courts of claims – in which such lawsuits must be heard. Many state legislatures have set dollar limits on the amount a patient can recover from a government agency if he wins his suit.

Financial burdens

If you choose to make your career in an alternative setting, take time to investigate your benefits as an employee. Your benefits and liability coverage may be somewhat different than if you had chosen to work in a hospital setting.

Purchasing professional liability insurance

Most private medical employers have coverage that includes the nurses they employ, but private industrial employers, especially small companies, may not. Check your employer's coverage thoroughly: If you have a doubt about whether you're fully protected, consider buying your own insurance.

You may also need your own professional liability insurance if you work for a peer review organization or a state or federal government agency,

unless the law grants you complete immunity from job-related lawsuits.

Union eligibility

You usually retain the right to join a union. In fact, if you work as an occupational health nurse in a factory with a closed shop, you may be required to join a union.

If you work for a state or local government, state laws may permit you to join a union but may forbid your union to strike. Remember that the National Labor Relations Act exempts state and local governments and doesn't protect government nurses — such as community health nurses and public school nurses — in unionization disputes.

Termination of employment

Whether you work in an alternative setting or a hospital, nothing but a contract clause, a union agreement, or a civil service law can legally protect you from being fired. Even if you have such protection, you may be vulnerable to discretionary firing until the end of an initial probationary period. After this period, any of these forms of protection guarantees you the right to appeal your employer's decision.

Workers' compensation

If you work in an alternative setting, you should know what coverage your employer and your state, federal, or Canadian jurisdictional government provide for on-the-job injuries. Workers' compensation will usually cover you — but not always.

Most states and jurisdictions require many privately owned businesses to participate in workers' compensation plans. If you work for such a business, you'll probably receive workers' compensation for job-related injuries. However, you should be aware that, if the money you receive from this fund is inadequate, workers' compensation laws prevent you from suing your employer for additional compensation.

If you work for a small office

Some states don't require employers with few employees or limited income (for example, a physician with a small practice) to participate in the workers' compensation plan, so if you work in such a setting, be aware that you may not be covered by workers' compensation for job-related injuries. In the event that you are injured on the job, keep in mind that you can sue your employer directly.

Most small employers buy their own insurance to cover workers' injuries. If your employer doesn't have such insurance, you can buy your own insurance.

If you work for the government

If you work for a state or federal government agency, you may receive compensation from the state workers' compensation plan or by filing a claim under a state or federal tort claims act, depending on the applicable laws. However, if the sovereign immunity doctrine applies, you may not be eligible for compensation.

If you're eligible for workers' compensation, it usually covers any on-the-job injury. For example, if you're a school nurse and a student kicks you, workers' compensation will normally cover you. You also usually have the legal right to sue the person who caused the injury. If you win your lawsuit, the court, depending on state or territory statute, may consider any money you've already received, either from workers' compensation or from other insurance, in deciding the amount of damages you should receive. Because lawsuits are costly and can take years to resolve, most nurses don't sue.

Professional challenges

Nurses working in an alternative health care setting will face many challenges unlike those faced in the traditional hospital setting. Depending upon the setting the nurse has chosen, she will have to meet and overcome these challenges. She will have to understand and meet the needs of culturally and ethnically diverse clients, stay current with emerging trends, and be responsible in continuing her professional education.

WORKING IN HOME HEALTH CARE

More patients are receiving nursing care in their homes. What's more, nursing care measures implemented in the patient's home are becoming more sophisticated. Whereas every hospital has similar characteristics, every home is unique. Each represents a different pattern of legal risks and an unknown constellation of interpersonal relationships.

Scope and limits of home health care nursing

Home health care nursing makes it possible for patients to obtain nursing care in their own homes. Unlike what patients receive with home health care aid service, RNs can provide skilled nursing care for all patients, regardless of their age or disease state. However, it's important for the home health care nurse to follow the federal and state laws that regulate home health care nursing as well as her state's nurse practice act.

Liability

One factor that clearly affects your potential liability as a home health care nurse is your degree of control over the home environment, which is much less controlled than the hospital environment. For example, situations such as safety hazards that result in liability in the hospital may have a different outcome in home health care litigation because the health care provider has little control over the home setting.

If you work for a home health care agency and your responsibilities include managing other home health care workers, keep in mind that it's more difficult to evaluate personnel who work in the patient's home. Negligent training of a home health care worker may form the basis for a legal action. In *Loton v. Massachusetts Paramedical Inc.* (1989), a personal care worker employed by a home health care company left the patient unattended in a shower. The worker left the apartment to go to another part of the building to do laundry. While the patient was alone, the temperature of the water became very hot. As the patient tried to readjust the water, she fell from the shower seat and inadvertently moved the temperature control to the hot zone. Because of her underlying disability, she was unable to move away from the scalding water. When the worker returned, she was unable to reach her supervisor. She then applied ice to the burns and waited before calling an ambulance. The patient suffered third-degree burns over a large portion of her body, requiring numerous operations and skin grafting.

The plaintiff alleged that the home health care agency was negligent in failing to educate personnel in managing patients with disabilities and also in not training staff for the appropriate response in emergency situations. The jury rejected the agency's defense and awarded the plaintiff $1 million.

Along with civil claims for malpractice and negligence, a home health care provider or agency may be held liable for criminal actions in cases of serious neglect. In one case involving neglect, a patient had been receiving home health care service. She was admitted to the hospital with numerous pressure ulcers, some of which extended to the bone. The woman looked unwashed and had a necrotic odor. An indictment was brought against the home health care agency, the administrator of one of its offices, a visiting nurse employed by the company, and an LPN in the agency's nursing and supportive care program. The charge involved knowingly and willfully neglecting the patient, causing serious mental and physical injury. After a jury trial, the company was convicted of a Class A misdemeanor and fined more than $8,000.

Financial burdens

Most home health care nurses must own their own vehicle or provide their own transportation to their clients' homes; however, most home health care agencies reimburse nurses for gas and mileage.

Professional challenges

Over the past couple of years, home health care has had many setbacks. The industry's main obstacles have been increased government regulation and the cuts in Medicare reimbursement. For example, Medicare will pay for skilled services such as wound care in the home, but not for long-term care for the chronically ill, which is tragic for this aging population. Home health care nurses must also continually prove the "cost-effectiveness" of their services and care to the government and to the insurers. Much of a nurse's time is spent on paperwork, proper billing and coding, and getting reimbursed for supplies and services.

The challenges for home health care nurses aren't all financial. When the nurse enters a patient's home, she must assess the patient's living situation, the physical environment, and family support, and figure how it affects her care and the patient's activities of daily living. She alone must assess the patient's status at home, his well-being, and his ability to stay at home or his need for acute care, and she's usually the first person to assess a patient following discharge from a hospital or after a surgical procedure.

The home health care nurse is also required to keep up with technological advances in nursing care and provide the patient with appropriate patient teaching.

WORKING AS AN AGENCY NURSE

Temporary nursing service agencies represent an innovative approach to the delivery of nursing services — one response to the constant demand for practical, efficient, and cost-effective nursing care. Many nurses decide to work for a temporary nursing service agency to achieve greater work schedule flexibility and the right to choose their own hours. What's more, most agencies pay higher salaries than hospitals.

When you work for an agency, you have an employee-employer relationship with that agency. The agency charges a fee for your services from which it pays your salary. It may also provide such benefits as social security and other tax deductions, workers' compensation, sick pay, and professional liability insurance. Traditional nursing registries don't enter into employee-employer relationships with private-duty nurses when they provide client referrals.

Scope and limits of agency nursing

Agency nurses work for a health care agency. The agency contracts with a health care facility to provide RN coverage in a capacity that fulfills the facility's needs. As an agency nurse, you may work in a hospital as a staff nurse, in a home as a home health care nurse, in a clinical research study for a university or pharmaceutical company, or wherever else the agency places you. Your scope is that of an RN, and the agency can't contract you for a job that's beyond your credentials. For example, if you haven't been certified in telemetry, you can't work on a telemetry floor. Keep in mind that you're obligated by your state's nurse practice act and the contractual agreement between you and your employer-agency.

Few clear-cut policies

A nurse's professional responsibilities as an agency worker are typically vague. No set of uniform policies and procedures has been formally identified or administratively defined. For example, if an RN and an LPN are assigned to care for the same patient in his home but on different shifts, what responsibility does the RN have for the LPN's work? Is the RN responsible for supervising home health care aides? Also, should communication between the RN and the patient's physician be direct or channeled through an agency supervisor?

Large agencies, especially those with nationwide placement, may have specific policies to deal with situations like these. But smaller, more regional agencies may not. Without clear-cut guidelines, you may have to rely heavily on your professional nursing judgment. However, remember that the courts apply the same legal principles governing staff nurse malpractice cases to agency nurse malpractice cases.

Liability

A nurse is liable for her own wrongful conduct. However, if an agency nurse is judged to have been working within the legally permissible scope of her employment, then the agency may be held vicariously liable and may be required to pay any damages awarded to the plaintiff. The court may use the doctrine of *respondeat superior* to interpret the nurse's legal status. This doctrine makes an employer responsible for the negligent acts of his employees — so the agency is responsible for the actions of the nurses it employs. If the court finds that the nurse exceeded the scope of her employment, she may be solely responsible for any damages.

As an agency employee, you may be assigned to work in a patient's home, to care for a single patient in a hospital or other health care facility, or to temporarily supplement a facility's staff. These different practice circumstances can influence how a court determines liability. A malpractice lawsuit that involves an agency nurse will probably name as defendants the nurse, the temporary-nursing service agency and, if applicable, the health care facility in which the alleged malpractice happened. When you work as an agency nurse in a patient's home, your agency-employee status is usually clear-cut. The same is true when you care for a single patient in a health care facility.

The courts have more difficulty assigning legal liability in cases that involve agency nurses working as supplemental facility staff. In this situation, you're still an agency employee, but you're also in the "special service" of another "employer" — the facility.

Courts may apply the borrowed servant (or *ostensible agent*) doctrine, holding that the regular employer (the agency) isn't liable for injury negligently caused by the nurse-employee (the "servant") while in the special service of another employer (the hospital). Although the legal liability shifts from the agency to the hospital or facility when a court interprets a case this way, the nurse may be held to be the agent of both the agency and the hospital, under the doctrine of dual agency, making both potentially liable.

Professional guidelines

To help protect yourself against a lawsuit, make sure you fully understand what's expected of you when you accept an agency job. Be prepared to adjust to different policies and procedures. This requires review of policy manuals and a clear understanding of what they contain. When you work in a patient's home, for example, your agency's policies and procedures govern your actions. Make sure you understand them thoroughly and follow them carefully. How competently you follow procedure may affect such matters as whether a claim for workers' compensation is allowed or whether your agency will be included as a defendant with you in a malpractice suit. Don't perform any nonnursing functions when you work in a patient's home or arbitrarily change his nursing regimen policies and procedures from what your agency has specified. If you do and the patient or his family decides to sue, you may find yourself solely liable.

ANA guidelines

The ANA has issued guidelines outlining the responsibilities of temporary-nursing agencies and agency nurses. These guidelines say that an agency has a duty to select, orient, evaluate, and assign nurses and to provide them with professional development. According to these guidelines, agency nurses should:

♦ keep their licenses current
♦ select reputable employers
♦ maintain their nursing skills
♦ observe the standards of professional nursing practice
♦ document their nursing practice
♦ adhere to the policies and procedures of their agencies and clients.

The last point is particularly important if an agency assigns you to work in a hospital or other health care facility. As always, you must make sure you understand the policies and procedures of the facility for the nursing tasks you're expected to perform. Get to know the head nurse or unit supervisor, and seek clarification from her whenever you're in doubt.

The hospital or facility, in turn, is obligated to supply any equipment you need for patient care and to keep its premises and equipment in safe condition.

Financial burdens

Although agency nurses are paid a higher salary because of the flexibility and skill they're willing to offer, agencies don't have to offer benefits (such as health, pension, and savings plans) because these nurses are temporary employees. To obtain such benefits, agency nurses must either bear the cost on their own (for example, by purchasing private health insurance) or seek additional, part-time employment with an employer that offers such benefits.

Professional challenges

Agency nurses must have years of acute care experience and be comfortable and confident with their acute care skills. You must be flexible with where you work and be willing to travel or work in different capacities (such as a home health care nurse, a staff nurse, or a critical care nurse) and in different settings. As an agency nurse, you're expected to keep up with the most current information and technology. Although the agency for which you're working may offer additional classes, it's up to you to keep up with certifications and continuing education.

Also, because new graduate nurses typically don't receive an "orientation" period, you must quickly adjust to your working environment, almost as soon as you start your first shift. You must be able to work well with others with whom you haven't yet built a rapport. Lastly, because of the nursing shortage crisis, many health care facilities are turning to agency nurses to help solve their staffing problem. You, as an agency nurse, will have to be prepared for whatever challenges you may face: heavy patient loads, the absence of more experienced nurses to whom you may turn for support, and low morale.

Despite the challenges that agency nursing presents, many agency nurses find their role fulfilling because it offers them flexibility as well as the opportunity to put their wide range of nursing skills to use.

Working with an agency nurse

If you're a hospital staff nurse and an agency nurse is assigned to your unit, your responsibilities as a coworker are the same as those when you're working with a nonagency nurse. For example, if you see the agency nurse performing a procedure in a way that may harm the patient, you have a responsibility to stop the procedure, just as you would if you saw a nonagency nurse performing that same procedure. If you see an agency nurse performing a procedure incorrectly but without potential harm to the patient, simply report your observation to your nursing supervisor.

Controversy over agency nursing

When a nursing shortage exists, many health care facilities suffer imbalances in the number of nurses available to work regularly scheduled shifts. Temporary nursing service agencies provide a valuable service by supplying skilled nurses on short notice. However, use of agency-provided RNs and LPNs as supplemental staff in hospitals, nursing homes, and extended-care facilities is a fairly new and controversial practice.

On the one hand, critics point out that inequities in salaries between hospital and agency nurses performing the same functions can lead to morale

problems. Proponents of agency-based supplemental staffing, on the other hand, stress the cost-effectiveness of the practice and believe that its flexibility helps to keep nurses working and prevents nurse burnout. Proponents and critics urge that nursing administrations plan supplemental staffing programs instead of bringing in agency nurses on a few hours' notice before a shift begins. Adequate planning helps to maintain quality and continuity of patient care.

Potential legal precedent

Although no plaintiff has ever charged a hospital with inadequate staffing caused by a failure to obtain available supplemental staff from an agency, observers of the nursing profession believe that this may happen soon. In a Louisiana case, *McCutchon v. Mutual of Omaha Insurance Co.* (1978), a court required an insurance company to pay the agency fees of two LPNs recruited to care for a critically ill patient whose physician had ordered RNs (and whose insurance policy allowed payment for only RNs). The court reached its decision after reviewing evidence that neither the temporary-nursing service agency, the hospital, nor the insurance company could locate any available RNs at the time the LPNs were assigned. The court also considered the fact that the assigned LPNs were closely supervised by an RN at all times.

Selected references

Bowers, B.J., et al. "How Nurses Manage Time and Work in Long-term Care," *Journal of Advanced Nursing* 33(4):484-91, February 2001.

Carson, W.Y. "Nursing Malpractice: Protect Yourself," *AJN* 101(12):81, December 2001.

Cashin, D., et al. "The Complex Role of the School Nurse. Promoting Who We Are and What We Do," *School Nurse News* 20(3):24-27, May 2003.

"Did Nurse Call Dr. Twice: Did Dr. Have Duty to Check Pt.? Case on Point: *Stubbs v. Ray,* 2000 WL 125325 S.E.2d-GA (2000)," *Nursing Law's Regan Report* 41(4):4, September 2000.

"Dr. Fails to Leave Post-op. Orders: Nurses Fail to Timely Call Dr. Case on point: *Lupinacci v. Med. Center of Delaware,* 2002 WL 31006263 N.E.2d-DE (2002)," *Nursing Law's Regan Report* 43(4):2, September 2002.

Dyck, M.J. "A Public Policy Problem: Access to Long-term Health Care," *Journal of Gerontological Nursing* 27(7):13-22, July 2001.

"In Cases of Malpractice, Are Nurse Practitioners Held to the Same Medical Standard of Care When Prescribing Medications for Clients, or Would They be Held to a Standard of Care Applicable to Advanced Practice Nurses?" *JONAS Healthcare, Law, Ethics & Regulation* 3(1):9, March 2001.

Madsen, W. "Working for Herself: Case Study of a Private Duty Nurse, 1965-1974," *International History of Nursing Journal* 7(3):23-31, Spring 2003.

Morrison, C.A. "Unlicensed Personnel Issues," *Advanced Practice Nurse* 9(8):29, August 2001.

Mueller, C. "A Framework for Nurse Staffing in Long-term Care Facilities," *Geriatric Nursing* 21(5):262-67, September-October 2000.

Northcott, N. "The Expectation and Reality of Bank and Agency Nursing," *Nursing Management (Harrow)* 9(7):10-11, November 2002.

Parker-Conrad, J.E. "A Century of Practice. Occupational Health Nursing. 1988," *AAOHN Journal* 50(12):537-41, December 2002.

Rantz, M.J., et al. "Statewide Strategy to Improve Quality of Care in Nursing Facilities," *Gerontologist* 43(2):248-58, April 2003.

Raymond, L. "Is a Legal Career for You?" *RN* 65(3):63-66, March 2002.

"RNs Accused of Negligence: Must Panel Interview Pt.? Case on Point: *Gerber v. Juneau Bartlett Memorial Hospital,* 2000 W. 641057-AK (2000)," *Nursing Law's Regan Report* 40(12):4, May 2000.

Salazar, M.K. "Applying Research to Practice. Practical Guidelines for Occupational Health Nurses," *AAOHN Journal* 50(11):520-27, November 2002.

Schipske, G. "The Difference Between Negligence and Malpractice," *Advance Practice Nurse* 10(5):26, May 2002.

"Spotlight on Transport/Flight Nursing," *Nursing* 32(7):78, July 2002.

Turkoski, B.B. "Home Care and Hospice Ethics: Using the Code for Nurses as a Guide," *Home Healthcare Nurse* 18(5):308-16, May 2000.

3

Patients' rights

At one time, nurses were forbidden to give patients even the most basic information about their care or health. Only physicians could answer questions about a patient's condition.

In the 1960s, attitudes changed. Patients began demanding more information about their care and turned to nurses to assist them in getting the information.

This chapter will help you apply sound legal principles when confronted with questions about patients' rights in everyday nursing practice. It begins with a discussion of the evolution of patients' rights and goes on to outline your responsibilities in ensuring informed consent, the patient's right to refuse treatment, and upholding his right to privacy. You'll find summaries of major U.S. Supreme Court rulings on the right to die and reproductive rights issues. You'll learn when you can disclose confidential information, what steps to take when the patient leaves the health care facility against medical advice, and how to avoid false imprisonment charges. Finally, you'll learn how to take responsibility for upholding the patient's dignity in regard to his decisions about death.

Documents upholding patients' rights

Patients' bills of rights, endorsed by major health care providers and consumer groups, have helped to reinforce the public's expectation of quality care. These documents define a person's rights while receiving health care.

For years, hospitals and extended-care facilities have had their own published patients' bills of rights and those of the American Hospital Association (AHA) to inform consumers of some of their rights in the health care setting. These privately drafted bills of rights are designed to protect such basic rights as human dignity, privacy, confidentiality, and refusal of treatment. They also assert the patient's right to receive a full explanation of the cost of medical care, to be fully informed, and to be required to give consent before participating in experimental treatments because the patient exercises control over his own health care. These bills emphasize the patient's right to acquire information about *all aspects* of his care.

EARLY BEGINNINGS OF PATIENTS' RIGHTS

The concept of a formal document setting forth patients' rights has been around since 1959, when the National League for Nursing (NLN) issued its position paper, which outlined seven key points to help patients better understand nursing care. It was entitled "What People Can Expect of Modern Nursing Practice" and referred to the patient as a partner in health care, whose ultimate goal was self-care. (See *Landmarks in the evolution of patients' rights,* page 72.) Patients' rights received increasing public support during the 1960s as more people became aware of their rights as consumers. In a 1962 message to Congress, President John F. Kennedy further heightened this awareness when he outlined four basic consumer rights: the right to safety, the right to be informed, the right to choose, and the right to be heard.

The AHA, in 1973, issued its "Statement on a Patient's Bill of Rights." The statement — the result of a study the AHA had conducted with consumer groups — listed 12 patient rights. (See *AHA patient's bill of rights,* pages 73 and 74.) Also in that year, Minnesota became the first state to enact a law protecting a patient's rights. That law requires all state health care facilities to post Minnesota's patient's bill of rights conspicuously and to distribute it to their patients.

Since these early milestones, all states, many advocacy groups, and health care organizations have developed their own patients' bills of rights. In 1990, the Advisory Board of Directors of the Hospice Association of America approved a bill of rights for hospice patients. (See *ACLU patient's bill of rights,* pages 75 and 76, and *Hospice patient's bill of rights,* pages 77 and 78.)

Congressional action

In 1973, Congress passed the Rehabilitation Act. This act guarantees the physically or mentally disabled person the right to any service available to a nondisabled person. In 1990, an expanded version of this act, called the Americans with Disabilities Act, was passed. The act prohibits discrimination on the basis of disability by employers with 15 or more employees, and restricts employers' medical testing of employees and job applicants.

Other laws passed by Congress to protect the rights of the disabled include the Community Mental Health Amendment of 1975, the Rehabilitation Comprehensive Services and Development Disability Amendment of 1978, the Personal Responsibility and Work Opportunity Reconciliation Act of 1996, and the Individuals with Disabilities Education Act of 1997.

In 1980, Congress enacted the Mental Health Systems Act (MHSA), a comprehensive federal law on mental health services. Although much of this statute was later repealed, the MHSA Patient's Bill of Rights, which recommended that states review their mental health laws in light of patients' rights, survived. Since then, several states have used the bill as a model when revising their laws concerning the rights of patients suffering from mental illness.

In 1987, Congress enacted the Omnibus Budget Reconciliation Act, which included provisions that imposed dozens of new requirements on extended-care facilities and home health agencies, to protect the rights of residents receiving long-term care. This law established minimum standards for the presence of registered nurses and

Landmarks in the evolution of patients' rights

A spirit of paternalism dominated health care until the 1970s and severely limited the rights of patients. Due in part to the growth in consumer activism, more attention is being paid to the rights of consumers of health care. It's interesting to note that despite the progress that has been made, nowhere in the United States is a person guaranteed an absolute right to health care.

1959: The National League for Nursing issues the first patient's bill of rights, outlining seven points to help patients understand nursing care.

1973: The American Hospital Association (AHA) draws up a patient's bill of rights, listing 12 patient "rights."

That same year, Minnesota passes a patient's bill of rights, modeled after the AHA bill, becoming the first state to establish a bill of rights as law.

1973 to 1978: Congress enacts a series of laws designed to protect the rights of the disabled. These laws include the Rehabilitation Act of 1973, the Community Mental Health Amendment of 1975, the Education for Handicapped Children Act of 1975, the Developmentally Disabled Assistance and Bill of Rights Act, and the Rehabilitation Comprehensive Services and Development Disability Amendment of 1978.

1976: The New Jersey Supreme Court rules in the *Quinlan* case, granting the parents of Karen Ann Quinlan, who was in a persistent vegetative state, permission to remove her ventilator. This is the first court case to use the constitutional right to privacy as a basis for withdrawing life support.

1980: The U.S. Government passes the Mental Health Systems Act, which includes a bill of rights for patients receiving mental health services. Although much of this statute is later repealed, several states adopt recommendations found in the act.

1990: The U.S. Supreme Court rules in the *Cruzan* case. The parents of Nancy Cruzan requested their daughter's feeding tube be removed after she spent several years in a persistent vegetative state. The Court refuses, saying that under the Constitution, a state has the right to require clear and convincing evidence that the patient wanted life-sustaining treatment withheld. The ruling implies that when such evidence exists, the patient's desires will be respected.

1991: The Patient Self-Determination Act goes into effect. This federal law calls for hospitals, nursing homes, health maintenance organizations (HMOs), hospices, and home health care agencies that participate in Medicare and Medicaid to inform patients of their right (under state law) to draft advance directives, such as living wills, durable powers of attorney for health care, and any other document that states the patient's wishes with regard to health care should he become incapacitated. Facilities must honor the directives within the limits of existing state law.

1999 to 2003: The U.S. House of Representatives and the U.S. Senate, unable to come to bipartisan agreement, pass differing versions of a patient's bill of rights. None are enacted into law, but Congress continues working toward a national patient's bill of rights.

the training of nursing assistants. Patients also were granted the right to immediate access to relatives and to federal and state officials who investigate complaints of abuse or neglect.

Under the law, nursing homes can be fined up to $10,000 a day for violating a patient's rights.

AHA patient's bill of rights

This document outlines the rights of the hospitalized patient as defined in 1992 by the American Hospital Association (AHA). Although this bill of rights had no enforcement mechanism, many hospitals have used it as a model when establishing guidelines for patient care.

A patient's bill of rights

1. The patient has the right to considerate and respectful care.

2. The patient has the right to obtain from his doctor complete current information about his diagnosis, treatment, and prognosis in terms the patient can be reasonably expected to understand. When it isn't medically advisable to give such information to the patient, it should be made available to an appropriate person on his behalf. He has the right to know, by name, the doctor responsible for coordinating his care.

3. The patient has the right to receive from his doctor information necessary to give informed consent prior to the start of any procedure or treatment. Except in emergencies, such information for informed consent should include but not necessarily be limited to the specific procedure or treatment, the medically significant risks involved, and the probable duration of incapacitation. Where medically significant alternatives for care or treatment exist, or when the patient requests information concerning medical alternatives, the patient has the right to such information. The patient has the right to know the name of the person responsible for the procedures or treatment.

4. The patient has the right to refuse treatment to the extent permitted by law and to be informed of the medical consequences of his action.

5. The patient has the right to every consideration of his privacy concerning his own medical care program. Case discussion, consultation, examination, and treatment are confidential and should be conducted discreetly. Those not directly involved in his case must have the permission of the patient to be present.

6. The patient has the right to expect that all communications and records pertaining to his care should be treated as confidential.

7. The patient has the right to expect that within its capacity a hospital must make reasonable response to the request of a patient for services. The hospital must provide evaluation, service, or referral as indicated by the urgency of the case. When medically permissible, a patient may be transferred to another facility only after he has received complete information and explanation concerning the needs for and alternatives to such a transfer. The institution to which the patient is to be transferred must first have accepted the patient for transfer.

8. The patient has the right to obtain information as to any relationship of his hospital to other health care and educational institutions insofar as his care is concerned. The patient has the right to obtain information as to the existence of any professional relationships among individuals, by name, who are treating him.

9. The patient has the right to be advised if the hospital proposes to engage in or perform human experimentation affecting his care or treatment. The patient has the right to refuse to participate in such research projects.

10. The patient has the right to expect reasonable continuity of care. He has the right to know in advance what appointment times and doctors are available and where. The patient has the right to expect that the hospital will provide a mechanism whereby his doctor or a delegate of the doctor informs him of the continuing health care requirements following discharge.

(continued)

AHA patient's bill of rights *(continued)*

11. The patient has the right to examine and receive an explanation of his bill, regardless of source of payment.

12. The patient has the right to know what hospital rules and regulations apply to his conduct as a patient.

Reprinted with permission from the American Hospital Association.

LEGAL STATUS

Bills of rights that have become laws or state regulations carry the most authority because they give the patient specific legal recourse. If a patient believes a health care facility has violated his legal rights, the patient can report the violation to the appropriate legal authority, usually the state health or licensing department. If an investigation shows that the facility violated the patient's rights, the state will demand that the facility modify its practices to conform to state law.

Bills of rights issued by health care facilities and professional associations aren't legally binding. However, facilities may jeopardize federal funding, such as Medicare and Medicaid reimbursement or research funding, if they violate federal regulations or the standards of the Joint Commission on Accreditation of Healthcare Organizations.

You should regard bills of rights for patients as professionally binding where they exist as a facility's stated policy, and you're required to uphold those rights. You're also expected to uphold the bills of rights published by professional organizations.

INTERPRETING PATIENTS' RIGHTS

The theory of patients' rights is clear, but the practice is inherently full of conflict. What happens if defending a patient's rights requires that you exceed the bounds of nursing practice?

Consider the case of *Tuma v. Board of Nursing* (1979). A patient with myelogenous leukemia was admitted to a hospital in Idaho for chemotherapy. Although she had agreed to this treatment, she was openly distressed about it. Instead of asking her physician about alternative treatment, she asked Jolene Tuma, RN, MSN, a nursing instructor at the College of Southern Idaho who supervised nursing students at the hospital. Ms. Tuma had asked to be assigned to the patient because of her interest in the needs of dying patients.

Ms. Tuma told the patient, in detail, about alternative treatments. She discussed Laetrile therapy and various natural food and herbal remedies, comparing their adverse effects with those of chemotherapy. She also gave the patient the name of a therapist who practiced alternative treatments and offered to arrange an appointment.

Ms. Tuma didn't encourage the patient to alter her treatment plan or indicate that alternative treatments were better than the prescribed therapy or would cure her.

At the patient's request, Ms. Tuma also discussed the alternative treatments with the patient's son and

ACLU patient's bill of rights

The American Civil Liberties Union (ACLU) developed this patient's bill of rights as a model for health care institutions.

Preamble

As you enter this health care facility, it's our duty to remind you that your health care is a cooperative effort between you as a patient and the doctors and hospital staff. During your stay a patient's rights advocate will be available to you. The duty of the advocate is to assist you in all the decisions you must make and in all situations in which your health and welfare are at stake. The advocate's first responsibility is to help you to understand the role of all who'll be working with you and your rights as a patient. Your advocate can be reached at any time of the day by dialing _____. The following is a list of your rights as a patient. Your advocate's duty is to see to it that you're afforded these rights. You should call your advocate whenever you have any questions or concerns about any of these rights.

Patient rights

◆ The patient has a legal right to informed participation in all decisions involving his health care program.

◆ We recognize the right of all potential patients to know what research and experimental protocols are being used in our facility and what alternatives are available in the community.

◆ The patient has a legal right to privacy regarding the source of payment for treatment and care. The right includes access to the highest degree of care without regard to the source of payment for that treatment and care.

◆ We recognize the right of a potential patient to complete and accurate information concerning medical care and procedures.

◆ The patient has a legal right to prompt attention, especially in an emergency situation.

◆ The patient has a legal right to a clear, concise explanation in layperson's terms of all proposed procedures, including the possibilities of any risk of mortality or serious side effects, problems related to recuperation, and probability of success, and will not be subjected to any procedure without his voluntary, competent, and understanding consent. The specifics of such consent shall be set out in a written consent form, signed by the patient.

◆ The patient has a legal right to a clear, complete, and accurate evaluation of his condition and prognosis without treatment before being asked to consent to any test or procedure.

◆ We recognize the right of the patient to know the identity and professional status of all those providing service. All personnel have been instructed to introduce themselves, state their status, and explain their role in the health care of the patient. Part of this right is the right of the patient to know the identity of the doctor responsible for his care.

◆ We recognize the right of any patient who doesn't speak English to have access to an interpreter.

◆ The patient has a right to all the information contained in his medical record while in the health care facility, and to examine the record on request.

◆ We recognize the right of a patient to discuss his condition with a consultant specialist, at the patient's request and expense.

◆ The patient has a legal right not to have any test or procedure, designed for educational purposes rather than his direct personal benefit, performed on him.

◆ The patient has a legal right to refuse any particular drug, test, procedure, or treatment.

◆ The patient has a legal right to privacy of both person and information with respect to

(continued)

ACLU patient's bill of rights (continued)

hospital staff, other doctors, residents, interns, and medical students, researchers, nurses, other hospital personnel, and other patients.
◆ We recognize the patient's right of access to people outside the health care facility by means of visitors and the telephone. Parents may stay with their children, and relatives with terminally ill patients 24 hours a day.
◆ The patient has a legal right to leave the health care facility regardless of his physical condition or financial status, although the patient may be requested to sign a release stating that he is leaving against the medical judgment of his doctor or the hospital.
◆ The patient has a right not to be transferred to another facility unless he received a complete explanation of the desirability of and need for the transfer. If the patient doesn't agree to transfer, the patient has the right to a consultant's opinion on the desirability of transfer.
◆ A patient has a right to be notified by his impending discharge at least 1 day before it's accomplished, to insist on a consultation by an expert on the desirability of discharge, and to

have a person of the patient's choice notified in advance.
◆ The patient has a right, regardless of the source of payment, to examine and receive an itemized and detailed explanation of the total bill for services rendered in the facility.
◆ The patient has a right to competent counseling from the hospital staff to help in obtaining financial assistance from public or private sources to meet the expense of services rendered in the institution.
◆ The patient has a right to timely prior notice of the termination of his eligibility for reimbursement by any third-party payer for the expense of hospital care.
◆ At the termination of his stay at the health care facility we recognize the right of a patient to a complete copy of the information contained in his medical record.
◆ We recognize the right of all patients to have 24-hour-a-day access to a patient's rights advocate, who may act on behalf of the patent to assert or protect the rights set out in this document.

Reprinted with permission from the American Civil Liberties Union.

daughter-in-law. They told the patient's physician and, as a result, he interrupted the chemotherapy until he could discuss the situation with the patient. The next day the patient again agreed to undergo chemotherapy. Two weeks later, she went into a coma and died.

The patient's physician demanded that the hospital remove Ms. Tuma from her position as clinical instructor at the College of Southern Idaho.

At the hospital's request, the board of nursing conducted an investigation and hearing. The board interpreted Ms. Tuma's behavior as unprofessional.

They agreed that she had interfered with the physician-patient relationship and suspended her nursing license for 6 months.

Ms. Tuma appealed, lost the appeal, and appealed again. This time, 3 years after the incident, the Idaho State Supreme Court declared her not guilty of unprofessional conduct. The Court ruled that the Idaho Nurse Practice Act neither clearly defined unprofessional conduct nor provided guidelines for avoiding it.

Hospice patient's bill of rights

In 1990, the Hospice Association of America issued a bill of rights for hospice patients.

Introduction

Patients have a right to be notified in writing of their rights and obligations before their hospice care begins. Consistent with state laws, the patient's family or guardian may exercise the patient's rights when the patient is unable to do so. Hospice organizations have an obligation to protect and promote the rights of their patients, including the following:

Dignity and respect

Patients and their hospice caregivers have the right to mutual respect and dignity. Caregivers are prohibited from accepting personal gifts and borrowing from patients, families, or primary caregivers.

Patients have the right:
◆ to have relationships with hospice organizations that are based on honesty and ethical standards of conduct
◆ to be informed of the procedure they can follow to lodge complaints with the hospice organization about the care that is, or fails to be, furnished and regarding a lack of respect for property (to lodge complaints with us, call _____)
◆ to know about the disposition of such complaints
◆ to voice their grievances without fear of discrimination or reprisal for having done so.

Decision making

Patients have the right:
◆ to be notified in writing of the care that is to be furnished, the types (disciplines) of caregivers who'll furnish the care, and the frequency of the services that are proposed to be furnished
◆ to be advised of any change in the plan of care before the change is made

◆ to participate in the planning of care and in planning the changes in the care, and to be advised that they have the right to do so
◆ to refuse services and to be advised of the consequences of refusing care
◆ to request a change in caregiver without fear of reprisal or discrimination.

Privacy

Patients have the right:
◆ to be informed of the extent to which payment may be expected from Medicare, Medicaid, or any other payer known to the hospice organization
◆ to be informed of any changes that won't be covered by Medicare
◆ to be informed of the charges for which the patient may be liable
◆ to receive this information, orally and in writing, within 15 working days of the date the hospice organization becomes aware of any changes in charges
◆ to have access, upon request, to all bills for the service the patient has received regardless of whether they are paid out-of-pocket or by another party
◆ to be informed of the hospice's ownership status and its affiliation with any entities to whom the patient is referred.

Quality of care

Patients have the right:
◆ to receive care of the highest quality
◆ in general, to be admitted by a hospice organization only if it's assured that all necessary palliative and supportive services will be provided that are necessary to promote the physical, psychological, social, and spiritual well-being of the dying patient; however, an organization with less than optimal resources may nevertheless admit the patient if a more appropriate hospice organization isn't available, but only after fully informing the patient of its

(continued)

Hospice patient's bill of rights (continued)

limitations and the lack of suitable alternative arrangements
◆ to be told what to do in case of an emergency.

The hospice organization will assure that:
◆ all medically related hospice care is provided in accordance with doctors' orders and that a plan of care developed by the patient's doc-

tor and the hospice interdisciplinary group specifies the services to be provided and their frequency and duration
◆ all medically related personal care is provided by an appropriately trained homemaker-home health aide who is supervised by a nurse or other qualified hospice professional.

Reprinted with permission from the Hospice Association of America.

Unanswered questions

The decision failed to define the nurse's specific role in upholding a patient's right to information. This leaves several troubling questions unanswered.

For example, Ms. Tuma's patient asked her, not the physician, for information about alternative therapies. The physician testified that he wasn't knowledgeable about these therapies, so what recourse did his patient have? If a physician can't or won't answer such questions, does a patient have the right to obtain answers from a nurse? Until the courts or legislatures address such questions, you won't find easy answers.

GUIDELINES FOR UPHOLDING PATIENTS' RIGHTS

The best guideline you can follow to protect your patient's interests is to become familiar with your employer's stated policy on patients' rights. If no such policy exists, consider the NLN's position statement on the role of nursing in patients' rights. (See *NLN patient's bill of rights.*)

The NLN encourages you to view your patient as a partner in the health care process. In planning your patient's care, recognize his right to participate in decisions. Help him set realistic goals for his health care, and teach him the various approaches he can use to achieve them.

Throughout the decision-making process, keep assessing the patient's understanding of his illness. When he needs and wants more information, first determine whether you or the physician should provide it. Then let the patient participate in the development of his care plan, which must address that patient's unique needs as well as his rights.

Added benefits

Upholding patients' rights provides additional benefits such as opening health care to new ideas. For example, nurse-midwives and other maternity nurses have acted as advocates for patients who challenge traditional childbirth practices. As a result, many health care facilities have introduced changes, such as:
◆ using birthing rooms as an alternative to traditional delivery rooms
◆ using less intervention and medication during delivery

NLN patient's bill of rights

In 1977, the National League for Nursing (NLN) published its patient's bill of rights. In it, it states that the NLN believes that nurses are responsible for upholding these rights of patients:

◆ People have the right to health care that is accessible and that meets professional standards, regardless of the setting.

◆ Patients have the right to courteous and individualized health care that is equitable, humane, and given without discrimination as to race, color, creed, sex, national origin, source of payment, or ethical or political beliefs.

◆ Patients have the right to information about their diagnosis, prognosis, and treatment — including alternatives to care and risks involved — in terms they and their families can readily understand, so that they can give their informed consent.

◆ Patients have the legal right to informed participation in all decisions concerning their health care.

◆ Patients have the right to information about the qualifications, names, and titles of personnel responsible for providing their health care.

◆ Patients have the right to refuse observation by those not directly involved in their care.

◆ Patients have the right to privacy during interview, examination, and treatment.

◆ Patients have the right to privacy in communicating and visiting with persons of their choice.

◆ Patients have the right to refuse treatments, medications, or participation in research and experimentation, without punitive action being taken against them.

◆ Patients have the right to coordination and continuity of health care.

◆ Patients have the right to appropriate instruction or education from health care personnel so that they can achieve an optimal level of wellness and an understanding of their basic health needs.

◆ Patients have the right to confidentiality of all records (except as otherwise provided for by law or third-party payer contracts) and all communications, written or oral, between patients and health care providers.

◆ Patients have the right of access to all health records pertaining to them, the right to challenge and to have their records corrected for accuracy, and the right to transfer of all such records in the case of continuing care.

◆ Patients have the right to information on the charges for services, including the right to challenge these.

◆ Above all, patients have the right to be fully informed as to all their rights in all health care settings.

Reprinted with permission from the National League for Nursing.

◆ allowing patients to use a birthing chair or walk at will during labor

◆ encouraging the company and support of a "coach" — husband, other relative, or friend — during labor and delivery

◆ allowing families, including other children and grandparents, to participate in or attend the delivery.

Hospitals employ full-time patient advocates, or ombudsmen, to mediate between the patient and the hospital when a patient is dissatisfied with care. Patient advocates may help you uphold your responsibilities to your patient, but advocates don't diminish those responsibilities. Whether you're a registered nurse (RN), licensed practical nurse (LPN), or licensed vocational nurse (LVN), you must respect and safeguard your patient's rights. It's the law.

Informed consent

Being adequately informed about proposed treatment, procedures, surgery, or research in order to properly consent is a patient's legal right. So, it isn't surprising that the topic of informed consent appears in all current medical and nursing texts and must be evidenced in the patient's records when invasive or experimental procedures, treatment, or surgery are contemplated.

In the 1960s, physicians were primarily responsible for obtaining the patient's consent. Since then, nurses have also come to play a role in obtaining informed consent. It's a basic rule that the responsibility for obtaining a patient's informed consent rests with the person who'll carry out the procedure. This procedure may be delegated to an appropriate person under certain circumstances (for example, to another physician who'll participate in the procedure).

Informed consent basically involves the patient — or someone acting on his behalf — having enough information to know what the patient is risking should he decide to undergo the proposed treatment or surgery or the anticipated consequences should consent to the treatment be refused or withdrawn. Nurses may provide patients and their families with information that's within a nurse's scope of practice and knowledge base. However, a nurse can't substitute her knowledge for a physician's input.

Under certain circumstances, people with mental disorders may be held competent to consent. When there's a question about an individual's capacity to give consent, a legal determination may be sought from the appropriate court (for example, probate court) or an ethics committee of the facility.

The bottom line in determining capacity must be whether the person giving consent is impaired in his capacity or judgment so as not to know what he's getting into before the treatment begins.

To assess capacity to consent, a nurse may need to rely on her instincts as well as professional judgment. If she believes the patient doesn't understand, she should reassess and discuss the consent issue with the patient, his guardian if applicable, and the physician before the treatment begins.

INFORMED CONSENT STANDARDS

Generally, informed consent can be viewed legally from two different perspectives. The first, from the physician's standpoint, is known as the majority rule, or malpractice model: what a reasonable physician would have disclosed to his patient regarding proposed treatment under the same or similar circumstances as the case in question (*Karp v. Cooley* [1974]). See also *Nathanson v. Kline* (1960), in which the physician allegedly failed to inform the patient of the adverse effects of cobalt radiation therapy. The court ruled that the physician had a duty to disclose information that "a reasonable medical practitioner would disclose under the same or similar circumstances." Therefore, under the majority rule, the information is viewed from what a reasonable health care professional would tell a patient or patient's family about the procedure.

The second perspective, known as the minority rule, looks at disclosure of the material information that a *reasonable patient* in the situation *would deem significant to know* in making a decision to undergo the proposed treatment.

Negligent nondisclosure

Consider *Canterbury v. Spence* (1972). In this case, a patient had a laminectomy and then fell and developed paralysis. The patient sued the physician for failing to warn him of the inherent risks. The court ruled that the physician had a duty to disclose as much information as he knew — or should have known — a reasonable patient would need to make an informed decision.

So, what should the patient be told? First, it's well accepted that a duty of reasonable disclosure of risks, incident to the medical diagnosis and treatment, is required. The patient must be given an opportunity to evaluate the options, alternatives, and risks, and then exercise his choice. In medical malpractice cases that involve consent issues, expert testimony is usually required to establish whether or not the information given to the patient was reasonable, understandable, presented at a time when the patient was functionally able to process the information (as opposed to being sedated or medicated), and complete enough to allow the patient to knowledgeably agree to proceed. However, not every single or remote risk or benefit must be raised or addressed. It's generally agreed that the risks and benefits that arise frequently or regularly need to be discussed with the patient or the decision maker for the patient. Alternatively, if the health care practitioner knows that specific consequences are particularly significant to this patient, those

must be discussed before true informed consent may be obtained. Professional judgment must be exercised by all health care practitioners involved at this point.

A landmark case from Texas, *Karp v. Cooley*, is a good example of how informed consents are raised and added to other allegations in malpractice cases. Mr. Karp was offered a mechanical heart transplant when it was obvious that his medical condition was deteriorating and he was near death. Many consultants evaluated Mr. Karp. One, Dr. Beasley, wrote in Mr. Karp's chart that he didn't recommend the procedure because he thought the patient wasn't a suitable candidate for the surgery. Dr. Cooley, the surgeon, admitted at trial that he didn't tell Mr. Karp of Dr. Beasley's note, which was made during initial workups and was actually directed and related to Beasley's reservation about the patient's psychological or emotional acceptance of a less-than-perfect outcome.

Mrs. Karp testified to what Mr. Karp's physicians said in her presence. However, Mr. Karp also spoke with his physicians on several occasions about the proposed treatment when his wife wasn't present, and it was Mr. Karp who signed the consent form. The consent form matched the details Dr. Cooley testified to as being the basis of discussions with Mr. Karp before he signed the form.

No expert testimony was offered to indicate that what Dr. Cooley discussed with Mr. Karp was inadequate or breached Dr. Cooley's duty to obtain informed consent.

The court dismissed the informed consent issue on that basis and also raised the issue that the plaintiff, the estate of Mr. Karp, didn't present substantial evidence that there was any causal connection between their claimed lack of informed consent and Mr. Karp's death. To address this proximate cause relationship, the court looked at Texas case law (previous cases on this issue) and noted that for a finding of proximate causation between the alleged omissions of informed consent and injury (in this case death), certain factors must be present:

◆ A hidden risk that should have been made known, and wasn't, must materialize.

◆ The hidden risk must be harmful to the patient.

◆ Causality exists only when disclosures of significant risks incidental to treatment would have resulted in the patient's decision against the treatment.

What the court relied upon, then, in discussing the case on the proximate cause issue was testimony that Mr. Karp was near death before the wedge excision operation to which he gave consent. There was no dispute by Mrs. Karp about the validity of that consent. After the excision, Mr. Karp was also near death. Therefore, no one testified that to a reasonable degree of medical certainty the mechanical heart caused Mr. Karp's death. Finally, no proof was offered at trial that Mr. Karp wouldn't have agreed to proceed with the mechanical-heart surgery had alleged undisclosed material risks been disclosed. On appeal, the dismissal on the informed consent issue was upheld.

Basic elements of informed consent

Informed consent should include:

◆ a description of the treatment or procedure

◆ a description of inherent risks and benefits that occur with frequency or regularity or specific consequences known by the health care practitioner to be particularly significant to this patient or his designated decision maker

◆ an explanation of the potential for death or serious harm (such as brain damage, stroke, paralysis, or disfiguring scars) or for discomforting adverse effects during or after the treatment or procedure

◆ an explanation and description of alternative treatments or procedures

◆ the name and qualifications of the person who'll perform the treatment or procedure

◆ a discussion of the possible effects of not having the treatment or procedure.

Patients must also be told that they have a right to refuse the treatment or procedures without having other care or support withdrawn and that they can withdraw consent after giving it. (See *Informed consent: A landmark ruling.*)

If you witness a patient's signature on a consent form, you attest to three things:

◆ The patient voluntarily consented.

◆ The signature of the patient or the patient's designated decision maker is authentic.

◆ The patient appears to be competent to give consent.

However, there are many more consent and privacy issues now, particularly because of such procedures as human immunodeficiency virus (HIV) testing, drug and alcohol treatment, and sterilization. Your facility's risk manager should define your responsibilities, your employer's policies, and your state's legal requirements. Each state has specific statutes governing informed consent issues that are subject to change as tort reform evolves and as case law interprets existing statutes or legal concepts.

Informed consent under state law

Many state legislatures have passed laws supporting the standards of in-

Informed consent: A landmark ruling

The right of informed consent didn't exist at the beginning of the century. A patient had no legal right to information about his medical treatment. If a physician performed surgery without the patient's consent, the patient could sue for *battery* – legally defined as one person touching another without consent. A patient could claim battery only if he had refused consent or wasn't asked to give it, but not if he didn't have enough information to make an appropriate decision.

Rare exceptions

Most battery lawsuits were unsuccessful because courts usually took the physician's word over the patient's. Two cases in which patients did win were *Mohr v. Williams* (1905), in which the patient consented to surgery on one ear but the physician performed it on both, and *Schloendorff v. Society of New York Hospitals* (1914), in which the patient consented to an abdominal examination but the physician performed abdominal surgery.

Establishing a patient right

The right to receive informed consent wasn't expressed legally until 1957, when the California Supreme Court introduced the theory in the case of *Salgo v. Leland Stanford, Jr., University Board of Trustees*. This case involved a patient who had acute arterial insufficiency in his legs. The physician recommended diagnostic tests but failed to describe the tests or their risks. The day after the patient underwent aortography, his legs became permanently paralyzed. The court found the physician negligent for failing to explain the potential risks of aortography.

This decision established a basic rule: A physician violates "his duty to his patient and subjects himself to liability if he withholds any facts that are necessary to form the basis of an intelligent consent by the patient to the proposed treatment."

Since this landmark ruling, a patient can sue for negligent nondisclosure if his physician fails to provide enough information to enable him to make an informed decision.

---

formed consent set by the courts. States have procedural laws on informed consent—laws that describe, for example, the tort of negligent nondisclosure. A few states have laws that are *substantive*, meaning they actually define what must be present for informed consent to have been established. These laws define who can give consent and for what, and what type of documentation is required. These laws define exemptions to documented consent and when consent becomes invalid. Although the physician or practitioner is primarily involved with explaining the treatment, the nurse plays an important role in document-

ing the patient's decision. (See *When a patient doesn't understand,* page 84.)

INABILITY TO CONSENT

Informed consent relies on an individual's capacity, or ability, to make decisions at a particular time under specific circumstances. To make medical decisions, people must possess not only the capacity to make such decisions, but also the competence to make decisions. Consider these three elements of decision making:

◆ The ability to understand and communicate information relevant to the decision

LEGAL TIP

When a patient doesn't understand

Suppose you're caring for a patient scheduled for surgery. He has talked to his physician and signed the consent form. However, the night before surgery, he doesn't seem to understand the implications of the procedure. What should you do?

As the nurse assigned to the patient, you should page the physician who's scheduled to perform the surgery and express your concern that the patient isn't properly informed. Also, if your facility provides institutionally-approved guidelines or pamphlets on the procedure, you may review these with the patient before the patient talks to the physician.

◆ The ability to reason and deliberate concerning the decision
◆ The ability to apply a set of values to the decision.

If you have reason to believe that a patient is incompetent to participate in giving consent because of medication or sedation, you have an obligation to call that to the practitioner's attention immediately. If you learn that the practitioner discussed consent issues with the patient at a time when the patient was heavily sedated or medicated, you need to bring your concerns to the attention of the practitioner. If the practitioner isn't available, discuss your concerns with your supervisor. Document attempts to reach the practitioner and attending physician in the medical record before allowing the patient to proceed with the surgery or invasive procedure.

Along with discussing the matter with the practitioner and the supervisor, you must assess the patient's understanding of the information provided by the practitioner. Nurses are trained to make professional assessments about patient understanding, and this is the proper time and place to use those professional skills, without, of course, interfering with the practitioner-patient relationship in the process.

However, if you do nothing, and the patient undergoes the procedure without giving proper consent, you might find yourself as a codefendant in a battery lawsuit. Patient's attorneys, judges, and juries will look closely at the medication records to see when, in relation to the signing of the consent form, the patient was last medicated, and the patient's response to the medication as documented in the record. You could be held jointly responsible for the patient undergoing a procedure that he didn't consent to, if:
◆ you took part in the battery by assisting with the treatment
◆ you knew it was taking place and didn't try to stop it.

If the practitioner fails to provide adequate information for consent because of the patient's medicated status, the patient may sue the practitioner for lack of informed consent due to temporary incapacitation. The courts might hold you responsible if, knowing the practitioner hasn't provided adequate information to a patient, you fail to try to stop the procedure until proper consent can be obtained.

So, if you see that a patient is confused or medicated, you can't provide the information the patient needs, or you assess that the patient wasn't competent to provide consent when speaking with the practitioner because of medication or sedation, notify the practitioner in a timely manner. Document your observations in the patient's chart, and make sure the patient gets information from his practitioner or another appropriate source. Your actions and documentation will be key evidence in the case of a lawsuit. What's more, by briefly delaying the surgery, you just might be saving the practitioner from a battery claim, as well.

Consent discrepancies

Just how far does the nurse's duty to protect the patient's interest in informed consent cases extend? Consider the following two cases.

In a Georgia case, Charlotte Butler sought relief for chronic pain, which she believed to be caused by breast cancer treatments. Her oncologist referred her to an anesthesiologist, who was working as an independent contractor at the South Fulton Medical Center in East Point, Georgia. The anesthesiologist, Dr. Kim, used epidural steroid injections on several occasions. Because the patient failed to obtain long-term relief, he administered a neurolytic block injection. At one point, the medication was injected too close to the spinal cord, and the patient became quadriplegic.

The patient sued and settled with Dr. Kim, but the patient also pursued litigation against South Fulton Medical Center, alleging that the nursing staff was negligent for filling out the consent form incorrectly and not noticing the error—that the procedure listed on the form was an epidural steroid injection, not a neurolytic block.

The court found in favor of the hospital (and its staff nurses) in a 6-to-3 decision, holding that the direct cause of her injury was the physician's negligence, not the nurses'. The patient's deposition testimony played a key role. She acknowledged that she didn't understand the difference between the treatments she received. Further, although she had signed consent forms for the steroid injections and for a prior neurolytic block, *"she had never read any of them."* The court reasoned that she probably would have signed no matter what procedure had been listed. The court also held the physician solely responsible for failing to tell the patient what he was doing and what risks were involved. The dissenting judges felt the nurses had violated their duties to the patient because they violated their own policies, which required them to check that the consent form was complete and accurate and, if it wasn't, to notify the physician or administration, before the procedure was administered.

This case (*Butler v. South Fulton Medical Center* [1994]) highlights the importance of communicating with the patient. A few simple questions to the patient would have revealed that she didn't understand the complicated procedure or its risks.

In a Wisconsin case (*Mathias v. St. Catherine's Hospital* [1997]), the court held that simply notifying the physician that there was no signed consent form was enough for the nurses to fulfill their duty. In that case, a physician performed a postdelivery tubal ligation on a patient after being told by the nurses that there was no signed consent form in the patient's chart. The physician reportedly replied, "Oh, okay," then performed the surgery. A few days after the tubal ligation had been performed, one nurse approached the patient with a consent form for the procedure and told the patient that the form was "just to close up our records." The nurse with the form then signed another nurse's name and backdated the form to the date of the procedure.

When the patient sued the physician and the hospital, claiming that the nurses should have stopped the physician from performing the surgery, the appeals court disagreed. It held that the nurses' only duty under these circumstances was to make the physician aware that there was no signed consent. The reason behind the decision apparently was that the court believed the nurses had no way of knowing the physician hadn't obtained the patient's consent and had no reason to think the absence of a signed form in the chart was anything more than a clerical error. The court wasn't swayed by the nurse's forging of another's signature, by the backdating of the form, or by the circulating nurse's testimony that she was an "advocate" for the patient.

Not all courts, however, would have reasoned as the Wisconsin Appeals Court did. Some courts would have taken the actions of the nurses in obtaining the patient's signature on the consent form several days after the procedure as evidence of "consciousness of guilt," fraud, or as a betrayal of the patient's trust. Some courts would have considered the nurse's conduct unethical, illegal, and unconscionable.

Even in cases in which the patient says he understands, this must be documented because it could save you from assault and battery charges for violating the patient's rights, should you participate in the procedure without consent being properly obtained. You also should document any teaching you do, in conjunction with answering questions the patient asks.

If special circumstances exist, such as a patient speaking a different language or being unable to read (and the form was read to the patient), they should be documented as well. If the patient can't sign his name, have him make an X on the form and note on it by whom the mark was made. Also, record the patient's verbal consent in the chart.

Incompetent patients

A patient is deemed mentally incompetent if he can't understand the explanations or can't comprehend the results of his decisions. When the patient is incompetent, the practitioner has two alternatives. She may seek consent from the patient's next of kin, usually a spouse. (Legal definition of next of kin varies from state to state.)

Alternatively, other interested family members or people, the physician, or the hospital may petition the court to appoint a legal guardian for the patient. Sometimes, a Probate Court may decide who the proper legal guardian should be after reviewing petitions and taking testimony. This works well if there's time to appoint a proper guardian.

However, that isn't always possible in the case of a potentially dangerous or deadly medical condition. Under those circumstances, the courts will look to the reasonableness of the actions by the health care providers, before proceeding with the treatment, in determining if there was informed consent by a proper party, or whether the informed consent requirement was properly waived.

Mental illness isn't the same as incompetence. People suffering from mental illness have been found competent to consent because they are alert and, above all, able to understand the proposed treatment, risks, benefits, and alternatives as well as the consequences of refusing the treatment. Consider a patient who has been hospitalized involuntarily but remains alert and oriented. His mental status and education enable him to understand the information presented by the practitioner but he lacks freedom from incarceration. Should this patient be allowed to make medical decisions that will affect his life or future health? Why should a court-appointed person assume this authority? On the other hand, shouldn't the patient have the right to refuse treatment even if it might ease his mental illness (for example, electroconvulsive therapy)?

Since the late 1980s, practitioners have had to reexamine medical restraint issues that involve elderly, confused, and infirm patients. It's now well established that a confined patient, mentally or physically disabled, may be forcibly medicated only in an emergency when he may cause harm to himself or others. In such cases, documentation in the patient record regarding the actual mental status of the patient and competency to give consent is critical.

Minors

Over the past 25 years, as nurses, we've witnessed a great social and legal challenge involving the rights of minors, especially their right to seek health care. As concerns for the rights of minors regarding consent to health care have developed, all states have looked at the issue of just who can give consent for minors to receive what care and what information a minor may keep confidential in regard to that care. Certain rules have evolved.

Usually, the person giving consent for care and treatment of a minor is a parent or other designated adult. This isn't always the case, however, as you'll see here. The practitioner must disclose all relevant information to the person giving consent to ensure that the consent is informed.

The patchwork of rights and limitations of the various state laws governing when minors can and can't consent give us alternating perceptions of teenagers. They're viewed as adultlike and childlike, and there's a desire to protect and respect both these qualities.

For example, a teenage mother must give consent before her baby can receive treatment but in general isn't permitted to determine the course of her own health care. Under federal law, adolescents can be tested and treated for HIV without parental involvement. However, parental consent is required to set an adolescent's broken arm in most cases.

Every state will allow an emancipated minor to consent to his own medical care and treatment. So far, state definitions of emancipation vary, but it's generally recognized that to be emancipated, the individual must be a minor by state definition (less than the legal age of majority in that state) and must have obtained a legal declaration of freedom from the custody, care, and control of his parents. In doing so, emancipated minors forgo the right to financial support from their parents and also any protection from lawsuits. When declared emancipated, minors gain the right to enter binding contracts, to sue, and to consent to medical, dental, or psychiatric care without parental approval. They also assume all the financial obligations for this care, just as an adult would if he entered into such contracts. In granting emancipated status to minors, the courts look for employment, demonstrated fiscal responsibility, and other evidence of support systems the minor has available as well as to the individual circumstances that underlie the request for legal determination of emancipation.

Most states allow teenagers to consent to treatment, even though they haven't been determined emancipated, in cases involving pregnancy and sexually transmitted diseases. Privacy issues are involved as well, so the nurse must understand the specific circumstances allowing a minor to consent and when to contact the parent or legal guardian. Your risk manager should be able to help you. Contact with a parent or legal guardian and disclosure of confidential information has resulted in lawsuits for breach of confidentiality.

An unemancipated minor, in mid-to-late teens, who shows signs of intellectual and emotional maturity, is considered a "mature minor." In some cases, a mature minor is allowed to exercise health care rights that are generally reserved for adults. Because there's no consensus about when maturity occurs and, thus, no clear guidelines for those who must make such assessments, the issue of maturity must be decided on a case-by-case basis.

It's an accepted practice to allow children, to the extent they may participate, to be involved in the decision-making process regarding life-sustaining medical treatment. In making the ultimate decisions, there must be a weighing of "the best interests" standard, which involves considering the benefits and the burdens to the child. Some benefits to be considered are prolonging life and improving quality of life after treatment. Burdens of the proposed treatment may include intractable pain, irremediable disability or helplessness, emotional suffering, and invasiveness of the procedure, which could severely detract from the quality of life. Keep in mind that the quality of life to be considered is from the child's perspective, not that of the

parent, the decision-maker, or even the health care providers. However, the assumption, without evidence to the contrary, is that life-sustaining medical treatment will be provided in accordance with existing medical, ethical, and legal norms.

Right to refuse treatment

It's generally held that parents have the right to refuse life-sustaining medical treatment for unemancipated children who lack the capacity or statutory criteria for maturity to make such decisions for themselves.

Decisions to limit, withhold, discontinue, or forgo treatment must be carefully documented and must be specific in nature. The collaborative process must occur between patient, parent (or legal guardian), and practitioner. Young children deserve to hear the general conclusions of a decision that will affect their survival, especially when the clinician believes treatment will no longer benefit the patient and should be withdrawn.

Emancipated or mature minors are presumed to have the capacity to give consent. Regarding younger children, however, it might be helpful to consider what the Tennessee State Supreme Court did in a 1987 case. It used the "Rule of Sevens." The court presumed that up to age 7 the child lacked capacity to consent. From ages 7 to 14, the presumption of incapacity can be rebutted (by evidence demonstrating that the child, in fact, possesses maturity); age 14 and older, the individual should be presumed to have capacity.

Remember that informed consent is a process, not a document. Hospitals generally address informed consent in policy and procedure manuals to ensure consistency and thorough implementation and documentation. Current Joint Commission on the Accreditation of Healthcare Organizations (JCAHO) "hot spots" include issues of restraints, informed consent (especially for participating in research), advance directives, and confidentiality. Regarding informed consent issues, evidence is required that the consent is voluntary and that sufficient information regarding the treatment was given. This includes an explanation of alternatives, differences in effectiveness of alternatives, consequences of not having the proposed treatment, risk and benefits, impact on daily living, likelihood of success, responsible practitioners, and any possible conflicts of interest. In addition, this information must be presented in a manner that the patient understands, including appropriate language, reading level, cognitive ability, and ethnic orientation. Lastly, the appropriate documentation must be completed properly.

EVIDENCE OF CONSENT

Consent can be demonstrated by a signed, witnessed document; a note in the medical record detailing communications between the physician and patient; or the patient willfully undergoing the procedure by appearing at the appointed time and place. Some states (such as Georgia) have statutes stating that a signed consent form disclosing the treatment in general terms is deemed conclusive proof of a valid consent. Of course, the validity of the signature may be challenged. However, if the patient is legally competent to sign the form and does so, he waives the right to a later claim that he didn't. He also waives the right to a later claim that he didn't understand the medical treatment or that the physician didn't explain to him information in the consent form.

Other states take the position that a signed consent form is evidence of informed consent, but that may be refutable if the patient offers sufficient evidence to the contrary. The patient may challenge his consent by attacking the substance of the consent form. He may claim the practitioner didn't explain the medical terms in a manner that a patient could understand or (given the medical diagnosis, the patient's condition, or the surgery contemplated) that relevant information significant to the patient wasn't provided.

A signed consent form may not be required in your state. However, there must still be evidence that the patient has been provided with the required information and that he has evidenced his consent to proceed. This may be done by a physician's notation in the progress notes indicating that the patient has been told of specific risks, benefits, and alternatives; has had an opportunity to have questions answered; and understands and agrees to the procedure. The evidence of informed consent is further enhanced if the medical record documents other family members who were present with the patient when the consent was obtained, such as "Wife present and concurs with patient's decision to proceed with the surgery."

If you work in a facility that uses investigational drugs or engages in research (RI.1.2.1.1), your policies and procedures must state that the patient or surrogate receives a clear explanation of experimental treatment. This includes the procedures to be followed (RI.1.2.1.4), a clear description of potential discomforts and risks (RI.1.2.1.2), a list of alternative treatments (RI.1.2.1.3), and a clear explanation that patients may refuse to participate in the research project without compromising their access to care and treatment (RI.1.2.1.5).

Most JCAHO type 1 recommendations given after the site visit involve informed consent and result from inadequate or incomplete documentation. (Health care organizations must resolve insufficient or unsatisfactory compliance with standards in a specific performance area within a specific time to maintain accreditation.) It's easier to comply with JCAHO standards if forms are user-friendly and include the required criteria, if an audit system is in place to validate that forms are consistently completed appropriately, and if the forms are included in the medical records. The nurses' notes or progress notes must also include an entry that the health care practitioner has discussed these issues with the patient or surrogate decision maker and that he understands and gives consent or refuses it.

EXCEPTIONS TO OBTAINING INFORMED CONSENT FIRST

Emergency treatment (to save a patient's life or to prevent loss of organ, limb, or a function) may be done without first obtaining consent in specific circumstances. If the patient is unconscious or a minor who can't give consent, emergency treatment may be performed. The presumption is that the patient would have consented had he been able, unless there's reason to believe otherwise. For example, to sustain the life of unconscious patients in the emergency department, intubation has been held to be appropriate even if no one is available to consent to the procedure.

Children brought to the emergency department after serious injury in school whose parents can't be located in time may be provided with emer-

gency medical care without consent while attempts are made to locate the parents. Even though consent can be legally presumed in these cases, health care facilities may still face lawsuits. For example, if blood is given to a severely injured, unconscious person, the patient or family could still sue if such an action were against their religious convictions. Courts will uphold emergency medical treatment as long as reasonable effort was made to obtain consent and no alternative treatments were available to save life or limb. The courts won't uphold treatment in the absence of informed consent if the practitioner has had prior contact and has been told that such treatment would be refused. If the practitioner has time to locate family members or to obtain proper consent from the patient, the courts will require the practitioner to do so.

Before proceeding, a prudent nurse will make certain that the medical emergency, the assumptions to obtain proper consent, and any information that has been conveyed to the patient is documented in the medical record. If the practitioner wants to provide care to the patient without consent, but you feel the care could wait, discuss this with the practitioner. If the practitioner insists on proceeding anyway, evaluate the situation. If your refusal to help would harm the patient or create an unsafe situation (a practitioner caring for a patient without assistance), you should assist. If you refuse to participate, make sure you notify your nursing supervisor. The incident should also be reported to hospital administration.

Patients may also waive their rights to additional information by appointing someone else as their medical decision maker. Advance directives are one way to have another person par-

Right to consent: From birth to adulthood

From birth, everyone has medical rights to:
◆ confidentiality concerning medical records
◆ privacy during treatment
◆ reasonable and prudent medical care.

A person attains more medical rights as he reaches the age of majority, defined as the age when a person is considered legally responsible for his activities and becomes entitled to the legal rights held by citizens generally.

Minors

Anyone younger than the age of majority (18 or 21 depending on the state in which he lives) has the right to consent to treatment for sexually transmitted diseases, serious communicable diseases, and drug or alcohol abuse (although state law may require that the minor's parents be notified).

Mature minors

In certain instances, a physician or judge may decide that a minor is sufficiently mature – has a sufficiently developed awareness and mental capacity – to consent to medical treatment. If so, the minor has the right to make decisions about medical care.

Adults

Anyone who has reached majority or who is a legally emancipated minor has the right to:
◆ consent to or refuse medical treatment
◆ consent to or refuse medical treatment for his children (in most circumstances).

---

ticipate and be responsible for one's medical care and treatment. If this has been decided beforehand, proper documentation must appear in the medical record.

WHEN INFORMED CONSENT BECOMES INVALID

Informed consent can become invalid if a change in the patient's medical status alters the risks and benefits of treatment. In such situations, the practitioner must explain the new risks and benefits to make sure the patient will consent to the treatment.

THERAPEUTIC PRIVILEGE

The controversy over informed consent centers on medical and surgical treatments and procedures that are invasive, risky, experimental, or have low likelihood for a successful outcome. We've come a long way since the concept of silence, or therapeutic privilege. In that situation, the physician was allowed to withhold information from a patient at the sole discretion of the physician and the patient's family, who believed that the information would jeopardize the patient's health. In some instances, patients weren't told that they were dying or that the treatment would have no benefit. Now, therapeutic privilege is viewed narrowly because withholding significant information from patients or their designated decision makers is frowned upon by the courts as a violation of a patient's right to self-determination, a right that the nurse is charged with protecting. (See *Right to consent: From birth to adulthood*.)

The patient who refuses treatment

Any mentally competent adult may legally refuse treatment if he's fully informed about his medical condition and about the likely consequences of his refusal. As a professional, you must respect that decision.

When your patient refuses treatment, you must understand more than his rights and your responsibilities. (See *When a patient says no.*)

RIGHT TO REFUSE TREATMENT

Most court cases related to the right to refuse treatment have involved patients with a terminal illness, or their families, who want to discontinue life support. In one of the best known cases, Karen Ann Quinlan's parents argued that unwanted treatment violated their comatose daughter's constitutional right to privacy. *In re Quinlan* (1976), the Quinlans successfully petitioned the New Jersey Supreme Court to discontinue her life support.

In another landmark case, *Cruzan v. Director, Missouri Department of Health* (1990), the parents of Nancy Cruzan petitioned to have their comatose daughter's tube feedings discontinued. In 1990, the U.S. Supreme Court held that the state of Missouri has the constitutional right to refuse to permit termination of life-sustaining treatment *unless "clear and convincing evidence" exists about a patient's wishes.* Because this standard wasn't met, the Court didn't allow removal of the feeding and hydration tube. Significantly, the Court implied that when clear and convincing evidence exists, the patient's wishes will be respected.

Two months after the Supreme Court ruling, the Cruzans petitioned the local court with new evidence. A Missouri judge granted them the right to remove Nancy's feeding and hydration tube. She died shortly thereafter. Publicity about Nancy Cruzan's legal ordeal heightened the awareness of millions of Americans to the need to prepare ahead for critical medical decisions.

More and more, health care providers consider quality end-of-life care as an ethical obligation. But what does end of life mean, and how do you measure it? Some researchers have viewed decisions from the patient's perspective based on five domains, or focal points, that study participants viewed as end-of-life issues. By understanding these domains from the patient's perspective, nurses can improve the quality of end-of-life care.

◆ The problem with pain and other symptoms is still of concern for some patients. Therefore, greater attention may be warranted to attitudes of nurses toward pain and symptom control and skill in delivering it. Clearer guidelines that separate appropriate pain management from euthanasia (thus alleviating the concerns of health care providers as well) are needed.

◆ Many patients fear "being kept alive" after life could no longer be enjoyed and loss of "dignity in death." This indicates health care providers need to focus not only on specific treatment decisions but also on consent issues.

◆ Sense of control is also critical, and some patients are adamant about controlling their end-of-life care decisions.

◆ Patients tend to focus more on psychological outcomes rather than precise treatment decisions. For example, some patients feel their loved ones will be relieved of the burden that difficult end-of-life care decisions entail.

◆ Many patients express an overwhelming need to communicate with

When a patient says no

A patient must give his consent before you can perform any treatment. If the patient refuses, take these steps:

1. Explain the risks involved in not having the treatment performed.

2. If the patient understands the risks but still refuses, notify your supervisor and the physician.

3. Record the patient's refusal in your nurses' notes.

4. Ask the patient to complete a refusal of treatment form, like the one shown below. The signed form indicates that appropriate treatment would have been given had the patient consented.

5. If the patient refuses to sign the release form, document this in your nurses' notes and write "refused to sign" on the patient's signature line. Initial it with your own initials and date it.

6. For additional protection, facility policy may require you to get the patient's spouse or closest relative to sign a refusal of treatment form. Document whether or not the spouse or relative does this in the same manner as above.

Refusal of Treatment Release Form

I, [patient's name], refuse to allow anyone to [insert treatment].
The risks attendant to my refusal have been fully explained to me, and I fully understand the results for this treatment and that if the same isn't done, my chances for regaining my normal health are seriously reduced and that, in all probability, my refusal for such treatment or procedure will seriously affect my health or recovery.

I hereby release [name of hospital] its nurses and employees, together with all physicians in any way connected with me as a patient, from liability for respecting and following my expressed wishes and direction.

_____
Witness

_____
Date

_____
Patient or Legal Guardian

_____
Patient's Date of Birth

loved ones at this stage of their life. Dying offers important opportunities for growth, intimacy, reconciliation, and closure.

Nurses can use these domains of end-of-life care to clarify treatment goals and provide a conceptual framework for teaching the care of dying patients to others. The domains can also serve as a checklist to review the adequacy of the care being provided. Clinicians may ask themselves: Am I adequately treating pain and other symptoms? Am I inappropriately prolonging life? Am I helping patients achieve a sense of control, relieve burdens on their families, and strengthen relationships with loved ones?

ADVANCE DIRECTIVES

The Patient Self-Determination Act of 1990 ensured the rights of patients to author or execute *advance directives* — written or verbal instructions by the patient about his wishes for medical treatment in the event he becomes "incapacitated." Examples include living wills, durable powers of attorney for health care, and any document that states the patient's wishes. JCAHO standard RI.1.2.4 mandates that each hospital assure patients older than age 18 the opportunity to initiate an advance directive. The hospital must also honor the directives within the limits of the law and their capabilities.

Consider the following tips for implementation:

◆ Information about the patient's rights and the opportunity to draft an advance directive should be initiated during the admission process and documented on the admission form.

◆ Regular chart audits should ensure that.an advance directive or a statement that a patient was told about his right to draft such an advance directive is included in the medical record.

◆ All employees of the facility must be told, during orientation and annual updates, that patients have rights to an advance directive.

◆ Policy and procedures must be drafted to include procedures in which conflicts regarding advance directives will be resolved such as by referral to the bioethics committee.

Not all advance directives are black and white and may not address all contingencies or medical situations that a patient may encounter. For example, the patient may not realize that advanced life support may only be necessary for a brief time to help him regain sufficient strength or to support breathing during surgery.

Although the health care proxy (that is, one authorized to act for another) is supposed to be the ultimate decision maker, the physician has a legitimate role in the decision-making process and may refuse to comply with any decision that he believes is contrary to the patient's wishes or best interests. If that happens, the proxy may ask that the patient be transferred to a physician who will honor the patient's or the proxy's requests. Alternatively, the proxy may request the ethics committee of the hospital to mediate. As a last resort, the proxy may seek a court order to stop the unwanted care or treatment.

FREEDOM OF RELIGION

Jehovah's Witnesses may refuse treatment on the grounds of freedom of religion. Members of this sect oppose blood transfusions, based on their interpretation of a biblical passage that forbids "drinking" blood. Some sect members believe that even a lifesaving transfusion given against their will deprives them of everlasting life. The courts usually uphold their right to refuse treatment because of the constitutionally protected right to religious freedom. In the case of *In re Osborne* (1972), for example, the court respected a Jehovah's Witness' right to refuse consent.

Most other religious freedom court cases involve Christian Scientists, who oppose many medical interventions, including medicines. For example, in *Winters v. Miller* (1971), a psychiatric patient claimed she involuntarily received treatment and medications at a New York state hospital. After her discharge, she sued for damages based on a violation of her religious freedom as a Christian Scientist. The trial court dismissed her complaint, but an appeals court ordered a new trial on the grounds that the unwanted treatment might have violated her rights.

Besides court rulings, most patients' bills of rights support the right to refuse treatment, starting with the bill of rights adopted by the AHA.

When a Jehovah's Witness refuses blood because of religious beliefs, health care professionals are challenged to provide optimal care without using standard medical treatment. Health care, legal, ethical, and management issues of how to treat blood loss when it occurs must be carefully considered. Some strategies are currently available that minimize blood loss during cardiac surgeries, for example, as well as methods to increase endogenous production. With more than 3.9 million Jehovah's Witnesses worldwide and about 1 million in the United States, more health care providers are facing situations in which blood transfusion isn't a treatment option.

Using a cardiac-surgery example, some suggested blood-conserving strategies as effective treatments include:
◆ preoperative adequacy of hemoglobin levels, administration of erythropoietin, and use of iron and folic acid supplements
◆ intraoperative hemodilution to decrease blood viscosity and to improve systemic and pulmonary circulation, preservation of clotting factors and platelets to reduce the likelihood of postoperative bleeding, hypothermia to reduce tissue oxygen requirements, desmopressin to control bleeding in the presence of platelet defects and in patients with decreased level of factor VIII, and aprotinin to reduce blood loss by inhibiting fibrinolysis and the turnover of coagulation factors
◆ postoperative use of protamine sulfate to bind with heparin and to neu-tralize the anticoagulant effect; use of aminocaproic acid to enhance fibrinogen activity and clot formation; erythropoietin, iron, and folic acid to accelerate erythropoiesis; and the use of blood reservoir devices and the smaller collection tubes for blood sampling in children, to minimize the volume of blood lost with phlebotomy and to preserve the hemoglobin level.

The use of blood-conserving techniques during surgery has been validated by several investigations and allows patients to adhere to their religious beliefs while resolving the dilemmas associated with the unacceptability of standard, accepted treatments. Of course, physicians would have the ethical and legal rights to refuse to care for any patient in a nonemergency situation when standard medical care isn't acceptable to the patient. Court orders can also be obtained, requiring the patient to undergo the standard treatment against the patient's wishes. Health care providers could also honor the patient's request under all circumstances. By looking at the available alternatives and trying to honor the patient's wishes, nurses may be able to comply with the Code of Nurses of the American Nurses Association (ANA), which specifies that nurses are obligated to support and protect each patient's right of self-determination, to respect the patient's individuality, to adhere to standards of care, and to maintain the patient's safety.

RIGHT TO DIE

Most states have enacted right-to-die laws (also called *natural death laws* or *living will laws*). These laws recognize the patient's right to choose death by refusing extraordinary treatment when he has no hope of recovery.

Whenever a competent patient expresses his wishes concerning extraordinary treatment, health care providers should attempt to follow them. If the patient is incompetent or unconscious, the decision becomes more difficult.

In some cases, the next of kin may express the patient's desires for him, but whether this is an honest interpretation of the patient's wishes is sometimes uncertain.

Written evidence of the patient's wishes provides the best indication of what treatment he would consent to if he were still able to communicate. This information may be provided through:
◆ a living will—This is an advance directive document that specifies a person's wishes with regard to medical care if he should become unable to communicate. (See *Living will.*) In some states, living wills don't address the issue of discontinuing artificial nutrition and hydration.
◆ a durable power of attorney for health care—In this document, the patient designates a person who will make medical decisions for him if he can't do so. This differs from the usual power of attorney, which requires the patient's ongoing consent and deals only with financial issues. (See *Durable power of attorney for health care,* page 99.)

Most states recognize living wills as legally valid and have laws authorizing durable powers of attorney for initiating or terminating life-sustaining medical treatment.

REQUIREMENTS OF THE SELF-DETERMINATION ACT

The Patient Self-Determination Act of 1990 requires that health care facilities ask whether the patient has completed an advance directive. This law includes the following requirements:

◆ Each patient must be given written information about his rights under state law to make decisions concerning medical care, including the right to accept or refuse medical or surgical treatment and to formulate advance directives.
◆ The patient's decision whether to execute an advance directive must be documented in the medical record.
◆ The facility must ensure that the patient's decision about the execution of an advance directive doesn't influence the provision of care. Furthermore, health care providers can't discriminate against a patient in any way based on his decision.
◆ The health care facility must provide education for the staff and community on issues concerning advance directives.

CHALLENGING THE PATIENT'S RIGHT TO REFUSE TREATMENT

There are two grounds for challenging a patient's right to refuse treatment: You can claim that the patient is incompetent, or you can claim that compelling reasons exist to overrule his wishes. (See *Overruling the patient,* page 100.)

The courts consider a patient incompetent when he lacks the mental ability to make a reasoned decision such as when he's delirious.

Compelling circumstances

The courts also recognize several compelling circumstances that justify overruling a patient's refusal of treatment. These include:
◆ when refusing treatment endangers the life of another—for example, a court may overrule a pregnant woman's objection to treatment if it endangers her unborn child's life.

Living will

The living will is an advance care document that specifies a person's wishes with regard to medical care, should he become terminally ill, incompetent, or unable to communicate. The will is commonly used in combination with the patient's durable power of attorney.

All states and the District of Columbia have living will laws that outline the documentation requirements for living wills. The sample document below is from Ohio.

Living will

If my attending doctor and one other doctor who examines me determine, to a reasonable degree of medical certainty and in accordance with reasonable medical standards, that I am in a terminal condition or in a permanently unconscious state, and if my attending doctor determines that at that time I no longer am able to make informed decisions regarding the administration of life-sustaining treatment, and that, to a reasonable degree of medical certainty and in accordance with reasonable medical standards, there is no reasonable possibility that I will regain the capacity to make informed decisions regarding the administration of life-sustaining treatment, then I direct my attending doctor to withhold or withdraw medical procedures, treatment, interventions, or other measures that serve principally to prolong the process of my dying, rather than diminish my pain or discomfort.

I have used the term "terminal condition" in this declaration to mean an irreversible, incurable, and untreatable condition caused by disease, illness, or injury from which, to a reasonable degree of medical certainty as determined in accordance with reasonable medical standards of my attending doctor and one other doctor who has examined me, both of the following apply:

1. There can be no recovery.

2. Death is likely to occur within a relatively short time if life-sustaining treatment is not administered.

I have used the term "permanently unconscious state" in this declaration to mean a state of permanent unconsciousness that, to a reasonable degree of medical certainty, is determined in accordance with reasonable medical standards by my attending doctor and one other doctor who has examined me, as characterized by both of the following:

1. I am irreversibly unaware of myself and my environment.

2. There is a total loss of cerebral cortical functioning, resulting in my having no capacity to experience pain or suffering.

Nutrition & Hydration

I hereby authorize my attending doctor to withhold or withdraw nutrition and hydration from me when I am in a permanent unconscious state if my attending doctor and at least one other doctor who has examined me determine, to a reasonable degree of medical certainty and in accordance with reasonable medical standards, that nutrition or hydration will not or no longer will serve to provide comfort to me or alleviate my pain.

[Sign here for withdrawal of nutrition or hydration]

(continued)

Living will *(continued)*

I hereby designate [Print name of person to decide] as the person who I wish my attending doctor to notify at any time that life-sustaining treatment is to be withdrawn or withheld pursuant to this Declaration.

_____   _____
[Sign your name here]   [Today's date]

Witness by:
[Living will person's name] voluntarily signed or directed another individual to sign this Living Will in the presence of the following who each attests that the Declarant appears to be of sound mind and not under or subject to duress, fraud, or undue influence.

_____
[First witness signs here]

_____
[Second witness signs here]

◆ when a parent's decision to withhold treatment threatens a child's life — for example, a court may overrule the parents' religious objections to their child's treatment when the child's life is endangered. When the child's life isn't in danger, the courts are more likely to respect the parents' religious convictions.

◆ when, despite refusing treatment, the patient makes statements indicating that he wants to live — for example, some Jehovah's Witnesses who oppose blood transfusions say or imply that they won't prevent the transfusions if a court takes responsibility for the decision. In *Powell v. Columbia-Presbyterian Medical Center* (1965), the court authorized transfusions when a Jehovah's Witness indicated that she wouldn't object to receiving blood, although she refused to give written consent.

◆ when the public interest outweighs the patient's right — for example, the law requires school-age children (with few exceptions) to receive a polio vaccine before they can attend classes.

RESPONDING TO THE PATIENT'S REQUEST TO STOP TREATMENT

When a patient plans to refuse treatment, you may be the person he tells first. Whether he tells you he's going to refuse treatment or he simply refuses to give consent, stop preparations for any treatment at once. Immediately notify the physician and report your patient's decision to your supervisor. Never delay informing your supervisor, especially if a delay could be life-threatening. Any delay you're responsible for will greatly increase your legal risks.

Durable power of attorney for health care

The sample document below is an example of a durable power of attorney, which allows a competent patient to delegate to another person the authority to consent to or refuse health care treatment. This helps the patient ensure that his wishes will be carried out if he should become incompetent.

Each state with a durable power of attorney for health care law has specific requirements for executing the document. The sample form below is from Nebraska.

Power of Attorney for Health Care

I appoint _____

whose address is_____

and whose telephone number is _____

as my attorney in fact for health care. _____

I appoint_____

whose address is_____

and whose telephone number is _____

as my successor attorney in fact for health care. _____

I authorize my attorney in fact appointed by this document to make health care decisions for me when I am determined to be incapable of making my own health care decisions. I have read the warning which accompanies this document and understand the consequences of executing a power of attorney for health care.

I direct that my attorney in fact comply with the following instructions or limitations (optional):

I direct that my attorney in fact comply with the following instructions on life-sustaining treatment (optional):

I direct that my attorney in fact comply with the following instructions on artificially administered nutrition and hydration (optional):

I have read this power of attorney for health care. I understand that it allows another person to make life and death decisions for me if I am incapable of making such decisions. I also understand that I can revoke this power of attorney for health care at any time by notifying my attorney in fact, my physician, or the facility in which I am a patient or resident. I also understand that I can require in this power of attorney for health care that the fact of my incapacity in the future be confirmed by a second physician.

_____   _____
[Signature of person making designation]   [Date]

Overruling the patient

Even when a patient's decision to refuse treatment rests on constitutionally protected grounds, such as religious beliefs, the court will intervene in certain circumstances. Becoming familiar with court rulings in this area will help you better cope if you're ever caught between a patient and his family and a court. Here are some delicate legal situations the courts have ruled on. Keep in mind that each case is binding only in its own jurisdiction. A court where you practice may hold differently.

Incapacitated patient

If an adult patient becomes physically or mentally incapacitated, a relative can't always refuse treatment for him. The court reserves the right to overrule even a spouse on the patient's behalf if the decision seems to be medically unreasonable. For example, in *Collins v. Davis* (1964), the court overruled a wife's refusal of surgery for her unconscious husband.

Patient responsible for child

If a patient who's responsible for the care of a child refuses lifesaving treatment, the court may reverse the patient's decision. In *Application of the President and Directors of Georgetown College, Inc.* (1964), the New York Supreme Court ordered a blood transfusion for a Jehovah's Witness who was the mother of an infant and who refused to give consent for her own transfusion. In the case of *In re Melideo* (1976), the court said that it might have ordered a lifesaving transfusion for the patient if she had had a child.

Pregnant patient

If a patient who's pregnant refuses treatment, thereby threatening not only her own health but also that of her unborn child, the courts can reverse the patient's decision. In *Jefferson v. Griffin Spalding County Hospital Authority* (1981), the court awarded temporary custody of an unborn child to a state agency. The mother had a complete placenta previa but had refused to consent to a cesarean birth. The court's custody award included full authority to give consent for a surgical delivery.

Patient who's a minor

If a patient is a minor, the court will allow his parents or legal guardian to consent to medical treatment but it will not allow them to deny him lifesaving treatment. *In re Sampson* (1972) was such a case.

The physician and hospital have the responsibility to take action, such as trying to convince the patient to accept treatment or asking him to sign a release form. This form relieves the hospital and the health care team of liability for any consequences the patient suffers by refusing treatment. It doesn't, however, release the health care team from its obligation to continue providing other forms of care.

Don't ignore the patient

Never ignore a patient's request to refuse treatment. A patient can sue you for battery — intentionally touching another person without authorization to do so — for simply following physician's orders. (See *Is this nurse liable?*)

To overrule the patient's decision, the physician or your hospital must obtain a court order. Only then are you legally authorized to administer the treatment.

If the physician or hospital tries to convince the court to overrule the patient on the grounds that he's incompetent, they'll need proof that he lacks the mental ability to make a reasoned decision. Your documented observations about your patient's mental status may be used as evidence.

No matter how serious the patient's condition, refusing treatment doesn't constitute evidence of incompetence. In *Lane v. Candura* (1978), for example, a patient with diabetes first agreed to have her leg amputated and then changed her mind and refused the surgery. After attempting to persuade the patient that the amputation was necessary, the physicians applied for a court order, arguing that by changing her mind, the patient had shown incompetence. The court disagreed, and upheld the patient's right to withdraw her consent.

RIGHT TO REFUSE EMERGENCY TREATMENT

A competent adult has the right to refuse emergency treatment. His family can't overrule his decision, and his physician may not give the expressly refused treatment, even if the patient becomes unconscious.

If there are no grounds for overruling your patient's decision, you have an ethical duty to defend his right to refuse treatment in the face of all opposition, even his family's. Try to explain the patient's choice to family members. Emphasize that the decision is his as long as he's competent.

Respecting the patient's autonomy

A patient may refuse any treatment — whether ordinary or extraordinary.

Is this nurse liable?

In the course of providing daily care, you may easily overlook the potential legal consequences of ignoring a patient who refuses treatment. Consider the fictional case below.

A battle of wills

Albert Proxmire, age 69, is hospitalized with a GI disorder. He's also depressed and uncooperative. His day-shift nurse, Bernice Bransted, reads on his chart that the physician ordered an enema.

Disgruntled and surly, Mr. Proxmire has other ideas. He bluntly tells the nurse, "Leave me alone. I'm not getting an enema now!"

Despite his protests, Ms. Bransted insists. She gently turns him in his bed and administers the enema.

Later, Mr. Proxmire's son becomes angry when his father tells him what happened. The son confronts the nursing supervisor and warns her that he intends to pursue the matter.

A battle in the courts?

Does Mr. Proxmire have a case for battery against the nurse? Yes. As a conscious, coherent adult, even though depressed, Mr. Proxmire has the right to refuse treatment. After he — or any other adult patient — refuses any nursing treatment, giving it will make the nurse liable for battery.

However, the decision to refuse ordinary treatment presents an especially complex ethical dilemma. This dilemma hinges on the conflict between beneficence and autonomy. If a patient can make an informed decision, he has a right to refuse treatment. But what if his decision doesn't serve his best interests? Which moral principle, autonomy or beneficence, should take precedence? (See *Saying "no" to rehabilitation.*)

AUTONOMY AND ITS LIMITS

One of the cornerstones of ethical decision making, autonomy refers to the right to make decisions about one's health care. However, external and internal pressures can limit the patient's autonomy.

External pressures

Family members and health professionals can exert appreciable influence over the patient. Typically, this influence takes the form of persuasion or encouragement. Infrequently, it takes the form of coercion, in which the patient comes to believe he has no free choice.

Physician–patient relationships are inherently imbalanced. The physician possesses knowledge and skill; the patient, a need for care. Because the patient has a need, he assumes a dependent and potentially vulnerable position. He must trust the caregiver. In doing so, he may think that assertiveness is inappropriate. You, however, can counteract this thinking by encouraging the patient to be informed and to ask questions.

Internal pressures

Doubt and illness itself can sap autonomy. For instance, the patient may see himself as too ignorant to make crucial decisions about his health. If he does, bolster his self-esteem; encourage him to take an active role in decision making, and support him in his efforts. The patient's signs and symptoms, such as dyspnea and pain, may distract him. If they do, try to relieve them so that the patient can make thoughtful decisions.

BENEFICENCE

When dealing with children or patients who can't make informed decisions, beneficence outweighs autonomy. Young children, for instance, don't understand the implications of not being vaccinated for measles or mumps and would simply prefer to avoid the pain of an injection.

For patients who can make an informed decision, though, the burden of proof for beneficence lies with the health care provider. Typically, a health care provider can advance these arguments in support of beneficence:
◆ The patient is under excessive stress and can't think rationally.
◆ The patient may change his mind later, when little or nothing can be done to restore his health.
◆ The patient needs to be protected from acting irrationally.

Underlying all of these arguments is a spirit of paternalism, of possessing superior or clearer knowledge than the patient. Of course, the patient could and might change his decision, but this uncertainty doesn't constitute grounds for overruling a competent patient's decision.

FUTILITY

Medical futility refers to treatment that can't benefit a patient, not necessarily because the treatment itself has no merit but more commonly because the condition of the patient makes the medical action futile. A futile intervention differs from one that's harmful, ineffective, or impossible, and it shouldn't be equated with hopelessness. Hope may be maintained by patients even in impossible situations.

A futile treatment differs from an ineffective or a highly improbable treatment in that it may achieve a short-term gain (such as improving carbon

Saying "no" to rehabilitation

One reward of rehabilitation nursing is watching a patient with severe injuries come to terms with an altered body image and eventually go on to live a fulfilling life with a disability. But what happens when a patient turns down the help that nurses and therapists offer? Nurses may experience a bitter ethical conflict between the principle of patient autonomy – which includes the right to refuse treatment – and the principle of beneficence. Consider the case of Philip Munson, a young quadriplegic who refused rehabilitative treatment, deciding that he preferred to die.

Wanting to die

Mr. Munson, age 30, was left a C3 quadriplegic after he broke his neck in an automobile accident. First admitted to the intensive care unit (ICU), Mr. Munson was totally dependent on others for all activities and all aspects of his care. His only relatives were a brother and a sister-in-law, who visited regularly and planned to have him live with them after rehabilitation.

During his month in the ICU, Philip told the nurses that he wanted to live. Shortly after being transferred to the rehabilitation unit, however, he changed his mind. He wanted to die and insisted on discontinuing his rehabilitation program. His brother made it clear that he wanted Mr. Munson's wishes respected. A psychiatrist evaluated Mr. Munson and concluded that he was competent and showed no evidence of psychosis or thought disorder.

Mr. Munson understood his condition and his prognosis; he was aware that after rehabilitation he would be able to operate a wheelchair and a computer. He also understood that he would be paralyzed from the neck down and would always need assistance with activities of daily living. Mr. Munson said that he wasn't afraid of death and wanted no heroic measures taken. His brother helped him draft an extensive legal statement establishing the right to refuse specific treatments, including antibiotic and I.V. therapy. Plans were made to discharge him to a nursing home.

Ethical considerations

Many of the nurses and therapists on the rehabilitation unit were distressed by the decision to stop Mr. Munson's program. Depression, anger, and refusal of treatment are common among young accident victims, and these health care professionals were skilled at encouraging, bargaining with, and even coercing patients to comply. They argued that Mr. Munson's decision was misguided and that there was justification for intervention based on the principles of paternalism and beneficence.

Jim DiFrancesco, RN, a nurse on the rehabilitation team, pointed out that there was a significant difference between a young, recently injured quadriplegic and a terminal cancer patient who finally decides to "pull the plug." He believed that Mr. Munson was under too much stress from the initial impact of the injury and would probably later change his mind and view life as worth living once again. He pointed out to members of the health care team that there are many examples of patients reversing their decision to die. Elizabeth Bouvia, a young woman incapacitated by cerebral palsy, received national publicity when she requested that the hospital discontinue her tube feedings and allow her to starve herself to death, but she later changed her mind and stated that she wanted to live.

Mr. DiFrancesco pointed out that many factors, such as depression, fear of treatment, hidden family dynamics, and ambivalence, complicated Mr. Munson's ability to make an autonomous decision. Furthermore, Mr. Munson was clearly ambivalent about his desire to die. His behavior wasn't always consistent with his expressed wish for death. For example, Mr.

(continued)

Saying "no" to rehabilitation *(continued)*

Munson was cheerful on many days and took great interest in the positioning of his joints and measures taken to prevent joint contractures.

In fact, for a brief period, Mr. Munson reneged on his wish to die. His best friend from high school learned about the accident and decided to devote a long visit to helping Philip. When he learned his friend would be arriving soon, Mr. Munson asked to start full therapy again. Although his high school buddy helped out tirelessly and offered to stay even longer, Mr. Munson quickly became overwhelmed by the pain and hardship of his existence and requested that his previous statement outlining his wish to die be reactivated.

Respecting patient autonomy

Another nurse on the unit, Christina Walsh, RN, pointed out that the rehabilitation unit's mission was to serve the patient's best interest, not meet the emotional needs of the staff. She believed that members of the health care team had their own vested interest in keeping Mr. Munson alive. For example, the occupational therapist was excited about experimenting with the latest wheelchair control devices. Many of her coworkers, accustomed to seeing their patients readjust to life, couldn't accept that they would inevitably fail some of their patients. It wasn't right, asserted Ms. Walsh, to pursue every technological intervention regardless of the cost or burden to the patient.

An ethical struggle

During the time Mr. Munson remained on the rehabilitation unit, the nurses who cared for him experienced an intense ethical struggle. It was difficult to agree not to perform routine tracheostomy care or range-of-motion exercises or to care for the pressure ulcer that developed on the back of Mr. Munson's head. It also was difficult, however, to do these things in good conscience for a patient who asked that they not be done. It seemed like a total usurpation of what little power and control Mr. Munson still had. Each nurse had to struggle with questions about the rights of a patient who doesn't have the ability to leave the hospital against medical advice, protest his treatment, or even complain without the assistance of another person.

Mr. Munson's ordeal finally came to an end when he was transported to a nursing home near the residence of his brother's family. After 2 months, he slipped into a coma and died. His existence was a lesson to the rehabilitation team: Most patients are grateful for the opportunity for a second chance at life; for some, however, the pain is too great. Ultimately, the decision to accept treatment belongs to the patient.

---

dioxide excretion in a ventilated patient who has chronic obstructive pulmonary disease), but it remains fruitless because it doesn't lead to a true personal benefit (restoration of health).

Often, health care teams don't render care they deem futile, but with the growing importance of patient autonomy and self-determination, such choices aren't so readily made. Patients believe that they have a right to determine what constitutes a "benefit" to them. At the same time, nurses and physicians should be able to decide when a treatment is futile based on their knowledge of the treatment and its probable effect on the patient's quality of life. The patient's right to choose is limited by the nurses and physicians whose duty it is to provide

> **Right to privacy** *(continued)*
>
> She's also willing to arrange to be in Mr. Gordon's room during morning care. If, for example, she opens his drawer to get his toothbrush and finds a medicine bottle, she can then ask about it. However, that's as far as she will go. She won't participate in a search without the patient's consent, even in his presence. She realizes that, as Dr. Stein said, this might limit the ability of the health care team to help Mr. Gordon, but a competent patient has the right to forgo help.

BREACHES OF CONFIDENTIALITY

Confidential information can ethically be disclosed in certain circumstances such as when failure to disclose information could cause serious physical harm to the patient, his family, facility staff, or another third party. However, knowing when confidentiality may be appropriately breached isn't always easy. Consider the three case studies here. For each case, decide whether you agree with the ethical decision made by the nurse.

Preventing harm to the patient

Kitisha Jefferson, RN, was caring for Will Cooke, a 33-year-old electrician who fractured his femur in a fall at a construction site. She had established a good nurse-patient relationship with him. However, Mr. Cooke had seemed bored and edgy for the past day or so. When Ms. Jefferson checked his room, she found his curtain drawn halfway around his bed. She walked to the open side and saw Mr. Cooke hurriedly closing a plastic bag that contained white powder. "What are you doing?" she asked him.

"All right," Mr. Cooke replied. "Because you're a good nurse, I'll level with you. I was doing cocaine. I know I shouldn't, but it gets boring when you're in traction with nothing to do but watch the tube. Please, don't tell anybody. If my wife finds out, I'm finished."

Ms. Jefferson patiently explained that cocaine can have severe effects, especially when taken with other drugs. She advised Mr. Cooke to discontinue using cocaine — at least while he's hospitalized.

After taking these measures, Ms. Jefferson still faced ethical dilemmas. What should she write in the patient's chart? Should she tell Mr. Cooke's physician? Should she recommend that Mr. Cooke tell the physician?

After careful consideration, Ms. Jefferson decided to tell Mr. Cooke that she had an obligation to let the physician know about his cocaine use — unless Mr. Cooke wanted to tell the physician himself. Her decision was based on the ethical principle of beneficence; she believed that the risk of cardiac arrest caused by the combination of cocaine and other medications was an overriding factor.

Protecting staff

Steve Walcott, RN, was reviewing Tamara Smith's chart before giving her a preoperative sedative when he realized that one of his colleagues had been discussing her at lunch the day before. This colleague, who worked in the laboratory, didn't mention Ms. Smith by name, but the age and admission date gave away the patient's identity. She had said that Ms. Smith tested positive for HIV infection but that the results weren't being noted on the chart. Should Mr. Walcott inform the surgical team of Ms. Smith's test results?

Mr. Walcott felt a strong temptation to protect his coworkers as the first consideration. However, he also realized that his colleague was remiss in discussing Ms. Smith's test results. Therefore, he reasoned that he would be remiss in further violating the confidentiality of this information. He also feared stigmatizing the patient. He further reasoned that the surgical team should use standard precautions for all patients, not just those who test positive for HIV. After all, patients who haven't had the test can also carry the antibody.

Protecting the patient's family

Jenny Chu, RN, was caring for Susan Schaffer, a 32-year-old mother of five scheduled for a tubal ligation. She wanted to make sure her patient understood the effects of this surgery, so she asked Mrs. Schaffer to explain the procedure. Mrs. Schaffer did so eagerly and added, "I'm so happy I won't have to worry about getting pregnant again. Five kids is more than I can handle as it is."

Satisfied, Ms. Chu left Mrs. Schaffer and continued her rounds. Later that day, she met Mrs. Schaffer's husband, Matt, at the nurses' station. He asked for a box of tissues and said, "I hope the surgery fixes Susan's problem. Did she tell you we've been trying to have another baby for over 1 year? I really want to have a few more kids."

What should Ms. Chu do: protect Mrs. Schaffer's confidentiality or tell

Mr. Schaffer the truth? Ms. Chu believed that her first obligation was to protect Mrs. Schaffer's confidentiality. The urge to tell Mr. Schaffer about his wife's deception was compelling, but he wasn't in danger of physical harm from her action. Ms. Chu felt badly that Mr. and Mrs. Schaffer couldn't talk to each other frankly, but she also believed that this wasn't an excuse for breaching confidentiality. Nonetheless, Ms. Chu decided to discuss the matter with the surgeon, especially because hospital policy required a spouse's signature on the consent form for a sterilization procedure.

Patient's right to privacy

Obtaining highly personal information from a patient can be uncomfortable and embarrassing. Reassuring the patient that you'll keep information confidential may help to put you both at ease. But stop to think about the legal complexities of this responsibility. What do you do when your patient's spouse, other health care professionals, the media, or public health agencies ask you to disclose confidential information?

IS THERE A CONSTITUTIONAL RIGHT TO PRIVACY?

Privacy and confidentiality were first proposed as basic legal rights in 1890 in a *Harvard Law Review* article titled "The Right to Privacy."

The U.S. Constitution doesn't explicitly sanction a right to privacy. But in several court cases, including *Roe v. Wade* (1973), the U.S. Supreme Court cited several constitutional amendments that imply the right.

The right to privacy essentially is the right to make personal choices without outside interference. In the landmark case of *Griswold v. Connecticut* (1965), for example, the Supreme Court recognized a married couple's right to privacy in contraceptive use. In *Eisenstadt v. Baird* (1972), the Supreme Court extended the right to privacy in contraceptive use to include unmarried people. In *Carey v. Population Services International* (1977), the Supreme Court said a state law that prohibited the sale of contraceptives to anyone younger than age 16 was unconstitutional.

The U.S. Department of Health and Human Services tried to modify the *Carey* ruling by publishing a regulation, "Parental Notification Requirements Applicable to Projects for Family Planning Services." Also known as the "squeal rule," this regulation proposed that any federally funded clinic or health agency giving contraceptives to a minor be required to inform the minor's parents or guardian. A New York federal district court, however, declared that divulging such confidential information invades the minor's privacy and is unconstitutional.

Right to privacy and abortion law

The Supreme Court ruling in *Roe v. Wade* (1973) protects a woman's right to privacy in a first-trimester abortion. After the first trimester, a state may regulate abortion to protect the mother's health and prohibit an abortion if the fetus is judged viable. However, state legislators have complicated access to abortion services in different ways. In 1999 alone, President George W. Bush, then governor of Texas, passed several laws affecting abortion rights. One law mandates parental notification and a 48-hour waiting period for minors. Another prohibits licensed medical professionals from performing third-trimester abortions. Another law excludes organizations that offer abortion procedures from receiving family planning funding and mandates that funds for prescription contraceptives for minors be given only with parental consent; another denies tax-exemption to nonprofit organizations that perform, refer for, or assist other organizations that perform or refer for abortion. Yet another law prohibits the state Child Health Plan from covering any services that prevent conception or birth. Another prohibits school-based health centers from providing reproductive services, counseling, or referrals if they receive certain grants. Other states have passed similar laws, including Virginia, Arizona, Iowa, and Florida.

Restrictions on the right to abortion

Since *Roe v. Wade* (1973), the Supreme Court has handed down more than 20 major opinions related to the abortion issue.

A 1989 Supreme Court decision, *Webster v. Reproductive Health Services*, placed certain aspects of *Roe v. Wade* into doubt. Although viability of the fetus remains the guideline, the Supreme Court now appears more willing to allow states to regulate abortion. For example, in 1992, in *Planned Parenthood of Southeastern Pennsylvania v. Casey*, the Supreme Court let stand Pennsylvania's Abortion Control Act of 1989. This act requires that a woman wait 24 hours between consenting to and receiving an abortion, except in narrowly defined medical emergencies, and that a woman seeking an abortion be given state-mandated abortion information and offered state-authored materials on fetal development. The Supreme Court struck down the requirement that a married woman inform her husband of her intent to have an abortion. Overall, the decision reaffirmed a woman's right to abortion, but suggested that the Court had revised its longstanding definition of that right as fundamental.

In May 1991, antiabortion groups won a victory on another front. In *Rust v. Sullivan* (1991), the Supreme Court upheld federal regulations prohibiting health care workers at more than 4,000 government-subsidized family planning clinics from providing any information about abortion. Under the regulations, if you work in a subsidized clinic you may not advise a pregnant woman that abortion is a possibility, nor may you help her find a private abortion clinic. You are obligated to refer pregnant women for prenatal care. (See *Money and contraception.*)

Abortion rights for minors

Roe v. Wade (1973) played an important role in extending abortion rights to minors. In *Planned Parenthood of Central Missouri v. Danforth* (1976), the Supreme Court overruled a law that prevented first-trimester abortions for minors without parental consent. This decision was based on *Roe v. Wade*.

In *Bellotti v. Baird II* (1979), the Supreme Court acknowledged that the privacy rights of a minor aren't equal to those of an adult. The Court held, however, that a state law requiring a minor to obtain parental consent for an abortion infringed on the minor's rights.

In *H.L. v. Matheson* (1981), the Supreme Court upheld a Utah law requiring a physician to notify the parents of an unemancipated minor before an abortion. However, in *Hodgson v. Minnesota* (1990), a Minnesota statute that required notification of both biological parents before a mi-

nor's abortion, after a wait of at least 48 hours, was held unconstitutional. The chief difference between the two cases is that the Utah law required notification of only one parent, where feasible; the Minnesota law required notification of both parents, even if they were divorced or separated. In *Hodgson*, the Supreme Court decreed that the rule requiring notification of both parents was too burdensome on the right to abortion because it could create exceptional difficulties for one-parent families. The Court also stated that the 48-hour waiting period required under the Minnesota law would not, by itself, render the statute unconstitutional.

By letting stand Pennsylvania's Abortion Control Act in 1992, the Supreme Court allowed the state to require that one parent or guardian give consent in person for a minor seeking an abortion, unless the minor obtains a judicial waiver.

In *Hodgson* and *Ohio v. Akron Center for Reproductive Health* (1990), the Supreme Court set forth its position on judicial bypass statutes. Judicial bypass statutes allow a minor to avoid notifying parents or obtaining consent for an abortion by going before a judge. The Court stated that judicial bypass satisfies the requirement that parents or other third parties can't have an absolute veto over the minor's abortion decision.

PRIVILEGE DOCTRINE

The state courts have been strong in protecting a patient's right to have information kept confidential. Even in court, your patient is protected by the privilege doctrine. People who have a protected relationship, such as a physician and patient, can't be forced (even during legal proceedings) to reveal

Money and contraception

Contraception and abortion are heavily restricted through legislation. A federal directive issued July 2, 1998, by the Clinton administration specifically mandates payment by Medicaid and insurance companies for the drug sildenafil (Viagra), which treats impotence. However, there are no laws mandating any type of payment for birth control, and about 50% of large insurance companies won't pay for it.

Birth control for pay

A controversial, privately funded program designed to decrease the number of drug-addicted newborns, started in Anaheim, California, and is now operating in Chicago, Dallas, Minneapolis, and Fort Pierce, Florida. The program provides money ($200 in at least one state) for people who undergo long-term birth control procedures. To be eligible, the person must have a form signed by a physician listing the form of birth control the person is using. Acceptable forms of long-term birth control include intrauterine devices, levonorgestrel (Norplant) arm implants, and sterilization. The most controversial is sterilization because it's potentially irreversible.

Opponents of the program question whether most addicts have the judgment to make such a decision and whether the program has racial undertones. However, to date, the majority of participants have been Caucasian. Interestingly, men have sought details about the program, but none have participated.

---

communication between them, unless the person who benefits from the protection agrees to it. This means that the patient must agree before confidential information is revealed in court. The purpose of the privilege doctrine is to encourage the patient to reveal confidential information that may be essential to his treatment. State law determines which relationships are protected by the privilege doctrine. Most states include husband–wife, lawyer–client, and physician–patient relationships.

Nurse-patient relationships

Only a few states (including New York, Arkansas, Oregon, and Vermont) recognize the nurse–patient relationship as protected. However, some courts have said that the privilege exists when a nurse is following a physician's orders. Whether the privilege applies to LPNs and LVNs as well is uncertain.

Extent of privilege

State laws also determine the extent of privilege in protected relationships. In *Hammonds v. Aetna Casualty and Surety Co.* (1965), the court reinforced the privilege doctrine by declaring that protecting a patient's privacy is a physician's legal duty. It further ruled that a patient could sue for damages any unauthorized person who disclosed confidential medical information about him. Similarly, a patient can sue for invasion of privacy any unauthorized personnel such as student nurses who observe him without his permission. The only hospital personnel who have a right to observe a patient are those involved in his diagnosis, treatment, and related care.

Exceptions

In some states, a patient automatically waives his right to physician-patient privilege when he files a personal injury or workers' compensation lawsuit.

A hospital or physician can't invoke the privilege doctrine if the motive is self-protection. In *People v. Doe* (1978), a nursing home was being investigated for allegedly mistreating its patients. The court ruled that the nursing home's attempt to invoke patient privilege was unjust because the issue at hand was the patients' welfare.

Patient privilege and Canadian law

In all Canadian jurisdictions, privilege doctrine applies only to solicitor-client communications. Physicians and nurses are bound by codes of ethics as well as legislation concerning confidentiality. Cases that suggest the physician-patient privilege include *Dembie* (1963), *Re SAS* (1977), and *Geransy* (1977). The Canadian Nurses Association has its own code of ethics, which has been largely adopted in nurse practice acts in Canadian jurisdictions. The code requires nurses to keep confidential any personal information they receive from a patient during nursing care. Consequently, although violation of a patient's right to privacy isn't subject to criminal prosecution in Canada, it's deemed professional misconduct. A nurse who violates a patient's right to privacy could lose her nursing license.

YOUR RESPONSIBILITIES IN PROTECTING PATIENT PRIVACY

Despite legal uncertainties regarding your responsibilities under the privilege doctrine, you have a professional and ethical responsibility to protect your patient's privacy, whether you're an RN or an LPN.

This responsibility requires more than keeping secrets. You may have to educate your patients about their privacy rights. Some of them may be unaware of what the right to privacy means, or that they even have such a right. Explain to the patient that he can refuse to allow pictures to be taken of his disorder and its treatment, for example. Tell him that he can choose to have information about his condition withheld from others, including his family. Make every effort to ensure that the patient's wishes are carried out.

WHEN YOU MAY DISCLOSE CONFIDENTIAL INFORMATION

Under certain circumstances, you may lawfully disclose confidential information about your patient. For example, the courts allow disclosure when the welfare of a person or a group of people is at stake. Consider the patient who's diagnosed as an epileptic and asks you not to tell his family. Depending on the circumstances, you may decide that this isn't in the patient's and his family's best interest, particularly in terms of safety. In that situation, inform the patient's physician; he may then decide to inform the patient's family to protect the patient's well-being. In most states, the physician is required to inform the Department of Motor Vehicles of uncontrolled epilepsy.

You're also protected by law if you disclose confidential information about a patient that's necessary for his continued care or if your patient consents to the disclosure.

Be careful not to exceed the specified limit of a patient's consent. Taking pictures is the largest single cause of invasion of privacy lawsuits. In *Feeney v. Young* (1920), a woman consented to the filming of her cesarean birth for viewing by medical societies, but the physician incorporated the film into a generally released movie titled *Birth*. The court awarded damages to the woman under the state's privacy law.

Protecting the public

The courts have granted immunity to health care professionals who, in good faith, have disclosed confidential information to prevent public harm. In *Simonsen v. Swenson* (1920), a physician who thought that his patient had syphilis told the owner of the hotel in which the patient was staying about the patient's contagious disease. The court ruled that physicians are privileged to make disclosures that will prevent the spread of disease.

A controversial California case established a physician's right to disclose information that would protect any person whom a patient threatened to harm. In *Tarasoff v. Regents of the University of California* (1976), a woman was murdered by a mentally ill patient who had told his psychotherapist that he intended to kill her. The victim's parents sued the physician for failing to warn their daughter. The Supreme Court found the physician liable because he didn't warn the intended victim. The Court ruled similarly in *McIntosh v. Milano* (1979).

WHEN YOU MUST DISCLOSE CONFIDENTIAL INFORMATION

In some situations, the law requires you to disclose confidential information.

Child abuse

All 50 states and the District of Columbia have disclosure laws for child abuse cases. Except for Maine and Montana, all states also grant immunity

from legal action for a good faith report on suspected child abuse. In fact, there may be a criminal penalty for failure to disclose such information.

Courts may also order you to disclose confidential information in cases of child custody and child neglect. One case involving such an order was *D. v. D.* (1969). Despite the physician-patient privilege, the court ordered the physician to turn the mother's medical records over to the court for a private inspection. The mother had a history of illness, and the court said that the inspection would help to decide which parent should be granted custody. The courts made a similar ruling in *In re Doe Children* (1978). The court stated that the children's welfare outweighed the parents' right to keep their medical records private.

Criminal cases

Some laws create an exemption to the privilege doctrine in criminal cases so that the courts can have access to all essential information. In states where neither a law nor an exemption to the law exists, the court may find an exemption to the doctrine in criminal cases.

Government requests

Certain government agencies can order you to reveal confidential information, including federal agencies such as the Internal Revenue Service, the Environmental Protection Agency, the Department of Labor, and the Department of Health and Human Services. State agencies that may order you to reveal confidential information include revenue or tax bureaus and public health departments. For example, most state public health departments require reports of all communicable diseases, births and deaths, and gunshot wounds.

Public's right to know

The newsworthiness of an event or person can make disclosure acceptable. In such circumstances, the public's need for information may outweigh a person's right to keep his medical condition private. For example, newspapers routinely publish the findings of the President's annual physical examination in response to the public's demand for information. Even the First Lady's health may become a matter of public record.

Other events for which the public's right to know may outweigh the patient's right to privacy include breakthroughs in medical technology (the first successful hand transplant) and product tampering cases, for example. In 1999, the national media gave wide exposure to an incident in New York State in which nine people died after being bitten by a mosquito that transmitted a flavivirus that causes St. Louis encephalitis.

Even when the public has a right to know about a confidential matter, the courts won't allow public disclosure to undermine a person's dignity. In *Barber v. Time, Inc.* (1942), *TIME* magazine was sued by a woman whose name and photograph were published in an article that revealed she suffered from an illness that caused her to eat as much food as 10 people could eat. The court ruled that publishing the patient's name and picture was an unnecessary invasion of her privacy, and that ethics required keeping such information confidential.

Doe v. Roe (1977) is a similar case. A patient sued his psychiatrist for publishing the patient's biography and thoughts verbatim. Even though the physician didn't use the patient's name, the court stated that the patient was readily identifiable by the article. It found the physician liable for violating the physician-patient privilege.

When the patient demands his chart

Suppose the patient says to you, "I'm paying for the tests; I have a right to know the results." Does the patient have the legal right to know what's in his medical records?

Yes — and because patients increasingly want explanations about what's being done to them and why, you should know how to respond when your patient asks to see his medical records.

Disclosure debate

For years, health care experts have debated the merits of letting a patient see his medical records. Proponents argue that knowing the information helps the patient to better understand his condition and care and makes him a more cooperative patient.

Opponents, usually physicians and hospitals, argue that the technical jargon and medical abbreviations found in medical records may confuse or even frighten a patient. In addition, opponents claim that opening medical records to a patient will increase the risks of malpractice lawsuits. No evidence exists to support this contention.

The "right to access" issue has spawned an important legal debate. The first issue the courts had to answer involved ownership.

Determining ownership

The hospital owns the hospital medical records, and the physician owns his office records, according to court decisions. Most courts have decided that a patient sees a physician for diagnosis and treatment, not to obtain records for his personal use.

Right to access

The second issue the courts had to resolve involved access. While granting ownership of medical records to physicians and hospitals, the courts have expressed their rights to get a patient's records anytime they need to have them for a case review.

For this reason, any patient in any state can file a lawsuit to subpoena his medical records. However, some court decisions and some states' laws have given patients the right to direct access. Many states guarantee a patient's right to his medical information.

In *Cannell v. Medical and Surgical Clinic* (1974), the court ruled that a physician had the duty to disclose medical information to his patient. The court also ruled, however, that physicians and hospitals need not turn over the actual files to the patient. Instead, they need only to show the complete medical record — or a copy — to the patient.

The court based the patient's limited right to access on two important concepts:

◆ A patient has a right to know the details about his medical treatment under common law.

◆ A patient has a right to the information in his records because he pays for the treatment.

Setting up roadblocks

Despite the laws and court decisions, hospitals don't always make access to records easy. Some hospitals discourage a patient from seeing his medical records by putting up bureaucratic barriers. For example, requiring the patient to have an attorney make the request can stifle a patient's attempt to gain access and encourage visits to malpractice lawyers. Other hospitals charge high copying fees to discourage patient record requests.

Some states, such as Pennsylvania, have laws setting maximum fees that can be charged for copying a patient's medical records.

How to respond to your patient's request

A patient's request should make you question whether you and your colleagues have done enough to communicate with him. Assess why the patient wants to see his records. He may simply be curious, or his request may reflect hidden fears about his treatment.

Many hospitals have established policies that deal with this issue. These policies may include notifying your nursing supervisor that the patient has asked to see his medical records and notifying the risk manager, if your facility has one, to alert administrative staff and legal counsel, if necessary.

After your patient gets approval to see his records, stay with him while he reads them. Explain to him that state laws prohibit him from changing or erasing information on his records, even information he considers incorrect. Tell him to show you any information he considers incorrect. Offer to answer any of his questions you can; assure him that his physician will answer questions, too. In fact, encourage the patient to write down specific questions for his physician, and offer to contact his physician for him.

While your patient reads, help him to interpret the abbreviations and jargon used in medical charting. One patient hospitalized for hypertension was greatly relieved when her nurse explained that the "malignant hypertension" notation on her chart had nothing to do with cancer.

Observe how the patient responds while he reads. If he becomes apprehensive, puzzled, or angry, try to provide him with calm, professional explanations about what he has read in his records. Some patients want to read their records just to make sure you and the physicians aren't hiding information. For example, one patient who demanded to see her medical records merely flipped through the pages. The hospital's willingness to share information about her treatment apparently satisfied her.

WHEN A RELATIVE REQUESTS MEDICAL RECORDS

A relative may see a patient's medical records under any of these conditions:
◆ The relative or next of kin is the patient's legal guardian, and the patient is incompetent.
◆ The relative has the patient's approval.

Patient discharge against medical advice

The patient's bill of rights and the laws and regulations based on it give a competent adult the right to refuse treatment for any reason without being punished or having his liberty restricted.

Some states have turned these rights into law. And the courts have cited the bill of rights in their decisions.

The right to refuse treatment provides patients with the right to leave the hospital against medical advice (AMA) any time, for any reason. As a nurse, all you can do is try to talk the patient out of it.

RECOGNIZING A POTENTIAL PATIENT WALKOUT

Because you have more contact with your patient than any other health care professional, you're likely to be the first person to suspect that a patient is contemplating leaving AMA.

Complaints or hostile behavior may indicate the patient's extreme dissatisfaction with hospital routine or with the care he's receiving. By carefully observing, listening, and talking with him, you may be able to resolve the problems by offering him a fresh perspective and perhaps change his mind about leaving.

If you discover that a specific problem has caused his dissatisfaction, try to resolve it. If the problem lies outside the scope of your practice, call the patient's physician.

A patient may tell you that he has changed his mind about leaving just to divert your attention. If you suspect this, check on him more often and ask colleagues to do the same. Stay with him when you escort him to another part of the hospital.

WHEN THE PATIENT INSISTS ON LEAVING

If your patient still insists on leaving AMA and your hospital has a policy on managing the patient who wants to leave, follow it exactly. Following policy will help to protect the hospital, coworkers, and you from charges of unlawful restraint or false imprisonment. If your employer doesn't have such a policy, take these steps:
◆ Contact the patient's family (if he hasn't already called them), and explain that the patient is getting ready to leave. If you can't reach the family, contact the person listed in the patient's records responsible for him or

for his body and valuables if he should die.

◆ Explain the hospital's AMA procedures to the patient if hospital policy delegates this responsibility to you.

◆ Give the patient the AMA form to sign. (See *Documenting a patient's decision to leave AMA,* page 118.) His decision to leave is the same as a refusal of treatment. Inform the patient of his medical risks if he leaves the hospital, and explain the alternatives available at the hospital and at other locations, such as regular visits to the hospital's outpatient clinic or admission to another facility. His signature on the AMA form is evidence of his refusal of treatment. You should witness the signature.

◆ Provide routine discharge care. Even though your patient is leaving AMA, his rights to discharge planning and care are the same as those for a patient who's signed out with medical advice. So if the patient agrees, escort him to the door (in a wheelchair, if necessary), arrange for medical or nursing follow-up care, and offer other routine health care measures. These procedures will protect the hospital as well as the patient.

When the patient refuses to sign out

If the patient refuses to sign the AMA form, you should document his refusal in a note stating that all risks have been explained to the patient. One innovative nurse routinely told emergency department patients that she would like them to indicate their refusal to sign by signing the back of the form. Most patients complied with her request.

Dealing with an escape

If you discover that a patient is missing from the hospital, notify the nursing supervisor and security immediately. If the patient was in police custody or poses a threat to anyone outside the hospital, the administration should contact the police. The hospital administration subsequently may ask you to notify the patient's family or friends, collect the patient's belongings, and document the escape in the patient's medical chart and incident report.

False imprisonment

Never attempt to detain a competent adult who has a right to leave. Any attempt to detain or restrain him may be interpreted as unlawful restraint or false imprisonment, for which you can be sued or prosecuted.

Your hospital's policy should reflect state law. It should specifically answer such questions as:

◆ How long and for what reasons may a patient be detained?

◆ When can you use forcible restraints?

◆ Who may order the use of restraints?

◆ Who may apply the restraints?

Knowing the policies will reduce your liability exposure.

Court cases

Most courts disapprove of detaining a patient arbitrarily or for an unreasonably long time, which may be ruled false imprisonment. (See *Patient or prisoner,* page 119.)

Court cases that involve false imprisonment charges have occurred when facilities threatened to hold patients or their personal belongings until bills were paid. In most cases, the courts ruled against the facilities.

Documenting a patient's decision to leave AMA

An against-medical-advice (AMA) form is a medical record as well as a legal document. It's designed to protect you, your coworkers, and your facility from liability resulting from the patient's unapproved discharge or escape.

To document an AMA incident, begin by getting your facility's AMA form. The form may look like the one shown below. The form clearly states that the patient:

◆ knows he's leaving AMA
◆ has been advised of, and understands, the risks of leaving
◆ knows he can come back.

Discuss this form with the patient and ask him to sign it. Don't try to force the patient to sign, if he's unwilling to do so. You should sign as a witness.

Add the AMA form to the patient's medical chart. Then write a detailed description of how you first learned of the patient's plan to leave AMA, what you and the patient said to each other, and what alternatives to the patient's action were discussed.

Also, check facility policy concerning incident reports. If the patient leaves without anyone's knowledge or if he refuses to sign the AMA form, you'll probably be required to file an incident report. Be sure to include the names of any other employees involved in the discovery of the patient's absence. The administration or your nurse-manager also may want to solicit corroborating reports from other employees, including other registered nurses, licensed practical nurses, nurses' aides, orderlies, and clerical staff.

Responsibility Release

This is to certify that I, _____ ,

a patient in _____ ,

am being discharged against the advice of my doctor and the hospital administration. I acknowledge that I have been informed of the risk involved and hereby release my physician and the hospital from all responsibility for any ill effects that may result from such a discharge. I also understand that I may return to the hospital at any time and have treatment resumed.

_____   _____
[Patient's signature]   [Date]

_____   _____
[Witness' signature]   [Date]

RE: _____   _____
[Name of patient]   Patient #

A hospital or nursing home can delay a patient's discharge, for a reasonable period of time, until routine paperwork is complete. *Bailie v. Miami Valley Hospital* (1966) was a case in which the court ruled in favor of a hospital.

An exception

In a few cases, because of extenuating circumstances, the courts have ruled against patients who sued on grounds of false imprisonment. The case of *Pounders v. Trinity Court Nursing Home* (1979) is one such example.

Mrs. Pounders, age 75, was a disabled widow. When her niece and nephew no longer wanted her to live with them, the niece arranged for her to move to Trinity Court Nursing Home. Mrs. Pounders didn't object.

During her 2 months at Trinity Court, Mrs. Pounders complained only once to a nurses' aide that she wanted to leave. Unfortunately, the aide failed to report the complaint to anyone in authority at the home.

Mrs. Pounders was finally released, through the aid of an attorney, into another niece's care. She eventually sued the nursing home.

However, because Mrs. Pounders couldn't prove she had been involuntarily detained, the court absolved the nursing home of the false imprisonment charges.

LAWFUL DETENTION

The right to leave the hospital AMA isn't absolute. Certain patients who pose a threat to themselves or to others can't legally leave the hospital. Restraint through the use of physical means or medication, when necessary, is lawful with psychiatric patients, prisoners, and violent patients.

Patients from psychiatric hospitals or prisons

If a patient transferred to your hospital for medical care from a prison or psychiatric hospital threatens to escape, notify the custodial facility immediately. They're responsible for sending personnel to guard the patient and for

COURT CASE > Patient or prisoner?

The case of *Big Town Nursing Home v. Newman* (1970) provides a good example of how a health care facility can become vulnerable to charges of false imprisonment.

Mr. Newman, age 67, had Parkinson's disease, arthritis, heart trouble, hiatal hernia, a speech impediment, and a history of alcoholism. Four days after his nephew signed him into a nursing home, Mr. Newman decided to leave.

No exit

Employees at the nursing home stopped Mr. Newman, locked away his suitcase and clothes, restricted his use of the phone, and restricted his right to visitors. When Mr. Newman tried to walk off the grounds, employees locked him in a wing with severely emotionally disturbed patients and patients addicted to drugs and alcohol. He made other unsuccessful escape attempts, so the staff tied Mr. Newman to a chair for long periods. Twenty-two days after his admission, Mr. Newman escaped. Eventually, he sued.

The court ruled in favor of Mr. Newman. Despite his physical infirmities, Mr. Newman hadn't legally been declared incompetent and was, therefore, legally entitled to exercise his rights.

making new arrangements for his care. Restrain the patient only if his medical condition warrants it or if the police or psychiatric hospital authorities instruct you to do so.

If the prisoner or psychiatric patient escapes, you or your hospital or nursing administration should call the authorities at the custodial facility or the police.

Violent patients

If you suspect that a patient with a history of violence or violent threats is planning to leave AMA, notify hospital and nursing administrators immediately. If state law allows it, your hospital administrators may decide to get police assistance to restrain the patient.

If the violent patient has escaped, notify your nursing or hospital administration immediately. They'll contact the police and mental health authorities. If the patient ever expressed an intention to harm a known person, the administration also should contact that person.

When a patient dies

When a patient dies, his rights are transferred to his estate. However, in recent years, legally determining when death occurred has become difficult. That, in turn, complicates your role.

How can you be sure a patient is legally dead? Who has the right to pronounce death? What are your responsibilities after the patient dies?

CONTROVERSY OVER THE DEFINITION OF DEATH

Determining death used to be simple — when a person's circulation and respiration stopped, he was dead. However, advances in medical technology have made death pronouncements more complicated. Because medical equipment, such as ventilators, pacemakers, and intra-aortic balloon pumps, can maintain respiration and circulation, patients may continue to "live" even after their brains have died.

Criteria for brain death

To help physicians determine death in such cases, an ad hoc committee at

Harvard Medical School published a report in 1968, establishing specific criteria for brain death, including:
◆ failure to respond to the most painful stimuli
◆ absence of spontaneous respirations or muscle movements
◆ absence of reflexes
◆ flat EEG.

The committee recommended that all these tests be repeated after 24 hours, and that hypothermia and the presence of central nervous system depressants such as barbiturates be ruled out.

In 1981, the American Medical Association, the American Bar Association, and the President's Commission for the Study of Ethical Problems in Medicine and Behavioral Research collaborated to derive a working definition of brain death. The result of this effort, the Uniform Determination of Death Act (UDODA), has gained wide acceptance among the health care and legal communities.

In general terms, the UDODA defines brain death as the cessation of all measurable functions or activity in every area of the brain, including the brain stem. This definition excludes comatose patients as well as those in a persistent vegetative state. Current debate centers on whether to expand the definition to include certain patients who still have brain stem function such as anencephalic infants.

Court cases

Several court decisions have been based on such definitions.

In the case of *State v. Brown* (1971), an Oregon court was among the first to recognize brain death. In this case of second-degree murder, the defendant argued that he hadn't caused the victim's death by inflicting a gunshot wound to the brain. Instead, he claimed, a physician killed the victim by removing artificial life support. The court ruled that the defendant caused the victim's death because the gunshot wound resulted in brain death.

In 1975, in *New York City Health and Hospitals Corporation v. Sulsona*, several New York hospitals initiated a lawsuit to get a legal ruling on the definition of death when the patient was a potential organ donor. Expert testimony showed that the common law definition of the term (cessation of circulation and respiration) raised the failure rate of organ transplants. The incidence of renal failure in kidney recipients was about 88%. However, using the brain death standard, the incidence of renal failure in recipients was only about 15%. (Medical advances have since improved the success rate of almost all types of transplant surgeries.)

The court ruled that it would recognize brain death in transplantation cases to encourage anatomic gifts even though the state had no law defining brain death. Its ruling applied only to transplantation cases, however.

In 1979, a Colorado court also accepted the criteria for brain death. In *Lovato v. Colorado* (1979), a mother was charged with abusing her child. The child was comatose, with a flat EEG and fixed and dilated pupils, and lacked spontaneous respiration or reflexes or responses to painful stimuli. The mother petitioned the court to keep the child on a ventilator. The court ruled that the child was dead because he met the criteria for brain death.

Know your state's law

In states without laws defining death or without judicial precedents, the common law definition of death (cessation of circulation and respiration) is still used. In these states, physicians are understandably reluctant to discontin-

ue artificial life support for brain-dead patients. If you're likely to be involved with patients on life-support equipment, protect yourself by finding out how your state defines death.

Canadian law

In Canada, pinpointing the moment of death has traditionally been left to medical professionals. Human tissue gift legislation may vary from one jurisdiction to another, although generally the state of death is determined by accepted medical practice.

PRONOUNCING DEATH

Only a physician or a coroner can legally pronounce a person dead. In some health care facilities, such as nursing homes, nurses pronounce death when a physician isn't available. The state board must indicate that this is an appropriate nursing practice. If you work in such a facility, you should understand that pronouncing death typically isn't a nursing responsibility.

The attending physician is usually responsible for signing the death certificate, unless the death comes under the jurisdiction of a medical examiner or coroner. State laws specify when this occurs. The coroner or medical examiner usually has jurisdiction over deaths with violent or suspicious circumstances. These include suspected homicides and suicides, and deaths after accidents.

Canadian law

The Canadian provincial laws on autopsies are similar. Any death that occurs in violent or suspicious circumstances comes under the jurisdiction of a medical examiner or coroner. Depending on the province, other types of death — including a prisoner's death, a sudden death, or a death not caused by a disease — come under the jurisdiction of a medical examiner or coroner.

YOUR RESPONSIBILITY WHEN A PATIENT DIES

When a patient dies, you're responsible for accurately and objectively charting all of his signs and any actions you take. For example, an appropriate entry in the nurses' notes would be: "Midnight. No respirations or pulse, pupils fixed and dilated. Notified Dr. York." Don't write a conclusion that borders on a medical diagnosis such as "patient seems dead."

You're also responsible for notifying the physician who can be reached most quickly. If this is the physician on call, he should notify the patient's physician, who should notify the family. Find out who will be notifying the family, and document it.

At the appropriate time, you should prepare the body for removal to the morgue, according to facility procedure. When doing this, carefully identify the body. In *Lott v. State* (1962), a nurse mistagged two bodies, causing a Roman Catholic to be prepared for an Orthodox Jewish burial and an Orthodox Jew to be prepared for a Roman Catholic burial. The court found her liable.

OBTAINING CONSENT FOR AN AUTOPSY

If a death comes under the jurisdiction of a medical examiner or coroner, the decision to perform an autopsy rests solely with him, despite the family's wishes. In all other cases, the patient's family has a right to give or withhold consent. In some states, the patient can give written consent to an autopsy before he dies.

When a physician or other hospital representative seeks consent from a patient's family, you can help by explaining why the autopsy is needed and how autopsy arrangements are made.

Who may give consent

Most states have laws that specify who has the right to give consent to autopsies. Some laws list which relatives can give consent. Others list relatives in descending order, according to their relationship to the deceased. The usual order is spouse, adult children, parents, brothers or sisters, grandparents, uncles or aunts, and cousins. The person with the right to consent may withhold consent or impose limits on the autopsy. If the autopsy exceeds these limits, the consenting relative may sue.

The relative with the right to consent may also sue if an autopsy is performed without any consent. The grounds for such lawsuits are usually mental or emotional suffering.

OBTAINING CONSENT FOR ORGAN DONATION

Depending on the facility where you work and the patient's physical condition at the time of death, you may be asked to assist with obtaining consent for organ donation from the deceased's next of kin. This can be a delicate procedure. Carefully explain to the next of kin what can be donated and how the organs are distributed. Alleviate his fears by reassuring him that organ donation doesn't disfigure the body or cost anything. Also, ensure that the next of kin knows that he won't receive financial compensation for giving consent because it's illegal to sell human organs or tissues.

It's important to remember that in most states, a donor's card or a driver's license with the donor box checked

Organ/tissue donor card

In recent years, various governmental and nonprofit organizations have developed programs to raise awareness about the importance of organ and tissue donation. One of their initiatives has been to promote organ/tissue donor cards (such as the one shown below), which people can keep on their person to signify their willingness to donate their organs in the case of an accident. While not a legally binding document, donor cards are helpful in getting a victim's next of kin to consent to donation.

I wish to donate my organs and tissues. I wish to give:

❏ Any needed organs and tissues   ❏ Only the following organs and tissues:

_____

Donor signature: _____   Date: _____

Witness: _____

Witness: _____

isn't a legally binding document. (In December 2002, Minnesota passed a law stating otherwise.) Consent must still be obtained from the next of kin, unless the deceased had made it perfectly clear of his intention to donate his organs, such as through a living will, an advance directive, and a donor registry. Check with your local organ procedure organization for more details and procedures specific to your area. (See *Organ/tissue donor card*.)

EXPERIMENTAL PROCEDURES

The family has a right to give or withhold specific consent to practice medical procedures on a corpse. In teaching hospitals, residents and medical students practice such procedures as intubation on corpses. However, if a hospital doesn't obtain proper consent, the family member responsible for consent may sue. In many states, the hospital may even face criminal charges.

RESPONSIBILITY FOR BURIAL

In the United States, the family member who has the right to consent to autopsy usually has the responsibility to bury the body as well. In Canada, regulations vary by jurisdiction. However, in one Canadian case, *Hunter v. Hunter* (1930), the court ruled that the deceased's son, who was the executor of the will, had this responsibility—not the wife, who was the next of kin.

If no one claims the body despite the hospital's effort to contact the person responsible, a state or county official must dispose of it. Laws in many states direct this official to deliver unclaimed bodies to an appropriate educational or scientific facility unless the person is a veteran or has died of a contagious disease. In these situations, the state pays for burial or cremation.

Selected references

Basanta, W.E. "Advance Directives and Life-sustaining Treatment: A Legal Primer," *Hematology/Oncology Clinic of North America* 16(6):1381-96, December 2002.

Chan, Z. "Informed consent — 'NURSE'," *Nursing Ethics* 10(3):333, May 2003.

Harris, J. "Consent and End of Life Decisions," *Journal of Medical Ethics* 29(1):10-15, February 2003.

"Know Your Rights. ANA's Bill of Rights Arms Nurses with Critical Information," *American Nurse* 34(6):16, November-December 2002.

LaDuke, S. "Nurses and the Attorney-Client Relationship," *JONAS Healthcare, Law, Ethics & Regulation* 2(4):117-23, December 2000.

Luce, J.M. "Three Patients Who Asked that Life Support be Withheld or Withdrawn in the Surgical Intensive Care Unit," *Critical Care Medicine* 30(4):775-80, April 2002.

McKee, D. "The Legal Framework for Informed Consent," *Professional Nurse* 14(10): 688-90, July 1999.

Michael, J.E. "Stay In-The-Know Regarding Informed Consent," *Nursing Management* 33(5):22-23,56, May 2002.

Moore, J. "End-of-life Care Legislation Signed into Law," *Michigan Nurse* 75(3):4, March 2002.

"Patient Safety Bill Updates," *Hospital Outlook* 5(5):4-5, September-October 2002.

Pennels, C. "The Data Protection Act and Patient Records," *Professional Nurse* 16(8): 1291-93, May 2001.

Rockett, L.R. "Legal Issues Affecting Confidentiality and Informed Consent in Reproductive Health," *Journal of American Medical Women's Association* 55(5):257-60, Fall 2000.

Stein, J. "The Ethics of Advance Directives: A Rehabilitation Perspective," *American Journal of Physical Medicine and Rehabilitation* 82(2):152-57, February 2003.

Chapter 4

Understanding malpractice liability

No legal issue sparks as much anxiety among nurses as malpractice, which can be emotionally harrowing and financially devastating. Unfortunately, more nurses are being named in lawsuits, and this trend shows no sign of changing. Several reasons for this phenomenon exist:

◆ Patients are more knowledgeable about health care, and their expectations are higher.

◆ The health care system is more reliant on nurses and providers other than physicians to help contain costs.

◆ Nurses are more autonomous in their practice.

◆ The courts are expanding the definition of liability, holding all types of medical professionals to higher standards of accountability.

Losing a malpractice lawsuit can jeopardize your nursing career. Prospective employers and insurance companies will ask if you've been found liable for nursing malpractice, been named a defendant in a lawsuit, or been disciplined by your state's board of nursing. If you answer "yes" to any of these queries, you may find job hunting more difficult or have an extended probation period or restrictions placed on your nursing practice. (See *National Practitioner Data Bank,* pages 126 and 127.) Also, your insurance company may refuse to renew your professional liability coverage. Other insurance carriers may refuse to insure you or require you to pay higher premiums for coverage.

Fortunately, you can take steps to help limit your risk of malpractice litigation. Your best protection against malpractice litigation is giving your patients the best possible nursing care, according to the highest professional standards. To do this, you must be familiar with and follow the standards of care that apply to your specific area of nursing as well as state and federal regulations, accreditation standards promulgated by the Joint Commission on Accreditation of Healthcare Organizations or the Community Health Accreditation Program, standards adapted by the American Nurses Association (ANA), standards of clinical specialty nursing organizations, and policies set forth by your employer.

You can further protect yourself by becoming familiar with malpractice law. This chapter describes malpractice issues, defines key legal terms, and explains legal doctrines that may be used as a defense during a malpractice lawsuit. You'll find extensive information on steps to take to avoid malpractice

National Practitioner Data Bank

In 1990, the National Practitioner Data Bank began operation. As a result, physicians, dentists, nurses, and other health care practitioners who are forced to pay malpractice judgments are going to have a much harder time concealing their professional histories from potential employers. The data bank, which stores malpractice data on a nationwide scale, was created under the Health Care Quality Improvement Act of 1986 and the Medicare and Medicaid Patient and Program Protection Act of 1987.

Reporting requirements

The National Practitioner Data Bank collects information about practitioners who have paid judgments, entered into settlements, or have adverse action against their license or privileges to practice. All hospitals and health care facilities, professional health care societies, state licensure boards, and insurance companies are now required to report the following information about nurses to the data bank:

◆ a nurse's malpractice payments (including judgments, arbitration decisions, and out-of-court settlements)

◆ actions taken against a nurse's clinical privileges

◆ adverse licensure actions, including revocations, suspensions, reprimands, censure, or probation.

Failure to report a nurse's malpractice payment of any amount — no matter how small — carries a $10,000 fine. However, the filing of a suit isn't, by itself, reportable; only the making of a payment is. Adverse clinical privilege actions against nurses may be reported at the discretion of the reviewing health care agency.

Federal agencies

Under the law, federal agencies aren't required to report to the National Practitioner Data Bank. However, the Department of Defense, the Drug Enforcement Administration, and the Department of Health and Human Services have voluntarily agreed to observe the regulations.

Availability of information

The information in the data bank isn't available to the general public nor is it available to attorneys, except in a specific context. If a practitioner is sued and it's determined that the employer didn't check the data bank, the attorney can send verification that the employing institution didn't check, along with the pending charges. If a similar case is in the data bank, notification will be sent. State licensing boards, hospitals, professional societies, and health care facilities involved in peer review may access the data bank. Individual nurses have access to records that pertain to themselves.

All hospitals must check the data bank when a nurse applies for clinical privileges. The hospital must request information on the nurse again every 2 years. The courts will presume that the hospital is aware of any information the data bank contains on any nurse or other practitioner in its employ. If knowledge of the information contained in the data bank would have resulted in denial of clinical privileges, the hospital could be held vicariously liable for negligence performed by the nurse as well as negligence in hiring the nurse in a malpractice lawsuit.

Information in the data bank

Reports made to the data bank typically include:

◆ the nurse's full name, home address, date of birth, professional schools attended and graduation dates, place of employment, Social Security number, and license number and state

National Practitioner Data Bank *(continued)*

◆ name, title, and phone number of the official submitting the report

◆ relationship of the reporting official to the practitioner

◆ dates of judgment or settlement or amount paid

◆ description of judgment, settlement, or action.

Disputing a report

If a report about you is submitted to the data bank, you'll receive a copy for your review. If you believe the report is in error, ask the official submitting the report to correct it. The official making the report must submit corrections to the data bank.

If you fail to get satisfaction from the reporting official, you'll have to follow a detailed procedure for disputing the report. This must be done within 60 days of the initial processing of the report. Ultimately, you may request review from the Secretary of Health and Human Services.

---

suits and advice on how to shop for professional liability insurance.

Even if you're meticulous in your practice and carefully avoid unnecessary legal risks, you can't completely escape the risk of being named in a lawsuit. To prepare you for this reality, you'll find guidelines in this chapter for facing a malpractice law suit and a court appearance with less anxiety.

Understanding malpractice law

Our legal system's view of malpractice evolved from the premise that each person is responsible, or *liable,* for the consequences of his actions. Malpractice law deals with a professional's liability for negligent acts, omissions, and intentional harms. (See *Understanding tort law,* pages 128 and 129.)

CASE LAW

Case law, or *judicial precedent,* may set a standard of care in nursing or may impact the outcome of a specific malpractice case. Case law arises when a lawsuit has gone to trial and someone, either the plaintiff or defendant, has been unhappy with the verdict and filed an appeal. After the appeals court has rendered a decision about the issues raised in the appeal, the written decision of the court is published and becomes case law.

Generally, the case law that applies to an individual nurse's practice is the case law for the state in which she practices and any applicable federal case law. A seminal case from another state may also establish a standard of care because of the national acceptance of its ruling.

HOSPITAL AND CORPORATE LIABILITY

Employers have the overall responsibility and liability for the actions of their employees under the doctrine of vicarious liability or *respondeat superior.* This means your employer may be responsible for your actions, even if

Understanding tort law

Most lawsuits against nurses fall into the tort category. If you're ever a defendant in a lawsuit, understanding the distinctions in this broad category may prove especially important.

A tort is a civil wrong or injury resulting from a breach of a legal duty that exists by virtue of society's expectations regarding interpersonal conduct or by the assumption of a duty inherent in a professional relationship (as opposed to a legal duty that exists by virtue of a contractual relationship). More generally, you may define a *tort* as "any action or omission that harms somebody." Malpractice refers to a tort committed by a professional acting in his professional capacity.

Unintentional vs. intentional torts

The law broadly divides torts into two categories: unintentional and intentional. An *unintentional tort* is a civil wrong resulting from the defendant's negligence. If someone sues you for negligence, he must prove four things in order to win:
◆ You owed him a specific duty. (In nursing malpractice cases, this duty is equivalent to the standard of care.)
◆ You breached this duty.
◆ The plaintiff was harmed. (The harm can be physical, mental, emotional, or financial.)
◆ Your breach of duty caused the harm.

An *intentional tort* is a deliberate invasion of someone's legal right. In a malpractice case involving an intentional tort, the plaintiff doesn't need to prove that you owed him a duty. The duty at issue (for example, not to touch people without their permission) is defined by law, and you're presumed to owe him this duty. The plaintiff must still prove that you breached this duty and that this breach caused him harm.

Tort claim   Actions that lead to claim

Unintentional tort

Negligence
◆ Leaving foreign objects inside a patient after surgery
◆ Failing to observe a patient as the physician ordered
◆ Failing to obtain informed consent before a treatment or procedure
◆ Failing to report a change in a patient's vital signs or status
◆ Failing to report a staff member's negligence that you witnessed
◆ Failing to provide for a patient's safety
◆ Failing to provide the patient with appropriate teaching before discharge

Intentional tort

Assault
◆ Threatening a patient

Battery
◆ Assisting in nonemergency surgery performed without the consent of the patient
◆ Forcing a patient to ambulate against his wishes
◆ Forcing a patient to submit to injections
◆ Striking a patient
◆ Inappropriately restraining a patient

Understanding tort law *(continued)*

Tort claim	Actions that lead to claim
Intentional tort *(continued)*	
False imprisonment	◆ Confining a patient in a psychiatric unit without a physician's order ◆ Refusing to let a patient return home
Invasion of privacy	◆ Releasing private information about a patient to third parties ◆ Allowing unauthorized persons to read a patient's medical records ◆ Allowing unauthorized persons to observe a procedure ◆ Taking pictures of the patient without his consent
Slander	◆ Making false statements about a patient to a third person, which causes damage to the patient's reputation

you weren't following its policies and procedures.

Because of the potential for corporate liability, health care facilities and agencies must be especially diligent in their hiring processes. They have to verify identity, training (including certificates, diplomas, transcripts, and licensure), and references, and they have to perform a background check (with the applicant's permission). Employers also have to thoroughly interview applicants, test basic nursing skills that are applicable to the open position, and check driving records. Then they must make sure that their findings are properly documented.

PHYSICIAN LIABILITY

As a nurse, you're responsible for following the nursing process in the care and treatment of your patients and for recognizing deviations from the standard of care. Furthermore, you're a patient advocate who's expected to question the appropriateness of every order

you receive. For orders that you know to be potentially detrimental to your patient, you must question the order, seek alternative treatment, and seek advice or intervention from your nursing supervisor, in addition to documenting the actions you took. For example, if a physician orders a drug that your patient is allergic to, you must question the physician's order and obtain an order for a different drug, one that the patient isn't allergic to. Doing otherwise puts you and the physician at risk of liability. This is known as *joint responsibility*.

A classic example of joint responsibility would be that of a foreign object (such as a sponge) being left in a patient during surgery. The surgeon is responsible for not leaving a foreign object in the patient during surgery; the nurses assisting in the operating room are responsible for making sure that all equipment, supplies, and sponges used are accounted for before the surgeon closes. If the surgeon and the nurses fail in their responsibilities and the patient is harmed, then the surgeon as well as the nurses are responsible for their negligence. (Keep in mind that there have been a few cases in which only the nurses doing the surgical counts were held liable for a foreign object being left in the patient.)

NURSE LIABILITY

Educational and licensing requirements for nurses increased after World War II. Nursing tasks became more complex, which lead to specialization.

These changes meant that nurses began to make independent judgments. Although this increased responsibility provides a sense of autonomy and a more rewarding working environment, it also makes nurses more liable for errors and increases their likelihood of being sued.

Causes of lawsuits against nurses

Patient falls and drug errors are the two most common causes of lawsuits against nurses. Other problems that prompt lawsuits include:

♦ operating room errors such as a foreign object (for example, a sponge or an instrument) being left inside a patient because counts weren't performed or were performed inaccurately before the surgeon closed

♦ communication breakdown between nurses and physicians or between nurses on different shifts

♦ inadequate observation or assessment of patients leading to a delay in diagnosis or treatment, permanent injury, or death

♦ failure to know and follow a facility's or agency's chain of command policy, thus causing injury to a patient because of a lack of appropriate intervention.

In addition to the above-mentioned areas of liability, nurses who work in special practice areas may be vulnerable to other areas of liability. (See *Liability in special practice settings*.)

Negligence vs. malpractice

The court's view of nursing liability has changed significantly over the years. At one time, nurses were charged only with negligence. Today, however, all courts recognize nursing negligence as a form of malpractice.

Negligence is the failure to exercise the degree of care that a reasonable person of ordinary prudence would exercise under the same circumstances. A claim of negligence requires that there be a duty owed by one person to another, that the duty be breached, and that the breach of duty results in injury. Although nurses always have a duty to their patients, *malpractice* is a more restricted, specialized kind of negligence, defined as a violation of professional duty or a failure to meet a standard of care or failure to use the skills and knowledge of other professionals (nurses) in similar circumstances.

The distinction shows that the courts recognize nursing as its own profession. This professional status may affect the statute of limitations applicable in a particular case. The *statute of limitations* defines the time period in which a lawsuit may be filed. Many states have statutes of limitations specifically pertaining to medical malpractice claims, which may be shorter than those for ordinary negligence actions. Generally, one statute of limitations applies to adults (usually 2 to 3 years) and one applies to minors (up to 21 years depending on the state). However, additional statutes may limit or extend the statute of limitations, depending on the claim, the entity being sued, and the state where the harm was done.

Liability in special practice settings

Although errors can be made in virtually any practice setting, nurses who work in certain settings are more vulnerable to malpractice charges because their errors usually prove more costly for patients. Also, the courts may expect a higher standard from a nurse who practices a specialty.

Critical care nursing

Compared with nurses in other units, critical care nurses spend more time in direct contact with their patients, thus increasing the opportunity for errors and the number of potential lawsuits. Because of the many invasive and potentially harmful procedures performed in this setting, critical care nurses are especially vulnerable to charges of negligence and battery. Furthermore, if they perform duties or procedures that are outside their scope of practice, they may be accused of practicing without a license.

Additional tort claims that may be filed against critical care nurses include:
◆ abandonment – the unilateral severance of a professional relationship with a patient without adequate notice and while the patient still needs attention (a critical care nurse who fails in her duty to observe the patient closely for any subtle changes in condition is vulnerable to this charge)
◆ invasion of privacy, intentional infliction of emotional distress, or battery – such cases usually involve a patient who was placed on or removed from life support
◆ failure to obtain informed consent – this is more likely to occur in a critical care setting because of the inherent pressure and urgency for immediate treatment (a critical care nurse who denies a competent patient the right to refuse treatment – even if lack of treatment results in the patient's death – exposes herself to charges of various intentional torts).

Emergency department nursing

Many day-to-day practices of emergency department (ED) nurses fall into a legal gray area because the law's definition of a *true emergency* is open to interpretation – for example, health care workers who treat a patient for what they regard as a true emergency may be liable for battery or failure to obtain informed consent if the court ultimately concludes that the situation wasn't a true emergency.

One of the most common charges filed against ED nurses is failure to assess and report a patient's condition. Inadequate triage may be considered negligence.

All too often, the use of high-tech equipment combined with a hectic daily pace increases the potential for lawsuits.

Other tort claims made against ED nurses include:
◆ failure to instruct a patient adequately before discharge
◆ discounting complaints of pain from a patient who's mentally impaired by alcohol, medication, or injury
◆ failure to obtain informed consent, giving rise to claims of battery, false imprisonment, and invasion of privacy.

Psychiatric nursing

Malpractice cases involving psychiatric care usually involve failure to obtain informed consent. A nurse may wrongly assume she doesn't need informed consent, especially if the patient's condition interferes with his awareness or understanding of the proposed treatment or procedure. Violation of a patient's right to refuse treatment may stem from the mistaken belief that all mentally ill patients are incompetent. The right to refuse treatment isn't absolute, however, and can be abrogated if a drug or treatment is required to prevent serious harm to the patient or others. Generally, a

(continued)

Liability in special practice settings *(continued)*

physician, not a nurse, makes this decision, and in many cases, a court makes the decision.

A nurse who reveals personal information about a patient to someone not directly involved in the patient's care also is vulnerable to malpractice charges. Violation of a patient's right to privacy and confidentiality is a common complaint in lawsuits against psychiatric health care workers, probably because of the stigma associated with mental illness.

Malpractice allegations may also stem from failing to protect a patient from inflicting foreseeable harm to himself or others. Protecting a patient or his potential victims from harm may include a duty to warn the patient's family that he's a threat to himself or a duty to warn a potential victim. This duty to warn is a standard of care in mental health practice that has been incorporated as either case law, statutory law, or both in many states.

If a nurse fails to report information given by the patient, even in confidence, that could have prevented the harm, she may be held liable for breaching her duty to appropriately assess the patient and for failing to comply with her duty to warn.

Obstetric nursing

Cases involving labor and delivery may have at least two plaintiffs: mother and infant. Monetary damages may be substantial, especially if the neonate sustained permanent and long-term injuries and is expected to live a long or near-normal life expectancy despite the injuries. An obstetric nurse may be held liable for:

◆ negligence through participation in transfusion of incompatible blood, especially in relation to rhesus factor incompatibility

◆ failure to attend to or monitor the mother or the fetus during labor and delivery

◆ failure to recognize labor symptoms and to provide adequate support and care

◆ failure to monitor contractions and fetal heart rate, particularly in obstetric units that have internal monitoring capabilities

◆ failure to recognize high-risk labor patients who show signs of preeclampsia or other labor complications

◆ failure to warn parents of the risks of diagnostic tests – or the consequences of refusing such tests – if the failure contributes to maternal or fetal injury

◆ abandonment of a patient in active labor

◆ failure to exercise independent judgment, such as knowingly carrying out medical orders that will harm the patient

◆ failure to ensure that a patient has given informed consent for various procedures or treatments, including physical examinations, administration of a medication, type of delivery method, sterilization, and postdelivery surgical procedures.

Other common sources of malpractice suits filed against obstetric and neonatal nurses include failure to attend to the infant in distress, failure to monitor equipment, use of defective equipment, failure to monitor oxygen levels, and failure to recognize and report neonatal jaundice during the immediate postnatal period.

In some states, parents can file a *wrongful birth* lawsuit if a nurse failed to advise them of contraceptive methods or the methods' potential for failure, potential genetic defects, the availability of amniocentesis to detect defects, or the option of abortion to prevent birth of a defective child. A child with a genetic defect can file a *wrongful birth* lawsuit if a nurse failed to inform the parents of amniocentesis and the option of abortion. Failure to provide adequate genetic counseling and prenatal testing when the mother has a history of Down syndrome can also result in a wrongful birth or wrongful life lawsuit. (Keep in mind that many states don't allow recovery for wrongful birth.)

Criminal liability

Although most legal actions arising out of nursing practice are civil actions, nurses occasionally face criminal charges. When this happens, prosecutors need to prove criminal intent. Showing such intent involves proving that the nurse knew or should have known that what she was doing or failing to do would cause the patient harm and that she intentionally failed to take the necessary actions. A nurse can also be held criminally liable if she intentionally harms a patient.

An example of failing to take the necessary actions might involve a registered nurse (RN) ignoring the observations of a licensed practical nurse (LPN) regarding the severity of a patient's condition and failing to appropriately observe and assess the patient, ensure the necessary intervention, and follow up. If the registered nurse's inaction leads to a severe worsening of the patient's condition, she could face criminal action.

An example of intentionally acting to harm the patient would include a violent act that caused either physical or mental harm to a patient such as wrongfully restraining him in a way that caused injury. Another example is abuse that causes the patient physical or mental harm.

Understanding the statute of limitations

The statute of limitations specifies the number of years within which one person can sue another. For malpractice lawsuits, the statute of limitations is specified in each state's medical malpractice law. These limits vary widely from state to state, so you should know the limits in your state. Contact the attorney, lobbyist, or legislative committee members of your state nurses' association for information about the statute of limitations in your state. (For a list of state nurses' associations, see pages 5 to 10.) Statutes of limitations also vary widely from jurisdiction to jurisdiction in Canada, and even within a jurisdiction.

RECOGNIZING ITS PURPOSE

As time passes, evidence vanishes, witnesses' memories fail, and witnesses die. A time limit for bringing a lawsuit ensures that enough relevant evidence exists for a judge or jury to decide a case fairly.

The statute of limitations for general negligence usually gives a person 3 years to sue another for damages. Defendants may invoke these limits as a defense in general personal-injury lawsuits. However, in response to pressure from medical and insurance groups, states have established shorter statutes of limitations for professions that require independent judgments and frequent risks. The statutes of limitations of medical malpractice laws, for example, usually give the patient 2 years or less to sue for damages.

DETERMINING WHICH STATUTE APPLIES

In many states, only physicians and dentists are expressly subject to medical malpractice statutes of limitations. These states view the nurse as someone carrying out orders, not making independent, risk-taking judgments.

If a nurse alleges a patient's claim is invalid because he didn't file suit until after the statute of limitations expired, the court must determine whether the statute of limitations for state medical malpractice law or the statute of limitations for general personal-injury lawsuits applies. (The statute of limitations for malpractice law is usually shorter.) The court bases its decision on two considerations:

◆ *The amount of limitation protection the court believes the defendant-nurse's job warrants.* If the nurse's job forces her to make many independent patient-care judgments, the court may apply a strict, or short, statute of limitations. A short time limit offers more protection for the nurse because the patient has less time to seek damages.

◆ *The type of negligent act the plaintiff-patient claims the nurse committed.* An injured patient may sue a nurse for one or several charges that constitute negligence or malpractice. The patient's attorney determines which charge has the best chance of winning the most damages for his client and structures his case accordingly. Then, if a statute of limitations is used as part of the nurse's defense, the court decides which statute of limitations to apply in relation to the patient's charges.

Court case
In an Alaska case, *Pedersen v. Zielski* (1991), the plaintiff-patient argued that a 6-year statute of limitations for controlled claims applied to a physician's negligence because the physician had a contract to provide care to that patient. The Alaska court disagreed and held that the 2-year statute of limitations for medical malpractice claims was applicable because the plaintiff's claims arose in tort (personal injury) law, not in contract law.

APPLYING THE STATUTE OF LIMITATIONS
Even if a patient files suit long after the statute of limitations has expired, that statute may not necessarily protect you from liability. Remember that the patient's attorney knows about the stat-

ute of limitations, and the suit is being filed anyway. That means he believes the court may set aside the statute of limitations because of the case's special circumstances.

Normally, the statute begins to run on the date the plaintiff's injury occurred. However, what if the plaintiff doesn't know he was injured or doesn't find out he has grounds for a suit until after the normal limitation period expires? Determining when the applicable statute begins to run has become the pivotal question whenever a defense attorney invokes the statute of limitations.

Legislatures and the courts, which are continually struggling with this question, have devised a series of rules to help decide, in individual malpractice cases, when a statute should begin to run. A court can apply these rules, when a plaintiff-patient's attorney requests that it do so, to extend the applicable statute of limitations beyond the limit written in the law. That means that the nurse's use of a statute of limitations as a defense may be invalidated, and the plaintiff-patient would still be allowed to sue.

Occurrence rule
Under the occurrence rule, the statute of limitations begins to run on the day the patient is injured. The occurrence rule generally leads to the shortest time limit. In several states, the courts have interpreted the occurrence rule strictly, so even badly injured patients have been prevented from bringing suit after the applicable statute of limitations had expired.

Termination-of-treatment rule
The courts may apply the termination-of-treatment rule when a patient's injury results from a series of treatments extended over time, rather than from a single treatment. The termina-

tion-of-treatment rule states that a statute of limitations begins on the date of the last treatment. In devising this rule, the courts reasoned that for the patient, a series of treatments could obscure just how and when the injury occurred.

The Supreme Court of Virginia applied this rule in *Justice v. Natvig* (1989). In this case, a patient filed a lawsuit 8 years after an allegedly negligent operation. The patient had continued to receive treatment during this interval. The defendant-physicians argued that the statute of limitations had lapsed. The court ruled, however, that the statute didn't begin to run until the treatment had ended, so the patient's lawsuit was allowed.

Constructive-continuing-treatment rule

The constructive-continuing-treatment rule is essentially the same as the termination-of-treatment rule, but it applies even after the patient leaves a nurse's or a physician's care. For example, suppose a patient you cared for is injured later, in someone else's care, and sues. Under the constructive-continuing-treatment rule, if the subsequent health care providers relied on decisions you made earlier in caring for the patient, the court may extend the statute of limitations in malpractice cases.

Discovery rule

Under the discovery rule, the statute of limitations begins to run when a patient discovers the injury. This may take place many years after the injury occurred. The discovery rule considerably extends the time a patient has to file a malpractice lawsuit.

Two types of cases in which the discovery rule is usually applied are foreign object and sterilization cases. When a nurse or a surgeon leaves a scalpel, sponge, or clamp inside a patient, the patient might not discover the error until long after his surgery. Under the discovery rule, the applicable statute of limitations wouldn't begin to run until the patient found out about the error.

A court's decision to apply the discovery rule depends on whether it believes the patient could have discovered the error earlier. If evidence indicates the patient should have recognized that something was wrong (for example, if he had chronic pain for months after the surgery but didn't take legal action until long afterward), the court could apply the termination-of-treatment rule instead.

Time limits for applying the discovery rule in foreign-object cases vary from state to state. Missouri allows the longest period, which is up to 10 years after discovery of injury; California, the shortest period, which is 1 year from discovery of injury.

In lawsuits involving tubal ligations or vasectomies, the courts have sometimes allowed the discovery rule to apply when a subsequent pregnancy occurs. In these cases, the courts' reasoning is that a patient can't discover the negligence until the procedure proves unsuccessful, no matter how long after the surgery this proof appears.

Because the discovery rule is so generous to plaintiffs, some states, notably Texas, have restricted its application. A number of states have adopted separate statutes of limitations, one for readily detected injuries and one for injuries discovered later. Other states permit statute of limitations extensions only in foreign-object cases.

Proof of fraud

Courts, in most states, will extend the limitation period indefinitely if a plaintiff-patient can prove that a nurse or physician used fraud or falsehood to conceal from the patient information about his injury or its cause. In most cases, the law says that the concealment must be an overt act, not just the omission of an act. The most flagrant frauds involve concealing facts to prevent an inquiry, elude an investigation, or mislead a patient. (See *Extending the statute of limitations.*)

Consider, for example, *Garcia v. Presbyterian Hospital Center* (1979). In this case, a patient who sued was operated on for cancer of the prostate gland twice in 1972 and once again in 1973. He'd repeatedly asked his physician and attending nurses why the third operation was needed, but he hadn't received any explanation. He later learned that the third operation had resulted from retention of a catheter in his body during the second operation. The court held that the applicable statute of limitations didn't prevent the patient from bringing suit.

Minor or mentally incompetent patients

In most states, laws give special consideration to minors and mentally incompetent patients because they lack the legal capacity to sue. Some states postpone applying the statute of limitations to an injured minor until he reaches the age of majority, which may be age 18 or 21, depending on the state. Some states have specific rules about how statutes of limitations apply to minors.

Cases involving mentally incompetent patients who file after the statute of limitations has expired usually follow the discovery rule or a special law. Most special laws state that a statute of limitation doesn't begin until the patient recovers from his mental incompetence.

USING THE STATUTE OF LIMITATIONS AS A DEFENSE

When a defendant-nurse and her attorney use a statute of limitations as a defense, they're making, in legal terms, an affirmative defense. The defendant must prove that the statute of limitations has run out. If the court decides the statutory time limit has expired, the plaintiff-patient's case is dismissed.

For example, in the Wisconsin case *Claypool v. Levin* (1997), the 3-year statute of limitations covering malpractice actions was determined to begin running when a plaintiff obtains actual or constructive notice of injury and its cause even though the first attorney they went to for legal advice said they didn't have a viable claim. Because a separate cause or the delay in bringing a lawsuit may exist doesn't toll (or pause) the statute. Thus, a patient can't argue that because he sought legal advice that indicated no viable claim the statute is tolled.

RETAINING MEDICAL RECORDS

Because a patient may file a malpractice suit years after he claims his injury occurred — and because you may be called on to recall specific clinical facts and procedures — accurate medical records should be kept on file for several years. Complete documentation of your care is usually found only in these medical records. These records provide your best defense. Without them, you're legally vulnerable.

Few states have laws setting precise time periods, but many legal experts urge hospitals and other health care facilities to maintain medical records long after patients are discharged. New Jersey, for example, requires hospitals to keep medical records for at least 7 years.

Extending the statute of limitations

If a plaintiff-patient can prove that a nurse or physician willfully deceived him, the court may lengthen the statute of limitations for filing a lawsuit.

Painful overtreatment

Consider the case of *Lopez v. Swyer* (1971). Mary Lopez, age 32, underwent a radical mastectomy after discovering a lump in her breast. Several physicians prescribed postsurgical radiation treatments, which a radiologist performed.

These treatments occurred six times a week for more than a month, and left painful radiation burns over most of her body. When Mrs. Lopez asked why the complications were so severe, her physician assured her that the burns weren't unusual. They never suggested that the treatments could have been too numerous or too long.

Mrs. Lopez's condition worsened. Over the next several years, she was hospitalized 15 times, including twice for reconstructive surgery made necessary by the radiation treatment. She didn't file a malpractice suit until she heard a consulting physician tell other physicians, gathered near her hospital bed, that she was a victim of negligence.

Extra time for the plaintiff

A lower court dismissed the suit because the 2-year statute of limitations for malpractice had expired. The New Jersey Supreme Court ruled that the statute of limitations didn't begin to run until Mrs. Lopez learned that her physicians had concealed the truth from her. This effectively lengthened the statute of limitations by nearly 10 years. The Supreme Court ruling allowed Mrs. Lopez to bring the facts of her case before a jury.

Some states have adopted the Uniform Business Records Act. This act calls for keeping records for no less than 3 years. Some states allow microfilm copies of medical records to be admitted as evidence in malpractice cases, but other states insist that only the original records can be used in court.

Avoiding malpractice liability

You can take steps to avoid tort liability by using caution and common sense and by being aware of your legal responsibilities. Follow the guidelines described here. (See *Everyday situations that can trigger lawsuits,* page 138 and 139.)

MAKE A FAVORABLE FIRST IMPRESSION

The patient's first impression of a nurse is lasting and can set the tone for the nurse–patient relationship. Because a patient is less likely to sue someone he likes and trusts, a favorable first impression can help prevent a malpractice suit. Convey a caring attitude, give your full attention to the patient, try to avoid interruptions, and create a trusting relationship.

ESTABLISH YOUR BASELINE

Nurses frequently find themselves in trouble because they fail to obtain adequate information about a patient before attempting to care for him. To avoid problems caused by lack of knowledge, each nurse should establish

Everyday situations that can trigger lawsuits

Everyday nursing situations can present legal hazards. These examples of nursing liability, based on actual court decisions, show how deviating from accepted standards can harm a patient and result in lawsuits. By being aware of how certain common situations can cause you legal entanglements, you can avoid making similar mistakes.

Failing to perform a proper assessment

When a man traveling between cities began having chest pain and numbness in his left shoulder and arm, he and his companion stopped at a small hospital for help. The nurse on duty in the emergency department (ED) advised him to travel to a larger hospital 24 miles away. She failed to perform a physical assessment or to obtain a formal history. On his way to the other hospital, the man had a massive myocardial infarction and died.

Clearly, the nurse failed to accurately assess her patient. Her mistake cost the patient his life and resulted in a landmark decision that established a nurse's independent relationship with her patient.

The court held the nurse responsible and accountable for her omissions, stating that she had failed to meet her duty to protect the patient from harm.

Federal law (Emergency Medical Treatment and Active Labor Act) also prohibits an emergency department to refuse treatment or discharge a patient without medical screening and stabilization. Hospitals are subject to fines and liability for failure to comply. Moreover, the plaintiff-patient may file suit under federal law as well as state negligence law for any injury that occurred as a result of the nurse's failure to screen the patient and stabilize his condition.

Failing to take appropriate precautions

An elderly senile patient with a history of falling down was left in bed with the side rails down. She fell out of bed and hurt herself.

Another patient, an alert 28-year-old, was instructed by a nurse to call for help before getting out of bed. After the nurse left the room, the patient got herself out of bed and fell.

In the first case, the nurse was found liable for failing to raise the side rails. When a patient is at clear risk for injury, the nurse must take extra measures to protect her.

In the second case, the nurse wasn't held liable for the patient's injuries. Her patient, a competent adult, had received appropriate instructions and chose to ignore them. In such circumstances, a court will hold the patient responsible.

Neglecting to document and communicate information

A mother took her two sons to an ED with head and chest rashes and high fevers. The mother gave the nurse an accurate history, which included the recent removal of two ticks from one of the boys.

The nurse didn't tell the physician about the ticks or record the information in the chart. The physician diagnosed measles in both boys and sent them home.

Two days later, one boy died of Rocky Mountain spotted fever, which is transmitted by ticks.

Although neither the hospital nor the physician was held responsible for the boy's death, the nurse's omission was found to be a contributing cause of death.

Everyday situations that can trigger lawsuits *(continued)*

Performing nursing procedures incorrectly

A nurse administered an I.M. injection in the wrong quadrant of a patient's buttocks. He later developed footdrop from sciatic nerve damage.

In this case, both the nurse and the hospital were found negligent. The law expects a nurse to administer drugs and treatments without injuring patients by following set standards of care. (Drug errors are one of the most common sources of negligence claims against nurses.)

The hospital's liability was established under the legal doctrine *respondeat superior,* which holds an employer responsible for an employee's errors.

Failing to report another's mistakes

While delivering a patient's baby, an obstetrician made an incision in the patient's cervix to relieve a constrictive band of muscle. After delivery, he failed to suture the incision.

The patient was sent to the postpartum unit for care and observation. The patient's nurse, noticing that the patient was bleeding

heavily, called the obstetrician three times. He assured the nurse that the bleeding was normal. Within 2 hours, the patient went into shock and died.

Even though the nurse contacted the patient's physician, the court held the nurse negligent for failing to intervene further. The courts expect nurses to exercise professional, *independent* judgment and to object when a physician's orders are inappropriate. In this case, the nurse should have reported the facts to her manager or the unit's medical director, insisting that the patient receive proper care.

Being involved in a surgical team's error

During a cholecystectomy, the surgical team accidentally left a sponge in the patient's body. When the sponge was discovered later, the patient needed another operation to remove it.

When the court awarded damages, both the surgeon and the nurse paid. At one time, the surgeon would have been fully responsible under the "captain of the ship" doctrine. Today, all members of the surgical team are responsible for their actions.

---

her own baseline for each of her patients by:
◆ reviewing each patient's medical records and noting significant information
◆ reading all pertinent information contained in the care plan
◆ discussing the care plan and past and current problems with the patient
◆ revising the care plan as needed
◆ appropriately reporting and documenting the patient's condition.

KNOW YOUR STRENGTHS AND WEAKNESSES

Don't accept responsibilities for which you aren't prepared. For example, if you haven't worked in pediatrics for 10 years, accepting an assignment to a pediatric unit without orientation only increases your chances of making an error. If you do make an error, claiming you weren't familiar with the unit's procedures won't protect you against liability.

As a professional, you shouldn't accept a position if you can't perform as a reasonably prudent nurse would in a similar setting. Courts may, however, be more lenient when dealing with nurses who work in emergency settings, such as in a fire or a flood. However, simply being told "We need you here today" doesn't constitute an emergency.

EVALUATE YOUR ASSIGNMENT

You may be assigned to work on a specialized unit, which is reasonable, as long as you're assigned duties you can perform competently and as long as an experienced nurse on the unit assumes responsibility for the specialized duties. Assigning you to perform total patient care on the unit is unsafe if you don't have the skills to plan and deliver that care.

Therefore, before you accept an assignment, make sure that you're competent to complete the assignment. If you're in the process of being oriented to a new unit or a new facility, don't take an assignment that puts you in over your head. Whenever an assignment requires skills that you don't have, make sure that another nurse with the necessary skills is available to help you with that portion of the care.

Nurses working in acute-care facilities are sometimes asked to float to units on which they aren't qualified to work. For example, a medical-surgical nurse might be asked to float to an orthopedic unit. If the nurse knows nothing about orthopedic nursing, she should insist that she be paired with an experienced orthopedic nurse and that she work alongside that experienced nurse in caring for orthopedic patients. However, if a nurse is asked to work in a critical-care area or an emergency department (ED), it may not be feasible to pair her with another nurse in that type of setting; therefore, the nurse should refuse to be floated to that unit.

DELEGATE CAREFULLY

An RN may delegate patient-care responsibilities to another RN, an LPN, or an unlicensed assistive person (UAP), such as a nursing assistant or a medical technician. However, before she delegates a given responsibility, she must know the skills and abilities of the delegatee and which patient-care needs may be met by LPNs and UAPs and which require the intervention of an RN.

For example, if a nurse wants a nursing assistant to take a blood pressure reading on a patient who has an arteriovenous fistula, her state's nursing practice act must allow it. The nurse must also make sure that the assistant knows how to properly take and record the blood pressure reading and understands special considerations that must be observed.

Nurses can be held liable if they fail to appropriately delegate responsibilities. It's important for every delegating nurse to remember to:
◆ make sure staff members are competent
◆ teach and direct staff members
◆ evaluate staff members on an ongoing basis
◆ rectify any incompetent actions
◆ reassess patients
◆ take responsibility for all delegated tasks
◆ ensure accurate documentation.

A delegating nurse should check her state's nurse practice act to learn which tasks may and may not be delegated. She should then delegate nursing tasks only to individuals who are appropriately trained. Report incompetent health care personnel to superiors through your facility's chain of command.

CARRY OUT ORDERS CAUTIOUSLY

Never treat any patient without orders from his physician, except in an emergency. Don't prescribe or dispense any drug without authorization. In most cases, only physicians and pharmacists may perform these functions legally.

Don't carry out any order from a physician if you have any doubt about its accuracy or appropriateness. Follow your facility's policy for clarifying ambiguous orders. Document your efforts to clarify the order, and whether or not the order was carried out.

If, after you carry out an order, the treatment adversely affects the patient, discontinue it. Report all unfavorable signs and symptoms to the patient's physician. Resume treatment only after you've discussed the situation with the physician and clarified the orders. Document your actions.

Keep in mind that a physician can change his orders at any time, including while you're off duty. A patient may know something about his prescribed care that no one has told you. If a patient protests a procedure, drug dosage, or drug administration route — saying that it's different from "the usual" or that it has been changed — give him the benefit of the doubt. Question the physician's orders, following your facility's policy.

If you're an inexperienced nurse, you should take steps to clarify all standing orders. Contact the prescribing physician for guidance, or tell your supervisor you're uncertain about following the order, and let her decide whether to delegate the responsibility to a more experienced nurse.

ADMINISTER DRUGS CAREFULLY

Drug errors are the most common type of nursing error. They typically occur because nurses fail to appropriately check the drug order or are unfamiliar with the drug they're giving.

Nurses can avoid drug errors by using the six "rights" to medication administration: right patient, right drug, right dose, right time, right route, and right documentation. Also, when a nurse is unfamiliar with a drug she's administering, she has the duty to look up the drug to understand its intended effects, any contraindications, and potential adverse effects or drug interactions. Finally, the nurse needs to be able to evaluate and document the patient's response to the drug administered.

Mistakes in dosage, patient identification, or drug selection by nurses have lead to vision loss, brain damage, cardiac arrest, and death. In *Norton v. Argonaut Insurance Company* (1962), an infant died after a nurse administered injectable digoxin at a dosage level appropriate for elixir of Lanoxin, an oral form of the drug. The nurse was unaware that digoxin was available in an oral form. The nurse questioned two physicians who weren't treating the infant about the order, but failed to mention that the order was written for elixir of Lanoxin. She also failed to clarify the order with the physician who wrote it. The nurse, the physician who originally ordered the drug, and the hospital were all found liable.

MAINTAIN RAPPORT WITH THE PATIENT

Trial attorneys have a saying: "If you don't want to be sued, don't be rude." Failing to communicate with patients is the cause of many legal problems.

Who's looking for litigation?

Patients who are more likely to file lawsuits against nurses share certain personality traits and behaviors. Furthermore, nurses who are more likely to be named as defendants also have certain common characteristics.

Beware of these patients

Although not all persons displaying the behaviors listed here will file a lawsuit, a little extra caution in your dealings with them won't hurt. Providing professional and competent care to such patients will lessen their tendency to sue.

A patient who's likely to file a lawsuit may:
◆ persistently criticize all aspects of the nursing care provided
◆ purposefully not follow the care plan
◆ overreact to any perceived slight or negative comment, real or imagined
◆ unjustifiably depend on nurses for all aspects of care and refuse to accept any responsibility for his own care
◆ openly express hostility to nurses and other health care personnel
◆ project his anxiety, or anger onto the nursing staff, attributing blame for all negative events to health care providers
◆ have filed lawsuits previously.

Nurses at risk

Nurses who are more likely to be named as defendants in a lawsuit display certain characteristic behaviors. If you recognize these attributes in yourself, changing your behavior will reduce your risk of liability.

A nurse who's likely to be a defendant in a lawsuit may:
◆ be insensitive to the patient's complaints or fail to take them seriously
◆ fail to identify and meet the patient's emotional and physical needs
◆ refuse to recognize the limits of her nursing skills and personal competency
◆ lack sufficient education for the tasks and responsibilities associated with a specific practice setting
◆ display an authoritarian and inflexible attitude when providing care
◆ inappropriately delegate responsibilities to subordinates
◆ fail to advocate for the patient.

Always remain calm when a patient or his family becomes difficult. Patients must be told the truth about adverse outcomes, but this information should be communicated with discretion and sensitivity. (See *Who's looking for litigation?*)

THINK BEFORE YOU SPEAK

Avoid offering your opinion when a patient asks you what you think is the matter with him. If you do, you could be accused of making a medical diagnosis, which would be practicing medicine without a license. Don't volunteer information about possible treatments for the patient's condition or about possible choices of physicians, either.

Avoid making any statement that could be perceived by the patient as an admission of fault or error. Don't criticize other nurses or health care practitioners, or the care they provide, if the patient can hear you. Don't discuss with the patient or visitors which members of the health care team are covered by malpractice insurance.

Be careful not to discuss a patient's confidential information with anyone except when doing so is consistent with proper nursing care. Also, avoid such discussions in public areas, such as waiting areas, elevators, or cafeterias.

DOCUMENT CARE ACCURATELY

From a legal standpoint, documented care is as important as the actual care. If a procedure wasn't documented, the courts assume it wasn't performed. Documentation of observations, decisions, and actions is considered to be more solid evidence than oral testimony.

The patient's chart, when taken into the jury room, is a nurse's "best evidence" of the care given. The chart should follow the FACT rule — that is, it should be factual, accurate, complete, and timely.

Use incident reports to identify and report accidents, errors, or injuries to a patient. A long period may elapse between an incident and subsequent court proceedings, and this documentation may contain pertinent facts of the incident that may have been left out of the patient's medical record.

Don't ever correct or revise a patient's medical record after he has filed a lawsuit. The case of *Carr v. St. Paul Fire and Marine Insurance Company* (1974) illustrates the liability a hospital can incur when nurses or other employees alter or destroy patient records. In this case, the patient came to the hospital ED suffering severe pain. One nurse on duty refused to call a physician for the patient, so he returned home and died a short time later. The nurses on duty in the ED that night testified that they had taken the patient's vital signs, but this couldn't be

proved or disproved because the patient's records had been destroyed. When instructing the jury, the judge indicated that they could find the hospital negligent.

In the case of *Sweet v. Providence Hospital* (1995), the court held that a rebuttable presumption of negligence arises if a health care facility's records are unavailable to a plaintiff and the plaintiff can demonstrate that the missing records are necessary to prove his negligence claim.

EXERCISE CAUTION WHEN ASSISTING IN PROCEDURES

Don't assist with a surgical procedure unless you're satisfied the patient has given proper informed consent. Never force a patient to accept treatment he has expressly refused. Don't use equipment that you are unfamiliar with or aren't trained to use or that seems to be functioning improperly. And, if you're an operating room nurse, always check and double-check to ensure that no surgical equipment, such as sponges or instruments, are unaccounted for after an operation is completed.

DOCUMENT THE USE OF RESTRAINTS

Restraints need to be applied correctly and checked according to your facility's policy. Documentation must be exact about the reason for restraint, the need for restraint, the amount and kind of restraint used, and the status of the restrained patient. Generally, there must be a physician's order for restraints to be used. Restraining patients without a proper order may be a claim for patient abuse or false imprisonment. An omission or failure to properly monitor a restrained patient may also result in a malpractice claim.

TAKE STEPS TO PREVENT PATIENT FALLS

Patient falls are a common area of nursing liability. Patients who are elderly, infirm, sedated, confused, agitated, or mentally incapacitated are the most likely to fall. Often, there's no way to predict if and when a patient is going to fall. However, if the nurse has any reason to suspect that a patient is at an increased risk for falling, she must take appropriate measures to safeguard the patient. The case of *Stevenson v. Alta Bates* (1937) involved a patient who had a stroke and was learning to walk again. As two nurses, each holding one of the patient's arms, assisted her into the hospital's sunroom, one nurse let go of the patient and stepped forward to get a chair for her. The patient fell and sustained a fracture. The nurse was found negligent. The court reasoned that the nurse should have anticipated the patient's need for a chair and made the appropriate arrangements before bringing the patient into the sunroom.

COMPLY WITH LAWS ABOUT ADVANCE DIRECTIVES

The Patient's Self-Determination Act, a federal law, requires that every patient, upon admission to a hospital, be given information about living wills and durable power of attorney. Follow your facility's policy for providing the required information. Don't, as one of the patient's health care providers, become a witness to a living will or a durable power of attorney. You should also be aware of state laws concerning living wills and advance directives.

ADHERE TO YOUR FACILITY'S POLICIES

You have a responsibility to adhere to your facility's policies. If they're sound and you follow them carefully, they can protect you against a malpractice claim. The court in *Roach v. Springfield Clinic* (1992) held that "hospital policies are admissible as standards of care for the treatment of patients within that hospital."

Your facility's drug policy may involve checking all drug cards against a central Kardex. If you do this and the Kardex is in error, you may not be liable for a resulting drug error because you followed the appropriate procedure and acted responsibly.

Inexperienced nurses are at high risk for liability. The RN must be able to recognize her limitations and admit to them, especially if the safety of the patient is at issue. If the nurse doesn't know how to perform a nursing function or doesn't understand the reason for a particular treatment, it's her duty to obtain assistance that's timely and appropriate.

KEEP POLICIES UP TO DATE

As the nursing profession changes, so should a health care facility's policies. As a professional, you're responsible for keeping these policies up to date. For example, does your facility have a written policy on dealing with emergency situations? "We've always done it this way" isn't an adequate substitute for a clearly written, officially accepted policy.

If administrators are reluctant to make policy changes based on one nurse's suggestion, join with colleagues to address the legal implications.

PROVIDE A SAFE ENVIRONMENT

When providing care, avoid using faulty equipment. Clearly mark the equipment as defective and unusable. Even after repairs are done, don't use the repaired equipment until technicians demonstrate that the equipment is operating properly. Document steps you took to handle problems with faulty equipment to show that you followed the proper procedure.

Maintaining professional liability insurance

In any work setting, you're at risk for malpractice suits, and the risk may increase if you work in an area that requires a high level of skill, specialized knowledge, or independent functioning. Because of this risk, you should consider obtaining your own nursing malpractice policy. (See *Choosing liability insurance,* pages 146 and 147.) It can provide you with an extra layer of security should you find yourself on the wrong end of a lawsuit and alleviates the stress of having to worry whether or not your employer is making a change in its coverage or failing to maintain adequate coverage.

Many nurses mistakenly believe that purchasing an individual malpractice policy invites lawsuits. Unfortunately, this false belief deters some nurses from obtaining individual insurance coverage. The reality? A plaintiff's attorney won't know if a nurse has malpractice insurance unless he has begun a lawsuit and asked questions about insurance coverage via interrogatories or at a deposition.

UNDERSTANDING LIABILITY INSURANCE

When you buy professional liability insurance, you get protection under contract for a designated period from the financial consequences of certain professional errors. The type of insurance policy you buy determines the amount that the insurance company will pay if the judgment goes against you in a lawsuit.

You may purchase a policy designated with "single limits" or "double limits." In a single-limits policy, you buy protection in set dollar increments — for example, $100,000; $300,000; or $1,000,000. The stipulated amount will shield you if a judgment, arising out of a single nursing malpractice occurrence, goes against you.

In the double-limits policy, you buy protection in a combination package, such as $100,000/$300,000; $300,000/$500,000; or $1,000,000/$3,000,000. The smaller sum is what your insurance company will make available to protect you from any one injury arising out of a single nursing malpractice occurrence. The larger sum is the maximum amount that will be paid for all claims under that policy in a given year. Although the single-limits policy will also protect you against injuries to more than one patient, the double-limits policy makes considerably more money available to protect you if you're involved in multiple lawsuits.

Occurrence policies and claims-made policies

The two main types of insurance policies available to nurses are occurrence policies and claims-made policies. If you purchase an occurrence policy that begins on January 1, 2005, and ends December 31, 2005, you're covered for any incident that occurs in this period that later results in a malpractice suit or board of nursing complaint, regardless of when it's reported. When you cease to practice nursing for any reason, you don't have to purchase additional coverage.

Choosing liability insurance

To find professional liability coverage that fits your needs, compare the coverage of a number of different policies. Make sure your policy provides coverage for in-court and out-of-court malpractice suits and expenses and for defense of a complaint or disciplinary action made to or by your board of nursing. Understanding insurance policy basics will enable you to shop more aggressively and intelligently for the coverage you need. You should work with an insurance agent who's experienced in this type of insurance. If you already have professional liability insurance, the information below may help you better evaluate your coverage.

Type of coverage

Ask your insurance agent if the policy covers only claims made before the policy expires (claims-made coverage) or if it covers any negligent act committed during the policy period, regardless of when it's reported (occurrence coverage). Keep in mind that the latter type offers better coverage.

Coverage limits

All malpractice insurance policies cover professional liability. Some also cover representation before your board of nursing, general personal liability, medical payments, assault-related bodily injury, and property damage.

The amount of coverage varies, as does your premium. Remember that professional liability coverage is limited to acts and practice settings specified in the policy. Be sure your policy covers your nursing role, whether you're a student, a graduate nurse, or a working nurse with advanced education and specialized skills.

Options

Check whether the policy would provide coverage for these incidents:

◆ negligence on the part of nurses under your supervision
◆ misuse of equipment
◆ errors in reporting or recording care
◆ failure to properly teach patients
◆ errors in administering medication
◆ mistakes made while providing care in an emergency, outside your employment setting.

Also, ask if the policy provides protection if your employer sues you.

Definition of terms

Definition of terms can vary from policy to policy. If your policy includes restrictive definitions, you won't be covered for actions outside those guidelines. Therefore, for the best protection, seek the broadest definitions possible and ask the insurance company for examples of actions the company hasn't covered.

Duration of coverage

Insurance is an annual contract that can be renewed or canceled each year. Most policies specify how they can be canceled – for example, in writing by either you or the insurance company. Some contracts require a 30-day notice for cancellation. If the company is canceling the policy, you'll probably be given at least 10 days' notice.

Exclusions

Ask the insurer about exclusions – areas not covered by the insurance policy. For example, "this policy doesn't apply to injury arising out of performance of the insured of a criminal act" or "this policy doesn't apply to nurse anesthetists."

Other insurance clauses

All professional liability insurance policies contain "other insurance" clauses that address payment obligations when a nurse is covered by more than one insurance policy, such as

Choosing liability insurance (continued)

the employer's policy and the nurse's personal liability policy:

◆ The *pro rata* clause states that two or more policies in effect at the same time will pay any claims in accordance with a proportion established in the individual policies.

◆ The *in excess* clause states that the primary policy will pay all fees and damages up to its limits, at which point the second policy will pay any additional fees or damages up to its limits.

◆ The *escape clause* relieves an insurance company of all liability for fees or damages if another insurance policy is in effect at the same time; the clause essentially states that the other company is responsible for all liability.

If you're covered by more than one policy, be alert for "other insurance" clauses and avoid purchasing a policy with an escape clause for liability.

Additional tips

Here's some additional information that will guide you in the purchase of professional liability insurance.

◆ The insurance application is a legal document. If you provide false information, it may void the policy.

◆ If you're involved in nursing administration, education, research, or advanced or nontraditional nursing practice, be especially careful in selecting a policy because many policies don't cover these activities.

◆ After selecting a policy that ensures adequate coverage, stay with the same policy and insurer, if possible, to avoid potential lapses in coverage that could occur when changing insurers.

◆ No insurance policy will cover you for acts outside of your scope of practice or licensure, nor will insurance cover you for intentional acts that you know will cause harm.

◆ Be prepared to uphold all obligations specified in the policy; failure to do so may void the policy and cause personal liability for any damages. Remember that an act of willful wrongdoing on your part renders the policy null and void and may lead to a breach of contract lawsuit.

◆ Check out the insurance company by calling your state division of insurance to inquire about the company's financial stability.

If you purchase a claims-made policy that begins on January 1, 2005, and goes through December 31, 2005, you're covered only for the incidents that both occur and are reported during the indicated time period. However, if you continue your claims-made coverage with a new policy the following year and in the subsequent years during which you're practicing, you'll be covered for any incident that occurs and is reported during any consecutive policy period. If you retire

from nursing or if you don't renew a claims-made policy, you need to purchase a reporting endorsement, commonly referred to as "tail" coverage, so that you'll be able to later report and have coverage for an incident that occurred when the policy was in effect. If you change insurance carriers and go from one claims-made policy to another, you need to obtain prior-acts coverage, which allows you to report incidents that occurred during a previous policy period and have resulted in a lawsuit or board of nursing complaint during your new policy period with your new insurance carrier.

Excess judgment

A judgment that exceeds policy limits is known as *excess judgment*. However, if you've purchased your own policy to supplement the coverage your employer is providing, it's unlikely that there will be an excess judgment. Also, if the insurance carrier or carriers providing coverage think that a verdict in excess of your policy limits is possible, they're obligated to try to get the case settled within your policy limits.

If your attorney has told you that the case might result in an excess judgment and the insurance company isn't moving to get it settled, your attorney should write a letter demanding that the case be settled within your policy limits. Once such a letter is written, the insurance carrier may become responsible for any excess judgment if it fails to make a good faith effort to settle the case. If a good faith effort to settle the case is unsuccessful and there's an excess judgment, then you may end up being personally responsible for the excess judgment.

Depending on the laws in your state, almost everything you own, except for a limited portion of your equity in your home and the clothes on your back, can be taken to satisfy the uninsured portion of a judgment.

SUBROGATION

Subrogation is defined as the act of substituting another (that is, a second creditor) with regard to a legal right or claim. Employers (or other defendants such as physicians) who have been found liable for damages can subsequently sue another involved in the incident to recoup their losses.

In a Pennsylvania case, *Mutual Insurance Company of Arizona v. American Casualty Company of Reading* (1997), a patient underwent angioplasty and had a complication, which was treated. However, during nurse-to-nurse report, the incident wasn't mentioned. The patient went into cardiac arrest and died within 12 hours. The patient's family sued the hospital and the physician, but the nurses weren't named in the lawsuit. After the hospital was found liable, the hospital's insurer filed suit against the nurses involved, saying the patient would have been more closely monitored if the staff had known it hadn't been a routine angioplasty. The court ruled that the suit was permissible.

INSURANCE COSTS

Fortunately, premiums for insurance coverage of $1 million aren't much more than they are for smaller limits. The reason is a substantial part of the premium pays for the insurance company's assumption of risk; higher limits don't increase the premium disproportionately.

General duty RNs usually pay less for coverage than critical care nurses, operating room nurses, ED nurses, postanesthesia care nurses, and advanced practice nurses. In recent years, nurses specializing in obstetrics have typically paid the highest insurance premium rates, in part because of the large number of lawsuits filed against obstetricians.

Insurance companies offer various liability insurance policies. If possible, choose an agent who's experienced in professional liability coverage. Organizations such as the ANA and your state nurses' association offer group plans at attractive premiums. You need to review the extent of coverage with your agent to make sure it's adequate for your needs.

INSURER'S ROLE IN A LAWSUIT

Professional liability insurance can supply you with more than just financial protection. The insurance company may also provide a defense counsel to represent you for the entire course of litigation if it's included in your insurance contract. Remember: Insurance companies aren't in business to lose money; they'll retain highly experienced attorneys with considerable experience in defending malpractice lawsuits.

When preparing your defense, attorneys will investigate the subject of the lawsuit, obtain expert witnesses, handle motions throughout the case, and prepare medical models, transparencies, photographs, and other court exhibits, if necessary. The cost incurred in preparing a defense and defending you through trial and appeals will be covered by your insurance policy.

Out-of-court settlements

During litigation — and even before a lawsuit is filed in court — your insurance company may seek an out-of-court settlement from the plaintiff's attorneys. Although this saves time and money, it may not be in your best interest professionally. In the United States, if you believe your professional reputation is at stake, you may be able to refuse to agree to an out-of-court settlement. If your policy contains a threshold limit, your insurer can't settle a case out of court for an amount greater than the threshold limit without your permission. Without a threshold limit, your insurer has control over out-of-court settlements.

If the lawsuit against you goes to court and the insurance company is

defending you, the insurer has the right to control how the defense is conducted. The insurer's attorney, however, makes all decisions regarding the case's legal tactics and strategy.

You have a right to be kept informed about every step in the case because you, not the insurance company, are the client, so the attorney must perform his legal duties according to what's in your best interest, not the insurance company's. After all, the insurer knows that a successful defense depends in part on the defendant's cooperation. Also, you can sue the insurance agency if it fails to provide a competent defense.

If you lose a malpractice lawsuit, the insurance company will cover you for jury-awarded general and special damages. Basic damages that can be verified in terms of past, present, and future expenses include but aren't limited to:
- medical expenses
- lost wages
- loss of earning potential
- other related expenses, such as:
  - modifications that need to be made to a home or vehicle
  - equipment that needs to be purchased or leased
  - homemaker or housekeeping services.

Other monetary damages that also may be added to the settlement or verdict value of a case include damages awarded for pain and suffering; loss of consortium; or emotional harm, now and in the future. Such damages can't be defined in verifiable monetary terms but are given values by those negotiating a settlement or by a judge or jury before rendering a verdict.

In states where tort law has undergone tort reform, there may be caps on the amount of recovery legally allowable for such things as pain and suffering or loss of consortium.

Punitive damages

Some states allow a plaintiff-patient to recover punitive damages from a defendant-nurse (or other health care provider) if that defendant did something to intentionally harm the patient or knowingly failed to take steps to prevent harm to the patient.

Some insurance carriers have provisions in their policies that specifically state they won't indemnify a policy holder for punitive damages if the policy holder is shown to have acted with malice or reckless disregard. Why? Punitive damages are meant to punish the defendant, and the defendant isn't really being punished if such damages are paid. However, many insurance carriers have decided to indemnify their insured health care provider for punitive damages that have been included in a settlement or verdict. Such decisions are generally made on a case-by-case basis. Additionally, if an insurance carrier doesn't have a specific exclusion in the policy for punitive damages, it's clear that the insurance carrier will be responsible for payment of any and all damages up to the limits of liability in any given policy.

MULTIPLE INSURERS

If you have more than one insurance policy — for example, malpractice coverage through your employer as well as your individual insurance policy — both insurance companies might well become involved in defending or settling a patient's claim against you. Determining who pays is complex. Generally, the coverage provided by your employer would be the primary policy if the lawsuit involves actions you performed at your place of employment

within your scope of practice. The coverage provided by your individual policy would be secondary and would take effect only after the primary policy was exhausted.

Your secondary policy would cover you up to its policy limits for any excess verdicts or settlements that weren't covered by your primary policy. However, you must promptly notify each insurance company you have a policy with that you're the target of a malpractice lawsuit. If you fail to notify your insurance companies of this or if you delay in notifying them, they can use such policy defenses to avoid responsibility for providing coverage.

INDEMNIFICATION SUITS

If several insurance companies are representing different parties in a malpractice lawsuit, they'll typically file counteractions against the other parties, seeking compensation, or *indemnification,* for all or part of any damages the jury awards.

Many states now permit damages to be apportioned among multiple defendants, the extent of liability depending on the jury's determination of each defendant's relative contribution to the harm done. This is called comparative negligence. For example, suppose you were the nurse responsible for the instrument count during surgery in a foreign-object case, and the court found you to be 75% responsible. Your insurance company would pay 75% of the total award. The other insurance companies would be held liable for the remaining 25%, in proportion to the percentage of harm attributed to each remaining defendant.

Also, a plaintiff's acts or omissions (for example, failure to follow a physician's order) may be considered by a jury in determining where liability lies. A judgment would be reduced by the plaintiff's own negligence. If one codefendant, such as the surgeon, decided that he had been judged negligent only because of your negligence, he could instruct his insurance attorneys to file a new, separate lawsuit in his name against you.

Indemnification suits are becoming more common. Your own hospital, a fellow nurse, or a laboratory technician — as long as each has individual professional liability insurance — can file an indemnification suit against you. This possibility strengthens the argument for having your own professional liability insurance.

LIABILITY COST CONTAINMENT

Many states are taking steps to decrease malpractice litigation and the size of potential jury verdicts. Besides establishing special statutes of limitations, some states have imposed a maximum limit on the monetary sums a jury can award for certain damages, such as loss of consortium, wrongful death, and pain and suffering. The federal government has also been debating a proposed award cap of $250,000 for pain and suffering, but the proposal has met stiff resistance; it has been called unconstitutional by certain members of Congress and various special-interest groups.

Medical associations and insurance companies are trying to limit malpractice awards by forcing malpractice claims into arbitration, thus removing them from the province of lay juries, and by requiring that claims be screened by a medical malpractice screening panel. A few states, such as Ohio, provide for submission to non-binding arbitration panels if all parties agree. State laws may also provide for binding arbitration if specified by a

written contract between a patient and the physician or hospital.

If a malpractice screening panel decides the plaintiff's claim is invalid, the plaintiff can't file suit unless he posts a bond to cover his defense costs in advance. Although more than half the states have set up screening panels, these panels have been criticized by consumer groups and plaintiffs' attorneys and challenged in court as being unconstitutional. In *Keyes v. Humana Hospital, Alaska, Inc.* (1988), Alaska courts upheld the constitutionality of the panels.

YOUR EMPLOYER'S INSURANCE

Virtually all health care facilities carry insurance to protect against their liability for an employee's mistakes. Without professional liability insurance, the facility would have to pay damages awarded in a lawsuit out of its own funds, which could lead it to bankruptcy.

To help you to more wisely assess your own professional liability insurance needs, find out the degree of professional and financial protection you're entitled to under your employer's liability insurance. To do this, consider obtaining and reviewing a copy of your employer's insurance policy. If you don't understand something in the policy, contact the insurer.

Coverage limits

Although each health care facility's professional liability insurance policy has a maximum dollar coverage limit, your employer can purchase coverage that exceeds the basic limit. Many hospitals do so for extra protection.

Deductible limit

Most hospitals also have a deductible provision that makes them responsible for damages under a certain figure. The higher the deductible limit, the lower the premium the insurer charges. You should pay careful attention to the deductible limit because your employer may be able to settle a claim against you, for which they may be held financially responsible, under that figure without ever consulting you or the insurer. Because you won't have a chance to defend yourself and because many people interpret a settlement as an admission of guilt, such an action could tarnish your professional reputation. A tarnished reputation, in turn, could jeopardize your ability to obtain your own professional liability insurance or a new job. Therefore, in the event of a lawsuit, you should maintain close contact with your employer's legal staff and insist on being informed about every step in the case.

Provisions for your defense

If you're sued and your employer's insurance covers you, the insurer may have a duty to provide a complete defense, including assigning an attorney to handle the entire case. The insurer will pay attorney fees as well as any investigation costs and expert witness fees.

Keep in mind that you're a player in the lawsuit, but the defense counsel is for the hospital first and the nurse incidentally. If there's ever a conflict between your best interest and your employer's best interest, you should obtain your own attorney who will be concerned with your defense. This attorney may work closely with hospital counsel, but his loyalty is to you. He'll provide you with an opportunity to confer with him and give your side of the story.

If your employer grants written consent to settle the case, the insurer may do so or it may decide to try the case in court if its legal advisors overrule the employer. If the plaintiff wins the lawsuit, the insurer is obliged to pay damages awarded to the patient up to the insurance policy's coverage limit.

Stipulations for denying coverage

Insurance companies that provide professional liability coverage for hospitals and other health care facilities reduce the risk they assume under *respondeat superior* in several ways. One way is by stipulating a precise coverage period, typically 1 year. Another way is by defining the type of coverage they provide, whether, for example, it's an occurrence policy or a claims-made policy. A third way is by putting exclusions into malpractice policies. These exclusions vary considerably from policy to policy, but all list specific acts, situations, or personnel that the insurance doesn't cover.

Besides exclusions, insurers may deny coverage to you or your employer because of other circumstances, including:

◆ The insurance policy lapses because your employer failed to pay the premiums.

◆ Your employer refuses to cooperate with the insurance company, for whatever reason.

◆ The insurer discovers that your employer made misstatements on the insurance application.

In some malpractice situations, an insurer could agree to provide you with a defense but refuse to pay damages awarded to a patient. The insurer agrees to defend you in this situation because he doesn't want to be accused of breach of contract. However, he must notify you of his intention not to pay damages in a reservation-of-rights letter. This letter informs you and your employer that the insurer believes the case falls outside what's covered by the insurance policy.

When your employer and the insurer disagree about whether insurance coverage exists, the dispute may have to be resolved through separate legal action. Similarly, you have the right to bring such action against your employer's insurance company if it refuses to cover you.

Special considerations

Keep in mind a few more concerns when reviewing your employer's policy. First, is the policy purchased for you as an employee benefit? In that case, the insurer protects you and not the hospital. Second, the policy may provide coverage only for incidents that occur while you're on the job. You may be held liable for nursing actions off the job, unless your actions are covered under a Good Samaritan act, a state law that protects health care professionals who act in an emergency.

Third, many employers provide only a claims-made policy. If a suit is filed against you for work you performed while working for a *former* employer, you probably won't be covered by your former employer's insurance plan.

Fourth, if you're an independent contractor such as a private-duty nurse, the court likely won't consider you to be under the hospital's direct supervision and control. Consequently, the hospital won't be considered responsible for your actions, and its insurance probably won't cover you. However, if the policy is yours with the hospital paying the premiums as an employee benefit, you're still covered.

Finally, with regard to intentional acts of harm, such as striking a patient, you would be responsible for any criminal or civil penalties levied against you. Simply keep in mind that intentional acts of harm usually aren't covered by any professional liability policy.

Selected references

American Hospital Association's Quality Agenda; American Society of Health-System Pharmacists; Hospital & Health Networks. "Medication Safety Issue Brief: A Fully Stocked Toolkit. Series II, part 1," *Hospitals & Health Networks* 77(6):supp 2 p. following 24, June 2003.

Berwick, D.M. "Errors Today and Errors Tomorrow," *New England Journal of Medicine* 348(25):2570-72, June 2003.

Clark, A.P. "Malpractice Prevention and Technology Expertise," *Clinical Nurse Specialist* 17(3):126-27, May 2003.

Clement, R. "Liability Awards and Nurses," *Hospitals & Healthcare Networks* 77(1):12, January 2003.

Denney, C. "Safe, Secure Staff Provides Better Care," *Nursing Management* 34(3):18, March 2003.

Haugh, R. "Surviving Medical Malpractice Madness," *Hospitals & Healthcare Networks* 77(5): 46-50, 52, May 2003.

Mello, M.M., et al. "The New Medical Malpractice Crisis," *New England Journal of Medicine* 348(23):2281-84, June 2003.

"Professional Liability Insurance. Myth vs. Fact," *Colorado Nurse* 102(1):18, March 2002.

Rosenbaum, S. "Medical Errors, Medical Negligence, and Professional Medical Liability Reform," *Public Health Reporter* 118(3):272-74, May-June 2003.

Walsh, P. "We Must Accept that Health Care is Risky Business," *British Medical Journal* 326(7402):1333-34, June 2003.

5

Lawsuits and the legal process

Before the early 1970s, health care providers seldom thought about their potential for being sued for medical malpractice because patients and their families were generally unaware of their rights within the heath care system. Patients didn't know their options when dealing with less-than-satisfactory outcomes. However, the malpractice crisis that erupted in the late 1970s — spurred on by greater patient awareness of disorders (and their specific treatments) and higher patient awards — quickly taught all health care providers that patients now expect higher quality of care and will sue if they feel they don't receive it. Today, specialization and daily advances in technology coupled with the consumers' expanding knowledge of medical techniques and therapies, has culminated in a glut of medical malpractice lawsuits that's threatening the foundation of the entire health care system.

The medical malpractice lawsuit

Most malpractice lawsuits against nurses are filed under the auspices of tort law. *Torts* are personal, civil injuries that reside outside a contractual relationship. *Malpractice* is a type of tort

that's defined as a professional person's wrongful conduct, improper discharge of professional duties, or failure to meet standards of care that results in harm to another person.

Patients typically file malpractice lawsuits against nurses when they perceive their nursing care to be substandard or the cause of foreseeable injuries. Keep in mind, however, that malpractice is more than an undesired outcome: in order for a patient to *successfully* file a malpractice lawsuit against a nurse, there must be evidence that some action or inaction that the nurse was obligated to perform resulted in harm to the patient. If the patient doesn't have compelling evidence, he may still file suit, but the court may find the suit to be frivolous and the suit will generally be unsuccessful.

Remember, every patient can sue, but not every patient can win a lawsuit.

THE FOUR ELEMENTS

In court, four elements must be shown before a nurse is said to be liable for malpractice: duty owed the patient, breach of duty owed the patient, causation, and injury and damages.

Duty owed the patient

The patient-plaintiff must show that the nurse-defendant owed him a specific duty and to what level the duty was owed. The nurse-patient relationship, showing that the patient was relying on the professional judgment of the nurse to deliver safe and competent care, forms the basis for this element. Standards of care become the main issue. The patient's attorney and the nurse's attorney will both present their views of what a reasonably prudent nurse, with like training and experience, would have done under similar circumstances.

Breach of duty owed the patient

Attorneys for the patient-plaintiff will present testimony concerning the nurse-defendant's failure to competently deliver quality nursing care. Attorneys for the nurse will present contradictory testimony. This portion of the lawsuit can be lengthy and usually involves the use of expert witnesses. (See *Courtroom controversy: Nurses as expert witnesses,* pages 156 and 157.)

Causation

Causation, the concept that certain events may reasonably be expected to cause specific results, is usually the most difficult element to prove at trial. The law states that the specific outcome must be foreseeable before there can be liability.

Causation may be further divided into cause-in-fact and proximate cause. Cause-in-fact involves the concept that what the nurse does or fails to do must be directly attributable to the harm that the patient incurs. It isn't enough that a patient is harmed; there must be a direct relationship to the harm and what the nurse did or failed to do. This element, like breach of duty owed the patient, is commonly argued

at court through the use of expert witnesses.

Finally, there can be proximate cause for which nurses are held liable. Proximate cause actually builds on foreseeability and attempts to determine how far the liability of the individual extends for consequences following negligent actions. If a nurse administers an overdose of a known nephrotoxic medication and the patient develops renal failure 2 years later, is the nurse liable for the renal failure? Under the concept of proximate causation, the answer could be yes. However, if a patient is deemed partially responsible for her injury, proximate causation may not apply. (See *Proximate causation,* page 158.)

Injury and damages

In order for a nurse to be held liable for malpractice, the patient must prove physical injury and significant monetary damages. Although courts allow some award of damages for pain and suffering, damages are generally awarded to compensate the patient for expenses incurred (actual and projected) as a direct or indirect result of the injury sustained. These damages may be apportioned among the various health care providers that are named as defendants in the case.

Sometimes the court awards punitive damages, which are meant to punish the nurse or other health care provider for harms that were the result of malicious or wanton disregard for the patient's safety. For example, in *Manning v. Twin Falls Clinic and Hospital* (1992), a decision was made to move a terminally ill patient to another room on the same unit. The patient, who was projected to have less than 24 hours to live, was on oxygen. His family requested that supplemental oxygen be given during the transfer. His nurses

Courtroom controversy: Nurses as expert witnesses

Testimony by experts is an essential ingredient in malpractice cases for both plaintiff and defendant. In lawsuits against nurses, the court's position is that a nurse is the appropriate expert witness when dealing with the actions or decisions of a nurse. Before 1980, it was common for physicians to testify about the standards for nursing care.

No double standard

In the case of *Young v. Board of Hospital Directors, Lee County* (1984), the court concluded that physicians may not determine nursing standards of care. The physician, being unfamiliar with the daily practices of nurses, is unable to set a standard or to testify as to deviation from common nursing practice. The expert witness nurse can explain technology or nursing care in the language jurors can understand. This type of testimony is crucial to dispel common misconceptions or to explain scientific facts as they pertain to nursing care and the care at hand.

Qualifications of an expert

A nurse expert witness testifying for the plaintiff in a malpractice case must be able to describe the relevant standard of care, describe how the nurse deviated from the acceptable standard, and explain how failure to meet acceptable nursing standards caused or contributed to the patient's injury. Defense counsel will also provide a nurse expert who will testify to the standard and whether the defendant nurse met the standard.

A nurse must meet certain criteria to be considered an expert witness. The first and only absolute criterion is current licensure to practice nursing. Also, the expert witness' credentials must match or exceed the defendant's. This includes clinical expertise in that specialty area, certification in the clinical specialty, and recent education relevant to the nursing specialty at issue. However, the expert witness may hold licensure in another state. Another criterion is a lack of bias; the expert witness must not have any relationship, professional or personal, with any parties involved in the suit.

Expert witness or legal consultant?

There's a difference between being a legal consultant and an expert witness. A legal consultant may be an expert, but her name and the information and opinions she gives aren't disclosed to the opposition. However, when a nurse agrees to become an expert witness, her name is given to opposing counsel and she may have to testify in court. Also, any comments, notes, or reports she makes may be discovered and reviewed by opposing counsel.

The nurse expert witness faces two dilemmas: the changing standard of care, and being trapped into saying that only one opinion is correct. As the nurse expert witness, she must consider the possibility that the standard of care may have changed by the time the case goes to trial, and thus it's crucial to know what was acceptable at the time of the incident. Furthermore, when there's more than one acceptable choice, the expert witness must repeatedly emphasize that more than one approach could have been selected and still be appropriate.

On occasion, a nurse may testify as an expert about a physician's care, when the physician performs an act that's also a nursing function, such as drawing blood or inserting a nasogastric tube.

Case study

In *Prairie v. University of Chicago Hospitals* (1998), an Illinois appellate court held that expert testimony wasn't needed to establish that a nurse acted negligently. A patient underwent

---

Courtroom controversy: Nurses as expert witnesses (continued)

a laminectomy; 2 days later a nurse forced the patient out of bed in spite of complaints of severe pain. The patient sued. The trial court ruled in favor of the nurse because of the plaintiff's failure to present expert testimony on the standard of care. However, the appellate court overturned the ruling. It said the fact existed that the nurse had acted negligently and that it was unnecessary for expert testimony to establish the standard because the propriety of the nurse's conduct could be evaluated by the jury on the basis of common knowledge.

---

declined the request because "the patient was a no-code." The patient went into cardiac arrest about 15 feet from his original room and was pronounced dead by the attending physician.

In the subsequent malpractice court case, the court allowed punitive damages because the nurses' action was an extreme deviation from standards of care.

BURDEN OF PROOF

The plaintiff in a medical malpractice lawsuit has to meet a burden of proof in order to collect damages. This means that he must not only prove the four above-mentioned elements exist but also that they meet an evidentiary standard called the *preponderance of the evidence*. The preponderance of the evidence standard (the least stringent of the evidentiary standards) requires that the fact finder — the judge or jury — believe that the evidence presented to prove each of the four elements is more than 50% likely to be true. If the fact finder believes that the plaintiff's attorney has proved the four required elements to be true by a preponderance of the evidence, then the fact finder should rule in favor of the plaintiff.

Another evidentiary standard that's used in civil litigation is clear and *convincing evidence,* which requires that there be substantial proof that the evidence presented is true. In states that require this level of evidence, a plaintiff's attorney would have to convince the fact finder that there's about a 75% chance that the evidence is true for each required element for him to prevail at trial. A third standard of evidence, beyond a *reasonable doubt,* is used in criminal cases and requires the fact finder to believe that each element of the prosecution's case has a 90% or greater chance of being true.

In a malpractice case, the only time that the plaintiff doesn't have the burden of proof is when evidence important to the plaintiff's case has been destroyed (or *spoliated*). For example, if a malpractice case involved issues related to the appropriate management of a patient in labor, and it was shown that the fetal monitor strips taken during labor were missing from the medical record, this would be considered a spoliation of evidence; the burden of proof would then shift from the plaintiff to the defendant. Although this doesn't happen often, it's just another reason why you should try to carefully preserve the medical record.

Proximate causation

In *Moore v. Willis-Knighton Medical Center* (1998), a patient was discharged to her home after hip replacement surgery. She was ordered to use a walker after discharge and to have an elevated toilet seat installed in her home. Part of the discharge planning included teaching the patient how to use a walker.

About 70 days after her discharge, the patient fell off the elevated toilet seat and reinjured her hip. She sued the health care facility for failure to provide adequate discharge planning instructions for using an elevated toilet seat with a walker, under the theory of proximate causation. The court found on behalf of the nurses. It's conclusion? The longer a patient has been living independently, with limitations but without problems, the more she's responsible for her own safety.

Whether the court would have made the same conclusion if the patient had fallen within the first few days after discharge is uncertain.

MALPRACTICE DEFENSES

Over the years, the law has developed special doctrines, or theories, to apply to cases involving subordinate-superior relationships. These doctrines may be used in a nurse's defense during a lawsuit. Exactly how much protection they offer, however, depends on the circumstances of the case and the development of the law in the nurse's state or province.

Respondeat superior

One of the most important malpractice defenses is the doctrine of *respondeat superior* (Latin for "let the master answer"), also called *the theory of vicarious liability*. This doctrine holds that when an employee is found negligent, the employer must accept responsibility if the employee was acting within the scope of his employment. The doctrine applies to all occupations, not just health care—a utility company, for instance, is liable for injuries that result if one of its on-duty truck drivers negligently hits a pedestrian.

To the extent that a nurse is working as the hospital's functionary, she can claim some protection under this theory. This doctrine is attractive to plaintiffs as well as employees because hospitals usually have much more money available to pay claims than nurses do (a reality facetiously known as the "deep pocket" doctrine).

Consider, for example, *Nelson v. Trinity Medical Center* (1988). A nurse delayed placing a woman who was in labor on a continuous fetal heart rate monitor, despite standing orders to do so. The child was born severely brain damaged, a condition that might have been prevented if the monitor had been operating to alert the physician to the need for a cesarean delivery. It was the hospital, not the nurse, who was found liable for the actions of its employee. (The physician settled out of court before the trial.) The parents were awarded $5.5 million.

In another case, *Crowe v. Provost* (1963), a mother returned with her child to her pediatrician's office one afternoon after having been there earlier that morning. She said her child was convulsing. The physician was at lunch, so the office nurse briefly examined the child. The nurse then called the physician, told him that she didn't feel the child's condition had changed since he had examined her, and advised that he need not rush back. After the nurse left the office, the child vomited violently, stopped breathing, and died before the receptionist could contact the physician.

The mother filed negligence charges against the nurse. At the trial, the court found the nurse's negligence was indeed the proximate cause of the child's death. However, the physician was also liable, according to the doctrine of *respondeat superior,* because the nurse was working as his employee.

Borrowed servant

A concept closely related to *respondeat superior* is the borrowed-servant or captain-of-the-ship doctrine. It's still applied in malpractice lawsuits, but not as often as it was in the past. The borrowed-servant doctrine might apply when you, as a hospital employee, commit a negligent act while under the direction or control of someone other than your supervisor such as a physician in the operating room. Because the physician is an independent contractor and you're responsible to him during surgery, you're considered his borrowed servant at the time. If you're sued for malpractice, his liability is vicarious, meaning that even though the physician didn't direct you negligently, he's responsible because he was in control.

Many states have moved away from strict application of the borrowed-servant theory. One reason for this shift is that operating room procedures are becoming so complex that they're beyond the direct control of any one person, thus making it too difficult for courts to determine responsibility under the borrowed-servant doctrine.

Res ipsa loquitur

In some cases, injured parties who aren't fully able to meet the element of causation may still be successful in a subsequent lawsuit. *Res ipsa loquitur,*

literally "the thing speaks for itself," is a rule of evidence that's applied when patients are injured in such a way that they can't show how the injury occurred or who was responsible for the injury. Malpractice may be inferred from the fact that the injury occurred. The principle underlying this doctrine is that the injury wouldn't have occurred in the absence of malpractice. The importance of applying the doctrine lies in the fact that expert witnesses aren't needed to assist the jury in understanding the facts of the case. Essentially, the rule of *res ipsa loquitur* allows a plaintiff to prove negligence with circumstantial evidence, when the defendant has the primary, and sometimes the only, knowledge of what happened to cause the plaintiff's injury.

Res ipsa loquitur derives from a 19th-century English case, *Byrne v. Boadle* (1863). In this case, the injured person had been struck by a flour barrel that fell from a second-floor window of a warehouse, but the plaintiff wasn't able to show which warehouse employee had been negligent in allowing the barrel to fall. The court applied the concept of *res ipsa loquitur* to the warehouse owners, who were found liable in the absence of proof that the employees weren't responsible for the plaintiff's injury.

Application of *res ipsa loquitur*

In most medical malpractice cases, the plaintiff has the responsibility for proving every element of his case against the defendant; until he does, the court presumes that the defendant has met the applicable standard of care. However, when a court applies the *res ipsa loquitur* rule, the burden of proof shifts from the plaintiff to the defendant. The defendant must prove that the injury was caused by something other than his negligence.

The case that set the precedent for this doctrine, *Ybarra v. Spangard* (1944), concerned a patient who suffered a permanent loss of neuromuscular control in his right shoulder and arm after an appendectomy. At trial, the patient's attorney was able to show that this wasn't the type of injury that normally occurs during an appendectomy but was unable to show how the injury occurred or who was responsible for it. The court in that case established three criteria that must be shown for *res ipsa loquitur* to apply:

◆ The injury must be the kind that ordinarily doesn't occur in the absence of some type of negligence.

◆ The injury must be caused by an action within the exclusive control of the defendant.

◆ The injury must not be the result of any voluntary action or contribution on the part of the plaintiff.

Usually, *res ipsa loquitur* is applied in lawsuits where the patient was unconscious and had no means of asserting any level of control in the situation such as a case involving an anesthetized surgical patient. Examples of court cases where *re ipsa loquitur* was successfully applied include those in which a foreign object was left in a surgical patient, infection was caused by unsterile instruments, surgical burns occurred, or a surgical operation was performed on the wrong part of a patient's body.

A recent case allowing for the application of *res ipsa loquitur* was *Babits v. Vassar Brothers Hospital* (2001). In that case, a patient awoke from surgery with third-degree burns on the back of her thighs. Although it wasn't clear how the burns got there, an expert witness gave two different hypothetical explanations. The court, acknowledging that the expert witness' theories were speculative, ruled that such an injury wouldn't have happened in the absence of negligence and applied the doctrine of *res ipsa loquitur.*

For and against *res ipsa loquitur*

Not all states that allow *res ipsa loquitur* apply this doctrine in the same manner. Some states limit its application, especially in cases where more detail is needed to assure the jury's understanding of the issues of the case, such as in instances of secondary infection. Other states have totally rejected the doctrine on the premise that negligence and malpractice must be proven, not presumed. *Garcia v. Bronx Lebanon Hospital* (2001) illustrates this point. In that case, a patient awoke in the emergency department (ED) with bruises over his entire body. He testified that he had been drinking, went to the ED because of chest pain, sat down to rest, and woke to find bruises over his body. The hospital security guards testified that the patient had come in highly intoxicated, picked up and swung a chair, and had to be physically restrained for the safety of staff and patients. The court refused to apply the doctrine of *res ipsa loquitur,* stating that the patient's injuries, in and of themselves, didn't prove that the hospital was negligent and that it would have to be shown that the security guards had used excessive force when the patient was restrained.

Canadian application

Canadian courts have allowed for the application of the *res ipsa loquitur* doctrine, though its application varies from province to province. Recent court cases indicate that although the doctrine is still in use, *res ipsa loquitur* may be less favored in the future (*Farrell v. Snell,* 1990; *McInnes,* 1998). The courts seem to want to ensure that the

Challenging a malpractice suit

If your attorney can establish one of the following malpractice defenses, the court will either dismiss the allegations or reduce the damages for which you're liable.

Defense	Rationale
False allegations	Does the plaintiff have legally sufficient proof that your actions caused his injuries? If he doesn't, the court may rule that the allegations against you are false and dismiss the case.
Contributory negligence	Did the plaintiff, through carelessness, contribute to his injury? If he did, some states permit the court to charge the plaintiff with failing to meet the standards of a reasonably prudent patient. Such a ruling may prevent the plaintiff from recovering damages. Many states permit the court to apportion liability, which prevents the plaintiff from recovering some, but not all, of the damages he claims.
Comparative negligence	Does the patient share a percentage of the blame for his injuries? If so, damages may be proportionately reduced.
Assumption of risk	Did the plaintiff understand the risk involved in the treatment, procedure, or action that allegedly caused his injury? Did he give proper informed consent and so voluntarily expose himself to that risk? If so, the court may rule that the plaintiff assumed some of the risk by knowingly disregarding the danger, thus relieving you of some or all of the liability, depending on your state's laws.

rule doesn't place too heavy a burden on the defendant.

Other malpractice defenses

Nurses and other health care providers aren't the only people who may have accountability for injuries that befall patients. Various circumstances may help to mitigate a health care providers' negligence and malpractice liability. (See *Challenging a malpractice suit*.) The three most commonly known mitigating defenses are contributory negligence, comparative negligence, and assumption of risk.

Contributory negligence and comparative negligence are essentially variations of the same concept. Both hold injured parties responsible for their own actions in creating or augmenting an injury. Examples of how patients contribute to injuries include failure to take prescribed medications, failure to keep follow-up appointments with health care providers, and giving misinformation to health care providers.

Contributory negligence, which is the older of the two doctrines, states that a patient who had any part in the adverse consequences of his medical or nursing care is barred from receiving compensation. Today, more states follow the comparative negligence concept, which reduces monetary awards by the percentage of harm that the injured party caused. For example, in a case in which $750,000 is the total monetary award and the patient's actions account for 20% of the harm, the final settlement to the patient would be $600,000. Some states disallow compensation for the injured party if he's found more than 50% accountable for the ultimate injury.

The third defense is assumption of risk, which states that patients are partially responsible for consequences if they understood the risks involved at the time they proceeded with the action. Many medical therapies, surgical interventions, and drug protocols have risks involved, and patients are made aware of these risks during the informed consent process. The doctrine of assumption of risk assists in allocating liability if untoward outcomes result.

Defending yourself in a lawsuit

Imagine you're at the nurses' station, catching up on paperwork, when a stranger approaches and asks for you. He thrusts some legal papers into your hands and starts to walk away. Baffled, you ask, "What's this all about?" He replies, "You've just been sued."

As you look over the papers, you recognize the name of a former patient listed as the plaintiff, and you see your name listed as the defendant. You learn that you've been accused of "errors and omissions." A nagging worry for most nurses has just become reality: You've been sued for nursing malpractice.

When and how should you respond? Your surest bet is to act immediately. Failing to respond to the complaint could result in a default judgment against you. However, how you respond depends on whether or not

you have professional liability insurance. (See *Responding to a malpractice summons.*)

NOTIFYING APPROPRIATE PERSONNEL

If you're covered by your employer's insurance, immediately contact your legal services administrators at work. They'll tell you how to proceed.

If you have your own professional liability insurance, consult your policy and read the section that tells you what to do when you're sued. Every policy describes whom you should notify and how much time you have to do it. Immediately telephone this representative, and tell him you've been sued. Document the time, his name, and his instructions. Then hand-deliver the lawsuit papers to him, if possible, and get a signed, dated receipt. Alternatively, send lawsuit papers by certified mail, return receipt requested, so you're assured of a signed receipt.

If you don't contact the appropriate representative within the specified time, the insurance company may refuse to cover you. To protect yourself, act quickly, document your actions, and get a receipt.

In addition, contact the National Nurses Claims Data Bank established by the American Nurses Association. Provide a full report of the incident in question, including the date, time, and persons involved. This contact will give you access to national data that may support your case, and your data will, in turn, help other nurses who are involved in lawsuits. Your name and address will be kept confidential.

Insurance company considerations

When you notify your insurance company that you've been sued, it will first consider whether it must cover you at

Responding to a malpractice summons

If you receive a summons notifying you that you're being sued, your immediate response can significantly affect the suit's outcome.

If you're contacted by the plaintiff, family members or friends of the plaintiff, or his attorney, don't speak to them. They should speak only through your attorney. If you're insured, you should politely insist to the insurer that your claim be handled by an attentive, experienced claims adjuster (the insurance company representative who investigates your claim and makes estimates for settlement) and a qualified attorney.

Be prepared to maintain your separate file on the case. Ask for copies of all relevant documents and reports from the claims adjuster, your attorney, and reports your attorney gets from the patient's attorney. Check the status of your case regularly with your attorney.

Selecting a defense attorney
One of your first concerns will be finding a qualified attorney to represent you.

If the patient names your hospital in the lawsuit, the hospital's insurance company may supply an attorney to defend you as the hospital's employee. If the hospital's attorney is representing the hospital's interest in the lawsuit, you should have a separate attorney to represent your interest. If you're sued alone, your insurance carrier may appoint a defense attorney to represent you. If you're uninsured, you'll have to find an attorney on your own.

If the dollar amount for which you're being sued exceeds your insurance coverage, consider hiring a private lawyer. This attorney will work exclusively for you. He'll notify your primary defense attorney and your insurer that, should the judgment exceed your coverage, the carrier may be held liable.

Shopping around
When seeking a qualified attorney, consider:
◆ consulting with your hospital's legal services department
◆ consulting with your state nurses' association or other appropriate professional organization
◆ asking friends or relatives with legal experience whose judgments you can trust
◆ calling your local bar association.

When you meet with a prospective attorney, ask him about his experience with malpractice cases. If he has little experience or if too many of his cases were decided for the plaintiff, you have the right to ask your insurance carrier for another attorney.

Working with your attorney
Establishing a good working relationship with your attorney is crucial. It's your job to educate the attorney about the medical information he needs to defend you. Be prepared to spend many hours reviewing charts, licensing requirements, hospital policies and procedures, journals, and texts as well as your professional qualifications and the details of the case. Here are some pointers:
◆ Provide your attorney and claims adjuster with all the information you can about the case, including anything relevant you remember that may not appear in the record.
◆ Supply your attorney with the nursing practice standards for your specialty.
◆ Discuss with your attorney how you feel about settling out of court.
◆ Develop a list of experts qualified to testify on the standards of care in your specialty, and present it to your attorney. Avoid recommending friends, because the jury may believe them to be less objective.
◆ Review all available records, including those obtained by your attorney that are normally inaccessible to you such as the records of the patient's private physician.

all. The insurer does this by checking for policy violations you may have committed. For example, your insurance company will check whether you gave late notice of the lawsuit, gave false information on your insurance application, or failed to pay a premium on time. If the company is sure you've committed such a violation, it will use this violation as a policy defense, and it can simply refuse to cover you. If the company thinks you've committed such a violation but isn't sure it has evidence to support a policy defense, it will probably send you a letter by certified mail informing you that the company may not have to defend you, but that it will do so while reserving the right to deny coverage later, withdraw from the case, or take other actions. Meanwhile, the company will seek a declaration of its rights from the court. If the court decides the company doesn't have to defend you, the company will withdraw from the case.

Usually, however, an insurance company takes this action only after careful consideration because denying coverage may provide you with grounds for suing the company. If you receive such a letter, find your own attorney to defend you in the lawsuit and to advise you in your dealings with the insurance company. If your case against the insurance company is sound, he may suggest that you sue the insurer.

If your insurance company doesn't assert a policy defense, your company representative will select and retain an attorney or a law firm specializing in medical malpractice cases as your attorney of record in the lawsuit. When so designated, this attorney is legally bound to do all that's necessary to defend you.

Your employer will almost certainly be named as a codefendant in the lawsuit. Even if that isn't the case, notify your employer that you're being sued. Your insurance company may try to involve your employer as a defendant.

FINDING AN ATTORNEY

If you don't have insurance — either your own or your employer's — you'll have to find your own attorney. Don't even consider defending yourself. You need an attorney who's experienced in medical malpractice because the case will be complex and experienced attorneys will be the opposition.

Make appointments with a few attorneys who seem qualified to defend you. In most cases, you won't be charged for this initial consultation. When you meet with each one, ask how long he thinks the lawsuit will take and how much money he'll charge. Also, try to get a feel for the attorney's understanding of the issues in your case. Then choose one as your attorney of record. Do this as soon as possible.

PREPARING YOUR DEFENSE

Your attorney will file the appropriate legal documents in response to the papers you were served. He'll ask you for help in preparing your defense. He should give you a chance to present your position in detail. Remember that all discussions between you and your attorney are *privileged communication,* meaning that your attorney can't disclose this information without your permission. Your attorney will also obtain complete copies of the pertinent medical records and other documents he or you feel are important in your defense.

Interrogatories, depositions, and examinations

Your attorney will use discovery tools to uncover every pertinent detail about the case against you. *Discovery tools* are legal procedures for obtaining information and may include:

◆ *interrogatories* — questions written to the other party that require answers under oath

◆ *depositions* — oral cross-examination of the other party under oath, either taken before a court reporter or recorded on videotape.

◆ *defense medical examination* — a medical examination of the injured party by a physician selected by your attorney or insurance company.

The plaintiff-patient's attorney will also use discovery tools, so you may have to answer interrogatories and appear for a deposition as well. Your attorney will carefully prepare you for these procedures.

Neither the interrogatories nor the deposition should be taken lightly. Don't speculate when answering a question. Work closely with your attorney in preparing your written answers to the interrogatories, and never submit interrogatories or other documents directly to the plaintiff's attorney; your attorney must review everything and submit the final copies to the opposing counsel.

That doesn't mean, however, that you must say or do anything your attorney asks. If you feel he's asking you to do or say things that aren't in your best interest, tell him so. You have the right to change attorneys at any time. If you believe an attorney selected by your insurance company is more interested in protecting the company than in protecting you, discuss the problem with a company representative. Then, if you still feel that he isn't properly defending you, hire your own attorney.

You may have grounds for subsequently suing the insurance company and the company-appointed attorney.

PREPARING FOR COURT

Plan on spending a considerable amount of time preparing your case before you appear in the courtroom. Make sure you dress nicely and present yourself professionally. This time can be stressful, and you need to be prepared.

Don't talk about the case

Don't try to placate the person suing you by calling him and discussing the case. Every word you say to him can be used against you in court. In fact, before the trial, don't discuss the lawsuit with anyone except your attorney. That will help prevent information leaks that could compromise your case. To protect your professional reputation, don't even mention to your colleagues that you've been sued.

Study copies of the medical records

Your attorney will ask you to study relevant medical records as soon as possible. Examine the complete medical chart, including nurses' notes, laboratory reports, and physicians' orders. If you must, on a separate sheet of paper, make appropriate notes on key entries or omissions about the records, but don't make any changes on the records. Such an action will undermine your credibility and hurt your case. Remember that you aren't the only person with a copy of these records. Also remember that once the plaintiff acquires your notes they may be used as evidence against you. Only your attorney's notes are safe from discovery.

Settling out of court

Only a small number of malpractice suits that are filed actually go to court; of those that do go to court, even fewer end with a final judgment. The rest are settled out of court.

Making a compromise

Settling your case out of court isn't an admission of wrongdoing. The law regards settlement as a compromise between two parties to end a lawsuit and to avoid further expense. You may choose to pay a settlement rather than incur the possibly greater expense, financial and emotional, of defending yourself at trial.

Determining your settlement rights

If you're covered by professional liability insurance, the terms of your policy will determine whether you and your attorney or the insurance company can control the settlement. Most policies don't permit the nurse to settle a case without the consent of the insurance company. In fact, many policies, especially those provided by employers, permit the insurance company to settle without the consent of the nurse involved.

Review your policy to determine your settlement rights. If the policy isn't clear on this point, call the insurance company representative and ask for clarification.

Evaluating a possible settlement

Offer your attorney and your insurance company's representative all the information you can about the case so they can evaluate not only your liabilities but also a possible settlement with the plaintiff.

Create your own legal file

Ask your attorney to send you copies of all documents and correspondence pertaining to the case. Try to maintain a file that's as complete as your attorney's. Also, make sure you understand all the items in your file. If you receive a document you don't understand, ask your attorney to explain it. Maintaining such a file should keep you current on the status of your case and prevent unpleasant surprises in court.

Take steps to protect your property

Many states have homestead laws that protect a substantial part of the equity in your house, as well as other property, from any judgment against you. Ask your attorney about the law in your state or province. If you don't have malpractice or professional liability insurance or if damages awarded to the plaintiff exceed your insurance coverage, you'll probably want to mount as aggressive a defense as possible.

NAVIGATING PRETRIAL EVENTS

While your attorney prepares your defense, he'll also explore the desirability of reaching an out-of-court settlement. If he decides an out-of-court settlement is in your best interest, he'll try to achieve it before your trial date. (See *Settling out of court.*)

If your case goes to trial, your attorney will participate in selecting the jury. During this process, attorneys for both sides will question prospective jurors, and your attorney will ask your opinion on their suitability. Either attorney may reject a small number of prospective jurors without reason (a peremptory challenge). Either attorney may reject an unlimited number of jurors for specific reasons. For example, an attorney may reject someone who knows the plaintiff or someone who has a personal interest in the lawsuit (*challenge for cause*).

To help prepare you to testify, your attorney will ask you to review the complete medical record, your interrogatory answers, and your deposition. You should also review the entire legal file you've been keeping, to make sure you understand all aspects of the case.

Deposition

Before the trial, you'll probably be called to testify at a deposition. (If you're called to testify as an expert witness at another defendant's trial, you should be aware that some states don't permit expert witnesses to give pretrial depositions.) The deposition can take place in an attorney's office or in a special room in the courthouse set aside for that purpose. Although the deposition takes place in a less formal atmosphere than a courtroom, don't forget that every word you and the attorneys say will be recorded. In a way, it's a rehearsal for the actual trial. At the trial, the plaintiff's and the defendant's attorneys have the right to use your pretrial testimony to bolster their respective cases, which is why you should work with your attorney to thoroughly prepare for your deposition.

PARTICIPATING IN THE TRIAL

Keep in mind that your trial may last several days or even weeks. After all witnesses have given their testimony, the jury, not the judge, will decide if you're liable unless both sides agree not to have a jury trial. If the jury finds you liable, it will also assess damages against you. (See *The trial process: Step-by-step*, page 168.) In some instances, an arbitration proceeding is used instead of a jury trial, but that's the exception and not the rule.

Testifying in court

When you're called to testify in a malpractice lawsuit, as a defendant or as an expert witness in another defendant's trial, you may be expected to respond quickly to a confusing presentation of claims, counterclaims, allegations, and contradictory evidence. You can use various techniques to help reduce stress and enhance the value of your testimony.

Maintaining proper courtroom demeanor

How you present yourself from the witness stand is very important. The jury may form its first, and sometimes lasting, impression of your credibility while you're testifying.

Your attorney will help prepare you to testify at the trial. He'll tell you how to dress—conservatively, as if you were going to an important job interview—and how to act. Your attorney may recommend, for example, that you sit with both feet on the floor with your hands folded in front of you and pay polite attention to other speakers. He'll also tell you to look at the jurors while you testify to help you appear more credible to them. Keep in mind that the purpose of these instructions is to help you win the case. Remember also that if you fail to cooperate with an attorney provided by an insurance company, the insurance company can use that information to deny coverage.

Malpractice lawsuits are notoriously slow moving. Interruptions occur in the form of recesses, attorneys' lengthy arguments in the judge's chambers, and the calling of witnesses out of turn. Be patient regardless of what happens. When you're asked to appear,

The trial process: Step-by-step

This list summarizes the basic trial process from complaint to execution of judgment. If you're ever involved in a lawsuit, your attorney will explain the specific procedures that your case requires.

Pretrial preparation

1. Complaint
Plaintiff files a complaint stating his charges against the named defendants, injuries sustained, and demand for award.

2. Service
Court issues defendant a service of the complaint stating plaintiff's charges.

3. Answer or counterclaim
Defendant files an answer and may add a counterclaim to plaintiff's allegations or those of other defendants. A motion for judgment may also be filed.

4. Discovery
Plaintiff's and defendant's attorneys develop their cases by gathering information by means of depositions and interrogatories and by reviewing documents and other evidence.

5. Pretrial hearing
Court hears statements from both parties and tries to narrow the issues.

6. Negotiation by settlement
Both parties meet to try to resolve the case outside the court and try to reach settlement.

7. Jury selection
Attorneys from both sides question prospective jurors and select a final panel of jurors.

8. Opening statements
Plaintiff's and defendant's attorneys outline for the jury what they intend to show during the trial.

9. Plaintiff presents case
Plaintiff's witnesses testify, explaining what they saw, heard, and know. Expert witnesses review any documentation and give their opinions about specific aspects of the case.

10. Cross-examination
Defendant's attorney questions plaintiff's witnesses.

11. Plaintiff closes case
Defendant's attorney may make a motion to dismiss the case, claiming plaintiff's evidence is insufficient.

12. Defendant presents case
Defendant's witnesses testify, explaining what they saw, heard, and know. Expert witnesses review any documentation and give their opinions about specific aspects of the case.

13. Cross-examination
Plaintiff's attorney questions defendant's witnesses.

14. Defendant closes case
Defendant's attorney may claim the plaintiff hasn't presented an issue for the jury to decide. Either side may move for a direct verdict.

15. Closing statements
Each attorney summarizes his case for the jury, making a final argument for the jury to consider.

16. Jury instruction
Judge instructs the jury in points of law that apply in this particular case and the specific charges.

17. Jury deliberation and verdict
Jury reviews facts and votes on verdict. Jury announces verdict before the judge and both parties. After the verdict is known, the losing side may request a new trial.

18. Appeal (optional)
Attorneys review transcripts. The party against whom the court ruled may appeal if he feels the judge didn't interpret the law properly, instruct the jury properly, or conduct the trial properly.

19. Execution of judgment
Appeals process is completed, and the case is settled.

be prompt. You may not score points with your punctuality, but you'll definitely lose a few if you aren't in court when you're called to testify.

When you testify, the jury doesn't expect you to be letter-perfect or to have instant or total recall. If you don't know the answer, say so. You may also refer to your prior deposition for answers that are specific, such as what was the patient's blood pressure at the time of the incident or how many milliliters of a drug you administered to the patient. Listen closely to questions, and answer only what the questioner has asked. Always answer the questions simply and in lay terms, and never elaborate or volunteer information. If you're going to be describing a piece of equipment that's unfamiliar to a lay audience, get your attorney's approval to bring it to the courtroom and show it to the jury.

Above all, be honest. When your testimony must be critical of a colleague or of your hospital's policies, you may be tempted to bend the truth a little — but don't.

During the trial, your professional reputation will be at stake. Project a positive attitude at all times, suggesting that you feel confident about the trial's outcome. Never disparage the plaintiff inside or outside the courtroom. Characterizing him as a gold digger, for example, can only generate bad feelings that may interfere with a possible settlement. If you happen to speak to him during the trial, make sure you are polite and dignified.

Undergoing cross-examination
During cross-examination, the opposing attorney will try to discredit your testimony. This may take the form of an attack on your credentials, experience, or education — especially if you're testifying as an expert witness.

Don't take the attacks personally or allow them to fluster you.

Another way of discrediting expert testimony is the "hired gun" insinuation. The cross-examining attorney may imply that because you accept payment for your testimony, you're being unethical and biased. Remember that as an expert witness you have the right to expect compensation for the time you spend on behalf of the case in and out of the courtroom, just as the attorney does. Say so if necessary.

Another ploy the opposing attorney can use to discredit your testimony is the "hedge." He may try to get you to change or qualify an answer you gave previously on direct examination or at the deposition. He may also try to confuse the issue by asking you a similar, but hypothetical, question with a slightly different — but significant — slant. Just remember that a simple but sincere "I don't know" can reinforce a jury's belief in your honesty and competence. You may also state that you don't understand a question and ask the attorney to clarify it. Your best protection against cross-examination jitters is adequate preparation and honest answers.

Understanding the judgment
The final stage of a lawsuit is the execution of the judgment, which occurs after all appeals have been exhausted. Two conclusions are possible: Monetary damages are awarded to the injured party, or all causes of action are dismissed against the defendant-nurse. If the injured party has prevailed, the individual will request that the award of damages be executed. This request is necessary because it gives legal relief if a losing defendant chooses to ignore the court order. In certain states, such a request allows for the garnishing of wages or for property to be confiscated

and sold to pay the amount of the award. Because states vary greatly with regard to such measures, attorneys guide their clients at this stage of the trial process.

Res judicata

Nurses may wonder, because there are different courts in which a lawsuit may be filed, if an injured party may attempt to bring a second lawsuit based on the same facts as an unsuccessful lawsuit. The doctrine of *res judicata,* literally "a thing or matter settled by judgment," prevents the same parties in a lawsuit from retrying the same issues as were involved in the original lawsuit, thus preventing duplication of litigation and the possibility of contradicting decisions. However, a word of caution about this doctrine: It doesn't apply to appeals, to parties not named in the original lawsuit, or to issues that weren't part of the original lawsuit. Therefore, it's possible for a losing party to file a second lawsuit if the issues at hand weren't part of the original trial.

Selected references

Ashley, R.C. "The Anatomy of a Lawsuit: Part 1," *Critical Care Nurse* 22(4):68-69, August 2002.

Ashley, R.C. "The Anatomy of a Lawsuit: Part 2," *Critical Care Nurse* 22(5):82-83, October 2002.

Culley, C.A., Jr., and Spisak, L.J. "So You're Being Sued: Do's and Don'ts for the Defendant," *Cleveland Clinical Journal of Medicine* 69(10):752, 755-56, 759-60, October 2002.

McCarter, W.D., and Hayek, T.J. "Expert Medical Testimony is Generally Required to Prove Medical Negligence," *Missouri Medicine* 98(10):488-89, October 2001.

Ramos, F., Jr. "Reducing Malpractice Exposure," *Advance Nurse Practitioner* 11(2):20, February 2003.

Regan, J.J., and Regan, W.M. "Medical Malpractice and *Respondeat Superior,*" *Southern Medical Journal* 95(5):545-48, May 2002.

Tingle, J. "Clinical Negligence and the Need to Keep Professional Updated," *British Journal of Nursing* 11(20):1304-306, November 2002.

Tingle, J. "The Professional Standard of Care in Clinical Negligence," *British Journal of Nursing* 11(19):1267-269, October 2002.

Wood, C. "The Importance of Good Record-keeping for Nurses," *Nursing Times* 99(2): 26-27, January 2003.

Chapter 6

Legal risks on the job

Harried and tense, you're struggling through your shift in an intensive care unit (ICU). You're already caring for more patients than one nurse can possibly handle, when the emergency department (ED) calls and says two more patients will be arriving soon. You know there's no way you can provide safe care. Your supervisor turns down your pleas for additional staff. Your first impulse is to walk out. How can you remedy this situation?

You're caring for a patient with a criminal record and a reputation for narcotics dealing. You're nervous enough as it is, but the situation gets worse when a stranger stops you in the hallway, flashes a detective's badge, and asks for articles of the patient's clothing and a blood sample. He says you're legally obligated to turn over this evidence. Should you do what he tells you?

A prestigious civic leader who's a candidate for local political office recently has made several trips to the ED. She has brought her daughter, whom she calls "Miss Clumsy." The child has had multiple hematomas. You think it *might* be child abuse. Fearful of wrongfully damaging the woman's reputation, you hesitate to make a report. What should you do?

Your patient has told you repeatedly that he doesn't want any "heroic measures" taken or "means" used to preserve his life if there's no reasonable chance of recovery. However, one evening after the patient has experienced a massive stroke, five members of his family march into your office demanding that everything be done to preserve his life. Should you fight to have the patient's wishes respected?

The situations described above are examples of the complex legal dilemmas you may encounter in daily practice. As the nursing profession grows and you take on greater responsibilities, you'll inevitably face increased legal vulnerability. Hardly any aspect of nursing practice is untouched by legal risk. It's important that you know how to avoid possible litigious or legally damaging situations. (See *Taking steps to prevent lawsuits*, pages 172 and 173.)

Reading this chapter will enable you to identify the legal responsibilities and risks of your profession. You'll find information on the legal consequences of violating your health care facility's policies and suggestions to help you cope with understaffing. You'll read about your responsibilities for witnessing and signing documents, maintaining patient safety, administering drugs

Taking steps to prevent lawsuits

Anytime you provide care that falls short of current legal and nursing standards, you make yourself a target for a malpractice suit.

In most situations, you can prevent this from happening to you by following these guidelines in your daily practice.

Defend the patient

Your first duty is to protect your patient, not his physician. If your judgment says your patient's condition warrants a call to his physician, don't hesitate – in the middle of the day or in the middle of the night – to fully communicate your concerns to the physician. If your judgment says to question a physician's order because you can't read it, don't understand it, think it's incomplete, or think it may harm your patient, don't hesitate.

If your hospital doesn't already have a policy covering nurse-physician communications, ask for one and keep asking until you get one. Meanwhile, for your own protection, carefully record all contacts with physicians, including the date, time, and the substance of the communication.

Stay current

Here are some effective ways to stay up-to-date on nursing practices: read nursing journals, attend clinical programs, attend in-service programs, and seek advice from nurse specialists. If your hospital doesn't offer needed in-service programs, ask for them. Check the Internet for on-line continuing education courses.

Remember, ignorance of new techniques is no excuse for substandard care. If you're ever sued for malpractice, your patient care will be judged against current nursing standards, regardless of whether your employer has offered you the necessary training. This is especially true if you're certified in a specialty area.

Use the entire nursing process

Taking shortcuts increases risks to your patient's well-being and your own. If you're charged with malpractice, and the court finds that you took a dangerous patient-care shortcut, the court may hold you liable for causing harm to your patient.

Document thoroughly

Document every step of the nursing process for every patient. Chart your observations as soon as possible, while facts are fresh in your mind; express yourself clearly; and always write legibly. When using charting forms, make certain they're complete and have no omissions or blank spaces. If you're ever involved in a lawsuit, a complete patient care record could be your best defense.

Audit your nursing records

Audit your records consistently and comprehensively, using specific criteria to evaluate the effectiveness of patient care. Ask for a charting class – or start one yourself – to encourage staff nurses to chart patient care correctly, uniformly, and legibly. Use problem-oriented charting (to be sure you're documenting all parts of the nursing process) and flow sheets (to record large volumes of data). Encourage other nurses to use these documenting aids. If certain charting forms, such as admission or evaluation forms, need the counter-signature of a supervisor or physician, be sure to have the form signed.

Use what you know

Use your nursing knowledge to make nursing diagnoses and give clinical opinions. You have a legal duty to your patient not only to make a nursing diagnosis, but also to take appropriate action to meet his nursing needs. Doing so helps protect your patient from harm and you from malpractice charges.

Taking steps to prevent lawsuits *(continued)*

Delegate patient care wisely
Know the legal practice limits of the people you supervise, and caution them to act only within those limits. If your delegation of skilled tasks to an unskilled person harms a patient, you can be held liable for violating your nurse practice act.

Know your nursing department policy manual
Review the policies at least yearly. If you think policies need to be added, amended, or omitted, ask for them. If you're ever involved in a malpractice lawsuit, a well-prepared manual and your knowledge of nursing policies could be important in your defense.

Show kindness and respect
Treat your patient and his family with kindness and respect. When you help relatives cope with the stress of the patient's illness and teach them the basics of home care, they'll more likely remember you with a thank-you card than with a legal summons.

(one of the riskiest aspects of nursing practice), and upholding a patient's living will (advance directive). You'll also learn about your responsibility under the law when you encounter victims of child abuse, are forced to use restraints on a psychologically disturbed patient, or are asked by police to turn over a patient's belongings or fluid and tissue samples for evidence. This chapter also covers the special legal risks incurred when working in the ED, operating room, ICU, and other special care units.

Basic standards
Whether you're an advanced practice nurse (APN), registered nurse (RN), licensed practical nurse (LPN), or licensed vocational nurse (LVN), you're always legally accountable for your nursing actions. In any practice setting, your care must meet minimum legal standards. Your care also should:
◆ reflect the scope of your state's nurse practice act

◆ measure up to established practice standards
◆ consistently protect your patient.

Upholding these standards should provide a base for sound legal practice no matter where you practice nursing.

Hospital policies

Every hospital and health care facility has *policies*—a set of general guidelines and principles by which it manages its affairs. You're obligated to know these policies and to follow the established procedures that flow from them.

However, never do this blindly. As a nurse, you're also obligated to maintain your professional standards, and these standards may sometimes conflict with your employer's policies and procedures. At times, you may be forced to make decisions and take actions that risk violating those policies and procedures. You must do what's best for your patient. If it's unsafe to follow the policy, then don't. Document the reasons you didn't follow policy and inform your nurse-manager and the nursing supervisor of your actions.

At times such as these, you may need help balancing your duty to your patient with your responsibility to your employer. Your best help is a nursing department policy manual that states relevant, clear guidelines based on up-to-date standards of care that are generally accepted by the profession. A typical problem with policies is that they aren't practical, are too restrictive, or involve standards too difficult to meet. In addition, there may be so many policies that nurses aren't familiar with all of them.

A policy manual that states relevant, clear guidelines based on the most up-to-date standards of care is the mark of a successful nursing department — one whose first concern is delivering safe, high-quality patient care.

QUALITIES OF A GOOD NURSING DEPARTMENT MANUAL

Although nursing department manuals will differ, they should:
◆ show how general policies apply to the nursing department
◆ outline the nursing department's roles and responsibilities, internally and in relation to other departments
◆ identify the expected limits of nursing action and practice
◆ offer guidelines for handling emergency situations
◆ contain procedures that show compliance with state and federal laws such as patient antidumping laws
◆ give standing orders for nurses in special areas, such as ICU and coronary care unit (CCU)
◆ show the steps to be taken before — and after — arriving at nursing care decisions. These steps provide the basis for the facility's nursing care standards.

The manual itself will be used as evidence in malpractice cases.

However, policies are typically:
◆ too specific
◆ too restrictive
◆ too idealistic
◆ irrelevant
◆ so voluminous that nurses don't know them
◆ not reviewed or discussed in regular staff meetings
◆ not updated or reviewed on a regular basis
◆ not communicated to the staff when changes are made.

Today, hospitals are rapidly revising and expanding their basic policies and procedures. Any good nursing department manual should undergo regular revision. Some of these procedure and policy changes result from efforts to streamline and standardize patient care. Others result from efforts to comply with new state, jurisdictional, territorial, and federal regulations or to implement recommendations of the Joint Commission on Accreditation of Healthcare Organizations (JCAHO) or the Canadian Council on Health Services.

HOW HOSPITAL POLICIES AFFECT COURT DECISIONS

Policies aren't laws, but courts generally have ruled against nurses who violated their employers' policies. Courts have also held hospitals liable for poorly formulated — or poorly implemented — policies. As previously discussed in chapters 1 and 2, other sources that describe nurses' duties include:
◆ nurse practice acts
◆ licensing board regulations
◆ state and federal laws
◆ case law
◆ professional organization standards.

Legally, if you practice within the scope of your job description and are sued for malpractice, the hospital will have to assume secondary responsibility under the theory of *respondeat superior*. Whether or not you've acted properly is determined, in court, by the patient's condition on admission, the hospital's nursing service policy, and the standard of care reasonably expected in your community.

How policy is applied in court

In *Utter v. United Health Center* (1977), nurses failed to report a patient's deteriorating condition to the department chairman after the physicians they notified failed to act, causing a critical 24-hour delay in the patient's treatment. A provision in the hospital's nursing manual said that if ever a physician in charge—after being notified—did nothing about adverse changes in a patient's condition or acted ineffectively, the nurse was to "call this to the attention of the Department Chairman."

The judge told the jury that it could label the nurses' failure to follow this provision as the proximate cause of the patient's injury. Because they failed to follow hospital policy, the nurses shared blame for the physicians' inaction.

HOW LAWS AFFECT HOSPITAL POLICIES

Many hospital policies and procedures are mandated by state or jurisdictional licensing laws or by such federal regulations that are the conditions for participation in Medicare or Medicaid.

Many such mandatory requirements exist. In the United States, for instance, the Patient Self-Determination Act, 42 U.S.C. § 1395 cc(f), is a federal law that requires hospitals, nursing homes, home health care agencies, and health maintenance organizations (HMOs) that are Medicare providers to inform patients about their rights to execute living wills. The Freedom of Information Act requires hospitals to give consumers and patients access to certain data previously considered privileged. In addition, U.S. Department of Health and Human Services regulations require that hospitals observe strict guidelines when using patients in research studies.

Canadian law

In Canada, each jurisdiction has its own laws governing hospitals. Although health care is the responsibility of the jurisdictions, the federal government outlines requirements for receiving federal funding. Since passage of the Canada Health Act of 1984, health care facilities are considered public institutions in Canada.

The jurisdictional legislatures also pass laws governing hospitalization in psychiatric facilities. Matters of criminal law, however, are in the hands of the federal parliament, so hospital policy makers look there for guidance on such issues as opioids and abortions.

COMPARING U.S. AND CANADIAN POLICIES

Hospital policies in the United States and Canada are similar in many ways; however, the differences are sometimes important. Always check the laws that prevail in your region.

Under English common law, people usually aren't obligated to help each other—not even in emergencies. However, where hospitals are concerned, Canadian jurisdictional legislatures have departed from this tradition. For example, the Public Hospitals Act of Nova Scotia states that if a qualified medical practitioner makes application for a patient and the hospital has room, it must admit the patient, even if he can't pay for his care.

Antidumping laws

In 1986, the U.S. Congress amended the Social Security Act to prevent hospitals from turning away uninsured or financially strapped patients. Called *patient anti-dumping laws,* the amendments require that hospitals participating in Medicare provide screening and stabilizing treatment for anyone who has an emergency condition or is in labor. Furthermore, the Act gives guidelines and requires documentation for transfers or for hospital discharge.

Failure to comply can lead to fines, loss of Medicare provider status, or both. This legislation has expanded regularly since 1989 and currently is known as the Emergency Treatment and Active Labor Act, or EMTALA.

How HOSPITAL POLICIES AFFECT YOUR JOB

Hospital administrators write policies to guide workers in the hospital's daily operations. These policies stem from the hospital's philosophy and objectives and are part of the hospital's planning process, so they affect your job directly.

If you're considering employment at a hospital, you can ask to see its policies. Study its policies carefully; if they're well defined, they may give you an indication of how satisfied and secure you can expect to be in your job.

If you're working in a specialized nursing area, such as the ICU or CCU, give special attention to any policies that directly or indirectly apply to you. Make sure your specialty is clearly defined in keeping with your state or jurisdictional nurse practice act — and with the standards recommended by

accrediting agencies and professional medical and nursing associations.

Besides reading policies — the general principles by which a hospital is guided in its management — read the hospital's rules too. These describe the actions that employees should or shouldn't take in specific situations. "No smoking in the patient's room," for example, is a rule that should be enforced without exception.

If you feel reasonably comfortable with the hospital's philosophy, objectives, policies, rules, and quality of care, you'll probably feel comfortable on the job. However, if the hospital's policy calls for nursing procedures that conflict with your personal nursing standards or ethics, then you should consider looking elsewhere for employment.

WHEN HOSPITAL POLICY AND YOUR NURSE PRACTICE ACT CONFLICT

You must refuse to follow hospital policy when it conflicts with your nurse practice act. A willful violation of rulings passed by the board of nursing, even with your hospital's knowledge and encouragement, could result in suspension or revocation of your nursing license.

The case of *O'Neill v. Montefiore Hospital* (1960) illustrates the dilemma a nurse faces when she must choose between hospital policy and her professional standards. This case involved a nurse who, following hospital policy, refused to admit a patient because he belonged to an insurance plan her hospital didn't accept. The man returned home and died. Although the trial court ruled in favor of the nurse, the New York Supreme Court reversed the decision and ruled the hospital nurse negligent for refusing to admit the patient.

HOSPITAL POLICIES THAT APPLY TO LPNs AND LVNs

LPNs and LVNs shouldn't be coerced to exceed limits that the law places on their practice, although practice may extend beyond the nurse's academic training. State law and national health commissions have recognized the rights of LPNs and LVNs to perform in an expanded role — for example, to administer drugs and I.V. fluids — if the LPN or LVN is properly trained for the task and it's one that other LPNs and LVNs perform in the hospital.

Get it in writing

Be careful to protect yourself. Make sure that the conditions for your doing this work are included in your hospital's written policies and that the policies have been established by a committee representing the medical staff, the nursing department, and the administration. The written version should be available to all medical and nursing staff members. If, for example, the policy that allows LPNs and LVNs to administer I.V. drugs isn't stated in writing, you had better not administer I.V. drugs. If you're sued on this basis and can't back up your actions with written hospital policy or state regulation, you may be found liable.

CHANGING HOSPITAL POLICY

When seeking to bring nursing policy problems to your hospital administration's attention, you can involve your health-team colleagues by discussing policy problems at committee meetings, conferences, and interdepartmental meetings. Many health care facilities require policy implementation to follow the chain of command. Your charge nurse or manager should be able to give you direction on where to start on a particular issue. Alternatively, you can communicate directly with your hospital administration via the grievance procedure, counseling, attitude questionnaires, and formal and informal unit management committees.

Legal risks caused by understaffing

Understaffing occurs when the hospital administration fails to provide enough professionally trained personnel to meet the patient population's needs. If you're like most nurses, you're familiar with understaffing and the problems it can cause.

Plaintiffs' attorneys frequently argue that understaffing is widespread and that it results in substandard bedside care, increased mistakes and omissions, and hasty documentation — all of which increase nurses' (and their employers') liability. For example, if during hospitalization a patient is harmed and can demonstrate that the harm resulted from the hospital's failure to provide sufficient qualified personnel, the hospital may be held liable.

WHAT CONSTITUTES ADEQUATE STAFFING?

You won't find many legal guidelines to help you answer this question unless you work in a nursing home or skilled nursing facility. Determining whether your unit has too few nurses or too few specially trained nurses may be difficult. The few guidelines that do exist vary from state to state and are limited mainly to specialty care units (such as the ICU). Even JCAHO offers little help. Its staffing standard sets no specific nurse-patient ratios. It just states generally that "The organization provides an adequate number of staff whose qualifications are commensurate with defined job responsibilities and applicable licensure, law and regulation, and certification."

Lawmakers have taken note of this issue. In October 1999, California passed a bill that requires hospitals to meet minimum nurse-patient ratios in all units, mandates additional staffing based on patient acuity, and prohibits nurses from being assigned to areas for which they lack adequate orientation or clinical training. In September 2002, the California Department of Health Services also announced nurse-patient ratios.

The courts have had no reliable standard for ruling on cases of alleged understaffing. Each case has been decided on an individual basis.

Important court rulings

The decision in the landmark case *Darling v. Charleston Community Memorial Hospital* (1965) was based partly on the issue of understaffing. A young man broke his leg while playing football and was taken to Charleston's ED, where the on-call physician set and cast his leg. The patient began to complain of pain almost immediately. Later, his toes became swollen and dark, then cold and insensitive, and a stench pervaded his room. Nurses checked the leg only a few times per day, and they failed to report its worsening condition. When the cast was removed 3 days later, the necrotic condition of the leg was apparent. After making several surgical attempts to save the leg, the surgeon had to amputate below the knee.

After an out-of-court settlement with the physician who had applied the cast, the court found the hospital liable for failing to have enough specially trained nurses available at all times to recognize the patient's serious condition and to alert the medical staff.

Since the Darling case, several similar cases have been tried — for example, *Cline v. Lun* (1973), *Sanchez v. Bay General Hospital* (1981), and *Harrell v. Louis Smith Memorial Hospital* (1990). Almost every case involved a nurse who failed to continuously monitor her patient's condition — especially his vital signs — and to report significant changes to the attending physician. In each case, the courts have emphasized:
◆ the need for sufficient numbers of nurses to continuously monitor a patient's condition
◆ the need for nurses who are specially trained to recognize signs and symptoms that require a physician's immediate intervention.

HOSPITAL LIABILITY

Courts have held hospitals primarily liable in lawsuits in which nursing understaffing is the key issue. A hospital can be found liable for patient injuries if it accepts more patients than its facilities or nursing staff can accommodate. The hospital controls the purse strings and, in the courts' view, is the only party that can resolve the problem.

Defending understaffing

Hospitals accused of failing to maintain adequate nursing staffs have offered various defenses. Some have argued they acted reasonably because their nurse-patient ratio was comparable to other area hospitals. This argument fails if any applicable rules and regulations contradict it.

Other hospitals have defended understaffing by arguing that no extra nurses were available. The courts have hesitated to accept this defense, however, especially when hospitals have knowingly permitted an unsafe condition to continue for a long period. One possible future scenario — a hospital may be held liable for failing to use the nursing personnel available from temporary-nursing service agencies or nurses' registries.

Still other hospitals have excused understaffing by pleading lack of funds. The courts have repeatedly rejected this defense.

Emergency defense

Hospital liability for understaffing isn't automatic. If the hospital couldn't have provided adequate staff by any reasonable means — because, for example, a nurse suddenly called in sick and no substitute could be found quickly — the hospital may escape liability. This is known as the *sudden emergency exception* when used as a defense during a trial. The emergency couldn't have been anticipated — in contrast to chronic understaffing.

Except for the sudden emergency exception defense, a hospital has only two alternatives for avoiding liability for understaffing: either hire sufficient personnel to staff an area adequately or else close the area (or restrict the number of beds) until adequate staff can be found.

CHARGE NURSE'S LIABILITY

A nurse put in charge of a unit, even temporarily, may find herself personally liable in understaffing situations, including these examples:

◆ She knows understaffing exists but fails to notify the hospital administration about it.

◆ She fails to assign her staff properly and then also fails to supervise their actions continuously. (See *When coworkers put you at risk,* page 180.)

◆ She tries to perform a nursing task for which she lacks the necessary training and skills.

Court cases

In *Horton v. Niagara Falls Memorial Medical Center* (1976), the charge nurse, one LPN, and one nurses' aide were responsible for 19 patients on a unit. During their shift, one patient became delirious and tried to climb down from a balcony off his room. The attending physician, when notified, ordered that someone stay with the patient at all times to keep him from going out on the balcony again.

The charge nurse, instead of calling for additional help from within the hospital or notifying the administration, called the patient's wife and summoned her to the hospital. The wife agreed to send her mother but said it would take time before her mother could arrive. During the interim, the charge nurse provided no supervision of the patient, who went out on the balcony again, jumped, and sustained injuries. In the lawsuit that followed, the court held the charge nurse liable.

In *Norton v. Argonaut Insurance Co.* (1962), a temporary staff shortage led the assistant director of nurses to volunteer her nursing services on a pediatric floor. Because she had been an administrator for several years and was unfamiliar with pediatric care, she proceeded to give a neonate 3 ml of digoxin in injectable, rather than elixir, form. The infant died of cardiac arrest, and the court held the assistant director liable. (See *Floating: Understanding your legal responsibility,* page 181.)

When coworkers put you at risk

To help you avoid legal dangers when working with a health care team, here are some questions and answers to clarify legal responsibilities.

Can I be held liable for mistakes made by a student nurse under my supervision?
Yes, if you have primary responsibility for instructing the student and correcting her mistakes.

If a student performs tasks that only a licensed nurse should perform and does so with my knowledge but without my supervision, am I guilty of breach of duty?
Yes, because as a staff nurse, you should know that a student nurse can perform nursing tasks only under the direct supervision of a nurse licensed to perform those tasks.

What should I do if I see another health team member perform a clinical procedure incorrectly?
If the incorrect procedure can harm the patient, you have a legal duty to stop the procedure – tactfully, when possible – and immediately report your action to your nursing supervisor. If the incorrect procedure doesn't threaten to harm the patient, don't stop the procedure – but report your observation to your supervisor.

Can I face legal action if I ask a hospital volunteer to help me give patient care and she does something wrong?
Yes. Don't ask a volunteer to participate in a task she isn't trained and professionally qualified to perform.

iable defenses

charge nurse isn't automatically li-
 for mistakes made by a nurse on
staff. Most courts won't hold the

charge nurse liable unless she knew, or should have known, that the nurse who made the mistake:
◆ had previously made similar mistakes
◆ wasn't competent to perform the task
◆ had acted on the charge nurse's erroneous orders.

Remember, the plaintiff-patient has to prove two things: that the charge nurse failed to follow customary practices, thereby contributing to the mistake, and that the mistake actually caused the patient's injuries.

COPING WITH A SUDDEN OVERLOAD

Like other nurses, you're probably all too familiar with understaffing. You begin your shift and suddenly find yourself assigned more patients than you can reasonably care for. What can you do to protect yourself?

First, make every effort to protest the overload and get it reduced. Begin by asking your supervisor or director of nursing services to supply relief. If they can't or won't, notify the hospital administration. If no one there will help either, write a memorandum detailing exactly what you did and said and the answers you received. Don't walk off the job (you could be held liable for abandonment); instead, do the best you can. After your shift is over, prepare a written report of the facts and file it with the director of nursing.

Keep in mind that filing a written report isn't guaranteed to absolve you from liability if a patient is injured during your shift. You may still be found liable, especially if you could have foreseen and prevented the patient's injury; however, a written report will impress a jury as a sincere attempt to protect your patients. The report could also provide you with a defense

Floating: Understanding your legal responsibility

For many nurses, an order to float to an unfamiliar unit triggers worry and frustration. It may cause worry about using skills that have grown rusty since nursing school or frustration at being pulled away from familiar or enjoyable work.

Unavoidable

Unfortunately, floating is necessary. Hospitals must use it to help solve their understaffing problems. The courts sanction it as being in the public's best interest.

Exceptions

Legally, you can't refuse to float simply because you fear that the skills you need for the assignment have diminished or because you're concerned about legal risks in the assigned unit. You'll have to go along with an order to float unless:

◆ you have a union contract that guarantees you'll always work in your specialty
◆ you can prove you haven't been taught to do the assigned task.

Tell your supervisor if you haven't been taught a task she's assigned you. Usually, she'll accommodate you by changing your assignment. However, if she insists that you perform the task that you don't know how to do, refuse the assignment. If the hospital reprimands or fires you, you may be able to appeal the action taken against you in a court of law.

---

if the alleged malpractice involves something you should have done but didn't because of understaffing.

Refusing to work

If conditions become intolerable and you refuse to work, you may be suspended from duty without pay. Consider the Canadian case, *In re Mount Sinai Hospital and Ontario Nurses Association* (1978).

This case involved three nurses in the hospital's ICU. Because they were already caring for many critically ill patients, they refused to accept still another from the ED. The nurses argued that admitting the new patient would endanger the patients already under their care. The hospital disagreed and suspended them for three shifts without pay.

The case was settled in favor of the hospital, on the premise that a hospital is legally obligated to provide care for patients it admits and can insist that certain instructions be carried out. If the hospital had to defer to its employees' opinions, the decision stated, it would be placed in an intolerable legal position.

CHRONIC UNDERSTAFFING

Chronic understaffing, if it occurs on your unit, presents you with a dilemma. On the one hand, your conscience tells you to try your best to help every patient. On the other hand, you feel compelled to protect yourself from liability.

Collective action

The best protection, as you might expect, is prevention — action taken to remedy the understaffing situation. Try to work with your institution to develop creative, workable solutions. The law will protect you in several important ways as long as you and your colleagues act responsibly and collectively to try to bring about institutional change.

A case in point is *Misericordia Hospital Medical Center v. N.L.R.B.* (1980), which involved a charge nurse who was discharged from her job because her employer found her activities "disloyal."

She belonged to a group of hospital employees called the Ad Hoc Patient Care Committee. The committee was formed after the JCAHO, which intended to survey the hospital, had invited interested parties—including hospital staff—to submit at a public meeting information on whether accreditation standards were being met. One complaint lodged by the nurse and her committee was insufficient coverage on many shifts—a situation the hospital had failed to remedy.

Even though JCAHO examiners approved the hospital, the nurse was fired shortly afterward. When the National Labor Relations Board (NLRB) ordered the hospital to reinstate the nurse, the hospital appealed. The appeals court upheld the NLRB order, citing a U.S. Supreme Court ruling that employees don't lose protection "when they seek to improve terms and conditions of employment or otherwise improve their lot as employees through channels outside the immediate employee-employer relationship."

Though this decision offers nurses some protection in conflicts with employers, especially those in which working conditions directly affect the care given patients, persons involved in the hiring, firing, scheduling, disciplining, or evaluation of employees are considered management and may not be included in the collective bargaining unit if a nurses' union exists in the hospital. Therefore, a nurse may be covered, depending on the court's interpretation of whether she's management.

Make sure you follow the appropriate channels of communication. If you can't get help to remedy a dangerous understaffing situation, first go through all hospital channels. Simply report what the problem is, the number of hours you've been forced to work without relief, the number of consecutive days you've been forced to work, and any other relevant facts. Then if you still can't get help and if your complaint involves an alleged unfair labor practice, consider contacting the NLRB.

Legal risks in special care units

In special care units, such as the ED, operating room, postanesthesia care unit (PACU), ICU, and CCU, nurses regularly perform tasks that only physicians used to perform. Here, patient care offers exciting nursing challenges, increased nursing responsibilities—and extra risk of liability.

For example, if you're an ED nurse, you'll have to employ triage—classifying patients according to the seriousness of their medical problems. If you make a mistake and a patient's treatment is needlessly delayed, you may be liable.

If the PACU, ICU, or CCU is your assignment, you know you must watch your patients for signs and symptoms of adverse anesthetic effects, of postoperative cardiac and pulmonary complications, and of shock caused by hypoxia, hemorrhage, or infection. In these units, you may also have to administer sophisticated drugs or perform difficult procedures such as operating an intra-aortic balloon pump. In these special care units, the patient's survival may depend on your judgment.

WHERE YOU STAND LEGALLY

If you work in a special care unit, take your increased liability seriously. Remember, even though hospital policy requires that you perform certain tasks, or you perform them under a physician's orders as a physician's borrowed servant or ostensible agent, your individual liability continues. If a patient sues for malpractice, all the persons involved can be held separately and jointly liable. That suggests that you carefully evaluate the jobs you're asked to do. If a task is beyond your training and expertise, don't attempt it. Even if you can do it, make sure you're permitted to do it according to hospital policy and your state or jurisdictional nurse practice act. (See *Self-protection for nurses in special care units,* page 184.)

Role expansion and the law

In general, a nurse can't legally make a medical diagnosis or prescribe medical, therapeutic, or corrective measures, *except as authorized by the hospital and the state where she's working.* This means that if you intubate a patient with an endotracheal tube while working on a postoperative orthopedic floor, you may be liable for performing a medical function, especially if you could have called a physician. However, you probably wouldn't be liable if you had been trained in Advanced Cardiac Life Support and performed endotracheal intubation in the ED during a disaster.

In Canada, several jurisdictions, including Ontario and Quebec, have passed medical practice acts that permit the delegation of specific medical functions to nurses. Some jurisdictions require that a nurse obtain special training or certification to perform these functions. In the United States, however, current laws provide little guidance for nurses who regularly face situations such as these.

Suppose, for example, you're working in an ICU and so must usually act on standing orders and without a physician's supervision. How can you be sure when you perform quasi-medical functions, even with standing orders, that you aren't violating your nurse practice act?

You can't be sure, of course, because nurse practice acts don't provide specific guidelines. They were written in general terms, probably to give discretion to the practitioner. The hospital needs to write specific, practical policies that comply with the nurse practice act.

Treating patients based on standing orders is a matter of judgment. In such situations, be sure you're qualified to recognize the problem; then follow established medical protocol.

HOW NURSING STANDARDS APPLY

In general, a nurse working in a special care unit is subject to the same general rule of law as her staff nurse colleagues: she must meet the standard of care that a reasonably well-qualified and prudent nurse would meet in the same or similar circumstances.

However, in a malpractice lawsuit, when deciding whether a specialty nurse has acted reasonably, the court won't consider what the average LPN, LVN, RN, or APN would have done. Instead, the court will seek to determine the standard of care that an LPN, LVN, RN, or APN specifically trained to work in the special care unit would have met. Thus, the law imposes a

LEGAL TIP — Self-protection for nurses in special care units

If you're working in a special care unit of a hospital – the emergency department, intensive care unit, operating room, or postanesthesia care unit – your expanded responsibilities make you especially vulnerable to malpractice lawsuits. To protect yourself, follow these precautions.

Know your role
Request a clear, written definition of your role in the hospital. Your hospital should have an overall policy and an individual, written job description for you that specifies the limits of your nursing role. You'll be better protected if guidelines for advanced nursing competencies are formally established.

Document thoroughly
Document everything you do, so there's no question later about your actions. Your nurses' notes, of course, should reflect the nursing process: document your assessment of the patient, your care plan, your actual care, and your evaluation of the plan's effectiveness. Be sure to accurately document the date and time.

Maintain skills
Make sure of your own competence. If your role expands, your skills have to grow, too. If that requires advanced courses and supervised clinical experience, make sure you get both.

Insure yourself
Damages awarded to patients can be very high, and high legal fees may mean you can't afford even to defend yourself in a lawsuit. If you don't have your own professional liability insurance, and your hospital doesn't help defend you against a lawsuit, you could face a startling bill even after all claims against you are proved groundless and dropped. (You might never even get to court – but you could still find yourself with a large bill for legal consultation.)

---

higher standard of conduct on persons with superior knowledge, skill, or training.

Courts' view of standards
Hunt v. Palm Springs General Hospital (1977) illustrates how the courts evaluate the reasonable nurse standard in light of prevailing practices.

The patient, Mr. Hunt, was rushed to the ED with seizures. When he was examined, his physician concluded that Mr. Hunt, a known drug addict, was experiencing seizures because he had gone without drugs for several days. The physician advised the hospital administration that the patient's condition wasn't critical, but he nevertheless requested hospitalization.

The hospital refused to admit Mr. Hunt because of a history of unpaid bills. During the next 4 hours, Mr. Hunt waited in the ED while the physician tried to find hospitalization for him elsewhere in the city. Eventually, Mr. Hunt was admitted to a neighboring hospital. He lived for 26 hours before dying of brain damage caused by prolonged seizures.

During the lawsuit that followed, the court examined the practice of ED nurses elsewhere and found that the Palm Springs General Hospital nurses had acted unreasonably. Their duty was

to monitor Mr. Hunt's condition periodically while he awaited transfer to
another hospital. If this duty had been
carried out, the court concluded, the
nurses would have noted his elevated
temperature — a clear indication that
he needed immediate hospitalization.

Similarly, in *Cline v. Lund* (1973), the
patient, Ms. Cline, was sent to a coronary care stepdown unit when problems developed after she underwent a
hysterectomy on July 10. Except for
one bout with nausea, she appeared to
be making satisfactory progress. At
about 2:30 p.m. on July 11, a nurse
dangled Ms. Cline's legs from the side
of her bed. The nurse charted that the
patient tolerated the dangling well. By
3:30 p.m., Ms. Cline was unresponsive,
her blood pressure was rising, and she
was vomiting.

At 9 p.m., when Ms. Cline's blood
pressure reached 142/90 mm Hg, the
attending nurse notified her supervisor, who at 9:40 p.m. notified the attending physician. He came to the
hospital, examined the patient, and —
suspecting an internal hemorrhage —
ordered blood work and vital signs
taken every 30 minutes. At 11:45 p.m.,
the patient's blood pressure was
160/90 mm Hg. Her arms and legs
were stiff and her fists were clenched.
Instead of summoning the physician
again, the attending nurse notified her
supervisor. At 12:15 a.m.
on July 12, when Ms. Cline's blood
pressure had reached 230/130 mm Hg,
the physician was called. The patient
stopped breathing at 12:40 a.m., suffered a cardiac arrest at 12:45 a.m., and
died at 4:45 a.m.

In the ensuing lawsuit, the court
found the nurse liable, stating that her
care had fallen below that of a reasonably prudent nurse in the same or similar circumstances. "Nurses," the court
decision said, "should notify the physi-

cian of any significant change or unre-
sponsiveness."

Canadian nursing standards

A Canadian nurse's performance is also
measured against the appropriate standard of care. For example, in *Laidlaw v.
Lions Gate Hospital* (1969), the court
held that both the PACU nurse who
left for a coffee break and the supervisor who permitted her to leave should
have anticipated an influx of patients
from the operating room.

When the nurse left on her break,
only two patients and the nurse supervisor were in the PACU. In a short
time, however, three more patients arrived — including the plaintiff, Mrs.
Laidlaw. Because only one nurse was
on duty to care for five patients, Mrs.
Laidlaw didn't receive appropriate care
and suffered extensive, permanent
brain damage as a result of anesthesia-
related hypoxia.

When the resulting lawsuit came to
trial, another nursing supervisor testified that usually two nurses were present in the PACU and that nurses
weren't permitted to take breaks after
new patients arrived. Other testimony
revealed that PACU nurses should
know the operating room schedule
and so should anticipate when new
patients will arrive.

The court found the nurse who left
and her supervisor negligent in leaving
only one nurse on duty in the PACU.

STAYING WITHIN NURSING PRACTICE LIMITS

When you work in special care units,
you must not presume that your increased training and broadened authority permit you to exceed nursing's
legal limits. That's especially important
in an area such as medical diagnosis, in
which you can easily cross the legal

boundary separating nursing from medicine.

One place where this sometimes happens is in the ED, where an on-call physician may refuse to see a patient himself, instead ordering care based on a nurse's observations of the patient. In another common ED situation, a patient asks an ED nurse for advice over the telephone. In such a case, she should respond carefully, telling the patient to come to the ED or see his physician if he has questions or his symptoms persist. Similar situations may occur in the PACU, ICU, and CCU, where split-second patient care decisions are sometimes made based on nurses' phone calls to attending physicians.

Keep in mind that all state and jurisdictional nurse practice acts prohibit you from medically diagnosing a patient's condition. You can tell the physician about signs and symptoms you've observed. You can't decide which medical treatments to administer. If you do, you'll be practicing medicine without a license and you'll be held at least partly liable for harm to the patient that results.

In *Methodist Hospital v. Ball* (1961), a young man, Mr. Ball, was brought to the ED with injuries sustained in an automobile accident. Because of a sudden influx of critically ill patients, the ED staff was unable to care for him immediately. While lying on a stretcher in the hospital hallway, Mr. Ball became boisterous and demanded care. Apparently, the attending nurse decided he was drunk. Instead of being treated, Mr. Ball was put into restraints and transported by ambulance to another local hospital. There, 15 minutes after arriving, he died from internal bleeding.

An autopsy revealed no evidence of alcohol in Mr. Ball's system. In the resulting lawsuit, the court found the attending nurse and medical resident negligent because they failed to diagnose Mr. Ball's condition properly, to give supportive treatment, and to alert personnel at the second hospital about Mr. Ball's critical condition.

A few precautions

If you practice in a special care unit, be sure you know — and follow — hospital policies and procedures. Know your own limitations, too — never perform a procedure you feel uncertain about. Remember, admitting to inexperience is never improper. However, performing a procedure that may exceed your capabilities could be, especially if it results in injury or death.

If you're an LPN or LVN working in a special care unit, the same precautionary watchword applies. As you help RNs care for acutely ill patients and carry out physicians' orders, remember that you assume a significant legal risk when you perform a task ordinarily assigned to an RN. If you injure the patient in the process and he sues you for malpractice, your care will be measured against what a reasonably competent RN would do in the same or similar circumstances.

If you work in an ED, remember to reassess the patient after treatment. It's both sound nursing care and a requirement of JCAHO to note and document a patient's response to care. If the patient hasn't had the expected response to treatment, you'll need to also document your subsequent intervention.

Legal responsibility for patient safety

One of your most important responsibilities is your patient's physical safety.

To prevent falls, for example, you have to make sure bedside rails are up for a debilitated, elderly, confused, or medicated patient. You also have to help a weak patient walk, use proper transfer methods when moving a patient, and sometimes use restraining devices to immobilize a patient.

In the interest of patient safety, you also have to keep an eye on your hospital's facilities and equipment. If you spot loose or improperly functioning side rails, water or some other substance on the unit floor, or an improperly functioning ventilator, you have a duty to report the problem and call for repairs or housekeeping assistance. Failure to do so may not only endanger patients, but also make you — and the hospital — liable if injuries occur.

PATIENT-SAFETY STANDARDS OF CARE

In a malpractice lawsuit against a nurse, she's judged on how well she performed her duty as measured against the appropriate standards of care. The court will analyze whether the defendant-nurse gave the plaintiff-patient care equal to that given by a reasonably well-qualified and prudent nurse in the same or similar circumstances.

With regard to patient safety, your duty includes anticipating foreseeable risks. For example, if you're aware that the floor in a patient's room is dangerously slippery, you must report the condition to the appropriate hospital department and place caution signs on the floor to warn of the dangers. If you don't, and a patient falls and is injured, you could be held liable.

In fact, you might be held liable even if you didn't know the floor was slippery. Using accepted standards of care, a court might reason that part of

your duty as a reasonable and prudent nurse was to check the floor of your unit regularly and report any patient hazard immediately.

The standards of care that you meet will vary with your job and the training you've had. A staff nurse's actions, for example, will be measured against staff nurse standards, and a gerontologic nurse's actions will be measured against standards that gerontologic nurses must meet.

National Patient Safety Goals

In July 2002, JCAHO approved its first set of National Patient Safety Goals, which will be reviewed and updated yearly. JCAHO established these goals to help accredited organizations better address patient safety. Current goals include:

◆ improving the accuracy of patient identification
◆ improving the effectiveness of communication among caregivers
◆ improving the safety of using high-alert medications
◆ eliminating wrong-site, wrong-patient, wrong-procedure surgery
◆ improving the safety of using infusion pumps
◆ improving the effectiveness of clinical alarm systems.

Failure to implement these safety goals will result in a special Type I recommendation.

SPECIAL SAFETY CONCERNS

In your practice, you need to recognize special safety concerns, such as patient falls, the use of restraints, the prospect of suicide attempts, the safety of equipment, and the risk of transmitting disease.

Patient falls

Almost anything can cause a patient to fall, particularly if he's elderly or receiving medication. Elderly patients are, in many instances, confused, disoriented, and weak. Medications can cause or increase confusion and lessen a patient's ability to react in situations in which he might fall. Here are some ways you can protect your patient from falls:

◆ Make sure the bed's side rails are kept up, when indicated.

◆ Orient him to where he is and what time it is, especially if he's elderly.

◆ Monitor him regularly — continually, if his condition makes this necessary.

◆ Offer a bedpan or commode regularly.

◆ Provide adequate lighting and a clean, clutter-free environment.

◆ Make sure that someone helps and supports him whenever he gets out of bed and that he wears proper shoes when walking.

◆ Make sure adequate staff are available to transfer him, if necessary.

◆ Make sure the call light is within his reach and in working order.

Elderly patients and patients taking medications that cause orthostatic hypotension, central nervous system depression, or vestibular toxicity need special nursing care when physicians' orders require them to be "up in chair for 15 minutes x 3 daily" or "up in chair for meals." If you can't supervise such a patient while he's sitting up, at least make sure another member of the health care team is available.

Restraints

Usually prescribed to ensure a patient's safety, restraints unfortunately can also endanger the patient. When a physician prescribes a restraining device, keep in mind that such devices don't remove your responsibility for the patient's safety. In fact, they increase it.

For example, when a patient wears a restraining belt, you have to make sure he doesn't undo it or inadvertently readjust it; if he does, it could choke or otherwise injure him. You also have to make sure the belt fits properly; if it's too tight, it could restrict the patient's breathing or irritate his skin. You may have to decide when the belt is no longer necessary. Check the governing laws and protocols for an automatic expiration of restriction orders. If you fail to handle patient restraints properly, you may be accused of false imprisonment.

Suicide prevention

Suicide prevention is another important aspect of patient safety. Keep in mind that self-destructive, suicidal patients are found in medical as well as psychiatric wards.

Your first obligation is to provide close supervision. A suicidal patient may require one-on-one, 24-hour-a-day supervision until the immediate threat of self-harm is over. Take from him all potentially dangerous objects, such as belts, bed linens, glassware, and eating utensils. Make sure he swallows pills when you give them; otherwise, he may retain them in his mouth, to save them for later.

Assess the hospital environment carefully for possible dangers. If he can easily open or break his room windows, or if escape from your unit would be easy, you may have to transfer him to a safer, more secure place — if necessary, to a seclusion room.

Remember, whether you work on a psychiatric unit or a medical unit, you'll be held responsible for the decisions you make about a suicidal patient's care. If you're sued because he's harmed himself while in your care, the court will judge you based on:

♦ whether you knew (or should have known) that the patient was likely to harm himself

♦ whether, knowing he was likely to harm himself, you exercised reasonable care in helping him avoid injury or death.

In *Woodword v. Myers, Dean, and Correctional Medical Services of Illinois* (2001), a nurse evaluated a jail detainee and documented "yes" to an intake question asking him if he had expressed thoughts about killing himself. Despite the affirmative answer, the nurse didn't obtain suicide precautions. Later, the man committed suicide while in custody. The nurse was sued on a claim that she deprived the detainee of his right to due process under the Fourteenth Amendment.

Equipment safety

You're responsible for making sure that the equipment used for patient care is free from defects. You also need to exercise reasonable care in selecting equipment for a specific procedure and patient and then helping to maintain the equipment. Here again, your patient care must reflect what the reasonably well-qualified and prudent nurse would do in the same or similar circumstances. This means that if you know a specific piece of equipment isn't functioning properly, you must take steps to correct the defects and document the steps you took. If you don't and a patient is injured because of the defective equipment, you may be sued for malpractice.

Selecting proper equipment and maintaining it also means making sure it isn't contaminated. When cleaning equipment, always follow hospital procedures strictly, and document your actions carefully. This will decrease the possibility that you could be held liable for using contaminated equipment.

You can also be held liable for improper use of equipment that's functioning properly. This liability frequently occurs with equipment that can cause burns – – for example, diathermy machines, electrosurgical equipment, and hot-water bottles. When using such equipment, carry out the procedure or therapy carefully, observe the patient continually until finished, and ask the patient frequently (if awake) whether he's experiencing pain or discomfort.

Disease transmission

Be careful not to cause contamination or cross-infection of patients. In *Widman v. Paoli Memorial Hospital* (1989), the hospital was found negligent because a preoperative patient was assigned to the same room as a patient infected with the *Klebsiella* organism. The court found that the hospital didn't make sure that personnel assigned to care for the patient followed established infection control procedures.

HOSPITAL'S RESPONSIBILITY FOR PATIENT SAFETY

Your hospital shares responsibility for the patient's safety. This institutional responsibility for patient safety rests on the two most frequently used doctrines of malpractice liability.

The first doctrine, *corporate liability,* holds the hospital liable for its own wrongful conduct — for breach of its duties as mandated by statutory law, common law, and applicable rules and regulations. The hospital's duty to keep patients safe includes the duty to provide, inspect, repair, and maintain reasonably adequate equipment for diagnosis and treatment. The hospital also has a duty to keep the facility reasonably safe. Thus, if a patient is injured because the hospital alone breached one of its duties, the hospital is responsible for the injury.

Over time, the courts have expanded the concept of an institution's liability for breaching its duties. In a landmark case, *Darling v. Charleston Community Memorial Hospital* (1965), the Illinois Supreme Court expanded the concept of hospital corporate liability to include the hospital's responsibility to supervise the quality of care given to its patients.

In *Thompson v. The Nason Hospital* (1991), the courts went even further and discussed four general areas of corporate liability. These include:
◆ a duty to use reasonable care to maintain safe facilities and equipment
◆ a duty to staff the hospital with only competent physicians
◆ a duty to oversee all individuals practicing medicine within the hospital
◆ a duty to develop and enforce policies and procedures designed to ensure quality patient care.

The second doctrine of institutional malpractice liability is respondeat superior. Under this doctrine, the facility is liable for an employee's wrongful conduct. This means that both the employee and the health care facility can be found liable for a breach of duty to the patient — including the duty of ensuring his safety.

DETERMINING LIABILITY

In a lawsuit involving failure to ensure patient safety, the hospital alone may be held liable or the nurse may share in the liability. The outcome depends on the facts involved.

If, for example, a court can determine that the duty to monitor patient care equipment and to repair any discovered defects rests with the hospital and the nurse, then both could be held liable for a breach of that duty. In *May v. Broun* (1972), the plaintiff-patient sued the hospital, the circulating nurse, and the physician for burns she sustained when an electric cautery machine's electrode burned her during a hemorrhoidectomy.

Although the machine had been used successfully earlier in the day, when the physician began to use it on the plaintiff, he noticed that its heat wasn't sufficient to cauterize blood vessels. He asked the circulating nurse to check the machine. She did, and after that it apparently worked properly. Nevertheless, the plaintiff was burned where the electrode had touched her body. She later sued the hospital, the circulating nurse, and the physician.

Because the hospital and the nurse settled with the plaintiff out of court, the physician was the only one to stand trial. The court held the physician not liable for the patient's injuries because the hospital had the duty to monitor the equipment and to provide trained personnel to operate it. This meant that the hospital had to bear responsibility for the defective equipment and wrongful conduct by the nurse. In this case, the hospital and the nurse were liable for the plaintiff's injury.

In *Story v. McCurtain Memorial Management, Inc.* (1981), the outcome was different. This case involved the delivery of one twin by the mother herself when she was left unattended in a shower room. The patient continuously called for help, but her calls went unanswered and the baby the mother delivered herself died.

The mother sued the hospital and the nurse on duty at the time. The court found the nurse not liable, but it held the hospital liable (under the doctrine of corporate liability) for failing to provide safeguards in the shower room and adequate supervision on the unit. Here, then, the hospital alone was liable for breaching its duty to protect patients from harm.

DECREASING YOUR LIABILITY

As a nurse, you have an important duty to ensure your patient's safety. Remember, all your actions directed toward patient safety must be in line with your hospital's policies and procedures, so be sure you know what these are. If no policies exist, or if they're outdated or poorly drafted, bring this to your supervisor's or head nurse's attention. Consider volunteering to help write or rewrite the policies. By getting involved in efforts to improve patients' safety, you may decrease your potential liability and, at the same time, improve the quality of patient care.

Legal risks when administering drugs

Administering drugs to patients continues to be one of the most important — and, legally, one of the most risky — tasks you perform.

Over time, nurses' responsibilities with regard to drug administration have increased. For many years, U.S. and Canadian nurses were permitted to give drugs only orally or rectally. Today, nurses give subcutaneous and intramuscular injections, induce anesthesia, and administer I.V. therapy. In some states, nurses may even prescribe drugs, within certain limitations.

U.S. and Canadian laws continue to strictly guard the nurse's role in drug administration. Within this limited scope, however, the law imposes exceptionally high standards.

SIX RIGHTS FORMULA

When administering drugs, one easy way to guard against malpractice liability is to remember the six rights formula:
♦ the right drug
♦ to the right patient
♦ at the right time
♦ in the right dosage
♦ by the right route
♦ and the right documentation.

DRUG-CONTROL LAWS

Legally, a drug is any substance listed in an official state, jurisdictional, or national formulary. A drug may also be defined as any substance (other than food) "intended to affect the structure or any function of the body…(or) for use in the diagnosis, cure, mitigation, treatment, or prevention of disease." N.Y. Educ. Law.

A *prescription drug* is any drug restricted from regular commercial purchase and sale. A state, jurisdictional, or national government has determined that this drug is, or might be, unsafe unless used under a qualified medical practitioner's supervision.

Federal laws

Two important federal laws governing the use of drugs in the United States are the Comprehensive Drug Abuse Prevention and Control Act and the Food, Drug, and Cosmetic Act. The Comprehensive Drug Abuse Prevention and Control Act (incorporating the Controlled Substances Act) seeks to categorize drugs by how dangerous they are and regulates drugs thought to be most subject to abuse. The Food, Drug, and Cosmetic Act restricts interstate shipment of drugs not approved for human use and outlines the process for testing and approving new drugs.

State laws

At the state and jurisdictional level, pharmacy practice acts are the main laws affecting the distribution of drugs. These are state and jurisdictional laws that mirror federal laws. Through these, criminal penalties attach under state or jurisdictional law for similar violations. These laws give pharmacists (in Canada, sometimes physicians as well) the sole legal authority to prepare, compound, preserve, and dispense drugs. *Dispense* refers to taking a drug from the pharmacy supply and giving or selling it to another person. This contrasts with administering drugs — actually getting the drug into the patient. Your nurse practice act is the law that most directly affects how you administer drugs.

Most nursing, medical, and pharmacy practice acts include:
◆ a definition of the tasks that belong uniquely to the profession
◆ a statement saying that anyone who performs such tasks without being a licensed or registered member of the defined profession is breaking the law.

In some states and jurisdictions, certain tasks overlap. For example, both nurses and physicians can provide bedside care for the sick and patient teaching.

In many states, if a nurse prescribes a drug, she's practicing medicine without a license; if she goes into the pharmacy or drug supply cabinet, measures out doses of a drug, and puts the powder into capsules, she's practicing pharmacy without a license. For either action, she can be prosecuted or lose her license, even if no harm results. In most states and Canadian jurisdictions, to practice a licensed profession without a license is, at the very least, a misdemeanor.

Court case

In *Stefanik v. Nursing Education Committee* (1944), a Rhode Island nurse lost her nursing license in part because she had been practicing medicine illegally: She had changed a physician's drug order for a patient because she didn't agree with what had been prescribed. No one claimed she had harmed the patient. However, to change a prescription is the same as writing a new prescription, and Rhode Island's nurse practice act didn't consider that to be part of nursing practice.

LAWSUITS RELATED TO MEDICATION ERRORS

Unfortunately, lawsuits involving nurses' drug errors are common. The court determines liability based on the standard of care required of nurses when administering drugs. In many instances, if the nurse had known more about the proper dose, administration route, or procedure connected with giving the drug, she might have avoided the mistake that resulted in the lawsuit.

In *Derrick v. Portland Eye, Ear, Nose and Throat Hospital* (1922), an Oregon nurse gave a young boy a pupil-contracting drug when the physician had ordered a pupil-dilating drug. As a result, the boy lost his sight in one eye; the nurse and the hospital were found negligent.

Getting the dose right is also important. In a Louisiana case, *Norton v. Argonaut Insurance Co.* (1962), a nurse inadvertently gave a 3-month-old infant a digoxin overdose that resulted in the infant's death. At the malpractice trial that followed, the nurse was found liable, along with the hospital and the attending physician.

Similarly, in *Dessauer v. Memorial General Hospital* (1981), an ED physician ordered 50 mg of lidocaine for a patient. However, the nurse, who normally worked in the hospital's obstetrics ward, gave the patient 800 mg. The patient died, the family sued, and the hospital was found liable.

In *Moore v. Guthrie Hospital* (1968), a nurse made a mistake in the administration route, giving the patient two drugs intravenously rather than intramuscularly. The patient suffered a seizure, sued, and won.

When reviewing these cases, one point becomes clear: The courts won't permit carelessness that harms the patient.

EMERGENCY DOSES

Some hospitals and extended care facilities have written policies that permit a nurse under special circumstances to go into the pharmacy and dispense an emergency drug dose. In the ED, physicians frequently write emergency orders for one to three doses — just enough to hold the patient until he can go to the pharmacy and have his prescription filled. If there's no pharmacist on duty, hospital policy may allow the nurse to obtain the required drug, bottle it, and label it.

Regardless of whether her employer has such a policy, a nurse who dispenses drugs is doing so unlawfully — unless her state's pharmacy practice act specifically authorizes her actions. If she makes an error in dispensing the drug and the patient later sues, the fact that she was practicing as an unlicensed pharmacist can be used as evidence against her.

Your options

If you need to dispense an emergency drug dose, you may choose to disregard the laws that govern your practice for the benefit of your patient's well-being. You do so at your own risk, however. Even if you don't harm your patient, you can still be prosecuted and you can still lose your license. When ethics and the law conflict and you have to weigh concern for your patient's life or health against concern for your license, you must make up your own mind about what action to take.

If your hospital policy requires you to dispense emergency medications and is in clear violation of your state's nurse practice act, consider taking steps to have your hospital policy changed. Start by approaching your nurse-manager with a copy of the nurse practice act and relevant hospital policies. Point out the inconsistencies and the professional risk nurses in the ED are taking. Then offer to accompany your nurse-manager when she approaches nursing administrators and the policy and procedure committee. Hospital administrators may designate an ED pharmacist, hire additional pharmacy staff, or prevail upon pharmacists or staff to take greater responsibility for distribution of ED medications.

YOUR ROLE IN DRUG EXPERIMENTATION

At times, you may participate in administering experimental drugs to patients or administering established drugs in new ways or at experimental dosage levels. Your legal duties don't change, but if you have any questions, you'll get your answers from the experimental protocol — not your usual sources (such as books and package inserts). Also, an institutional review board (IRB) probably reviewed and accepted the protocol before it was instituted. This is another resource for the nurse, especially if ethical concerns regarding the treatment develop. You'll also need to make sure no drug is given to a patient who hasn't consented to participate. (Note that if it's a federally funded experiment, consent should be in writing.)

YOUR RESPONSIBILITY FOR KNOWING ABOUT DRUGS

When you have your nursing license, the law expects you to know about any drug you administer. If you're an LPN or LVN, you assume the same legal responsibility as an RN once you've taken a pharmaceutical course or obtained authorization to administer drugs. More specifically, the law expects you to:
◆ know a drug's safe dosage limits, toxicity, potential adverse reactions, and indications and contraindications for use
◆ refuse to accept an illegible, confusing, or otherwise unclear drug order
◆ seek clarification of a confusing order from the physician and not to try to interpret it yourself.

Increasingly, judges and juries expect nurses to know what the appropriate observation intervals are for a patient receiving medication. They expect you to know this even if the physician doesn't know or if he doesn't write an order stating how often to check on the newly medicated patient. A case that was decided on this basis is *Brown v. State* (1977). After a patient was given 200 mg of chlorpromazine, the nurses on duty left him largely unobserved for several hours. When someone finally checked on the patient, he was dead. The hospital and the nurses the resulting lawsuit.

QUESTIONING A DRUG ORDER

If you question a drug order, follow your hospital's policies. Usually, they'll tell you to try each of the following actions until you receive a satisfactory answer:
◆ Look up the answer in a reliable drug reference.
◆ Ask your charge nurse.
◆ Ask the hospital pharmacist.
◆ Ask your nursing supervisor or the prescribing physician.
◆ Ask the chief nursing administrator, if she hasn't already become involved.
◆ Ask the prescribing physician's supervisor (service chief).
◆ Get in touch with the hospital administration and explain your problem.

WHEN YOU MUST REFUSE TO ADMINISTER A DRUG

All nurses have the legal right not to administer drugs they think will harm patients. You may choose to exercise this right in a variety of situations:
◆ when you think the dosage prescribed is too high
◆ when you think the drug is contraindicated because of possible dangerous interactions with other drugs, or with substances such as alcohol
◆ because you think the patient's physical condition contraindicates using the drug.

In limited circumstances, you may also legally refuse to administer a drug on grounds of conscience. Some states and Canadian jurisdictions have enacted right-of-conscience laws. These laws excuse medical personnel from the requirement to participate in an abortion or sterilization procedure. Under such laws, you may, for example, refuse to give a drug you believe is intended to induce abortion.

When you refuse to carry out a drug order, make sure you do the following:

◆ Notify your immediate supervisor so she can make alternative arrangements (assigning a new nurse, clarifying the order).

◆ Notify the prescribing physician if your supervisor hasn't done so already.

◆ If your employer requires it, document that the drug wasn't given, and explain why.

PROTECTING YOURSELF FROM LIABILITY

If you make an error in giving a drug, or if your patient reacts negatively to a properly administered drug, immediately inform the patient's physician, and protect yourself by documenting the incident thoroughly. Besides normal drug-charting information, include information on the patient's reaction and medical or nursing interventions taken.

In the event of error, you should also file an incident report. Identify what happened, the names and functions of all personnel involved, and what actions were taken to protect the patient after the error was discovered.

LPN/LVN ROLES IN ADMINISTERING DRUGS

Most nurse practice acts now permit LPNs and LVNs *with the appropriate educational background or on-the-job training* to give drugs under the supervision of an RN, physician, or dentist. What constitutes appropriate training or educational background? No clear-cut definitions exist, but most courts probably would be satisfied if an LPN or LVN could prove that her supervising RN or physician had watched her administer drugs and had judged her

competent. For tasks that require instruction and experience beyond the nurse's academic training, health care facilities usually develop didactic training with goals and proficiency tests. Additionally, skills testing should be documented through proficiency checklists. This provides objective documentation in case of a lawsuit. (Note, however, that some states prohibit LPNs and LVNs from inserting I.V. lines.)

Telephone triage

Telephonic medical advice traditionally has been a part of most primary care practices. This type of service, which has become known as telephone triage, generally operates with a clinician taking calls and processing requests for medical advice. As health care costs continue to rise, more managed care organizations, HMOs, and EDs are using these systems as a cost-saving and case management measure.

Most telephone triage systems are staffed with fully trained nurses who use computerized algorithms and their clinical judgment to analyze a patient's complaints and give advice. The algorithms, which are designed in a systematic, question-and-answer format, indicate what advice the nurse should give. The nurse may provide self-care instructions, or she may tell the caller to come to the emergency room or make an appointment with his primary care physician or a specialist.

If you dispense advice over the phone, keep in mind that a legal duty arises the minute you say, "OK, let me tell you what to do." You now have a nurse-patient relationship, and you're responsible for advice you give. After you start to give advice by telephone, you can't decide midway through that you're in over your head and simply hang up; that could be considered abandonment. You must give appropriate advice or a referral — for example, "After listening to you, I suggest that you go to the emergency department."

You also need to ensure that you complete the proper documentation for every call you take. Every telephone call that the unit receives should be logged in. The log should include the date and time of the call, the caller's name and address, the caller's chief complaint or request, the disposition of the call, and the name of the person who made the disposition. Make sure that you document this information properly. Take thorough notes during the call, and complete the call log immediately after the call has been completed — when the information is still fresh in your mind. That way, you're ensuring its completeness and accuracy.

As a telephone triage nurse, you'll run into challenges that don't exist in other units of your facility. A telephone call doesn't allow you to visually assess the caller. In addition, a caller may be reluctant to provide personal details over the phone. Language and cultural differences can also make evaluating a caller's symptoms difficult. Finally, processes to follow up with the caller's physician may not be adequate.

Standards

The Emergency Nurses Association (ENA) and the American Accreditation HealthCare Commission (URAC) have established guidelines and standards for telephone triage programs. ENA guidelines require telephone triage nurses to be experienced professional RNs with specialized education in triage, telephone assessment, and communication and documenta-

tion skills. Included in the ENA guidelines are mandatory continuing education requirements; defined protocols, policies, and procedures; and a continuous quality improvement program.

URAC's Health Call Center Standards apply to managed care organizations providing triage and health information services to the public when conducted by telephone, via Web site, or other electronic means. The standards assure that RNs, physicians, or other validly licensed individuals perform the clinical aspects of triage and other health information services in a manner that's timely, confidential, and medically appropriate. URAC also mandates that each telephone triage unit must have be a continuous staff management program, including orientation and training, written job descriptions, performance evaluations, and verification of licenses.

HIPAA
The Health Insurance and Portability and Accountability Act (HIPAA), passed by Congress in 1996, was designed to provide safeguards against the inappropriate use and release of personal medical information, including all medical records and identifiable health information in all forms (electronic, on paper, or oral). The telephone triage nurse needs to follow HIPAA's policies and procedures and inform callers of the scope of confidentiality that exists within the telephone triage program. Although the telephone triage nurse isn't likely to be in a position to violate HIPAA regulations, she must be made aware that protecting personal health information is a serious duty.

CASE LAW

In *Shannon v. McNulty and HealthAmerica Pennsylvania* (1998), the court held HealthAmerica, an HMO, vicariously liable for the negligence of its nursing telephone triage staff when it failed to quickly refer Mrs. Shannon to her physician or hospital when she called complaining of signs and symptoms of preterm labor. Mrs. Shannon lost her child. The Shannons also alleged that HealthAmerica was liable for its lack of appropriate procedures and protocols when dispensing telephonic medical advice to its subscribers.

In a Texas case, *Norman v. Good Shepard Medical Center* (2001), the court held the hospital liable for the actions of one of its LVNs who improperly performed telephone triage when Mrs. Norman called the ED looking for medical advice regarding her 10-year-old daughter's rash. The evidence established that the LVN disobeyed a hospital policy stating that LVNs were not to give medical advice in non–life-threatening situations. The LVN gave incorrect medical advice, which caused a delay in diagnosis and forced the child to undergo several limb amputations.

AVOIDING LIABILITY

To avoid liability while working as a telephone triage nurse, you need to know the policies and procedures of your telephone triage unit and uphold the privacy of protected health information. Proper training that includes orientation to protocols, proper documentation and follow-up communication, continuing education, and quality improvement monitoring is paramount for your own — and your patient's — protection.

Patient teaching and the law

Anytime you give a patient information about his care or treatment, you're involved in patient teaching — a professional nursing responsibility and a potential source of liability.

Patient teaching has taken on increased significance, largely because patients are routinely discharged much earlier from hospitals. Patients and their families need more understanding of patients' illnesses and how to manage them at home.

Patient teaching may be formal or informal. You teach formally when, for example, you prepare instructions on stoma care for a colostomy patient. When giving the patient this detailed information, you should follow these steps:

◆ assessing what the patient wants or needs to know
◆ identifying goals that you and the patient want to reach
◆ choosing teaching strategies that will help reach the goals
◆ evaluating how well you've reached the goals.

You teach *informally* when, for example, you calm a patient's fears by explaining an upcoming diagnostic test or when you answer a friend's questions about how to treat her child's fever.

For best results, patient teaching should include the family and others involved in the patient's care. If family members understand the reason for a patient's treatment, they'll be more willing to provide emotional support.

PATIENT-TEACHING STANDARDS

Most nurse practice acts in the United States and Canada contain wording about promoting patient health and preventing disease or injury. However, they don't specify a nurse's responsibility for patient teaching. Nurses can find this information in the practice standards developed by professional organizations, in nursing job descriptions, and in statements about nursing practice from national commissions.

JCAHO requires that the "patient and his or her family be provided with appropriate education and training to increase the knowledge of the patient's illness and treatment needs and to learn skills and behaviors that promote recovery and improve function." JCAHO requires patient teaching be done in an interdisciplinary manner, considering the patient's ability to learn and any cultural or emotional factors or any cognitive or physical limitations that would affect his ability to learn.

Patient teaching should be a dynamic process that changes to meet the patient's and his family's needs. It should include instruction in how to adapt to the illness as well as how to prevent future problems.

PATIENT'S RIGHT TO HEALTH CARE INFORMATION

Both statutory law and common law support the patient's right to have information about his condition and treatment. In fact, when a patient is admitted to a hospital, he may be handed a patient's bill of rights that clearly outlines his rights. The doctrine of informed consent further supports the patient's right to know.

Despite RNs' deep involvement in patient teaching, the courts have rarely addressed nurses' liability in this area of patient care. The issue typically arises in litigation when a patient sues and the defendant health care provider attempts to prove patient responsibility

for the bad outcome. For example, a patient is seen in the ED for an infection, is prescribed an antibiotic, is told to follow up with a specialist, and is discharged. The patient doesn't follow instructions and his infection worsens. To rebut his own negligence, the patient will argue that he wasn't told the risks if he didn't follow the physician's advice. However, some legal experts believe that as nurses take on greater patient-teaching responsibilities, they'll increasingly become the target of lawsuits dealing with the patient's right to information.

Suppose you're sued for malpractice, and your alleged wrongful act involves patient teaching. The court will consider whether patient teaching was your legal duty to the patient and whether you met or breached it.

Court case

The court in *Kyslinger v. United States* (1975) addressed the nurse's liability for patient teaching. In this case, a veteran's administration (VA) hospital sent a hemodialysis patient home with an artificial kidney. He eventually died (apparently while on the machine), and his wife sued the federal government — because a VA hospital was involved — alleging that the hospital and its staff had failed to teach either her or her late husband how to properly use and maintain a home hemodialysis unit.

After examining the evidence, the court ruled against the patient's wife, as follows: "During those 10 months that plaintiff's decedent underwent biweekly hemodialysis treatment on the unit (at the VA hospital), both plaintiff and decedent were instructed as to the operation, maintenance, and supervision of said treatment. The Court can find no basis to conclude that the plaintiff or plaintiff's decedent weren't properly informed on the use of the hemodialysis unit."

If the patient doesn't want to be taught

Suppose you begin teaching a patient about the medications he's taking, only to hear him say, "Oh, just tell my wife; she gives me all my pills." When something like this happens, be sure to document the incident. Include the patient's exact words; then describe what you taught his wife, and how.

LPN/LVN ROLES IN PATIENT TEACHING

Unlike RNs, LPNs and LVNs aren't typically taught the fundamentals of patient teaching as part of their school curriculum — nor is patient teaching included in their scope of practice. RNs are primarily responsible for patient teaching and may delegate to LPNs or LVNs only the responsibility to reinforce what has already been taught. For example, if an RN is preparing a patient for a barium enema, she could ask an LPN or LVN to tell the patient about the X-ray room and what to expect. The RN could add to the information as necessary.

COOPERATING WITH COLLEAGUES

Physicians, nurses, and other health team members sometimes disagree about how patient teaching should be done and who should do it. To avoid conflict, always consult physicians and other appropriate health team members when you're preparing routine patient-teaching protocols. A team approach to patient teaching not only decreases conflicts, but also ensures continuity in teaching — and a better-educated patient.

You can also avoid conflicts by listening to the instructions that physicians, respiratory therapists, dietitians, and others give the patient. Then you'll know exactly what has already been said to him, and you can structure your teaching accordingly.

Candor and diplomacy, of course, also help reduce conflict. Everyone profits when health team members share their patient-teaching approaches and work together to achieve patient-teaching goals.

Incident reports

An incident is an event that is inconsistent with the hospital's ordinary routine, regardless of whether injury occurs. In most health care facilities, an injury to a patient requires an incident report. Patient complaints, medication errors, and injuries to employees and visitors require incident reports as well.

An incident report serves two main purposes:
◆ to inform hospital administration of the incident so that it can monitor patterns and trends, thereby helping to prevent future similar incidents (risk management)
◆ to alert the administration and the hospital's insurance company to the possibility of liability claims and the need for further investigation (claims management).

Even when the incident isn't investigated, the report serves as a contemporary, factual statement of it. The report also helps identify witnesses if a lawsuit is started months or even years later.

To be useful, an incident report must be filed promptly and must be thorough and factual.

YOUR DUTY TO REPORT PATIENT INCIDENTS

Whether you're an APN, an RN, an LPN or LVN, a nursing assistant, a staff nurse, or a nurse-manager, you have a duty to report an incident of which you have first-hand knowledge. Not only can failure to report an incident lead to your being fired, it can also expose you to claims of malpractice — especially if your failure to report the incident causes injury to a patient.

If you're the staff member who knows the most about the incident at the time of its discovery, you should complete the incident report. When you do so, include only the facts: what you saw when you came upon the incident or what you heard that led you to believe an incident had taken place. If information is second-hand, place it within quotation marks and identify the source. After completing the incident report, sign and date it. You should complete it during the same shift the incident occurred or was discovered.

REPORTING AN INCIDENT

An incident report is an administrative report, and therefore doesn't become part of the patient's medical record. In fact, the record shouldn't even mention that an incident report has been filed because this serves only to deflect the medical record's focus. The record should include only factual clinical observations relating to the incident. (Again, avoid value judgments.)

Entering your observations in the nurses' notes section of the patient's record doesn't take the place of completing an incident report. Nor does completing an incident report take the place of proper documentation in the patient's chart.

Once an incident report has been filed, the nursing supervisor, the physician called to examine the patient, appropriate department heads and administrators, the hospital attorney, and the hospital's insurance company may review it. (See *Filing an incident report: Chain of events.*) The report may be filed under the involved patient's name or by the type of injury, depending on the hospital's policy and the insurance company's regulations. Reports are rarely placed in the reporting nurse's employment file.

If you're asked to talk with the hospital's insurance adjuster or attorney about an incident, be cooperative, honest, and factual. Fully disclosing what you know early on will help the hospital decide how to handle legal consequences of an incident and it also preserves your testimony in case you're ever called to testify in court.

What to include

An incident report should include only the following information:

◆ the names of the persons involved and witnesses

◆ factual information about what happened and the consequences to the person involved (supply enough information so the hospital administration can decide whether the matter needs further investigation)

◆ other relevant facts (such as your immediate actions in response to the incident; for example, notifying the patient's physician).

What not to include

Never include the following types of statements in an incident report:

◆ opinions (such as a reporter's opinion of the patient's prognosis or who's at fault)

◆ conclusions or assumptions (such as what caused the incident)

◆ suggestions of who was responsible for causing the incident

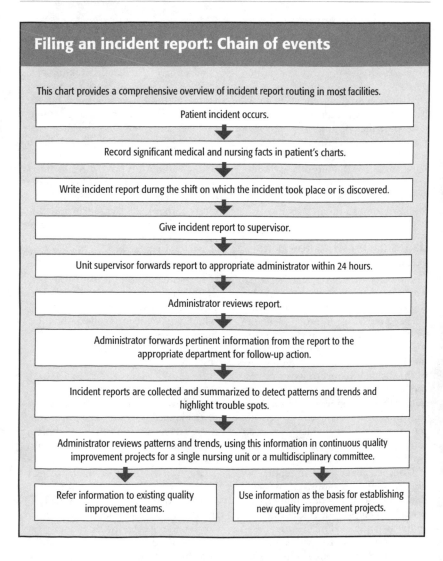

Filing an incident report: Chain of events

This chart provides a comprehensive overview of incident report routing in most facilities.

Patient incident occurs.

↓

Record significant medical and nursing facts in patient's charts.

↓

Write incident report durng the shift on which the incident took place or is discovered.

↓

Give incident report to supervisor.

↓

Unit supervisor forwards report to appropriate administrator within 24 hours.

↓

Administrator reviews report.

↓

Administrator forwards pertinent information from the report to the appropriate department for follow-up action.

↓

Incident reports are collected and summarized to detect patterns and trends and highlight trouble spots.

↓

Administrator reviews patterns and trends, using this information in continuous quality improvement projects for a single nursing unit or a multidisciplinary committee.

↓   ↓

Refer information to existing quality improvement teams.

Use information as the basis for establishing new quality improvement projects.

◆ suggestions to prevent the incident from happening again.

Including this type of information in an incident report could seriously hinder the defense in a lawsuit arising from the incident.

Remember, the incident report serves only to notify the administration that an incident has occurred. In effect, it says, "Administration: Note that this incident happened, and decide whether you want to investigate it further." Such items as detailed statements from witnesses and descriptions of remedial action are normally part of an investigative follow-up; don't include them in the incident report itself.

Potential pitfalls

Be especially careful that the hospital's reporting system doesn't lead to improper incident reporting. For example, some hospitals require nursing supervisors to correlate reports from witnesses and then file a single report. Also, some incident report forms invite inappropriate conclusions and assumptions by asking, "How can this incident be prevented in the future?" If your hospital's reporting system or forms contain such potential pitfalls, alert the administration to them.

USING INCIDENT REPORTS AS COURTROOM EVIDENCE

Controversy exists over whether a patient's attorney may "discover" (request and receive a copy of) an incident report and introduce it into evidence in a malpractice lawsuit. The law on this issue varies from state to state. To avoid discovery, the hospital may send copies of the incident report to its attorney, or the hospital attorney may write a letter stating that the report is being made for his use and benefit only, or the hospital may make the incident report an integral part of the quality assurance process and label it as such.

Concern about incident report discovery should be minimal if an incident report contains only properly reportable material. The information in a properly completed incident report is readily available to the patient's attorney through many other sources. Only when an incident report contains second-hand information, opinions, conclusions, accusations, or suggestions for preventing such incidents in the future does discovery of the incident report become an important issue for attorneys and the courts.

REPORTING YOUR OWN ERROR

If an incident results from your error, you still have the duty to file an incident report immediately. Making a mistake is serious and may invite corrective action by your hospital, but the potential consequences of attempting to cover it up are worse.

For one thing, the likelihood that an incident report will be used against you is slight. A hospital wants its nurses to report incidents and to keep proper records. Nurses may not do this consistently if they're always reprimanded for even small errors. Most hospitals, in fact, will reprimand a nurse for not filing an incident report if injury is done to the patient.

If an incident results from your act of gross negligence or irresponsibility or is one of a series of incidents in which you've been involved, then the hospital may take action against you; that possibility increases if the patient sustains injury because of your error.

Reporting a coworker's error

If a fellow employee's error causes a reportable incident, your safest course is to be factual and objective in reporting what you observed. This allows institutional review to be unbiased in its investigation. Remember, the truth isn't libel. If corrective action is taken, remember that the person who made the error is responsible, not the person who made the report. By properly fulfilling your duty to your patient and your hospital, you'll also minimize potential liability if the employee files a lawsuit against you.

Here's another point to remember: Most states have laws granting "qualified privilege" to those who have a duty to discuss or to evaluate coworkers, employees, or fellow citizens. This privilege means that no liability for libel exists unless the person giving the information knows it's false or has acted with a reckless disregard for the truth.

RISK MANAGEMENT STRATEGY

How can you minimize the chances that a patient will sue after an incident? And how can you protect yourself and your hospital in case he does? The best way is to follow the "three R's" of risk management strategy: rapport, record, and report.

Maintain rapport with the patient

Answer his questions honestly. Don't offer an explanation if you weren't personally involved in the incident; instead, refer the patient to someone who can supply answers. If you try to answer his questions without direct knowledge of the incident, inconsistencies could arise and the patient could interpret these as a cover-up.

If you feel uncomfortable talking to the patient or family, ask your supervisor, hospital patient–relations specialist, or an administrator for advice on how to answer questions or to participate and help you provide answers. Remember that patients usually respond favorably if they know you're being honest and show that you care about their well-being.

Don't blame anyone for the incident. If you feel someone was at fault, tell your charge nurse or supervisor — not the patient.

If an incident changes the patient's care plan (such as medication orders), tell the patient about it and clearly explain the reasons for the change.

Record the incident

Be sure to note the facts of the incident in the medical record. Remember, truthfulness is the best protection against lawsuits. If you try to cover up or play down an incident, you could end up in far more serious trouble than if you had reported it objectively. Never write in the medical record that an incident report has been completed. An incident report isn't clinical information but rather an administrative tool.

Report every incident

Some nurses think incident reports are more trouble than they're worth and, furthermore, that they're a dangerous admission of guilt. That's false. Here's why incident reports are important:

◆ Incident reports jog our memories. The medical chart is client-focused, and facts pertinent to the incident — but not the patient — may be left out. Much time may pass between an incident and when it comes to court. We simply can't trust our memories — but we can trust an incident report.

◆ Incident reports help administrators to act quickly to change the policy or procedure that seems to be responsible for the incident. An administrator can also act quickly to talk with patients' families and offer assistance, explanation, or other appropriate support. Sometimes helpful communication with an injured patient and his family can be the balm that soothes a family's anger and prevents a lawsuit.

◆ Incident reports provide the information hospitals need to decide whether restitution should be made. One example is tracking "lost" belongings.

Caring for a minor

A minor is a person under the age of majority, which is usually 18 or 21, depending on state or jurisdictional law. When you care for a minor, you should keep in mind the way minors' legal rights are structured. What legal rights a minor has depends largely on his age. He may also have special legal status.

MINOR'S RIGHTS

A minor's rights fall into three categories:
◆ *Personal rights that belong to everyone from birth.* Examples include the right to privacy and the right to protection against crimes.
◆ *Rights that can be exercised as a minor matures.* These fall into two groups. The first includes the right to drive a car, to work at a paying job, and to have sexual relations — as long as both partners are of legal age. These rights are granted at certain ages, according to state laws, whether or not the minor is mature enough to exercise the right intelligently.

The second group includes rights granted by the courts rather than by statutory law. These are given to a minor who shows the mental and emotional ability to handle them.
◆ *Rights that belong to adults and can be exercised only by adults and by emancipated minors.* Examples include many financial and contractual rights, such as the right to consent to medical treatment.

The law provides special protection for minors so that they may exercise certain rights after reaching the age of majority. For example, because a minor can't sue in court, most states give minors a grace period after they reach the age of majority to bring any lawsuit relating to when they were minors. This includes suing persons their parents could have sued earlier on the minor's behalf but chose not to. Because this can include a lawsuit for medical malpractice, the law generally requires that hospitals keep the records of pediatric patients longer than the records of adults.

MATURE MINOR

A mature minor is a nonemancipated minor in his middle to late teens who shows clear signs of intellectual and emotional maturity. A mature minor may be able to exercise certain adult rights, depending on laws in his state.

EMANCIPATION

Emancipation is the legal process whereby children may obtain freedom from the custody, care, and control of their parents before the age of majority. Under most state statutes, an emancipated minor loses his right to financial support from his parents in exchange for the ability to govern his own affairs. Emancipation may also enable a minor to enter into binding contracts and to sue and be sued in his own name. Some statutes also give an emancipated minor the ability to consent to medical, dental, or psychiatric care without parental consent.

Depending on the jurisdiction, emancipation may be addressed by common law or statutory law. Most state statutes require a hearing in emancipation cases.

Standards for emancipation may include:
◆ *best interests of the minor* (Many state statutes contain a provision allowing judges to use the best interests of the child as a standard for emancipation.)
◆ *ability to manage financial affairs* (Many state statutes have a provision requiring that a minor demonstrate the ability to manage financial affairs before becoming emancipated.)
◆ *living separate and apart from parents* (Many statutes require that minors who wish to be emancipated live separate and apart from their parents. Some require parental consent for separate living arrangements.)
◆ *parental consent* (Many states require parental consent for an emancipation

petition; others ignore this requirement altogether.)

◆ *age* (Most states require that children
be at least age 16 before initiating
emancipation proceedings. A few states
don't have an age requirement.)

Under most circumstances, you
should treat an emancipated minor the
same as if he were an adult.

Restrictions on rights

Note that even an emancipated minor
may not exercise some rights. If he's 18
and the drinking age in his state is 21,
he can't legally buy an alcoholic bever-
age. Some states set a minimum age for
making a will (usually the age of majority). In those states, even if the minor is married or has a child, a will he
draws up won't be valid.

GUARDIANS *AD LITEM*

A *guardian ad litem* is a person appointed by the court to protect the interest
of a minor in a legal proceeding. The
court may appoint a guardian *ad litem*
when these conditions coexist:

◆ A decision is needed for the minor.

◆ A "diversion of interest" exists. (The
court possesses evidence that the interest of the minor's parents or legal
guardians probably doesn't coincide
with the minor's welfare.)

The court may appoint a guardian
ad litem even if one or both parents
are still living and interested in the minor's welfare or if the minor already
has a guardian.

OBTAINING CONSENT

By far the most common problem
with minors is obtaining proper consent for their medical care. Although
the physician bears the legal responsibility for this, you'll commonly be involved in the process. Here are 11 dif-

ferent situations you may face in helping to obtain a minor's consent.

Nonemancipated minor

If the minor isn't emancipated, his
mother, father, or legal guardian has
the right to refuse or consent to treatment for him. Whenever possible, consent should be obtained from both
parents or both guardians when joint
guardians have custody of the minor.

If the parents are divorced or separated, the policy is to obtain consent
from the parent who has custody. If the
minor's parents are incompetent or
dead and he has no legal guardian, the
court will usually appoint a legal
guardian. The guardian can consent or
refuse, just as if he were a parent.

Mature, nonemancipated minor

In some Canadian jurisdictions under
certain circumstances, mature, nonemancipated minors may consent to
medical treatment themselves. Where
legislation exists, common law provides that if nonemancipated minors
understand the nature and consequences of treatment, they may give
their own consent. In the United
States, nonemancipated but mature
minors' rights aren't as broad. However, in some jurisdictions, parental consent is no longer necessary for various
types of medical and psychiatric care.
In California, for example, nonemancipated minors age 15 and older, who
live separate from their parents and
manage their own finances, may consent to their own medical care. Ask
your hospital attorney to check your
state's statutes in this area.

Emancipated minor

An emancipated minor can usually
refuse or consent to treatment himself.
However, if he can't do so (for example, he's unconscious after an accident),
you have to try to find someone who

can give consent for him. Talk to the hospital attorney to determine if there are laws in your state that designate surrogate decision makers when the patient becomes incompetent. Possibilities, in descending order of preference, include his spouse, parents or guardians, and nearest living relative. You may waive this requirement for consent only in an emergency situation when your failure to treat a minor immediately could result in further injury or in death.

When parents or joint guardians disagree

Problems can arise when parents (whether married, divorced, or separated) or joint guardians disagree about consenting to treatment for a nonemancipated minor. The hospital's only recourse may be to go to court, where a judge either decides or assigns responsibility to one parent or guardian. If you find yourself in a situation in which a minor's parents or guardians can't agree on consenting to his treatment, tell the hospital administrators immediately so they can talk to the parents or guardians and, if necessary, alert the hospital's attorney.

When a minor needs emergency care

The legal rule to follow when a minor needs emergency care is the same as that for adults: Treat first and get consent later. Some courts have held that a mature minor, emancipated or not, may give valid and binding consent to emergency treatment. For example, in *Younts v. St. Francis Hospital and School of Nursing* (1970), a nonemancipated but mature 17-year-old was held able to consent to surgical repair of a severed fingertip.

When a minor requests an abortion

Recent U.S. Supreme Court rulings, including *Ohio v. Akron Center for Reproductive Health* (1990) and *Hodgson v. Minnesota* (1990), indicate that state laws can't prevent a minor from seeking and obtaining a legal abortion; however, states can impose conditions on consent. The law in some states (such as Virginia, in which abortion-consent laws have been upheld by the Supreme Court) may require a minor seeking an abortion to notify her parents or to bypass this consent requirement by going before a judge, a procedure called *judicial bypass.*

For the rules your state requires you to follow when verifying consent for a minor's abortion, check with your facility's attorney.

When a minor asks for a contraceptive

In *Carey v. Population Services International* (1977), the U.S. Supreme Court ruled unconstitutional a state law prohibiting the sale of contraceptives to anyone younger than age 16. The court held that the decision to bear a child is a fundamental right and that state interference can be justified only if it protects a compelling state interest. As a result, a minor can obtain contraceptives without parental consent.

Again, consult the hospital's attorney if you have questions regarding restrictions on distributing contraceptives to minors. For example, your state may require you to notify a parent or guardian about the matter.

When a minor needs treatment for a communicable disease

Most states and Canadian jurisdictions have laws that permit minors to consent to treatment for serious communicable diseases, including sexually transmitted diseases, without parental approval.

If you must deal with a minor who's refusing diagnosis or treatment for a communicable disease, check your state's laws. Most states permit public health authorities to deal with a non-consenting minor as an adult, including deciding whether he should be quarantined.

When a minor needs treatment for drug abuse

State and federal laws generally permit minors to consent to take part in drug-abuse treatment and rehabilitation programs just as though they were adults. Like adults, minor patients in drug treatment programs are entitled to have their records kept confidential.

When religious beliefs conflict with a minor's treatment

If your patient or his parents or guardians are Jehovah's Witnesses or Christian Scientists, you may have special problems getting consent to treatment.

Although competent adults or emancipated minors may refuse treatment for religious reasons, nonemancipated minors may not. In most states in which the question has come before the courts, judges have ruled that parents and guardians can't stop a hospital from treating their child solely on religious grounds if a reasonable chance exists that the treatment will help the patient.

Note, however, that in this situation a court will have to appoint a guardian *ad litem* for the sick minor. This may take some time, so to avoid delaying the minor's treatment unnecessarily, notify your hospital administration as quickly as possible.

When a minor seeks or receives mental health care

Minors, like adults, may be treated at private and state-run mental health facilities. When the minor and his parents agree to seek such treatment for the minor, the facility will follow its normal medical guidelines and procedures in deciding whether to admit him. This usually involves informing the patient and his parents or guardian of their rights and then obtaining their informed consent for admission.

In many states, however, the rules controlling admission of minors to inpatient mental health facilities are more rigorous. The rules may call for a full-scale hearing, with attorneys present, within a set time after admission (if not concurrent with admission).

Caring for an abused patient

In the course of your career, you're likely to encounter victims of abuse. Sometimes abuse is physical battering such as when a son regularly beats his aging father. At other times, abuse involves verbal, sexual, or emotional attack, or neglect and abandonment.

PROFILE OF THE ABUSER

People who abuse others come from all socioeconomic levels and all ethnic groups. No specific psychiatric diagnosis encompasses the abuser's personality and behavior. However, many abusers have a history of being abused themselves when young or of having witnessed abuse of parents or siblings. (Such childhood experiences are usually profound and can influence a person's behavior throughout his adult life.) In many cases, abusive persons lack self-esteem and the security of being loved—qualities that help non-abusive persons cope with stress.

In times of crisis, abusers resort to the behavior learned in childhood. They abuse just as they were abused— all in an attempt to restore their own feelings of self-control and self-esteem. After all, if abuse was an acceptable behavior for their parents, why can't it be the same for them now?

Abusers are usually unable to tolerate personal failure or disapproval from spouses, children, or friends. When an abuser's self-esteem is low, he expects rejection and will act in ways that cause others to reject him. Rejection in turn provokes the abuser to commit further verbal or emotional abuse.

Abusers commonly have unrealistic expectations of the people they abuse. When an individual fails to live up to those expectations, the abuser feels a stronger compulsion to control, mortify, reject and, if necessary, physically injure that individual.

Cycle of abuse

Low self-esteem may prompt an abuser to choose a partner much like himself. Each will then feed into the other's forms of abuse. If the couple has children, in many cases they become targets of their parents' abusive behavior. What the children witness and suffer often begins another cycle of abused child-to-child abuser.

CHILD ABUSE

U.S. government studies indicate that abused children who die from their injuries are most likely to die before age 4. Studies have indicated that the majority of maltreatment fatalities occur in children younger than age 5. (See *Responding to suspected child abuse.*) Children with behavior problems are particularly vulnerable to abuse, as are malformed or developmentally dis-abled children and children born prematurely or to unmarried parents. From the abusive parent's perspective, such a child represents an unplanned disruption or a stress-producing crisis. If the child has mental or physical defects, the parent may see this as reaffirming his own inadequacy and weakness. If the child has severe defects, the parent may be unable to accept that the child is his: He may pour on abuse in an effort to be rid of the child.

Parents may also view children as extensions of persons they hate. Sometimes this results from similarities in physical appearance or similarities in behavior. If a child resembles a spouse who deserted the family, he may be blamed for the spouse's failures and abused accordingly.

ADULT ABUSE

Spouses, disabled persons, and elderly parents or relatives are the most common victims of adult abuse.

The abused spouse in many cases suffers from lack of self-esteem. An abused spouse's parents may have abused each other, or one parent may have abused the other. Having witnessed these attacks as a child, the present-day abused spouse accepts that she too will be abused. By behaving passively, spouses make it easy for their partners to abuse them repeatedly without fear of retaliation.

Like children, adults can become abuse victims if they're viewed as too dependent, too sickly, or too much like a hated person. Ill or elderly persons who make financial, emotional, or personal demands in many cases will end up injured when the stress they create becomes intolerable for their abusers. (See *Elder abuse,* page 210.)

Among abusers of adults, men who abuse women predominate, but sometimes the opposite happens. Abused

LEGAL TIP **Responding to suspected child abuse**

Suppose you're on duty in the emergency department when Mrs. Firth comes in with her son Billy, age 4. She tells you, "Billy was riding in a friend's car and they had an accident. I didn't think he was hurt at first, but later on his knee swelled up. I decided I'd better have a doctor look at it."

You examine Billy closely for head and neck injuries. You don't see any, but you do notice some bruises on his left arm and on his legs that look several weeks old. You question Mrs. Firth about the accident, but she offers few details. Then, when you ask her about Billy's injuries, she gets defensive. Although his injuries look painful, Billy sits quietly while you examine him.

How to respond

You suspect Billy has been abused. What should you do next? Follow these guidelines:
◆ Tell the physician your reasons for suspecting child abuse and ask him to order a total-body X-ray, especially if you detect multiple old and new fractures or suspicious-for-age fractures. Also, inform your supervisor of the situation.

◆ If you suspect the child has been forced to ingest drugs or alcohol, get an order for toxicology studies of the child's blood and urine.
◆ Document the location, size, and appearance of all bruises and wounds (old or fresh) on an intake form with a body profile, making sure to sign and date it. Pictures may be taken, but proper identification of the patient, date, and time needs to be included in the photograph.
◆ If the child is severely bruised, get an order for a blood coagulation profile.
◆ If X-rays or other studies suggest the child has been abused, talk with the physician about confronting the parents. Ask how you might help him do this.
◆ If a parent admits to abusing the child and appears to want help, give the address and telephone number of a local group, such as a local chapter of Parents Anonymous, and encourage the parent to call.
◆ Whether or not the parent admits to abusing the child, report all suspected abuse to the state-designated agency empowered to investigate the situation. Keep in mind that in many states, failure to report suspected abuse is a crime.

men, married or not, in most cases show the same low self-esteem and passivity as abused women. Sometimes an abused man is the less aggressive and more subservient member of the relationship and accepts a certain level of abuse in the hope that it won't get worse. At other times, he may be so ashamed by his inability to provide adequately that he invites abuse to give himself a feeling of atonement.

Also be aware that abuse occurs in same-sex relationships, but the abused person may fail to report it out of fear of homophobia.

ABUSE AND THE LAW

In 1874, grossly battered "Mary Ellen," age 9, was found chained to her bed in a New York City tenement. Etta Wheeler, a church worker, tried to find help for Mary Ellen, but she quickly discovered that New York had no laws to protect children. Her only recourse was the American Society for the Prevention of Cruelty to Animals, which agreed to intervene on Mary Ellen's behalf.

One year after Mary Ellen's case reached the courts, New York state adopted the country's first child-

Elder abuse

Elder abuse has reached alarming proportions, having increased 150% between 1986 and 1996. Estimates range from 700,000 to 2 million annual cases of mistreatment in the United States alone. A study by the Administration on Aging and the Administration for Children and Families estimates that more than 500,000 older persons in domestic settings were abused or neglected during 1996 and that for every reported incident, about five went unreported.

The greater an elderly person's disabilities, the more vulnerable he is to abuse or neglect by caregivers – usually his relatives. Family members provide about 80% of all care given to older people, and about 85% of all reported abuse involves a family member's behavior.

Defining abuse and neglect

Nearly every state has laws mandating that suspected elder abuse be reported to the authorities. However, not all states define elder abuse. Instead, they leave its diagnosis to health care professionals. One definition of abuse and neglect goes as follows:

◆ *Elder abuse* is destructive behavior that's directed at an older adult, carried out in a context or relationship of trust, and occurring intensely or frequently enough to produce harmful physical, psychological, social, or financial suffering and a decreased quality of life.

◆ *Elder neglect* is harm caused by failure to provide prudently adequate and reasonable assistance to meet the elderly person's basic physical, psychological, social, and financial needs.

Detecting abuse

As a nurse – especially if you're in an outpatient or acute care setting – you have more contact with patients than most other members of the health care team. You may be the first to notice or suspect mistreatment of an elderly patient. In fact, in hospitals with special Elder Assessment Teams, most abuse referrals are generated by nurses – especially those in the emergency department. If you suspect elder abuse, report it according to hospital or agency policy or as mandated by state law.

Signs and symptoms

Detecting abuse in a frail, elderly person with multiple health problems can challenge your assessment skills. A situation or condition that suggests mistreatment may actually represent the progression of disease. For example, you may suspect that an elderly woman covered with bruises is battered when in fact she has a coagulation disorder caused by the medication she takes for heart disease.

The following signs and symptoms, though not definitive for abuse, call for further investigation and reporting:

◆ unexplained bruises, fractures, or burns
◆ poor hygiene or nutritional status
◆ pressure ulcers or other evidence of skin breakdown or infection
◆ dehydration
◆ fear of a family member or a caregiver
◆ indications of overmedication or undermedication, such as grogginess or decreased level of consciousness
◆ unusual listlessness or withdrawal
◆ signs and symptoms of sexually transmitted disease.

protection legislation. This gave child-protection agencies a legal base, and it proved a breakthrough for other disadvantaged groups as well.

Since then, child abuse has gained increasing attention from the public, from legislators, and from concerned health care professionals. In 1946, for example, radiologists reported that subdural hematomas and abnormal X-ray findings in the long bones were commonly associated with early childhood traumatic injuries. In 1961, an American Academy of Pediatrics symposium on child abuse introduced the term "battered child."

The first statutes requiring mandatory reporting of child abuse resulted from a 1963 report by the Children's Bureau of the U.S. Department of Health, Education, and Welfare (now the Department of Health and Human Services). Most states, using the model in the report, developed protective legislation by the early 1970s. Unfortunately, the diversity of these laws made uniform interpretation impossible.

To help remedy this, Congress passed the Child Abuse Prevention and Treatment Act in 1973. This act requires states to meet certain uniform standards to be eligible for federal assistance in setting up programs to identify, prevent, and treat the problems caused by child abuse. The act also established a national center on child abuse and child neglect.

The act was amended in 1984 in response to "Baby Doe" cases. These cases involved parents who refused lifesaving treatment for mentally and physically handicapped infants. The amendments require the states to respond to reports of a child's medical neglect. States must respond to reports that medically indicated treatment (including appropriate nutrition, hydration, and medication) has been withheld from an infant. The law allows three exceptions under which treatment may be withheld:
◆ when the infant is chronically ill and irreversibly comatose
◆ when treatment would only prolong dying
◆ when treatment itself would be inhumane and futile in terms of survival.

According to interpretive guidelines to the regulations (which don't have the force of law), even when one of these exceptions is present, the infant must still receive appropriate nutrition, hydration, and medication.

State law
Two common features characterize most state child abuse legislation:
◆ empowering of a social welfare or law enforcement bureau to receive and investigate reports of actual or suspected abuse
◆ granting of legal immunity from liability, for defamation or invasion of privacy, to a person reporting an incident of actual or suspected abuse.

Laws protecting abused spouses are still being written. Although many domestic relations laws exist, additional legislation is required to help protect victims of domestic violence.

YOUR LEGAL DUTY TO REPORT ABUSE
As a nurse, you play a crucial role in recognizing and reporting incidents of suspected abuse. While caring for patients, you can readily note evidence of apparent abuse. When you do, you must pass the information along to the appropriate authorities. In many states, failure to report actual or suspected abuse constitutes a crime.

Protection from liability
If you've ever hesitated to file an abuse report because you fear repercussions, remember that the Child Abuse Prevention and Treatment Act protects you against liability. If your report is bona fide (that is, if you file it in good faith), the law will protect you from a suit filed by an alleged abuser.

FILING A REPORT

Make your report as complete and accurate as possible. Be careful not to let your personal feelings affect either the way you make out a report or your decision to file the report.

Abuse cases can raise many difficult emotional issues. Remember, however, that not filing a report can have more serious consequences than filing one that contains an unintentional error. It's better to risk error than to risk breaching the child abuse reporting laws — and, in effect, perpetuating the abuse.

RECOGNIZING ABUSE

Learn to recognize the events that trigger abuse and the signs and symptoms that mark the abused and the abuser. Early in your relationship with an abused patient, you'll need to be adept to spot the subtle behavioral and interactional clues that signal an abusive situation.

Examine the patient's relationship with the suspected abuser. For example, abused people tend to be passive and fearful. An abused child usually fails to protest if his parent is asked to leave the examining area. An abused adult, on the other hand, usually wants his abuser to stay with him.

Abused persons may react to procedures by crying helplessly and incessantly. They tend to be wary of physical contacts, including physical examinations.

Many facilities have a policy, procedure, or protocol that establishes criteria to help nurses and other health care providers make observations that will help identify possible victims of abuse. Learning these criteria will make spotting victims of abuse more objective and prevent cases from going unrecognized.

Assessing the abuser

Sometimes the abuser will appear overly agitated when dealing with health care personnel; for example, he'll get impatient if they don't carry out procedures instantly. At other times, he may exhibit the opposite behavior: a total lack of interest in the patient's problems.

Patient history

When you take an abuse victim's history, he may be vague about how he was injured and tell different stories to different people. When you ask directly about specific injuries, he may answer evasively or not at all. Sometimes he'll minimize or try to hide his injuries.

Physical examination

Look for characteristic signs of abuse. In most cases of abuse, you'll find old bruises, scars, or deformities the patient can't or won't explain. X-ray examinations may show the presence of many old fractures.

Documenting abuse

Always document your findings objectively; try to keep your emotions out of your charting. One way to do this is to use the SOAP technique, which calls for these steps:
◆ In the subjective (S) part of the note, record information in the patient's own words.
◆ In the objective (O) part, record your personal observations.
◆ Under assessment (A), record your evaluations and conclusions.
◆ Under plan (P), list sources of hospital and community support available to the patient after discharge.

OFFERING SUPPORT SERVICES

Many support services have become available for both abusers and their victims. For example, if a female victim is afraid to return to the scene of her abuse, she may find temporary housing in a women's shelter. If no such shelter is available, she may be able to stay with a friend or family member.

Social workers or community liaison workers may also be able to offer suggestions for shelter. Another possibility is a church, synagogue, or mosque, which may have members willing to take the patient in. If no shelter can be found, the patient may have to stay at the hospital for her safety.

Alert the patient to state, county, or city agencies that can offer protection. The police department should be called to collect evidence if the patient wants to press charges against the abuser. If the patient is a child, the law will probably require filing a report with a government family-service agency.

Help for the abuser

You need to evaluate the abuser's ability to handle stress. He'll probably pose a continued threat to others until he gets help in understanding his behavior and how to change it. In such a situation, you may attempt to refer him to an appropriate local or state agency that can offer help.

For abusive fathers or mothers, a local chapter of Parents Anonymous (PA) may be helpful. (See *Help for the abused and the abuser.*) PA, a self-help group made up of former abusers, attempts to help abusing parents by teaching them how to deal with their anger.

Besides helping short-circuit abusive behavior, a self-help group takes abusing parents out of their isolation and introduces them to individuals who can empathize with their feelings. It also provides help in a crisis, when members may be able to prevent an abusive incident.

Telephone hot lines to crisis intervention services also give abusers

---

Help for the abused and the abuser

These organizations offer support and counseling for the abuse victim and the abuser. Also, check the "Guide to Human Services" section of your phone directory under "Abuse" and "Child & Youth" for local or state agencies.

Childhelp USA
1-800-4-A-CHILD
www.childhelpusa.org

National Court Appointed Special Advocate Association
1-800-628-3233
www.nationalcasa.org

National Domestic Violence Hotline
1-800-799-SAFE
www.ndvh.org

National Sexual Assault Coalition Resource Sharing Project
(319) 339-0899
www.resourcesharingproject.org

Rape, Abuse and Incest National Network
1-800-656-HOPE
www.rainm.org

---

someone to talk with in times of stress and crisis and may help prevent abuse. Typically staffed by volunteers, telephone hot lines provide a link between those who seek help and trained counselors.

These and other kinds of help are also available through family-service agencies and hospitals. By becoming familiar with national and local resources, you'll be able to respond quickly and authoritatively when an abuser or his victim needs your help.

TEACHING THE PUBLIC

Besides your duty to report abuse, you also have the opportunity to teach the public about abuse. The Child Abuse Prevention and Treatment Act encourages health care facilities to develop programs to identify, report, and ultimately prevent abuse. You can help reduce the incidence of abuse by teaching people about its signs and symptoms, diagnosis, and treatment, not just in the workplace, but in health fairs, at school presentations, or other interactions with the public.

Caring for a mentally ill or developmentally disabled patient

Despite his usually dependent condition, a mentally ill or developmentally disabled patient has most of the same rights as other members of society. In fact, usually the law covers such a patient's rights in extra detail to ensure that he receives proper care and treatment. If you violate these rights, even unwittingly, you could face serious legal complications.

Much of today's concern for the rights of the mentally ill and developmentally disabled stems from attempts to correct past abuses. Under the U.S. Constitution, a person's rights can't be limited or denied merely because of his mental status. Many health care professionals still don't realize that the courts have generally interpreted the Constitution to mean that mentally ill and developmentally disabled persons have a right to fair and humane treatment, including during hospitalization.

Under most circumstances, such a patient can't be kept in a hospital against his will, for example. Nor can he be denied the right to refuse treatment or to receive information, so he can give informed consent to proposed surgery.

GOVERNMENT ACTION

State governments have tried to ensure the rights of this special population by enacting legislation specifically addressing the problems of the mentally ill and developmentally disabled. This legislation describes and authorizes specific services and provides the necessary funding.

The federal government also provides for the mentally ill and developmentally disabled. The Rehabilitation Act of 1973, for example, earmarked funds specifically for rehabilitative programs. It provides cash assistance for persons who, because of their disabilities, aren't able to provide adequately for themselves or their families. The act also outlines 14 patient's rights to ensure high standards of health care. Facilities that participate in Medicare must comply with these 14 rights and make sure that the patient, his guardian, next of kin, or sponsoring agency knows about them, too.

The Americans with Disabilities Act of 1990 (P.L. 101-336) further ensures a disabled citizen's rights by providing a "national mandate for the elimination of discrimination against individuals with disabilities." This act addresses discrimination in employment, public accommodations, and public services, programs, and activities.

Canada makes similar provisions for mentally ill and developmentally disabled persons. As in the United States, Canadian legislation seeks to prevent maltreatment and to fund programs that help these persons to function successfully in society.

ESTABLISHING LEGAL RESPONSIBILITY

When a mentally ill or developmentally disabled child is admitted to a hospital, legal responsibility for him must be established immediately. If a parent accompanies the patient, usually the parent will be legally responsible.

If the child has been institutionalized before entering the hospital, the institution may have responsibility. However, this is true only if the parents have waived responsibility and the institution has written evidence to prove it.

If the courts have found the parents unfit or unable to care for the child, a legal guardian will have been appointed. This person has the legal right to assume responsibility for the child.

When no guardian has been appointed for the child, the state may act as a guardian under the doctrine of *parens patriae*. This doctrine also applies to mentally ill or developmentally disabled adults, who must have guardians.

Adult guardianship

If your mentally ill or developmentally disabled patient is an adult, check his chart to see if he requires a legal guardian and to establish whom it is. It may be a parent. Or if the patient is married, it may be the patient's spouse.

Sometimes an adult patient and his guardian will seriously disagree about the patient's care. When this happens, get clarification by going through proper hospital channels.

Remember, you have no right to control the life of a mentally ill or developmentally disabled patient. Restricting his liberty for any reason is almost never legally permissible, except when he may otherwise harm himself or others. You must analyze each situation carefully to determine at what point the patient needs help in making health care decisions.

OBTAINING INFORMED CONSENT

When consent is required from a patient who's mentally ill or developmentally disabled, consider the following three questions:
◆ Can consent for treatment or a special procedure be obtained the same way it is from any other patient?
◆ Does the patient fully understand the procedure that he's to undergo, including the risks and alternatives?
◆ Does the patient have the authority to give his own consent, or must someone else give it?

The answers to these questions will vary with each patient. Clearly, if the patient is of unsound mind and can't understand the nature, purpose, alternatives, and risks of the proposed treatment, he can't legally consent. In such a case, consent must be obtained from the patient's legal guardian.

If the legal guardian is unavailable, a court authorized to handle such matters may authorize treatment.

Questioning a patient's ability to give consent

Sometimes a physician or nurse may doubt a patient's capacity to consent, even though he hasn't been judged incompetent. This commonly happens during an illness that causes temporary mental incompetence. In such a situation, you must follow your state laws to determine who can make health care decisions for the patient. Typically, the nearest relative's consent is often obtained or, if none can be found, the court must authorize treatment.

In the *New York case of Collins v. Davis* (1964), a hospital administrator sought a court order to permit surgery on an irrational adult whose life was considered to be in danger. The patient's wife had previously refused to give consent, allegedly for reasons she felt served the patient's best interest. The court, after considering the entire situation — especially the patient's prognosis if surgery wasn't performed — agreed that the hospital and the physician had only two choices: either let the patient die, or perform the operation against his wife's wishes. The court overruled the wife's refusal, holding that the patient had sought medical attention and that treatment normally given to a patient with a similar condition should be provided.

Nurse's role

You can best protect the mentally ill or developmentally disabled patient's legal rights to informed consent by making sure that a physician has provided him or his guardian with information. Find out if the patient's and guardian's questions have been answered to their satisfaction.

Unless your absence would place the patient in danger, you should refuse to assist with procedures on a patient whose informed consent hasn't been obtained. If you do participate, you can be held liable along with the physician and the hospital. In fact, if your patient is a minor, you could face double liability: his parents could sue you now, and he could sue you when he comes of age.

FORCED HOSPITALIZATION AND USE OF RESTRAINTS

Mentally ill or developmentally disabled persons may be involuntarily kept in hospitals if they're at risk of taking their own lives or if they pose a threat to other persons' property or lives. However, mental illness alone isn't a sufficient legal basis for detaining a patient.

Similar restrictions apply to physical restraint of patients. Most states require a physician to write the restraint order and place it in the patient's medical record before applying restraints.

Restraint (or seclusion) may be used only to prevent a patient from seriously injuring himself or others — and only when all other physical and psychological therapies would likely fail to prevent such injuries. Whenever possible, use minimal restraint — only that amount necessary to protect the patient and safeguard the staff and others. Restraint should never be used for punishment, for the convenience of staff, or as a substitute for treatment programs. Use of restraints is usually limited to a specific period. (See *Caring for a patient in restraints or seclusion*.)

If you make a decision to apply restraints, you should immediately request that a physician examine the patient and write an order to restrain him. In an emergency situation — such as a violent outburst with actual or potential harm to persons or property — a person may apply restraints to the patient. However, obtain an order for the restraint as soon as possible, and document the incident carefully.

Potential liability

As a nurse, you may be held liable in a lawsuit if you can't verify that — in your judgment — a patient needed to be restrained and that he was restrained only as long as necessary. If you restrain or seclude a patient simply for shouting obscenities, for example, you risk a lawsuit for false imprisonment.

Caring for a patient in restraints or seclusion

Before you can keep a patient in restraints or in seclusion, you must get an order from the patient's physician authorizing it. The Joint Commission on Accreditation of Healthcare Organizations (JCAHO) standards are specific regarding restraint and seclusion.

Guidelines

JCAHO requires that before restraints or seclusion are used:
◆ documentation shows that such interventions are clinically justified
◆ less restrictive interventions have been attempted
◆ the patient's current condition is considered.

Orders are to be time-limited and written for a specific episode, with start and end times, rather than for an unspecified time in the future. Established policy should specify the maximum length of time that each intervention may be used.

In an emergency, specially trained staff may initiate the use of restraints or seclusion and obtain the physician's order within a specified time (as established by the facility's policy).

Care requirements

When you're caring for a patient in restraints or seclusion, periodic monitoring and observation is essential (as required by your facility's policy).

For patients who require frequent or prolonged restraint or seclusion, the treatment team should meet to consider alternatives and changes in the care plan. Generally, 72 hours of continuous restraint or more than four episodes in 7 days is considered prolonged or frequent.

Document such items as the patient's hydration, feeding, toileting, and range of motion and condition of limbs. The facility should have policies or procedures for addressing these concerns; they should be followed and documented accurately.

You should also be sure you know how to use restraining devices safely and effectively. You may be held liable if your restraints don't prove effective and the patient is injured as a result. (See *Use of restraints and nursing liability,* page 218.)

If a competent patient makes an informed decision to refuse restraint, the facility may require the patient to sign a release that would absolve the facility of liability should injury result from the patient's refusal to be restrained.

How to apply restraints

When applying restraints, follow these guidelines:

◆ Restraint is a form of imprisonment, so it should only be used as a last resort. Before restraining a patient, consider alternatives, such as constant observation or walking with the patient.
◆ Take care to avoid undue force; otherwise, you may invite a lawsuit for battery. Even threatening to use force may be sufficient cause for legal action.
◆ When a physician isn't immediately available, you're responsible to see that restraints and seclusion are used only to the extent necessary to prevent injury. Make sure the staff contacts the physician as soon as possible.

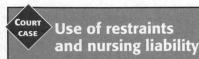

Use of restraints and nursing liability

COURT CASE

Improperly restraining a patient can leave the nurse vulnerable to a host of legal charges, such as negligence, professional malpractice, false imprisonment, and battery. This case provides an example of nurses who failed to use restraints effectively.

The patient who escaped

In *Rohde v. Lawrence General Hospital* (1993), police brought the patient into the hospital at 1 a.m. following an auto accident. The patient assaulted a clinician in the emergency department (ED) and was diagnosed as having an "acute psychotic episode." The physician ordered leather restraints.

Around 6 a.m., the patient escaped from four-point restraints, went into the parking lot, found a car that had been left running, and drove off. He crashed the car and was seriously injured.

The patient sued the hospital, the ED physician, and two nurses for medical malpractice, claiming that the staff didn't supervise him properly and that his restraints weren't securely fastened.

◆ Most states follow the *least restrictive principle,* which holds that no more restraint should be used than necessary. For example, a restraining vest shouldn't be used when simple wrist restraints will suffice.

◆ To avoid allegations of false imprisonment, document carefully the decision-making process that led to the use of restraints, and review the continuing need for restraints on a regular basis.

◆ Bedside rails are a form of restraint, and shouldn't be raised indiscriminately. The patient's age alone isn't a justification for raising the side rails.

◆ Tranquilizing drugs may provide an alternative to restraints. However, use them sparingly, with caution, and only with a physician's order. The patient's right to the least restrictive treatment or to an open-door policy that allows patients to move about "freely" means little if accompanied by indiscriminate drug use as a substitute for restraints.

RIGHT TO PRIVACY

The law has tried to protect all citizens from unwarranted intrusion into their private lives. Unfortunately, mentally ill and developmentally disabled patients' rights to privacy are easily violated. A good definition of privacy, first presented at the International Commission of Justice in 1970, reads: "Privacy is the ability to lead one's life without anyone:

◆ interfering with family or home life
◆ interfering with physical or mental integrity or moral and intellectual freedom
◆ attacking honor and reputation
◆ placing one in a false light
◆ censoring or restricting communication and correspondence, written or oral
◆ disclosing irrelevant or embarrassing information
◆ disclosing information given or received in circumstances of professional confidence."

Keep this definition in mind as you work with mentally ill and developmentally disabled patients, and do all you can to protect their right to privacy.

RIGHT TO WRIT OF *HABEAS CORPUS*

Institutionalization may, at times, breach a patient's rights, giving him cause to petition for a writ of *habeas corpus*. This writ seeks to ensure the timely release of a person who claims that he's being detained illegally and deprived of his liberty.

RIGHT TO TREATMENT

In *Wyatt v. Stickney* (1972), the court upheld the legal right of a mentally ill person hospitalized in a public institution to receive adequate psychiatric treatment. This decision suggests that when a patient is involuntarily committed because he needs treatment, his rights are violated if he doesn't receive proper care. Furthermore, if the underlying reason for a patient's commitment is that he's dangerous to himself or others, treatment must be provided to make him less so.

In the Wyatt decision, the court outlined a complete bill of rights for the mentally ill patient. Among the key points, the court said treatment should be given:

◆ by adequate staff
◆ in the least restrictive setting
◆ in privacy
◆ in a facility that ensures the patient a comfortable bed, adequate diet, and recreational facilities
◆ with the patient's informed consent before unusual treatment
◆ with payment for work done in the facility, outside of program activities
◆ according to an individual treatment plan.

If possible, ensure that a mentally ill or developmentally disabled patient knows what treatment he needs and how he'll get it. You must know what his major problems are and what he can do for himself—or what others must do for him—to help him get ready for discharge. You should also involve him in formulating his treatment plan, unless you have a documented reason why he can't or won't be involved.

SEXUAL RIGHTS

Many questions remain regarding the sexual rights of mentally ill and developmentally disabled patients. For example, should developmentally disabled persons be given sex education? Should they be allowed to reproduce, practice contraception, or undergo voluntary sterilization? Although the general inclination is to let guardians make these decisions, the issue of the individual's right to make his own decisions won't go away. If good care can be given to both the developmentally disabled and their offspring, who's to say that they should be denied the opportunity to enjoy the same satisfactions others do?

The U.S. Supreme Court has upheld the rights of mentally ill or developmentally disabled patients:

◆ to marry
◆ to have children
◆ to employ contraception, abortion, or sterilization, if desired
◆ to follow a lifestyle of their own choosing.

Several cases, such as *Sengstack v. Sengstack* (1958), *Wyatt v. Stickney* (1972), and *O'Connor v. Donaldson* (1975), have used the U.S. Supreme Court decisions as a basis for their rulings.

Involuntary sterilization

Involuntary sterilization of developmentally disabled patients isn't employed today as in the past. Although the U.S. Supreme Court upheld the constitutionality of involuntary sterilization in *Buck v. Bell* (1927), if a similar case were to come before the Supreme Court today, the precedent would likely be overturned.

In *Buck v. Bell,* the court held that the state has the right to sterilize a developmentally disabled or mentally ill person provided that:
◆ the sterilization isn't prescribed as punishment
◆ the policy is applied equally to all
◆ a potential child's interest is sufficient to warrant the sterilization.

Courts today can authorize such a procedure but only within specific guidelines. Generally, it must be shown that sterilization is the only workable means of contraception. In some cases, the court orders a separate, independent presterilization review of the case. (In New York state, unlike California, for example, an independent medical review board must review and approve every planned involuntary sterilization before it can be performed.) Even though the patient's guardian has requested sterilization, if the patient refuses to submit to surgery, the court may call for use of a less permanent birth control method.

PARTICIPATION IN RESEARCH

Another troublesome area involves using mentally ill and developmentally disabled persons as subjects for medical or other research — especially if risks are involved. Guidelines for consent to experimentation and drastic, questionable, or extreme forms of treatment are complicated and raise many unresolved questions. The so-called Willowbrook decision, *N. Y. State Association for Retarded Children, Inc. v. Carey* (1977), however, decreed that both voluntary and involuntary residents of a mental health facility have the constitutional right to be protected from harm. The proper authority (usually an institu-

tional review board) should allow the patient to participate in the research only if it's relevant to his needs and the needs of others like him and its potential benefits outweigh its potential risks. For example, a depressed patient shouldn't be asked to participate in research involving anxiety and schizophrenia.

Strict federal regulations guide how experimental treatment can be carried out. Such treatment must be given with extreme caution to mentally ill or developmentally disabled patients.

RESPONDING TO PATIENT REQUESTS

"Ordinary" requests made by mentally ill or developmentally disabled patients may require special consideration.

For example, a patient may demand to smoke a cigarette. His physician hasn't written an order for the request. If the patient should smoke only under supervision because of the danger of fire, you may decide to stay with him while he does so. If you have a duty to be elsewhere, you should refuse his request, explaining why and telling him when he'll be able to smoke. If you know a refusal will agitate and anger him, you can also ask another nurse to supervise the patient while he smokes.

Perhaps the patient is well aware that he's violating the hospital's no-smoking policy and his request is really a challenge to authority. If so, you may decide to refuse the request, explaining the need to follow the hospital's social and safety policies.

If the patient's behavior is part of a pattern that includes, for example, refusing to shower, refusing to go to bed by a certain time, and demanding to make an immediate phone call, then you need to refer the situation to the treatment team for a well-thought-out decision — one that serves the best interests of both the patient and the hospital. Once it's made, ask all the health team members to enforce this decision consistently.

Caring for a suspected criminal

Suppose you're asked to care for an injured suspect who's accompanied by police. Because the police need evidence, they ask you to give them the patient's belongings and also a sample of his blood. Should you comply? The answer to this question isn't simple. If you're ignorant of the law and fail to follow proper protocol, the evidence you turn over to police may not be admissible in court. Worse still, later on, the patient may be able to sue you for invasion of privacy.

CONSTITUTIONAL RIGHTS

The Fourth Amendment to the U.S. Constitution provides that "the right of the people to be secure in their persons, houses, papers and effects, against unreasonable searches and seizures shall not be violated, and no warrants shall issue, but upon probable cause." This means that every individual, even a suspected criminal, has a right to privacy, including a right to be free from intrusions that are made without search warrants. However, the Fourth Amendment doesn't absolutely prohibit all searches and seizures, only unreasonable ones.

Further, under constitutional law, when a magistrate issues a warrant authorizing a police officer to conduct a search, the warrant must be specific about the places to be searched and the items to be seized.

Probably the exclusionary rule is the most common rule affecting nurses in relation to suspected criminals and their victims. This rule stems from the Fourth Amendment's prohibition of unreasonable searches and seizures. In the landmark case of *Mapp v. Ohio* (1961), the U.S. Supreme Court held that evidence obtained through an unreasonable or unlawful search can't be used against the person whose rights the search violated.

Searches without a warrant

Under certain circumstances, a police officer may lawfully conduct a search and obtain evidence without a warrant:

◆ If an accused person consents to a search, any evidence found is considered admissible in court (*Schneckloth v. Bustamonte* [1973]).

◆ A search incidental to an arrest may be conducted without a warrant. Usually, such a search shouldn't extend beyond the accused person's body or an immediate area where he could reach for a weapon. However, in *Maryland v. Buie* (1990), the U.S. Supreme Court ruled that a search incidental to an arrest could extend to adjoining rooms and closets of a private residence from which an accomplice could attack. Police may even conduct a sweep of an entire area if they have reason to think they may be in danger. Although this Supreme Court case dealt with searches in a private home, the ruling could apply to searches conducted in a hospital.

◆ Police may search an area, even out of arm's reach, to recover a weapon that could pose a threat to their safety (*New York v. Class* [1985]).

◆ Police may enter a private area and seize items in plain view if they're in "hot pursuit" of a criminal suspect (*Warden v. Hayden* [1967]).

Evidence obtained as part of a blood test

Opinions differ as to whether a blood test, such as a blood alcohol test, is admissible in court if the person refused consent for the test. In *Schmerber v. California* (1966), the U.S. Supreme Court said that a blood extraction obtained without a warrant, incidental to a lawful arrest, isn't an unconstitutional search and seizure and is admissible evidence. Many courts have held this to mean that a blood sample must be drawn *after* the arrest to be admissible.

Further, the blood sample must be drawn in a medically reasonable manner. In *People v. Kraft* (1970), a suspect was pinned to the floor by two police officers while a physician drew a blood sample. In *State v. Riggins* (1977), a suspect's broken arm was twisted while a policeman sat on him to force consent to a blood test. In both cases, the courts ruled the test results inadmissible. The courts have also ruled as inadmissible — and as violative of due process rights — evidence gained by the forcible and unconsented insertion of a nasogastric tube into a suspect to remove stomach contents (*Rochin v. California* [1952]).

Courts have admitted blood tests as evidence when the tests weren't drawn at police request but for medically necessary purposes such as blood typing (*Commonwealth v. Gordon* [1968]). Some courts have also allowed blood work to be admitted as evidence when it was drawn for nontherapeutic reasons and voluntarily turned over to police.

Be careful, though. A physician or nurse who does blood work without the patient's consent may be liable for committing battery, even if the patient is a suspected criminal and the blood work is medically necessary.

Blood alcohol tests and drunk driving arrests

Many states have enacted so-called implied consent laws as part of their motor vehicle laws. These laws hold that by applying for a driver's license, a person implies his consent to submit to a blood alcohol test if he's arrested for drunken driving. Many of these laws state specifically that if an individual refuses to submit to the chemical test, it may not be given, but the driver then forfeits his license. Check to see whether such laws exist in your state.

Evidence obtained during a surgical procedure

A Massachusetts case, *Commonwealth v. Storella* (1978), involved a bullet that a physician removed during a medically necessary operation. After the operation, the physician turned the bullet over to the police. The court allowed the bullet to be admitted as evidence because the physician was acting according to good medical practice, and not as a state agent, in removing the bullet.

In 1985, the U.S. Supreme Court ruled that the constitutionality of such court-ordered surgery to acquire evidence must be decided on a case-by-case basis. The interest in individual privacy and security must be weighed against the societal interest in collecting evidence. Therefore, you should be wary if asked to assist in a highly invasive procedure to help the state obtain evidence if the suspect doesn't consent. If necessary, consult an attorney.

Swallowed contraband

Drug couriers have been known to carry contraband by swallowing it in small balloons, which can be recovered after elimination. As a nurse, you may become involved in efforts to detect and recover swallowed contraband. In

United States v. Montoya de Hernandez (1985), the U.S. Supreme Court ruled that the police could lawfully detain drug couriers until swallowed items could be recovered and seized.

Searches by a private party

In Burdeau v. McDowell (1921), the U.S. Supreme Court said that the Fourth Amendment protections applied only to governmental (such as police) action and not to searches conducted by private parties. Although several courts have criticized this rule, it has been repeatedly upheld.

In State v. Perea (1981), a nurse took a suspect's shirt for safekeeping, then turned it over to the police even though they hadn't requested it. A New Mexico court allowed the shirt to be admitted as evidence. The reason: Because no governmental intrusion was involved, the suspect's Fourth Amendment right wasn't violated.

The case of United States v. Winbush (1970) produced a similar result. In this case, the court ruled that evidence found during a routine search of an unconscious patient's pockets was admissible because the purpose of the search was to obtain necessary identification and medical information.

Evidence in plain view

As a nurse, if you find a gun, knife, drug, or other item that the suspect could use to harm himself or others, you have a right to remove it. You should, however, notify the administration immediately and maintain control over the evidence until you can give it to an administrator or law enforcement official.

When the suspect may sue

In general, searches that occur as part of medical care don't violate a suspect's rights. However, searches made for the sole purpose of gathering evidence — especially if done at police request — very well may. Several courts have said that a suspect subjected to an illegal private search has a right to seek remedy against the unlawful searcher in a civil lawsuit. One such case was Stone v. Commonwealth (1967). (See Conducting a drug search, page 224.)

Canadian law

The major difference between U.S. and Canadian law regarding searches is that, in Canada, evidence obtained during an illegal search may still be admissible in court. However, a police officer should have a search warrant before searching a suspected criminal to protect his rights.

A word of caution

The laws of search and seizure are complex and subject to change by new legal decisions. Consult with the administration or an attorney before complying with a police request to turn over a patient's personal property. Some state laws require that police obtain a warrant before they're legally entitled to this evidence.

DOCUMENTING YOUR ACTIONS

Be careful and precise in documenting all medical and nursing procedures when you care for a suspected criminal. Note blood work done, and list all treatments and the patient's response to them.

If you turn anything over to the police or administration, record what it was and the name of the person you gave it to. Record a suspect's statements that are directly related to his care. If a suspect says, "I shot a cop in the arm tonight," that isn't related to his care. However, if he says, "I think I

LEGAL TIP ▸ Conducting a drug search

If you suspect your patient is abusing drugs or alcohol, you have a duty to do something about it. If such a patient harms himself or anyone else, resulting in a lawsuit, the court may hold you liable for his actions.

When you know about drug abuse

Suppose you know for certain that a patient is abusing drugs – if you're an emergency department nurse, you may find drugs in a patient's clothes or handbag while looking for identification. Your hospital policy may obligate you to confiscate the drugs and take steps to ensure that the patient doesn't acquire more.

When you suspect drug abuse

When a patient's erratic or threatening behavior makes you suspect he's abusing drugs or alcohol, your hospital's policy may require that you conduct a search. Is your search legal? As a rule of thumb, if you strongly believe the patient poses a threat to himself or others and you can document your reasons for searching his possessions, you're probably safe legally.

Guidelines for searches

Before you conduct a search, review your hospital's guidelines on the matter. Then follow these guidelines carefully. Most hospital guidelines will first direct you to contact your supervisor and explain why you have legitimate cause for a search. If she gives you her approval, ask a security guard to help you. Besides protecting you, he'll serve as a witness if you do find drugs. When you're ready, confront the patient, tell him you intend to conduct a search, and tell him why.

Depending on your hospital's guidelines, you can search a patient's belongings as well as his room. If you find illegal drugs during your search, confiscate them. Depending on your hospital's guidelines, you may be obligated to report the patient to the police.

If you find alcoholic beverages during your search, hospital guidelines may require you to take them from the patient. Explain to the patient that you'll return them when he leaves the hospital.

Maintaining written records

After you've completed your search, record your findings in your nurses' notes and in an incident report. Your written records will be an important part of your defense (and your hospital's) if the patient decides to sue.

---

was shot in the leg by a cop," that relates directly to his medical care.

SAFEGUARDING EVIDENCE

Before any evidence can be admissible in court, the court must have some guarantee of where — and how — it was gathered. Someone must account for the evidence from the moment you collect it until it appears in court, a continuum known as the *chain of custody*. Evidence can't be left unattended because it might be tampered with.

If you discover evidence, use your facility's chain of custody form. First used when evidence is taken from the patient, this form should remain with the evidence until the trial. It documents the identity of each person handling the evidence as well as the date and times it was in their possession. In effect, the form should serve as an uninterrupted log of the evidence's whereabouts.

If your facility doesn't have a chain of custody form, keep a careful note as to exactly what was taken, by whom, and when. Give this information to the administrator when you deliver the evidence. Until such time as the evidence can be turned over, it should be kept in a locked area.

When a suspect dies, most states provide that the coroner can claim the body. Police are free to gather any evidence that won't mutilate the body. A dead body has no constitutional rights, so no rights are violated by a search.

NURSING BEHIND BARS

Even after conviction, an individual doesn't forfeit all constitutional rights. Among those retained is the Eighth Amendment's proscription against cruel and unusual punishment. This implies that prison officials and health care workers must not deliberately ignore a prisoner's medical needs.

The U.S. Supreme Court, in *Estelle v. Gamble* (1976), stated that the Eighth Amendment prohibits more than physically barbarous punishment. The amendment embodies "broad and idealistic concepts of dignity, civilized standards, humanity, and decency against which we must evaluate penal measures."

Right to medical care

The state has an obligation to provide medical care for those it imprisons. The Supreme Court has concluded that "deliberate indifference to serious medical needs of prisoners constitutes the unnecessary and wanton infliction of pain proscribed by the Eighth

Amendment. This is true whether the indifference is manifested by prison physicians in response to a prisoner's needs or by prison personnel in intentionally denying or delaying access to medical care or intentionally interfering with the treatment once prescribed."

In *Ramos v. Lamm* (1980), the court outlined several ways in which prison officials show deliberate indifference to prisoners' medical needs:
◆ preventing an inmate from receiving recommended treatment
◆ denying access to medical personnel capable of evaluating the need for treatment
◆ allowing repeated acts of negligence that disclose a pattern of conduct by prison health staff
◆ allowing such severe deficiencies in staffing, facilities, equipment, or procedures to exist that inmates are effectively denied access to adequate medical care.

Providing care

Working daily with prisoners is difficult and demanding, both professionally and emotionally. Along with exhibiting a host of other unpleasant behaviors, prisoners can be abusive, manipulative, and angry. In spite of this, health care professionals can't forget their ethical and legal duty to provide quality care.

Nurses working in a prison setting should be aware that the doctrine of *respondeat superior* doesn't apply to prison cases when the prisoner sues for violations of his constitutional rights. The nurse supervisor or manager can't be held responsible for accusations of "cruel and unusual punishment" unless she has personally acted to deprive the prisoner of medical care. *Vinnedge v. Gibbs* (1977).

When a prisoner refuses treatment

Several courts have stated that individuals have a constitutional right to privacy based on a high regard for human dignity and self-determination. That means any competent adult may refuse medical care, even lifesaving treatments. For instance, in *Lane v. Candura* (1978), an appellate court upheld the right of a competent adult to refuse a leg amputation that would have saved her life.

A suspected criminal may refuse unwarranted bodily invasions. However, an arrested suspect or convicted criminal doesn't have the same right to refuse lifesaving measures. In *Commissioner of Correction v. Myers* (1979), a prisoner with renal failure refused hemodialysis unless he was moved to a minimum security prison. The court disagreed, saying that although the defendant's imprisonment didn't divest him of his right to privacy or his interest in maintaining his bodily integrity, it did impose limitations on those constitutional rights.

As a practical matter, anytime a patient refuses lifesaving treatments, inform your facility's administration. In the case of a suspect or prisoner, notify law enforcement authorities as well.

Upholding a patient's living will

When a legally competent person draws up a living will, he declares the steps he wants or doesn't want taken when he's incompetent and no longer able to express his wishes. The will applies to decisions made after a patient is incompetent and has no reasonable possibility of recovery. Generally, a living will authorizes the attending physician to withhold or discontinue certain lifesaving procedures under specific circumstances.

The will is called *living* because its provisions take effect before death. By clearly stating his wishes regarding lifesaving procedures, the patient also helps relieve guilt his family and the health care team might otherwise feel for discontinuing life support.

A living will is considered a legal statement of the patient's wishes. Most states have statutes authorizing living wills and the appointment of a health care agent. The exceptions are states with legislation authorizing only the appointment of a health care agent (Massachusetts, Michigan, and New York) or authorizing only living wills (Alaska).

A patient may also choose to execute a durable power of attorney for health care. Should the patient become incompetent, this document designates a surrogate decision maker with authority to carry out the patient's wishes regarding health care decisions. Most states have laws authorizing only durable power of attorney for the purpose of initiating or terminating life-sustaining medical treatment.

CONTENT OF LIVING WILL LAWS

Living will laws usually include provisions, such as:
◆ who may execute a living will
◆ witness and testator requirements
◆ immunity from liability for following a living will's directives
◆ documentation requirements
◆ instructions on when and how the living will should be executed
◆ under what circumstances the living will takes effect.

WHEN LIVING WILLS DON'T APPLY

When the patient's condition is such that the living will isn't applicable, or in cases in which the patient hasn't executed a living will, the patient's surrogate will need to make decisions regarding the removal of life support systems and treatment.

The Supreme Court's ruling in *Cruzan v. Director, Mo. Dept. of Health* (1990) may influence future court rulings in this area. The U.S. Supreme Court held that the state of Missouri has the constitutional right to refuse termination of life-sustaining treatment unless "clear and convincing evidence" exists about a patient's wishes, implying that the patient's wishes will be honored. Because states differ on what they consider "clear and convincing evidence," consult your facility's ethics committee or attorney in cases of this type.

INTERPRETING THE WILL

A physician may also face real difficulties in determining when a living will should apply. Wording in many living wills is vague. What, for example, is a "reasonable expectation of recovery"? And what's a "heroic" or an "extraordinary" measure? When a patient actually enters a coma, it may be difficult to precisely interpret the intentions expressed in his living will. That's one reason why legislatures have been slow to make living wills binding.

States have tried to relieve patients and families from the burden of judicial involvement in medical decisions, encouraging decision making by the patient, family, and physician. Unfortunately, the more latitude provided for decision makers, the less protection for the patient. For instance, the original Illinois Health Care Surrogate Act,

effective January 1, 1998, expanded the boundaries of surrogate decision-making legislation to include general medical decisions, permitting the patient to remain uninformed about his loss of decision-making status and subsequent decisions. It's important to note that the Act applies to those who lack a living will or a chosen health care agent as well as to those with a living will that doesn't address the specific condition of the patient. This Act would allow a surrogate decision maker to refuse an abortion for a pregnant minor, for instance. The surrogate decision maker, a close family member, could be an abusive spouse, a child abuser, or another person that the patient would deem unacceptable, if he were informed. Because of the uncertainty in the judicial system today, it's important that a patient clearly state in his living will exactly what medical treatments he'd choose to receive and which he'd forgo to ensure that his wishes are honored.

Patients should be encouraged to review their living wills with their families and physicians, so that unclear areas can be discussed. Living wills also need to be reviewed periodically to keep pace with changes in technology. Some living wills are detailed, multi-page documents; some, a simple paragraph.

Immunity

If physicians, nurses, and other health care providers follow the wishes expressed in a living will authorized by law, they're generally immune from civil and criminal liability. No matter which state you work in, check your facility's policy and procedures manual and seek advice from the legal department as needed.

CHILDREN AND LIVING WILLS

Although minors can't make valid testamentary wills, and adults can't make such wills for them, living wills are another matter. In a few states, adults are authorized to make living wills for their minor children.

Parents don't normally plan for their child to die, so most are unlikely to make a living will before a child's terminal illness is diagnosed. Even then, a living will is usually legally unnecessary. If the parents and the child agree that no extraordinary means should be used to prolong life, or if the child is too young to understand, the parents have the legal right to act for the child. They can require that the health care team not use extraordinary means to prolong his life. The same principle also applies in reverse: if the child wants to die but his parents want him treated, the parents' wishes prevail.

If a terminally ill adolescent doesn't want extraordinary treatment but his parents do, and the adolescent has written a living will, a physician or health care facility may use the will to petition a court on his behalf. Even though the will itself is legally invalid because it was written by a minor, its existence may prompt the court to consult the adolescent and, in its ruling, grant the patient his wishes.

LIVING WILL FROM ANOTHER STATE OR COUNTRY

U.S. law applies to foreign citizens treated in the United States. That means a foreign citizen may execute a living will while in the United States, and it must be honored if executed in a state with a living will law.

What if a patient produces a living will executed in a foreign country? What about a patient who executes a living will in one state and later finds himself terminally ill in another state? The law of the state where the living will decision will be carried out prevails. Therefore, if a patient has an out-of-state living will, you should determine whether it matches the criteria required by the laws of the state you're in. When dealing with an out-of-state living will, consult your facility's legal counsel.

The same general legal principle applies to U.S. citizens in Canada or in another foreign country. A foreign country's law applies to all persons, whether citizens of that country or not, and determines the extent to which a living will be honored. Check with your facility's attorney.

WHEN A LIVING WILL BECOMES INVALID

A living will needn't be honored if it has been revoked or is out of date. State law may mandate that a living will is valid only for a limited number of years. If the patient's family and attending medical personnel find that the patient made the living will many years ago and his life circumstances have changed substantially since then, they may have legal justification for disregarding the will. For this reason, publishers of living will forms suggest reviewing the living will yearly, revising it if necessary, and redating and resigning it.

If the patient asks that the will be disregarded, or if a patient tells his physician to proceed with treatment that contradicts the will, such action effectively revokes the will.

WHEN THE FAMILY'S WISHES CONTRADICT THE WILL

The patient's family can't revoke a patient's living will unless they can prove the will is invalid. Some states provide penalties for concealing a patient's living will or for falsely reporting that it has been revoked.

DRAFTING A LIVING WILL

Like all legal documents, a living will must be written, signed, and witnessed. State laws specify the execution requirements. If the patient asks for help drafting a living will, refer him to your facility's legal department or the local legal aid agency.

Although it isn't required, a patient should be encouraged to file copies of his living will with his physician and with family members who would attend him in the event of a terminal illness.

You may be asked to witness a living will. Check to see if your state law allows this. If it doesn't, ask your nursing supervisor for the procedure you should follow.

If the patient drafts a living will while under your care, document this in your nurses' notes, describing factually the circumstances under which the will was drawn up and signed.

ORAL STATEMENTS

Patients may make oral statements expressing their wishes about further medical treatment before or during a terminal illness.

Before terminal illness

When a patient has made his treatment wishes known to his family and physician in advance, they'll usually respect his wishes even if he later becomes comatose or otherwise incompetent. If the physician and the family disagree about what's best for the terminally ill incompetent patient, they may have to settle the dispute in court.

During terminal illness

Every competent adult has the right to refuse medical treatment for himself, including the use of extraordinary means. If a competent terminally ill patient tells a physician or nurse to discontinue extraordinary efforts, his wishes are binding.

If a patient tells you his wishes about dying, first write what he says in your nurses' notes, using his exact words as much as possible. Next, describe the context of the discussion — for example, was the patient in pain, or had he just been informed of a terminal illness? Be sure you also tell the patient's physician about the discussion. Remember, *oral statements aren't legally enforceable,* although a patient's stated refusal of treatment is binding. Oral statements *should* be respected, however, as guidelines to how the patient feels about his treatment.

Dealing with living wills

Federal legislation, the Patient Self-Determination Act of 1990, requires hospitals, extended care facilities, HMOs, hospices, and home health care agencies that participate in Medicare and Medicaid to provide patients with written information about their rights under state law regarding living wills and durable power of attorney (together called *advance directives*) as well as about the facility's procedure for implementing them. The law also requires the health care facility or agency to document whether the patient has a living will or durable power of attorney.

If your patient has a living will, review your nursing or facility manual for directions on what steps to take. For instance, you may need to inform the patient's physician about it. Or you may need to ask your nursing supervisor to inform the administration and the legal affairs department. With the patient's permission, make sure that the family knows about the will; if they don't, show them a copy.

If the patient is able to talk, discuss the will with him, especially if it contains terms that need further definition. As always, objectively document your actions and findings in the patient's record.

Beyond these actions, your responsibilities for a patient's living will are determined by the circumstances involved — including the family's and physician's responses to the will. If there's conflict among the parties, work with family members and colleagues to come up with a unified care plan.

Personal conflicts over a living will

If implementing a living will conflicts with your personal ethics or beliefs, you may wish to discuss the matter with a clinical nurse specialist, your nursing supervisor, a nursing administrator, a chaplain, an administrator at your facility, or an ethics committee member. If you're still unable to accept the idea after talking over your feelings with one of them, you can ask for reassignment to another patient. Chances are your request will be honored and no disciplinary action will be taken against you.

Working as a quality management nurse

Quality management (QM) or continuous quality improvement focuses on processes of care delivery and not on individual blame. As a QM nurse, it's your job to monitor, evaluate, and correct potential quality of care issues — a complicated task, indeed. You have to make sure that your facility follows appropriate federal and state laws, complies with its own internal set of rules and regulations, and meets the accreditation requirements of various accrediting agencies, such as JCAHO and the National Committee for Quality Assurance. If you fail to perform your duties properly, you put yourself and your facility at professional and legal risk.

CONFIDENTIALITY

Confidentiality is every nurse's responsibility, but as a QM nurse, it's more than a responsibility — it's a mission. Usually, you're dealing with sensitive, privileged information. Withholding this information from friends and colleagues can be a burdensome duty, especially when you're dealing with adverse events, peer review, incident reporting, and record review for investigational purposes or focused quality improvement studies. Although various state and federal statutes for peer review afford some protection from liability, the legal realities of discovery and the absence of immunity put you at risk to testify should a lawsuit arise.

Selected references

Abraham, A. "Poor Systems and Staffing Problems Led to Poor Patient Outcomes," *Professional Nurse* 18(10):576-77, June 2003.

Baker, G.R., and Norton, P. "Making Patients Safer! Reducing Error in Canadian Healthcare," *Healthcare Paper* 2(1):10-31, 2001.

Barach, P. "The End of the Beginning: Lessons Learned from the Patient Safety Movement," *Journal of Legal Medicine* 24(1):7-27, March 2003.

Erdman, C. "The Medicolegal Dangers of Telephone Triage in Mental Health Care," *Journal of Legal Medicine* 22(4):553-79, December 2001.

Henrickson, T. "Telephone Triage and Consultation: An Emerging Role for Nurses,"

Nursing Outlook 48(2):92-93, March-April 2000.

Joint Commission on Accreditation of Healthcare Organizations. "National Patient Safety Goals." Online: *www.jcaho.org/accredited+organizations/ patient+safety/npsg/npsg.htm*

Larson-Dahn, M.L. "Tel-eNurse Practice: A Practice Model for Role Expansion," *Journal of Nursing Administration* 30(11):519-23, November 2000.

Leclerc, B.S., et al. "Recommendations for Appeal to Another Resource in a Health Case Brought by Nurses in the Info-Health Service CLSC: Convergence Between Utilization Declarations and Informants' Data," *Canadian Journal of Public Health* 94(1):74-78, January-February 2003.

Lee, T.J., et al. "Caller Satisfaction with After-hours Telephone Advice: Nurse Advice Service Versus On-call Pediatricians," *Pediatrics* 110(5):865-72, November 2002.

Liang, B.A., and Sorti, K. "Creating Problems as Part of the 'Solution': The JCAHO Sentinel Event Policy," *Journal of Health Law* 33(2):263-85, Spring 2000.

Meurier, C.E. "Understanding the Nature of Errors in Nursing: Using a Model to Analyze Critical Incident Reports of Errors Which Had Resulted in an Adverse or Potentially Adverse Event," *Journal of Advanced Nurses* 32(1):202-07, July 2000.

Pohlman, K., and Schwab, N. "Consent and Release," *Journal of School Nursing* 17(3): 162-65, June 2001.

Preston, F.A. "Telephone Triage," *Clinical Journal of Oncology Nursing* 4(6):294-96, November-December 2000.

Streger, M.R. "The Universal Truths of Writing Incident Reports," *Emergency Medical Services* 32(5):82-83, May 2003.

Chapter 7

Legal aspects of documentation

Just how important is good nursing documentation? Ask Lauren Ball, RN, a nurse at the Good Samaritan Hospital in West Islip, N.Y. In 1987, Ms. Ball failed to document in her nurses' notes that a patient, Gerolamo Kucich, reported seeing a bearded man in a white lab coat put "something" in his I.V. line. The bearded man, Richard Angelo, was subsequently convicted of assaulting Kucich and killing four others by injecting the drug pancuronium to paralyze their breathing. Ms. Ball saved Kucich's life and was a key witness in the trial against Angelo. Nevertheless, in 1991, she was charged with negligence and professional misconduct and faced possible revocation of her license and a $10,000 fine simply for failing to document the patient's observation.

Thankfully, incidents such as this are rare. Nevertheless, the fact that the state pressed charges against Ms. Ball underscores the seriousness of the nurse's responsibility to document in the eyes of the law. Nursing documentation has become increasingly scientific and complex, and its quality has taken on greater legal significance than ever before.

In this chapter, you'll learn about the legal significance of the patient's medical record—the principal tool used by the health care team to plan, coordinate, and document the care given to each patient. You'll also read about the importance of good nursing documentation, examine several court cases in which documentation quality affected the patient's outcome, and review guidelines for avoiding documentation errors. You'll find a discussion of computerized medical records and their legal implications. Finally, you'll learn about new documentation systems prompted by health care reform initiatives and the pressure to reduce costs. (See *Documentation systems.*)

Purpose of accurate documentation

The trend toward increasing specialization means that patients are being assessed, cared for, and treated by more health care professionals than ever before. Complete, accurate, and timely documentation is crucial to the continuity of each patient's care. The medical record is also a legal and business record with many uses. A well-documented medical record:

♦ reflects the patient care given
♦ demonstrates the results of treatment

Documentation systems

Properly documented, the medical record provides legal evidence that can be used to protect the patient, the health care facility, or the health care team. Here are the major record-keeping systems in use today.

Source-oriented system

Health care facilities have been using the source-oriented system since record keeping began. Under this system, each professional group kept a separate record.

This system was widely practiced until recently, with physicians charting the progress notes and nurses charting the nurses' notes. The drawback is that you must consult several sources to get an accurate picture of the patient's condition. Also, failure to consult all the individual records carries potentially serious consequences for both the patient and staff. For example, in a case from Louisiana, *Villetto v. Weilbaecher* (1979), nurses observed that a patient had developed several blisters 8 days after knee surgery. They recorded their observation in the nurses' notes and reported the problem to the physician. However, the physician didn't mention the blisters in his notes until 6 days later. The patient sued, and was awarded damages for pain and scarring; the physician was found liable for failure to treat the blisters. The nurses were found not liable because the record showed that they had met their standard of care.

Problem-oriented system

Many facilities have adopted problem-oriented records, which give a comprehensive picture of the patient's clinical status and response to therapy. All members of the health care team combine their data into a format known by the acronym **SOAP**. "S" is for subjective patient data. "O" is for objective findings on observation, assessment, and examination. "A" is for assessment of the subjective complaints and objective findings. "P" is for plan, both for present and future therapy.

For instance, if the problem is pain on ambulation, the nurse might record:
S – The patient says, "My side hurts when I walk."
O – Favoring left side, appendectomy performed 01/11/04. Approximately 2-cm erythematous area surrounding stitches.
A – Local inflammation of appendectomy stitches causing pain.
P – Report to physician. Assist when walking.

Traditional narrative format

In this approach, the nurse documents ongoing assessment data, nursing interventions, and patient responses in chronologic order. This system has several drawbacks. Writing narrative notes is time-consuming and repetitive. Also, tracking problems and trends can be difficult because you have to read the entire record to arrive at the patient outcome. Today, this system, when used, is typically combined with the source-oriented system.

FOCUS CHARTING

This technique makes patient care problems the focus of concern. A focus may be a nursing diagnosis, a sign or symptom, a patient behavior, a special need, or an acute change in the patient's condition. You identify a focus by reviewing assessment data, and then document the focus precisely by filling out a progress sheet.

PIE charting

In this system, information is grouped into three categories: **P**roblem, **I**ntervention, and **E**valuation. PIE charting integrates the care plan into the nurses' progress notes, omitting the need for a separate care plan. The nurse keeps a daily patient assessment flow sheet and progress notes.

(continued)

Documentation systems *(continued)*

Charting by exception

Gaining support in the current managed-care environment, charting by exception (CBE) requires you to document only abnormal or significant findings. It relies on written standards of practice that identify nurses' basic responsibilities to patients and protocols for interven-

tions. The CBE format includes a standardized care plan based on nursing diagnoses, as well as several types of flow sheets, which let you easily track trends.

The chart below compares the advantages and disadvantages of focus charting, PIE charting, and CBE.

SYSTEM AND ADVANTAGES	DISADVANTAGES
FOCUS CHARTING	
◆ Highlights patient concerns ◆ Provides structure for progress notes ◆ Enhances documentation of nursing process ◆ Promotes analytical thinking ◆ Can be adapted to all clinical settings	◆ Must be monitored regularly to ensure compliance with response component ◆ May require in-depth training to use ◆ Involves many checklists and flow sheets ◆ May be difficult for some nurses to write accurate, logical notes using this system
PIE charting	
◆ Encourages use of nursing diagnoses ◆ Simplifies charting by incorporating care plan in progress notes ◆ Calls for evaluation of each identified problem at least once every shift	◆ Time-consuming; may lead to repetitive entries by requiring reevaluation of each problem on every shift ◆ Eliminates planning step of nursing process ◆ Doesn't provide opportunity to document expected outcomes ◆ Eliminates care plan or protocol to guide care ◆ Not well suited to long-term care
Charting by exception	
◆ Eliminates need to document routine care through use of nursing standards ◆ Decreases charting time and report time ◆ Allows patient data to go directly to permanent record ◆ Reduces risk of transcribing errors ◆ Gives other caregivers access to most current patient data ◆ Standardizes assessments so that all caregivers evaluate and document findings consistently ◆ Makes trends in patient's care status obvious ◆ Markedly reduces chart size	◆ Requires large time commitment by the institution to develop clear guidelines and standards of care ◆ Requires major teaching effort for implementation ◆ Must be thoroughly understood and correctly used by all staff members to be effective ◆ Has questionable legal basis ◆ Requires well-formatted flow sheet

◆ helps to plan and coordinate the care contributed by each professional

◆ allows interdisciplinary exchange of information about the patient

◆ provides evidence of the nurse's legal responsibilities toward the patient

◆ demonstrates standards, rules, regulations, and laws of nursing practice

◆ supplies information for analysis of cost-to-benefit reduction

◆ reflects professional and ethical conduct and responsibility

◆ furnishes data for a variety of uses — continuing education, risk management, diagnosis-related group assignment and reimbursement, continuous quality improvement, case management monitoring, and research.

Legal significance of the medical record

The medical record provides legal proof of the nature and quality of care the patient received. The weight it carries in legal proceedings can't be overemphasized. The record may be the focus of inquiry in personal injury, professional malpractice, or product liability claims, as well as in workers' compensation, child custody, and employment disputes.

A factual, consistent, timely, and complete record defends you against allegations of negligence, improper treatment, and omissions in care. Health care professionals have a legal duty to maintain the medical record in sufficient detail, and inadequate documentation of care may result in liability or nonreimbursement by third-party payers.

In fact, documentation of care has become synonymous with care itself, and failure to document implies failure to provide care. Despite the recent introduction of charting by exception — a system that implies all standards have been met with a normal or expected response unless otherwise documented — the prevailing rule is: "If it isn't documented, it hasn't been done." (See *Legal risks of charting by exception,* page 236.)

In *Collins v. Westlake Community Hospital* (1974), a boy was hospitalized with a fractured leg, which was put in a cast and placed in traction. The evening nurse recorded the condition of the boy's toes several times during her shift. The night nurse, however, didn't record the condition of his toes until 6 a.m., when she noted that they were dusky and cold, and that his physician had been contacted. The leg required partial amputation, and the boy's family sued the hospital, claiming that the amputation was necessary because the night nurse had negligently failed to observe the condition of the toes in a timely fashion.

In her defense, the nurse testified that she had observed the toes periodically and that they were normal. Experts for the defense testified that only abnormal findings required documentation. However, the jury disagreed, concluding that failure to document implied failure to observe, and held the nurse liable for malpractice.

CONTENTS OF THE MEDICAL RECORD

Federal regulations, such as those governing Medicare and Medicaid reimbursement, partially determine the form and content of the medical record. Although state laws vary in their stringency and specificity, all states require health care facilities to maintain the medical record in sufficient detail.

Legal risks of charting by exception

Charting by exception (CBE) omits all charting related to routine nursing care. Instead, it relies on written standards of practice that identify the nurse's basic patient responsibilities. Of course, care must be consistently provided even though it's not documented.

Because this charting system requires the nurse to document only information that deviates from the expected, it can raise legal concerns. To ensure a legally sound patient record, well-defined guidelines and standards of care for its use must be understood by all nursing staff members and used consistently.

When CBE violates the law

Lama v. Boras (1994) illustrates what can go wrong when nurses don't follow accepted standards of care when using CBE. On May 15, 1985, Roberto Romero Lama had surgery for a herniated disk. Two days later, a nurse wrote in his chart that the bandage covering the surgical wound was "very bloody." An entry the next day indicated he had pain at the incision site.

On May 19, a nurse documented the bandage as "soiled again." The next day, Mr. Romero began to complain of severe back discomfort; he passed the night screaming in pain; on May 21, the physician diagnosed an infection in the space between the vertebral disks, and ordered antibiotics. The patient was hospitalized for several months to treat the infection.

Mr. Romero sued the hospital and the physicians who treated him, alleging that they failed to prepare and monitor proper medical records. The hospital didn't dispute the charge that nurses didn't supply the required notes; instead, it pointed out that they followed the hospital's official CBE policy.

The court ruled against the hospital on the grounds that Puerto Rico law requires qualitative nurses' notes for each nursing shift, and that violation of this regulation had caused Mr. Romero's injury. The court reasoned that a more complete picture of his evolving condition was unavailable because the hospital's CBE policy called for nurses to note qualitative observations only when needed to chronicle important clinical changes. Although objective aspects of the patient's care and condition (temperature, vital signs, medications) were charted regularly, important details, such as the changing condition of the surgical wound and the patient's reports of pain, weren't.

Playing it safe

Although CBE complies with legal principles, the system may be questioned in court until it becomes more widely known. If you believe your facility's CBE policy is unsafe or ambiguous, confer with your colleagues and supervisors, and then approach an administrator about clarifying it.

The following documents are usually included in the medical record:
◆ patient admission form and history
◆ physician's order form and progress notes
◆ nursing assessment and nursing diagnoses
◆ patient's medication record
◆ nurses' notes and progress notes
◆ diagnostic and laboratory test results
◆ X-ray and other radiologic reports
◆ operative and other treatment reports
◆ flow sheets, checklists, and graphic sheets (see *Using flow sheets*)

LEGAL TIP ▸ Using flow sheets

Flow sheets are record-keeping forms used for tracking information about the repetitive tasks you perform through the day, such as giving medication or monitoring your patient's vital signs or fluid balance. Using a flow sheet enables you to keep all routine measurements in one place and to compare data quickly. Flow sheets come in a variety of styles, including blank-ruled paper and graph paper, to suit various documenting needs.

Advantages

A flow sheet offers the following advantages:
◆ It displays a specific aspect of your patient's condition such as his temperature at a glance. You don't have to search through pages of notes to determine his temperature pattern during the past 48 hours.
◆ It saves you time. You can note the vital signs or medication given without having to write a full descriptive entry every time. You can use your nurses' notes to describe how the patient is responding to treatment.
◆ It documents that you're giving the patient continuous care.
◆ It provides a mechanism for nonlicensed personnel to record their care and observations. Because nonlicensed personnel usually aren't permitted to chart in the nurses' notes, information they have about patient care may be lost. Instead, you can ask them to describe

their care and initial each entry on a flow sheet. Then if you have a question about the status of your patient's skin, for example, you can check the flow sheet to identify the nursing assistant who administered that day's bed bath.

Common errors

Flow sheets can create a legal tangle if you don't avoid two common mistakes:
◆ The first mistake is to treat flow sheets casually. For instance, some nurses will routinely check off whatever the previous shift checked off on the flow sheet, or made checks at the beginning of the shift before the care is provided regardless of the care given, and then carefully chart the actual care in the nurses' notes. This creates an inconsistency. As part of the legal medical record, the flow sheet must accurately reflect the care provided.
◆ The second mistake is to depend too heavily on flow sheets. Flow sheets can help you document, quickly and accurately, what care was given and who provided it. However, don't neglect to record the patient's response to care in your nurses' notes. Like other chart forms, retain the flow sheet as part of the permanent chart so that you have a progressive picture of the patient's status and a record of your care.

◆ discharge summary (see *Documenting discharge planning,* page 238)
◆ referral summaries
◆ consent forms, such as advance directives, living wills, do-not-resuscitate orders, name of health care proxy or legal guardian, and patient privacy consent forms
◆ home care instruction sheet.

FAILURE TO PROPERLY MAINTAIN THE MEDICAL RECORD

As a general rule, the medical record is presumed to be accurate if there is no evidence of fraud or tampering. Evidence of tampering can cause the record to be ruled inadmissible as evidence in court. Medical records may be corrected if the portion in error re-

Documenting discharge planning

When planning a patient's discharge, be sure to document in his chart that he or his family is aware that treatment and care will be discontinued on a specific date. Also document the alternative resources and specific plans that must be organized to ensure continuity of care.

Writing a discharge summary
The final document in each patient's record, the discharge summary highlights the patient's condition, treatment, status at discharge, discharge nursing diagnoses, and all medications. It should also include a home care instruction sheet, the name of an escort, the patient's discharge address, and his transportation mode.

Document the names of family members or other caregivers who are present for discharge instructions, especially if competency issues are of concern. Also document their understanding of the discharge orders and instructions.

Make appropriate referrals for follow-up care and document the patient's status, discharge instructions, and other instructions or special considerations verbalized to the patient, family, or medical team.

Taking it step-by-step
When preparing a discharge summary, take the following steps:
◆ First, review the patient's nursing diagnoses or problem list, care plan, flow sheets, and progress notes to develop an overall impression of his hospital stay.
◆ Follow your facility's policies regarding the format and content of the summary.
◆ Include any exceptional details or unusual findings.
◆ Outline all patient teaching and provide, as a record, written instructions in a language the patient understands.

Reviewing the summary
Make sure that the discharge summary:
◆ summarizes the patient's care
◆ provides useful information for further teaching, evaluation, and readmission
◆ shows that the patient has information needed for self-care or to get further help
◆ shows that you've met Joint Commission on Accreditation of Healthcare Organizations documentation requirements for collaboration with other disciplines and for patient teaching
◆ helps safeguard you and your employer against malpractice charges.

mains legible; deleting or rendering the entry illegible can impose liability. Late entries are usually acceptable if they're clearly marked "late entry" when made. Loss of the medical record raises a presumption of negligence (which may be overcome by contrary evidence).

Nursing documentation

With a large number of health care professionals involved in each patient's care, nursing documentation must be complete, accurate, and timely to foster continuity of care. (See *Documentation tips.*) It should cover the following:
◆ initial assessment using the nursing process and applicable nursing diagnoses

LEGAL TIP   **Documentation tips**

If you're ever involved in a malpractice lawsuit, how you documented, what you documented, and what you didn't document will heavily influence the jury and the outcome of the trial. Following these tips can ensure that your records don't tip the scales of justice against you.

How to document

◆ Use the appropriate form, and document in ink.
◆ Record the patient's name and identification number on every page of his chart.
◆ Record the complete date and time of each entry.
◆ Document the care given in a timely manner.
◆ Include patient statements in quotations when significant.
◆ Be specific. Avoid general terms and vague expressions.
◆ Use standard abbreviations only.
◆ Use a medical term only if you're sure of its meaning.
◆ Document symptoms by using the patient's own words.
◆ Document objectively.

What to document

◆ Document all nursing actions you take in response to a patient's problem. For example: "8 p.m. medicated for incision pain." Be sure to include the medication name, dose, route, and site.
◆ Document the patient's response to medications and other treatment.
◆ Document safeguards you use to protect the patient. For example: "raised side rails" or "applied safety belts."

◆ Document the incident in two places: in your progress notes and in an incident report. Don't mention the incident report in the patient's record, unless your facility or state requires it.
◆ Document each observation. Failure to document observations will produce gaps in the patient's records. These gaps will suggest that you neglected the patient.
◆ Document procedures after you perform them, never in advance.
◆ Write on every line. Don't insert notes between lines or leave empty spaces for someone else to insert a note.
◆ If you have empty spaces, place a line through them so that someone else can't insert information in the middle of your notes.
◆ Sign every entry.
◆ Chart an omission as a new entry. Never backdate or add to previously written entries. Within the body of the note, reference the time and date of omission.
◆ Correct errors according to your facility's policies and procedures.
◆ Draw a thin line through an error and mark "error" above it, with the date and your initials. Never erase or obliterate an erroneous entry.
◆ Document only the care you provide. Never document for someone else.
◆ Understand and follow the documentation standards of your facility and your state or province. These standards are usually defined in state or provincial nurse practice acts (the statutes governing nursing practice) and in state or provincial administrative codes (the rules and regulations governing nursing practice).

◆ nursing actions, particularly reports to the physician
◆ ongoing assessment, including the frequency of assessment
◆ variations from the assessment and plan
◆ accountability information, including forms signed by the patient, location of patient valuables, and patient education
◆ notation of care by other disciplines, including physician visits, if practical
◆ health teaching, including content and response
◆ procedures and diagnostic tests
◆ patient response to therapy, particularly to nursing interventions, drugs, and diagnostic tests
◆ statements made by the patient
◆ patient comfort and safety measures.

SOURCES OF DOCUMENTATION DUTIES AND STANDARDS

Factors that influence nursing documentation standards include:
◆ federal statutes and regulations
◆ state regulations and statutes, including licensing statutes and nurse practice acts
◆ custom
◆ accrediting bodies
◆ standards of practice issued by professional organizations
◆ institutional policies and procedures.

Professional organizations and accrediting bodies have developed and refined recommendations and standards of practice for nursing documentation. Sometimes these standards are more stringent than those required by state law.

The American Nurses Association (ANA) has included documentation in its Standards of Nursing Practice. The ANA says documentation must be systematic, continuous, accessible, communicated, recorded, and readily available to all health care team members.

The Joint Commission on Accreditation of Healthcare Organizations (JCAHO) also sets standards. Current standards stress a change from source-oriented documentation to a fully integrated, multidisciplinary approach.

Documentation should reflect the collaborative planning and provision of care and treatment. JCAHO doesn't specify a format for medical record documentation. Thus, patient care, treatment, and rehabilitation may involve many forms, from preprinted forms to handwritten reports to electronic formats, which may include decision algorithms and care maps.

Many of the professional specialty societies, such as the American Association of Critical-Care Nurses, the Association of Operating Room Nurses, and the Emergency Department Nurses Association, have developed guidelines, standards, or recommendations concerning content and technique of nursing documentation.

Typically, a health care facility has integrated the appropriate laws, regulations, and standards into its own policy and procedure manual. Your best assurance of following the law may be to adhere to the facility's policy, which usually describes who's to maintain each portion of a patient's record and by which technique. (See *Managed care: Implications for documentation.*)

The courts and institution policy

In a dispute, the law will frequently support a health care facility's policies and procedures with regard to documentation. Consider the case of *Stack v. Wapner* (1976).

The plaintiff was admitted to the hospital to give birth. At 2:45 a.m., according to her chart, I.V. oxytocin was started to induce labor. Accepted medical practice requires continuous monitoring of patients receiving oxytocin to prevent complications of excessive uterine contractions, such as subsequent fetal distress or uterine rupture. However, the labor room record didn't document monitoring of her clinical status until 5:15 a.m.

After delivery, the patient developed heavy uterine bleeding. Unable to stop the bleeding, the physician performed a total hysterectomy. The patient later sued, claiming that her complications resulted from improper administration and monitoring of oxytocin.

Both the attending physicians testified that they had monitored the administration of the drug. However, they had no defense against evidence that hospital policy required them to document on the patient's chart all information that supported diagnosis and treatment, as well as the patient's response to treatment. The patient was awarded damages.

You must document the baseline assessment and clinically significant changes thereafter. Look to your health care facility's policy for what strips need to be saved. Fetal monitoring strips are usually part of the record. Document the time started on the strip as well as clinically significant activity that would correlate with changes in the strip.

HAZARDS OF IMPROPER NURSING DOCUMENTATION

In the following cases, nurses or other health care providers made documentation errors that contributed substantially to the legal outcome. The cases reviewed here include faulty record keeping, failure to include information, charting after the fact, misplaced records, and failure to follow set standards of care when using charting by exception. All these cases contain important lessons about the courts' determination to uphold standards of documentation.

Managed care: Implications for documentation

Because managed care balances the importance of a medical procedure or treatment against its cost, it requires greater standardization of care plans as well as continuous monitoring of health care outcomes. To improve outcomes, several tools have been developed.

Clinical practice guidelines are standards developed to help practitioners and patients make decisions regarding appropriate care in specific clinical circumstances.

Practice parameters are educational tools that enable physicians to obtain the advice of clinical experts, keep abreast of the latest clinical research, and assess the clinical significance of often conflicting research findings.

Clinical pathways and *critical paths* are clinical management tools that help to organize, sequence, price, and time the major interventions of nurses, physicians, and other health care providers for a particular case type, subset, or condition.

Care maps are elaborate critical pathways that show the relationships of sets of interventions to sets of intermediate outcomes along a time line. They merge standards of care with standards of practice in a cause-and-effect relationship.

Faulty record keeping

Rogers v. Kasdan (1981) involved a woman who died of brain damage 7 days after admission for injuries sustained in an accident. The Supreme Court of Kentucky ruled against the physician and the hospital, based on the patient's medical record: the emergency department records were incomplete, fluid intake and output was incorrectly tallied, and other records contained discrepancies or were illegible or incomplete.

Absence of information

St. Paul Fire and Marine Insurance Co. v. Prothro (1979) involved a claim in which the patient, after undergoing a total hip replacement, was injured while being lowered into a Hubbard tank by an orderly. The metal basket holding him collapsed, struck his hip, and reopened the wound. The orderly stopped the bleeding and took the plaintiff to his room, where a nurse treated the wound. However, the nurse failed to document the incident. The wound subsequently became infected, necessitating removal of the prosthesis and leaving the patient with a permanent limp. The court ruled in the patient's favor and noted that a determining factor was the absence of critical information on the patient's chart, which would have helped the physician and staff provide proper care.

Charting after the fact

In *Thor v. Boska* (1974), a rewritten copy of a patient's record was suspected of being an altered record. This lawsuit involved a woman who had seen her physician several times because of a breast lump. Each time, the physician examined her and made a record of her visit. After 2 years, the woman sought a second opinion and learned that she had breast cancer. She sued her first physician. Rather than producing his records in court, the physician brought copies of the records and said he had copied the originals for legibility. The court reasoned that he was withholding incriminating evidence, and held in favor of the plaintiff.

In a suspected case of notes written after litigation, handwriting experts are

retained by the plaintiff's attorney to determine when portions were written. An alteration in the record can make a defensible case indefensible.

Missing records

The case of *Battocchi v. Washington Hosp. Center* (1990) underscores the significance of missing records. In this case, parents brought a medical malpractice suit against the hospital and a physician for injury to their son during forceps delivery. The nurse had immediately documented the delivery and posted the record in the chart.

Later, the hospital's risk management personnel apparently lost the nurse's record. The court ruled in favor of the hospital and physician, saying the jury couldn't presume negligence and causation simply because the hospital lost the nurses' notes. The appeals court sent the case back to the trial court to determine whether loss of the record stemmed from negligence or impropriety.

Poor communication

Although thorough documentation is crucial, it isn't always enough. Unless you report significant findings you document, exemplary charting can be worthless. In a 1995 Nebraska case, a couple sued a hospital, claiming that the staff's negligence caused brain damage to their newborn son. Jeffrey Critchfield was born at 7:30 a.m., weighing 4 lb, 10 oz. According to the admission assessment, Jeffrey had chest wall retractions, cyanosis, pallor, weak cry, and flaccid muscles. He was admitted to the neonatal intensive care unit, where nurses documented his grunting, pallor, and chest retractions. At about 7:45 p.m., a nurse documented that Jeffrey was lethargic.

At the trial, a pediatric neurologist testifying for the Critchfields stated that lethargy was a sign of neurologic changes, and that nursing observations recorded throughout the night indicated that Jeffrey had signs of acute brain damage from lack of oxygen and blood to the brain. He also said that the nurses should have reported these findings to the attending physician during the night and the early morning hours. Another expert testified that the hospital should have had a policy requiring expert consultation, and that if nurses had reported Jeffrey's problems, his brain damage could have been ameliorated. The court ruled in favor of the Critchfields, reasoning that the hospital had a duty, through its nursing staff, to report medically significant changes in a patient's condition to the treating physician without delay.

AVOIDING DOCUMENTATION ERRORS

In addition to their potential impact on patient care, charting errors or omissions, even if seemingly harmless, will undermine your credibility in court. Especially avoid the following.

Omissions

Include all significant facts that other nurses will need to assess the patient. Otherwise, a court may conclude that you failed to perform an action missing from the record or tried to hide evidence.

Change in treatment

When an ordered treatment is no longer appropriate, which may occur after a change in the patient's condition, document why the treatment wasn't administered and any communications with the patient's physician regarding the need for new orders.

Personal opinions

Don't enter personal opinions. (See *Distinguishing between subjective and objective charting,* page 244.) Record only factual and objective observations and the patient's statements. *Brookover v. Mary Hitchcock Memorial Hospital* (1990).

Vague entries

Instead of "Patient had a good day," state why: "Patient didn't complain of pain."

Late entries

If a late entry is necessary, identify it as such, sign, and date it. Reference the date and time you're relating back to.

Improper corrections

Never erase or obliterate an error. Instead, draw a single line through it, label it "error," and sign and date it. Follow your facility's policy for correcting errors. Some facilities believe the word "error" raises red flags unnecessarily, but that it's appropriate to document "correction."

Unauthorized entries

Only you should be keeping your records. *Henry By Henry v. St. John's Hospital* (1987).

Erroneous or vague abbreviations

Use only standard abbreviations, and follow your facility's policies.

Illegibility and lack of clarity

Write so that others can read your entry. Use a dictionary if you're unsure of spelling or usage.

SIGNING YOUR DOCUMENTATION

Sign all notes with your first initial, full last name, and title. Place your signature on the right side of the page as

LEGAL TIP

Distinguishing between subjective and objective charting

The most common error most nurses make when they chart is writing value judgments and opinions — subjective information — rather than factual, or objective, information. Subjective information reflects how the nurse feels about the patient's condition, not the patient's condition. Here are some subjective entries, with their objective alternatives.

SUBJECTIVE CHARTING	OBJECTIVE CHARTING
She's drinking well.	Drank 1,500 ml liquids between 7 a.m. and noon.
She reported good relief from Demerol.	Pain in R hip decreasing, now described as "like a dull toothache."
Dorsalis pedis pulse present. Good pedal pulses.	Peripheral pulses in legs 2+/4+ bilaterally.
Moves legs and feet well.	Leg strength 5+/5+ bilaterally all major muscle groups. Sensation intact to light touch, pin; denies numbness or tingling. Skin warm and dry. No edema.
Voiding qs.	Voided 350 ml clear yellow urine in bedpan.
Patient is nervous.	Patient repeatedly asks about length of hospitalization, expected discomfort, and time off from work.
Breath sounds normal.	Breath sounds clear to auscultation all lobes. Chest expansion symmetrical — no cough. Nail beds pink.
Bowel sounds normal.	Bowel sound present in all quadrants — abdomen flat. NPO since 12:01 a.m.
Ate well.	Ate all of soft diet.

proof that you entered all the information between the previous nurse's signature and your own. If the last entry is unsigned, request that the nurse who made the entry sign it. Never sign for procedures completed by another care provider. (In rare instances, you may need to sign for another health care provider to maintain and update the record; in this situation, explain why you are signing and for whom.) Draw lines through empty or remaining spaces to prevent subsequent amendments or additions. (See *Signing your*

nurses' notes. See also *Countersigning: Important guidelines,* page 246.)

AVOIDING SUSPICIOUS CHANGES AND POTENTIAL LEGAL TRAPS

In the event of a legal challenge, or if the medical record has been requested for examination in a trial, avoid making changes, corrections, or additions. To do so would raise suspicion, even if you have legitimate reasons and the best intentions.

In addition, many lawyers advise against keeping personal notes about a

records of each dose dispensed and the remaining quantities.

The legal consequences of improper charting are especially significant when administering opioids and other controlled substances and maintaining controlled substance records. Be familiar with your facility's policy when you dispense these drugs. Also be aware of *controlled substance acts* — federal and state laws that control the distribution, classification, sale, and use of drugs. Consult your facility's policies or contact your state board of nursing for information about these laws. If you have a specific question about the propriety of a policy or procedure in your facility, talk to your facility's attorney or write to the state board of nursing and request a formal board opinion or a declaratory ruling.

Administering opioids

For proper, accurate documentation of opioids, use the special opioids records — the control sheet and the check sheet — provided by the pharmacy and follow the procedure described below.

Before you give an opioid:
◆ Verify the count in the opioids drawer.
◆ Sign the opioid control sheet to indicate you removed the drug.
◆ Get another nurse to sign the control sheet if you waste or discard all or part of a dose.

At the end of your shift:
◆ Record the amount of each opioid in the drawer on the opioid sheet while the nurse beginning her shift counts the opioids out loud.
◆ Sign the opioid check sheet only if the count is correct. Have the other nurse countersign.
◆ Identify and correct discrepancies before nurses leave the unit.

LEGAL TIP

Documenting spoken orders

When a physician writes an order for the patient and signs it – or when another health care professional writes an order and the physician countersigns it – the courts usually won't question the legality of the order. However, if a physician gives you a verbal order – either in person or by telephone – protect yourself legally, as follows:
◆ Write down the order exactly as he gives it, the date, and the time.
◆ Repeat the order back to him so that you're sure you heard the physician correctly.
◆ Follow up to ensure that the physician signs the order.

The danger of poor documentation

Here's what can happen if you don't document verbal orders:
◆ You could face disciplinary measures by your employer and state board of nursing for failing to document.
◆ You could damage your defense or your hospital's in a malpractice suit.
◆ Other nurses, not knowing what orders have been given, may follow prior orders that result in harm to the patient.
◆ If controlled substances are given, suspicions could be raised that you're diverting drugs for your own use.

For your own protection, conform to all facility, nursing department, and pharmacy policies and procedures if an ordered dose of a controlled substance isn't administered, or if it's wasted or discarded.

Witnessing and signing documents

As a nurse, you may be asked to witness the signing of documents, such as deeds, bills of sale, powers of attorney, contracts, and wills. You may also participate in witnessing oral statements made by patients and others that may have legal significance. Your actions at these times can influence whether what you witnessed has the force of law, and they can also expose you to legal consequences. Later, you may have to testify in court about the signing and the circumstances surrounding it.

SIGNIFICANCE OF YOUR SIGNATURE

When you sign as a witness, you're usually certifying only that you saw the person, known to you by a certain name, place his signature on the document. You're not necessarily certifying the presence or absence of duress, undue influence, fraud, or error. Also, keep in mind that you aren't validating that the patient has been told the significant risks, benefits, and options for treatment, which constitute informed consent. When you witness consent forms in a nursing capacity, your signature merely attests to the signer's:

◆ authenticity
◆ voluntariness
◆ capacity.

If you're called to testify about the signing, don't underestimate the importance of your testimony. A court looking into charges of fraud or undue influence used in executing a document will usually give great weight to a nurse's perception. You may be asked about the patient's physical and mental condition at the time of the signing, and the court may ask you to describe his interactions with his family, his attorney, and others.

RELEVANT LAWS

In the United States and Canada, nurse practice acts establish nurses' scope of professional and legal accountability. When you witness a document, other laws also apply. For example, all states have laws setting out the legal requirements for written and oral wills, dying declarations, living wills, powers of attorney, and gifts in expectation of death.

Wills

State laws establish requirements for wills, including:
◆ format requirements
◆ the number of witnesses needed
◆ who can be a witness
◆ what makes a will valid or invalid
◆ how to make a will inoperative
◆ how to contest a will.

Usually, an individual must be age 18 or older and have two witnesses present to make a valid will. In about two-thirds of all states, the will may be handwritten — such a document is called a holographic will.

In many states, your signature on a will certifies that:
◆ you witnessed the will signing
◆ you heard the maker of the will declare it to be his will
◆ all witnesses and the maker of the will were actually present during the signing.

By attesting to the last two facts, you help ensure the authenticity of the will and the signatures. Your signature doesn't certify, however, that the maker of the will is competent.

Precautions

If a patient asks you to serve as a witness when he draws up his will, follow these precautions:

◆ Don't forget to notify the patient's physician and your supervisor before you act as a witness.

◆ Don't give the patient any legal advice.

◆ Don't offer to assist him in phrasing the document's wording.

◆ Don't allow yourself to be named as a recipient in the will.

◆ Don't comment on the nature of his choices.

◆ Don't forget to document your actions in your nurses' notes.

The laws also cover dying declarations and gifts in expectation of death, specifying when they're valid and when they aren't.

In the case of a living will, your state law may prohibit you from acting as a witness because of your role in executing the instructions in a living will.

YOUR LIABILITY

You can be held liable and in violation of the prevailing standard of care if the signature you witness is false or if you sign knowing the patient is incompetent or has given uninformed consent. You can also be held liable if you knowingly allow a minor, nonguardian, or other ineligible person to sign a document.

If you're the only person who informs a patient about a planned medical procedure and you then witness his signature, you can be liable for practicing outside your nurse practice act, for practicing medicine without a license, or both. Your hospital may be liable for negligence under the doctrine of respondeat superior. If you give the patient false information in an attempt to deceive him, you may be guilty of fraud or misrepresentation.

READ BEFORE YOU SIGN

Before you sign any document, read at least enough of it to make sure it's the type of document the primary signer represents it to be. Usually, you won't have to read all the text, and legally that isn't necessary for your signature to be valid as a witness only. You should, however, always examine the document's title and first page and give careful attention to what's written immediately above the place for your signature. (The place for your signature should be clearly labeled.)

HOW TO SIGN

When signing a document, write legibly and use your full legal name. When signing on hospital forms, add your title. On other documents, the title is optional but adding it will establish why you're in the hospital.

WHEN TO SIGN

When you're asked to sign as a witness, do so only if you believe the patient to be mentally and physically competent. Legally, you don't need to have knowledge of exactly what's contained in the documents you witness. However, professionally you should be aware of the content, just as you should be aware of the content when witnessing the patient's signature to an informed consent form.

When to refuse

Here are some instances when you shouldn't witness a document:

◆ when the patient isn't legally able to give consent—for example, when he's a minor or a nonguardian

◆ when the patient isn't who he says he is, or you can't be sure
◆ when the patient has no power of free choice — for example, when he's being blackmailed or otherwise pressured into signing
◆ when the patient is uninformed about what he's consenting to because he has been given misleading information, doesn't understand the information given, or hasn't been told of the risks involved (Clarify with the physician why known risks haven't been disclosed.)
◆ when a patient is obviously incompetent — for example, when he's suffering from advanced dementia and is being pressured to sign a deed transferring a real estate title to someone else or if he's on medication
◆ when you feel uncomfortable about signing.

Keep in mind that you have no legal obligation to witness a will or other document. In such situations, simply explain that you choose not to act as a witness. Then record the incident in your nurses' notes, using a chronological format. Chart the setting, the patient's mental and physical condition, the reason for the refusal, what you saw and heard, and what happened after your refusal (for instance, that someone else witnessed or someone else gave consent).

Finally, report the incident to other concerned staff members — for example, your supervisor and the patient's physician.

WRITING THE NURSES' NOTES

When you record in your notes that you've witnessed a patient's signature on a document, always include something about his apparent perceptions of his health and general circumstances.

When you witness a written will, document that it was signed and witnessed, who signed it, who else was present, what was done with it after signing, and the patient's condition at the time.

When you witness oral statements, such as dying declarations and oral wills, document the names of other witnesses, the patient's physical and mental condition at the time, and the patient's reaction to the statements afterward. Make your notes carefully: remember, they could be used in court for probating the will, for resolving creditors' claims, or for prosecuting alleged criminals. The notes will also refresh your memory if you're called to testify in court.

CANADIAN PROCEDURES

Formalities of signing and witnessing documents in the United States and Canada may differ. Both countries, however, have legal systems based primarily on English common law, and both have essentially the same rules governing how a witness should sign legal documents.

Computerized medical records

As with the manual record system, the computerized medical record provides a detailed account of the patient's clinical status, diagnostic tests, treatments, and medical history. However, unlike the manual system, the computerized record stores all the patient's medical data in a single, easily accessible source.

Using computers to maintain and access records dramatically increases efficiency and precision. Computerization improves the quality and accuracy of the documentation, improves clarity and legibility, makes the patient record more complete, and keeps patient information more current. The computerized record also allows practitioners to rely less on human recall, which helps to increase accuracy. Computers prove especially useful in areas that benefit from automated patient monitoring, such as the intensive care unit and the coronary care unit.

HOSPITAL COMPUTER SYSTEMS

Senior hospital officials usually introduce computers for the sake of controlling health care costs. A hospital's computer system typically consists of a large, centralized computer to store information, linked to smaller video display terminals in each work area. Ideally, there should be a computer terminal at each bedside.

To use the system, a nurse signs in by typing onto the keyboard a signature code, or password, that gives her access to a patient's records. The computer recognizes by the signature code that the nurse has authorized access to the information stored in its memory. After a patient's code number is entered, the computer displays the patient's records on the screen. The nurse may access care plans, vital signs, medication records, general progress notes, laboratory and diagnostic test results, assessment findings, discharge plans, and other information. The nurse can also order a printed copy of the patient's record.

Benefits

Just how computer technology will change the nursing profession remains to be seen. Some experts predict a paperless chart. Health care reform may further transform the documentation process, with the creation of a universal medical record that follows a patient throughout his life. At best, integrating computers into your practice will free you to spend more time meeting the needs of your patients. The computerized medical record can save time spent filing, searching for, and retrieving information about a patient. By improving legibility, computers reduce the risk of misinterpretation. Computers also reduce misinterpretation by offering standardized, structured input formats and mandatory charting fields for assessment reports, flow charts, and care plans. Time-stamping minimizes scheduling errors. Correct spelling and legibility are major advantages of computerized systems.

Disadvantages

Many critics fear that computers will diminish the personal satisfaction that nurses derive from practicing their profession. They argue that technical advances tend to have a dehumanizing effect on the workplace. Relying on computers may mean less opportunity for interaction and communication with coworkers and patients. In addition, patients may be less truthful in providing medical histories and details about illnesses if they know that the information is going into a computer, which could be used to improperly divulge their medical information.

Some systems provide you with a selection of words and phrases from which you can quickly create a complete narrative note. Use of an incorrect descriptive prompt or phrase can give a misleading assessment. If the prompts aren't exactly descriptive, then it's important to type or write out your assessment.

Another disadvantage of a computerized medical record system is the need for backup records in case computers break down, making informa-

LEGAL TIP

Computer charting: Minimizing your legal risks

Your liability when working with computer documentation is exactly the same as when working with a manual system. You may be liable for any patient injuries associated with charting errors.

To minimize your legal risks:

◆ Always double-check all patient information.

◆ Don't divulge signature codes.

◆ Inform your supervisor if you suspect that someone is using your code.

◆ Indicate whether the physician's order is written, verbal (in person), or verbal (by telephone) and when the entry is made.

◆ Know your state's rules and regulations and your facility's policies and procedures regarding privileged data, confidentiality, and disclosure. To learn about state rules and regulations, consult your facility's policy and procedure manual, check with your facility's attorney, or consult your state board of nursing or the state statutory and administrative codes.

◆ Know the requirements of the Health Insurance Portability and Accountability Act concerning privacy, confidentiality, and security of medical information.

Verifying computerized records

Verification is one way of reducing errors in the computerized record. It serves the same purpose as signing off on the manual record of a physician's order. To use verification, the unit secretary enters the physician's order into the computer. The order is held in a "suspense file" until a nurse reviews the entry, verifies the order, and adds it to the active record file.

LEGAL CONCERNS

The legal implications of computerized medical records are evolving. (See *Computer charting: Minimizing your legal risks*.) Most computer records are legitimate substitutes for manual records. However, some state laws require written records as well. The most pressing legal questions concern the threat to patient privacy and confidentiality. With traditional records, information is restricted simply by keeping the record on the unit; computer records can be called up at any terminal in the facility. The primary safeguard is the signature code, limiting access to the records. For example, a nurse's code would call up a patient's entire record, but a technician's code would produce only part.

Various laws protect the privacy of a patient's medical records. The Federal Privacy Act of 1974 protects the confidential medical information of patients in veterans' hospitals. The Health Insurance Portability and Accountability Act (HIPAA) of 2003 protects the privacy, confidentiality, and security of medical information. (Under HIPAA, only those who have a need to know patient information for the care of the patient and those authorized by the patient to have access to his medical information can lawfully enter a patient's medical record.) Some state practice acts impose an ethical duty to

tion unavailable. Ensuring completeness and continuity in charting requires a backup system. Poorly designed computer systems or human error can also scramble entries and spread flawed data. Obviously, the key to avoiding these problems is for all members of the health care team to know how to use the system.

guard patients' privacy. However, no one can fully guarantee that unauthorized persons won't gain access to computerized records.

Care also must be taken to safeguard patient information sent by fax machine. In particular, policies and procedures should be established to prevent confidential patient information such as a positive result on a human immunodeficiency virus test from being transmitted by fax machine — especially one that's centrally located and easily seen by staff members or the general public. HIPAA requires that procedures be in place to reduce the exposure of patient information to anyone who doesn't have a need to know the patient's private information.

In addition, hospitals must show that their computer systems are trustworthy enough to be used in court. For example, they should use software that automatically records the date and time of each entry and each correction, as well as the name of the author or anyone who modifies a record. When an error is corrected, the software should preserve both the original and corrected versions and identify each author.

Challenging a computer record in court

In 1977, a patient in New York charged that a computerized record system was an invasion of his privacy. In *Whalen v. Roe* (1977), the patient challenged the constitutionality of a state law that required patients buying certain prescription drugs to list their name, address, age, the drug, dosage, and prescribing physician's name for a state database. The state then entered all the information into a computer. The Supreme Court upheld the law but acknowledged the threat to privacy implicit in the system. The Court reasoned that central storage and easy

accessibility of computerized data vastly increase the potential for abuse of that information.

Selected references

Apple, G., and Brandt, M. "Ready, Set, Access! An Action Plan for Conducting a HIPAA Privacy Risk Assessment," *Journal of the American Health Information Management Association* 72(6):26-32, June 2001.

Baker, S.K. "Minimizing Litigation Risk. Documentation Strategies in the Occupational Health Setting," *AAOHN Journal* 48(2): 100-105, February 2000.

Carelock, J., and Innerarity, S. "Critical Incidents: Effective Communication and Documentation," *Critical Care Nursing Quarterly* 23(4):59-66, February 2001.

Cutcliffe, J.R. "To Record or Not to Record: Documentation in Clinical Supervision," *British Journal of Nursing* (9)6:350-55, March-April, 2000.

Glondys, B. "Practice Brief. Ensuring Legibility of Patient Records," *Journal of the American Health Information Management Association* 74(5):64A-64D, May 2003.

Kurtz, CA. "Accurate Documentation Equals Quality Patient Care," *Insight* 27(1):8-10, January-March 2002.

Rodden, C., and Bell, M. "Record Keeping: Developing Good Practice," *Nursing Standard* 17(1):40-42, September 2002.

Streger, M.R. "Universal Truths of Patient Care Documentation," *Emergency Medical Services* 32(2):45-51, February 2003.

Taylor, H. "An Exploration of the Factors that Affect Nurses' Record Keeping," *British Journal of Nursing* 12(12):751-54, June-July 2003.

Wood, C. "The Importance of Good Record-Keeping for Nurses," *Nursing Times* 99(2):26-27, January 2003.

8

Legal risks while off duty

When you're on duty, numerous guidelines define the legal limits of your nursing practice. They include hospital policies, standards issued by nursing organizations, and state or jurisdictional nurse practice acts. Statutory law and common law provide additional direction. When you're off duty, however, you have few specific guidelines. Your legal responsibilities aren't as clear-cut.

For example, you probably wouldn't hesitate to perform an abdominal thrust maneuver to save a choking victim. However, what if you panic, make a mistake, and injure the patient? Can you be sued by the victim or his estate? Can your nursing license be suspended or revoked? Does the law protect you because of your good intentions?

Fortunately, thus far, lawsuits resulting from off-duty nursing actions have been extremely rare. However, whether you frequently provide off-duty care or just give free advice occasionally to your neighbor, it's important to act on sound legal footing.

LEGAL ISSUES

This chapter discusses legal issues related to off-duty nursing. You'll find information on:

♦ acting as a Good Samaritan—your liability when you give emergency care at an accident scene or in a disaster
♦ giving free health care advice—legal ramifications of giving advice to family members and friends
♦ donating nursing services—protecting yourself legally when you volunteer your nursing skills
♦ acting during disasters—legal aspects of providing nursing services during emergencies and declared disasters.

You'll learn to distinguish between what the law requires and what the law allows. You'll also find out how your nurse practice act and other state laws apply to off-duty actions.

Legal protection for Good Samaritans

Imagine yourself driving in heavy traffic. Not far ahead, you see an automobile accident and a bloodied motorist gesturing for help. Nearby, another victim lies sprawled at curbside. What should you do? Your conscience and compassion prompt you to help the victim in any health care emergency. Your common sense prompts you to ask if helping out means courting legal trouble.

YOUR OPTIONS

You have three options. You can:
◆ help the accident victim at the scene
◆ leave the scene, stop at the nearest phone, and call for an ambulance or other rescue service
◆ pass the scene and make no attempt to call for help.

In almost every state, you have the legal right to choose any of these options. In most cases, off-duty nurses in the United States and Canada have no legal duty to rescue anyone.

Obligation to rescue

In general, the only people with a legal duty to rescue others are individuals who perform rescues as part of their jobs — firefighters, police officers, emergency medical technicians, and a few others such as public transportation workers. However, in a few states, such as Vermont, Rhode Island, Minnesota, and Wisconsin, "duty to rescue" laws may apply to nurses. Unless you're covered by a duty-to-rescue law, your decision to help remains voluntary and personal.

Common and statutory law

If you choose to help the accident victim, two kinds of laws protect you: common law and statutory law, specifically the Good Samaritan acts.

Common law, also known as case law, is the cumulative result of court decisions over the years. These decisions may provide guidelines for acting in a similar situation.

Good Samaritan acts were enacted to encourage people to voluntarily help someone in need without the fear of being sued for any reasonable care rendered — even if some mistake in

treatment might occur. Every state has enacted a Good Samaritan act, but each state's statute varies. Some may apply specifically to nurses or other health care professionals, while others may apply to anyone who offers assistance. (See *State Good Samaritans acts*, pages 256 to 260.)

PROVING MALPRACTICE

Normally, to bring a malpractice suit to a jury trial, the patient must establish the following:
◆ you owed a duty, based on a nurse-patient relationship
◆ you breached that duty
◆ the patient was harmed
◆ your breach of duty caused the harm.

Consider these same points as they apply to the auto accident.

Your legal duty

As long as you pass the accident scene — whether you stop down the road to call for help — you owe the victim no legal duty unless you reside in a state that has a duty-to-rescue law. He isn't your patient, and he has no legal claim to your professional services.

However, just by stopping your car at the scene, you incur a legal duty. From that point on, you can't leave the victim until he's being cared for by another health care professional with at least as much training as you have or until the police order you from the scene.

When you stop your car at the scene, you give the appearance to other potential rescuers that you'll take care of the victim. At that point, you establish a nurse-patient relationship for that particular emergency. You owe the victim the normal duty you owe any patient — treatment that meets the

(Text continues on page 261.)

State Good Samaritan acts

	Alabama	Alaska	Arizona	Arkansas	California	Colorado	Connecticut	Delaware	District of Columbia	
Statute	6-5-332	9.65.090	32-1471	17-93-101	§2395	13-21-108	52-557b	16 §6802	2-1344	
Good Faith Effort	•		•	•	•	•		•	•	
Covers in-state nurses	•						•			
Covers in-state and out-of-state nurses			•				•			
Covers "any person" (4)		•	•	•	•	•			•	
Separate Good Samaritan act for nurses								•		
Covers only gratuitous services	•		•	•		•	•	•	•	
Covers emergencies occurring in health care facilities		•			•	•				
Specifically protects against failure to provide or arrange for further medical treatment	•		•							
Specifically covers transportation from the scene of the emergency to the destination for further medical treatment								•		
Specifically mentions that acts of gross negligence or willful or wanton misconduct aren't covered		•	•		•	•	•	•	•	
Includes duty-to-rescue statute										

(1) Florida: in hospitals only; (2) Kansas: applies only to health care practitioners; (3) Florida: requires consent by statute; (4) California: licensee.

Use this chart to familiarize yourself with your state's Good Samaritan act. You may want to check with your board of nursing to make sure your state hasn't passed amendments that would affect how this law pertains to your practice.

	Florida	Georgia	Hawaii	Idaho	Illinois	Indiana	Iowa	Kansas	Kentucky	Louisiana	Maine	Maryland
	21B §768.13	51-1-29	663.1.5	§5-330	745ILCS 4940	34-30-12.1	613.17	65-2891	411.148	37:1731	14§164	5-603
	•	•	•	•	•	•	•	•		•		
		•				•		•	•	•		
					•							
	•	•	•	•			•	•			•	•
					•	•						
	•	•	•		•	•	•	•	•	•	•	•
	•							•				
	•	•				•				•		
				•			•					•
	•		•	•	•	•	•	•	•		•	•

(continued)

State Good Samaritan acts (continued)

	Massachusetts	Michigan	Minnesota	Mississippi	Missouri	Montana	Nebraska	Nevada	New Hampshire
Statute	112:12B	691.1501	604A.01	73-25-37	537.037	27-1-714	25-21,186	41.500	508.12a
Good Faith Effort	•	•		•	•	•		•	•
Covers in-state nurses		•		•					
Covers in-state and out-of-state nurses	•				•				
Covers "any person"			•			•	•	•	•
Separate Good Samaritan act for nurses									
Covers only gratuitous services	•	•	•		•	•	•	•	•
Covers emergencies occurring in health care facilities									
Specifically protects against failure to provide or arrange for further medical treatment							•	•	
Specifically covers transportation from the scene of the emergency to the destination for further medical treatment			•	•					•
Specifically mentions that acts of gross negligence or willful or wanton misconduct aren't covered		•	•		•	•		•	•
Includes duty-to-rescue statute			•						

	New Jersey	New Mexico	New York	North Carolina	North Dakota	Ohio	Oklahoma	Oregon	Pennsylvania	Rhode Island	South Carolina	South Dakota
	2A:62A-1	24-10-3	30-300-a	90-21.16	32-03.1-02	2305.23	76§5	30.800	42-§8331	5-34-34	15-1-310	20-9-3
	•	•					•	•	•	•	•	
	•											•
				•			•	•	•	•		
		•	•	•		•					•	
	•						•	•	•	•		•
		•	•	•		•	•			•	•	
				•								
										•		
		•	•	•	•	•	•	•	•	•		
										•		

(continued)

State Good Samaritan acts (continued)

	Tennessee	Texas	Utah	Vermont	Virginia	Washington	West Virginia	Wisconsin	Wyoming
Statute	63-6-218	74.001	78-11-22	24§71	32.1-111.14.1	4.24.3000	55-7-15	895.48	1-1-120
Good Faith Effort	•	•	•		•		•	•	•
Covers in-state nurses	•								
Covers in-state and out-of-state nurses									
Covers "any person"	•	•	•	•	•	•	•	•	•
Separate Good Samaritan act for nurses	•								
Covers only gratuitous services	•	•	•	•	•	•	•	•	•
Covers emergencies occurring in health care facilities									
Specifically protects against failure to provide or arrange for further medical treatment	•								
Specifically covers transportation from the scene of the emergency to the destination for further medical treatment	•				•	•			
Specifically mentions that acts of gross negligence or willful or wanton misconduct aren't covered	•	•	•	•	•	•			
Includes duty-to-rescue statute				•				•	

standard of care of a reasonably prudent nurse in a similar situation.

Breach of duty

Once you've stopped to help, you can avoid breaching your duty by using the same good judgment that you use every day on the job. However, what if you *do* breach your duty in this unusual situation?

If your performance falls below the standard of care expected of a reasonably prudent nurse in a similar situation, the court will decide whether your act worsened the victim's condition. In most states your action or inaction has to be grossly negligent, intentional, or reckless for there to be a cause of action. If your act didn't make the victim measurably worse, the court may find that the harm committed doesn't warrant damages. Your act must cause measurable harm for the court to consider you legally responsible.

Causation

Some states consider the fact that a person has difficulty in proving causation and will allow an "increased risk of harm standard;" that is, your action or inaction increased the risk of harm and was a substantial factor in causing damages. The victim must prove that the probability is better than 50% that your error (whether an act of commission or omission) caused his injuries. Historically, the courts have recognized the 50% figure as the standard. Because the typical victim already has suffered injuries from the accident, he's likely to have a hard time proving that your error caused or worsened his injuries.

In making it hard for the accident victim to prove you negligent, the courts must balance the victim's right to justice with society's need to encourage trained professionals to assist in emergencies.

GOOD SAMARITAN ACTS

Good Samaritan acts limit your liability for any service you render at an accident or emergency scene unless it's proved that your care was grossly negligent or intentionally harmful or that you were the person who initially caused the emergent situation. Most states require your services to be performed in good faith, meaning that you sincerely intended to help. Also, a few states specifically require consent for the services you render. However, if someone is unconscious or unable to communicate, implied consent is assumed.

Good Samaritan acts don't prevent an accident victim from filing a malpractice suit, but to win such a suit the injury party must prove that you intentionally caused his injury or were grossly negligent in your care.

Determining gross negligence

No law can protect you if you commit an act of gross negligence — an extremely careless act or omission that seriously violates the applicable standard of care.

In court, jury members decide whether your negligent error constitutes "ordinary" negligence or "gross" negligence. To make this distinction, they measure your error against the local standard of care, which may vary from place to place. For example, what may qualify as ordinary negligence in rural Georgia may be gross negligence in metropolitan New York. However, as more nurses take certification examinations that are national in scope, members of the profession are held increasingly accountable to a national standard, like physicians.

Additionally, the court considers your training and experience to decide whether you've breached the standard of care and, if so, to what degree. This

LEGAL TIP

Care tips for Good Samaritans

When you stop at an emergency scene to offer assistance, always observe professional standards of nursing care, regardless of the setting. To reduce your malpractice risk, follow these guidelines:

◆ Ask the injured person, or family member, if available, for permission to help.

◆ Care for the victim in the vehicle or at the exact site, if you can do so safely.

◆ Assess the possibility of fractures.

◆ Move the victim if he's in danger and if conditions permit. Avoid moving him needlessly, and don't try to straighten his arms and legs.

◆ Let him lie or sit quietly. Don't carry him or force him to walk.

◆ Keep his airway open.

◆ Stop his bleeding.

◆ Keep the victim warm.

◆ Determine his level of consciousness.

◆ Ask the victim where he feels pain.

◆ Avoid speculating about who or what caused the accident.

◆ Allow only skilled personnel to attend or treat the victim.

◆ Stay at the accident site until skilled personnel arrive to assume care of the victim.

◆ Provide a complete picture of the care given.

◆ Guard the injured person's personal property. Release it to the police or members of his family.

Legal discrepancies

Good Samaritan protection varies. For example, some acts specifically include nurses, whereas other acts — those in Florida and Alaska, for example — protect any person who offers help to a victim. Some acts protect out-of-state nurses only if they're trained in cardiopulmonary resuscitation. In some jurisdictions, Good Samaritan acts include only "practitioners of the healing arts." The courts usually interpret this terminology to mean physicians and dentists. (See *Understanding Good Samaritan acts.*)

Compensated care

Keep in mind that most Good Samaritan acts apply only to uncompensated emergency care. If you charge or accept money for your services, the law usually says that you forfeit the special protections afforded by such acts.

INVOKING GOOD SAMARITAN LAW

Regardless of the kind of Good Samaritan act your state or jurisdiction has, accident victims rarely sue "Good Samaritans." Although nurses have been sued, when the Good Samaritan defense has been raised, no nurse has been found responsible. In addition, common law so far has served as a deterrent.

Ironically, though, auto accident victims sometimes claim that a Good Samaritan act *requires* a nurse or physician to respond at an accident scene. To date, the courts have accepted this argument only in those states that have enacted duty-to-rescue laws.

In some states, physicians have invoked a Good Samaritan act as a defense against malpractice suits, claiming that the act protects them from liability for emergency services they provided in a hospital. In Illinois, a physician re-

means that the court holds registered nurses (RNs) — even as Good Samaritans — to a higher standard than it holds licensed practical nurses (LPNs). (See *Care tips for Good Samaritans.*)

Understanding Good Samaritan acts

Am I covered by a Good Samaritan act if I respond to an emergency outside the hospital while I'm officially on duty?
That depends on two things: the wording of the act in your state and court decisions, if any, interpreting that act. All Good Samaritan acts cover aid at the scene of an emergency, accident, or disaster. If an emergency occurs just outside the hospital and you provide care while on duty, most likely this would be considered providing care in an emergency setting and, therefore, would be covered under Good Samaritan law. Note that some states' Good Samaritan statutes specifically cover emergencies outside of the hospital, physician's office, and other places that have medical equipment.

I live and work in Kansas. Every year, I go skiing in a different state. What if I help an accident victim while I'm vacationing? Does the Good Samaritan act of the state I'm in apply to me?
It does if that state's act says it applies to "any person." It may not, however, if the act specifically states that it applies only to "nurses." The designation "nurses" in a law or act may mean

a registered nurse, licensed practical nurse, or licensed vocational nurse licensed in that state.

Does the Good Samaritan Act apply if I accept money from the person I've helped?
Not usually. By accepting money in such a situation, you establish a professional relationship with the person you've helped.

For how long am I responsible to the person I've helped?
Statutory law doesn't address this subject, but common law does. The courts say your responsibility ends:
◆ when the emergency ends (when you're certain that the victim is no longer in danger)
◆ when an authorized rescuer or other qualified medical service takes over for you
◆ when the victim is pronounced dead.

If a physician and I respond to the same emergency, does the Good Samaritan act cover us equally?
Not necessarily. In some states, the Good Samaritan act for nurses differs completely from the Good Samaritan act for physicians. Contact your state nursing board to find out what's true for your state.

---

sponded to an in-hospital emergency in which both parties (mother and fetus) later died, and the estate brought suit. The physician successfully invoked, as part of his defense, the Illinois Good Samaritan Act. The appellate court found that the Act protected the physician from liability for a true hospital emergency in which the service was provided in good faith and without fee. Using this argument in California, physicians have met with mixed results. The same argument won't hold for nurses in California be-

cause the Good Samaritan act specifically covers nurses only during emergencies "outside both the place and course" of employment.

DUTY TO RESCUE

Four states and most Canadian jurisdictions (as well as most European countries) have taken the Good Samaritan principle a step further by requiring potential rescuers to help a victim. Vermont's law, the first of its type in the United States, defines a *rescuer* as a person who knows another is exposed to grave physical harm. The Vermont law requires that anyone (Vermont resident or not) who can help a victim must do so, provided he won't be endangering himself or interfering with important duties he owes to others. Minnesota has a similar law, as do Rhode Island and Wisconsin (which has a "duty to rescue crime victims" law).

These Duty to Rescue statutes provide penalties for failure to comply. The Rhode Island and Wisconsin statutes set fines of up to $500 and possible imprisonment for up to 6 months; the Vermont statute provides for a fine of up to $100; Minnesota doesn't set out specific penalties, but it does consider the violation a petty misdemeanor.

In contrast, some other states have Duty to Rescue statutes that apply specifically to criminal events causing injury. They generally provide for liability if someone on the scene fails to report the crime or call for assistance, but they don't specifically address the requirement to render aid to the victim. The Quebec statute provides no penalties for failure to comply.

How a duty-to-rescue law would apply to nurses remains uncertain. For example, if you pass an accident scene on the way to your dentist, the duty-to-rescue law requires you to stop and try to help. However, what if you're on your way to work? Would your nursing job be considered an important duty owed to others? The answer to this question eventually will come from the courts.

Giving free health care advice

Most likely, friends and family members rely on you for advice on health

matters. Respond cautiously, even though this may seem unnatural when speaking with individuals you know well. Keep in mind that you can be sued for giving inappropriate advice. If you decide not to give advice at all, be reassured: The law doesn't require it.

If you choose to offer advice, be aware of positions on the issue taken by your state's nurse practice act, common law, professional organizations, and your malpractice insurance coverage. (See *Minimizing legal risks when giving advice.*)

FREE ADVICE AND THE LAW

In a hospital setting, giving health care advice may be construed to be a part of patient teaching, a recognized nursing function. Outside of this setting, giving advice may subject you to liability if, in giving the advice, you don't act as a reasonably prudent nurse.

The person suing you for harm caused by inappropriate advice must prove that you owed him a specific duty, that you breached that duty, that he was harmed, and that the harm was a result of the breach of duty.

Establishing breach of duty

For a duty to exist, you must have a nurse-patient relationship with the person asking for your advice. This rarely occurs in everyday, short-lived conversations with other people. Suppose, for example, that you're a guest at a cocktail party. Another guest finds out that you're a nurse and bombards you with questions about his health. If you decide to answer, you have a duty to answer as correctly as a reasonably prudent nurse would, but you don't have a duty to follow up after the party is over or to monitor the outcome of your advice. The person who's asking your advice hasn't established (or clearly indicated to you that he intends to establish) an ongoing nurse-patient relationship with you.

Establishing probable reliance

The situation may be different if you decide to give advice to a neighbor. For instance, imagine that your neighbor calls across the yard and asks you about her child's fretfulness. You observe honestly that the child's activity doesn't appear to warrant a call to the physician. A day later, you see the mother and child together outdoors, and the child appears particularly listless. If you discover that the child has a fever or other signs and symptoms of illness, you're legally and professionally responsible for telling the mother to take the child to a physician as soon as possible. This holds true regardless of your original advice.

You must respond to the mother's probable reliance on you for further advice, even though your original intention wasn't to form a nurse-patient relationship with her and her child.

Again, if you realize that your neighbor now relies on you for further advice, you have an obligation — a legal and professional duty — to keep your advice current as the situation changes. Or you may opt to take formal steps to break off the relationship by telling the mother to look elsewhere for help.

Keep in mind that the principles that apply to your on-duty work also apply to off-duty advice. The help and advice you give your patient Monday morning may have to be changed by Tuesday afternoon. Furthermore, if a patient's questions reveal that his problem may be beyond the scope of nursing practice, you have a clear duty to advise the individual to seek the care of a physician. (See *Neighborly advice: Some legal safeguards,* page 266.)

LEGAL TIP

Minimizing legal risks when giving advice

Here are some steps to take to minimize your risk when giving health care advice to friends or family.

What to do

◆ Be sure that your advice reflects accepted professional and community standards.

◆ Check whether your (or your employer's) professional liability insurance covers such off-the-job nursing activities as giving advice.

◆ Remember that Good Samaritan acts exclude gratuitous actions not associated with an emergency. However, keep in mind that some state statutes specifically include illnesses.

◆ Know what – if anything – your state's nurse practice act says about giving advice to friends.

◆ Give advice only within the confines of your nurse practice act, education, and experience.

◆ Make sure that the advice you give is up-to-date. You'll be judged on current nursing standards if your advice results in a lawsuit.

What not to do

◆ Don't charge a fee or accept money for your advice.

◆ Avoid speculating about your friends' illnesses or ailments.

◆ Never suggest that friends change or ignore their physicians' orders.

◆ Steer clear of giving a medical diagnosis, medical opinion, or advice about medical care.

◆ Avoid giving directions that, if wrong or misinterpreted, could result in serious or permanent injury.

Law Q&A ▸ Neighborly advice: Some legal safeguards

My best friend Sara and I have babies the same age. Sara isn't a nurse, and I know she relies on my judgment a lot. How should I answer her when she asks questions? For instance, yesterday, she asked, "If your Richie had a rash like Tommy's, would you take him to the doctor?"

If you answer "yes," no harm will result from your advice, and you'll be on safe legal ground. If you answer "no," and if following your advice results in harm to the child, you may be liable. In such situations — best friend or not — conservative advice is legally safer, especially if you have doubts.

I seem to be the neighborhood ear-piercer. Of course, with children I require a parent's permission, and I warn everyone about the risks of infection and how to reduce them. Still, I'm worried: If someone got an infection and sued me, would this verbal warning protect me from malpractice liability?

Some states have legislation or regulations governing ear piercing, so check with your state licensing board. If your state doesn't have regulations on ear piercing, your warnings

about possible infection protect you only if infection results from piercing done according to accepted standards. The warning doesn't protect you if the infection results from your negligence. Written confirmation of the warning provides a little better protection.

One of my neighbors comes to see me whenever one of her family members gets sick or enters the hospital. She's a good friend and I'm glad to help, but I think she's making a habit of asking for my advice. I feel especially uncomfortable when she asks me to explain everything the physician tells her. Once she said, "The doctor says my husband might have adhesions from a previous operation. What does that mean? Is that common?" How can I answer her questions and protect myself too? Should I say, "I can tell you only what I know from my own experience?"

You'd be better off saying, "I can tell you what those terms usually mean, but not what they mean in your husband's case." You can best serve your neighbor, though, by encouraging her to ask the physician to explain anything she doesn't understand.

PROFESSIONAL STANDARDS

Whenever you establish a professional relationship with an individual seeking advice, you must provide an answer as good as any reasonably prudent nurse would give in similar circumstances.

Do this by applying the same standards that you're expected to apply in your regular work. If you feel confident that you know the answer — and your education and experience support you — you're legally free to give it. Naturally, you must make sure your answer is correct and that giving it falls within your scope of nursing practice.

To protect yourself, you might say something such as, "I think your problem sounds like arthritis, but it could be something more serious, and I'm not sure. You should ask a physician."

Remember, you're legally protected if you refer the questioner to his physician. However, the law doesn't require you to make that suggestion if you're honestly convinced that it isn't necessary and that a reasonably prudent nurse wouldn't make it either.

Guard against the temptation to say, "Don't worry," when family members or friends ask for advice. Reassure them only if you're certain that nothing is seriously wrong. The law requires you to apply this standard: If I were at work and one of my patients asked the same question, what would I tell him? Try to imagine that an inquiring family member or friend is a complete stranger. Then give your best professionally considered answer.

Medical advice

Giving health care advice can lead to legal problems if the advice can be interpreted as medical advice. Then you may be at risk for practicing medicine without a license. Instead, urge the person seeking medical advice to seek medical attention, either at a hospital or with a physician.

Donating nursing services

Many health care professionals, including nurses, donate their professional services to community organizations or activities.

Usually, when you volunteer your nursing services, no pay is involved. At times, you may "volunteer" services for pay by providing nursing care outside of your usual paid work. In such situations, you're volunteering your personal time while being paid for your nursing services.

You might donate your nursing services to family members, friends, or such community organizations and activities as the following:
◆ a community ambulance service
◆ a bloodmobile or hypertension outreach program
◆ a home and school association panel discussion on child health issues
◆ a community or sporting event.

As a nurse, your responsibilities to patients don't change when you do-

nate your services. However, your legal status does. It becomes less defined than when you're paid. In most states, nurse practice acts specify only the legal limits of paid nursing practice.

DONATED SERVICES AND THE LAW

Being exempt from your state's nurse practice act if you donate nursing services doesn't mean you'll be exempt from a lawsuit. In such a situation, the court can use the provisions of your state nurse practice act — together with expert witness testimony and applicable standards of nursing care — to determine if you acted as a prudent nurse would have acted in similar patient care circumstances. If the court finds that your care didn't conform to the requirements of your state's nurse practice act, you may be facing a malpractice suit. In addition, your malpractice insurance may or may not cover your voluntary services. Because insurance is a contract, you should review your insurance policy's language to determine its application and coverage. (See *Minimizing legal risks when volunteering,* page 268.)

Even if no lawsuit results, you may be subject to discipline by your state nursing board if the board finds that your services fall below the accepted standard of care. In such a situation, the board may suspend or even revoke your license.

Volunteering out of state

If you travel to a state in which you aren't licensed to practice, you aren't prohibited from donating your nursing services as long as that state's nurse practice act covers only paid nursing care. However, if you're sued, the court will probably evaluate your actions and their consequences against whatever

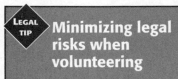

Minimizing legal risks when volunteering

When offering your time and skills for free, observe the same standards of care that you observe in your paid job. Consider these guidelines:

Have necessary orders

Obtain a physician's order or a standing order before giving any treatment or medication that requires such an order.

Document your actions

Document your donated care as carefully as you document the care you give on the job. Keep a copy of your nurses' notes so you have a permanent record of your actions should a question ever arise.

Check your coverage

Check your professional liability insurance and its limitations from every angle before agreeing to donate your services to any organization. Also check the coverage provided by the organization that receives your volunteer services. Does your or the organization's coverage include the volunteer nursing duty that you're considering? Is the coverage adequate in light of the potential damages and legal fees that you might have to pay if sued?

standard of nursing care would apply in that state rather than your home state.

Good Samaritan acts

Good Samaritan acts won't cover you in day-to-day situations in which you donate nursing services. These acts apply only to accidents or other emergency situations. In addition, not all state Good Samaritan acts extend coverage to all nurses.

Acting during a disaster

A tornado levels a part of your community. Spring floods take life and property at the south end of town. A freight train derails, blanketing the community with toxic vapor. The brakes fail on an airplane carrying 137 passengers, and the craft careens off the runway. Any of these disastrous events can overload local medical and nursing resources. In situations such as these, nurses have special responsibilities and legal rights.

CONTRACT DUTIES

When you give nursing care during a disaster, professional, ethical, and legal concerns figure heavily in every decision you make. In general, with the exception of declared emergencies, a nurse's responsibilities in a disaster don't differ legally from her everyday responsibilities. You may have specific duties to perform in specific kinds of disasters, and you may be legally bound to perform those duties, but that's likely to be based on your employment contract and not on laws or precedent-setting legal cases.

If you work in a city hospital, for example, your employment contract may contain a provision that you can be called to work whenever a government official declares a state of emergency. If you refuse to come in, you can be disciplined, suspended, or fired. This rule applies even if the work you're assigned to do isn't normally part of your job description.

If you're already on the job when a disaster occurs, the same contractual provisions may be invoked to keep you from going home at the end of your shift. And the same penalties apply if you refuse to cooperate.

Similarly, if you're an unpaid volunteer for a community service, such as the Red Cross or an ambulance unit, you may be expected to report for duty in any local disaster as long as your reporting doesn't conflict with your regular employment. If you refuse, the service can drop you from its roster; if you're a paid, part-time worker for such an organization, you can be dismissed. These duties apply even if your work arrangements are unwritten but are part of an oral agreement.

Contract defenses

Because reporting for work in an emergency, including a disaster, is usually a contract matter, specific contract defenses apply if you're disciplined for failing to fulfill your duties. One such contract defense is that of impossibility. If reporting is impossible for you and you can prove it—even if you're contractually required to do so and would be paid for the work—you can't be disciplined or prosecuted. For example, if a blizzard absolutely prohibits travel from your home to the job or disastrous flooding causes the governor to ban all travel in your area, what your contract says doesn't matter much. In addition, if you're disciplined, you have a legal defense. However, watch for exceptions to travel bans—for example, a ban may be announced for all but "required personnel" or "persons with medical or nursing training." In those situations, obviously you must report for duty.

Volunteering during a disaster

No law prevents you from voluntarily donating your services, and specific statutory or common laws may provide protection. If you want to volunteer your help in a disaster, do it, whether anyone in authority has asked you. (See *Minimizing legal risks during a disaster,* page 270.)

Suppose you're working in a hospital that doesn't have a policy mandating that health care personnel report to work when a disaster occurs. You can still volunteer to stay for extra shifts or to perform services outside your normal scope of employment. The hospital will almost certainly accept your offer, if they haven't already asked for help. That's especially likely if emergency conditions prevent other staff nurses from reporting to work.

You can't necessarily expect your pay to reflect the extra work performed during a disaster. Most facilities will try to pay for the overtime, but some may not. If you're curious, find out what your facility's policy is before a disaster occurs. The policy may depend on union rules, state fair labor employment laws, or, if you work in a city or state hospital, on city ordinances or state regulations.

Volunteering in another state

Nurse practice acts don't legally restrict you from volunteering during a disaster in an out-of-state location. For instance, suppose you're licensed in California and while you're on vacation in Oregon, a disaster occurs. You can give your nursing services during the disaster without concern that you're breaching California's or Oregon's nurse practice act. That's because most nurse practice acts have a special exemption for care given in emergen-

Minimizing legal risks during a disaster

By taking a few precautions, you can help assure protection from liability when working under disaster conditions.

Be prepared
Don't wait for a disaster to happen before you ask your charge nurse what you'll be required to do during a disaster. Keep equipment you're likely to need available and in working condition.

Follow instructions
In any disaster, public officials and other authorities – such as medical personnel, public health workers, or municipal staff – will probably issue orders. Even if these people aren't normally your superiors, follow their directions as much as possible. Offer advice only when you think necessary.

Know your limits
Don't work beyond the point of effectiveness. If you're so tired that you can't make correct decisions, no one will benefit from your care. Describe your fatigue to the person in charge, and ask for a break.

cies that usually includes disasters. Some state statutes specifically address nurses with out-of-state licenses, as the table on pages 256 to 260 reflects.

Right to refuse
If you don't want to volunteer, and your hospital policy or contract doesn't require it — or, as happens rarely, if you don't have a contract — in most states you have the right to refuse. Most nurse practice acts don't require you to provide emergency care in disasters, any more than they require you to perform care. They only permit such care. Similarly, Good Samaritan acts provide some legal immunity for giving emergency care but don't require you to provide that care — except in states with duty-to-rescue laws.

Civil defense laws, also known as disaster relief laws, don't apply in most states to nurses who aren't already involved in civil defense work — although in a declared national emergency, nurses (like anyone else) can be drafted. Alternatively, martial law may be imposed, which makes all citizens subject to public authority. Many civil defense laws authorize state or federal governing bodies to enforce special regulations dealing with the duties of medical and nursing personnel in a declared emergency. Some states already have such plans ready for use in a sufficiently serious disaster.

Deciding whether to volunteer
When deciding whether to help out in a disaster, assess your actual ability to help. Caring for the disaster victims may require particular skills — for example, knowledge of a special area such as toxicology. Alternatively, the skill required may be as simple as rowing a boat in a flood.

Also, consider whether you can get to the disaster site or to the place where care will be provided. If an airliner crashes, for example, and emergency departments throughout the city are treating victims, your ability to get to your hospital or another hospital quickly may figure in whether you decide to volunteer. What if, for example, the disaster involves a riot occurring during a total blackout in your city, and the mayor decrees, "Don't travel to work unless you're within walking distance"? If you try to drive into the city from your suburban home, you'll only complicate driving conditions — and you probably won't get to your hospital in time to be helpful.

You may also consider whether volunteering in the disaster will keep you from working and earning your regular salary. Find out, too, whether your professional liability insurance covers services provided in a disaster or other off-the-job activities.

WORKING OUTSIDE YOUR SCOPE OF PRACTICE

In a disaster, you may find yourself performing duties outside your usual scope of practice. If you're an LPN or a licensed vocational nurse, you may be asked to perform duties that ordinarily would be restricted to RNs, and nurses' aides may be asked to do work you usually do. If you're an RN, you may find yourself doing tasks usually reserved for medical residents. And either you or a resident may be asked to do work a nursing assistant would normally do. Provided you have the knowledge and skill to meet minimum safety requirements, you may be permitted to give such substitute care in disasters based on the same exemption in nurse practice acts that lets an out-of-state nurse volunteer her services in a disaster. This exemption may be construed as letting you expand the scope of your practice in a disaster. You'll want to check your state's nurse practice act to determine such exemption. Even if it can't be construed this way, statutory or common laws usually permit regulatory authorities to place the public welfare above strict enforcement of the letter of the law.

Selected references

Hampshire, M. "Aftershock," *Nursing Standard* 14(29):16-17, April 2000.

Sbaih, L.C. "Dilemma — Volunteering Help," *Accidental Emergency Nursing* 9(4):222-24, October 2001.

Tumolo, J. "To the Rescue. Considering the Risks and Rewards of Being a Good Samaritan," *Advanced Nurse Practitioner* 10(2):68-70, February 2002.

Walker, M. "To Stop or Not: Good Samaritan 2001," *Journal of Christian Nurses* 18(3):34-35, Summer 2001.

Chapter 9

Nurses' rights as employees

Decent wages mean financial security for you and your family. Optimal working conditions can mean improved job security, enhanced job satisfaction, and the opportunity to deliver the best possible care to your patients.

However, to achieve the wages, benefits, and working conditions you deserve, you need to understand your rights as an employee. You also need to be prepared to take appropriate action if your employee rights are violated.

Becoming familiar with the information in this chapter will help you assert your employee rights. The focus of this chapter is on two crucial issues: strategies for reading and understanding an employment contract and the pros and cons of joining a union.

You'll learn about types of contracts and implied conditions as well as what to do if your employer breaches your employment contract. You'll also learn about the strategies unions use to protect the rights of their nurse-members, including collective bargaining, grievance procedures, arbitration, and strikes, and how these strategies may affect you.

Understanding employment contracts

Most nurses are hired without the benefit of a written employment contract. Usually, an application or a résumé is submitted and an agreement is reached as to the start date, position, benefits, and starting pay. This arrangement is no less legal than a written contract. It does, however, present certain problems if, at a later date, some portion of the employment agreement is disputed by either party.

If you sign an employment contract, read it carefully to make sure it adequately defines your duties, authority, and benefits. Knowing what to look for in a contract will help you decide if a particular job is right for you. Learning to interpret contract terms will help you function within the contract's specified limits. Also, be sure to carefully read the procedure for terminating the contract.

Labor attorneys try to draft most employment agreements as *at-will contracts,* meaning that either party can end the agreement for any reason or for no reason. These contracts are in contrast to the less common just cause agreements, in which the employer must have just cause to fire you or risk penalties if a court finds that you were wrongfully terminated. Although the at-will contract has benefits for the employer, the employer risks having the employee quit at any time, without a reason.

RESTRICTIONS OF AT-WILL CONTRACTS

There are some important restrictions on an employer's ability to terminate an employee at will. Primarily, these restrictions arise if an employer's decision to terminate an employee violates a law — for example, firing someone based on race, religion, sex, or other factors addressed by antidiscrimination laws. (The scope of these laws differs depending on the state. Firing based on race, for example, is illegal in all states as well as under federal law. Firing someone based on sexual orientation, on the other hand, is illegal in some states, but not in others, and it isn't prohibited by federal law.)

In some states, legislation has recently been enacted that prohibits health care employers from firing nurses (and, in many cases, other employees) who act as whistle-blowers by reporting unsafe conditions or illegal activities to state or federal agencies. Employers also can't fire someone for exercising her legal right to join a union or to engage in collective bargaining.

In addition to situations where terminating an employee violates an existing law, most states (except Alabama, Florida, Georgia, Louisiana, Maine, Nebraska, New York, and Rhode Island) recognize a "public-policy" exception to at-will employment. Under the public-policy exemption, an employer wrongfully terminates an employee when said termination violates a state's well-established public policy, which can be found in the state's constitution, statutes, administrative rules, common laws, and any expansion thereof. For example, it would be against public policy if an employer fired an employee for filing a worker's compensation claim after being injured on the job or for refusing to break the law at the employer's request. However, states differ in terms of how they define them.

Some states also recognize an *implied covenant of good faith and fair dealing*, meaning that an employer can't fire an employee maliciously or in bad faith. Even among those states that recognize this exception to "at-will" employment there are differences in how far it extends and how to apply it.

TYPES OF CONTRACTS

A *contract* is a legally binding promise between two parties that can be enforced in court. According to U.S. and Canadian law, an employment contract is legally binding if all of these provisions apply:

◆ You've accepted an offer, verbally or in writing, to perform in a certain capacity.

◆ You and the other person are legally competent, of legal age, and without mental impairment.

◆ You both understand the agreement.

◆ The terms of the agreement are lawful.

◆ You receive something of value such as money for fulfilling the agreement or, in some cases, you give up something of value.

In general, agreements about conscience, morals, and social activities aren't legally binding. If you break a lunch date, you can't be fined or taken to court. If you violate any term in a legally binding contract, however, you might face consequences.

Written contract

Sometimes an employment contract is a formal, written contract. It may be an individual contract, which you negotiate, or a collectively bargained contract that was negotiated by a nurse negotiation committee and a labor organization or union. In either contract, wage increases may be awarded automatically or may be linked to merit or experience.

Oral express contract

Contracts need not be in writing to be legally binding. An employment agreement can be and is usually an oral contract, offered and accepted orally. Most states allow parties to orally agree to employment relationships, and those contracts are legal and enforceable in court (assuming state law allows them). However, because the judge and jury won't have a written contract to consider if a dispute about the terms of employment arises, other documents (such as an employee handbook, a notice of a physical examination, a welcoming letter, or pay stubs) would play a major role in proving that such an oral contract existed and outlining its terms.

Finally, witnesses who may have overheard the offer extended to the nurse and the nurse's acceptance may be called to testify at a hearing, deposition, or trial to prove the existence of an oral employment agreement.

Pitfalls of oral contracts

An oral contract can be problematic if the parties involved disagree about its terms. Memories fail and witnesses move away or may become otherwise unavailable. Consequently, if the original agreement isn't in writing, the subjective and fallible memories of the parties may have to reconstruct it. If the matter must be litigated, more time

and money will be spent to prove what simply could have been put into writing.

If an employer doesn't offer you a written contract, you can write a letter to the person with whom you spoke, confirming that you accept the offer and repeating the terms you heard. Confirm the start date and say that you look forward to working with that person. Be sure to put all important, agreed-to terms and conditions in the letter. At the end, write that if they have anything to add or disagree with the matters in your letter, they should contact you in writing at their earliest convenience. Send the letter, but first make a copy for your file. Hopefully, you'll never need to refer to it.

IMPLIED CONDITIONS

Most contracts contain *implied conditions*—elements that aren't explicitly stated but are assumed to be part of the contract. For example, your employer assumes that you'll practice nursing in a safe, competent manner as defined by your nurse practice act and the health care facility's standards and policies. You assume, based on implied conditions, that the employer will provide you with resources, supplies, and equipment necessary for you to perform your work and that the employer will ensure a safe working environment.

OFFER AND ACCEPTANCE

In any contract, there must be an offer and an acceptance. An offer must be definite and communicated by words or actions. If you fail to respond, the employer can't interpret your silence as acceptance, but can withdraw the other without penalty at any time before it has been accepted. Although you may orally accept an offer or simply report for duty, a written acceptance is generally best. The employment contract should be as specific as possible about wages, hours, and the terms and conditions of the relationship. (See *Components of an employment contract*.)

BREACH OF CONTRACT

Unjustified failure to perform all or part of your contractual duty is considered a breach of contract. If the breach is substantial, the entire agreement may have been broken and legal damages may result. (In the case of at-will employment, a likely consequence is that the employment relationship will terminate.) If only part of the agreement has been breached, the remaining contract may still be effective and both parties may want to continue the relationship, with some clarification. Breaches can be avoided if both parties carefully consider the terms and conditions of the contract and know what they're promising each other.

Employee breach of contract

When you agree to do (or not to do) something in an employment contract, and you don't perform as promised, you may be in breach of the contract and subject to litigation forcing you to perform as promised. You may even be required to reimburse your employer for the cost of hiring someone else to do the job that you were supposed to do.

It's rare, except in unusual circumstances, for a court to order an employee to perform services against his will. If the employment relationship is at-will, failure to perform may simply terminate the agreement. However, in other employment contracts — especially those involving specialized services — failure to perform as agreed

---

Components of an employment contract

For an employment contract to be legally binding, it must include the following components:

A promise
Two or more legally competent parties must promise each other to do or not do something.

Mutual understanding
The parties involved must clearly understand the terms and obligations the contract imposes on them.

Compensation
The parties involved must agree that, to fulfill the contract, lawful actions will be performed in exchange for something of value.

---

may result in legal consequences, which may require the person to perform as agreed in the contract.

Of course, the terms and conditions of a contract can be changed or modified by oral or written agreement — certainly, it's far better to change a contract than to breach it. Good communication may prevent a perceived breach, and renegotiation is cheaper than litigation.

Employer breach of contract

An employer may also breach a contract. If, for example, he fails to give you the vacation time agreed to, he has breached the contract. If you discover a breach, follow procedures outlined in your employee handbook.

Commonly, misunderstandings can be cleared up by talking with the proper people in the chain of command (always in a professional and unemotional manner). If documents are involved, they're important proof. If you have a union contract, tell your representative as soon as you're aware of a breach.

If you exhaust all channels of appeal, you may need to discuss the problem with an attorney with contract and employment law expertise, using a written log of your attempts to rectify the situation, including statements made, with dates and times.

Canadian law

Because the law varies by jurisdiction, it's best to check with local legal counsel about procedures and deadlines.

INVALID CONTRACTS

A nursing employment contract is considered invalid when the agreement concerns actions that are illegal or impossible to carry out, or when any of the following applies:
◆ An applicant has lied about qualifications.
◆ A nurse is forced into signing a contract.
◆ The agreement involves unlawful activity — for example, it requires you to bill for services that weren't actually performed.
◆ A minor or mentally incompetent person signs the contract.

Physical or mental inability to carry out the agreement may be a basis to set the agreement aside but not always. Both parties expect, from the start, that the nurse will be able to physically carry out the agreement.

If your health status changes, you may feel that your agreement no longer stands. If litigated, your obliga-

tion will be determined on an individual basis by the judge. Mere physical or mental disability won't void the contract. However, you may be protected under the Americans with Disabilities Act, which requires reasonable accommodations in certain instances.

TERMINATING A CONTRACT

When you terminate a contract, you've fulfilled or absolved yourself of all obligations. Because most employment contracts don't specify termination dates, you can end them at any time, if you follow proper notification procedures. You can also end contracts with termination dates if your employer agrees to the date. Follow the contract's procedures for giving written notice (most require 2 to 4 weeks) or, if your contract has an automatic expiration date, don't renew it.

Your employer can terminate your contract if he determines that you're incompetent or have behaved unprofessionally on the job. Before discharging you, he'll probably give you several warnings about the quality of your work. Then he might confront you with several examples of your shortcomings from previous written evaluations of your performance. If you don't want to lose your job, you should discuss areas of improvement with him.

If you disagree with your employer's complaints, you can request an evaluation by someone else who supervised your work, or you can request a transfer to another unit where you would be reevaluated after an agreed-upon length of time. However, your employer isn't obligated to agree to either request unless these steps are part of a disciplinary process stated in an employment contract or an employee manual. If he doesn't agree, you may seek written support from your coworkers who will refute your employer's complaints. You can also seek support from your union, if you have one. The union may file a grievance on your behalf.

Most hospitals operate on an employment-at-will basis, in which there's either no employment contract or the existing contract fails to specify the job's duration. However, the hospital can't violate a union bargaining agreement that mandates proof of just cause for discipline or discharge.

Unions

Although individual contracts provide significant legal protection, employees in many areas — from farm workers, laborers, and truck drivers to actors, teachers, and musicians — have found that they're better off signing a contract negotiated for them as a group. Their union representatives engage in collective bargaining for contract conditions. When necessary, they use arbitration, strikes, and threats of strikes to enhance their terms of employment and enforce contracts.

Before 1974, nurses' rights to form labor unions were limited primarily to employees of nursing homes, for-profit hospitals, and many public hospitals and health care agencies. Also, some state laws allowed for labor unions in nonprofit hospitals, and some private nonprofit hospitals voluntarily recognized nurses' unions. In 1974, Congress extended the National Labor Relations Act (NLRA) to cover private, nonprofit health care facilities and agencies. Since then, the number of unionized nurses has increased dramatically.

The NLRA now applies to employees of hospitals and other health care facilities with annual revenues of at least $250,000 and to nursing homes, visiting nurses' associations, and related nursing facilities with annual revenues of at least $100,000. Also, many states now have collective bargaining laws patterned after the NLRA that control public sector bargaining in the state.

A new window of opportunity for nurses to unionize was opened in 1991, when the U.S. Supreme Court decided, in *American Hospital Association v. National Labor Relations Board* (NLRB), that the NLRB had acted properly in defining eight bargaining units in acute-care hospitals, including one unit composed of only registered nurses. After the 1991 decision, unions stepped up campaign efforts to organize nurses.

THE SUPERVISORY ISSUE

Two U.S. Supreme Court cases — *NLRB v. Health Care & Retirement Corporation* (1994) and *NLRB v. Kentucky River Community Care* (2001) — have addressed the issue of whether and when nurses who direct the work of others should be considered "supervisors" within the meaning of the NLRA. This is an extremely important issue because supervisors aren't covered by the NLRA, and thus they aren't protected by it — meaning, among other things, that they have no right to form or join unions or to bargain collectively. Furthermore, because many registered nurses (RNs) may "direct" the work of others (for example, licensed practical nurses, licensed vocational nurses, unit clerks, and nurses aides) in the course of performing their own professional duties, the issue of where and how to draw the line in determining who is a "supervisor" has tremendous implications for the nursing community as a whole.

Before 1994, the NLRB generally found that nurses weren't considered supervisors because when they direct the work of others as an incidental aspect of providing patient care, they're acting in the interests of the patient and not of the employer. However, in *Health Care & Retirement Corporation,* the U.S. Supreme Court rejected this distinction, even though it didn't make a blanket decision as to whether nurses were supervisors. Instead, the Court found that the NLRB couldn't use this distinction to determine whether a nurse or a group of nurses worked in a supervisory role. After this case, the NLRB continued to examine each case individually, and RNs continued to organize despite disputes as to whether charge nurses (sometimes including nurses who are assigned charge duties on a rotating basis) were supervisors.

In 2001, the Supreme Court revisited the issue of nurses as supervisors in the case of *NLRB v. Kentucky River Community Care.* It rejected the NLRB's argument that nurses who direct other employees as part of their patient care duties are exercising professional judgment, and that this differs from exercising independent judgment as supervisors. However, the Court didn't specifically rule that all RNs who direct the work of others are supervisors. It left open other avenues for finding that nurses who direct the work of others aren't supervisors and, once again, the NLRB continued to evaluate each case individually. The Court also ruled that employers and not employees have the burden of proof in demonstrating that a nurse is a supervisor.

Nurses' unions objected to the Supreme Court's decision but emphasized that it didn't eliminate nurses' rights to organize, whereas employer groups supported the decision. Thus far, organizing among nurses continues, but the issue of whether and when nurses are supervisors is unlikely to be resolved anytime soon. (See *Nurses' unions and collective bargaining.*)

JOINING A UNION: PROS AND CONS

Union officials have targeted the hospital field as one of the last large industries ripe for organizing. Unionization continues to spark debate within the hospital setting and the nursing profession.

Pros

Union proponents argue that unionization gives nurses a strong voice in such issues as wages, benefits, and pensions. Unionization, they argue, assures fair grievance procedures and provides nurses with more influence in patient care decisions. Unionization also gives nurses more control over working conditions, such as staffing and overtime, and equalizes bargaining power between employer and employee.

Cons

Critics argue that unionization tarnishes the image of the nursing profession by shifting emphasis away from patient care to economic advancement. Many nurses are reluctant to depend on an organization for their economic and professional well-being. Some nurses fear the potential disruption of picketing and strikes. Others argue that unionization creates antagonism between nurses and their employers, preventing effective cooperation.

Nurses' unions and collective bargaining

The question of whom nurses should choose as their collective bargaining representative has been a hot-button issue among nurses for years. In July 2001, the American Nurses Association (ANA) addressed this issue when it published its *Code of Ethics for Nurses with Interpretive Statements,* which addressed collective bargaining in Provision 6. It states that nurses "participate in establishing, maintaining, and improving health care environments and conditions of employment conducive to the provision of quality health care and consistent with the values of the professional through individual and collective action." It also recommends that nurses address their concerns about the health care environment through the proper channels, preferably through a professional association such as their state nurses' association.

State nurses' associations

Many registered nurses choose their ANA-affiliated state nurses' association as their collective bargaining representative because they believe that their association can best advocate for them on practice and professional issues as well as wages and working conditions. Organizing through a state nurses' association also means that nurses are part of the ANA and, by extension, also part of the International Council of Nurses.

However, not all state nurses' associations have chosen to engage in collective bargain-

ing. Reasons for this vary. Association leadership may not want the association to get involved with collective bargaining activity, or the association may not possess the expertise or resources to effectively engage in collective bargaining.

Unionization

In 1999, the ANA formed the United American Nurses (UAN), a union composed of state nurses' associations that engage in collective bargaining, those associations' labor programs, or both. The following year, UAN joined AFL-CIO, the federation to which most labor unions belong. The UAN also provides a mechanism for organizing nurses in states where the state nurses' association doesn't engage in collective bargaining.

In addition to the UAN, several large unions that represent a wide range of workers in different industries have been active in organizing nurses. These include the Service Employees International Union; the American Federation of State, County, and Municipal Employees; and the American Federation of Teachers. In some instances, nurses are represented by independent unions, which operate only at one or two hospitals. There are also state-specific nursing unions. For example, the California Nurses Association and the Massachusetts Nurses Association are statewide labor unions that were affiliated with the ANA but decided to become independent.

Questions to consider

Before deciding whether to participate in collective bargaining, ask yourself these questions:

◆ Am I eligible? (See *Joining a nurses' union,* page 280.)

◆ Will collective bargaining help my professional and economic status?
◆ Can I address my professional concerns through collective bargaining?
◆ Can I change my working conditions as an individual, or do I need to organize with other nurses?

LAW Q&A

Joining a nurses' union

For most nurses, the decision to join a union is a difficult one. Here are some answers to frequently asked questions about unionization.

Can I join a labor union?
A nurse who works as an employee can join a labor union. However, under the National Labor Relations Act, some nurses may be excluded from the definition of "employee" – for example, nurses who are managers or supervisors. The courts and the National Labor Relations Board (NLRB) continue to wrestle with the circumstances under which a nurse is considered a "supervisor" because she responsibly directs the work of others. For the most part, the NLRB continues to examine this issue on a case-by-case basis.

Can I be forced to join a union?
If you're eligible to join the union and you work under a "union shop" contract, you must join the union within a specified time to remain employed. If the contract provides for an "open shop," you can choose not to join the union and still keep your job.

Can the hospital where I work fire me for helping to organize a union?
Federal regulations strictly forbid your employer from firing you or taking any other reprisal against you for helping to organize a union.

What consequences do I face if I refuse to participate in my union's strike?
As long as you continue working, your hospital or health care facility will pay your wages and benefits. Although no union can force you to strike, you might face some antagonism from those colleagues who do strike.

If you believe that organizing a union is necessary to improve the professional or economic status of the nurses in your facility, the full force of the law will protect your efforts.

PROTECTING THE RIGHT TO UNIONIZE

In the United States, regulations governing union organizing among nurses in private-sector employment come under the jurisdiction of the NLRB, the agency that enforces federal labor laws.

The NLRB protects eligible employees' rights to organize a union, join a union, or decertify a union (vote the union out), and may defend you against unfair labor practices. The NLRB also helps employers by enforcing regulations that control picketing and strikes, and by providing remedies for any unfair union practices.

If a nonsupervisor decides to organize a union, the NLRB supervises procedures for elections. These procedures enforce rules that both the union and management must follow. The NLRB works to investigate unfair labor practices that may arise during the election process. (See *Recognizing unfair labor practices*.)

INITIATING A UNION DRIVE

To organize a collective bargaining unit at your facility, begin by contacting your state nurses' association, if it engages in collective bargaining, or the union of your choice. The union will assign a union staff member to help you organize your campaign. The union may support your efforts by supplying stationery, printing, legal advice, organizational guidance, and encouragement. The union can also arrange for meeting halls and publicity,

Recognizing unfair labor practices

If eligible, you have a legal right to participate in union activities. If your work involves supervising others, you may be ineligible to join the union. However, you still have some protection under Sections 7 and 8 of the National Labor Relations Act regarding the organization of a union in your facility and management's practice. If your employer infringes on that right – through interference, domination, discrimination, or refusal to bargain – you can charge unfair labor practices.

Interference

Employers may interfere with a union election by unilaterally improving wages or benefits to encourage votes against the union. This is considered an unfair labor practice. Other unfair practices include:

◆ helping employees withdraw from union membership

◆ making coercive statements about participation in union activities

◆ libeling or slandering union officials

◆ threatening to close down the facility

◆ questioning employees about union activities or organizers

◆ spying on – or implying the possibility of spying on – union meetings

◆ creating an atmosphere of fear.

Domination

The National Labor Relations Board (NLRB) doesn't allow management to dominate a union by paying a union's expenses, giving union leaders special benefits, or taking an active part in organizing a union.

Discrimination

Discrimination is an unfair labor practice that can involve discharging, disciplining, or threatening an employee for joining a union or for encouraging others to join. Other types of discrimination include:

◆ refusing to hire anyone who belongs to a union

◆ refusing to reinstate or promote an employee because she testified at a NLRB hearing

◆ enforcing rules unequally between employees who are involved in union activities and those who aren't.

Refusal to bargain

To weaken union participation, management may refuse to take part in collective bargaining. It's an unfair labor practice to take unilateral action to alter employment conditions that either are covered in an existing contract or are included among legally mandated areas of bargaining. Other unfair labor practices include:

◆ refusing to meet with a union representative

◆ refusing to negotiate a mandatory issue

◆ demanding to negotiate a voluntary issue.

---

and can file the proper election petitions with the NLRB.

Management's rights and limitations

During a union drive, the NLRB also protects the rights of management.

Under the law, management is allowed to:

◆ tell you the disadvantages of belonging to a union

◆ explain to you your election rights, such as your right to refuse to sign an authorization card

LEGAL TIP

The NLRB:
Protecting your right to organize a union

If your hospital punishes you solely because you're involved in organizing a union, the federal agency known as the National Labor Relations Board (NLRB) will protect you. This board enforces the National Labor Relations Act, the federal labor laws that explicitly sets forth your rights to form and join a union.

An example

Suppose you're working as a hospital pediatrics nurse, and you support unionization of the hospital's nurses. Union organizers ask you to distribute prounion pamphlets to your colleagues. You begin giving out pamphlets in the nurses' lounge, but a hospital administrator orders you to stop. He says the hospital solicitation policy prohibits anyone from distributing literature inside the hospital. You remind him that the hospital has allowed nurses to distribute other information, such as literature to solicit volunteers for the local cancer society. You ignore the administrator's order and resume handing out pamphlets. You are suspended or intimidated by management staff.

You file an unfair labor practice charge with the NLRB. After a hearing, the board concludes that the hospital can't prevent you from distributing the pamphlets on your own time in a nonwork area. The board also concludes that the hospital was discriminatory in applying the nonsolicitation policy.

A likely ruling

In this situation, the board would order the hospital to reinstate you, pay your back wages, and refrain from punishing you or any other nurse who was active in the union drive.

◆ encourage you to vote "no" in a union election (provided they don't use threats or coercion of any kind).

However, to protect your right to organize and belong to a union, the NLRB places the following limitations on management:

◆ Management can't interfere with your organizing activities.

◆ Management can't discriminate against you for participating in union activities, for testifying against management, or for filing a grievance.

◆ Management can't dominate a union by gaining undue influence over it, such as by paying union expenses or giving union leaders special benefits.

◆ Management can't refuse to bargain in *good faith* (an honest desire to reach an agreement).

◆ Management must assume responsibility for any unfair labor practice committed by a supervisor. (See *The NLRB: Protecting your right to organize a union.*)

Union's rights and limitations

Neither management nor the union can interfere with your individual rights as guaranteed by federal or state law. Federal laws that help protect employee rights include the Fair Labor Standards Act, the Civil Rights Act, and the Age Discrimination in Employment Act. States also enact protective legislation, such as so-called whistle-blower statutes, equal employment opportunity acts, and public employee collective bargaining laws.

However, just like management, the union must also comply with certain limitations. The NLRB ensures that the union:

◆ bargains in good faith
◆ assumes responsibility for any unfair labor practice committed by union officials
◆ doesn't threaten or force you to support the union
◆ doesn't demand that your employer do business only with companies that have unions.

ELECTING A UNION

In the initial step toward a union election, eligible nurses or union representatives distribute authorization cards. Nurses who want a union election sign an authorization card. In the United States, if at least 30% of eligible nurses sign the cards, the nurses or the union can ask the NLRB to authorize and supervise an election. If 50% or more of eligible nurses sign the cards, U.S. law allows the employer to forgo the election process and simply recognize the union, but this rarely occurs. In Canada, more than 50% of nurses must sign the cards to authorize an election. (See *What happens when nurses decide to unionize,* page 284.)

Union and management may disagree about which nurses are eligible to vote. Either side can challenge a nurse's eligibility. In the United States, the NLRB will settle an eligibility dispute by reviewing the individual nurse's job description, her duties and responsibilities, and her supervisory functions, if any.

To win the election, the union must get a majority of the votes of those nurses who actually voted, not those who are eligible to vote.

In some cases, more than one union may be on the ballot. This can happen when, after the first petitioning, the union demonstrates that 30% or more of the eligible nurses want an election. If this occurs, other unions can get on the ballot provided they can obtain a show of interest from 10% of the nurse–employees.

If elected, the union will negotiate a contract addressing mutually agreeable wages, benefits, and work rules and other professional issues. The contract will be devised by the negotiators and ratified by members of the bargaining unit.

Maintaining perspective

When making a commitment to a unionization drive, be prepared to continue to nurture good relations with supervisors and coworkers who oppose the union. Keep in mind that, regardless of the election's outcome, everyone will need to continue to work together. If the union wins, both management and labor will have to adjust to new rules spelled out in the contract. If the union loses, management should optimally correct the problems that led to the organizing campaign; otherwise, the same problems will resurface.

Legal issues in collective bargaining

In collective bargaining, the employer and the employees' representatives meet to confer about employment issues and put their agreements into writing. According to the NLRB, two or more people who share employment interests and conditions may constitute a bargaining unit. (See *Landmarks in the history of collective bargaining,* page 285.)

What happens when nurses decide to unionize

The decision to unionize initiates a step-by-step process. First, organizers distribute leaflets and authorization cards. At least 30% of all proposed union employees must sign those cards to authorize a union election.

Steps in the election process

After the employees sign the authorization cards, the following occurs:

1. The union notifies the National Labor Relations Board (NLRB), and an NLRB representative steps in to referee and organize the election.

2. The NLRB holds a hearing to decide who's eligible to join the bargaining unit. The employer may challenge any employee's eligibility. For example, the employer may argue that one or more employees are supervisors and are therefore ineligible.

3. The NLRB determines the place and election date. The employer and the union can then begin campaigning.

4. Within 7 days of the NLRB announcement of the election date and place, the employer provides the NLRB the names and addresses of all eligible employees. The NLRB gives this list to the union.

5. On election day, employees vote by secret ballot to accept or reject the union. If more than one union is on the ballot, employees can select one of the unions or vote for no representation at all.

6. The NLRB representative tallies the votes. The results depend on the majority of ballots cast, regardless of the percentage of eligible employees who actually vote. (If only a minority of eligible employees vote, those few employees will decide the question of unionization for all.)

The outcome

If most of the voting employees choose the union, that union is legally required to represent all eligible employees, even those who didn't vote. The NLRB will certify the union as the employees' collective bargaining representative.

If most of the voting employees reject the union, the law prohibits another election involving a union for 1 year.

THE NLRB'S ROLE IN COLLECTIVE BARGAINING

In the United States, the laws governing collective bargaining are outlined in the NLRA and the Labor Management Relations Act (LMRA), also known as the *Taft-Hartley Act*. The NLRB is the federal agency authorized to administer and enforce these laws. (See *Appealing to the NLRB,* page 286.)

The NLRB's responsibilities include determining appropriate bargaining units for employee groups, resolving disputes between labor and management, and conducting elections for employee bargaining representatives. The NLRB won't assert jurisdiction over labor laws for minimum wages, overtime pay, termination, or discrimination unless those issues have been written into the employees' labor contract and the contract doesn't provide for binding arbitration of alleged violations. If arbitration is provided for, the NLRB usually declines its jurisdiction and defers to the arbitrator.

Landmarks in the history of collective bargaining

The following is a summary of major legislative landmarks in the struggle for collective bargaining rights:

1935: Congress passes the National Labor Relations Act (NLRA). This act requires employers to bargain with employees and provides for the formation of the National Labor Relations Board (NLRB) to enforce the provisions of the act.

1946: The American Nurses Association (ANA) launches its Economic Security Program to establish national salary guidelines for nurses. ANA takes an active role in supporting nurses' rights to bargain collectively.

1947: The Labor Management Relations Act (LMRA), also known as the Taft-Hartley Act, says that nonprofit organizations, including nonprofit hospitals, don't have to bargain with their employees.

1962: An amendment to the LMRA gives federal employees, including nurses, the right to bargain collectively.

1974: Health care amendments to the NLRA explicitly grant employees of nonprofit health care facilities and agencies the right to bargain collectively.

1991: In *American Hospital Association v. NLRB,* the U.S. Supreme Court upholds NLRB regulations that make it easier for unions to organize nurses.

1994: In *NLRB v. Health Care & Retirement Corporation of America,* the U.S. Supreme Court rejects the NLRB's traditional grounds for finding that those nurses who direct the work of others aren't "supervisors." Because supervisors are excluded from the protections of the NLRA, this decision raises concerns that many registered nurses (RNs) would no longer be eligible to engage in collective bargaining.

However, the Court states that the NLRB should evaluate this issue on a case-by-case basis, and the NLRB continues to recognize RNs' right to union representation.

2001: In *NLRB v. Kentucky River Community Care,* the U.S. Supreme Court rejects the NLRB's argument that says nurses who direct other employees as part of their patient care duties are exercising professional judgment and not independent judgment as supervisors. However, the Court left open other avenues for finding that nurses who direct the work of others aren't supervisors, and the NLRB continues to evaluate each nurse on a case-by-case basis. The Court also rules that employers have the burden of proof in demonstrating that a nurse is a supervisor and thus excluded from the NLRA's protections.

State law

Before passage of the 1974 Health Care Amendments, several states had passed legislation requiring nonprofit hospitals to bargain with their employees. Consequently, nurses who worked for such hospitals in Connecticut, Idaho, Massachusetts, Michigan, Minnesota, Montana, New Jersey, New York, Oregon, Pennsylvania, and Wisconsin had some bargaining rights all along.

State legislatures have also passed laws defining the rights of nurses who work for state, county, and municipal health care facilities. Some states gave these government employees the right to organize and bargain, but not the right to strike. Other states assigned a specific arm of the state government to negotiate labor concerns or mandate pay scales for state-employed nurses.

Appealing to the NLRB

If you feel that management is engaging in unfair labor practices, begin by telling your union representative. If she believes your charges are valid, either you or the union can appeal to the National Labor Relations Board (NLRB).

NLRB response

The board will ask you for a sworn statement concerning the dates and times of the alleged events, the names and positions of management staff involved, and the names and addresses of other employee witnesses. Your statement will serve as a legal affidavit that will supply the NLRB with the information it needs to carry out an investigation.

Should the NLRB investigate and find that management is engaging in unfair labor practices, it will issue a formal complaint against your employer. The employer may appeal the NLRB's complaint, but if the court upholds it, the employer must comply with the NLRB's

penalty – usually reinstating employees, issuing back pay, or restoring other benefits.

An example

While nurses at Good Faith Hospital were organizing a union campaign, supervisors asked them for the names of nurses who attended meetings the organizers sponsored. Also, one supervisor suggested to her staff that if a nurses' union was organized, the union might try to force management to increase wages – which because of the hospital's precarious financial position, could result in layoffs. Several nurses complained about the supervisor's remarks at a subsequent union meeting. The union organizers agreed that management was interfering with union organization – an unfair labor practice – and consequently filed a complaint against the employer with the NLRB.

Canadian law

In Canada, the provincial or territorial labor relations boards handle local labor issues, and the Canada Labour Relations Board deals with labor issues at the federal level, as in the case of military hospitals.

Bargaining units

Bargaining units usually represent different groups of workers in the same hospital. The NLRA empowers the NLRB to decide what's an appropriate bargaining unit. This gives the NLRB considerable power. It's much easier to unionize employees if there's a bargaining unit for each kind of job classification; employees in each bargaining unit typically have more shared interests.

In 1987, the NLRB issued rules permitting eight bargaining units for acute-care hospitals. Since its establishment in 1935, this was the first time the NLRB had drafted rules defining permissible bargaining units for an entire industry. These bargaining units include:

◆ RNs in nonsupervisory positions
◆ physicians
◆ professionals other than RNs and physicians
◆ technical employees
◆ skilled maintenance employees
◆ business office clerical employees
◆ guards
◆ all other nonprofessional employees.

In response to these 1987 rules, the American Hospital Association (AHA) filed suit. In *AHA v. NLRB* (1991), the

AHA claimed that the NLRB rules were illegal, arguing that the Taft-Hartley Act requires determination of appropriate bargaining units in each individual hospital.

The U.S. Supreme Court unanimously rejected the AHA's interpretation and ruled that the NLRB has the power to promulgate rules for all hospitals, not just on a hospital-by-hospital basis. This ruling made it easier for unions to organize nurses and was considered a blow to management's efforts to resist.

Other NLRB functions

Along with rule making, the NLRB also resolves disputes by interpreting provisions of the LMRA. The NLRB hears cases on the supervisor's role and the employee's right to solicit new members or picket. The NLRB also determines whether labor or management has committed unfair acts during a campaign or the term of a contract. For example, in *NLRB v. Baptist Hospital* (1979), the NLRB upheld its rule against soliciting new members in upper-floor hospital halls and sitting rooms near patients, but upheld the employees' right to talk about the union in first-floor lobbies and other areas away from patients.

If a hospital or bargaining unit disagrees with an NLRB decision, either party can appeal in a federal appellate court.

Canada's courts are unlikely to interfere with a provincial labor relations board decision unless it acted outside its jurisdiction or violated common law.

Mandatory bargaining issues

The NLRB has interpreted the *mandatory bargaining issues* (issues an employer must address during bargaining) broadly to include wages and hours, seniori-ty, leaves of absence, work schedules and assignments, benefits, promotion and layoff policies, grievance and discipline procedures, and breaks, holidays, and vacations. (See *Perils of not bargaining,* page 288.)

Voluntary issues

Bargaining on other issues may occur if both parties voluntarily agree. The NLRB considers voluntary bargaining issues to include all other possible legal employment issues. It excludes illegal issues, such as requiring new employees to join a union in less than 30 days or job discrimination. Because nurses can't force an employer to bargain over voluntary issues, negotiating or not negotiating with the employer usually depends on how committed nurses are to their professional concerns and on management's willingness to be flexible.

NEGOTIATIONS

Before bargaining begins, union negotiators should prepare for the procedure by understanding the beliefs and attitudes of the people they represent and developing a system of communication between negotiators and the bargaining unit. They should also consider in advance how management might respond to various issues.

The actual bargaining involves good-faith negotiations (an honest desire to reach an agreement) between the union's and the management's negotiating teams. Proposals may be exchanged for study before the first session. Each proposal and counterproposal is discussed, and disagreements are debated in detail, sometimes with teams taking time-outs to privately reconsider positions. When disagreements persist and outside mediation fails, the union members may decide

Perils of not bargaining

A hospital can't avoid collective bargaining by refusing to recognize its nurses' union. The law, strengthened by court decisions, requires a hospital to bargain in good faith with duly elected unions. A key court case, *Eastern Maine Medical Center v. NLRB* (1981), illustrates this principle.

An antiunion stand

Nurses at Eastern Maine Medical Center voted 114 to 110 to be represented by the Maine State Nurses Association, the state's largest nurses' union. In response, the hospital administration adopted a strong antiunion stand, refusing to meet with the nurses for collective bargaining talks. Moreover, the administration gave substantial wage-and-benefit increases to nonunion employees and withheld the increases from the unionized nurses.

The administration's policy of not bargaining with the union made the union nurses bitter and frustrated. The union filed unfair labor practice charges against the hospital administration.

NLRB ruling

The National Labor Relations Board (NLRB) concluded that the hospital had violated the National Labor Relations Act by refusing to bargain in good faith and by discriminating against the unionized nurses. The board directed the hospital administration to negotiate with the union and to pay the wage-and-benefit increases withheld from members of the bargaining unit.

Appeals court ruling

In upholding the actions of the NLRB, an appeals court ruled that the hospital's refusal to negotiate violated the nurses' collective bargaining rights.

---

to strike. If all issues are resolved, however, the written agreement is taken to the union members with a recommendation that they ratify the terms.

DECISION TO STRIKE

Collective bargaining doesn't guarantee that the bargaining parties will reach an agreement. If the parties arrive at a stalemate, employees may decide to strike in hopes of forcing the employer to make concessions. A strike decision is an extreme measure, so labor laws have established provisions that require any curtailment of services to be orderly.

In the United States, negotiating parties must follow this timetable — and series of steps — before a strike can be called:

◆ The side wanting to modify or terminate the contract must notify the other side 90 days before the contract expires (or labor or management proposes that changes take place).

◆ If, 30 days later, the two sides don't agree, they must notify the Federal Mediation and Conciliation Service (FMCS) and the corresponding state agency of the dispute.

◆ Within 30 days, the FMCS will appoint a mediator and, in rare cases, an inquiry board. Within 15 days, the mediator or inquiry board will give both sides its recommendations.

◆ If, after 15 more days, the parties don't agree, the employees may plan to strike. If the union didn't have employees vote earlier, a vote will be held to decide whether or not to send a strike notice.

◆ If most employees vote to send a strike notice, the union must send management the strike notice at least 10 days before the scheduled strike, specifying the exact date, time, and place of the strike. The strike can't be scheduled before the contract expires.

In most cases, union and management representatives, with the assistance of a mediator, schedule additional negotiations during this period. A strike vote is held before the walkout is scheduled to begin.

Note that, in many states, public-sector employees are prohibited from striking. If an impasse occurs, labor and management must resolve their differences through binding arbitration.

Canadian law

Some Canadian jurisdictions prohibit health care employees from striking. In these jurisdictions, compulsory arbitration is imposed when employees and employer fail to reach an agreement. The arbitrator can then draft and impose contract terms.

Wildcat strikes

Employees who ignore the strike provisions and engage in illegal strikes lose the protection of the NLRA. They may be discharged by their employer. Unions that sanction or encourage illegal strikes may have their certification revoked by the NLRB.

Delaying a strike

Employees may delay a strike for up to 72 hours if they feel the extra time would enable them to come to terms with management.

To delay the strike, they must give management written notice at least 12 hours before the time the strike was

scheduled to start. If the initial strike date passes during the negotiations, the union must issue another 10-day strike notice. If the contract expires during the negotiations, the employer and employees remain bound by the contract.

Grievances and arbitration

When an employee's dispute isn't resolved, tempers flare, morale declines, and apparent injustices smolder. That's why union and management officials give grievance and arbitration procedures high priority when they negotiate collective bargaining agreements. Even if your workplace isn't unionized, understanding these procedures can help you create fair work rules and grievance procedures in your workplace.

RESOLVING DISPUTES

When unionized employees and management sign a labor contract, they agree to abide by certain rules and policies. A contract can't cite every potential dispute, so it includes grievance procedures — specific steps that both sides agree to follow. Usually, the process moves from discussions to formal hearings and written statements of times, dates, details, and even witnesses. If the matter can't be resolved, the aggrieved party requests arbitration.

Recognizing a grievance

The definition of *grievance* depends on the contract. Some contracts define the term as any complaint that reflects dissatisfaction with union or management policies. However, most contracts define it as a complaint that involves contract violations.

As a staff nurse, you or your union representative can file a grievance against your employer. Your union can file a grievance against management. Management can file a grievance—usually called a disciplinary action—against any employee. Most grievances are filed against management because of management's decision-making role.

Distinguishing between gripes and grievances

Smooth labor relations require both sides to honor the contract's terms and to show good faith in using the grievance procedures. Both parties need to know when to compromise and when to retreat on a disputed issue.

Union representatives must typically defuse complaints before they become formal grievances. An effective union representative will be able to distinguish between a legitimate grievance and a gripe. A grievance is a substantive complaint that involves a contract violation; a gripe is a personal problem unrelated to the contract.

Sometimes union or management representatives pursue a groundless grievance (that is, a gripe) for political or harassment purposes. A nurse's self-interest or her resentment of authority can lead to a groundless grievance. So can a supervisor's poor decision or misuse of her authority.

TYPES OF LEGITIMATE GRIEVANCES

Most grievances fall into one of two classifications:
◆ unfair labor practices
◆ violations of a contract, a precedent, or a past practice. (See *Legitimate grievances.*)

Unfair labor practices are tactics prohibited by state and federal labor laws. For example, under federal law,

an employer who discriminates against you because you're involved in union activities commits an unfair labor practice. Violations of a contract, precedent, or past practice are actions that break mutually accepted work rules. For example, suppose your contract says a supervisor must give you 2 weeks' notice before making you rotate to another shift. If a supervisor assigns you to another shift without giving you notice, you can file a grievance.

MOST COMMON GRIEVANCES

Grievances can involve an almost infinite number of complaints, but some are more common than others. Management usually takes disciplinary action against employees who:
◆ allow personal problems to interfere with their jobs
◆ fail to perform their assigned duties
◆ show poor work habits, such as tardiness or unreliability
◆ take an antagonistic attitude toward management in labor relations when serving in union positions.

Employees commonly file grievances against supervisors who dispense discipline inconsistently, show favoritism, or treat employees unfairly. Other common sources of grievances include management's selection policies for promotions, favored shift assignments, disciplinary actions, and merit salary raises. Staff nurses sometimes file grievances when they're temporarily assigned nurse-manager responsibilities without getting commensurate pay.

Many grievances result from unwitting contract violations (such as poorly thought-out workload decisions) by first-level or midlevel managers. Personnel and labor relations departments can resolve many actions that would otherwise lead to grievances by an-

Legitimate grievances

Not all complaints against an employer meet the definition of a "legitimate grievance." If your complaint fits into one of the following categories, chances are it's a legitimate grievance upon which your union can act.

Contract violations

Your employment contract is binding between you and your employer. If your employer violates it, you have a valid grievance. The following examples describe violations that would likely be prohibited by an employment contract:

◆ You're performing the charge nurse's job 2 to 3 days a week but still receiving the same pay as other staff nurses.
◆ You've had to work undesirable shifts or on Sundays more often than other nurses.
◆ Your supervisor doesn't post time schedules in advance.
◆ Your employer fires you without just cause.

Federal and state law violations

An action by your employer that violates a federal or state law would be the basis of a grievance, even if the employment contract permits the action. For example:

◆ You receive less pay for performing the same work as a male nurse.
◆ You don't receive the overtime pay to which you're entitled.
◆ Your employer doesn't promote you because of your race.

Past practice violations

A past practice—one that has been accepted by both parties for an extended time but that's suddenly discontinued by the employer without notification—may be the basis for a griev-

ance. The past practice need not be specified in the contract. If the practice violates the contract, either party can demand that the contract be enforced. If the practice is unsafe, an arbitrator may simply abolish it. Examples of past practice violations might include:

◆ Your employer charges you for breaking equipment when others haven't been charged.
◆ Your employer revokes parking lot privileges.
◆ Your employer eliminates a rotation system for float assignments.

Health and safety violations

Grievances pertaining to health and safety violations usually involve working conditions for which the employer is responsible. Legitimate grievances may be recognized even if the contract doesn't address the specific complaint. For example:

◆ You're required to hold patients during X-rays.
◆ You have no hand-washing facilities near patient rooms.

Employer policy violations

Employers have the right to establish *reasonable* work rules and policies. These rules and policies aren't usually specified in the employment contract. Your employer can't violate its own rules without being guilty of a grievance (note, however, that an employer can change rules unilaterally). For example:

◆ You haven't received a performance evaluation in 2 years, though your employee handbook states that such evaluations will be done annually.
◆ Your employer assigns you a vacation period without your consent, contrary to personnel policies.

swering labor questions and offering advice.

GRIEVANCE PROCEDURES

The elements of a grievance procedure vary from contract to contract. Key elements always include:

◆ reasonable time limits for filing a grievance and making a decision

◆ procedures to appeal a grievance to higher union–management levels if the grievance is unresolved

◆ assigning priority to crucial grievances (such as worker suspensions or dismissals)

◆ an opportunity for both sides to investigate the complaint.

The first step is usually an informal discussion between the nurse and her supervisor. The nurse may then submit her complaint in writing. If the supervisor doesn't or can't resolve the grievance, the nurse can ask for a union representative, or *steward*, to assist her. The representative will meet with the supervisor to discuss the grievance's merits. If the supervisor stands firm, the nurse can then file a written complaint within a contract-specified time period. Subsequent hearings move to higher levels of management. The number of steps in a grievance procedure varies with each contract's provisions.

ARBITRATION

When neither side can work out a settlement on a substantive issue, arbitration is indicated. During arbitration, the parties present evidence to a neutral labor relations expert. Parties who have negotiated a collective bargaining agreement or are covered by one with an arbitration clause are required to arbitrate contract disputes. Parties with no bargaining agreement (nonunion-

ized) may agree to independent arbitration, hoping to resolve a matter short of litigation or termination of the relationship.

The side requesting arbitration gives a written notice to the other party. The requesting party then contacts one of several national agencies that supply arbitrators, such as the FMCS or the American Arbitration Association. Both sides must agree on a specific arbitrator; the date, time, and place of the hearing; and the finality of the arbitrator's decision.

Arbitration hearing

An arbitration hearing resembles a courtroom proceeding, except that it's less formal. The party requesting arbitration has the burden of proof and must present evidence that the contract has been violated. (However, when a nurse challenges disciplinary action, management must prove its case first by presenting supporting evidence.) In an arbitration hearing, both sides may call and cross-examine witnesses. The requesting side makes a closing summary, followed by one from the opposing side. Each side can submit written briefs instead of making summary statements.

The arbitrator usually renders a written decision weeks or even months after the hearing. If both sides request an immediate response, the arbitrator can issue an oral decision and withhold a written explanation of the decision unless both parties request it.

In most cases, both sides prefer arbitration to a lengthy court fight because arbitration is speedier and less expensive, and may be conducted without attorneys. When a dispute goes to arbitration, both sides lose control of the outcome because, in the United States, the arbitrator's decision is binding. Although the losing party can challenge the decision in court, the court rarely overturns an arbitrator's decision.

In Canada, arbitrators' decisions are binding, and courts don't interfere with decisions unless there's a question of jurisdiction or the decision is patently unreasonable.

RESOLVING COMPLAINTS CAUSED BY UNFAIR LABOR PRACTICES

Most grievances arising from contract violations follow contract-stipulated grievance and arbitration procedures. The NLRB addresses allegations of unfair labor practices. If a nurse who isn't a member of a collective bargaining unit brings an allegation to the NLRB, the NLRB must determine if she's engaged in concerted action — that is, if her action is part of (or in concert with) a group effort. The NLRB will conduct a hearing to review evidence and then issue a decision. Either side can challenge an NLRB decision in court.

If a nurse has a complaint involving discrimination on the basis of race, religion, national origin, age, disability, or sex, she can file a charge of discrimination with the U.S. Equal Employment Opportunity Commission (EEOC) or a comparable state agency in addition to filing a grievance. The EEOC handles violations of:
◆ the Equal Pay Act of 1963, which forbids wage discrimination based on an employee's sex
◆ the Civil Rights Act of 1964, which forbids job and wage discrimination based on an employee's religion, race, sex, or ethnic background
◆ the Age Discrimination in Employment Act of 1967, which forbids discrimination based on an employee's age

◆ the Americans with Disabilities Act of 1990, which states that "no individual shall be discriminated against on the basis of disability in the full and equal enjoyment of the goods, services, facilities, privileges, advantages, or accommodations of any place of public accommodation...."

The EEOC will also prosecute disputes involving sexual harassment. Employees don't have to be union members to file a complaint with the EEOC.

DISCIPLINARY HEARINGS

A disciplinary hearing can be initiated by the complaint of an employer or a patient. The hearing may be based on allegations of incompetence or alleged violation of state law pertaining to nursing practice.

If you're ever served with notice that a state's licensing board is investigating you, seek legal counsel, plus emotional and professional support. Don't approach these proceedings lightly or unprepared. The hearing process and the outcome can have a major impact on how you view yourself, how you practice nursing, and how you view your profession.

Before the hearing, do your homework, be aware of recent state laws, muster witnesses and evidence, and be prepared to stand up for your rights and your nursing license. Learn everything you can from the experience. Finally, be prepared to support your colleagues who may also go through a disciplinary hearing.

Selected references

American Nurses Association. "2002 Legislation: Whistleblower Protection," American Nurses Association, December 2002. Available at *www.nursingworld.org/gova/state/2002/whistle.htm*

American Nurses Association. *Code of Ethics for Nurses with Interpretive Statements.* Washington, D.C.: American Nurses Publishing, 2001.

Burke, M.R. "Demystifying Common Terms in Employment Agreements," *Family Practitioner Management* 10(6):38-40, June 2003.

Crooks, L., and Rathbone, L. "Should Nurses Ever Strike?" *Nursing Times* 98(50):18-19, December 2002.

Forman, H., and Grimes, T.C. "Living with a Union Contract," *Journal of Nursing Administration* 32(12):611-14, December 2002.

Forman, H., and Kraus, H.R. "Decertification: Management's Role when Employees Rethink Unionization," *Journal of Nursing Administration* 33(6):313-16, June 2003.

Forman, H., and Merrick, F. "Grievances and Complaints: Valuable Tools for Management and for Staff," *Journal of Nursing Administration* 33(3):136-38, March 2003.

Gamroth, L., et al. "The Undergraduate Nurse Employment Project," *Canadian Nurse* 99(4):32-36, April 2003.

Haiven, L., and Haiven J. *The Right to Strike and the Provision of Emergency Services in Canadian Health Care.* Ottawa: Canadian Centre for Policy Alternatives, 2002. Available at *www.policyalternatives.ca/publications/right-to-strike.pdf*

Heitlinger, A. "The Paradoxical Impact of Health Care Restructuring in Canada on Nursing as a Profession," *International Journal of Health Services* 33(1):37-54, 2003.

Muhl, C.J. "The Employment-at-will Doctrine: Three Major Exceptions," *Monthly Labor Review* 124(1):3-11, January 2001.

Zimmerman, P.G. "Organizing in the Face of Increasing Demands on Nursing," *Journal of Emergency Nursing* 26(4):294-95, August 2000.

Internet resource

U.S. National Labor Relations Board: *www.nlrb.gov*

Chapter 10

Ethical decision making

Every day, nurses make ethical decisions in their nursing practice. These decisions may involve patient care, actions related to coworkers, or nurse-physician relations. At times you may find yourself trapped in the middle of an ethical dilemma, pulled in every direction by your duties and responsibilities to your patient, to your employer, and to yourself. Even after you make a decision, you may ask yourself, "Did I do the right thing?"

There are no automatic guidelines for solving all ethical conflicts. Although such conflicts may be painful and confusing, particularly in nursing, you don't have to be a philosopher to act ethically or to make decisions that fall within nursing's ethical codes. Nonetheless, you need to understand the principles of ethics that guide your nursing practice. Legally, nurses are responsible for using their knowledge and skills to protect the comfort and safety of their patients. Ethically, nurses are responsible, as patient advocates, for safeguarding their patients' rights.

Although a nurse isn't legally responsible, for example, for obtaining a patient's informed consent, the nurse is ethically responsible, as the patient's advocate, for reporting to the physician a patient's misunderstandings about treatment or withdrawal of consent. To be an effective advocate, a nurse must understand the ethical and legal principles of informed consent, and that the patient's consent isn't valid unless he understands his condition, the proposed treatment, treatment alternatives, potential risks and benefits, and relative chances of success or failure.

Law vs. ethics

Ethics is the area of philosophic study that examines values, actions, and choices to determine right and wrong. *Laws* are binding rules of conduct enforced by authority. In many situations, laws and ethics overlap. When they diverge, you have to identify and examine the fine lines that separate them.

RELATIONSHIP BETWEEN LAW AND ETHICS

When a law is challenged as unjust or unfair, the challenge usually reflects some underlying ethical principle. That's because, ideally, laws are based on what is right and good. Realistically, though, the relation between law and ethics is complex. Most nurses realize that most malpractice suits result from patients' dissatisfaction with care they received. When patients believe they haven't been treated with respect and dignity or that their needs and rights have been ignored or violated, they're more likely to initiate legal action. There's a strong connection between ethics and law regarding the nurse's role as patient advocate. (See *Nursing ethics and the law.*)

Moral dilemmas

A nurse who must decide whether to follow a physician's orders to administer an unusually high dose of an opioid faces a *moral dilemma*—an ethical problem caused by a conflict of rights, responsibilities, and values.

Such a dilemma carries with it a great deal of stress. As you grapple with the situation, trying to decide what to do, you'll probably experience internal psychological and emotional stress, such as fear or guilt. You may also experience stress caused by external factors that are political or interpersonal—for example, you may be nervous about confronting the physician with your doubts because you fear his anger.

Moral dilemmas call for ethical choices in the face of profound uncertainty. At times, you may not know what the right or ethical course of action should be. At other times, you may believe completely that a particular action is morally right and yet, for various reasons, find it difficult to act.

A moral dilemma may be further complicated by psychological pressures and personal emotions, especially when a choice is a forced one at best and, in many cases, results in an uncomfortable compromise. Many moral dilemmas in nursing involve choices about justice or fairness, when scant

resources (such as bed space or limited staffing) must be divided among patients with equal needs. In other cases, a choice must be made quickly because the patient's condition is fluctuating or rapidly deteriorating. Often, nurses who are compelled to make ethical decisions don't have the luxury of time.

TYPES OF DILEMMAS

Most moral dilemmas in nursing can be identified according to the following classifications:

◆ Dilemmas of beneficence—dilemmas that involve deciding what's good as opposed to what's harmful. Dilemmas often occur when health care providers, patients, or family members disagree about what course of action is "in the patient's best interest."

◆ Dilemmas of nonmaleficence—dilemmas that involve the avoidance of harm. These issues often involve a nurse's responsibility to "blow the whistle" if she sees others compromising the patient's safety.

◆ Dilemmas of autonomy—dilemmas that involve deciding what course of action maximizes the patient's right of self-determination. Autonomy issues are often closely related to beneficence issues, especially when individuals other than the patient must determine (or attempt to determine) what's best for the patient.

◆ Dilemmas of justice—ethical issues of fairness and equality, such as dilemmas that involve dividing limited health care resources fairly.

◆ Dilemmas of fidelity—those that involve honoring promises. These may include the extent and limits of a nurse's role and duties to a patient that might conflict with other duties such as duties to the physician.

Nursing ethics and the law

When you make decisions, your choices and actions should ideally fulfill *three* criteria:
◆ They should be the best practice *clinically*.
◆ They should be within the scope of policies, procedures, and practice acts *legally*.
◆ They should be the *right* things to do *morally*.

Sometimes ethics, law, and best practices don't always agree. Certain actions may be considered by some people to be morally or legally ambiguous. Each type of situation shown below can present potential moral dilemmas for nurses.

Nursing choices, decisions, and actions

	Ethical	Unethical
LEGAL	Type 1: Actions of this type are the ideal—they're ethical and legal, though not always without complications and inconveniences. *Example:* While prepping and medicating a patient for surgery, a nurse realizes that the patient doesn't want the operation but has given consent only because her husband insisted. Because this isn't a valid consent, the nurse contacts the patient's physician, even though this action will alter surgical schedules and planned outcomes.	Type 2: Actions of this type might be considered unethical but are, nevertheless, legal. *Example:* A nurse caring for a 12-year-old boy with cancer learns that he has accepted the fact that he's dying and wants to stop chemotherapy. His parents have consented to try a new, aggressive course of chemotherapy. The nurse goes ahead and administers the chemotherapy as ordered by the physician.
ILLEGAL	Type 3: Actions of this type might be considered ethical by some but are, nevertheless, illegal. *Example:* A nurse is caring for an elderly patient with dementia and cancer. The patient's husband asks for information about "terminal sedation"—what type and how much medication could be used to bring about a peaceful death. The nurse gives him this information and arranges for the patient to be discharged home in her husband's care.	Type 4: Actions of this type are neither legal nor ethical. *Example:* A physician informs a nurse that he routinely prescribes antidepressants for every new resident admitted to a nursing home. If residents ask about the medication, he instructs the nurse to say, "This is just a pill your physician ordered," because telling them more might upset them. The nurse follows the physician's orders because he's politically powerful and she doesn't want to cross him.

Ethical principles in conflict: A case study

Nurses often identify ethical principles—such as beneficence, nonmaleficence, autonomy, justice, and fidelity—and strive to honor them in making ethical decisions and choosing courses of action. This way of making ethical decisions, called principlism, deductively uses general ethical principles to logically determine the best resolution of an issue. It's effective only as long as ethical principles aren't in conflict. In the reality of a nurse's daily responsibilities, ethical principles can—and commonly do—conflict with each other.

Ethical principles	Ethical issue
The principle of beneficence	A 45-year-old patient is brought by ambulance to the emergency department. He's anxious, pale, and diaphoretic, and complaining of severe substernal pain. An assessment, electrocardiogram, and other initial tests are inconclusive to rule out a myocardial infarction. The patient receives medication for pain and is admitted to the cardiac care unit for further observation. After 30 minutes, the patient tells the nurse that he's pain-free.
The principle of autonomy	This patient insists that because he's now feeling fine again, he's leaving the hospital because he absolutely has to be at an important business meeting. He says that he has already called a taxi.
Beneficence and autonomy conflict	The nurse tells the physician, who orders her to convince the patient to stay in the hospital for his safety and well-being. How should the nurse interpret and carry out the physician's order while respecting her patient's autonomy? Does "convince" mean "coerce"? Even if the patient is willing to leave against medical advice, is letting him go the right thing to do?

Fidelity involves *confidentiality*—respecting privileged information; a patient's right to privacy must be balanced against society's right to be informed of potential threats to public health.

Fidelity also involves a commitment to *veracity*—telling the truth; fully informing a patient of his medical condition. (See *Ethical principles in conflict: A case study.*)

TYPES OF DECISIONS

In a moral dilemma, the types of decisions facing nurses usually can be grouped into four categories:
◆ Active decisions—ethical decisions and moral judgments that lead directly to actions and bring about change
◆ Passive decisions—decisions that deny, delay, or avoid action and maintain the status quo by denying or shifting responsibility to avoid change

Principles yardstick

In situations involving conflicting ethical principles, it's helpful to avoid the trap of "either/or" thinking. Instead, think of ethical principles as yardsticks, and strive for compromise rather than sacrificing one principle for another. For example, the principles yardstick would look like this:

| Abandonment of patient | ◄ ◄ AUTONOMY-BENEFICENCE ► ► | Paternalism |

If we move too far toward emphasizing autonomy without balancing it with beneficence, the result is abandoning the patient. If we move too far in the other direction by emphasizing doing good without balancing it with respect for the patient's autonomy, the result is paternalism.

◆ Programmed decisions—decisions that use precedents, established guidelines, procedures, and rules to resolve anticipated, routine, and expected types of moral dilemmas
◆ Nonprogrammed decisions—decisions that require a unique response to complex and unexpected moral dilemmas.

Most commonly, a nurse's programmed decisions are also active ones. For example, when a nurse and a physician tell a patient what to expect in surgery and then ask the patient to sign a consent form, they're participating in a programmed decision process that involves ethical and legal practices (such as truth telling) as well as patients' rights (such as self-determination).

The patient facing surgery—feeling unprepared to make a complex decision—may respond passively, saying, "I don't know what's best. Should I risk the complications of having surgery or the danger of not having it? I'll do whatever you tell me."

In such a situation, the physician and nurse must make a choice. They must either relieve the patient's stress by telling him what's "best" for him or ensure the patient's autonomy by removing themselves from the decision-making process. By providing education and assistance to the patient throughout the process of informed consent (or refusal of consent), the nurse is able to balance the principles of autonomy and beneficence without "taking over" the decision for the patient. (See *Principles yardstick*.)

Whenever you're faced with a moral dilemma, you must make moral judgments that lead to decisions about right and wrong courses of action. Even passive decisions—for example, deciding to protect oneself by remaining silent or not taking a stand on an issue—are based on moral judgments. (See *Approaching ethical decisions*, page 300.)

LEGAL TIP **Approaching ethical decisions**

When faced with an ethical dilemma, consider the following questions:
◆ What health issues are involved?
◆ What ethical issues are involved?
◆ What further information is necessary before a judgment can be made?
◆ Who will be affected by this decision? (Include the decision-maker and other caregivers if they'll be affected emotionally or professionally.)
◆ What are the values and opinions of the people involved?
◆ What conflicts exist between the values and ethical standards of the people involved?
◆ Must a decision be made and, if so, who should make it?
◆ What alternatives are available?
◆ For each alternative, what are the ethical justifications?
◆ For each alternative, what are the possible outcomes?

Values and ethics

Values are strongly held personal and professional beliefs about worth and importance. (The word *value* comes from the Latin *valere* — to be strong.) The remarks that follow are examples of value statements:
◆ "Nursing is a meaningful profession."
◆ "Nurses make a difference to their patients by comforting, caring, and teaching."
◆ "Nurses should be paid more for what they do."

◆ "The nursing profession must change radically to survive in today's health care system."
◆ "HMOs put too much pressure on professional health care employees."
◆ "Physicians, not hospital administrators, should make important health care decisions."
◆ "A new emphasis on preventive medicine will make nursing a more valuable and respected profession."

Not all nurses would agree with every one of these value statements. Value conflicts are common among nurses, physicians, patients, families, and health care facility administrators.

Clarifying your own values is an important part of developing a professional ethic. A person may become more aware of his values by consciously examining his statements and behavior. (See *Developing value awareness.*)

MORAL RELATIVISM

The question arises: Are certain values intrinsically best, or are values always a matter of personal interpretation? A theory of ethics known as *moral relativism* holds that there are no ethical absolutes, that whatever a person believes is right is right for him or her at that moment.

Consider what would happen if everyone practiced moral relativism.
◆ There would be no objective way to resolve moral dilemmas.
◆ A person could never question or disapprove of another's moral judgment.
◆ Professional standards, such as nursing standards, would become meaningless.
◆ Law and order in society would disappear.
◆ People and cultures would be unable to grow morally.

Developing value awareness

Nurses, like all people, sometimes tend to rely on hearsay, opinions, or prejudice, instead of developing a strong sense of their own values. Only infrequently do they stop to reflect on the values that are mirrored in their conversation and behavior.

Consider the following dialogue, in which three nurses express various value judgments. As you read, ask yourself: What values does each nurse express? Do the values of the three conflict? Are individual nurses expressing consistent values? Do they show a high regard for patient autonomy?

Shop talk

Kate: I can't believe it. I have to float to the ICU – and it's only my second week on the job. I hate floating, especially to intensive care.

Dean: So do I. The last time I floated to ICU, I was assigned to a 300-pound patient who had been driving drunk and wasn't wearing a seat belt. The guy was badly hurt, and I had to do all the positioning myself because the unit was so short-staffed. I just about killed my back. It isn't fair that they always assign male nurses to obese patients.

Pat: Floating is really a tough issue. I try to see it from the patient's side, though. I mean, maybe you were assigned to care for this patient because you're a good nurse and could give him the best care.

Kate: What bugs me is having to care for patients such as that drunk driver, who obviously don't care how they live. They don't watch their weight, they drive drunk, they don't use seat belts – and we get pulled from the work we're comfortable with to care for them. I can't even find time for a cigarette break.

Pat: Don't forget, Kate, we're supposed to take care of patients, regardless of their health habits or lifestyle. No one's perfect, after all.

Kate: Yeah, I guess you're right, but floating makes me nervous anyway. I'm scared I'll really mess up because everything's so unfamiliar.

Dean: Let me give you some advice. No matter what you think about floating, don't say anything. If you're pegged as a complainer around here, your career is over.

Pat: You sound like you think nurses shouldn't ever speak out if something is wrong with the system. I think nurses do have the power to change things for the better, but that won't happen if we aren't willing to take some risks.

Dean: You're an idealist. I'm a realist. I ask, what's worth risking your job?

Pat: I think being a nurse means not being willing to compromise your standards of care just to keep a job.

Kate: What happened to the 300-pound patient? Is he still in ICU? Do you think I might get assigned to him?

Dean: Well, no. It's the craziest thing. He was a quadriplegic after the accident. So we put all this time and effort into stabilizing his condition and keeping him infection-free, and one day he decides it isn't worth it, so the physicians just turned everything off. Now I ask you, is that right?

Examining values

The nurses in this scenario make various moral judgments. By analyzing their attitudes, you can come to a better understanding of your own values.

◆ Kate criticizes the health habits of an obese trauma patient but insists on her own right to have time for a cigarette break. What values are guiding her opinions? Do you think her outlook is consistent?

◆ Dean thinks that Kate should take an assignment for which she isn't prepared rather than risk losing favor with the administration. Do you think this attitude is irresponsible or merely realistic?

(continued)

Developing value awareness *(continued)*

◆ Pat is accused of being an idealist. Is that a fair judgment?

◆ What values are mirrored in each nurse's attitude about floating?

◆ At the end of the conversation, Dean mentions that the physician decided to withdraw treatment from the quadriplegic patient. If the three nurses were to discuss the ethical questions raised by the physician's decision, how do you think each nurse would respond?

◆ Would these three nurses have similar or conflicting views about what it means to be a patient advocate?

Values clarification

Values clarification refers to the process of raising unconscious values to consciousness so that value conflicts can be resolved. Exercis-

es (such as analyzing the dialogue among Kate, Dean, and Pat) offer one way to clarify values. Reflecting on one's own statements and actions is another. You're likely to encounter many conflicting sets of values in the course of your professional career. You must choose among competing values to establish your own ethical beliefs. Then you need to incorporate chosen values into your everyday thoughts and actions. You'll then be better prepared to act on chosen values when you're confronted with difficult ethical choices.

Making ethical decisions need not be haphazard. By clarifying your own values and checking to see if they're consistent with the established ethical standards of the nursing profession, you can enhance your ability to make responsible moral judgments.

Although different people and cultures have different values, moral relativism doesn't provide an adequate basis for ethical decision making. Because you'll probably face numerous moral conflicts in the course of your career, you need to develop consistent ethical standards to guide your behavior.

Ethical theories

As the basis for professional codes of ethics, ethical theories attempt to provide a system of principles and rules for resolving ethical dilemmas. Ethical theories consist of fundamental beliefs about what's morally right or wrong, and propose reasons for maintaining those beliefs. (See *Ethical codes for nurses.*)

TELEOLOGY AND DEONTOLOGY

In nursing, two types of ethical theories — teleology and deontology — are commonly used as guides in ethical decision making. (For a description of some other types of ethical theories, see *Alternative ethical theories,* page 306.)

Teleologic ethical theories determine what's right or wrong based on an action's consequences. (One such teleologic theory, called utilitarian ethics, requires decision-makers to determine and choose those actions that will result in maximized good — that is, the greatest good for the greatest number of people.)

In teleologic theories, ethical decisions are usually made through a process called risk-benefit analysis. For example, you may help patients and their families evaluate several courses

Ethical codes for nurses

Two of the most important ethical codes for registered nurses are the American Nurses Association (ANA) code and the Canadian Nurses Association (CNA) code. Licensed practical nurses (LPNs) also have an ethical code. The International Council of Nurses (ICN), an organization based in Geneva, Switzerland, which seeks to improve the standards and status of nursing worldwide, has also published a code of ethics.

American Nurses Association code of ethics

The ANA views nurses and patients as individuals who possess basic rights and responsibilities and whose values and circumstances should command respect at all times. The ANA code provides guidance for carrying out nursing responsibilities consistent with the ethical obligations of the profession.

According to ANA code, the nurse:
◆ provides services with respect for human dignity and the uniqueness of the patient, unrestricted by considerations of social or economic status, personal attributes, or the nature of health problems
◆ safeguards the patient's right to privacy by judiciously protecting information of a confidential nature
◆ acts to safeguard the patient and the public when health and safety are affected by incompetent, unethical, or illegal practice of any person
◆ assumes responsibility and accountability for individual nursing judgments and actions
◆ maintains competence in nursing
◆ exercises informed judgment and uses individual competence and qualifications as criteria in seeking consultation, accepting responsibilities, and delegating nursing activities to others
◆ participates in activities that contribute to the ongoing development of the profession's body of knowledge

◆ participates in the profession's efforts to implement and improve standards of nursing
◆ participates in the profession's efforts to establish and maintain conditions of employment conducive to high-quality nursing care
◆ collaborates with members of the health professions and other citizens in promoting community and national efforts to meet the health needs of the public.

Canadian Nurses Association code of ethics

The CNA code consists of eight primary values that form the basis of nursing obligations:

Safe, competent, and ethical care
Nurses value the ability to provide safe, competent, and ethical care that allows them to fulfill their ethical and professional obligations to the people they serve.

Health and well-being
Nurses value health promotion and well-being and assisting persons to achieve their optimum level of health in situations of normal health, illness, injury, or disability, or at the end of life.

Choice
Nurses respect and promote the autonomy of persons and help them to express their health needs and values and also to obtain desired information and services so they can make informed decisions.

Dignity
Nurses recognize and respect the inherent worth of each person and advocate the respectful treatment of all persons.

Confidentiality
Nurses safeguard information learned in the context of a professional relationship and ensure that it's shared outside the health care

(continued)

Ethical codes for nurses *(continued)*

team only with the person's informed consent, as may be legally required, or where the failure to disclose would cause significant harm.

Justice
Nurses uphold principles of equity and fairness to assist persons in receiving a share of health services and resources proportionate to their needs and in promoting social justice.

Accountability
Nurses are answerable for their practice, and they act in a manner consistent with their professional responsibilities and standards of practice.

Quality practice environments
Nurses value and advocate for practice environments that have the organizational structures and resources necessary to ensure safety, support, and respect for all persons in the work setting.

Code for Licensed Practical Nurses
The code for LPNs seeks to provide a motivation for establishing, maintaining, and elevating professional standards. This code requires these nurses to:
◆ regard conservation of life and disease prevention as a basic obligation
◆ promote and protect the physical, mental, emotional, and spiritual well-being of the patient and his family
◆ fulfill all duties faithfully and efficiently
◆ function within established legal guidelines
◆ take personal responsibility for actions and seek to earn the respect and confidence of all members of the health care team
◆ keep confidential all information about the patient obtained from any source
◆ give conscientious service and charge reasonable fees

◆ learn about and respect the religious and cultural beliefs of all patients
◆ meet obligations to patients by staying abreast of health care trends through reading and continuing education
◆ uphold the laws of the land and promote legislation to meet the health needs of its people.

International Council of Nurses code of ethics
According to the ICN, the fundamental responsibility of the nurse is fourfold: to promote health, to prevent illness, to restore health, and to alleviate suffering.

The ICN further states that the need for nursing is universal. Inherent in nursing is respect for life, dignity, and the rights of man. It's unrestricted by considerations of nationality, race, color, age, gender, politics, or social status.

Nurses and people
◆ The nurse's primary responsibility is to people who require nursing care.
◆ The nurse, in providing care, respects the beliefs, values, and customs of the individual.
◆ The nurse holds in confidence personal information and uses judgment in sharing this information.

Nurses and practice
◆ The nurse carries personal responsibility for nursing practice and for maintaining competence by continual learning.
◆ The nurse maintains the highest standards of nursing possible within the reality of a specific situation.
◆ The nurse uses good judgment in relation to individual competence when accepting and delegating responsibilities.
◆ The nurse, when acting in a professional capacity, should at times maintain standards

Ethical codes for nurses *(continued)*

of personal conduct that would reflect credit upon the profession.

Nurses and society
◆ The nurse shares with other citizens the responsibility for initiating and supporting actions to meet the health and social needs of the public.

Nurses and coworkers
◆ The nurse sustains a cooperative relationship with coworkers in nursing and other fields.

◆ The nurse takes appropriate actions to safeguard the patient when his care is endangered by a coworker or another person.

Nurses and the profession
◆ The nurse plays the major role in determining and implementing desirable standards of nursing practice and nursing education.
◆ The nurse is active in developing a core of professional knowledge.
◆ The nurse, acting through the professional organization, participates in establishing and maintaining equitable social and economic working conditions in nursing.

---

of treatment to decide which one will produce the greatest amount of relief (benefit) with the least danger of suffering (risk).

The fact that teleologic theory assumes that good and harm can be quantified and evaluated can make it a less than ideal approach to resolving health care issues. Determining the "greatest good" is highly subjective and can result in inconsistent decisions.

Deontologic ethical theories emphasize moral obligation or commitment. Deontologic theories give most weight to obeying moral laws, such as "Always tell the truth" and "Never harm a patient." According to deontologic theories, honoring ethical obligations ensures the greatest good, even though actions may be difficult and consequences painful.

Because deontology centers on duty or obligation to others, many experts consider it the only acceptable theory for ethical decision making in health

care. Nevertheless, complications can arise when duties conflict with one another and you have to decide which duty takes precedence.

For example, suppose someone proposes keeping a brain-dead patient on a ventilator while recipients for a kidney transplant are found. Several staff members object because the patient had expressed a wish to die naturally, without artificial support.

On the one hand, you may favor maintaining the patient on a ventilator because you recognize how useful his kidneys will be to others. On the other hand, if you resolve this dilemma by deciding which course of action best supports the patient's rights, you would probably give more weight to his right of self-determination. This would lead you to oppose maintaining the patient on a ventilator. So, as you can see from this example, duties can conflict, and you'll have to determine which duty takes precedence.

Alternative ethical theories

In addition to deontology and teleology, other ethical theories may guide decision making, but each has its limitations.

Egoism

Egoism considers self-interest and self-preservation as the only proper goals of all human actions, insisting that the only right decision is the one that maximizes the autonomy of the decision maker.

Limitations

◆ Egoism ignores moral principles or rules outside the individual's point of view.
◆ Inconsistencies arise from one decision to the next, even in similar situations.
◆ Social chaos can result when individuals act solely in their own interests.
◆ Because it ignores the rights of others, egoism is unacceptable for most ethical decisions in health care.

Obligationism

Obligationism attempts to resolve ethical dilemmas by balancing distributive justice (dividing equally among all) with beneficence (doing good and not harm). This theory holds that benefits and burdens should be distributed equally, according to merits and needs.

Limitations

◆ The two basic principles of obligationism – justice and beneficence – may conflict in certain situations.
◆ The theory can be useful in determining public policy, but it's impractical for decisions that affect one person.

Social contract theory

Social contract theory is based on the concept of original position. The least advantaged people (such as children and the disabled) are considered the norm. Whether an act is right or wrong is determined from the norm's point of view.

Limitations

◆ Without specific guidelines, the theory is useless in day-to-day health care decisions.
◆ Social inequalities are persistent.

Theological ethics

Ethical theories and moral-legal principles can be based in religious traditions – for example, Good Samaritan acts are based on the biblical concept of altruism and selflessness.

Limitations

◆ It may be difficult for someone who doesn't share a particular religious faith to understand its beliefs or to apply its teachings to health care situations.

Virtue ethics

Virtue ethics encourages and focuses on traits of character, such as trustworthiness, loyalty, helpfulness, friendliness, kindness, bravery, generosity, cleanliness, reverence, and the like.

Limitations

◆ Virtue ethics tend to neglect conduct and outcome. It also doesn't provide a formula for resolving conflict cases.

Nurses usually combine aspects of both teleologic and deontologic theories when making ethical decisions. To avoid becoming confused, you should develop orderly, systematic, objective decision-making methods. Otherwise, your decision making becomes subjective and arbitrary, and results in moral relativism.

Basis of ethical decisions

Ethical decision making most commonly involves reflection on the following:
◆ options or courses of action available
◆ options that seem unavailable
◆ consequences, both good and bad, of all possible options (teleology)
◆ rules, obligations, and values that should direct choices (deontology)
◆ who should make the choices
◆ desired goal or outcome.

Equally important is the process of self-reflection. This involves uncovering, sharing, and discussing:
◆ personal and professional values relevant to the situation (values clarification)
◆ cultural considerations (ethnic groups may have different perceptions as to what constitutes acceptable treatment; however, this must be balanced with notions of moral relativism — discussed on page 300)
◆ prejudices or biases that affect objectivity
◆ previous experiences with similar situations and decisions
◆ limitations that affect skills or understanding
◆ motives and intentions, particularly those of self-interest and convenience.

All these elements should come together when you're making an ethical decision. The best way to ensure this may be to use a method with which every nurse is familiar: the nursing process adapted to ethical decision making.

HOW TO APPLY THE NURSING PROCESS

The nursing process is a continuous, interdependent, systematic organization of cognitive behaviors designed to resolve problems and promote well-being. The essential steps of the nursing process include assessment, planning, implementation, and evaluation.

Assessment begins with the nurse's initial contact with a patient. It involves collecting systematic data, identifying the patient's needs, and determining the nursing diagnosis.

Planning includes assigning priorities to nursing diagnoses based on acuity, determining goals of nursing actions, identifying appropriate nursing actions necessary to attain goals, establishing outcome criteria, and developing a nursing care plan.

Implementation involves coordinating, performing, or delegating activities specified in the nursing care plan and recording results.

Evaluation includes collecting data, measuring outcomes against outcome criteria, and altering the nursing care plan by continuation of the nursing process.

You can effectively use the same type of continuous, systematic, rational approach when making ethical decisions.

Assessment
◆ Gather facts, perceptions, and opinions about the ethical problem. Read the patient's chart. Talk with the patient and his family, other health care providers, and anyone who may be familiar with the patient's values.
◆ Identify the people involved in the problem, and assess their roles, responsibilities, authority, and decision-making abilities.
◆ Identify available resources. These may include the ethics committee,

chaplain, nurse ethicist, counselors, and facilitators. Resources may also include institution policies, as well as literature on similar cases.
◆ Help decision makers participate in values clarification.

Planning
◆ Identify the types of moral dilemmas involved—beneficence, autonomy, justice, fidelity, nonmaleficence, confidentiality, or veracity. Identify the specific issues involved by examining the rights, duties, and values that are in conflict.
◆ Identify possible courses of action, along with their probable and possible risks and benefits (teleology).
◆ Formulate and assign priorities to the ethical goals or objectives desired by the people involved.
◆ Determine the ethical obligations of those involved and the ethical principles that shape their actions (deontology).

Implementation
◆ Develop an ethical goal that maximizes the greatest good; work with others involved, as appropriate.
◆ Determine the course of action that will produce results closest to those of the ethical ideal.
◆ Determine if that course of action violates legal or moral principles. (If so, modify or change the course of action until it doesn't do so.)
◆ Carry out the agreed-on course of action.

Evaluation
◆ Determine if the results approximate the ethical ideal.
◆ If the results fall short of the ideal, determine what new moral dilemmas have been created.

◆ Reenter the decision process in the assessment phase to resolve additional moral dilemmas.

Although this process imposes the structure and objectivity necessary for resolving a moral dilemma, it doesn't provide all the answers. Because human beings are fallible, it's impossible for anyone to gather all the facts or to be completely without bias. Psychological and emotional factors can wreak havoc on fairness and impartiality. (See *The nurse's role on the ethics committee.*)

HOW TO SKILLFULLY COMMUNICATE
When it comes to making fair and ethical decisions, personality conflicts, political forces, and power plays can sabotage even the best intentions. For this reason, you should use communication skills and management techniques to help promote collaboration and prevent divisiveness. In addition, you should observe the following rules of behavior:
◆ Act within professional bounds, following the appropriate codes of ethics.
◆ Don't make ethical decisions alone. Seek counsel and advice from other professionals.
◆ Validate information. Don't base ethical decisions on rumors, innuendo, hearsay, first impressions, or snap judgments.
◆ If religious faith and spiritual values are important to you or others involved in the ethical dilemma, include prayer in the decision-making process.

ACTING AS A PATIENT ADVOCATE
One of your most important moral obligations is your role as a patient advocate. When a patient must make an ethical decision, you should help him

The nurse's role on the ethics committee

If your organization *doesn't* have an ethics committee, you may be able to help start one. If one already exists, you may be able to play a vital role as a committee member or by educating patients, residents, or clients and their families about the existence and work of the ethics committee. It's of no value for an organization to have an ethics committee, if patients, residents, or clients and their families don't know how the committee can help them.

Make sure that when your organization informs those it serves about their rights as patients, residents, or clients it also tells them about their right to access an ethics committee for help in making difficult choices about care and treatment. All patients, residents, or clients should receive written information about their rights that includes at least a simple paragraph such as this:

The ethics committee is available to help you and your family as you deal with difficult decisions about your care and what's right and fair. There's no charge for this service. To find out more about the ethics committee, ask your nurse.

Committee makeup
The ethics committee is usually multidisciplinary. Membership includes nurses, physicians, allied health care professionals, and other key members of the care team (respiratory therapists, registered dietitians, licensed clinical social workers, chaplains), administrators, ethics experts such as a nurse ethicist, and a community representative familiar with the role of the ethics committee who's a strong patient advocate. Nurse members should include staff, advance practice nurses or clinical experts, and nurse administrators.

Key committee functions
The ethics committee has three key functions:
◆ Develop and revise policies and procedures relevant to ethics (such as policies and procedures on patient rights, advance directives, confidentiality, informed consent, and forgoing treatment and resuscitation).
◆ Educate committee members to develop a level of competency consistent with the guidelines of the American Society for Bioethics and Humanities Core Competencies for Health Care Ethics Consultation, and then educate staff, administration, trustees, patients, families, and the community about issues of importance in health care ethics.
◆ Develop a team to do case consultation through facilitation, discussion, research, negotiation, resolution, and documentation of difficult cases and evaluation of outcomes to monitor and improve quality.

---

resolve his moral dilemma in ways that enhance personal values, priorities, freedom, dignity, and the quality of life.

As an advocate, you must never impose personal agendas or values on a patient. By listening carefully to the patient and asking thoughtful questions, you may be able to help the patient and his family make ethical decisions with which they are most comfortable. Consider asking the patient to describe the problem to you, and then ask him the following questions to help him clarify his thoughts.
◆ What has the physician told you about the situation?
◆ What options are you considering?
◆ Have you considered making a list of the best and worst things for each option you're considering?

◆ What else would it help you to know as you're making the decision?
◆ Is there anyone you'd like to speak with about this decision (for example, clergy, counselor, social worker, trusted friend, or lawyer)?
◆ What is the hardest part about coping with this decision?
◆ What things in the past have helped you cope with difficult decisions or situations?
◆ What would make it easier for you and your family to talk about this situation?
◆ What do you think is the best thing to do?

Selected references

Berggren, L., and Severinsson, E. "Nurse Supervisors' Actions in Relation to their Decision-making Style and Ethical Approach to Clinical Supervision," *Journal of Advanced Nursing* 41(6):615-22, March 2003.

Bosek, M.S. "Ethical Decision Making for Emergency Nurses: A Descriptive Model," *Journal of Nursing Law* 7(4):31-41, March 2001.

Cooper, R.W., et al. "Ethical Helps and Challenges Faced by Nurse Leaders in the Healthcare Industry," *Journal of Nursing Administration* 33(1):17-23, January 2003.

Hadjistavropoulos, T., et al. "Ethical Orientation, Functional Linguistics, and the Codes of Ethics of the Canadian Nurses Association and the Canadian Medication Association," *Canadian Journal of Nursing Research* 34(2):35-51, September 2002.

King, C.A., and Broom, C. "Ethics in Perioperative Practice — Values, Integrity, and Social Policy," *AORN Journal* 76(6):1047-53, December 2002.

Skott, C. "Storied Ethics: Conversations in Nursing Care," *Nursing Ethics* 10(4):368-76, July 2003.

Smith, K.V., and Godfrey, N.S. "Being a Good Nurse and Doing the Right Thing: A Qualitative Study," *Nursing Ethics* 9(3): 301-12, May 2002.

Vittone, S.B. "Ethics in the ICU," *Critical Care Nursing in Clinics of North America* 14(2): 157-63, viii, June 2002.

Volker, D.L. "Is There a Unique Nursing Ethic?" *Nursing Science Quarterly* 16(3): 207-11, July 2003.

Wong, F.W., and Anderson, S.M. "Team Approach in Cross-cultural Ethical Decision Making: A Case Study," *Progress in Transplantation* 13(1):38-41, March 2003.

Internet resources

Albert Association of Registered Nurses: *www.nurses.ab.ca/profconduct/ethics.html*

Canadian Nurses Association: *www.cna-nurses.ca*

Ethical conflicts in clinical practice

Rapid advances in medical research have outpaced society's ability to solve the ethical problems associated with new health care technology. For nurses, ethical decision making in clinical practice is complicated by sociocultural factors, legal controversies, growing professional autonomy, and consumer involvement in health care.

This chapter describes six major areas of ethical conflict—the right to die, organ transplantation, critically ill neonates, human immunodeficiency virus (HIV) and acquired immunodeficiency syndrome (AIDS), abortion and reproductive technology, and genetic engineering and screening. No matter what your nursing specialty, you'll probably encounter at least one of these conflicts during your career.

Ethical dilemmas resist easy resolution. The choice is typically between two desirable or two undesirable alternatives. By learning as much as possible about the underlying ethical principles, you'll be better equipped to participate in the decision-making process. The more you practice ethical thinking, the more confident you'll become in your ability to make decisions.

Getting help

When ethical problems arise, discuss them candidly with other members of the health care team, especially the patient's physician. Also, consider calling on social workers, psychologists, the clergy, and ethics committee members to help you resolve difficult ethical problems.

By learning as much as possible, you can facilitate the decision-making process for the patient, his family, his physician, and for yourself. (See *The ethics committee,* page 312.)

Right to die

The most difficult ethical decisions in health care involve whether to initiate or to withhold life-sustaining treatment for patients who are irreversibly comatose or vegetative or suffering with end-stage terminal illness. Treatment decisions for these patients can be morally troubling. The patient, his family, and the health care team may be asked to choose between a potentially painful extension of life and immediate death. Surrogate decision makers—people who are designated to act when a patient is no longer capable of deciding his own fate—also

The ethics committee

The ethics committee addresses ethical issues regarding the clinical aspects of patient care. It provides a forum for the patient, his family, and health care providers to resolve difficult conflicts.

The functions of an ethics committee include:

◆ policy development (such as developing policies to guide deliberations over individual cases)

◆ education (such as inviting guest speakers to visit your health care facility and discuss ethical concerns)

◆ case consultation (such as debating the prognosis of a patient who's in a persistent vegetative state)

◆ addressing a single issue (such as reviewing all cases that involve a no-code, or do-not-resuscitate [DNR] order)

◆ addressing problems of a specific population group (for example, the American Academy of Pediatrics recommending that hospitals have a standing committee called the "infant bioethical review committee")

◆ addressing issues of organization ethics (such as business practice, marketing, admission, and reimbursement).

Pros and cons

Properly run, an ethics committee provides a safe outlet for venting opposing views on emotionally charged ethical conflicts. The committee process can help to lessen the bias that interferes with rational decision making. It allows for members of disparate disciplines, including physicians, nurses, clergy, social workers, hospital administrators, and ethicists, to express their views on treatment decisions.

Critics of the ethics committee think that committee decision making is too bureaucratic and slow to be useful in clinical crises. They also point out that one dominating committee member may intimidate others with opposing

views. Furthermore, they contend that physicians may view the committee as a threat to their autonomy in patient-care decisions. For these reasons, many ethics committees use a "rapid response team" of committee members who are on call to respond quickly in emergent ethical dilemmas. The rapid-response team usually consists of three or four committee members, including a physician, who have had special training in negotiation and mediation. The entire committee will retrospectively review each case.

Selection of committee members

Committee members should be selected for their ability to work cooperatively in a group. The American Hospital Association recommends the following ratio of committee members: one-third physicians, one-third nurses, and one-third others, including laypersons, clergy, and other health professionals. Regulations of the Joint Commission on Accreditation of Healthcare Organizations require that nursing staff members participate in the hospital ethics committee.

The nurse's role on a hospital ethics committee

Because of the nurse's close contact with the patient, his family, and other members of the health care team, she's frequently in a position to identify ethical dilemmas such as when a family is considering a DNR order for a relative. In many cases, the nurse is the first to recognize conflicts among family members or between the physician and the patient or his family.

Before ethics committees were widely used, nurses had no official outlet for voicing their opinions in ethical debates. In many situations, physicians made ethical decisions about patient care behind closed doors. Nurs-

The ethics committee *(continued)*

ing supervisors frequently would call meetings to alert nursing staff on treatment decisions and to discourage protest. Now, ethics committees provide nurses with a means to ex-press their views, hear the opinions of others, and understand more deeply the rationale behind ethical decisions.

---

face tremendous moral and emotional pressures.

Sometimes, the patient's expressed wishes to withhold life-sustaining treatment are ignored or overridden by physicians and family members. As a nurse, you may feel that you're caught in the middle, frustrated and demoralized by the demands of caring for an unresponsive patient who had expressly wished to withhold life-sustaining treatment.

DEFINING DEATH

Part of the problem stems from a lack of consensus about what constitutes death. Some people define *death* as the loss of all vital functions, whereas others define it by neurologic criteria such as *brain death* — the irreversible cessation of brain functioning accompanied by ongoing biological functioning in all other parts of the body that's only maintained by life-support measures.

Some people maintain a strong ethical belief in the absolute sanctity of life. Others argue that it's wrong and wasteful to continue life support when a patient's life is devoid of dignity. To function effectively when caring for critically ill patients, you'll need to be aware of your personal feelings about death and quality-of-life issues.

ORDINARY VS. EXTRAORDINARY TREATMENT

Ordinary means of medical treatment are medications, procedures, and surgeries that offer the patient some hope of benefit without incurring excessive pain or expense. In contrast, extraordinary means, sometimes called heroic measures, merely maintain or prolong a patient's life, usually at great expense and suffering for the patient and his family. Because of continuing advances in medicine and technology, the distinction between "ordinary" and "extraordinary" treatments is becoming less defined.

In 1983, the President's Commission for the Study of Ethical Problems in Medicine and Behavioral Research defined *ordinary* and *extraordinary* treatments: "The Commission believes that extraordinary treatment is that which, in the patient's view, entails significantly greater burdens than benefits and is therefore undesirable and not obligatory, while ordinary treatment is that which, in the patient's view, produces greater benefits than burdens."

The commission further stated that health care professionals aren't obligated to provide treatment that's considered useless or futile.

Discontinuing treatment

Despite the commission's recommendations, countless terminally ill patients continue to receive treatment that's unlikely to benefit them. Determining whether a particular treatment is futile is highly subjective. Many such decisions aren't based only on incomplete information but may also involve value judgments about quality of life. One method being considered to help with these subjective decisions is a computerized mortality prediction system called the Acute Physiology and Chronic Health Evaluation System.

When deciding whether to terminate life-sustaining treatment, health care providers face incredible emotional pressure; a patient can't be brought back after he stops treatment. Nurses do have one ethically sound option: helping patients determine their own fate by educating them about their right to refuse extraordinary treatment.

RIGHT TO REFUSE TREATMENT

The right to refuse treatment is grounded in the ethical principle of respect for the autonomy of the individual. This principle of autonomy has led to the concept of informed consent — the obligation of health care providers to inform the patient of the risks and benefits of a procedure and to obtain permission before the procedure is carried out. Terminally ill patients who receive life-sustaining treatment have an equal right to informed consent.

Because the nursing profession is oriented to saving and prolonging lives, you may find it difficult to go along with a patient's decision to withhold life-sustaining treatment. Keep in mind that limiting treatment doesn't mean abandoning the patient. Supportive measures aren't considered extraordinary treatment. A patient who has chosen to forgo life-sustaining

treatment still has the right to receive care that preserves his comfort, hygiene, and dignity. In particular, he has the right to adequate pain control.

Health care workers' rights

Although patients have the right to decide whether to accept or forgo heroic measures, they don't have the right to insist on treatments that provide no medical benefit. If you believe that you'll violate your own values by implementing a certain treatment, you have an obligation to arrange for the transfer of the patient's care to another provider. Likewise, if you believe that you'll violate your values by withholding treatment, you should request the transfer. This right, also known as *the conscience clause* or *conscientious objection,* applies to assisting in abortions as well as to noninitiation or withdrawal of life-sustaining treatment or euthanasia.

DOCUMENTING A PATIENT'S WISHES

A patient who has a strong desire to request or reject aggressive treatment measures should document his wishes. He should also designate a surrogate decision maker to speak for him if he can no longer make his own health care decisions. Statements that indicate a patient's wishes in the event he loses his decision-making capability are known as *advance directives,* the patient's best means of ensuring that his wishes will be respected. The advance directive includes a living will, which goes into effect when the patient can't make decisions, and the durable power of attorney, which authorizes another person to make those decisions. If a patient has both, the person with durable power should be in complete support of the patient's wishes. No family member or health care provider can then override the person with the durable power of attorney.

Although specific treatments can be requested in an advance directive, most people execute a living will to ensure that no extraordinary procedures are used to sustain or prolong life. A durable power of attorney designates a surrogate decision maker who will have full authority to carry out the patient's wishes regarding health care decisions. The authority of this surrogate decision maker is based on the principle of substituted judgment — allowing the surrogate to make the same decisions the patient would, if he were able.

Advance directives, although useful, haven't ended the controversy over a patient's right to limit treatment. Critics contend that they represent the first step toward active euthanasia, or *mercy killing*. These people believe that advance directives such as living wills should be restricted to a narrow range of circumstances. (See *When family members contest a living will,* page 316.)

Although many states have enacted so-called natural death acts to encourage practitioners to abide by a living will by granting statutory enforcement, these laws vary from state to state. Several require a "reasonable effort by the physician" to transfer the patient to a physician who will abide by the living will.

Helping the patient plan ahead

Of the many professionals who care for the critically ill, nurses probably have the best chance to act as true patient advocates. The patient will probably look to you as well as his physician for guidance. You can't make the ultimate medical decisions to initiate or limit treatment, but you can help the patient express his wishes about his health care and guide him in translating these desires into advance directives.

When you're discussing limiting treatment with a patient, consider these suggestions:
◆ Present options, such as do-not-resuscitate (DNR) orders, in a realistic but positive context. Reassure the patient that he'll continue to receive supportive care and pain medication. (See *DNR and slow codes,* page 317.)
◆ Pay attention to the patient's questions and misunderstandings. Be especially alert for unexpressed fears.
◆ During your discussions with the patient, note his nonverbal cues and emotional responses.

Despite your best efforts to provide objective advice, the patient may not be able to reach a decision about initiating or terminating care. Remember that you must respect the patient's explicit refusal to participate in health care decisions.

WHEN THE PATIENT SHOULDN'T DECIDE

At times you may question whether a particular patient should be allowed to decide to refuse life-sustaining treatment. Consider whether the patients described below are capable of making life-and-death decisions.
◆ Joe Ryan suffered a stroke 2 years ago that left him paralyzed on the right side and unable to speak. He was admitted to the hospital with sepsis caused by infected stasis ulcers of his lower legs. Mr. Ryan's physician recommended bilateral above-the-knee amputations. As he was being prepared for the surgery, Mr. Ryan became visibly agitated.
◆ Mary Kane suffered a severe head injury in a traffic accident that also left her a quadriplegic and dependent on a ventilator. About 3 months after the

When family members contest a living will

A living will isn't a guarantee that the patient's expressed wishes will be honored. The language in many living wills is vague and unclear. Patients who have added specific requests to a standardized form (for example, requesting termination of tube feedings) may not realize that such requests may conflict with state law. Nurses and physicians sometimes find it difficult to carry out wishes expressed years before current treatment options became available.

The family's response to the living will can also create problems. Family members may not know about the living will or may choose to ignore it in their turmoil over "letting go." As the following case history demonstrates, health care workers, including nurses, can be caught in the crossfire.

Conflicting demands

Esther Summerson was brought to the emergency department (ED) in respiratory distress after a long history of chronic obstructive pulmonary disease (COPD). The ED staff asked Mrs. Summerson if she wanted help breathing, but they couldn't get a clear response before she lost consciousness. She was intubated and transferred to the intensive care unit.

When Mrs. Summerson's older daughter, Jean, arrived at the hospital, she was upset to find that her mother had been placed on a ventilator. She showed the staff a copy of her mother's living will, specifying that her mother not be placed on a ventilator or receive supplementary nutrition. Miss Summerson also produced a form giving her durable power of attorney. As her mother's designated decision maker, she demanded that her mother be removed from the ventilator.

Susan Johnson, Mrs. Summerson's younger daughter, reached the hospital about an hour after her sister. Although her mother was still unresponsive, Mrs. Johnson didn't want her removed from the ventilator. "I don't know what I'd do without Mom," she sobbed. "I want you to do everything you can for her."

Implementing hospital policy

Fortunately, the hospital had developed procedures for resolving this sort of conflict. Mrs. Summerson's physician, her primary nurse, her priest, and a representative of the hospital's ethics committee called a meeting with Miss Summerson, Mrs. Johnson, and Mrs. Johnson's husband. They explained the living will and Miss Summerson's role as the surrogate decision maker, emphasizing that Mrs. Summerson's living will clearly specified her opposition to the ventilator. Mrs. Johnson and Miss Summerson were informed that without the ventilator their mother might breathe on her own or she might die. If she did die, however, it would be from lung damage caused by her long-standing COPD – as a result of their desire to honor her living will. Each step of the procedure was carefully reviewed.

As a result of this discussion, Mrs. Johnson changed her mind and agreed to removal of the ventilator. All three family members decided to be present when this occurred. After they had a chance to talk to Mrs. Summerson and express their love for her, the balloon was deflated and the tube removed. Mrs. Summerson died quietly 2 days later, with her daughters and her son-in-law by her side.

accident, she insisted that the ventilator be removed. A hospital psychiatrist determined that Mrs. Kane was seriously depressed.

◆ George Bowen has Alzheimer's disease. He can't remember a recent conversation, the names of his three children, or how to find his bedroom, although he's still continent and responsive. When Mr. Bowen was admitted to the hospital with his third heart attack, his wife told the physician he had begged to be allowed to "meet his maker."

The concept of informed consent creates ethical dilemmas in situations in which the patient's ability to make an informed judgment about his treatment options is questionable. If the patient is nonverbal, depressed, demented, or semiconscious, can he truly consent to or refuse life-sustaining treatment?

It's important to remember that some patients may remain capable of expressing health care preferences even when they can't manage in other areas, such as personal care, eating, or speaking.

Standards for judging decision-making ability

Commonly used standards for judging decision-making capability include:
◆ the ability to indicate a choice
◆ a clear understanding of the issues at hand
◆ the ability to reason based on the information given
◆ an appreciation of the true nature of the situation.

If a patient is incapable of making a decision, it becomes the duty of a surrogate decision maker or the health care team to act in his best interest.

MAKING DECISIONS FOR THE PATIENT

Two ethical principles can be used in making decisions for an incapacitated patient. The *substituted judgment* test professes to make the same decision the patient would, if he were capable (the principle of autonomy). Alternatively, the decision may be based on

the best interest standard, or deciding what's best for the patient, given his current circumstances (the principle of beneficence). Both principles are ethically valid. If the two are at odds, they can create dilemmas for family members, physicians, and nurses.

DNR and slow codes

Cardiopulmonary resuscitation (CPR) is widely used to treat victims of heart failure, despite its limited usefulness in prolonging life. For example, a study of the resuscitations carried out at a major medical center over 1 year revealed that only 14% of those who received CPR actually survived to leave the hospital. Nonetheless, it isn't uncommon for a patient to undergo several CPR attempts during a single hospitalization.

Most U.S. hospitals require CPR unless a specific medical order, known as a do-not-resuscitate (DNR) order (also called a *no-code situation*), is written to prevent this. In addition, the physician usually must notify the patient and his family before issuing a DNR order.

Slow codes

In the past, physicians who wanted to issue a DNR order but couldn't persuade the patient or his family to agree sometimes assisted staff to perform a slow code. Slow codes are considered unethical and probably illegal and, as a nurse, you shouldn't participate in going through the motions of a code with no intention of saving the patient. If a patient doesn't have a DNR order, you must make every effort to revive him.

FOSTERING COMMUNICATION

Effective communication is essential when helping families decide whether to limit or withhold treatment. If you're helping family members or surrogates while they're making life-and-death decisions, the following guidelines can improve communication.

◆ Create a quiet, private, and unhurried environment—keep all communication simple, factual, and direct.
◆ Encourage decision makers to ask questions.
◆ Express medical information in simple, clear language.
◆ Ask decision makers to summarize and check their responses.
◆ Clarify missing or misunderstood information.

Keep in mind that this may be the most heartrending decision family members or surrogates will ever be asked to make. They need plenty of time, care, and understanding.

EUTHANASIA

Euthanasia, also known as *mercy killing,* and assisted suicide further confuse the right-to-die issue. Although DNR orders and other decisions to limit treatment are sometimes referred to as passive euthanasia, euthanasia usually refers to active intervention such as lethal injection to bring about death. The issue of whether nurses or other health care professionals can ever ethically assist in taking a life is hotly debated in professional journals and the mass media.

In 1994, Oregon voters legalized physician-assisted suicide. Enactment of the law was delayed in the courts, but similar bills were introduced in other states. The Oregon law states (with qualifying safeguards) that a terminally ill person can ask a physician to prescribe a lethal dose of oral medication, which the patient will take when he deems it appropriate. Although assisted-suicide laws remain on the books in Oregon and several other states, the federal Assisted Suicide Funding Restriction Act of 1997 has, to a large extent, negated the effects of these laws. This act forbids the use of federal funds to cause or assist suicide or mercy killing. Several states considering assisted-suicide legislation have dropped it, and other states that had passed assisted-suicide laws have since withdrawn them. Check with your state board of nursing about the legal status of assisted suicide in your state.

Proponents of euthanasia and assisted suicide base their argument on the right to self-determination. They argue that if a terminally ill patient is in unendurable pain that can't be controlled, physician-assisted suicide might be seen as a more humane alternative. Public reaction to highly publicized cases of assisted suicide indicates that many people support a patient's right to control his own fate. Dr. Jack Kevorkian, who has assisted the suicides of more than 130 terminally ill persons, has numerous supporters, including jurors who have acquitted him of criminal charges brought by the state of Michigan in 1995. However, in fall 1998, Dr. Kevorkian raised the legal and ethical stakes.

On the nationally broadcast network news show *60 Minutes,* Dr. Kevorkian not only admitted to administering a lethal drug to a patient without the patient's assistance but also made and played a videotape that showed the incident. The patient, who had amyotrophic lateral sclerosis (Lou Gehrig disease), had requested that Dr. Kevorkian kill him and had signed a consent form and release. Dr. Kevorkian admitted that his motivation for the act was to be tried in a test case for active euthanasia. He was convicted of second-degree murder and, in April 1999, was sentenced to up to 25 years in prison. (See *End-of-Life Choices: Euthanasia advocates.*)

Many critics, however, find the mercy killing concept repugnant. Although many nurses would agree with allowing the family of a comatose patient to withdraw food and fluids, most oppose more active forms of euthanasia. Allowing euthanasia, many argue, would eventually lead to patients selectively being put to death without consent. The potential object of mercy killing—a patient with Alzheimer's disease or a patient in a persistent vegetative state, for example—has lost the capacity to express his wishes. Family members and health care providers don't know if the patient truly desires to die and don't have the moral right to make the decision for him.

All major professional nursing and medical organizations have taken positions against assisted suicide. The American Nurses Association (ANA) has reaffirmed this position repeatedly through its publications. American Medical Association (AMA) policy contains the following: "It is understandable, though tragic, that some patients in extreme duress—such as those suffering from a terminal, painful, debilitating illness—may come to decide that death is preferable to life. However, allowing physicians to participate in assisted suicide would cause more harm than good. Physician-assisted suicide is fundamentally incompatible with the physician's role as healer, would be difficult or impossible to control, and would pose serious societal risks."

End-of-Life Choices: Euthanasia advocates

End-of-Life Choices, formerly known as The Hemlock Society, supports the option of active voluntary euthanasia for patients with advanced terminal or severe, incurable illnesses. Founded in 1980, the group is purported to have 28,000 members. Its goals include promoting a climate of public opinion tolerant of the terminally ill person's right to end his own life in a planned manner. It also seeks to improve existing laws on assisted suicide.

End-of-Life Choices doesn't encourage suicide for any primary emotional, traumatic, or financial reasons in the absence of terminal illness. The group, in fact, approves of suicide prevention work. To obtain further information, contact End-of-Life Choices at *www.endoflifechoices.org.*

COST CONSIDERATIONS

You may find the mention of cost considerations in the context of limiting treatment for the terminally ill offensive. Such considerations, however, are ethically legitimate. The necessity of conserving resources eventually will force the public to consider this issue. Health care resources—including organs available for transplants, beds in the intensive care unit (ICU), and experimental drugs—are limited in quantity and are costly. Some individuals have begun to debate the equity of giving a disproportionate share of the most expensive medical treatments and procedures to elderly patients who are gravely ill. Medicare pays out $21 billion, or 28% of its budget, for bills incurred in the final year of life. Some policy makers believe that the patient's

age should be a valid ethical consideration in the delivery of medical care, especially when so much money is spent
to achieve relatively small gains in life
expectancy.

Health care in the United States is
already rationed to a degree through
policies that discourage the poor from
seeking medical attention. Unafford-
ably high insurance rates, underfi-
nanced state medical programs, and
crowded clinics, in effect, ration care.

Deciding how to ration lifesaving
technology is an ethical dilemma of
huge proportions. It ultimately will
have to be resolved by society at large
using the ethical principle of justice.

Organ transplantation

The benefits of organ transplantation
are widely recognized by health care
professionals and the general public.
Nevertheless, organ transplantation
poses serious ethical concerns. Transplant procedures affect families of the
donor and the recipient, nurses, physicians, and even ambulance attendants
at the deepest emotional level. In such
a highly charged atmosphere, conflicts
of rights easily can develop.

◆ If the potential donor is a child,
questions may arise as to the validity of
informed consent.
◆ Controversy may occur over when
to declare a potential donor dead.
◆ The wishes of a potential donor's
family may conflict with the needs of a
transplant patient.
◆ Because the number of available
donor organs is limited, difficult choices must be made about which patients
should receive transplants.
◆ Many transplants are prohibitively
expensive; questions arise as to whether
subsidizing the procedure is a just allocation of health care resources.

◆ In light of the limited number of
available donor organs and the high
cost of the procedure, questions arise as
to the patient's right to multiple transplants.

Even if you don't make the ultimate
medical decisions about an organ
transplant, you may play a critical role
in resolving ethical conflicts.

PROTECTING THE RIGHTS OF POTENTIAL DONORS

Some transplantation procedures pose
few ethical problems. An autograft, in
which tissue is transplanted from one
part of the patient's body to another
(such as a skin graft to treat a third-
degree burn), is a good example. Certain types of transplants from one person to another (allograft), including
blood transfusions and cornea or bone
marrow transplants, also are widely accepted and ethically untainted.

The most difficult ethical issues surround the procurement of essential organs, such as hearts, kidneys, livers, and
lungs. In these instances, organ procurement remains ethical only if steps
are taken to ensure that the donor's life
and functional integrity aren't compromised.

Nonmaleficence

At first glance, removing an organ
from a healthy person who has nothing to gain from the procedure seems
to violate the ethical principle of *nonmaleficence*— the obligation to "do no
harm." However, when providing care,
there are many instances in which the
principle of nonmaleficence can't be
strictly applied. Some harm, in the
form of an invasive or a potentially
risky procedure, must be incurred in
diagnosing and treating many diseases.

When a living person donates the
organ, the key issue is informed con-

sent. From both an ethical and a legal standpoint, informed consent requires the donor to be fully aware of all risks and benefits that can result from the transplant procedure. Because relatives, particularly identical twins or full siblings, typically provide the closest match for a transplanted organ, a great deal of emotional pressure can be exerted on a potential donor. Extreme guilt feelings and emotional distress may disturb a potential donor's ability to render informed consent.

Child donors
Special problems arise when the potential donor is a child. Because, in most cases, a minor's consent is legally invalid, the parents or legal guardians must give substitute consent. Sometimes the wishes of the child and the parents are clearly the same. A 13-year-old girl whose parents support her wish to donate a kidney to her 5-year-old brother can probably give valid informed consent. But what about a 3-year-old child, who can't express his opinion? Can his parents ethically "volunteer" this child to donate a kidney? Parents have a moral obligation to protect the life and well-being of all their children. Sometimes it's unclear how to best uphold this obligation. Which are more important—the rights of the healthy child or the rights of the child who needs the kidney?

In a widely publicized 1991 case, physicians at the City of Hope Medical Center in Duarte, California, transplanted bone marrow into Anissa Ayala, a 19-year-old woman with potentially fatal leukemia. The marrow came from her infant sister, Marissa. The parents said that they conceived Marissa to provide bone marrow to save Anissa's life. This marked the first time a family publicly admitted to

conceiving a child to serve as an organ or a tissue donor.

The case raised troubling ethical questions. Does conceiving a child as a source of donated organs violate the principle that children should be brought into the world and cherished for their own sake and no other motive? If prenatal tests indicate that the fetus has the wrong tissue type to serve as a donor, is an abortion justifiable? Selling organs is both unethical and illegal in many countries, but the legal and ethical status of conceiving potential donors remains unclear.

CADAVERIC DONORS
Harvesting organs from a deceased donor poses a different set of ethical problems. Perhaps the most fundamental issue involves the actual definition of *death*. Although some organs and tissues, such as bone, skin, corneas, and even kidneys, can be transplanted after complete cardiac arrest, other organs, including the heart, lungs, liver, and pancreas, aren't viable unless they're taken from a brain-dead, or "beating heart," cadaver.

Most states recognize the definition of brain death set forth by the Uniform Determination of Death Act as the legal definition of death. In general terms, a patient is pronounced brain-dead when all functional activity in every area of the brain, including the brain stem, stops. Significantly, this definition isn't universally accepted by health care workers, ethicists, or laypersons. Many find it difficult to declare death when other aspects of bodily function continue, even if by artificial support.

The issue of declaring brain death must be approached cautiously. The determination that a person is brain-dead should be made by neurologic

National Organ Transplant Act

In response to widespread public interest in organ transplantation, Congress enacted the National Organ Transplant Act of 1984 (PL 98-507). This act:
◆ prohibits the sale of organs
◆ provides funding for grants to organ procurement agencies
◆ establishes a national organ-sharing system.

Task Force on Organ Transplantation

This act also convened the 25-member Task Force on Organ Transplantation, with members representing medicine, law, theology, ethics, allied health, the health insurance industry, and the general public. Representatives from the Office of the Surgeon General, the National Institutes of Health, the Food and Drug Administration, and the Health Care Financing Administration also were appointed to the task force. This task force examined the medical, legal, ethical, economic, and social issues created by organ transplantation.

In its final report, the task force concluded that the best way to close the gap between the small number of organ donors and the large number of potential transplant recipients was to actively solicit donations from bereaved families. As a result, the task force recommended that all state legislatures introduce and enact legislation requiring health care professionals to present organ donation as an option to families ("required request").

Assertive approach

Required request policies are legally mandated in many states. This assertive approach to organ procurement has proved highly successful; as many as 80% of families given the option to become donor families ultimately do so. Significantly, studies show that organ donation can facilitate the grieving process and speed recovery for the bereaved family.

consult and never by a physician who's involved in organ removal. No request for organ donation should be made until the potential donor's family understands what brain death is as well as that it's a final state.

Informed consent

The Uniform Anatomical Gift Act allows a person to donate specific organs or even his entire body for organ transplantation. A patient who before death indicated his willingness to be an organ donor could be considered to have given informed consent. True informed consent, however, requires that the patient have the option to withdraw consent at any time before a medical procedure. Therefore, the final decision is left up to the potential donor's family, even if it results in the loss of an organ donation.

Approaching a potential donor's family

All states have enacted required request acts. These laws require hospitals to ask families of potential organ donors to permit donation. The required request laws are intended to increase organ availability. (See *National Organ Transplant Act*.)

Most required request laws are fair to the families of potential donors. Family members are under no compulsion to grant permission to donate organs. Most required request acts grant an exclusion if the request will cause the family severe emotional distress.

These laws may create serious ethical conflicts, however, for a nurse who opposes organ transplantation or who finds the idea of approaching a grieving family offensive. Should a nurse be forced to request organ donation regardless of her feelings? One solution to this dilemma is assigning the job of approaching the donor's family to a specially trained organ procurement team, whose members have been specially trained to deal with emotional situations.

If you're making the request for an organ donation from a patient's family, approach family members tactfully and be sufficiently informed to answer their questions. You should be able to explain the potential good to others. Remember that the decision of the family must be respected.

Fetal tissue

Because the mother and the health care team carrying out an abortion are responsible for the death of the fetus, the transplantation of fetal tissue is far more controversial than transplantation where the donor is a cadaver. (See *Fetal tissue transplant debate*, page 324.)

Caring for a potential donor

If you're caring for a patient who's a potential donor, your ethical responsibility includes maintaining his dignity as a human being until he's declared legally dead. You'll want to follow normal cleaning and skin maintenance procedures and keep the body properly covered. You'll also need to adhere to the physician's instructions for discontinuing medication and avoiding procedures that could damage the organ.

Maintaining a brain-dead patient until preparations for the transplant are complete raises additional ethical questions. If *death* is defined as "brain death," doesn't the patient have the right to die when this determination is made? If not, how long can he be ethically maintained on a life-support system? One day? One week? Is this a justifiable allocation of resources? The effort and money spent to maintain a brain-dead organ donor for any appreciable period might be better spent helping living patients.

USING ORGANS FROM ANENCEPHALIC INFANTS

Anencephaly is the congenital absence of most or all of the cerebral hemispheres. Many anencephalic infants are stillborn, but others have a functional brain stem and live for a short time after birth.

Anencephalic infants might seem to be ideal organ donors. Their immune systems are still immature, reducing the chance of rejection. Also, their small organs can be readily used in children, who commonly encounter the most trouble locating a suitable donor.

The anencephalic infant, however, isn't a "beating heart" cadaver. Although severely debilitated, an infant with a functioning brain stem must be considered to be in a persistent vegetative state or a coma, not brain-dead. Until an anencephalic infant meets the clinical criteria for brain death, his organs can't ethically be used for transplantation.

Laws have been proposed that would increase the supply of organs available for donation from anencephalic infants by broadening the definition of *brain death* (to discount brain stem function). Another, called presumed consent, would presume every

Fetal tissue transplant debate

Although still in the research phase, transplants using tissue from aborted fetuses offer new hope for treating Parkinson's disease, Alzheimer's disease, diabetes, and other degenerative disorders. The immaturity of the fetal immune system reduces the chances of rejection, making fetal tissue ideally suited to transplantation. However, from an ethical standpoint, fetal tissue transplants are a cause for concern.

Obtaining fetal tissue

When family members give permission for the donation of organs from a deceased loved one, death has already occurred and they aren't responsible for the person's death. With fetal tissue transplants, however, the mother and members of the health care team carrying out the abortion are responsible for the death of the fetus. This makes questions about when and how tissue is obtained much more problematic.

Opponents of fetal tissue transplants point to the high risk of ethical abuses. For example, suppose a woman can no longer watch her father, who has Alzheimer's disease. She decides to conceive and then abort a fetus to supply brain tissue for a transplant for her father. Although it's easy to understand her motives, few people would agree that this is ethical.

Clearly, guidelines need to be developed to ensure that women who provide tissue from abortions are adequately informed about fetal tissue transplants, yet not encouraged to consent to an abortion they might not otherwise have.

Second-trimester abortions

The timing of the abortion is another critical issue. Most elective abortions take place during the first trimester, almost as soon as the mother finds out she's pregnant. Unfortunately, the best tissue for transplantation comes from second-trimester fetuses. Is it ethical for the mother to postpone the abortion? Some fetuses may be viable by the last stages of the second trimester.

Research ban

In 1988, the Department of Health and Human Services banned federal funding for research in which healthy cells from fetal tissue are transplanted in adults to replace defective cells. However, former President Bill Clinton addressed the issue early in his presidency and, in 1993, lifted the ban on federal funding.

---

person would donate unless they carried a card stating otherwise. (See *Organ donation and the concept of consent.*)

SELECTING TRANSPLANT RECIPIENTS

The number of potential transplant recipients far exceeds the number of available donors. How should one determine who receives a transplant and who is turned down?

Medical and physical factors rule out some matches. For example, the donor and the recipient must have compatible blood and tissue types and be fairly close in size and age (it would be impossible to place a 30-year-old accident victim's heart in the chest cavity of a 5-year-old patient). Beyond these limitations, the selection of transplant recipients depends on value judgments. As a result, the potential for serious value conflicts and unethical behavior is tremendous. For example, the high cost of transplantation raises questions about the fair distribution of organs. Should a wealthy or well-insured patient be given priority over an indigent patient with a similar need? (See *Choosing between potential transplant recipients,* page 326.)

Recipients with unhealthy lifestyles

Another concern is transplanting organs into people whose unhealthy lifestyles have destroyed their health. Mickey Mantle's 1995 liver transplant is a case in point. He had admitted causing damage through years of alcohol and drug abuse. When he died quickly of lung cancer, his long-term smoking became an issue as well. Considering his lifestyle, should he have been a successful transplant candidate?

Ethically, the principle of distributive justice could work both ways in lifestyle cases. Underlying the principle is the belief in equal treatment, which suggests that Mr. Mantle should have had an even chance at a new liver. In the other view, distributive justice applied to scarce resources says the organs should go to people more likely to sustain them with a healthy lifestyle.

To ensure that transplant recipients are selected as fairly as possible, most medical centers have adopted certain guidelines, which are discussed below.

Coordinating transplants

A regional organ donation center should coordinate the matching of transplant recipients and potential donors. The principle of "first come, first served" should form one criterion for selection.

All transplant decisions should be made by a committee under the auspices of an impartial organization such as the American Red Cross that in-

---

Organ donation and the concept of consent

Recent legislative initiatives to increase the supply of organs available for donation have sought to broaden the definition of consent. One recent proposal is based on the concept of presumed consent – the assumption that all sane and rational people would consent to donate organs if they had the chance to do so.

Under this legislation, each person would be considered an organ donor unless he carried a card stating that he did *not* want to donate his organs. Rather than being asked if they wanted to have their loved one's organs transplanted, family members would be asked if they had any objections to transplantation.

A violation of informed consent?

Although the doctrine of presumed consent is applied to other aspects of health care law, when applied to organ donation, presumed consent is a controversial idea. Opponents argue that it's coercive and violates the right to informed consent. It contradicts the widely held belief that a person should have free choice in all decisions related to his own body.

---

cludes a physician, nurse, lawyer, religious leader, and well-informed layperson. The committee should take every precaution — including the institution of policies and procedures — to prevent transplanting the wrong organ or other deleterious events.

Determining need

The selection procedure should be based on need as well as the potential

Choosing between potential transplant recipients

One concern about organ transplantation is the potential for elitism when choosing one recipient over another. Consider the following situation, in which the committee on organ donation and transplantation at a major teaching hospital had to choose between two potential liver recipients.

Patron's daughter

Jodi Morgan, a 5-year-old girl, received a liver transplant 18 months ago. Although her initial response was promising, she has recently been hospitalized again with signs of irreversible hepatic failure.

Jodi was born with multiple birth defects. In addition to biliary atresia, which led to her need for a transplant, she has only one functioning kidney and a cyanotic heart defect. She's mildly retarded and can't speak and has only recently mastered toilet training.

Jodi's father, Jack, is a prominent local businessman, politician, and patron of the hospital. He wants Jodi placed at the head of the registry for a second liver transplant. She spent 4 months on the registry before her first transplant. Nonetheless, rumors spread that Mr. Morgan had "bought" Jodi's first transplant by making a sizable donation to the hospital's new cardiology wing.

Mother of three

Brenda DeStefano, a 22-year-old mother of three young children, heads the list of potential liver recipients. In chronic hepatic failure for nearly 2 years, she has been on the transplant list most of that time and is now near death. She's unemployed and has no health insurance. Because the federal government won't reimburse for a liver transplant, the hospital stands little chance of being paid for her surgery.

Committee decision

According to state law, Jodi couldn't receive a second transplant unless she was returned to the registry. But should she be placed at the head of the list?

The committee struggled with many ethical questions:
◆ Mr. Morgan would probably exert a great deal of political and financial pressure on the hospital. Could committee members realistically ignore this factor?
◆ How might past rumors that Mr. Morgan bought Jodi's first transplant influence the present thinking of committee members?
◆ Mrs. DeStefano's inability to pay would probably create a financial hardship for the hospital. Should this influence its decision?
◆ Do risk-benefit calculations justify another procedure for Jodi Morgan? Because of her underlying cardiac pathology and renal dysfunction, even if the transplant is successful, her prognosis is poor. The potential for success of the transplant is less than it would be for healthier patients.
◆ Should a child such as Jodi be given automatic preference over an adult? What about Mrs. DeStefano's children? Should their right to have a mother be an overriding consideration?

After much debate, the committee decided to return Jodi to the transplant list, behind Mrs. DeStefano. After a donor was found for Mrs. DeStefano, Jodi could have a second chance at life.

for survival. Patients with the greatest need (those closest to death) and best survival potential are assigned the highest priority.

Determining potential for survival
Survival is a more complex issue than need. For example, the potential for survival doesn't necessarily decrease as

a patient ages. A health-conscious elderly patient may represent a better transplant risk than a younger patient who has neglected his health.

A patient's willingness to comply with lifestyle changes, drug regimens, and dietary restrictions can also influence survival. Lifestyle factors may raise questions about a patient's suitability as a transplant recipient. Should a heavy smoker who refuses to quit be given a heart-lung transplant? Because of the controversy created by Mickey Mantle's liver transplant and subsequent debate over the fairness of organ donation, the United Network for Organ Sharing (UNOS) began, in 1998, to develop a new system, including a way to make donor livers available on a nationwide basis.

UNOS has moved from a local to a regional allocation system. In 1998, categories of potential recipients were revised: status 4, the least serious, was eliminated, and status 2 was divided into 2A and 2B. The 1999 naturalistic data on regional and state sharing reveal that:

♦ sharing increases the most serious status 1 transplantation rates
♦ sharing decreases status 2B pretransplantation mortality
♦ sharing decreases transplantation rates of status 3 patients, thereby providing more organs for seriously ill patients
♦ sharing, which decreased transplantation rates for status 3 patients, didn't provide a concomitant increase in mortality of status 3 patients.

Determining potential value to the community

The selection procedure can also take into account a potential recipient's value to the community. A good case could be made for assigning a higher priority to a mother of two young children than to a convicted drug dealer. Note that value is the last criterion, to be used only if a decision can't be made based on need or potential for survival.

Avoiding manipulation

Neither the donor nor his family ought to play a role in the selection procedure. Because of the potential for manipulation (a payoff by the recipient), such participation isn't compatible with an ethical selection procedure.

Last resort

When other criteria fail to establish priority, the final selection should be made by lot. Although imperfect, this method is unbiased.

COST CONSIDERATIONS

Organ transplants can be prohibitively expensive. A kidney transplant costs about $35,000; a heart transplant may exceed $100,000. Either procedure is much more affordable than a liver or pancreas transplant. The federal government will pay up to 80% of the costs for kidney and heart transplants but refuses to subsidize liver or pancreas transplants, which are still considered experimental. For the patient whose life depends on receiving a liver transplant, the current reimbursement policy would appear unjust.

Along the same line, one might pose an even more challenging question: Is it fair for one person to receive that great a share of the limited funds available for health care? The $100,000 cost of a heart transplant would finance inoculations for several thousand children or prenatal care for hundreds of women. Utilitarian ethical theory would claim that the rights of hundreds of potential patients to a quality life exceed the right of one person to a heart transplant.

MULTIPLE TRANSPLANTS

The issue of multiple transplants is closely related to the concept of distributive justice. At first glance, it might seem unethical, or at least unfair, for the same person to receive three or four transplants. The nurses and physicians caring for a transplant recipient, however, may believe that everything possible must be done to keep the patient alive, including another transplant.

Perhaps the most equitable course of action is to place a repeat-transplant patient back on the regional transplant center register for a fair evaluation.

TRANSPLANT APPENDAGES

A new wrinkle has been added to the debate over transplant ethics. In January 1999, a man in the United States had a hand transplant to replace the one he lost some 13 years before in a firecracker accident; a man in Italy underwent a testicular transplant in the spring of the same year. Although the initial procedures were successful, it's still much too early to determine the long-term outcome of these transplants.

The ethical issues involved revolve around beneficence and maleficence. Before the procedures, these transplant recipients were healthy. It's accepted that all surgeries have risks, but transplant surgeries are riskier than most because of the length of time they take and the possible damage they may cause to the vascular system. Also, there are many possible complications, including embolus formation in the attached appendage, the possibility of infection due to the use of antirejection drugs posttransplant, and the transmission of diseases, such as hepatitis and HIV.

The fundamental question becomes, "Does the health care provider violate the principle of beneficence by changing an otherwise healthy person (who's missing a hand or other body part) into an immunocompromised patient who will need to take antirejection drugs for the rest of his life?" We justify the dangers of transplantation and antirejection drugs in kidney, heart, and liver transplants because these transplants are performed for life-threatening conditions. However, missing a hand or set of testes, although inconvenient, definitely isn't life-threatening.

Perinatal ethics

Twenty years ago, a neonate born at 26 weeks' gestation had almost no chance of surviving, yet today such neonates can survive. Thanks to spectacular advances in neonatology, such as intrauterine surgery, synthetic lung surfactant, and new antibiotics, physicians can save increasingly smaller and sicker infants.

Many people argue that this lifesaving technology has gone too far. Physicians and nurses who treat critically ill neonates, they say, act too aggressively, frequently overriding the wishes of the neonate's parents. Treatment leads to even greater suffering for the neonate and places an enormous financial burden on society. Ethical questions are complicated by lack of knowledge about the long-term outcome of heroic measures.

SANCTITY OF LIFE VS. QUALITY OF LIFE

Without life, other values are irrelevant. As a result, society holds the sanctity of life in high regard. The belief that all human lives have meaning and ought to be respected supports the notion that a critically ill infant should be kept alive at any cost.

But what about the quality of life? A utilitarian ethic would support a decision to withhold treatment for a severely disabled neonate when the prospect for an acceptable quality of life is poor. But what's an "acceptable quality of life"?

One measure of the value of a person's life is his ability to achieve certain goals. Thus, if a neonate has little hope of achieving anything but sheer survival, it may be ethically acceptable to terminate treatment.

The best-interest criterion is another measure of the quality of life. Unfortunately, not everyone agrees its exact meaning. Is death ever in anyone's best interest?

Still another definition considers the patient's potential to establish some type of human relationship. According to this view, an infant who has little chance of recognizing and relating to his family has such a poor quality of life that withholding treatment is both compassionate and ethical. There are two objections to the human-relationship standard. First, the standard suggests that medical treatment be withheld from adults who have a limited capacity for human relationships. You would almost certainly find it morally unacceptable to refuse to perform an emergency appendectomy on a psychotic patient or to withhold medication from a comatose automobile accident victim.

Some experts argue that the infant isn't the only one with a right to an acceptable quality of life. The financial and emotional cost of sophisticated perinatal technology places an enormous burden on the infant's family as well as society in general. Is this too great a price for a few extra months or years of life?

Who should decide

The best-qualified person to make a quality-of-life decision is the patient himself. But who's best qualified to give proxy consent for a premature neonate born at 25 weeks' gestation?

Parents

Although no one knows the neonate's true desires, legal and ethical precedent suggests that his parents ought to be the chief decision makers. Others argue that the parents' ability to make a wise and rational decision on short notice in such an emotionally charged atmosphere is limited. Furthermore, few parents have the necessary medical knowledge to make an informed decision. The combination of time pressures, ignorance, prejudice, and religious or moral beliefs can force parents into a decision that's at odds with the opinions of the medical team caring for their neonate.

Health care team

Members of the health care team are more objective and better informed about the potential outcomes of the various treatment options. Ethically, however, this paternalistic approach is unacceptable. After all, the health care team won't bear the burden of raising the child.

Hospital ethics committee

Unfortunately, the slow pace of most committee decisions is incompatible with the rapid decisions required when treating seriously ill neonates. Also, using this approach might simply substitute the biases of the committee members for the biases of the parents, physicians, and nurses

Critically ill neonate

If you care for extremely premature or severely disabled infants or their mothers, family members will look to you to assist them in life-and-death decisions. Consider the nurse's role in this case study.

Grim prognosis

Matthew Klein, a microcephalic infant with transposition of the great arteries, was born more than 6 weeks prematurely. He also had spina bifida. The news of his condition was devastating to his parents, an older professional couple who had eagerly anticipated their first child.

The attending pediatrician asked a noted neurosurgeon and a pediatric cardiologist to consult on Matthew's case. These experts concurred that without immediate corrective surgery, he might live as long as 1 month on life support. Even with surgery, he probably wouldn't live past age 20. During that time, physicians explained to Mr. and Mrs. Klein that Matthew could be expected to suffer from seizure disorders, paralysis, and episodes of heart failure. He would be highly susceptible to infection and severely retarded. In fact, he faced a grave risk just from the surgery.

Treatment options

Mr. and Mrs. Klein were given two options. They could choose aggressive surgical intervention for their child. If Matthew survived, he would need additional surgery at age 4 and again at age 10. Alternatively, the Kleins could elect a conservative treatment plan, which included antibiotics, nutrition, and comfort measures but no heroic treatment.

Angelica Perez, a registered nurse with more than 3 years of experience in caring for

seriously ill neonates, was assigned as Matthew's primary nurse. Ms. Perez soon realized that Matthew's parents were overwhelmed. She knew that, as a result, their decision-making ability was compromised.

Ms. Perez strongly believed in the sanctity of life, but her practical experience gave her an appreciation for quality-of-life issues. In her professional opinion, the quality of Matthew's life was likely to be poor, and the conservative treatment option would be the best.

She carefully reviewed both treatment plans with Matthew's parents, analyzing the possible outcomes and explaining unfamiliar medical terms. Ms. Perez pointed out that even with surgical intervention, Matthew might be too severely brain damaged to ever recognize or interact with them. Mrs. Klein would have to quit her job to care for Matthew, and his medical expenses would pose an enormous financial burden. Eventually, he was almost certain to require institutional care.

Ms. Perez recognized that the conservative option presented problems for the Kleins as well. Deeply religious, both husband and wife strongly opposed mercy killing. They had difficulty seeing the distinction between allowing their son to die and actually causing his death.

Even after extensive counseling, the Kleins couldn't reach a decision. At this point, Ms. Perez suggested that the couple discuss their feelings with the physician, a social worker, and their minister. As a result of these discussions, Mr. and Mrs. Klein accepted the conclusion that conservative treatment was best for Matthew. The baby survived 2 weeks and died in his mother's arms.

Courts

As the designated protector of individual rights, the legal system typically

takes a narrow view of the issues. For example, up to the time of birth, greater weight is given to the rights of the mother. However, during or after birth, the courts usually have decided that the rights of the neonate supersede those of the parents.

"BABY DOE" REGULATIONS

Court-mandated settlements to perinatal ethical conflicts have created significant debate. The best-known case involved a neonate born with Down syndrome and a tracheoesophageal fistula. The family opted to forgo surgical treatment of the fistula and withhold supplemental nutrition, reasoning that the child's quality of life was too severely compromised. A nurse caring for the child disagreed. She contacted the authorities, but during the ensuing legal battle, the neonate died.

On the basis of this and similar cases, the federal government instituted regulations standardizing the care of critically ill or severely disabled neonates. Enacted under the umbrella of the Child Abuse Protection and Treatment Act, these "Baby Doe" regulations prohibited physicians and nurses from denying treatment to disabled infants. The only exceptions were infants in an irreversible coma; those for whom treatment would prolong dying, not life; and those for whom treatment would be futile or even inhumane. Violators could be prosecuted for negligence or malpractice.

Some lawmakers opposed the constitutionality of the Baby Doe regulations. The Supreme Court agreed and, in June 1986, struck down federal laws requiring the treatment of all disabled neonates. Furthermore, it reinforced the right to privacy by denying access to Baby Doe's medical records. Unfortunately, because many states backed up the federal laws with their own Baby Doe regulations, it's still possible

to be prosecuted for withholding treatment.

The major ethical problem with these regulations is their failure to address the quality-of-life issue. Also, they're based on the mistaken assumption that a set of rigid laws can take the place of the ethical decision-making process.

NURSE'S ROLE

The repeal of federal Baby Doe regulations hasn't clarified the ethical issues surrounding the care of critically ill infants. If anything, by creating a conflict between the federal government and state and local laws, it has made the situation even more complicated.

To help the parents of an extremely premature or critically ill neonate reach ethically sound decisions, you'll need to present all available options in a compassionate, unbiased manner using simple terms. By carefully considering the pros and cons of both initiating and withholding treatment, you can help family members come to terms with their child's condition and reach a decision with which they'll be able to live. (See *Critically ill neonate.*)

HIV and AIDS

Nurses have always honored their professional responsibility to care for all patients, regardless of personal attributes, lifestyle, or the nature of the illness. Today, HIV and AIDS challenge this long-standing professional ethic. No other contagious illness incites such emotionally charged ethical debate.

HIV and AIDS touch on two highly controversial social issues: sexuality and drug use. It isn't surprising that many nurses experience value conflicts when working to meet their professional

Ethical issues and AIDS: Where do you stand?

Acquired immunodeficiency syndrome (AIDS) raises numerous ethical issues for nurses and other health care professionals. These issues range from personal safety to societal obligations. Read and answer the questions below to help you articulate your ethical position on AIDS.

◆ Should all health care professionals have the right to refuse to treat patients who are human immunodeficiency virus (HIV)–positive?

◆ Should patients with AIDS receive "heroic" life-sustaining treatments?

◆ Should patients who are pregnant and who are also HIV-positive have abortions rather than risk the chance of passing the virus to their unborn children?

◆ Should health departments obtain lists of all sexual contacts of people diagnosed as HIV-positive and notify those on the lists of their risk of exposure?

◆ Should the U.S. government provide free medical insurance to patients who are HIV-positive and who are no longer able to buy health insurance?

◆ Should pregnant drug abusers who acquire HIV and infect their infants be charged with child abuse?

◆ Should costly, limited intensive care unit (ICU), neonatal ICU, and pediatric ICU resources be tied up in the care of patients with AIDS if other patients with better prognoses for survival are being deprived?

◆ Should health care facilities test all current and new employees for HIV infection?

◆ Should states and jurisdictions enact special laws allowing terminally ill patients with AIDS to request and receive a lethal, painless injection?

obligations. (See *Ethical issues and AIDS: Where do you stand?*)

Prejudice, fear, and misunderstanding surround HIV and AIDS. An HIV-positive test result may mean the loss of a job, medical insurance, financial security, and even housing. Family, friends, and even the public may shun the HIV or AIDS patient. As a result, maintaining confidentiality is a serious concern for people with HIV and AIDS.

MANDATORY TESTING

Although there has been a major effort at education about HIV transmission, the Centers for Disease Control and Prevention (CDC) estimate that most of the 1.5 million Americans infected with HIV don't know about it. Lack of awareness can seriously undermine both patient care and prevention efforts. (See *Do you know the facts about AIDS?*)

Testing for HIV isn't the same as testing for other infectious diseases. The patient with a positive gonorrhea culture doesn't face the same likelihood of discrimination as the patient who's HIV-positive.

Some organizations, including the military and prisons, and many insurance companies insist on mandatory testing. Several states attempted to institute mandatory testing to obtain a marriage license and then abandoned the policy because of high costs and the low percentage of positive results. Most states now mandate written consent for testing and mandate pretest and posttest counseling.

Does mandatory testing violate the ethical principles of autonomy (the patient's right to control his own fate) and justice (his right to be treated fairly)? Does it violate his right to privacy? Many nurses believe that it doesn't.

Health care workers, they argue, have a right to protect themselves and need a complete picture of the patient's health status to deliver quality care.

Public health officials contend that mandatory testing would improve our understanding of the spread of the disease and aid in prevention. Hospital administrators say that knowing a patient's HIV status could lower health care costs by pinpointing those who require extra precautions.

Opponents of mandatory testing emphasize the risk of discrimination and the high cost of screening all patients. They also believe that testing drives away patients who need care because many people fear being tested.

Mandatory testing can also backfire. An exposed person can take 12 weeks or longer to develop HIV antibodies. During this time, he's contagious but seronegative.

Case study

The following example illustrates some of the ethical problems raised by mandatory testing.

Karen Owen, a trauma nurse, was accidentally exposed to a patient's blood during emergency surgery to treat a gunshot wound. Many AIDS patients are treated at Ms. Owen's inner-city hospital. Although, as a precautionary measure, hospital policy dictated HIV testing of the patient because the hospital employee was exposed to blood or body fluids, Ms. Owen's patient strongly objected. She argued that she was equally likely to have contracted AIDS from Ms. Owen. She demanded that Ms. Owen be tested as well.

Is this a legitimate request and must the hospital honor it? What about Ms. Owen's right to privacy? If she proved to be HIV-positive, would she lose her job? If she was HIV-negative, did she

> ### Do you know the facts about AIDS?
>
> Answer true or false to the following statements:
> ◆ The first documented case of acquired immunodeficiency syndrome (AIDS) was in 1952.
> ◆ It's possible to prevent the spread of human immunodeficiency virus (HIV).
> ◆ Casual contact doesn't spread HIV.
> ◆ No cure for HIV or AIDS exists.
> ◆ HIV-infected people who show no symptoms can infect others.
> ◆ HIV is spread primarily through sexual contact.
> ◆ HIV survives outside the human body for a short time.
> ◆ People can't get HIV from insect bites.
> ◆ Most people infected with HIV don't know that they have the infection.
> ◆ It may take up to 12 weeks before a person infected with HIV tests positive.
>
> (All answers are true.)
>
> Source: Stone, J.G. (1998), *AIDS Update*, Prentice Hall, New Jersey.

have to consent to be retested at a later date?

Out of concern for her own health, Ms. Owen agreed to be tested. To provide further reassurance, the hospital noted on the patient's consent form that the test was necessary because of worker exposure, not because that patient was part of a high-risk group.

PUBLIC'S RIGHT TO KNOW

Many people believe that all health care providers should be routinely tested for HIV. The public, they argue, has the right to know a nurse's or physician's HIV status.

After at least three patients contracted HIV from a Florida dentist, the AMA and the American Dental Association recommended that physicians and dentists who are HIV-positive perform no invasive procedures and tell their patients that they're infected.

State and federal lawmakers have considered proposals to prevent physicians who are HIV-positive from performing surgery and other risky procedures. Such proposals are highly controversial. In April 1991, a New Jersey court upheld the right of a Princeton hospital to prohibit a surgeon with AIDS from performing surgery. Some people question the need for restrictions based on status alone. Rules about impaired health care workers, whether based on addiction, mental status, or physical illness, seem fairer and minimize the chance of HIV-based discrimination.

TESTING GUIDELINES

Following the guidelines below can help to ensure that HIV testing is carried out in an ethically responsible manner.
◆ The sole purpose of any screening program should be to prevent the spread of HIV.
◆ The confidentiality of the test results must be ensured. If it's necessary to disclose the results (when a blood donor tests positive), the affected person should be notified.
◆ The patient should receive adequate pretest and posttest counseling.
◆ The diagnostic laboratory must be reliable.
◆ Informed consent should be obtained before a patient is allowed to participate in a voluntary screening

program. (See *Correcting a flawed HIV testing policy.*)

STANDARD PRECAUTIONS

The CDC contends that mandatory testing isn't necessary to protect nurses if health care workers follow standard precautions for all patients. This means using gloves, gowns, and goggles to prevent contact with a patient's blood or body fluids and strictly adhering to safety measures when handling needles, scalpels, and other sharp instruments.

Unfortunately, few nurses follow these precautions all the time. Some hospitals fail to provide enough supplies. Some nurses complain that gloves and gowns make it more difficult to perform certain procedures. Nurses working in the emergency department may not have time to adhere meticulously to standard precautions. Furthermore, many white, middle-class patients are automatically assumed to be seronegative.

Standard precautions are time-consuming, expensive, and obstructive. Nonetheless, following these precautions means that nurses can protect themselves without forcing patients to undergo mandatory testing.

REFUSING TO PROVIDE CARE

Dorothy Smith, a critical care nurse, struggled for many months with her prejudices against AIDS patients. Although she was deeply committed to her career, her religion taught that homosexuality and drug use were sins. She also was apprehensive about the danger of contracting AIDS. Finally, she begged her supervisor to avoid assigning her to AIDS patients.

Marie James, who worked on the surgical floor of a large teaching hospi-

Correcting a flawed HIV testing policy

Regardless of whether human immunodeficiency virus (HIV) testing is voluntary or mandatory, careless procedures can ruin lives and increase liability. Consider this case study.

Surgeon's request

Mike Robertson, a robust, athletic 25-year-old, suffered a herniated disk in a bicycling accident. When bed rest and anti-inflammatory drugs didn't relieve his pain, he was referred to an orthopedic surgeon. The physician recommended surgery but insisted that Mr. Robertson undergo HIV testing before the operation.

"I don't understand why I need an HIV test," Mr. Robertson told Sherry Water, the nurse-counselor who performed his preadmission counseling.

She explained that the physician's request was legal and that it was probably a routine practice. She reviewed the details of the test procedure, emphasizing that a positive result didn't mean that he had acquired immunodeficiency syndrome, although it would mean that he faced a high risk of developing the disease and could infect others. Finally, she pointed out that his test results would remain confidential but, if he preferred, she could refer him to an anonymous testing site.

"No, that's OK," Mr. Robertson replied. "I want to get this done and get my back fixed next week. It's really been killing me."

Devastating results

Mr. Robertson's surgery was scheduled for the following Tuesday. Ms. Water set up an appointment for Monday afternoon to give him the test results. To her dismay, he was HIV-positive. Then, making things worse, he didn't keep his appointment. Later that day, he called to reschedule the appointment for the morning of the surgery.

Ms. Water became frantic. Should she tell Mr. Robertson the test results just before surgery, when the information could be dangerously upsetting? Should she wait until after surgery, when he would still be somewhat sedated and might not really understand?

Ms. Water finally reached Mr. Robertson's surgeon just an hour before the operation. Even though Mr. Robertson had already received preoperative sedation, the physician immediately canceled surgery. He recommended that Ms. Water explain Mr. Robertson's test results as soon as he woke up. She agreed, knowing that Mr. Robertson would need an explanation for the cancellation.

Mr. Robertson was disappointed and angry that the surgery hadn't taken place and horrified to learn that he was HIV-positive. He felt that his physician had abandoned him, leaving him with two untreated medical problems: his back and his HIV status.

Changing hospital policy

Ms. Water also was disappointed and angry. Fortunately, she capitalized on her feelings to improve her hospital's HIV testing program. She discussed Mr. Robertson's case with the director of nursing, and stressed that, in the future, she would refuse to carry out a test unless ample time was provided for posttest counseling. In response, the hospital established new guidelines. Physicians who requested the HIV antibody test before any medical procedure had to verify that posttest counseling had taken place before the procedure could be performed. In addition, the physician was required to specify whether he would continue to care for a patient who tested positive. If not, he would need to designate another physician who would do so.

Legal Tip

ANA guidelines: Your obligation to provide care

If you work in a hospice, be aware of these special legal responsibilities toward your patient, as outlined by the American Nurses Association (ANA).

Standing orders
A hospital staff nurse can follow standing orders for pain medication. When working in a hospice, however, never rely on standing orders as authorization to administer pain medication. Always obtain specific orders signed by the patient's physician.

Advice on making a will
In a hospice, never give your patient advice concerning his will. If he asks for advice, tell him you can't help him. Suggest that he discuss the matter with his attorney or his family.

Living wills
The nurse who works in a hospice must respect the patient's living will. Unless it contains illegal obligations such as assisted suicide or violates a court order, don't violate it in any way.

tal, also wanted to avoid AIDS patients, but for a different reason. She had just learned that she was pregnant, and she wanted to avoid exposure to cytomegalovirus (CMV), a common opportunistic infection associated with AIDS. The infection causes severe and overt disease in fetuses.

Ethical solutions

The ANA Code for Nurses states that "the nurse provides services unrestricted by considerations of social or economic status, personal attributes, or the nature of health problems." Thus, Ms. Smith's refusal to care for AIDS patients because this duty conflicts with her religious beliefs isn't ethically viable. No matter how strong your personal feelings, you can't allow them to interfere with your moral obligation to provide care.

This obligation isn't absolute, however. If the risk to you is greater than the potential benefit to the patient, you can ethically refuse to take that risk. Mrs. James, for example, was justified in refusing to treat patients with CMV infection because of the risk to her unborn child. However, she couldn't avoid caring for patients with *Pneumocystis carinii* pneumonia, where subclinical infection is common and antibodies are present in 75% of 4-year-olds in the United States, or patients with Kaposi's sarcoma, which is a cancer and not infectious.

You may also refuse to perform procedures on a patient who deliberately puts you at risk. For example, if a patient deliberately moves his arm while you're drawing blood, you have the right to refuse to carry out the procedure. You may even be justified in refusing altogether to care for this patient, but you can't abandon the patient. Ethically and legally, you're required to find someone else to care for him. (See *ANA guidelines: Your obligation to provide care.*)

What if a patient with AIDS becomes violent or threatens to bite you? If the patient's decisional capability is in doubt, the use of chemical or physical restraints may be justified. If the patient makes threats because of anger, warn him that his aggressive behavior must stop or treatment can't continue. You and the physician should document the patient's behavior, stating, if necessary, that because treatment can't be administered at this time, the patient is being discharged.

CONTACT NOTIFICATION

The patient's right to privacy may conflict with your duty to prevent the spread of the disease. Although the patient may balk when you request that he inform his partner that he's HIV-positive, you must respect the patient's right to confidentiality. You should try to impress on him, however, how crucial it is for the other person to know about exposure to the AIDS virus. Anonymous contact notification programs may provide assistance. For example, with the patient's consent, you can refer the problem to the county health department, which will attempt to locate and inform contacts of exposure.

Many married patients are reluctant to notify their spouses, especially if the infection can be traced to an extramarital affair. Legally, you can't compel the patient to tell his wife, but you can explore options that may make it easier for him to do so. For example, ask the patient if he would feel more comfortable if a family physician gave her the news. A counselor could also work with the patient to reduce his anxiety about informing his wife as well as to support him when he tells her.

Laws dealing with contact notification continue to evolve and vary widely from state to state. For example, a Utah law that was effective until 1993 barred those with HIV from marrying. In 1998, New York lawmakers passed a law requiring medical personnel to report identifying information of those patients with HIV infec-

tion, HIV-related illness, and AIDS to the state health department for the purposes of monitoring, tracking, and notifying sexual partners whom the patient may have infected. Since then, other state legislatures have passed similar laws.

As of May 1, 2003, Canadian law requires public health officials to be notified when a person tests positive for HIV, but it doesn't require HIV-positive persons to divulge the names of sexual partners or notify others of a positive test result.

Many states charge HIV-infected individuals with murder when they have unprotected sex with partners whom they didn't inform of their infection. In 1991, a man in Oakland, California, was sentenced to 3 years in prison for this offense. In Florida, a 22-year-old man was convicted of attempted second-degree murder for knowingly engaging in intercourse while infected with HIV. He was sentenced to 4 to 5 years in jail and 13 years of probation.

AIDS AND THE PREGNANT PATIENT

Mandatory testing of pregnant women gained support when it was learned that giving a woman zidovudine (Retrovir) significantly lessened the chance of HIV transmission to her fetus. Giving zidovudine to the neonate of an HIV-positive woman also helps the at-risk baby.

Those who favor mandatory testing say the potential reduction in transmission is so important that the woman's autonomy should be set aside. Others condemn forced testing or forced medication and, again, raise the specter of women who fear the test and who then avoid seeking prenatal care and harm more babies in the long run.

Economic burden of AIDS

With the AIDS population rapidly growing, the cost of providing care will cause society to rethink questions about whether health care is a right or a privilege. Nurses must provide care regardless of the patient's ability to pay for it. But what about the rest of the health care system? Must hospitals and government agencies bear the burden of AIDS patients who can't handle the financial burdens imposed by their illness?

The right to health care is, at best, a tentative and an unenforceable right with no legal foundation, although most agree that a patient who enters the health care system has a right to receive treatment appropriate to his illness. Still, health care resources are limited, especially for lower- and middle-income and uninsured patients. With such limitations, the best you can do is to refer patients to the appropriate social service agencies and support legislation that guarantees equal access to health care.

Abortion and reproductive technology

Abortion poses a complex and painful ethical dilemma for nurses and their patients. Consider the cases described below.

◆ Ashley Adams, a pregnant 14-year-old, quietly wept with her mother sitting next to her. They were waiting in the short procedure unit for Ashley's turn in the operating room. When the nurse took her aside to talk privately, Ashley began to cry harder. She told the nurse that she didn't really want an abortion but her parents had placed so

much pressure on her that she had no real choice.

◆ Loretta Hofmann was pregnant with her fourth child. Recently fired from his job, her husband had begun drinking heavily and on more than one occasion had become emotionally abusive. One of her three children was hyperactive and having trouble in school. Mrs. Hofmann believed that she couldn't handle another child or cope with going through a pregnancy and placing the child for adoption. To get to the abortion clinic, she had to pass through a picket line of pro-life protesters, who harassed and taunted her. During her initial interview with the nurse, she was visibly shaken and said that she could no longer cope with the stress in her life.

◆ Lynnette Mack worked in a women's health center that provided general family planning, treatment for vaginal infections, counseling, health care for adolescents, and abortion services. Although she was fervently prochoice when she took the job, over the months her feelings about abortion changed. She wanted to continue working at the center but without participating in abortions. She feared that this would create tension as well as extra work for her colleagues. Mrs. Mack, who was the primary wage earner for her family, considered resigning for ethical reasons.

The U.S. Supreme Court has handed down more than 20 decisions related to the abortion issue. Court rulings, however, can't answer the ethical questions about abortion that nurses encounter in their daily practice.

Is the fetus a human being?

The status of the fetus as a human life is an important element in the abortion controversy. Should the fetus be considered a human being or a potential human being? Even if the early embryo isn't considered a human being (at least not in the same sense as a neonate), does its potential to become a human being guarantee a right to life?

This confusion is complicated by the fact that the age of *fetal viability* — the age at which a fetus can survive outside the womb — has decreased to between 20 and 24 weeks.

Many bioethicists use measurable criteria of human body development, such as fetal movement and the existence of a heart and nervous system, to determine when the fetus is alive, but this hasn't ended the debate.

POLITICAL BATTLE

Abortion has become the focal point of a long and bitter political struggle.

Pro-life position

The pro-life position cuts across all religions and philosophies. Opponents of legal abortion argue that human life begins at conception and, therefore, abortion is murder. In 1869, Pope Pius IX of the Roman Catholic Church condemned all abortions as a form of murder. Before then, the church had imposed no penalties for abortions within the first 40 days of pregnancy.

Antiabortion groups also contend that tolerance for the murder of unborn children implies tolerance for assisted suicide, death by neglect, and murder of other categories of "undesirable" people, such as the mentally disabled, seriously ill, and deformed.

Pro-choice position

Those who support legal abortion argue that an embryo or a young fetus represents the potential for human life but shouldn't be considered a human

being at the time. They view abortion as a type of surgery necessary for the physical and psychological well-being of certain women. Abortion, they point out, will always be part of human society, regardless of whether it's legal. Legal abortions reduce the number of mutilations and deaths associated with illegal abortions. Further, they argue that legal abortions help reduce the number of unwanted children and forced marriages as well as the economic stress on some families.

Some take a third position: Abortions should be allowed only when the life of the pregnant woman is in danger or when the woman is a victim of incest or rape.

Continuing debate

The furor over abortion is unlikely to go away anytime soon. An abortion-inducing pill, mifepristone (RU-486; Mifeprex) has sparked new controversy. Taken in the first 7 weeks of pregnancy, mifepristone blocks progesterone receptors, allowing prostaglandins to stimulate uterine contractions and detach the conceptus. Mifepristone has been marketed in France since 1989 and is used in Britain and Sweden. In the United States, the drug obtained Food and Drug Administration (FDA) approval for use on July 19, 1996.

In 1995, two more drugs were found to induce abortion safely and effectively. They're common prescription drugs to fight cancer (methotrexate) and ulcers (misoprostol). Methotrexate is injected and stops the division of cells — malignant or fetal. Then, 5 to 7 days later, a misoprostol suppository is given to induce contractions and expel the fetus. One researcher suggests that the procedure could be administered by a nurse practitioner under a physician's supervision, increasing availability and lowering costs of abortion. This treatment regimen received FDA approval in 1997.

Although many manufacturers may not supply mifepristone for fear of reprisals from pro-life organizations, the cancer- and ulcer-fighting drugs are too valuable to be forced off the market. Antiabortion leaders, meanwhile, have made mifepristone a prime target and won't ignore the newest method.

The ethical principle of autonomy (self-determination) is an important part of the abortion debate. This principle upholds a woman's right to control her own body. From the mother's point of view, that right includes choosing whether to have an abortion. Many women may think that they shouldn't be forced into the physical, emotional, and financial hardships of pregnancy.

Opponents of abortion maintain that pregnancy involves two persons with a right to autonomy — the mother and the fetus.

RESOLVING YOUR VIEWS ABOUT ABORTION

A nurse who's ethically or morally opposed to abortion can't be forced to participate in the procedure. On the other hand, her employer can insist that she provide nursing to all in her care.

To reach your own ethical resolution to the abortion issue, you'll need to examine your views honestly and carefully. You'll also want to periodically reevaluate your position in light of new medical information and your own experience. If you feel strongly one way or the other, you should work for a facility that matches your views on abortion.

Postabortion care

Every nurse has an ethical obligation to provide competent, compassionate care. Even nurses who strongly oppose abortion shouldn't allow their personal feelings to interfere when caring for a postabortion patient. Nor is it appropriate to impose your values on the patient. If the patient expresses guilt or regret over her decision, an appropriate therapeutic response might be: "You made a decision that you thought was right. I want to help you live with your decision and rebuild your life." Offering to find a clergy member is another way to help.

PRENATAL SCREENING

Because of diagnostic procedures, such as amniocentesis, ultrasound, alpha-fetoprotein screening, and chorionic villus sampling, it's now possible to detect inherited disorders and congenital abnormalities well before birth. In a few cases, the diagnosis has paved the way for repair of the defect in utero. However, because it's easier to detect genetic disorders than to treat them, prenatal screening may force a patient to choose between having an abortion and taking on the emotional and financial burden of raising a severely disabled child.

Even those who are opposed to abortion may waver after seeing a child afflicted with Tay-Sachs disease or Duchenne muscular dystrophy. Is the quality of these children's lives so poor that it would be more compassionate to prevent their births? Is death ever more beneficial than life?

Some ethicists worry that this line of reasoning could cater to a desire for "perfect" children. How would this affect attitudes toward the disabled? How severe must a defect be for abortion to be considered an ethically acceptable option? For example, should a fetus with cleft palate, a surgically correctable defect, be aborted because of the disability? What about a girl conceived by parents who desperately want a boy?

The diagnostic procedures themselves involve some risk to the fetus. Amniocentesis, for example, causes serious complications or death about 0.5% of the time. This risk creates a conflict between the rights of the fetus and the parents' right to know his health status. If testing is to be conducted ethically, patients must understand the associated risks before the procedure.

Patients must also comprehend what the test can and can't tell them as well as all the available options. Thus, just as in HIV testing, effective pretest and posttest counseling are essential parts of an ethical prenatal screening program.

IN VITRO FERTILIZATION

Infertility can have devastating effects on the emotional well-being of a couple who yearn for children. As a result, many couples will spend a great deal of time and money trying to conceive or adopt a child. When medical procedures (such as fertility drugs, hysterosalpingostomy [opening blocked fallopian tubes], and artificial insemination) fail and adoption is impossible, infertile couples may turn to controversial techniques, including in vitro fertilization (IVF).

IVF refers to the process of removing ova from a woman's ovaries, placing them in a Petri dish filled with a sterilized growth medium, and covering them with healthy motile spermatozoa for fertilization. Three to five ova are implanted in the woman's uterus 10 to 14 days after fertilization, and the remaining fertilized ova are frozen for future use or discarded.

IVF can use the partner's sperm (homologous) or a donor's sperm (heterologous) to fertilize the ova.

Complicated and expensive, IVF has resulted in the birth of hundreds of healthy test-tube babies since the first successful attempt in 1978. The parents of these babies have no doubts about the procedure; they're thankful for the opportunity to have children. Yet egoism isn't an acceptable basis for ethical decision making·in health care. Worthy ends don't always justify the means, and many people question the morality of IVF.

Medical miracle or unnatural act?

Some people hail scientific manipulation of the ova and sperm as a medical miracle, but others denounce it as circumvention of the natural process of procreation. By concentrating on conception, IVF enables couples to sidestep other important aspects of a normal sexual relationship, including pleasure, respect, and love. Many religions maintain that a Supreme Being participates in the act of procreation. People with strong religious beliefs may contend that IVF diminishes the spiritual value of family life.

It's ethically acceptable to modify normal body functions to enhance natural actions. Thus, procedures such as hysterosalpingostomy pose few ethical problems. Is IVF the next logical step in fertility modification, or is it an unnatural act that oversteps the bounds of standard medical intervention?

IVF and conflicts of rights

The long-term effects of IVF on the children, their parents, and society in general represent another serious ethical concern. Human society depends on the strength and integrity of the family. By distancing parents from the physical act of procreation, IVF could have a harmful impact on family life.

Leftover embryos. IVF would pose fewer ethical problems if only one embryo were needed to guarantee a successful pregnancy. Unfortunately, it doesn't work that way. About 15 to 20 embryos may result from a single fertilization effort, but only 3 to 5 are implanted in the mother's uterus. The question arises: What should be done with the leftover embryos? Is it ethical to discard them, destroy them, or perform experiments on them?

In practice, leftover embryos usually are frozen. This raises questions with regard to parental responsibility for the frozen embryos. In 1989, for example, a divorcing Tennessee couple fought a custody battle over seven fertilized eggs that were frozen at an IVF clinic in Knoxville. Mary Sue Davis wanted custody for future implantation; her estranged husband, Junior Davis, insisted on having a joint say in the future of the embryos. In a controversial decision, a circuit court judge ruled that the embryos are people, not property, and should go to the mother.

Effects on child development. Parents may feel less responsible for IVF children born with congenital defects or conceived with donor sperm. Test-tube babies themselves may develop identity or adjustment problems after they learn the facts surrounding their conception. They're likely to feel insecure about their position in the family, especially if they have naturally conceived siblings.

Sperm and egg banks
One of the results of the widespread use of IVF is an increased number of sperm and egg banks in which to store semen and ova until they're ready for use in the IVF procedure. Sperm banks

have existed for many years. In the past, stored semen was primarily used for artificial insemination of women whose husbands were infertile and unable to make adequate quality or amounts of semen to produce fertilization.

Egg banks are a new development. To obtain ova, a woman is given a hormone preparation that hyperstimulates the ovaries to produce 30 times the usual number of mature ova. The ova are then removed by laparoscopy or vaginal ultrasound-guided aspiration. The ova can be fertilized immediately or frozen and stored in an egg bank for later use. Since the increase of IVF procedures, egg banks are experiencing shortages and couples desiring IVF have to wait from weeks to a year.

The ethical and legal issues involved with stored semen and ova are similar to those in the storage of in vitro–fertilized ova. One obvious ethico-legal question is, "Who owns the ova and semen after they're deposited for storage in the bank?" Traditionally, after semen was donated and the donor paid for his services, the semen was considered the property of the storage facility to be sold at a later date to an appropriate customer. The donor couldn't find out the names of the women who used the semen for fertilization.

By similar logic, it would seem that women who donate ova to an egg bank and are paid for their services would also lose their possession rights to the ova. But most women undergo the ova stimulation and harvesting procedure for their own IVF, thus retaining ownership of their ova.

Several complicated legal and ethical dilemmas have surfaced from the storage of semen and ova. In a landmark case, a man who knew he was dying donated semen to a sperm bank. After his death, his wife wanted to be fertilized with his semen to have his children. But the husband's family, who didn't like the wife, sued to prevent her from becoming pregnant using his semen. The decedent's parents claimed that the semen belonged to them because the man was their son and that the wife had no legal right to use it for insemination. The court held that the wife had ownership rights to her husband's semen because he intended for her to use it after his death.

Consider this issue: How long can the semen and ova be stored? Almost indefinitely, with current cryotechnology, but no one knows how long-term storage affects semen and ova. Would it be ethical to fertilize ova that have been stored for a decade or two only to produce children who have major birth defects?

Another question that arises from the procedure is beyond comprehension: Who do the children of stored semen and ova belong to? Obviously, they belong to the couple if their semen and ova are used in IVF. However, what about the couple who benefits from semen and ova donated by strangers? If the child has a birth defect, is mentally disabled, or is of the wrong sex, the couple could claim that the child really wasn't theirs anyway. What happens to the child? Can they give it back? Does it become a ward of the state, like an abandoned child? Where do we apply the principles of distributive justice in this case?

Although nurses aren't usually responsible for the technical process of obtaining semen and ova, you may have to teach and counsel patients about the risks and complications involved in the procedures. Assess their awareness and understanding of the ethical and legal issues involved in the process. Equally critical are their feelings about sexuality and reproduction.

If they're to receive ova that don't belong to them, how will they feel about the resulting child? Even though the IVF procedure is technical and artificial, the result of the process is hardly so. Producing a child is a human event, not a manufacturing process.

Government regulation
Although the federal government has several proposals for legislation to regulate the use of IVF, none have become law. Several states have proposed regulations, but there seems to be a lack of consensus about what should be included in the regulations. The inability of government agencies to pass laws regulating IVF and sperm and egg banks points to the fact that the legal system is poorly equipped to deal with ethical issues regarding reproduction.

Court decisions made on actual cases involving IVF and reproductive controversies have produced a small amount of case law. However, the cases are dissimilar and the decisions tend to be inconsistent. In some situations, the courts support the property rights of self-determination and choice of the mother or patients. In other cases, the courts uphold the child's right to life and nurturing.

In practice, most decisions about IVF and sperm and egg banks are made outside the legal system by the couples and their lawyers. Some facilities have developed internal guidelines to determine who would be acceptable candidates for IVF. If you work in a facility that performs IVF or maintains a sperm or an egg bank, it's important that, as a nurse, you become involved in the development of policies and guidelines based on your knowledge of ethical standards. (See *What would you do?* page 344.)

Conversely, if IVF becomes a medically essential procedure, the ethical

What would you do?

Marjie May, RN, has worked at the Reproductive Sciences Center (RSC) of the University Research Hospital in a large city for 6 years. The RSC has a reputation for using cutting-edge technology and has received many public and privately funded grants for developing innovative procedures and techniques to help couples with infertility problems. The RSC has sperm and egg banks that provide semen and ova for the artificial inseminations and in vitro fertilization (IVF) procedures conducted at the center. As a circulating nurse at RSC, she's exposed to routine IVF procedures. Although initially she had ethical issues regarding IVF and artificial insemination, she resolved those concerns and now feels comfortable with most of the activities at the center.

One day, Ms. May's closest friend, a technician in the IVF laboratory where the eggs are fertilized, tells her that Dr. Floral, head of RSC and the person most responsible for its funding, has been experimenting with somatic cell nuclear transfer technique, and that he's planning to use cloned embryos for one of the IVF procedures that Ms. May is to assist the next morning. The woman to be implanted with the cloned embryo thinks that she's getting an IVF embryo from one of her own eggs harvested earlier and fertilized by the sperm of an unknown donor. The woman is an admitted lesbian but wants to have a child without having intercourse with a man.

Ms. May hasn't resolved the ethics of cloning humans but generally believes it's un-ethical and probably immoral. She also believes that not telling the truth to the woman is a violation of the principle of veracity and informed consent. Before the center closes for the day, Ms. May expresses her concerns about the ethics of the procedure to the nurse-manager. The nurse-manager states her belief that all forms of unnatural reproduction are basically the same and, if IVF is OK, so is cloning. Because the woman didn't know the semen donor, not knowing it was a cloned embryo was basically the same thing, she reasoned.

The nurse-manager also reminds Ms. May that Dr. Floral is the main authority at the center and that questioning him and going against his wishes by telling the woman the truth might result in Ms. May losing her job. Furthermore, revealing the cloning technique's use at RSC might jeopardize the center's funding and close it permanently because the government has banned human cloning. The nurse-manager reasons: "If the center shuts down, we won't be able to help those sad couples who come here with infertility problems. Do you want that to happen?"

What's the basis of Ms. May's ethical dilemma? Are her concerns legitimate? What action can she take? What ethical system seems to guide the nurse-manager's reasoning? Are Dr. Floral's actions ethical? What would you do if you were Ms. May?

---

principle of distributive justice holds that everyone — regardless of socioeconomic status — should have access to it. But the cost of a publicly supported infertility treatment program based on IVF would be astronomical.

Cloning

With the successful birth of Dolly, the sheep, in 1996 in Scotland, the world has awakened to the reality of cloning as a viable reproductive method. The concept of cloning, however, has existed since the discovery of deoxyribonucleic acid (DNA) by Watson and Crick. It's based on the fact that every cell in an animal's body contains all the genetic information needed to reproduce every other cell in the body. In the strict scientific meaning of the word, the cloning process occurs when a cell in the animal's body is removed and placed in an appropriate growth environment where it develops into an identical reproduction of the animal from which the cell came. However, scientists still don't know what triggers some parts of the DNA strand to become active and reproduce and others to remain dormant. If a human skin cell is removed and placed in a growth medium, it will grow new skin — not an identical person.

Although popularly referred to as cloning, the scientific name for the process used to produce Dolly and other identical animals (so far, cows, mice, and monkeys) is somatic cell nuclear transfer technique. The process starts by removing unfertilized ova from an animal and then removing all genetic material (DNA) from the ova. Next, the scientists remove the DNA from a cell in the animal they wish to clone and insert it into the unfertilized, DNA-free ova. The ova with the new DNA is then implanted in the uterus of an appropriate animal, and it grows into an identical twin of the DNA donor. In the case of Dolly, the DNA donor was her mother (the sheep in whose uterus she was implanted). That makes Dolly an identical twin of her mother even though she's 6 years younger.

Another technique that's commonly referred to as cloning is really embryo splitting. After an ovum is fertilized by a sperm, naturally or with IVF, a single cell (called a zygote) results, containing a combination of genetic material

(DNA), half each from father and mother. Left alone to develop, that single cell will eventually develop into an individual who shares some of the inherited features of both parents because of the combination of DNA. Within 12 hours after the zygote is formed, it begins to divide into 2, then 4, then 8, and then 16 identical cells. When it reaches 16 cells, it enters the morula stage.

While the embryo is dividing, up to and including the morula state, the cells can be divided and separated. Because the cells are identical, contain all the genetic material necessary to produce a new individual, and have fully active DNA, each cell is essentially a zygote. After the cells are divided and separated, they can be implanted into several appropriate females and will continue to divide and develop into identical twins, or triplets, or more. Also, when the embryo is in the four- to eight-cell stage, the cells can be separated, the DNA material removed from them, and new genetic material inserted. The cell with the new DNA will then grow into a twin of the animal from which the DNA was taken. It appears that by using the embryo-splitting technique, scientists could produce an unlimited supply of ova for the somatic cell nuclear transfer procedure.

With the IVF procedure, embryo splitting, and DNA transfer, the fertilization and early development process occurs in a Petri dish in the laboratory. After the cells begin to develop, they're implanted into an appropriate female for the remainder of the pregnancy. Although the cloning or embryo-splitting process is relatively simple, its success rate is at best marginal. For instance, to produce Dolly, more than 1,000 ova were genetically created. Of these, only 29 began to develop and only one actually produced Dolly. Although it's theoretically possible to reproduce humans using this technique, so far it has been used to produce only animals.

Legal and ethical issues of cloning

Shortly after the news of Dolly reached the United States, a crucial debate developed over whether cloning of humans was ethical or even legal. The three most troubling ethical issues were the loss of uniqueness of the individual, the potential misuse of the technology by diabolical scientists, and degeneration of society as it now exists. Other, more traditional ethical concerns — such as medical risks to the mother or child (beneficence and nonmaleficence), life status of the embryo produced by the procedure, distributive justice issues of cost and availability of technology, and autonomy issues of using humans as incubators or sources of organs for donation — are also part of the debate.

The concern for loss of individuality and uniqueness stems from the fact that clones are exact copies of their DNA donors. For many people, it conjures up an Orwellian image of rows of tanks in which identical babies are being grown and incubated, giving rise to genetic determinism and the production of inferior humans through mass photocopying.

The belief that genetic determinism will produce individuals who not only look the same but also act identically is flawed. Although every cell in one twin body is genetically identical to that of the other twin body, experience shows that twins develop individual personalities and character traits. Personality development is influenced by a wide range of environmental and experiential elements — not just genetic composition. If and when it happens, cloned human babies born to mothers who live in different situations, although they may look the same, will probably have different personalities.

Similarly, experience doesn't support the belief that each time an individual is cloned, quality is lost. In many cases, photocopies may be of higher quality than the original. However, cloning is more than making photocopies because the process is quite different. The danger of "bad copies" from cloning that may result in inferior-quality offspring or offspring with congenital defects arises from the mechanical collection and transfer of the fragile DNA strands. Damaging even one gene sequence can produce birth defects.

In most ethical dilemmas, motivation is an important element in determining if the act was right or wrong. There are several possible motivations to clone human beings, ranging from egoism to helping an infertile couple have a child.

The egoistic motivation conjures up images of the diabolical scientist or a political leader who wants to create a "super race" by the repeated cloning of physically and mentally superior individuals. It isn't hard to imagine what Hitler might have done with this technology. How about cloning genius inventors, brilliant leaders, and superb athletes? Could embryo factories be far behind?

A somewhat more altruistic, although no less diabolical motive, is cloning humans for organ donation. In theory, a person who needs a heart transplant could donate his DNA and, after some time, have an individual who has a heart with a perfect genetic match. Most people, however, detest the idea of using cloned children as a means to an end, especially if harvesting the organ (as in a heart transplant) would result in the child's death. Scientists in Texas have cloned mice without heads whose organs were then transplanted into DNA donor mice. What if human clones could be created without heads? Would these headless beings truly be human? Or would they just be biological storage units for organs to be used for donation when the need arose? At first glance, this practice might seem abhorrent. However, is it any different from the sperm, egg, embryo, or organ banks that exist today?

In the past few years, parents who have children with leukemia have gone on to have more children for the primary purpose of providing bone marrow for the sick child. In many cases, the younger children were identical six-antigen matches, and the bone marrow was harvested from the infant and transplanted into the sick child who recovered from the disease. Is having children for this purpose different from cloning children for organ transplantation? What if scientists are able to clone one organ or a specific tissue? If a person needed a liver, the DNA from his or her liver could be transferred to an ovum and then a new liver grown in the laboratory. A similar procedure is being used already, without ethical objections, for growing new skin to graft onto burn patients.

Some parents might be tempted to clone a replacement child for one who's dead or dying. These parents could "set aside" a clone through the embryo-splitting technique that could be stored in an embryo bank to be implanted and grown if the child died. The underlying motivation would seem to be selfish and self-serving, to create a replacement child for the relief of grieving patients. However, is the cloned child really a replacement for the child who died? Physical appearance may be identical, but experience has shown that the child's personality and temperament could be radically different.

Similarly, an infertile couple who had tried all other methods and were unable to have a child might seek a cloned embryo as a last resort. Perhaps this motivation could pose the fewest ethical objections. Rather than using semen or ova from strangers, they might provide their own DNA, either from the father or the mother, to produce a child.

Legal update

In 1997, President Clinton issued an executive order banning any federal funding for cloning involving humans. He also proposed legislation that would outlaw human cloning for at least five years, but Congress defeated the legislation in February 1998. As a result, human cloning remains banned in all publicly funded institutions in the United States, but remains legal in privately funded institutions.

The issue however isn't being ignored by Congress. In February 2003, the House of Representatives passed a bill banning all human cloning, but it has yet to pass through the Senate. Critics of the bill claim that, as it stands, it would limit or prevent vital health research into the use of genetics for disease prevention or cure. Currently, the U.S. Senate has been unable to agree on legislative action over human cloning because they can't agree uniformly as to what merits legal protection.

SURROGATE MOTHERHOOD

A surrogate mother is a woman who gives birth after carrying the fertilized ovum of another woman or, more commonly, after being artificially inseminated with sperm from the bio-logical father. In this case, the infant is then legally adopted by the wife of the biological father. Since the first surrogate birth in England in 1976, more than 2,500 babies have been born through this arrangement.

Surrogate motherhood offers hope to the 60% to 70% of infertile couples in which the woman is the infertile partner. It's also an option for women whose age or health makes pregnancy risky. A surrogate birth poses no greater risk to the fetus (or the surrogate mother) than does a normal birth.

Surrogate motherhood vs. conventional motherhood

One concern about surrogate motherhood involves the true nature of mothering. Is "motherhood" merely the biological act of bearing children? Many people believe that motherhood also implies a long-term commitment to the care and nurture of the child. By agreeing to give the baby to the contracting couple, is a surrogate mother defaulting on a moral commitment? The advertising of services by potential surrogate mothers, with fees ranging from $50,000 to $150,000, suggests to some that surrogate motherhood represents a form of baby selling.

Conflicts of rights

Surrogate motherhood can also produce conflicts among the rights of the surrogate mother, the infertile couple, the fetus, and society.

The basic dispute revolves around who has the strongest claim to the child. Is it the surrogate mother by virtue of her biological connection? Or does the surrogate contract guarantee the infertile couple the right to the child? Courts of law usually have ruled in favor of the couple.

Surrogate mother contracts seemingly violate adoption laws, which prohibit a mother from surrendering parental rights before the infant is born. Such laws, enacted to protect a biological mother from undue pressure, typically specify an initial waiting period of a few days. In many cases, she can't terminate all parental rights until 6 months after the birth.

What if no one wants the child? This can become an issue if the infant is born with a disability. Can the infertile couple or the surrogate mother refuse to take responsibility for such a child? What if the defect isn't apparent until the child is 4 years old? Can the infertile couple return the child to his biological mother?

Clearly, the rights of the child to a normal family life must not be lost in the debate over custody. (See *Orphaned ova*.)

Exploitation

The infertile couple and the surrogate mother are highly vulnerable to exploitation. The couple, blinded by a longing for a child, are easy victims for financial and emotional blackmail. On the other hand, surrogate motherhood can be used to exploit poor women, who have few marketable skills other than their ability to bear children. "Womb renting" is as ethically unacceptable as baby selling.

YOUR ROLE IN IVF AND SURROGATE MOTHERHOOD

You're unlikely to be directly involved in the IVF procedure or in drawing up a surrogate mother contract, but you may be called on to care for patients who choose these options. Before you can do so effectively, you'll need to examine your views on these controversial procedures and become familiar

Orphaned ova

Unanswered questions about in vitro fertilization (IVF) and surrogate motherhood may soon come to haunt society. Consider this case study, which explores what could happen if a surrogate motherhood arrangement doesn't go as planned.

Orphaned before birth

Howard Belmont, age 39, owned a successful manufacturing company. He and his wife, Marsha, age 35, had been trying to have a baby for 2 years without success. After the Belmonts underwent a battery of infertility tests, their physician concluded that Mrs. Belmont could ovulate and produce mature ova but couldn't conceive or bear children. On the physician's suggestion, the couple began to explore the possibility of IVF and surrogate motherhood.

After lengthy consideration, Mrs. Belmont had her ova fertilized in vitro using her husband's sperm. When some of the fertilized ova were frozen for implantation, the Belmonts located a surrogate mother, Hazel Towers. Ms. Towers agreed to sign a long-term contract saying that she would bear three children for Mr. and Mrs. Belmont. The contract stated that Ms. Towers would be paid $100,000 for the first child and $75,000 (already placed in trust) for the subsequent two children. Ms. Towers was successfully implanted with Mr. and Mrs. Belmont's fertilized ova. When Ms. Towers was near the end of the first trimester of pregnancy, Mr. and Mrs. Belmont were killed in an automobile accident.

Making an offer

Mr. Belmont's two brothers and one sister stood to inherit his company and assets worth $15 million. However, according to the will of the deceased couple, if Ms. Towers had the baby, the child would inherit the estate.

Mr. Belmont's brothers and sister offered Ms. Towers $500,000 if she would abort the fetus and refuse to be implanted with any more fertilized ova. In addition, the brothers and sister offered to make a $1 million donation for the construction of a new pediatric wing to the hospital where the fertilized ova were stored if the administrator agreed to have the ova destroyed.

Ms. Towers's dilemma

Ms. Towers was placed under a great deal of stress. She realized that she could base her actions only on her own ethical principles. The $500,000 offer was a temptation she would have to ignore; she didn't think that financial gain justified an abortion. According to the contract, she was to surrender the child to Mr. and Mrs. Belmont at its birth. She had serious misgivings, however, about surrendering it to the brothers or sister in light of the offer they made for her to have an abortion.

When they learned that Ms. Towers refused to surrender the child, the brothers and sister accused her of having the child for financial gain. They pointed out that the child would be heir to a large fortune; Ms. Towers would probably benefit from the estate in caring for the child.

Preborn siblings

Questions remained about production of the two other children agreed on in the contract. Was the contract binding after the death of Mr. and Mrs. Belmont? Because the money had already been set aside, could Ms. Towers be implanted with the ova, bear the children, and expect to be paid?

What about the hospital administrator and his role in the destruction of fertilized ova? If he believes that the ova aren't human, he probably wouldn't hesitate to carry out this re-

(continued)

Orphaned ova *(continued)*

quest. However, what if he believes that human life starts at the moment of conception? Then it would be betraying his ethical beliefs to destroy the ova.

Outcome

Over time, Ms. Towers began to think of the child in her womb as her own. She realized that her child would need to be loved and cherished for its own sake. She accepted the fact that she would probably lose her surrogate mother's fee because the contract stipulated that she must turn the child over to the

Belmonts. She decided to raise the child, regardless of the financial consequences.

Because of the severe emotional stress she experienced, Ms. Towers decided to forgo having more fertilized ova implanted. The Belmont family immediately initiated a legal action contesting her child's inheritance; eventually, an out-of-court settlement was reached.

Ms. Towers experienced a bitter lesson in the moral uncertainty that surrounds IVF and surrogate motherhood. Existing laws aren't sufficient to answer the many questions raised by reproductive technology; future court rulings may provide better guidelines.

---

with the legal and ethical pitfalls they present.

You can't be forced to participate in procedures you find ethically and morally objectionable. But according to the ANA Code for Nurses, you're obligated to care for all patients assigned to you, regardless of your beliefs or feelings. In any event, you have an ethical obligation to be aware of and report abuses of IVF and surrogate motherhood.

Genetic engineering and screening

Genetic engineering, also known as genetic manipulation, continues to contribute significantly to medical progress. Scientists are discovering new ways to identify and manipulate the genetic material of everything from single-celled organisms to human beings.

Each cell of an animal or a plant carries a genetic blueprint for the entire organism. This information is encoded by the DNA in its nucleus. By removing or adding DNA, scientists can program the cell or the entire organism to carry out new functions. Such manipulation can be highly beneficial. For example, it has yielded new antibiotics and hormones (such as human insulin) and increased our understanding of cancer cells. But genetic manipulation also gives researchers the potential to alter the gene pool in unethical ways and to create terrifying biological weapons.

Each of the estimated 100,000 genes found in nearly every human cell codes for a single protein involved in a specific body function. Even a small error in the gene produces a defective protein that can result in disease or deformity. More than 4,000 inherited disorders result from such genetic mistakes. Gene therapy, the introduction of healthy genes to overcome an inherited defect, may someday provide cures for diseases, such as cystic fibrosis, muscular dystrophy, and hemophilia.

The identification of the genes responsible for inherited diseases and congenital malformations has spurred the development of screening tests. Genetic testing is now a fairly common component of prenatal care, facilitating the identification of fetuses with disorders, such as Down syndrome and Tay–Sachs disease. The screening of neonates for phenylketonuria is legally required by most states.

Potential for discrimination

Researchers have also identified the genes responsible for adult-onset disorders such as Huntington's disease, polycystic kidney disease, and some forms of cancer. Ideally, the results of genetic screening could encourage patients to make lifestyle changes that reduce their risk of developing the disease. At the least, the knowledge can help them prepare to deal with the disease. Unfortunately, this information can also lead to genetic discrimination, preventing people from obtaining health or life insurance or jobs and adopting children.

ETHICS OF GENETIC ENGINEERING

Genetic engineering has tremendous potential for altering the course of human development. By themselves, genetic engineering techniques, including cloning, somatic alteration, germ cell alteration, recombinant DNA synthesis, and gene therapy, are ethically neutral. It's the application of these techniques that creates ethical problems. (See *Language of genetic manipulation*.)

Language of genetic manipulation

The following terms are associated with the science of genetic manipulation.

Cloning: production of an entire organism from a single cell

Eugenics: science of improving a species through control of hereditary factors by manipulation of the gene pool

Gene: fragment of deoxyribonucleic acid (DNA) that encodes a single protein

Gene splicing: technique by which recombinant DNA is produced and made to function in an organism

Gene therapy: insertion of a normal gene into the nucleus of a cell to compensate for a defective one

Genetic marker: dominant gene or trait that serves to identify genes or traits linked with it

Germ cell alteration: changes in DNA structure during the earliest stages of cell growth (before differentiation)

Recombinant DNA synthesis: insertion of DNA segments from one species into the DNA of another species

Restriction fragment length polymorphism: genetically variable DNA fragments usually used as markers for a nearby disease gene

Somatic alteration: in vitro isolation of a specific gene that's then synthetically reproduced in the laboratory

---

Control over future generations

Do researchers have a greater obligation to help those currently alive or, alternatively, to protect the interests of future generations? It would appear that the most ethical applications of genetic engineering should do both, and research should concentrate on solving long-term medical and environmental problems, such as hereditary disease, cancer, pollution, and hunger.

Safety

Genetic researchers have a moral obligation to take all necessary precautions to recognize and prevent harmful consequences of their work, such as the accidental release of new pathogens. Patients who participate in gene therapy trials must be fully informed of the potential risks as well as the benefits. For example, the retroviral vectors used to introduce new genes may also increase a patient's risk of developing cancer.

Potentially dehumanizing effects

In the past, medical research has been limited to efforts to repair or halt the damage caused by disease and injury. But genetic engineering gives science the ability to re-create the human body. Is this unethical? If genetic engineering techniques are used to cure disease and improve the quality of life, society stands to benefit. Imagine a society, however, in which genetically "perfect" children or genetically inferior servants could be created in the laboratory. Such unethical applications clearly violate human dignity and integrity.

VOLUNTARY VS. MANDATORY GENETIC SCREENING

Screening for genetic disorders isn't new. Progress in mapping defective genes to particular chromosomes has led to more sophisticated tests that probe directly for the faulty gene or a nearby "marker" gene. Moreover, scientists are learning more about the genetic basis of such diseases as diabetes, cancer, and hypertension.

Like genetic engineering, genetic screening is ethically neutral. Applications of this technology, however, may be acceptable. Prenatal, neonatal, and adult screening can be used to improve treatment, guide personal decisions, and initiate prevention programs. Other applications are an ethical Pandora's box.

Mandatory screening

The ethical principle of beneficence requires that a procedure help the patient. Mandatory genetic screening can be beneficial, such as in the case of neonatal screening for phenylketonuria, in which early detection prevents mental retardation. But what about mandatory testing for incurable diseases such as Huntington's disease? Although some patients want to know this information for constructive reasons, others could be seriously harmed psychologically. In this instance, voluntary screening is ethically acceptable, and mandatory screening isn't.

Creation of a "biological underclass"

Insurance companies have been among the first to be charged with genetic discrimination. From the company's point of view, it's a sound business decision to increase premiums or deny coverage to anyone with a serious medical condition or at high risk for developing such a condition. Unfortunately, predictive tests don't always tell the whole story. A single faulty gene may not cause trouble unless other related genes are also defective, or the gene may never be expressed unless it's set off by an environmental trigger. A patient who's seen as "certain to become disabled" rather than "at risk" could easily join the ranks of the uninsured—with little legal recourse.

Employers represent another source of potential genetic discrimination. In times of increasing health care costs, employers may avoid hiring someone who is likely to incur large medical bills. Industry officials also argue that genetic screening can identify workers who might be especially sensitive to industrial toxins. A more ethical approach would be to clean up the workplace so that all workers face a decreased risk.

Patient confidentiality

Preserving patient confidentiality may help to guard against abuses of genetic information. However, confidentiality isn't an absolute right. The confidentiality of health-related information, in particular, is protected by law only when the health and well-being of others aren't threatened. For example, the law requires a physician or nurse to report sexually transmitted diseases, gunshot wounds, and suspected child abuse.

It's unclear whether the disclosure of genetic information represents a breach of confidentiality. Certainly, the right to treatment of a child with phenylketonuria supersedes the parents' right to confidentiality. But what about a patient who has a positive test result for the Huntington's disease gene? Here, confidentiality should be preserved, but the widespread use of computerized records makes this task increasingly difficult.

JUSTICE AND GENETIC SCREENING

Justice, as an ethical principle in health care, requires equal sharing of the risks and benefits of diagnostic tests and treatments offered to patients. Genetic screening programs haven't always adhered to this principle. When large-

scale screening programs for sickle cell carriers were initiated in the 1970s, for example, participants received little or no posttest counseling or follow-up care. In contrast, similar programs set up to screen for Tay-Sachs disease included teaching programs, support groups, and financial aid. All genetic screening programs need to incorporate this sort of thorough follow-up care.

The justice principle also impinges on the issue of health insurance coverage. Because serious chronic diseases raise everyone's premiums, it would seem that justice is best served by asking those who pose a greater risk to bear more than the average share of the cost. The danger is that these people may never develop the disease. If so, they have been unfairly overcharged.

YOUR ROLE IN GENE THERAPY

Genetic manipulation, including gene therapy, is still experimental. As a result, few nurses are directly involved in this aspect of genetic research. Nonetheless, you have an ethical obligation to stay informed and to support efforts to establish legal and technological safeguards.

If you're more likely to be involved in genetic screening, you have an important role to play in dealing with the related ethical conflicts. Your ethical responsibilities may involve:
◆ making sure that the patient understands the procedure and gives informed consent before the test
◆ thoroughly reviewing options for treatment or prevention of a genetic disease during posttest counseling
◆ refusing to take part in compulsory screening programs
◆ refusing to disclose test results to unauthorized people

◆ actively supporting legislation to prevent genetic discrimination by employers and insurance companies.

RIGHT TO KNOW VS. RIGHT TO SAFETY

Seeking new knowledge is an essential part of human nature. Yet society tends to oppose the scientist's right to uncontrolled experimentation. This is particularly true with regard to genetic research. Many people believe in the sanctity of life and view genetic screening and manipulation as violations of that principle, especially when human beings are involved. The public also has a right to protection and personal safety. Thus, it seems likely that the federal government will be involved in regulating genetic research.

Scientists will remain suspicious of attempts to control their work, and a large segment of the public will oppose unregulated tinkering with the building blocks of life. Our hope is that both sides will remember that the dignity, value, and worth of human life must be preserved at all costs.

Personal safety in the workplace

Health care workers are entitled to work in a safe environment. The ethical principle of justice or fairness supports the position that employers should provide security measures, whether in an institution or in the community. Without those safeguards, an ethical dilemma arises. Although nurses must provide care to patients (nonabandonment and fidelity), they also need to protect themselves.

Policies that address appropriate staffing levels, adequate training, and security escorts minimize the ethical conflicts between providing care and ensuring safety. Federal safety and health standards require that all employers develop injury and illness prevention programs for hazards unique to their facility or program. However, it remains up to the individual nurse to recognize and protect herself from on-the-job hazards, such as the following:

◆ *Infection:* A particularly serious threat to nurses is the patient whose infection hasn't yet been diagnosed. In many cases, the infections of patients with obviously noninfective conditions, such as heart failure, aren't guarded against or detected for several days. Nurses in high-contact areas, such as emergency departments, are particularly at risk for diseases such as tuberculosis.

HIV has triggered a new era in the care of patients with communicable diseases. The CDC has mandated the use of standard precautions to prevent the spread of HIV. Although it's up to the nurse to follow the precautions, employers must provide the gloves, eye covers, sharps containers, and other equipment for this form of protection.

◆ *Hazardous chemicals:* Many potentially hazardous chemicals are routinely used in health care. For example, anesthetic gases increase the risk of birth defects and spontaneous abortions. New standards attempt to control the anesthetic in the operating room, but many hospitals move pregnant nurses out of areas in which these gases are used. Chemotherapeutic drugs, radiation, and powerful cleaning solutions and disinfectants are common hazards for health care workers. They all require knowledge and vigilance from the nurse and strict supervision by the facility.

◆ *Back injuries:* The most common physical reason nurses lose time from work is back injuries, typically a herniated disk. Because the nurse is required to lift, turn, and support patients who may be much larger than herself, each situation should be evaluated. Although a "can-do" attitude is important, the nurse must learn how to be assertive about her own safety. Getting enough help to work with patients demonstrates sound nursing judgment.

◆ *Latex allergies:* As the use of latex gloves has increased, more nurses are becoming sensitized to the allergenic proteins in the latex. This growing problem is compounded by the lack of knowledge many nurses have about latex allergies. These nurses tend to dismiss the symptoms as a simple rash or hay fever and treat it with lotion or creams.

Latex allergy follows a predictable progression of symptoms that continue as long as the person is in contact with the allergen. The symptoms usually begin as local irritation and itching on the skin of the hands. The irritation gradually progresses to hives and open lesions. Repeated exposure to the allergen leads to asthma, watery eyes, and recurrent sinusitis and may eventually produce anaphylactic shock with continued exposure.

The initial allergy-producing culprit seems to be the latex-laden powder in the glove rather than the glove itself. The powder contains microscopic particles of the latex protein that over time and with continued exposure enter the pores and are absorbed into the body, where the immune system reacts to them. After there has been a primary immune reaction to the powder, further exposure to any type of latex triggers an ever-increasing immune response that can eventually produce a massive release of histamine, causing anaphylactic shock. Unless treated quickly and aggressively, anaphylactic shock can cause respiratory arrest and can be fatal.

A secondary problem is that after a person develops a latex allergy, exposure to even the microscopic particles of latex powder that become airborne whenever a coworker puts on or takes off a pair of powdered gloves can trigger a severe reaction. The powder can be carried through the ventilation system in the hospital and circulate to parts of the building in which gloves aren't being used. Sensitized people working in these areas, although away from the actual glove use, can suffer severe reactions.

An associated problem is the development of latex allergies by patients. The allergy development process is identical to what happens to the health care provider and can be triggered by one of the large number of latex products used in patient care today, such as surgical drains, catheters, tourniquets, and gloves. You should consider latex allergy whenever you see unexplained rashes in hospitalized patients.

WORKPLACE VIOLENCE

Workplace violence is a serious problem in the United States. How serious? A 2002 survey reported that workplace violence accounts for 1,000 deaths and more than 1.5 million nonfatal injuries each year. Unfortunately, hospitals, long-term care facilities, hospices, and other health care facilities aren't immune from this growing trend. The violent behaviors occurring in health care facilities today simply mirror those of the larger society.

Nurses are particularly vulnerable to workplace violence. On average, 30% of nurses report experiencing assault, abusive language, emotional or mental abuse, or sexual harassment. Patients and physicians are the most common perpetrators of physical violence against nurses; physicians, nurse managers, or other supervisors are the most common perpetrators of verbal and emotional abuse.

Studies indicate that drugs, poor staffing, hospital type and location, gangs, easy access to a hospital emergency area, long hours worked, inadequate training, power and control issues, and stress contribute to violence in health care settings. A history of abuse can also be a contributing factor: More than 50% of all abused nurses report being victims of childhood or adult abuse.

Creating a safe work environment

Health care officials and nursing leaders have an ethical and legal responsibility to create and maintain a safe, healthy work environment. In order to do this, they need to develop policies and procedures detailing behavioral expectations, reporting mechanisms that don't further victimize victims of workplace violence, and effective security policies and systems. Some of the initiatives that they can take include:

◆ documenting required employee safety and self-protection training provided for all employees by the organization

◆ teaching proven strategies of intervention for situations of escalating violence

◆ teaching caregivers to work as a team when responding to violence

◆ clearly stating behavioral expectations for employees, medical staff, patients, and visitors

◆ stating the organization's expectations for reporting instances of violence or abuse and describing appropriate documentation

◆ establishing a mechanism (such as the organizational ethics committee)

for investigating, negotiating, and resolving conflicts and disputes

How to properly intervene

Interventions should be immediate and appropriate to the level of violence. Ignoring the angry or belligerent patient, physician, or coworker can heighten violence by increasing the violent individual's suspicions, paranoia, fear, anxiety, and feelings of being out of control.

Employee rights

When violence occurs in the workplace, employees may have claims against their employer under federal or state law. Employees may have additional legal remedies against their abusers and their employer under legal principles involving tort or contract issues. Tort cases may occur if an employer or manager intentionally or negligently violates an employee right. Cases involving contract issues may occur if the employer was negligent in providing contracted security safeguards.

NEEDLE STICKS

Needle sticks are one of the most commonly reported occupational hazards nurses face. With an estimated 600,000 to 1 million needle-stick injuries occurring per year, it's paramount that nurses take every precaution when handling sharps and using needle delivery systems. All it takes is one mistake for a nurse to become infected with HIV, AIDS, hepatitis C, or any of the other deadly diseases that can be transmitted via needle stick.

Although safer needle delivery devices have been available for many years, many employers have failed to provide them until recently. However, the Needlestick Safety and Prevention

Act, which took effect in April 2001, strengthened the requirement for employers to provide safer needle delivery devices. It also required employers to maintain a sharps injury log of all needle sticks and to consult employees when reviewing, evaluating, and selecting devices.

Nurses who work in settings in which needle sticks are a risk need to understand their rights. You can demand that your employer provide safer equipment by requesting a meeting with your employer to discuss this issue or by getting coworkers to sign a petition demanding safer needles. If you're a member of a union, you can contact your union representative.

SEXUAL HARASSMENT

Sexual harassment in the workplace isn't new, nor is it unique to health care facilities. Anecdotal evidence suggests that the problem is related in part to nurses' traditionally subservient role to that of the physician in health care and the sexism underlying this problem. However, sexism and sexual harassment can and do involve same-sex advances as well as female-male situations.

From coworkers, sexual harassment is best understood as a form of violence in the workplace. It's much less about sex than it is about abuse and control issues. For this reason, sexual harassment is experienced in two forms: *quid pro quo* and *hostile workplace.*

The Latin term *quid pro quo* means "this for that." *Quid pro quo* sexism occurs when a manager, supervisor, or individual in a "dominant" role (such as a physician) indicates or hints to an employee or person in a "nondominant" position that he'll trade job advancement, job benefits, or other special considerations for sexual favors.

Sexual harassment may also be defined as any form of sexual hostility in the workplace. Sexual hostility can include sexually offensive jokes, pictures, innuendoes, or behaviors. Although this type of sexual harassment is commonly repeated in the work environment, with the intent to shock, annoy, and degrade the recipient, it may sometimes take only one incident to provoke a charge of sexual harassment. For example, a vice president for nursing, the hospital's only female senior manager, brought suit against the hospital when the other senior manager hired a male stripper to "perform" at a management birthday party for her.

From patients and visitors

Harassment may also include any unwelcome or offensive verbal or physical conduct from a patient or visitor. Such acts may intimidate or threaten the nurse, be offensive, or undermine the therapeutic relationship. Such acts may be gestures or physical acts, slurs, taunting, verbal abuse or epithets, comments or jokes, or the displaying of derogatory objects, cartoons, posters, drawings, or pictures.

Legality

Sexual harassment is a violation of Title VII of the 1964 Federal Civil Rights Act, which was amended by the Civil Rights Act of 1991. It's now easier for employees to prove discrimination and receive higher awards in damages.

Hospitals and other health care organizations should establish fair policies and procedures that clearly define sexual harassment. Nurses should receive consistent education about sexual harassment in the workplace, including how to recognize it and how to avoid causing it. Some of the ways to protect

yourself from becoming a victim of sexual harassment include:
◆ refraining from talking or joking with employees about sex, including remarks you feel are innocent
◆ stopping sexually oriented conduct among employees, such as joke telling and gestures
◆ keeping sexually oriented materials (such as posters, cartoons, or E-mails) from being posted in the workplace
◆ calling employees by their name or title
◆ refraining from expressing sexual interest or feelings for another employee.

WHISTLE-BLOWING

Whistle-blowing refers to an employee's disclosure of illegal, immoral, or illegitimate practices under an employer's control. The ANA's Code for Nurses outlines the nurse's obligation to report acts of negligence and incompetence by other health care providers. It states that "the nurse acts to safeguard the patient and public when health care and safety are affected by incompetent, unethical, or illegal practice by any person."

The ANA guidelines on reporting incompetent, unethical, or illegal practices identify helpful parameters for judging problematic conduct. Incompetent nursing practice is measured by nursing standards, unethical practice is evaluated in light of the Code for Nurses, and illegal practice is identified in terms of violations of the law. As a patient advocate, you must be willing to take appropriate action — in short, to blow the whistle.

The Canadian Nurses Association also has a Code for Nurses that conveys the same message: "The nurse, as a member of the health care team, is obliged to take steps to ensure that the patient receives competent and ethical care."

WHEN TO BLOW THE WHISTLE

A health care professional who makes a mistake usually wants to ensure that it won't happen again. Correcting an error usually involves admitting the mistake, expressing honest regret, and completing an incident report. At times, though, you may encounter a health care professional who makes repeated mistakes, attempts to cover them up or minimize them, and engages in suspect or misleading behavior. To uphold the ethical standards of your profession, you need to blow the whistle. (See *Is whistle-blowing warranted?*)

IMPLICATIONS OF WHISTLE-BLOWING

Many nurses equate whistle-blowing with heroic self-sacrifice: a moral victory in the midst of a professional defeat. In fact, some nurses have had their reputations tarnished, lost their jobs, or been named in libel suits after reporting professional misconduct. Fortunately, such bitter retaliation isn't the norm. Keep in mind, however, that the higher the professional standing of the health care professional who commits misconduct, the greater the risk you face when blowing the whistle. (See *Whistle-blowing: A systematic approach,* page 361.)

REPORTING NURSE MISCONDUCT

Usually, institutional channels exist through which you can report the misconduct of another nurse or nursing assistant without fear of reprisal. Typically, a nurse-manager and the personnel office assume joint responsi-

Is whistle-blowing warranted?

How do you know whether to blow the whistle on a colleague? The decision may require careful deliberation and judgment. Review these two case studies. Do you think that each nurse's decision to blow the whistle is justified?

Habitually late colleague

An hour after her shift began, Sylvia Myers, RN, can't locate her coworker Mary Calvo, RN. She checks Ms. Calvo's time card; it shows that she punched in on time. A few minutes later, Ms. Myers sees Ms. Calvo with her coat and gloves on, getting off the elevator.

Ms. Myers approaches Ms. Calvo and asks where she has been. Ms. Calvo impatiently tells her to mind her own business and adds, "You have no idea how hard it is to raise three kids and have to work."

Upset and confused, Ms. Myers decides that she had better find out what's going on. After some investigation, she realizes that Allison Henkel, RN, a mutual friend, has been punching in Ms. Calvo. Ms. Henkel tells her that Ms. Calvo arrives up to an hour late two to three times per week. She goes on to say, "Don't worry. I'll keep covering for Ms. Calvo. What's important is that we're helping Ms. Calvo out and no one's getting hurt."

Ms. Myers is faced with an ethical dilemma: Should she report Ms. Calvo's lateness and Ms. Henkel's cover-up? Or should she remain quiet; after all, Ms. Calvo's lateness hasn't affected patient care thus far, and blowing the whistle might undermine her friendship with Ms. Henkel.

After careful consideration, Ms. Myers decides that there's no getting around the fact that Ms. Calvo is jeopardizing her patients' well-being and that Ms. Henkel shares partial responsibility. Although sympathetic to Ms. Calvo's child-care problems, Ms. Myers recognizes her overriding obligations to ensure the health and safety of patients.

Ms. Myers decides that her first step is to talk directly to Ms. Calvo about the situation. If Ms. Calvo's behavior persists, Ms. Myers will explain that she's ethically obligated to report Ms. Calvo to the nurse-manager. Before taking action, Ms. Myers is careful to document specific circumstances of Ms. Calvo's lateness.

Questioning medical protocol

Rachel Kirkwood, RN, is the nurse-manager of a small oncology unit that develops treatment protocols for the National Cancer Institute. She has worked for several years on the unit, finds her position rewarding, and enjoys a good relationship with the medical staff. However, the latest protocol of the chief oncologist troubles her. None of the patients are improving with the experimental therapy. Ms. Kirkwood knows from her own extensive clinical experience that patients with the same condition fare much better with conventional therapy.

Ms. Kirkwood decides to share her concerns with the oncologist. He responds curtly, saying only that his research brings a large grant for the unit. He makes it clear that he doesn't want to discuss the matter with her further.

Ms. Kirkwood is faced with a choice: Should she defer to the oncologist's knowledge and trust his sense of professional responsibility? Or should she pursue her concerns?

Ms. Kirkwood realizes that her options are limited: She's in no position to make charges against the chief oncologist, but she can still take steps to correct the situation. She decides to discuss the matter confidentially with another oncologist and see what insight he can provide. In addition, she begins keeping accurate records of each patient's treatment and its re-

(continued)

Is whistle-blowing warranted? *(continued)*

sults. If the evidence she gathers indicates that the patients are suffering harm and the chief oncologist continues to ignore her, Ms. Kirkwood is ready to blow the whistle.

Ms. Kirkwood is committed to preparing herself for the long haul. She gathers numerous articles on whistle-blowing and arranges to meet with a lawyer experienced in representing whistle-blowers. Aware that her actions may jeopardize her job, she has begun to search for alternative employment, and she also realizes that she must emotionally prepare to deal with the wrath of coworkers, especially those who disagree with her conclusions.

---

bility for investigating allegations of misconduct. For you, the only drawback is animosity from the affected staff member — and possibly from her acquaintances or sympathizers. The benefits, though, include correcting an injustice, preventing future harm, and strengthening your sense of moral integrity.

REPORTING MEDICAL OR MANAGEMENT MISCONDUCT

If you report the misconduct of a physician, a nursing supervisor, a nurse-manager, or a member of the institution's administration, expect stiffer resistance and, possibly, more severe retaliation, especially if management has cooperated in concealing the misconduct. Be prepared for a lengthy and hard-fought battle. That's because the accused professional may attempt to discredit you — or have you fired — rather than face the allegations honestly.

Consider the case of Barry Adams, a registered nurse in Boston, who was fired after reporting allegedly unsafe working conditions to the administration of the now-closed Youville Health Care Center in Cambridge. The National Labor Relations Board validated his complaints of retaliation, and now he has a complaint pending with the Massachusetts Board of Nursing against one of the center's executives, Ann Poster, alleging unprofessional and unethical conduct in connection with allegedly unsafe patient conditions at the center. If you risk significant personal losses, you may want to make a thorough moral assessment before taking action. If these losses extend to your dependents, consider the situation carefully. You may have moral grounds for not blowing the whistle if your dependents could be harmed emotionally, financially, or even physically.

Working through channels
Whistle-blowing can be pursued by one of two ways: by going public or proceeding through the institution's chain of command. You should make every effort to correct the situation internally before going public. If you work successfully through the chain of command, you'll be able to accomplish your goals with a minimum of exposure. Ethically, you owe management an opportunity to change the situation before going public. For your own legal protection, you should maintain a

Whistle-blowing: A systematic approach

As with other nursing actions, whistle-blowing can be carried out successfully if it's planned, systematic, and purposeful.

Gathering facts

Begin by gathering all the facts. Then put in writing the misconduct you want to report. Be sure to include the incident's date and time, the person or people involved, and the source of your information. Above all, avoid accusations and personal opinions.

Stating the problem

Clearly state the problem and identify causative factors. Was incompetence or negligence involved? Were supplies adequate? Did equipment malfunction? Was facility policy at fault?

When answering these questions, try to eliminate your personal biases. If possible, review the problem with a trusted colleague.

Determining your objective

State your objective in confronting the problem. For example, you may want to eliminate threats to patient safety; eliminate illegal, immoral, or illegitimate practices; uphold professional ethical standards; or put into effect changes in facility policy.

Confronting the problem

Confront the person who committed the misconduct in a constructive, nonthreatening way. Express your concerns and ask for an explanation of the incident. Seek reassurance that the problem will be addressed.

Making your decision

After a reasonable duration, determine if the problem has been corrected. If it hasn't, identify the pros and cons of whistle-blowing. The pros include correction of a harmful or potentially harmful situation, retained moral integrity, and an enhanced sense of moral accountability. The cons include alienation, stress and, possibly, loss of reputation, professional standing, and job. After you weigh the pros and cons, talk over the issue of whistle-blowing with your lawyer or another knowledgeable person.

Next, realistically appraise your situation. Will you be able to cope if you blow the whistle? Are you secure professionally and financially? Do you have the support of your family, colleagues, or administration? How much help can you count on?

Now make your decision based on your analysis of the severity of the incident, the consequences of whistle-blowing, and your resources. If you elect to blow the whistle, carefully devise a strategy that follows facility channels.

If you're fearful of losing your job as a result of your actions, consider taking a position in another facility before you blow the whistle. If you fail to get satisfaction through facility channels, consider consulting professional organizations, regulatory agencies and, as a last resort, the press. Be sure to document each step you take.

record of your efforts to work through channels before considering more drastic measures.

If you fail to get satisfaction from the institution's chain of command,
contact the appropriate regulatory agencies. Contact the media only as a last resort.

Providing adequate documentation

Document your disclosure carefully. Write a clear, objective summary of the relevant facts. Explain why the information is significant and what needs to be done. Avoid focusing on personalities. Personal accusations detract from the disclosure and may invite a lawsuit for libel or slander. Have other professionals verify the information, if possible. This will lend objectivity to the information and may shield you from retaliation.

Surviving the setbacks

Prepare yourself for possible retaliation. Management may find it more convenient to attack the whistleblower than to address the problem. Colleagues may start giving you the cold shoulder, or you may experience overt harassment. Rumors that you're dishonest or incompetent may spread through the institution. To protect yourself and to maintain pressure on management, meticulously document everything, including continued incidents of incompetence or negligence. Consider photocopying all the incident reports you file. Be especially vigilant in your practice, and document your nursing actions carefully. Your employer may try to distract attention from the disclosure by portraying you as a troublemaker; to counter this tactic, maintain diplomatic relations with as many colleagues as possible.

If you anticipate that whistleblowing will cause severe personal hardship, consider mapping out a self-protection strategy. Find new employment before you blow the whistle, and retain a lawyer who will provide you with competent legal advice throughout your ordeal. Seek out friends and colleagues who have the moral integrity to stand behind you.

REPORTING MEDICAL MALPRACTICE

Consider the case of Beth Madison, a registered nurse with 8 years of experience in critical care. According to ICU policy, critical care nurses may remove an arterial line if a complication is assessed. In the middle of the night shift, Ms. Madison was assessing a patient who was complaining of pain. She noted redness, swelling, drainage, and hematoma at the arterial line site. She removed the line and applied pressure to the site. She paged the resident on call, obtained a standard order set for central and hemodynamic lines, and gathered necessary equipment for an arterial line insertion, all according to her facility's policy.

When the resident arrived, he appeared irritated and questioned Ms. Madison repeatedly about why she had removed the line as she prepared for new line insertion, flushed the pressure tubing, and zeroed the arterial line transducer. The resident then asked her to prep the site he had chosen. Ms. Madison asked, "Do you want to do a modified Allen's test to verify a patent palmar arch first and administer the local anesthetic before I prep?"

The resident said, "Oh, right," and then gave the patient a local but didn't verify a patent palmar arch. As the resident attempted to insert the arterial guide wire catheter, the patient continued to complain of severe pain. The resident looked stressed. He turned to Ms. Madison and asked, "Can you get this thing in?" Then he handed the guide wire to her. Ms. Madison inserted and advanced the guide wire into the patient's artery. She then offered to call the chief resident to complete the procedure. The resident was so irate that he insisted that she leave the room while he completed the procedure himself.

The next day the on-call resident filed an incident report accusing Ms. Madison of being insubordinate and practicing outside her scope of nursing practice by inserting a guide wire. Now Ms. Madison is wondering what she should do. Should she also file an incident report and include her doubts about the resident's ability to correctly perform the arterial line insertion? Or should she just do nothing for fear her report will sound like "sour grapes"?

Difficult dilemma

Nurses are, by their professional code of ethics and licensure standards, required to act as patient advocates. (See *Patient advocacy and medical malpractice*.) Whenever nurses see other health care providers acting in a way that could endanger the health or safety of a patient, they should make a report of what they witnessed. (In many states, state law *requires* nurses to report patient endangerment.)

The concept of moral agency should guide nurses, not only in situations of whistle-blowing, but also in reporting witnessed or suspected malpractice. Some states have regulations and case law that protect nurses who speak up in cases of suspected or confirmed medical malpractice.

Substance abuse among nurses

The ANA estimates that 6% to 8% of nurses in the United States are addicted to alcohol or drugs. In one state study, researchers found that more than 90% of disciplinary hearings for nurses in the state were related to alcohol and drug abuse. These statistics aren't surprising in light of the high stress levels in nursing today. Nurses can experience frustration and feelings of power-

---

Patient advocacy and medical malpractice

Nursing policies and procedures must clarify the circumstances under which nurses, as advocates for their patients, are required to report suspected or witnessed malpractice. Nurses must know the method by which such reports are to be made, to whom they should be made, and whether they can be considered discoverable and are protected under quality assurance protocols.

Of course, there can be problems with reporting instances of witnessed or suspected malpractice. Nurses may confuse issues of malpractice with other ethical or legal issues. For example, a nurse sees a physician lose his temper and slap a patient. Is this an instance of medical malpractice? No. But it's an example of violence in the workplace and the nurse's reporting procedure should be addressed in the facility's policy on managing violence in the hospital. Suppose a nurse witnesses a physician giving a dying patient an excessive dose of morphine? Is this an instance of medical malpractice? Possibly, but it's also an ethical issue and should be reported to and addressed by the facility's ethics committee.

---

lessness when trying to act as patient advocates. Frequent floating to unfamiliar units, unrealistic workloads, and long or double shifts may bring on fatigue and loneliness. Many nurses today must shoulder tremendous family and financial obligations while trying to meet professional demands. And, of course, nurses aren't immune to the harsh social realities of modern life. Combined with the availability of controlled substances, such stressors can lead a nurse to substance abuse.

PAST ATTITUDES TOWARD SUBSTANCE ABUSE

In the past, nurses who were caught abusing drugs or alcohol were punished. The prevailing ethic held that a nurse who abused drugs violated the public trust and the standards of her profession and deserved to be subject to strong disciplinary action.

Nursing administrators were expected to report suspected substance abusers to their state nursing board. The board would then investigate the allegation, and if it found the nurse guilty, it would impose punishment such as revocation of her license.

In practice, though, many administrators didn't report substance abuse but chose instead to fire the offending nurse. Furthermore, colleagues of suspected substance abusers commonly didn't report their suspicions because they knew the nurses' job would be in jeopardy. Aware of the harsh treatment that awaited them, nurses who abused drugs or alcohol switched jobs frequently, rather than endure the repercussions that would follow an admission of abuse.

Ethical perspectives

From an ethical viewpoint, this punitive approach to substance abuse left much to be desired. Administrators who simply fired a substance abuser abnegated their ethical responsibility to help nurses in need and to prevent qualified nurses from dropping out of their profession. Colleagues who didn't report substance abuse abandoned the best interests of both the addicted nurse and her patients. The substance abuser usually switched jobs rather than ask for help. She had little moti-

vation to change, knowing that she was unlikely to receive understanding or rehabilitation.

A MORE ENLIGHTENED VIEW

Fortunately, society is learning to view substance abuse as a treatable disorder, and the emphasis is on rehabilitating chemically dependent nurses. Within the nursing profession, there's a greater understanding of the importance of peer support for the nurse struggling with addiction. Nurse practice acts may include provisions that encourage chemically dependent nurses to complete a treatment program. Many facilities now have policies for dealing with substance abuse among employees, from initial reporting through rehabilitation and returning to work. Also, treatment programs have become commonplace, and associations for recovering nurses are available to provide needed support.

WHEN YOU SUSPECT SUBSTANCE ABUSE

Because of the high rate of chemical dependency among nurses, chances are you'll encounter this problem sometime during your career. Like many nurses, you may experience confusion, guilt, anger, and remorse if faced with the responsibility of confronting and reporting a nurse-addict. Numerous potential ethical conflicts may arise from this situation.

◆ You may resent the increased workload, risk to patients, and stress created by the nurse's drug or alcohol problem.

◆ You may be torn between your obligation to protect patients and your loyalty to a fellow nurse.

◆ You may think that you contributed to the addiction by not acting sooner.

◆ If you aren't entirely certain your suspicions are correct, you may fear the damage you could do to an innocent nurse's reputation and career.

◆ You may have difficulty accepting the addict's self-destructive behavior as part of her addiction.

◆ You may think that you're betraying a friendship.

Though the decision to report a coworker is never an easy one, you have an ethical obligation to intervene if you suspect that a colleague is abusing drugs or alcohol. Intervening enables you to fulfill your moral obligation to your colleague: By reporting abuse, you compel her to take the first step toward regaining control over her life and undergoing rehabilitation. You also fulfill your obligation to patients by protecting them from a nurse whose judgment and care don't meet professional standards.

Recognizing substance abuse

Be aware that allegations of substance abuse are serious and potentially damaging. To make an accurate assessment, you need to be familiar with the signs of substance abuse.

Signs of drug or alcohol abuse may include:

◆ rapid mood swings, usually from irritability or depression to elation

◆ frequent absences, lateness, and use of private quarters such as bathrooms

◆ frequent volunteering to administer medications

◆ excessive errors or problems with controlled substances, such as reports of broken vials or spilled drugs

◆ illogical or sloppy charting

◆ inability to meet deadlines or minimum job requirements

◆ avoidance of new and challenging assignments

◆ increased errors in treatment, particularly in dosage computation

◆ poor personal hygiene and appearance

◆ inability to concentrate or remember details

◆ alcohol on the breath

◆ slurred speech, unsteady gait, flushed face, or red eyes

◆ discrepancies in narcotics supplies detected at the end of the nurse's shift

◆ narcotics signed out to patients only on the nurse's shift

◆ patient complaints of no relief from narcotics supposedly administered when the nurse is on duty

◆ preference for working alone or on the night shift, when supervision is minimal

◆ social withdrawal

◆ memory loss

◆ alcohol-induced complications, including jaundice, bruises (from falls), and delirium.

Reporting substance abuse

If you detect signs of substance abuse, your first step is to document them. Include the time, date, and place of the incident; a description of what happened; and the names of any witnesses. Be sure to leave out personal opinions and judgments. For example, "At about 9 p.m. on November 15, 2003, Mrs. Fox in room 501 told me that my injections of morphine were much better than those the other nurse gives. I asked what she meant. She told me that June Barrett's injections never seemed to take away her pain but that mine always did. Two nights later, at 10:15 p.m., I went to the restroom. When I opened the door, I saw June Barrett injecting some solution into her thigh using a hospital syringe. She told me to get out. I did. We didn't talk about it afterward."

Never confront or accuse the suspected nurse on your own. After you've documented the incident, dis-

Steps to helping an impaired colleague

Colleagues can take steps to put a stop to a nurse-addict's self-destructive behavior. By using an effective, nonpunitive, group-oriented approach, they can break the cycle of addiction. In this approach, group members confront the nurse-addict, help her to acknowledge her condition, and motivate her to seek rehabilitation before she harms a patient or herself.

Intervention team
The team includes 2 to 10 carefully selected persons who are personal and professional associates of the nurse-addict. If possible, the team also includes a colleague who has successfully entered rehabilitation and a nurse who possesses experience in treating drug and alcohol addiction.

   Team members must share a nonjudgmental attitude. Each must accept that the nurse's self-destructive behavior represents an aspect of her illness and doesn't indicate that she's morally deficient. Furthermore, each should avoid expressing judgments about her.

Confronting the colleague
◆ Team members document all evidence of the nurse's chemical dependence, including the date, time, and place of relevant incidents.

◆ They should be careful not to include any judgmental remarks in their documentation.
◆ The team leader reviews all important documentation, including patient charts, nurses' notes, physician's orders, medication administration and narcotics records, and the impaired nurse's personnel file.
◆ Team members meet with the impaired nurse in a private room away from the nurses' station. The group leader explains why the team has gathered. Participants present their evidence, always prefacing their testimony with positive remarks.
◆ The impaired nurse is given a chance to respond.
◆ The team leader makes clear the options available to the impaired nurse. The impaired nurse is given an opportunity to voluntarily enter a treatment program; otherwise, she may lose her job and be reported to the state board of nursing.
◆ Arrangements are made for the team leader to monitor how the nurse is progressing in therapy.
◆ Events of the meeting are documented.
◆ To ease the tension stirred up by the confrontation, the team leader may arrange for follow-up discussions.

cuss it with your nurse-manager. She'll need to gather additional information by examining patient charts, medication records (especially for narcotics), and reports from patients and other nurses. After the nurse-manager completes this review, she'll try to determine if the evidence corroborates your incident report.

Confronting the substance abuser
If the nurse-manager concludes that substance abuse is likely, she'll need to confront the nurse with the facts and explain the options. It's hoped that these options will include treatment and perhaps eventual reinstatement in her position. (See *Steps to helping an impaired colleague.*) If you're asked to be present for this confrontation, keep in mind that you best fulfill your moral obligation to the substance abuser by

being honest, compassionate, and non-judgmental and by expressing your willingness to help. Expect that she'll feel threatened and may attempt to deny her condition, even if the facts are fully substantiated.

In most substance abuse cases, if the nurse is willing to enter a treatment program and successfully completes it, no disciplinary action is taken against her. If the nurse refuses to enter treatment, she may be reported to the state board of nursing, suspended, or dismissed.

The road back

In most instances, the recovering nurse is able to return to work. She may be placed under a special contract that stipulates conditions for continued employment. These conditions may include:
◆ attending weekly meetings with a counselor
◆ participating in a 12-step program and meetings with other recovering nurses
◆ submitting to random blood and urine screenings
◆ remaining drug-free.

The nurse-manager who's responsible for the recovering nurse should carefully document all meetings and keep a copy of all contracts.

The chemically dependent nurse's colleagues must use their professional training to try to understand her condition. Coworkers play a crucial role in the recovering nurse's ultimate success or failure. When recovering from addiction, a person's needs include:
◆ finding ways to improve self-esteem, including assertiveness training
◆ developing a stronger support system
◆ developing stress management and coping techniques

◆ learning to come to terms with past traumatic experiences, such as physical or sexual abuse.

Welcoming a recovering nurse back to the work setting and offering support during the critical transition period is as important as detecting and reporting signs of abuse. From an ethical point of view, working with a colleague who's a substance abuser can be frustrating and uncomfortable, but helping a nurse recognize her problem and begin the process of recovery is an act of significant moral courage and humanity.

Selected references

American College of Physicians. *Ethics Manual,* 4th ed. Philadelphia: American College of Physicians, 1998.

American Nurses Association. *Nursing's Social Policy Statement,* 2nd ed. Washington, D.C.: American Nurses Association, 2003.

Anderson, C. "Workplace Violence: Are Some Nurses More Vulnerable?" *Issues in Mental Health Nursing* 23(4):351-66, June 2002.

Botes, A., and Otto, M. "Ethical Dilemmas Related to the HIV-Positive Person in the Workplace," *Nursing Ethics* 10(3):281-94, May 2003.

Clark, S.P., et al. "Effects of Hospital Staffing and Organizational Climate on Needlestick Injuries to Nurses," *American Journal of Public Health* 92(7):1115-19, July 2002.

Dean, J.A. "The Resuscitation Status of a Patient: A Constant Dilemma," *British Journal of Nursing* 10(8):537-43, April-May 2001.

Dierckx de Casterle, B., et al. "Ethics Meetings in Support of Good Nursing Care: Some Practice-based Thoughts," *Nursing Ethics* 9(6):612-22, November 2002.

Fetter, M.S. "End-of-life Care: The Nursing Role," *Medsurg Nursing* 9(5):230-31, October 2000.

Goodman, B. "Ms B and Legal Competence: Examining the Role of Nurses in Difficult Ethico-legal Decision-making," *Nursing in Critical Care* 8(2):78-83, March-April 2003.

Haiduven, D.J. "Planning a Hepatitis C Post Exposure Management Program for Healthcare Workers. Issues and Challenges," *AAOHN Journal* 48(8):370-75, August 2000.

Lipscomb, J., et al. "Perspectives on Legal Strategies to Prevent Workplace Violence," *Journal of Law and Medical Ethics* 30(3 supp):166-72, Fall 2002.

Moloughney, B.W. "Transmission and Postexposure Management of Bloodborne Virus Infections in the Health Care Setting: Where Are We Now?" *Canadian Medical Association Journal* 165(4):445-51, August 2001.

Robinson, J.R., et al. "Workplace Stress Among Psychiatric Nurses. Prevalence, Distribution, Correlates, and Predictors," *Journal of Psychosocial Nursing and Mental Health Services* 41(4):32-41, April 2003.

Sinclair, R.C., et al. "Prevalence of Safer Needle Devices and Factors Associated with their Adoption: Results of a National Hospital Survey," *Public Health Report* 117(4):340-49, July-August 2002.

Sylvester, B.J., and Reisener, L. "Scared to go to Work: A Homecare Performance Improvement Initiative," *Journal of Nursing Care Quality* 17(1):71-82, October 2002.

Tiedje, L.B. "Moral Distress in Perinatal Nursing," *Journal of Perinatal Neonatal Nursing* 14(2):36-43, September 2000.

Wilder, M.A. "Ethical Issues in the Delivery Room: Resuscitation of Extremely Low Birth Weight Infants," *Journal of Perinatal Neonatal Nursing* 14(2):44-57, September 2000.

Worthington, K. "Violence in the Health Care Workplace," *AJN* 100(11):69-70, November 2000.

Wright, L., and Daar, A.S. "Ethical Aspects of Living Donor Kidney Transplantation and Recipient Adherence to Treatment," *Progress in Transplantation* 13(2):105-09, June 2003.

Yoder, A.D. "Laws Protect Whistle Blowers," *Oregon Nurse* 65(3):9, September 2000.

Bioethics Discussion Pages: *www-hsc.usc.edu/~mbernste*

Center for the Study of Bioethics, Medical College of Wisconsin: *www.mcw.edu/bioethics/index.html*

GeneLetter: *www.geneletter.com*

The Institute for Genomic Research: *www.tigr.org*

National Human Genome Research Institute: *www.genome.gov*

Office of Genomics and Disease Prevention: *www.cdc.gov/genomics/default.htm*

Internet resources

AIDS Info BBS Database: *www.aidsinfobbs.org*

AIDS Information Global Education Service: *www.infoweb.org*

Glossary,
Appendices,
and Index

Glossary

A

AA *abbr* Alcoholics Anonymous

abuse of process A civil action in which it's alleged that the legal process has been used in an improper manner. For example, an abuse of process action might be brought by a physician attempting to countersue a patient or by a psychiatric patient attempting to demonstrate wrongful confinement.

ad hoc committee A committee commissioned for a specific purpose.

adjudicated incompetent Declared incompetent by exercise of judicial authority. Note that a patient who has been adjudicated incompetent may still have the mental capacity to make an informed decision about his medical care. Compare *incompetence* and *mental incompetence*.

administrative review An investigation conducted by the state board of nursing when a nurse is accused of professional misconduct. The board first reviews the complaint and then may hold a formal hearing at which evidence is presented and witnesses examined and cross-examined. Court proceedings — and possibly legal penalties — may result from the board's findings.

admissible evidence Authentic, relevant, reliable information that's present during a trial and may be used to reach a decision.

ADN *abbr* associate degree in nursing

adult 1. One who's fully developed and mature and who has attained the intellectual capacity and the emotional and psychological stability characteristic of a mature person. 2. A person who has reached legal age (in most states, age 18 or 21).

advance directive A document (or documentation) allowing a person to give directions about future medical care or to designate another person(s) to make medical decisions if and when the individual patient loses decision-making capacity.

advance directive system A system implemented by health care institutions (including hospitals, extended-care facilities, and hospices) to ensure that every patient, at admission, is informed of his right to execute a living will or durable power of attorney for health care decisions.

advanced practice nurse (APN) An individual whose education and certification meet criteria established by each state's board of nursing, including current licensure as a registered nurse and a master's degree or post-basic program certificate in a clinical nursing specialty with national certification.

adverse reaction A harmful, unintended reaction to a drug administered at normal dosage.

affidavit A written statement sworn to before a notary public or an officer of the court.

affirmative defense A denial of guilt or wrongdoing based on new evidence rather than simple denial of a charge. For example, a nurse who pleads immunity under the Good Samaritan law is making an affirmative defense. The defendant bears the burden of proof in an affirmative defense.

against medical advice A patient's decision to leave a health care facility against his physician's advice.

age of majority 18 or 21 years, depending on the laws of each state or Canadian province.

agency A relationship between two parties in which the first party authorizes the second to act as an agent on behalf of the first.

agent A party authorized to act on behalf of another and to give the other an account of such actions.

AHA *abbr* American Hospital Association

Alcoholics Anonymous (AA) An international nonprofit organization founded in 1935 that consists of abstinent alcoholics whose purpose is to help other alcoholics stop drinking and maintain sobriety through group support, shared experiences, and faith in a power greater than themselves.

alcoholism The extreme dependence on excessive amounts of alcohol, associated with a cumulative pattern of deviant behaviors. Alcoholism is a chronic illness with a slow, insidious onset, which may occur at any age. The cause is unknown, but cultural and psychosocial factors are suspect. Also, families of alcoholics have a higher incidence of alcoholism. See also *drug addiction*.

AMA *abbr* against medical advice; American Medical Association

amendment An alteration to an existing law or complaint.

American Hospital Association (AHA) Founded in 1898, the AHA is a national association comprised of individuals and health care institutions, including hospitals, health care systems, and preacute and postacute health care delivery organizations. The AHA is dedicated to promoting the welfare of the public through its leadership and assistance to its members in the provision of better health services for all people.

American Medical Association (AMA) A professional association including practitioners in all recognized medical specialties as well as general primary care physicians. The AMA is governed by a Board of Trustees and House of Delegates. Trustees and delegates represent various state and local medical associations as well as such government agencies as the Public Health Service and medical departments of the Army, Navy, and Air Force.

American Nurses Association (ANA) The national professional association of registered nurses in the United States. It was founded in 1896 to improve standards of health and the availability of health care given in order to foster high standards for nursing, to promote the professional development of nurses, and to advance the economic and general welfare of nurses. The ANA is made up of 53 constituent associations from 50 states, the District of Columbia, Guam, and the U.S. Virgin Islands, representing more than 900 district associations. Members may join one or more of the five Divisions on Nursing Practice: Community Health, Gerontological, Maternal and Child, Medical-Surgical, and Psychiatric and Mental Health Nursing. These divisions are coordinated by the Congress for Nursing Practice. The Congress evaluates changes in the scope of practice, monitors scientific and educational developments, encourages research, and develops statements that describe ANA policies regarding legislation that affects nursing practice. Other commissions within the association include the Commission on Nursing Education, the Commission on Nursing Services, the Commission on Nursing Research, and the Economic and General Welfare Commission.

American Red Cross A nationwide organization that seeks to reduce human suffering through various health, safety, and disaster relief programs in affiliation with the International Committee of the Red Cross. The Committee and all Red Cross organizations evolved from the Geneva Convention of 1864, following the example and urging of Swiss humanitarian Jean-Henri Dunant, who aided wounded French and Austrian soldiers at the Battle of Solferino in 1859. The American Red Cross (one of more than 120 national Red Cross organizations) has more than 130 million members in about 3,100 chapters throughout the United States. Volunteers constitute the entire staffs of about 1,700 chapters. Other chapters maintain small paid staffs and some professionals but depend largely on volunteers. See also *International Red Cross Society.*

ANA *abbr* American Nurses Association

answer The response of a defendant to the claims of a plaintiff. The answer contains a denial of the plaintiff's allegations and may also contain an affirmative defense or a counterclaim. It's the principal pleading on the part of the defense and is prepared in writing, usually by the defense attorney, and submitted to the court.

APN *abbr* advanced practice nurse

appellant The party who lost the case in lower court and is appealing the appellate court to change the lower court's decision.

appellate court A court of law that has the power to review the decision of a lower court. An appellate court

doesn't make a new determination of the facts of the case; instead, it reviews the way in which the law was applied to the case.

appellee The party in an appeal who won the case in a lower court. The appellee argues that the decision of the lower court shouldn't be modified by the appellate court.

arbitration The settlement of a dispute by an impartial person chosen by the disputing parties.

arbitrator An impartial person appointed to resolve a dispute between parties. The arbitrator listens to the evidence as presented by the parties in an informal hearing and attempts to arrive at a resolution acceptable to both parties.

assault An attempt or threat by a person to physically injure another person.

associate degree in nursing (ADN) An academic degree obtained after satisfactory completion of a 2-year course of study, usually at a community or junior college. The recipient is eligible to take the national licensing examination to become a registered nurse. An associate degree in nursing isn't available in Canada. Compare *bachelor of science in nursing.*

attending physician The physician who's responsible for a specific patient. In a university setting, an attending physician usually also has teaching responsibilities and holds a faculty appointment. Also called the *attending* (informal), *physician of record.*

attorney of record The attorney whose name appears on the legal records for a specific case as the agent of a specific client.

audit A methodical examination; to examine with intent to verify. Nursing audits examine standards of nursing care.

authorization cards Cards employees sign to authorize a union election.

autonomy The principle of self-determination. The right to make decisions about one's own health care.

autopsy A postmortem examination of a body to determine the cause of death.

B

bachelor of science in nursing (BSN) An academic degree awarded upon satisfactory completion of a 4-year course of study in an institution of higher learning. The recipient is eligible to take the national licensing examination to become a registered nurse. A BSN degree is prerequisite to advancement in most systems and institutions that employ nurses. Compare *associate degree in nursing.*

bargaining agent A person or group selected by members of a bargaining unit to represent them in negotiations.

bargaining unit A group of employees who participate in collective bargaining as representatives of all employees.

BASIC abbr Beginners' All-purpose Symbolic Instruction Code, a programming language widely used on personal computers and small business systems.

battered woman syndrome (BWS) This syndrome is the "learned helplessness" that results from repeated but failed attempts to escape a batterer's violence. Eventually, the woman stops trying to escape the violence. Such violence tends to follow a predictable pattern. The first phase is characterized by the abuser's increased irritability, edginess, and tension. These feelings are expressed in the form of verbal criticism and abuse as well as physical shoves and slaps. The second phase is the time of acute, violent activity. As tension mounts, the woman becomes unable to placate the male abuser and she may argue or defend herself. The man uses this as justification for his anger and assaults her, usually saying that he's "teaching her a lesson." The third stage is characterized by apology and remorse with promises of change on the part of the abuser. The calm continues until tension builds again. BWS occurs at all socioeconomic levels and one-half to three-quarters of female assault victims are the victims of an attack by a lover or husband. It's estimated that up to 2 million women are beaten by their husbands each year.

battery The unauthorized touching of a person by another person. For example, a physician who has treated a patient beyond what the patient has consented to has committed battery.

beneficence The promotion of good and prevention of harm.

benefits Nonsalary forms of compensation an employer provides for employees — for example, medical and dental insurance.

binding arbitration A process of settling disputes in which all parties agree to be bound by the determination of an arbitrator.

block charting A method of charting in which procedures carried out during a block of time are detailed in paragraph form.

BMA abbr British Medical Association

board of health An administrative body acting on a municipal, county, state, province, or national level. The functions, powers, and responsibilities of boards of health vary with the locale. Each board is generally concerned with the recognition of the health needs of the people and the coordination of projects and resources to meet and identify those needs. Among the tasks of most boards of health are prevention of disease, health education, and implementation of laws pertaining to health.

borrowed–servant doctrine A legal doctrine that courts may apply in cases in which an employer "lends" his employee's services to another employer who, under this doctrine, becomes solely liable for the employee's wrongful conduct. Also called *ostensible agent doctrine.* Compare *captain-of-the ship doctrine* and *dual agency doctrine.*

brain death Final cessation of activity in the central nervous system, especially as indicated by a flat electroencephalogram for a predetermined length of time. The cessation of all measurable function or activity in every area of the brain, including the brain stem. Compare *death.*

breach of contract Failure to perform all or part of a contracted duty without justification.

breach of duty Neglect or failure to fulfill in a proper manner the duties of an office, job, or position.

British Medical Association (BMA) A national professional organization of physicians in the United Kingdom.

BSN *abbr* bachelor of science in nursing

BWS *abbr* battered woman syndrome

C

Canadian Association of University Schools of Nursing (CAUSN) A national Canadian organization of nursing schools affiliated with institutions of higher learning.

Canadian Nurses Association (CNA) This official national organization is a federation of professional nurses associations from 11 jurisdictions and territories. It represents more than 110,000 members and is the national voice of the profession in Canada.

capitation A per-member, monthly payment to a provider that covers contracted services and is paid in advance of delivery. In essence, a provider agrees to provide specified services to enrollees for this fixed payment for a specified term, regardless of how many times the member uses the service.

captain-of-the-ship doctrine A legal doctrine that considers a surgeon responsible for the actions of his assistants when those assistants are under the surgeon's supervision. Compare *borrowed-servant doctrine.*

care plans A charting format that shows the relationships of sets of interventions to sets of intermediate outcomes along a time line.

case management The process by which a designated health care professional, usually a nurse, manages all health-related matters of a patient. Case managers coordinate and ensure continuity of care. They develop a plan to use health care resources efficiently and achieve the optimum patient outcome in the most cost-effective manner. They also match the appropriate intensity of services to the patient's needs.

causa mortis Latin phrase meaning "in anticipation of approaching death." The state of mind of a person approaching death.

CAUSN *abbr* Canadian Association of University Schools of Nursing

CCU *abbr* coronary care unit; critical care unit

CDC *abbr* Centers for Disease Control and Prevention

Centers for Disease Control and Prevention (CDC) An agency of the U.S. government that provides facilities and services for the investigation, identification, prevention, and control of disease.

central processing unit (CPU) In data processing, the group of physical components of a computer system containing the logical, arithmetical, and control circuits for the system. Also called *hardware.*

certification A statement recognizing that a nurse is specially qualified, based on predetermined standards, to provide nursing care in a particular area of nursing practice.

CGFNS *abbr* Commission on Graduates of Foreign Nursing Schools *certified nurse-midwife* See *midwife*.

chain of custody An evidentiary rule requiring that each individual having custody of a piece of evidence be identified and that the transfer of evidence from one custodian to another be documented so that all evidence is accounted for. Also called *chain of evidence*.

challenge An objection by a party (or his lawyer) to the inclusion of a particular prospective juror as a member of the jury that's to hear the party's cause or trial, with the result that the prospective juror is disqualified.

challenge for cause A challenge based on a particular reason (such as bias) specified by law or procedure as a reason that a party (or his lawyer) may use to disqualify a prospective juror.

charting by exception A shorthand method for documenting normal findings, based on clearly defined standards of practice and predetermined criteria for nursing assessments and interventions.

child abuse The physical, sexual, or emotional mistreatment of a child. It may be overt or covert and commonly results in physical or psychological injury, mental impairment or, sometimes, death. Child abuse results from complex factors involving both parents and child, compounded by various stressful environmental circumstances, such as poor socioeconomic conditions; inadequate physical and emotional support within the family; any major life change or crisis, especially those crises arising from marital strife; or a combination of these factors. Also called *battered child syndrome* for children younger than age 3. Compare *child neglect*.

child neglect Failure by parents or guardians to provide for the basic needs of a child by physical or emotional deprivation that interferes with normal growth and development or that places the child in jeopardy. Compare *child abuse*.

child welfare Any service sponsored by the community or special organizations that provides physical, social, or psychological care for children in need of that service.

chronic care A pattern of medical and nursing care that focuses on the long-term care of people with chronic diseases or conditions, either at home or in a medical facility. It includes care specific to the problem and measures to encourage self-care, promote health, and prevent loss of function.

circumstantial evidence Testimony based on inference or hearsay rather than actual personal knowledge or observation of the facts in question.

civil defense laws The body of statutory law that's invoked when the jurisdiction is under attack — for example, during a war.

civil penalty Fines or money damages imposed as punishment for a certain activity.

claims-made policy A professional liability insurance policy that covers the insured only for a claim of malpractice made while the policy is in effect.

claims review agency An agency that investigates claims for payment made to an insurance company. It determines whether the claim is legitimate, assesses how severe the loss is, and determines the amount the insurance company is required to pay.

clinical nurse specialist (CNS) A registered nurse who holds a master of science degree in nursing (MSN) and who has acquired advanced knowledge and clinical skills in a specific area of nursing and health care.

clinical pathways A clinical tool used by case managers to achieve better quality and cost outcomes by outlining and sequencing the usual and desired care for particular groups of patients. Clinical pathways incorporate care requirements from preadmission through postdischarge. Also called *critical paths*.

clinical practice guidelines A decision-making tool used to help practitioners determine how diseases or disorders can most effectively and appropriately be prevented, diagnosed, treated, and managed clinically. These guidelines include advice and information from recognized clinical experts.

closed shop See *union shop*.

CNA *abbr* Canadian Nurses Association

CNM *abbr* certified nurse-midwife; see *midwife*.

CNS *abbr* clinical nurse specialist

code 1. A published body of statutes, such as a civil code. 2. A collection of standards and rules of behavior, such as a dress code. 3. A symbolic means of representing information for communication or transfer, such as a genetic code. 4. *Informal*. A discreet signal used to summon a special team to resuscitate a patient without alarming patients or visitors. See also *no-code order*.

codes A system of assigned terms designed by a medical institution for quick and accurate communication during emergencies or for patient identification.

collective bargaining A legal process in which representatives of unionized employees negotiate with employers about such matters as wages, hours, and conditions.

collectively bargained contract A contract negotiated by a labor organization or union. Also called a *collective contract*.

Commission on Graduates of Foreign Nursing Schools (CGFNS) An organization established in 1977 to ensure safe nursing care for the American public and to protect graduates of foreign nursing schools from employment exploitation.

commitment 1. The placement or confinement of an individual in a specialized hospital or other institution-

al facility. 2. The legal procedure of admitting a mentally ill person to an institution for psychiatric treatment. The process varies from state to state but usually involves judicial or court action based on medical evidence certifying that the person is mentally ill. 3. A pledge or contract to fulfill some obligation or agreement, used especially in some forms of psychotherapy or marriage counseling.

common law Law derived from previous court decisions as opposed to law based on legislative enactment (statutes). Also called *case law*. In the absence of statutory law regarding a subject, the judge-made rules of common law are the law on that subject.

comparative negligence Determination of liability in which damages may be apportioned among multiple defendants. The extent of liability depends on each defendant's relative contribution to the harm done as determined by the jury.

complaint 1. In a civil case, a pleading by a plaintiff made under oath to initiate a suit. It's a statement of the formal charge and the cause for action against the defendant. In a criminal case, a serious felony prosecution requires an indictment with evidence presented by a state's attorney. 2. *Informal*. Any ailment, problem, or symptom identified by the patient, member of the patient's family, or other knowledgeable person. The chief complaint is usually the reason the patient has sought health care.

computerized medical record system A system that stores medical records in the memory bank of a computer.

confidentiality A professional responsibility to keep all privileged information private. In some instances, confidentiality is mandated by state or federal statutes and case law.

consent form A document that's prepared for a patient's signature, disclosing his proposed treatment in general terms.

consequential damages See *special damages*.

consumer A person who buys goods or services for his own needs and not for resale or to use in the production of other goods or services for resale.

continuum of care The full range of health care services, from health promotion and disease prevention through delivery of primary care, acute care, home health care, and long-term care.

contract defense An answer to an allegation that a breach of contract has occurred. Compare *impossibility defense*.

contract duties Duties defined in a contract such as an employment contract.

contract violations Actions that break mutually accepted contract provisions such as those of an employment contract.

controlled substance Any substance that's strictly regulated or outlawed because of its potential for abuse or addiction. Controlled substances include cannabis, depressants, hallucinogens, opioids, and stimulants. Compare *prescription drug*.

convalescent home See *extended-care facility*.

cooperation strategy A plan for bringing about change in which the person who initiates change influences others to adapt to the change, using open communication and interpersonal skills.

coronary care unit (CCU) A specially equipped hospital area designed for the treatment of patients with sudden, life-threatening cardiac conditions. Such units contain resuscitation and monitoring equipment and are staffed by personnel specially trained and skilled in recognizing and immediately responding to cardiac emergencies with cardiopulmonary resuscitation techniques, administration of antiarrhythmics, and other appropriate therapeutic measures.

coroner A public official who investigates the causes and circumstances of a death occurring within a specific legal jurisdiction or territory, especially a death that may have resulted from unnatural causes. Also called *medical examiner*.

corporate liability The legal responsibility of a corporation and its officers. A corporation's liability is normally limited to its assets; the shareholders are thus protected against personal liability for the corporation.

counterclaim A claim made by a defendant establishing a cause for action in his favor against the plaintiff. The purpose of a counterclaim is to oppose or detract from the plaintiff's claim or complaint.

countersignature A signature obtained from another health care professional to verify that information is correct and is within the verifier's personal knowledge.

CPU *abbr* central processing unit

critical care unit (CCU) A hospital unit in which patients requiring close monitoring and intensive care are housed for as long as needed. A critical care unit contains highly technical and sophisticated monitoring devices and equipment, and the staff in the unit is educated to provide intensive care, as needed by the patients. See also *intensive care unit*.

critical paths See *clinical pathways*.

CRNA *abbr* certified registered nurse anesthetist; see *nurse anesthetist*.

cross-examination The questioning of a witness by the attorney for the opposing party.

custodial care Services and care of an unskilled nature provided on a long-term basis, usually for convalescent and chronically ill individuals. Custodial care may include providing board and personal assistance.

D

damages The amount of money a court orders a defendant to pay the plaintiff when the case is decided in favor of the plaintiff.

DEA *abbr* Drug Enforcement Administration

death 1. The final and irreversible cessation of life as indicated by the absence of heartbeat or respiration. 2. The total absence of meaningful activity in the brain and the central nervous, cardiovascular, and respiratory systems, as observed and declared by a physician. Also called *legal death*. Compare *brain death*.

declared emergency Situation in which a government official formally identifies a state of emergency.

decree of educational equivalency An official decision stating that a person's experience is of equal value to an academic degree.

default judgment A judgment rendered against a defendant because of the defendant's failure to appear in court or to answer the plaintiff's claim within the proper time.

defendant The party that's named in a plaintiff's complaint and against whom the plaintiff's allegations are made. The defendant must respond to the allegations. See also *answer* and *litigant*.

defense independent medical examination In malpractice litigation, a medical examination of the injured party by a physician selected by the defendant's attorney or insurance company. Compare *discovery device*.

delinquency 1. Negligence or failure to fulfill a duty or obligation. 2. An offense, fault, misdemeanor, or misdeed; a tendency to commit such acts.

delinquent 1. Characterized by neglect of duty or violation of law. 2. Behavior characterized by persistent antisocial, illegal, violent, or criminal activity; a juvenile delinquent.

deontology An ethical theory based on moral obligation or commitment to others.

dependent nursing function A function the nurse performs following another health care professional's written order on the basis of that professional's judgment and for which that professional is accountable.

deposition A sworn pretrial testimony given by a witness in response to oral or written questions and cross-examination. The deposition is transcribed and may be used for further pretrial investigation. It may also be presented at the trial if the witness can't be present or changes his testimony. Compare *discovery device* and *interrogatories*.

direct access The right of a health care provider and a patient to interact on a professional basis without interference.

direct contract model HMO A managed-care organization that contracts directly with individual physicians to provide services to its members.

directed verdict A verdict given by a jury at the direction of the trial judge.

direct examination The first examination of a witness called to the stand by the attorney for the party the witness is representing.

direct patient care Care of a patient provided in person by a member of the staff. Direct patient care may involve any aspect of the health care of a patient, including treatments, counseling, self-care, patient education, and administration of medication.

disclosure laws Legislation requiring that potentially confidential information be reported — for example, laws that mandate nurses report suspected child abuse or neglect.

discovery device A pretrial procedure that allows the plaintiff's and defendant's attorneys to examine relevant materials and question all parties to the case. Compare *deposition, defense inde-*

pendent medical examination, and *interrogatories.*

discovery rule A rule stating that the time period for a statute of limitation begins when a patient discovers the injury. This may take place many years after the injury occurred and after the applicable statute of limitation has formally run out.

discretionary powers The freedom of a public officer to choose courses of action within the limits of his authority.

disease state management An effort to provide cost-effective care for a chronic condition by emphasizing treatment protocols and changes in personal habits. It's a comprehensive approach to lowering costs and improving patient outcomes that's applied on a disease-by-disease basis.

dismiss To discharge or dispose of an action, suit, or motion trial.

dispense To take a drug from the pharmacy and give or sell it to another person.

distributive justice The principle that advocates equal allocation of benefits and burdens to all members of society.

DO *abbr* Doctor of Osteopathy; see *physician.*

Doctor of Medicine (MD) See *physician.*

Doctor of Osteopathy (DO) See *physician.*

documentation The preparation or assembly of written records.

drug abuse The use of a drug for a nontherapeutic effect, especially one for which it wasn't prescribed or intended. Some of the most commonly abused substances are amphetamines, barbiturates, tranquilizers, and cocaine. Drug abuse may lead to organ damage, addiction, and disturbed patterns of behavior. Some illicit drugs, such as lysergic acid diethylamide, phencyclidine hydrochloride, and heroin, have no recognized therapeutic effect. Use of these drugs can incur criminal penalties in addition to the potential for physical, social, and psychological harm. See also *drug addiction.*

drug addiction A condition characterized by an overwhelming desire to continue taking a drug to which one has become habituated through repeated consumption because it produces a particular effect, usually an alteration of mental activity, attitude, or outlook. Addiction is usually accompanied by a compulsion to obtain the drug, a tendency to increase the dose, a psychological or physical dependence, and detrimental consequences for the individual and society. Common addictive drugs are barbiturates, cocaine, crack, and morphine and other opioids, especially heroin, which has slightly greater euphorigenic properties than other opium derivatives. See also *alcoholism* and *drug abuse.*

Drug Enforcement Administration (DEA) An agency of the federal government empowered to enforce regulations regarding the import or export of narcotic drugs and certain other substances or the traffic of these substances across state lines.

dual agency doctrine A legal doctrine stating that both the agency and the "borrowing" party may be held liable for the actions of the agent. Under this doctrine, a nurse from a nurses' registry may be held to be the agent of both the registry and the hospital. Compare *borrowed-servant doctrine.*

due process rights Personal rights based on the principle that the government may not deprive an individual of life, liberty, or property unless certain rules and procedures required by law are followed.

durable power of attorney A legal document enabling an individual to designate another person, called *an attorney-in-fact,* to act on the individual's behalf, even if the principal person becomes disabled or incapacitated. This power is revoked when the principal person dies. Compare *power of attorney.*

duty A legal obligation owed by one party to another. Duty may be established by statute or another legal process, such as by contract or oath supported by statute, or it may be voluntarily undertaken. Every person has a duty to avoid causing harm or injury to others by negligence.

duty-to-rescue laws Legislation that requires certain people — those who perform rescues as part of their jobs — to rescue people in need. These people include firefighters, police officers, and emergency medical technicians. Only a few states apply duty-to-rescue laws to nurses.

E

egoism An ethical theory that considers self-interest to be the goal of all human actions.

emancipated minor A minor who's legally considered free from the custody, care, and control of his parents before the age of majority. To be considered emancipated, a minor must meet one of three conditions: be living separate from parents or guardian and managing his or her own financial affairs for any length of time (with or without permission), be married, or be the birth mother of a child. Emancipated minors lose the right to parental support but may gain certain other rights, such as the right to consent to their own medical care and the right to enter into binding contracts.

Emergency Medical Service (EMS) A network of services coordinated to provide aid and medical assistance from primary response to definitive care, involving personnel trained in the rescue, stabilization, transportation, and advanced treatment of trauma or medical emergency patients. Linked by a communications system that operates on both a local and regional level, EMS is usually initiated by a citizen calling an emergency number. Stages include the first medical response; involvement of ambulance personnel, medium and heavy rescue equipment, and paramedic units, if necessary; and continued care in the hospital with emergency department nurses and physicians, specialists, and critical care nurses and physicians.

EMS *abbr* Emergency Medical Service

endorsement 1. The act of giving approval, support, or sanction. 2. A policy whereby the state board of nursing will accept an out-of-state license to practice nursing.

EPO *abbr* exclusive provider organization

ethical diagnosis The determination that a moral dilemma exists, followed by classification of the dilemma by type.

ethics An area of philosophy that examines values, actions, and choices to determine right and wrong. The study of standards of conduct and moral judgments.

euthanasia Deliberately bringing about the death of a person who's suffering from an incurable disease or condition, either actively (for example, by administering a lethal drug) or passively (for example, by withholding treatment).

evaluation Determining the extent to which nursing care has achieved its goals.

exclusionary rule A constitutional rule of law that states that otherwise admissible evidence may not be used in a criminal trial if it was obtained as a result of an illegal search and seizure.

exclusive provider organization (EPO) EPOs limit health care benefits to participating providers. EPOs are regulated under insurance laws.

executing a contract Carrying out all the terms of a contract.

exemplary damages See *punitive damages.*

expert witness A person who has special knowledge of a subject about which a court requests testimony. Special knowledge may be acquired by experience, education, observation, or study and isn't possessed by the average person. An expert witness gives expert testimony or expert evidence. This evidence usually serves to educate the court and the jury about the subject under consideration. Compare *witness*.

express contract A verbal or written agreement between two or more people to do or not do something.

extended-care facility An institution devoted to providing medical, nursing, or custodial care for an individual over a prolonged period of time, such as during the course of a chronic disease or during the rehabilitation phase after an acute illness. Kinds of extended-care facilities are intermediate care facilities and skilled nursing facilities. Also called *convalescent home* and *nursing home*.

extraordinary life-support measures Resuscitative efforts and therapies that maintain or prolong a patient's life, usually at great expense and suffering.

F

false imprisonment The act of confining or restraining a person without his consent for no clinical or legal reason.

family nurse practitioner (FNP) A nurse practitioner possessing skills necessary for the detection and management of acute self-limiting conditions and the management of chronic stable conditions. An FNP provides primary ambulatory care for families in collaboration with primary care physicians.

FDA *abbr* Food and Drug Administration

Federal Tort Claims Act (FTCA) A federal law that regulates how and under what circumstances the U.S. government can be sued. Sections of the law include the statute of limitations for filing suits, the procedure for filing suits, and causes of action that may be alleged against the government.

fee-for-service 1. A charge made for a professional activity such as a physical examination. 2. A system for the payment of professional services in which the practitioner is paid for the particular service rendered rather than receiving a salary for providing professional services as needed during scheduled hours of work or time on call.

fidelity Faithfulness to agreements that one has accepted.

fiduciary A person having a duty, created by his undertaking, to act primarily for the benefit of another in matters connected with that undertaking.

fiduciary relationship A legal relationship of trust and confidence that exists whenever one person relies on another, as in a physician–patient relationship.

first aid The immediate care given to an injured or ill person. It includes self-help and home care measures.

flexible staffing patterns Work schedules that vary — for example, 10- and 12-hour shifts, shorter work weeks, and special weekend schedules.

flextime, flexitime A system of staffing that allows flexible work schedules. A person who works 7 hours daily might choose to work from 7 to 3, 10 to 5, or other hours. Use of this system tends to improve morale and decrease turnover.

FNP *abbr* family nurse practitioner

Food and Drug Administration (FDA) The federal agency responsible for the enforcement of federal regulations regarding the manufacture and distribution of food, drugs, and cosmetics.

forensic medicine The application of medical science to legal problems and issues.

fraud Intentional deception resulting in damage to another, whether to his person, rights, property, or reputation. Fraud usually consists of a misrepresentation, concealment, or nondisclosure of a material fact, or at least misleading conduct, devices, or contrivance.

FTCA *abbr* Federal Claims Tort Act

G

gatekeeper Usually a physician or nurse who screens people seeking medical care and eliminates costly and sometimes needless medical intervention and referrals to specialists for diagnosis and management.

general damages Compensation for losses that are directly referable to a legal wrong but abstract in nature, such as pain and suffering and a worsening change in lifestyle. Compare *punitive damages* and *special damages*.

gerontologic nursing Nursing care that provides for the physical, intellectual, and emotional needs of elderly people. As defined by the American Nurses Association, gerontologic nursing is the care and treatment of an older adult holistically, not just as a diseased or sick person. Nurses may choose gerontologic nursing as an area of clinical specialty.

good faith Total absence of intention to seek unfair advantage or to defraud another party; an intention to fulfill one's obligations.

Good Samaritan acts State or provincial laws that provide civil immunity from negligence lawsuits for individuals who stop and render care in an emergency.

grace period In general, any period specified in a contract during which payment is permitted, without penalty, beyond the due date of the debt.

grandfather clause A provision permitting persons engaged in an activity before passage of a law affecting that activity to receive a license without having to meet the new requirements.

grievance A complaint about working conditions or contract violations brought by an employee or union against an employer.

grievance procedure Steps agreed upon by employees and their employer to settle disputes in an orderly fashion. A labor contract may outline grievance procedures.

gross negligence The flagrant and inexcusable failure to perform a legal duty in reckless disregard for the consequences.

ground rules Rules governing a particular situation that describe legitimate behavior.

group model HMO A managed-care organization that contracts with a multispecialty group of physicians to provide all physician services to its members. The physicians are employed by the group practice—not the HMO—and may treat other patients.

guardian ad litem A person appointed by the court to safeguard a minor's or other incompetent person's legal interest during certain kinds of litigation.

H

health care consumer Any actual or potential recipient of health care, such as a patient in a hospital, a client in a community mental health center, and a member of a prepaid health maintenance organization.

health care industry The complex of preventive, remedial, and therapeutic services provided by hospitals and other institutions, nurses, physicians, dentists, government agencies, voluntary agencies, noninstitutional care facilities, pharmaceutical and medical equipment manufacturers, and health insurance companies.

health care professional Any person who has completed a course of study in a field of health care — for example, a nurse. The person is usually licensed by a government agency, such as a board of nursing, and becomes registered or licensed in that health care field. In some instances, as in a certified nursing assistant, the person is certified by a state regulatory body.

Health Insurance Portability and Accountability Act (HIPAA) A federal law that requires the Department of Health and Human Services to adopt national standards for electronic health care transactions and code set compliance.

health maintenance organization (HMO) An organization that provides basic and supplemental health maintenance and treatment services to voluntary enrollees who prepay a fixed periodic fee that's set without regard to the amount or kind of services received. Individuals and families who belong to an HMO are cared for by member physicians with limited referral to outside specialists.

health provider Any individual who provides health services to health care consumers.

HIPAA *abbr* Health Insurance Portability and Accountability Act

HIS *abbr* hospital information system

HMO *abbr* health maintenance organization

homestead laws Laws protecting any property designated as a homestead (any house, outbuildings, and surrounding land owned and used as a dwelling by the head of a family) from seizure and sale by creditors.

hospice A system of family-centered care designed to assist the chronically ill person to maintain a satisfactory lifestyle through the terminal phases of dying. Hospice care is multidisciplinary and includes home visits, professional medical help

available on call, teaching and emotional support of the family, and physical care of the patient. Some hospice programs provide care in a center as well as in the home.

hospital information system (HIS) A computer-based information system with multiple access units to collect, organize, store, and make available data for problem solving and decision making.

hospital quality assurance program A program, developed by a hospital committee, that monitors the quality of the hospital's diagnostic, therapeutic, prognostic, and other health care activities.

hospital quality improvement program An approach to continuous study and improvement of the processes of providing health care services.

human investigations committee A committee established in a hospital, school, or university to review applications for research involving human subjects in order to protect the rights of the people to be studied. Also called *human subjects investigation committee.*

human subjects investigation committee See *human investigations committee.*

I

ICN *abbr* International Council of Nurses

ICU *abbr* intensive care unit

illegal abortion Induced termination of a pregnancy under circumstances or at a gestational time prohibited by law. Many illegal abortions are performed under medically unsafe conditions. Also called *criminal abortion.* Compare *legal abortion* and *therapeutic abortion.*

immunity from liability Exemption by law of a person or institution from a legally imposed penalty.

immunity from suit Exemption by law of a person or institution from being sued.

implementation 1. A deliberate action performed to achieve a goal, as in carrying out a plan in caring for a patient. 2. In the nursing process, a category of nursing behavior in which the actions necessary for accomplishing the health care plan are initiated and completed.

implied conditions Elements of a contract that aren't stated but are assumed to be part of the contract.

implied contract A contract manifested by conduct rather than words. An implied contract is based on an obligation created by law for reasons of justice and fairness. Also called *quasicontract*.

implied-in-law contract Obligations imposed upon a person by the law without his agreement and against his will or design because the circumstances between the parties render it just that the one should have a right and the other a corresponding liability similar to those that would arise from a contract between them.

impossibility defense A contract defense that says circumstances rendered the violation of a contract (such as not showing up for work) impossible to avoid. Compare *contract defense*.

incident An event that's inconsistent with ordinary routine, regardless of whether injury occurs.

incident report A formal, written report that informs a health care facility's administration (and its insurance company) about an incident and serves as a contemporary, factual statement of the incident in the event of a lawsuit.

incompetence The inability or lack of legal qualification or fitness to discharge the required duty. Compare *adjudicated incompetent* and *mental incompetence*.

indemnification Repayment or compensation for a loss. A person who has compensated another for injury, loss, or damage caused by a third party may file a suit seeking indemnification from the third party.

independent contractor A self-employed person who renders services to clients and independently determines how the work will be done.

independent practice association (IPA) model HMO A managed-care organization that contracts with an association of physicians to provide physician services to its members. The physicians maintain their independent practices.

independent provider organization (IPO) A hybrid form of managed-care organization with characteristics of both IPAs and medical associations. They're commonly organized by community physicians to provide a mechanism for evaluating and negotiating participation in HMOs.

individual contract A contract negotiated with an employer by an individual employee.

informed consent Permission obtained from a patient to perform a specific test or procedure after the patient has been fully informed about the test or procedure.

injunction A court order restraining a person from committing a specific act or requiring the individual to do something.

in loco parentis Latin phrase meaning "in the place of the parent." The assumption by a person or institution of the parental obligations of caring for a child without adoption.

inpatient 1. A patient who has been admitted to a hospital or other health care facility for at least an overnight stay. 2. Pertaining to the treatment of such a patient or to a health care facility to which a patient may be admitted for 24-hour care.

insurance adjuster One who determines the amount of an insurance claim and then makes an agreement with the insured as to a settlement.

intensive care Constant, complex, detailed health care as provided in various acute, life-threatening conditions. Special training is necessary to provide intensive care. Also called *critical care.*

intensive care unit (ICU) A hospital unit in which patients requiring close monitoring and intensive care are housed for as long as needed. An ICU contains highly technical and sophisticated monitoring devices and equipment, and the staff in the unit is educated to give critical care, as patients need it. See also *critical care unit.*

intermediate care A level of medical care for certain chronically ill or disabled individuals at which room and board are provided but skilled nursing care isn't.

International Council of Nurses (ICN) The oldest international health organization, the ICN is a federation of nurses' associations from 93 nations and was one of the first health organizations to develop strict policies against discrimination based on nationality, race, creed, color, politics, sex, or social status. The objectives of the ICN include promoting national associations of nurses, improving standards of nursing and the competence of nurses, improving the status of nurses within their countries, and establishing an authoritative international voice for nurses.

International Red Cross Society An international philanthropic organization, based in Geneva, concerned primarily with the humane treatment and welfare of the victims of war and calamity and with the neutrality of hospitals and medical personnel in times of war. See also *American Red Cross.*

interrogatories A series of written questions submitted to a witness or other person having information of interest to the court. The answers are transcribed and are sworn to under oath. Compare *deposition* and *discovery device.*

intervention 1. Any act performed to prevent harm from occurring to a patient or to improve the mental, emotional, or physical function of a patient. A physiologic process may be monitored or enhanced, or a pathologic process may be arrested or controlled. 2. The fourth step of the nursing process. This step includes nursing actions taken to meet patient needs as determined by nursing assessment and diagnosis.

invalid contract Any contract concerning illegal or impossible actions; no legal obligation exists.

JK

JCAHO *abbr* Joint Commission on Accreditation of Healthcare Organizations

job description A written statement describing responsibilities of a specific job and the qualifications an applicant for that job should have.

Joint Commission on Accreditation of Healthcare Organizations (JCAHO) A private, nongovernmental agency that establishes guidelines for the operation of hospitals and other health care facilities, conducts accreditation programs and surveys, and encourages the attainment of high standards of institutional medical care. Members include representatives from the American Medical Association, American College of Physicians, and American College of Surgeons.

joint practice 1. The (usually private) practice of a physician and a nurse practitioner who work as a team, sharing responsibility for a group of patients. 2. In inpatient nursing, the practice of making joint decisions about patient care by committees of physicians and nurses working in a division.

joint statement A statement, opinion, or recommendation issued jointly by two or more organizations or committees.

judicial bypass statutes Statutes that allow a minor to go before a judge to avoid a strict requirement of parental notification or consent to obtain an abortion.

just cause A lawful, rightful, proper reason to act. A defendant establishes a cause for action in his favor.

L

law 1. In a field of study: a rule, standard, or principle that states a fact or a relationship between factors, such as Dalton's law regarding partial pressures of gas and Koch's law regarding the specificity of a pathogen. 2. *a.* A rule, principle, or regulation established and promulgated by a government to protect or to restrict the people affected. *b.* The field of study concerned with such laws. *c.* The collected body of the laws of a people derived from custom or from legislation.

lay jury A jury made up of people who aren't from a particular profession. For example, a lay jury in a medical malpractice trial wouldn't include physicians, nurses, or other members of the medical profession.

lay-midwife See *midwife.*

legal abortion Induced termination of pregnancy by a physician before the fetus has developed sufficiently to live outside the uterus. The procedure is performed under medically safe conditions prescribed by law. Compare *illegal abortion* and *therapeutic abortion.*

legal death See *death.*

legal guardian An officer or agent of the court who's appointed to protect the interests of minors or incompetent persons and provide for their welfare, education, and support.

liability Legal responsibility for failure to act or action that fails to meet standards of care that causes another person harm.

liable Legally bound or obligated to make good any loss or damage; responsible.

liaison nurse A nurse who acts as an agent between a patient, the hospital, and the patient's family and who speaks for the entire health care team.

libel A tort consisting of a false, malicious, or unprivileged written publication aiming to defame a living person or to damage the memory of a deceased person. Compare *slander.*

licensed practical nurse (LPN) A person trained in basic nursing techniques and direct patient care who practices under the supervision of a registered nurse or other health care provider. An LPN must complete a course of training that usually lasts 1 to 2 years, pass the NCLEX-PN examination, and meet the requirements set forth by the board of nursing for licensure in her state. In Canada, an LPN is called a *nursing assistant.* In the United States, an LPN is also called a *licensed vocational nurse.*

licensed vocational nurse (LVN) See *licensed practical nurse.*

licensure Permission granted by a competent authority (usually a government agency) to an organization or person to engage in a practice or activity that would otherwise be illegal. Kinds of licensure include the issuing of licenses for general hospitals or nursing homes, for health care professionals such as physicians, and for the production or distribution of biological products. Licensure is usually granted on the basis of education and examination rather than performance. It's usually permanent but a periodic fee, demonstration of competence, or continuing education may be required. Licensure may be revoked by the granting agency for incompetence, criminal acts, or other reasons stipulated in the rules governing the specific area of licensure.

lie detector An electronic device or instrument used to detect lying or anxiety about specific questions. A commonly used lie detector is the polygraph recorder, which senses and records pulse, respiratory rate, blood pressure, and perspiration. Some experts hold that certain patterns indicate the presence of anxiety, guilt, or fear, emotions that are likely to occur when the subject is lying.

litigant A party to a lawsuit. See also *defendant* and *plaintiff.*

litigate To carry on a suit or to contest a suit.

living will A witnessed document indicating a patient's desire to be allowed to die a natural death, rather than be kept alive by heroic, life-sustaining measures. The will applies to decisions that will be made after a terminally ill patient is incompetent and has no reasonable possibility of recovery. Compare *testamentary will.*

living will laws Laws that help to guarantee that a patient's documented wishes regarding terminal illness procedures will be carried out. Living will laws may set forth testator and witness requirements for executing a living will and medical requirements for terminating treatment. Living will laws may also address other issues, such as authorization of a proxy for health care decisions, immunity from liability for following a living will's directives, and the withholding or withdrawal of life-sustaining treatment. Also called *natural death laws* and *right-to-die.*

locality rule Allowance made, when considering evidence in a trial, for the type of community in which the defendant practices his profession and the standards of that community.

LPN *abbr* licensed practical nurse

LVN *abbr* licensed vocational nurse; see *licensed practical nurse.*

M

malfeasance Performance of an unlawful, wrongful act. Compare misfeasance and nonfeasance.

malpractice A professional person's wrongful conduct, improper discharge of professional duties, or failure to meet standards of care that results in harm to another person.

managed-care organization (MCO) A system that integrates the financing and delivery of appropriate health care services to covered individuals by means of contracts with selected providers.

mandatory bargaining issues Issues, such as wages and working conditions, that an employer must address during collective bargaining.

master's degree program in nursing A post-baccalaureate program in a school of nursing based in a university setting that grants the degree Master of Science in Nursing (MSN) to successful candidates. Nurses with this degree usually work in leadership roles in clinical nursing, as consultants in various settings, and in faculty positions in certain schools of nursing. Some programs also prepare the nurse to function as a nurse practitioner in a specific specialty.

MCO *abbr* managed-care organization

MD *abbr* Doctor of Medicine; see *physician.*

Medicaid A program that subsidizes medical care for low-income women and children, some men, and people with certain disabilities. Although passed by Congress in 1965, Medicaid is a state-level program, with each state defining income levels and other standards of eligibility and the federal government subsidizing a portion of the expenses.

medical directive A comprehensive advance care document that covers preferred treatment goals and specific scenarios of patient incompetence. It also includes the option to designate a proxy decision maker or power of attorney for the event of incompetence, the option to record a personal statement, and a place to designate wishes for organ donation. Also called *physician's directive*.

medical record A written, legal document that includes every aspect of the patient's care. A record of a person's illnesses and treatment.

medical release form The form an institution asks a patient to sign when he refuses a medical treatment. The form protects both the institution and the health care professional from liability if the patient's condition worsens because of his refusal.

Medicare Federally funded national health insurance authorized by the Social Security Act for persons age 65 and older.

medicolegal Of or pertaining to both medicine and law. Medicolegal considerations are a significant part of the process of making many patient care decisions and in setting policies about the treatment of mentally incompetent people and minors, the performance of sterilization or therapeutic abortion, and the care of terminally ill patients. Medicolegal considerations, decisions, definitions, and policies provide the framework for informed consent, professional liability, and many other aspects of health care practice.

mental competence The ability to understand information and act reasonably. A mentally competent person is capable of understanding explanations and is able to comprehend the results of his decisions.

mental incompetence The inability to understand the nature and effect of the action a person is engaged in. A mentally incompetent person is incapable of understanding explana-

tions and is unable to comprehend the results of his decisions. Compare *adjudicated incompetent* and *incompetence*.

mental status examination A diagnostic procedure for determining the mental status of a person. The trained interviewer poses certain questions in a carefully standardized manner and evaluates the verbal responses and behavioral reactions.

midwife 1. In traditional use: a person who assists women in childbirth. 2. According to the International Confederation of Midwives, the World Health Organization, and the Federation of International Gynecologists and Obstetricians: "a person who, having been regularly admitted to a midwifery educational program fully recognized in the country in which it's located, has successfully completed the prescribed course of studies in midwifery and has acquired the requisite qualifications to be registered or legally licensed to practice midwifery." Among the responsibilities of the midwife are supervision of pregnancy, labor, delivery, and puerperium. The midwife conducts the delivery independently, cares for the neonate, procures medical assistance when necessary, executes emergency measures as required, and may practice in a hospital, clinic, maternity home, or in a woman's home. Also called *lay-midwife, nurse-midwife*, and *certified nurse-midwife (CNM)*.

minor A person not of legal age; below the age of majority. Minors may not be able to consent to their own medical treatment unless they are legally emancipated. However, in many jurisdictions, parental consent is no longer necessary for certain types of medical and psychiatric treatment.

misdemeanor An offense that's considered less serious than a felony and carries with it a lesser penalty, usually a fine or imprisonment for less than 1 year.

misfeasance An improper performance of a lawful act, especially in a way that might cause damage or injury. Compare *malfeasance* and *nonfeasance.*

misrepresentation The statutory crime of giving false or misleading information, usually with the intent to deceive or be unfair.

moral dilemma An ethical problem caused by conflicts of rights, responsibilities, and values.

moral relativism An ethical theory that holds there are no ethical absolutes and whatever an individual feels is right for him at that moment is indeed right.

moral turpitude Vileness, intentional violence, deceit, fraud, or dishonesty of a high degree. A crime of moral turpitude demonstrates depravity in the private and social duties a person owes to others, contrary to what's accepted and customary. The act is considered intentionally evil.

MSN abbr Master of Science in Nursing; see *master's degree program in nursing.*

N

National Council of Licensure Examination (NCLEX) An examination, administered separately by licensing authorities of each state, that measures competency to practice as a licensed RN or LPN. The test is commonly referred to as the "state boards." All 50 states (and some Canadian jurisdictions) require candidates for RN licensure to take the NCLEX-RN test. Candidates for LPN licensure must take the NCLEX-PN test. The NCLEX-RN consists of about 375 multiple-choice and alternative-format items involving multiple-response—multiple-choice, fill-in-the-blank, and point-and-click diagrams, which appear as case situations. Most test questions require the ex-

aminee to apply nursing knowledge to patient-care situations.

National League for Nursing (NLN) An organization concerned with the improvement of nursing education, nursing service, and the delivery of health care in the United States. Its members include nurses and other health care professionals, nursing educational institutions, agencies, departments of nursing in hospitals and other health care facilities, home and community health services, and community members interested in health. Among its many activities are accreditation of nursing programs at all levels, provision of preadmission and achievement tests for nursing students, and compilation of statistical data on nursing manpower and on trends in health care delivery.

natural death laws See *living will laws.*

negligence Failure to act as an ordinary prudent person would under similar circumstances. Conduct that falls below the standard established by law for the protection of others under the same circumstances.

negligent nondisclosure The failure to completely inform a patient about his treatment.

negotiation A meeting at which an employer and employees confer, discuss, and bargain to reach an agreement.

network model HMO A managed-care organization that contracts with more than one group practice to provide physician services to its members.

next of kin One or more persons in the nearest degree of relationship to another person.

NLN abbr National League for Nursing

no-code order An order, written in the patient record and signed by a physician, instructing staff not to attempt to resuscitate a patient if he suffers cardiac or respiratory failure.

nonfeasance Failure to perform a task, duty, or undertaking that one has agreed to perform or that one has a legal duty to perform. Compare *malfeasance* and *misfeasance.*

nonmaleficence An ethical principle based on the obligation to do no harm.

NP *abbr* nurse practitioner

nurse 1. A person educated and licensed in the practice of nursing. The nurse acts to promote, maintain, or restore the health of the patient. The American Nurses Association defines nursing as the "diagnosis and treatment of human responses to actual and potential health problems." The nurse may be a generalist or a specialist and, as a professional, is ethically and legally accountable for the nursing activities performed and for the actions of others to whom the nurse has delegated responsibility. 2. To provide nursing care. 3. To breastfeed an infant. See also *nursing* and *registered nurse.*

nurse anesthetist A registered nurse qualified by advanced training in an accredited program in the specialty of nurse anesthetist to manage the anesthetic care of the patient in certain surgical situations.

nurse clinician A nurse who's prepared to identify and diagnose patient problems by using the expanded knowledge and skills gained by advanced study in a specific area of nursing practice. The specialist may function independently within standing orders or protocols and collaborates with associates to implement care plan that's focused on the patient.

nurse-midwife See *midwife.*

nurse practice act A law enacted by a state's legislature outlining the legal scope of nursing practice within that state.

nurse practitioner (NP) A nurse who, by advanced training and clinical experience in a branch of nursing (as in a master's degree program in nursing or a certification program), has ac-

quired expert knowledge in a specialized branch of practice.

nurses' notes A means of documenting the care the nurse provides and the patient's response to that care; a legal document that can be submitted as admissible evidence in a court of law.

nurses' registry An employment agency or listing service for nurses who wish to work in a specific area of nursing, usually for a short period of time or on a *per diem* basis.

nursing 1. The professional practice of a nurse. 2. The process of acting as a nurse and providing care that encourages and promotes the health of the person being served. 3. According to the American Nurses Association, the "diagnosis and treatment of human responses to actual and potential health problems." 4. Breastfeeding an infant. See also *nurse* and *registered nurse.*

nursing administrator A nurse who's responsible for overseeing the efficient management of nursing services.

nursing assessment The first step of the nursing process, which involves the systematic collection of information about the patient from multiple sources, including the history, physical examination, and laboratory findings. This information is analyzed and used by the nurse to formulate inferences or impressions about the patient's needs or problems.

nursing audit A thorough investigation designed to identify, examine, or verify the performance of certain specified aspects of nursing care using established criteria. A concurrent nursing audit is performed during ongoing nursing care. A retrospective nursing audit is performed after discharge from the care facility, using the patient's record. In many instances, a nursing audit and a medical audit are performed collaboratively, resulting in a joint audit.

nursing care plan A plan devised by a nurse and based on a nursing assessment and a nursing diagnosis. It has four essential components: the identification of the nursing care problems and a statement of the nursing approach to solve those problems; the statement of the expected benefit to the patient; the statement of the specific actions taken by the nurse that reflect the nursing approach and the achievement of the goals specified; and the evaluation of the patient's response to nursing care and the readjustment of that care as required. See also *nursing assessment* and *nursing diagnosis.*

nursing diagnosis Descriptive interpretations of collected and categorized information indicating the problems or needs of a patient that nursing care can affect. According to the North American Nursing Diagnosis Association, "a clinical judgment about individual, community, or family responses to actual or potential health problems or to life processes. Nursing diagnoses provide the basis of selection of nursing interventions for which the nurse is accountable."

nursing home See *extended-care facility.*

nursing process An organizational framework for nursing practice, encompassing all the major steps a nurse takes when caring for a patient. These steps are assessment, diagnosis, planning, implementation, and evaluation.

nursing skills The cognitive, affective, and psychomotor abilities a nurse uses in delivering nursing care.

nursing specialty A nurse's particular professional field of practice, such as surgical, pediatric, obstetric, and psychiatric nursing. Compare *subspecialty.*

O

obligationism An ethical theory that attempts to resolve ethical dilemmas by balancing distributive justice with beneficence.

occurrence policy A professional liability insurance policy that protects against an error of omission occurring during a policy period, regardless of when the claim is made.

ombudsman A person who investigates complaints, reports findings, and helps to achieve equitable settlements.

open shop A place of employment where employees may choose whether to join a union.

oral contract Any contract that isn't in writing or isn't signed by the parties involved.

ordinary negligence The inadvertent omission of the care that a reasonably prudent nurse would ordinarily provide under similar circumstances.

original position The underlying principle of the social contract theory, which states that people in a society determine the principles of justice by which all members are bound to live.

ostensible agent doctrine See *borrowed-servant doctrine.*

outcomes management A process of systematically tracking a patient's clinical treatment and responses. The system encourages caregivers to follow a set of guidelines (practice guidelines or clinical pathways) that research has shown to be the "one best way" to treat a medical condition.

P

PA *abbr* Parents Anonymous; physician's assistant

parens patriae A doctrine that appoints the state as the legal guardian of a child or incompetent adult when a person hasn't been appointed as guardian.

Parents Anonymous (PA) An international organization, founded in 1970, dedicated to the prevention and treatment of child abuse.

patient 1. A health care recipient who's ill or hospitalized. 2. A client in a health care service.

patient advocate A person (typically a nurse) who seeks to protect a patient's rights from infringement by institutional policies.

patient antidumping laws Amendments to the Social Security Act intended to prevent hospitals from turning away patients who are uninsured or unable to pay. They require that hospitals participating in Medicare provide medical screening and stabilizing treatment for any patient who has an emergency condition or is in labor and provide guidelines and require documentation for transfers to other facilities or for hospital discharge.

patient classification systems Ways of grouping patients so that the size of the staff needed to care for them can be estimated accurately.

patient overload The situation that occurs when the number of patients exceeds an institution's medical, nursing, and support staff resources to care for them properly. Also called *staffing shortage.*

patient record A collection of documents that provides a record of each time a person visited or sought treatment and received care or a referral for care from a health care facility. This confidential record is usually held by the facility and the information in it is released only to the person or with the person's written permission, except in certain situations, such as when release is required by law. It contains the initial assessment, health history, laboratory reports, and notes by nurses, physicians, and consultants as well as order sheets, medication sheets, admission records, discharge summaries, and other pertinent data. A problem-oriented medical record also contains a master problem list. The patient record is usually a collection of papers held in a folder but, increasingly, hospitals are computerizing the records after every discharge, making the past record available on visual display terminals. Also called *patient's medical chart* (informal).

patient's bill of rights Documents that define a person's rights while receiving health care. Bills of rights for patients are designed to protect such basic rights as human dignity, privacy, confidentiality, informed consent, and refusal of treatment. The American Hospital Association, the National League for Nursing, the American Civil Liberties Union, and other organizations and health care institutions have prepared patient's bills of rights. Concepts expressed in these documents may be incorporated into law. Although bills of rights issued by health care institutions and professional organizations don't have the force of law, nurses should regard them as professionally binding.

PC *abbr* professional corporation

pediatric nurse practitioner (PNP) A nurse practitioner who, by advanced study and clinical practice, has gained expert knowledge in the nursing care of infants and children.

peremptory challenge A right given to attorneys at trial to dismiss a prospective juror for no particular reason; the number of times an attorney can invoke this right is usually limited.

persistent vegetative state A state of severe mental impairment in which only involuntary bodily functions are sustained.

physician 1. A health professional who has earned a degree of Doctor of Medicine (MD) after completion of an approved course of study at an approved medical school and satisfactory completion of the National Board Examinations. 2. A health professional who has earned a degree of Doctor of Osteopathy (DO) by satisfactorily completing a course of education in an approved college of osteopathy.

physician of record See *attending physician*.

physician assistant (PA) A person who's trained in certain aspects of the practice of medicine and provides assistance to a physician. A physician's assistant is trained by physicians and practices under the direction and supervision and within the legal license of a physician. Training programs vary in length from a few months to 2 years. Health care experience or academic preparation may be a prerequisite for admission to some programs. Most physician's assistants are prepared for the practice of primary care but some practice subspecialties, including surgical assisting, dialysis, or radiology. National certification is available to qualified graduates of approved training programs. The national organization is the American Association of Physician's Assistants (AAPA). Also called *physician's associate*.

physician's associate See *physician assistant*.

physician's directive See *medical directive*.

plaintiff A person who files a civil lawsuit initiating a legal action. In criminal actions, the prosecution is the plaintiff, acting on behalf of the people in the jurisdiction. See also *litigant*.

PNP abbr pediatric nurse practitioner

policy A definite course or method of action selected from among alternatives and in the light of given conditions to guide, and usually determine, present and future decisions. Compare *rule*.

policy defense Rationale for denying coverage given by professional liability insurance carriers when a client submits a claim. Reasons for denial may include failure to pay a premium on time or failure to renew the policy.

power of attorney A legal document enabling an individual to designate another person, called an *attorney-in-fact*, to act on the individual's behalf as long as the individual doesn't become disabled or incapacitated. Power of attorney continues to operate only with the continued consent of the person who granted it. If the grantor of the power should become incompetent, the power of attorney is automatically revoked. It's also revoked when the grantor dies. Compare *durable power of attorney*.

PPO abbr preferred provider organization

practicing medicine without a license Practicing activities defined under state or provincial law in the Medical Practice Act without medical supervision, direction, or control.

practicing pharmacy without a license Practicing activities defined under state or provincial law in the Pharmacy Practice Act without pharmacist supervision, direction, or control. These laws give pharmacists the sole legal authority to prepare, compound, preserve, and dispense drugs.

practitioner A person qualified to practice in a special professional field such as a nurse practitioner.

preferred provider organization (PPO) Entity through which an employer health benefit plan and insurance carrier purchase health care service for members from a select group of providers.

prescription drug Any drug restricted from regular commercial purchase and sale. Compare *controlled substance*.

presumed consent A legal principle based on the belief that a rational and prudent person would consent in the same situation, if able to. Applies primarily to emergency care of unconscious patients but may be expanded to cadaver organ donors.

privacy One's private life or personal affairs. The right to privacy refers to the right to be left alone and to be free from unwanted publicity.

privileged communication A conversation in which the speaker intends the information given to remain private between himself and the listener.

privilege doctrine A doctrine that protects the privacy of persons within a fiduciary relationship, such as a husband and wife, a physician and patient, or a nurse and patient. During legal proceedings, a court can't force either party to reveal communications between them unless the party who would benefit from the protection agrees.

probate 1. The act of proving that a purported will was signed and executed in accordance with the law and of determining its validity. 2. The combined result of all procedures necessary to establish the validity of a will.

probation period A period of time during which an individual is observed and evaluated to ascertain fitness for a particular job or duty.

problem-oriented medical record A record-keeping system in which all members of the health care team combine their information in a special format that goes by the acronym SOAP. Each note combines Subjective data, Objective data, Assessment data, and Plans. Also, the patient's active and inactive problems are documented on a master problem list. See also *SOAP.*

pro-choice The philosophy that a woman has the right to choose to either continue or terminate her pregnancy.

professional corporation (PC) A corporation formed according to the law of a particular state for the purpose of delivering a professional service.

professional liability A legal concept describing the obligation of a professional person to pay a patient or client for damages caused by the professional's act of omission, commission, or negligence, after a court determines that the professional was negligent. Professional liability better describes the responsibility of all professionals to their clients than does the concept of malpractice, but the idea of professional liability is central to malpractice.

professional liability insurance A type of liability insurance that protects professional persons against malpractice claims.

professional organization An organization created to deal with issues of concern to its members, who share a professional status.

professional RN Defined by the American Nurses Association as a registered nurse who has graduated from a baccalaureate or higher degree program. Professional RNs develop policies, procedures, and protocols and set standards for practice. Compare *technical RN.*

pro-life The philosophy that an unborn fetus has the right to develop to term and to be born.

proprietary hospital A hospital operated as a profit-making organization. Many are owned and operated by physicians primarily for their own patients, but they also accept patients from other physicians. Others are owned by investor groups or large corporations.

protocol A code providing and prescribing strict adherence to guidelines for and authorization of particular practice activities.

Provincial Territorial Nurses Association (PTNA) An association of nurses organized at the provincial or territorial level. The Canadian Nurses Association is a federation of the 11 PTNAs.

proviso A condition or stipulation. Its general function is to except something from the basic provision, to qualify or restrain its general scope, or to prevent misinterpretation.

proximate cause A legal concept of cause and effect, which says a sequence of natural and continuous events produces an injury that wouldn't have otherwise occurred.

proxy The recipient of a grant of authority to act or speak for another.

psychiatric nurse practitioner A nurse practitioner who, by advanced study and clinical practice, has gained expert knowledge in the care and prevention of mental disorders.

PTNA *abbr* Provincial Territorial Nurses Association

punitive damages Compensation in excess of actual damages that are a form of punishment to the wrongdoer and reparation to the injured. These damages are awarded only in rare instances of malicious and willful misconduct. Also called *exemplary damages*. Compare *general damages* and *special damages*.

Q

qualified privilege A conditional right or immunity granted to the defendant because of the circumstances of a legal case.

quality of life A legal and ethical standard that's determined by relative suffering or pain, not by the degree of disability.

R

RCP *abbr* Royal College of Physicians

RCPSC *abbr* Royal College of Physicians and Surgeons of Canada

RCS *abbr* Royal College of Surgeons

reasonably prudent nurse The standard a court uses to judge a nurse being sued for negligence. The court considers whether another nurse would have acted similarly to the defendant under similar circumstances.

rebuttable presumption A presumption that may be overcome or disputed by contrary evidence.

Red Cross See *American Red Cross* and *International Red Cross Society*.

redefinition A rewriting of the fundamental provision of a nurse practice act. This changes the basic premise

of the entire act without amending or repealing it.

registered nurse (RN) 1. In the United States: A professional nurse who has completed a course of study at an approved school of nursing, passed the NCLEX-RN, and met the requirements for licensure set forth by the board of nursing in her state. A registered nurse may use the initials RN following her signature. RNs are licensed to practice by individual states. 2. In Canada: A professional nurse who has completed a course of study at an approved school of nursing and who has taken and passed an examination administered by the Canadian Nurses Association Testing Service. See also *nurse* and *nursing*.

registered nursing assistant In Canada, a person trained in basic nursing techniques and direct patient care who practices under the supervision of a registered nurse.

registry 1. An office or agency that maintains lists of nurses and records pertaining to nurses seeking employment. 2. In epidemiology: a listing service for incidence data pertaining to the occurrence of specific diseases or disorders, as in a tumor registry.

remand To send back. An appellate court may send a case back to the lower court that considered the case, ordering that further action be taken there.

res ipsa loquitur Latin phrase meaning "the thing speaks for itself." A legal doctrine that applies when the defendant was solely and exclusively in control at the time the plaintiff's injury occurred, so that the injury wouldn't have occurred if the defendant had exercised due care. In addition, the injured party couldn't have contributed to his own injury. When a court applies this doctrine to a case, the defendant bears the burden of proving that he wasn't negligent.

respondeat superior Latin phrase meaning "let the master answer." A legal doctrine that makes an employer indirectly liable for the consequences of his employee's wrongful conduct while the employee is acting within the scope of his employment.

resuscitative life-support measures Actions taken to reverse an immediate, life-threatening situation (for example, cardiopulmonary resuscitation).

review committee A group of individuals delegated to inspect and report on the quality of health care in a given institution.

right-of-conscience laws Based on freedom of thought or of religion, these laws allow a health care provider to refuse to care for a patient when an objection to the care or lack of care exists.

right-to-access laws Laws that grant a patient the right to see his medical records.

right-to-die law Law that upholds a patient's right to choose death by refusing extraordinary treatment. Also called *living will law* and *natural death law*.

right to notice 1. A due process right requiring that the accused receive timely notification of both the pending charges and the hearing date. 2. An employee's right to receive sufficient notification or warning before termination. This allows the employee time to protest or appeal the termination and to seek employment elsewhere.

risk management The identification, analysis, evaluation, and elimination or reduction—to the extent possible—of risks to an organization's patients, visitors, or employees. Risk management programs are involved with both loss prevention and loss control and handle all incidents, claims, and other insurance- and litigation-related tasks.

risk manager A person who identifies, analyzes, evaluates, and eliminates or reduces an organization's potential accidental losses. This job entails systematically and continually answering three questions: "What can go wrong in this situation?", "What are the options?", and "Which option minimizes adverse effects for the organization?" Almost always, a risk manager deals with situations in which the only possible outcome is a loss or no change in the status quo. Examples of the responsibilities of a risk manager include purchasing and managing insurance policies, inviting engineering professionals to examine the structural integrity of a building, and examining policies and procedures to eliminate unnecessary risks.

RN *abbr* registered nurse

Royal College of Physicians (RCP) A professional organization of physicians in the United Kingdom.

Royal College of Physicians and Surgeons of Canada (RCPSC) A national Canadian organization that recognizes and confers membership on certain qualified physicians and surgeons.

Royal College of Surgeons (RCS) A professional organization of surgeons in the United Kingdom.

rule A guide for conduct that describes the actions that should or shouldn't be taken in specific situations. Compare *policy*.

S

school nurse practitioner (SNP) A registered nurse qualified by postgraduate study to act as a nurse practitioner in a school.

scope of practice In nursing, the professional nursing activities defined under state or province law in each state's (or Canadian province's) nurse practice act.

service of process The delivery of a writ, summons, or complaint to a defendant. The original document is shown; a copy is served. Service of process gives reasonable notice to allow the person to appear, testify, and be heard in court. See also *summons*.

settlement An agreement made between parties to a suit before a judgment is rendered by a court.

signature code A code of letters or numbers that are entered into a computer to identify the user.

skilled nursing facility (SNF) An institution or part of an institution that meets criteria for accreditation established by the sections of the Social Security Act that determine the basis for Medicaid and Medicare reimbursement for skilled nursing care, including rehabilitation and various medical and nursing procedures.

slander Spoken words that may damage another person's reputation. Compare *libel*.

slippery slope principle An ethical principle based on the belief that, when an ethical or legal barrier has been lowered, desensitization to the ethical or legal principle occurs.

slow-code order An illegal verbal or implicit order from a physician instructing staff to refrain from resuscitating a patient until cardiopulmonary resuscitation is unlikely to be successful.

SNF *abbr* skilled nursing facility

SNP *abbr* school nurse practitioner

SOAP An acronym for the format used in problem-oriented record keeping; it represents Subjective data, Objective data, Assessment data, and Plans. See also *problem-oriented medical record*.

socialized medicine A system for the delivery of health care in which the government bears the expense of care.

source-oriented records A record-keeping system in which each professional group within the health care team keeps separate information on the patient.

sovereign immunity doctrine A privilege granted to the elected government and its appointed agents — government employees — giving them immunity from lawsuits.

special damages Compensation for indirect loss or injury, such as present and future medical expenses, past and future loss of earnings, and decreased earning capacity. Also called *consequential damages*. Compare *general damages* and *punitive damages*.

specialty standard The standard of care that applies to a given nursing specialty.

staff 1. The people who work toward a common goal and are employed or supervised by someone of higher rank such as the nurses in a hospital. 2. A designation by which a staff nurse is distinguished from a head nurse or other nurse. 3. In nursing education: the nonprofessional employees of the institution, such as librarians, technicians, secretaries, and clerks. 4. In nursing service administration: the units of the organization that provide service to the "line," or administratively defined hierarchy, such as the personnel office is "staff" to the director of nursing and the nursing service administration.

staffing pattern In institution or nursing administration: the number and kinds of staff assigned to the particular units and departments of an institution. Staffing patterns vary with the unit, department, and shift.

staffing shortage See *patient overload*.

staff model HMO A managed-care organization in which the physicians who serve the HMO are its salaried employees.

standard 1. A criterion that serves as a basis for comparison for evaluating similar phenomena or substances, such as a standard for the practice of a profession. 2. A pharmaceutical preparation or a chemical substance of known quantity, ingredients, and strength that's used to determine the

constituents or the strength of another preparation. 3. Of known value, strength, quality, or ingredients.

standard death certificate A form for a death certificate commonly used throughout the United States. It's the preferred form of the U.S. Census Bureau.

standards of care Criteria that serve as a basis of comparison when evaluating the quality of nursing practice. In a malpractice lawsuit, a measure by which the defendant's alleged wrongful conduct is compared — acts performed or omitted that an ordinary, reasonably prudent nurse, in the defendant's position, would have done or not done.

standing orders A written document containing rules, policies, procedures, regulations, and orders for the conduct of patient care in various stipulated clinical situations.

state of emergency A widespread need for immediate action to counter a threat to the community.

statute of limitation Law that sets forth the length of time within which a person may file a specific type of lawsuit.

statutory law A law passed by a federal or state legislature.

statutory rape Sexual intercourse with a person below the age of consent. (Age of consent varies from state to state; usually age 18.)

steward A union representative.

subacute care Designed for patients who don't need acute-care hospitalization but instead more hours of nursing care per day than the typical nursing home resident.

subpoena A writ issued under authority of a court to compel the appearance of a witness at a judicial proceeding; disobedience may be punishable as contempt of court.

subspecialty A subordinate field of specialization. For example, dialysis nursing might be considered a sub-specialty of renal care. Compare *nursing specialty*.

substantive laws Laws that define and regulate a person's rights.

substitute consent Permission obtained from a parent or legal guardian of a patient who's a minor or who has been declared incompetent by the court.

substitute judgment A legal term indicating the court's substitution of its own judgment for that of a person the court considers unable to make an informed decision such as an incompetent adult.

sudden emergency exception Defense used by hospitals in liability cases involving understaffing when staffing shortages couldn't have been anticipated, as opposed to chronic understaffing.

summary judgment A judgment requested by any party to a civil action to end the action when it's believed that there's no genuine issue or material fact in dispute.

summons A document issued by a clerk of the court upon the filing of a complaint. A sheriff, marshal, or other appointed person serves the summons, notifying a person that an action has been begun against him. See also *service of process*.

support group People in whom a person confides and draws on for support, either as individuals or in a group setting.

T

technical RN Defined by the American Nurses Association as a nurse who has graduated from an associate degree program. Technical RNs follow policies, procedures, and protocols developed by professional RNs. Compare *professional RN*.

teleology An ethical theory that determines right or good based on an action's consequences.

temporary practice permit Permission granted by a state board of nursing to an out-of-state nurse enabling her to legally practice nursing until she can obtain a license from that state.

terminate In contract law, to fulfill all contractual obligations or to absolve oneself of the obligation to fulfill them.

termination The procedure an employer follows to fire an employee.

testamentary Any document, such as a will, that doesn't take effect until after the death of the person who wrote it.

testamentary will A will whose provisions take effect after death. Compare *living will*.

testator One who makes and executes a testament or will.

therapeutic abortion Induced termination of pregnancy to preserve the health, safety, or life of the woman. Compare *illegal abortion* and *legal abortion*.

therapeutic privilege A legal doctrine that permits a physician to withhold information from the patient if he can prove that disclosing it would adversely affect the patient's health.

third-party reimbursement Reimbursement for services rendered to a person in which an entity other than the giver or receiver of the service is responsible for the payment. Insurance plans commonly pay third-party reimbursement for the cost of a subscriber's health care.

time charting A method of charting in which the care administered to a patient at a particular time is detailed at regular time intervals — for example, every half-hour.

tort A civil wrong outside of a contractual relationship.

traditional staffing patterns Work schedules that follow 8-hour shifts, 7 days per week, including evening and night shifts.

trial de novo A proceeding in which both issues of law and issues of fact are reconsidered as if the original trial had never taken place. New testimony may be introduced, or the matter may be determined a second time on the basis of the evidence already produced.

U

unfair labor practices Actions taken by an employer that are prohibited by state and federal labor laws. This term commonly refers to tactics used by an employer to discourage employees from participating in union activities. For example, under the National Labor Relations Act, unfair labor practices include interfering with, restraining, or coercing employees who exercise their right to organize.

Uniform Anatomical Gift Act A law in all 50 states that allows anyone older than age 18 to sign a donor card, donating some or all of his organs after death.

union shop A place of employment in which employees must join a union.

U.S. Public Health Service (USPHS) An agency of the federal government responsible for the control of the arrival from abroad of any people, goods, or substances that may affect the health of U.S. citizens. The agency sets standards for the domestic handling and processing of food and the manufacture of serums, vaccines, cosmetics, and drugs. It supports and performs research, aids localities in times of disaster and epidemics, and provides medical care for certain groups of Americans.

USPHS *abbr* United States Public Health Service

utilization management Evaluation of the necessity, appropriateness, and efficiency of the use of medical services, procedures, and facilities. This includes review of admissions, services ordered and provided, length of stay, and discharge practices on a concurrent and retrospective basis.

V

values Strongly held personal and professional beliefs about worth and importance. The social principles, goals, or standards held by an individual or society.

verbal order A spoken order given directly and in person by a physician to a nurse.

voluntary bargaining issues Issues such as noneconomic fringe benefits that an employer or union may or may not address during collective bargaining.

WXYZ

witness 1. One who gives evidence in a case before a court and who attests or swears to facts or gives testimony under oath. 2. To observe the execution of an act, such as the signing of a document, or to sign one's name to authenticate the observation.

workers' compensation Compensation to an employee for an injury or occupational disease suffered in connection with his employment, paid under a government-supervised insurance system contributed to by employers.

writ of habeas corpus Literally means "you have the body"; a process whereby an individual detained or imprisoned asks the court to rule on the validity of the detainment or imprisonment. If the person is granted the writ, he must be released immediately.

wrongful death statute A statute existing in all states that provides that the death of a person can give rise to a cause of legal action brought by the person's beneficiaries in a civil suit against the person whose willful or negligent acts caused the death. Prior to the existence of these statutes,

a suit could be brought only if the injured person survived.

wrongful life action A civil suit usually brought against a physician or health care facility on the basis of negligence that resulted in the wrongful birth or life of an infant. The parents of the unwanted child seek to obtain payment from the defendant for the medical expenses of pregnancy and delivery, for pain and suffering, and for the education and upbringing of the child. Wrongful life actions have been brought and won in several situations, including unsuccessful tubal ligations and vasectomies. Failure to diagnose pregnancy in time for abortion and incorrect medical advice leading to the birth of a defective child have also led to malpractice suits for a wrongful life.

Understanding the judicial process

The judicial process in the United States is based on court jurisdiction and consists of state and federal court systems. Court jurisdiction refers to a court's authority to hear a case and determine judicial action in a given place at a given time. Jurisdiction is determined by several factors, including the type of case (for

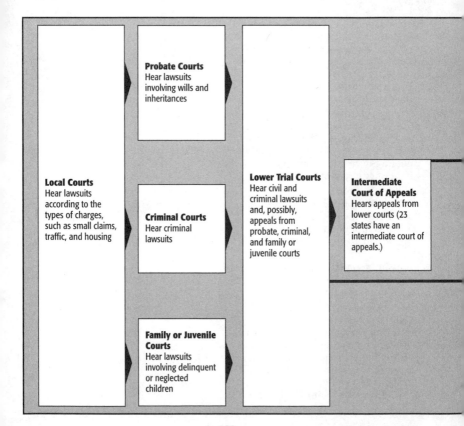

Local Courts
Hear lawsuits according to the types of charges, such as small claims, traffic, and housing

Probate Courts
Hear lawsuits involving wills and inheritances

Criminal Courts
Hear criminal lawsuits

Family or Juvenile Courts
Hear lawsuits involving delinquent or neglected children

Lower Trial Courts
Hear civil and criminal lawsuits and, possibly, appeals from probate, criminal, and family or juvenile courts

Intermediate Court of Appeals
Hears appeals from lower courts (23 states have an intermediate court of appeals.)

example, a tort action or a criminal case) and the location of the transgression or dispute.

Appeal is a legal process whereby a party dissatisfied with the decision of a lower court can seek a more favorable decision from a higher court. Either the plaintiff or the defendant can appeal an unfavorable decision from a lower court.

JUDICIAL PROCESS FLOWCHART

This flowchart depicts selected courts within the federal and state judicial systems. The arrows indicate pathways for appeal. Note that this flowchart doesn't include the complete federal court structure and that not all states follow the model depicted here.

State Supreme Court
Hears appeals from lower state courts; makes final decisions except when lawsuits involve constitutional rights or a federal question

Supreme Court of the United States
Consists of a chief justice and eight associate justices appointed by the President with advice and consent of the U.S. Senate; hears lawsuits between states, appeals from the U.S. Court of Appeals, and appeals from state supreme courts if cases involve federal law or constitutional rights

U.S. Court of Customs and Patent Appeals
Hears appeals from the U.S. Customs Court

U.S. Customs Court
Hears lawsuits involving the U.S. Patent and Trademark Office and other federal agencies

U.S. Tax Court
Hears lawsuits involving tax disputes

U.S. Court of Appeals
Hears appeals from U.S. district courts and the U.S. Tax Court

U.S. District Courts
Hear federal, criminal, and civil lawsuits

U.S. Court of Appeals for the Federal Circuit
Hears appeals from all federal circuit courts

U.S. Court of Claims
Hears lawsuits against the federal government that involve a constitutional right, federal laws or regulations, or government contracts

Types of MCOs

The era of the managed-care organization (MCO) is upon us. Created as a method to deliver health care by integrating resource utilization, financial spending, and desired patient outcomes through strict regulations on the provider used and the procedures performed, MCOs are controversial. However, their huge growth makes it likely that you work for an MCO-associated physician or hospital and that most of the patients you provide care for belong to an MCO.

MCOs often create guidelines for patient care; if health care providers want to be paid for their services, they must follow these guidelines, which are usually based on what's most cost-effective rather than what's best for the individual patient. This makes it necessary for all nurses to be aware of the types of MCOs, such as the health-maintenance organization (HMO), preferred provider organization (PPO), exclusive-provider organization (EPO), and point-of-service (POS) provider, and how their differences may affect nursing practice.

HMOs are the most well-known of the MCOs. The most popular models of HMOs in use today are the *staff model,* the *group model,* the *network model,* and the *independent practice association (IPA).* Additionally, some HMOs are formed on the basis of direct contract.

Kaiser Permanente is a classic example of a staff model HMO, in which physi-cians who serve the HMO enrollees are employed by the HMO. Staff model HMOs are having difficulty maintaining their profitability because they're unable to reduce the compensation to their physicians rapidly enough to keep up with the declining payments being made to physicians in group, network, and IPA-model HMOs.

Group, network, and IPA-model HMOs are in a much better competitive position in the marketplace. They require that the HMO contract with physicians, either individually or on a group or network basis, for the services needed to cover those enrolled in the HMO. The HMOs are left with the upper hand as physicians struggle to respond in a competitive marketplace.

Somewhere between the traditional fee-for-service program and the HMO is the PPO. PPOs are the most popular form of managed-care organizations, with 50% of all workers insured by large and medium-sized companies enrolled in this type of insurance plan. In a PPO, an employer or a health care insurance carrier contracts with a group of preferred or selected participating providers. These providers typically agree to accept the PPO's discounted reimbursement structure and payment levels, in return for which the PPO limits the size of its participating provider groups and provides incentives for its covered individuals to use the participating providers instead of other providers. Most recently, PPO plans for Medicare beneficiaries (Medicare combined with choice private fee-for-service plans) have been developed to help control Medicare costs.

EPOs are similar to PPOs and HMOs, but in EPOs, patients must select their provider from a list given to them by the EPO. In contrast are the POS organizations, which allow patients to select out-of-network providers at a reduced reimbursement rate.

Disease-management companies

Some HMOs contract with disease-management companies, which manage all aspects of treating a specific disease. Major pharmaceutical companies (including Merck, Eli Lilly, and SmithKline Beecham), major providers of health care (including The Johns Hopkins Hospital, Mayo Clinic, and Memorial Sloan-Kettering Cancer Center), third-party payers, and others have joined forces or have gone into disease management on their own.

In a typical disease-management arrangement, an HMO, employer, or insurance company contracts with a disease-management company for coverage of its enrollees when they're diagnosed with a specific disease, such as cancer. Components of a disease-management program include clinical pathways or treatment guidelines designed to provide the best possible care in the most streamlined environment. Disease-management companies usually guarantee that payments won't exceed a maximum amount. At best, the arrangement may provide high-quality care at the lowest possible cost.

Health care networks

Conceptually, health care networks are similar to disease-management companies. A typical health care network includes a major hub hospital; several smaller, community-based hospitals; a long-term-care facility; and perhaps a rehabilitation center, home health care agency, and subacute-care center.

In smoothly functioning health care networks, patients benefit from the reduction or elimination of fragmented delivery of care. Such networks can provide a continuum of care from one stage of illness to the next. Duplication of services is limited, and both preventive and outpatient care can be encouraged.

However, health care networks may become so powerful that they eliminate competition from alternative health care providers. This can cause substantial controversy. Ethical issues regarding patient referrals may be raised when there is cross-ownership of different components of the health care network.

Interpreting legal citations

You may obtain information on a specific court case or law (statute or regulation) from your county courthouse law library or local law school library. If you're looking for an overview or summary of a court case or law, look up the citation in a standard legal reference, such as a legal encyclopedia *(Corpus Juris Secundum)* and a legal text *(Restatements of Law)*.

If you have a full citation, you can locate the complete text of a court case. A full citation includes the name of the court case and a series of identifying numbers and letters. If you're missing some or all of the identifying information, you can look up the case name in the index of a legal reference.

In the court case citation index of this handbook, most of the court cases on the state level will have two complete series of identifying numbers. The first series is the *official citation,* indicating where the case can be found in that state's set of court case decisions. The second series is the *unofficial citation,* indicating where the case can be found in a commercially published set of court case decisions grouped by region. Keep in mind that an "unofficial" legal reference doesn't have any less authority than an "official" legal reference.

Each citation includes an abbreviation for the legal reference that contains the law or case. For example, "U.S.L.W."

stands for *United States Law Week.* To find out what the abbreviations used in the *Nurse's Legal Handbook,* Fifth Edition, stand for, see the list of legal reference abbreviations at right. For more information on legal citations, see *The Bluebook: A Uniform System of Citation*, 17th Edition. (The Harvard Law Review Association, 2000).

The number that precedes the abbreviation indicates either a volume number or title classification within the legal reference. A title classification is a body of laws or cases on a particular subject such as malpractice. A title can be one book or many books, depending on the amount of cases that bear on the titles.

Two sets of numbers follow the abbreviation. The first set indicates the page where you'll find the case. The second set, in parentheses, indicates the year of the decision.

Law or case	Legal reference	Abbreviation
Federal court decisions	*United States Law Week* (unofficial reporter containing recently issued Supreme Court decisions)	U.S.L.W.
	United States Reports (official reporter containing Supreme Court decisions)	U.S.
	Supreme Court Reporter (unofficial reporter containing Supreme Court decisions)	S. Ct.
	Lawyers Edition, United States Supreme Court (unofficial reporter containing Supreme Court decisions)	L. Ed.
	Federal Reporter (contains court of appeals decisions)	F., F. 2d
	Federal Supplement (contains Federal District Court of Appeals decisions)	F. Supp.
State court decisions	Published state court decisions in official state sets for about two-thirds of U.S. states (The *Uniform System of Citation* lists all state reporters and instructs how to cite them.)	Standard state abbreviations
	Commercially published National Reporter System, which includes all state and group state court decisions by region:	
	North Eastern Reporter	N.E., N.E. 2d
	Atlantic Reporter	A., A. 2d
	South Eastern Reporter	S.E., S.E. 2d
	Southern Reporter	So., So. 2d
	North Western Reporter	N.W., N.W. 2d
	South Western Reporter	S.W., S.W. 2d
	Pacific reporter	P., P. 2d
Miscellaneous abbreviations	*New York Supreme Court, appellate division*	A.D.
	New York Miscellaneous Reports	Misc. 2d
	West's New York Supplement	N.Y.S. 2d
	Dominion Law Reports (Canada)	D.L.R.
	Western Weekly Reports (Canada)	W.W.R.
	Ontario Reports	O.R.
	Ontario Law Reports	O.L.R.
	Labour Arbitration cases (Canada)	L.A.C.
	Canadian Cases on the Law of Torts	CCLT
	Reports of Family Law (Canada)	RFL
	National Labor Relations Board	N.L.R.B.
Federal statutes	*United States Law Week* (contains chronologic list of recently enacted statutes)	U.S.L.W.
	United States Statutes at Large (contains chronological lists of all statutes enacted during a single legislative session)	STAT. or STAT. AT L.
	United States Code (contains all statutes arranged by title)	U.S.C.
State statutes	Published state statutes in official state sets	Standard state abbreviations
Federal regulations	*Code of Federal Regulations* (contains federal regulations arranged by title)	C.F.R.
	The Federal Register (contains updates to the C.F.R.)	F.R.
State regulations	Published state regulations in official state sets	Standard state abbreviations

Court case citations

A

American Hospital Association v. NLRB, *111 S. Ct. 1539, 59 U.S.L.W. 4331 (1991)*

Application of the President and Directors of Georgetown College, Inc., *331 F.2d 1000 (D.C. Cir. 1964); cert. denied, 377 U.S. 978 (1964)*

Ashley v. Nyack Hospital, *412 N.Y.S.2d 388, 67 A.D.2d 671 (1979)*

B

Babits v. Vassar Brothers Hospital, *732 N.Y.S. 2nd 46 (N.Y. App. 2001)*

Bailie v. Miami Valley Hospital, *8 Ohio Misc. 193, 221 N.E.2d 217 (1966)*

Barber v. Reinking, *68 Wash. 2d 139, 411 P. 2d 861 (1966)*

Barber v. Time, Inc., *348 Mo. 1199, 159 S.W.2d 291 (1942)*

Battocchi v. Washington Hosp. Center, *581 A.2d 759 (D.C. App. 1990)*

Bellotti v. Baird II, *443 U.S. 622, 99 S. Ct. 3035 (1979)*

Big Town Nursing Home v. Newman, *461 S.W.2d 195 (Tex. Civ. App. 1970)*

Brookover v. Mary Hitchcock Memorial Hospital *893 F. 2d 411 (1st Cir. 1990)*

Brown v. State, *391 N.Y.S.2d 204, 56 A.D.2d 672 (1977)*

Burdreau v. McDowell, *256 U.S. 465, 41 S. Ct. 574 (1921)*

Butler v. South Fulton Medical Center, Inc., *215 Ga. App. 809, 452 S.E.2d 768 (1994)*

Byrne v. Boadle, *159 Eng. Rep. 299 (1863)*

C

Cannell v. Medical and Surgical Clinic S.C., *21 Ill. App. 3d 383, 315 N.E.2d 278 (1974)*

Canterbury v. Spence *464 F.2d 772 (D.C. Cir. 1972)*

Carey v. Population Services International, *431 U.S. 678, 97 S. Ct. 2010 (1977)*

Carr v. St. Paul Fire and Marine Insurance Co., *384 F. Supp. 821 (W.D. Ark. 1974)*

Cline v. Lund, *31 Cal. App.3d 755, 107 Cal. Rptr. 629 (1973)*

Claypool v. Levin, *Wis. 562 N.W.2d 584, 209 Wis. 2d 284 (1997) No. 94-2457*

Collins v. Davis, *254 N.Y.S.2d 666, 44 Misc. 2d 622 (1964)*

Collins v. Westlake Community Hospital, *57 Ill. 2d 388, 312 N.E.2d 614 (1974)*

Colorado State Board of Nurse Examiners v. Hohu, *129 Colo. 195, 268 P.2d 401 (1954)*

Commissioner of Correction v. Myers, *379 Mass. 255, 399 N.E.2d 452 (1979)*

Commonwealth v. Gordon, *431 Pa. 512, 246 A.2d 325 (1968)*

Commonwealth v. Porn, *196 Mass. 326, 82 N.E. 31 (1907)*

Commonwealth v. Storella, *6 Mass. App. 310, 375 N.E.2d 348 (1978)*

Cooper v. National Motor Bearing Co., *136 Cal. App. 2d 229, 288 P.2d 581 (1955)*

Crowe v. Provost, *52 Tenn. App. 397, 374 S.W.2d 645 (1963)*

Cruzan v. Director, Mo. Dept. of Health, *110 S. Ct. 2841, 111 L. Ed. 2d 224 (1990)*

D

D. v. D., *108 N.J. Super. 149, 260 A.2d 255 (1969)*

Darling v. Charleston Community Memorial Hospital, *33 Ill. 2d 326, 211 N.E.2d 253 (1965)*

Dembie, *21 RFL 46 (1963)*

Derrick v. Portland Eye, Ear, Nose and Throat Hospital, *105 Ore. 90, 209 P.2d 344 (1922)*

Dessauer v. Memorial General Hospital, *96 N.M. 92, 628 P.2d 337 (N.M. Ct. App. 1981)*

Doe v. Roe, *400 N.Y.S.2d 668, 93 Misc. 2d 201 (Sup. Ct. 1977)*

In re Doe Children, *402 N.Y.S.2d 958, 93 Misc. 2d 479 (1978)*

Dowey v. Rothwell, *[1974] 5 W.W.R. 311 (Alberta)*

E

Eastern Maine Medical Center v. NLRB, *658 F.2d 1 (1st Cir. 1981)*

Edith Anderson Nursing Homes, Inc. v. Bettie Walker, *232 Md. 442, 194 A.2d 85 (1963)*

Eisenstadt v. Baird, *405 U.S. 438, 92 S. Ct. 1029 (1972)*

Emory University v. Shadburn, *47 Ga. App. 643, 171 S.E. 192 (Ct. App. 1933)*

Estelle v. Gamble, *429 U.S. 97, 97 S. Ct. 285 (1976)*

F

Farrell v. Snell, *2 S.C.R. (Ct. App., New Brunswick, 1990)*

Feeney v. Young, *181 N.Y.S. 481, 191 A.D. 501 (1920)*

G

Garcia v. Bronx Lebanon Hospital, *731 N.Y.S. 2nd 702 (N.Y. App., 2001)*

Garcia v. Presbyterian Hospital Center, *92 N.M. 652, 593 P.2d 487 (1979)*

Geransy, *13 R.F.L.2d 202 (1977)*

Griswold v. Connecticut, *381 U.S. 479, 85 S. Ct. 1678 (1965)*

Gugino v. Harvard Community Health Plan, *380 Mass. 464, 403 N.E.2d 1166 (1980)*

HI

Hammonds v. Aetna Casualty and Surety Co., *237 F. Supp. 96 (D.C. Ohio 1965)*

Harrell v. Louis Smith Memorial Hospital, *3975 E.2d 746 (Ga. 1990)*

Henry By Henry v. St. John's Hospital, *512 N.E.2d 1044 (Ill. App. 4 Dist. 1987)*

Hernicz v. Fla. Dept. of Professional Regulation, *390 So. 2d 194 (Dist. Ct. App. 1980)*

Hiatt v. Groce, *215 Kan. 14, 523 P. 2d 320 (1974)*

H.L. v. Matheson, *450 U.S. 398, 101 S. Ct. 1164 (1981)*

Hodges v. Effingham County Hospital, *355 S.E.2d 104 (Ga. 1987)*

Hodgson v. Minnesota, *110 S. Ct. 2926, 111 L. Ed. 2d 344 (1990)*

Horton v. Niagara Falls Memorial Medical Center, *380 N.Y.S 2d 116, 51 A.D.2d 152 (1976)*

Hudock v. Children's Hospital of Philadelphia, *Civil Action No. 98-929, 1999 U.S. Dist. LEXIS 19269 (3d Cir. 1999)*

Hunt v. Palms Springs General Hospital, *352 So. 2d 582 (Fla. Dist. Ct. App. 1977)*

Hunter v. Hunter, *65 O.L.R. 586 (1930)*

J

Jefferson v. Griffin Spalding County Hospital Authority, *247 Ga. 86, 274 S.E.2d 457 (1981)*

Jones v. Hawkes Hospital, *175 Ohio 503, 196 N.E.2d 592 (1964)*

Justice v. Natvig, *178, 381 S.E.2d 8 (Va. 1989)*

K

Kansas State Board of Nursing v. Burkman, *216 Kan. 187, 531 P. 2d 122 (1975)*

Karp v. Cooley, et al., *493 F.2d 408, 419 (1974)*

Keyes v. Humana Hospital, Alaska, Inc., *750 P.2d 343 (Alaska 1988)*

Kyslinger v. United States, *406 F. Supp. 800 (W.D. Pa. 1975)*

L

Laidlaw v. Lions Gate Hospital, *[1969] 70 W.W.R. 727 (B.C. 1969)*

Lama v. Boras, *16 F.2d 473 PR (1994)*

Lane v. Candura, *6 Mass. App. 377, 376 N.E.2d 1232 (1978)*

Larrimore v. Homeopathic Hospital Association, *176 A.2d 362, aff'd, 54 Del. 449, 181 A.2d 573 (1962)*

Leib v. Board of Examiners for Nursing, *177 Conn. 78, 411 A.2d 42 (1979)*

Leigh v. Board of Registration in Nursing, *395 Mass. 670, 481 N.E.2d 1347 (1985)*

Lopez v. Swyer, *115 N.J. Super. 237, 279 A.2d 116 (1971)*

Loton v. Massachusetts Paramedical, Inc., *Mass. Sup. Ct. 1987, 4 National Jury Verdict Review and Analysis 5 (1989)*

Lott v. State, *225 N.Y.S.2d 434, 32 Misc. 2d 296 (1962)*

Lovato v. Colorado, *198 Colo. 419, 601 P.2d 1072 (1979)*

M

Manning v. Twin Falls Clinic and Hospital, *830 P. 2nd 1185 (Idaho, 1992)*

Mapp v. Ohio, *367 U.S. 643, 81 S. Ct. 1684 (1961)*

Maryland v. Buie, *494 U.S. 325, 110 S. Ct. 1093 (1990)*

Mathias v. St. Catherine's Hospital, *212 Wis. 2d 540, 569 N.W.2d 330 (1997)*

May v. Broun, *261 Ore. 28, 492 P.2d 776 (1972)*

McCarl v. State Board of Nurse Examiners, *39 Pa. Cmwlth. 628, 396 A.2d 866 (1979)*

McCutchon v. Mutual of Omaha Insurance Co., *354 So. 2d 759 (La. Ct. App. 1978)*

McInnes v. Dillard Department Stores, Inc., *736 So. 2d 1190; 1999 Fla. App. LEXIS 6322*

McIntosh v. Milano, *168 N.J. Super. 466, 403 A.2d 500 (1979)*

In re Melideo, *390 N.Y.S. 2d 523, 88 Misc. 2d 974 (Sup. Ct. 1976)*

Methodist Hospital v. Ball, *50 Tenn. App. 460, 362 S.W.2d 475 (1961)*

Misericordia Hospital Medical Center v. NLRB, *623 F.2d 808 (2d Cir. 1980)*

Mohr v. Jenkins, *393 So. 2d 245 (La. Ct. App. 1980)*

Mohr v. Williams, *95 Minn. 261, 104 N.W. 12 (1905)*

Moore v. Guthrie Hospital, *403 F.2d 366 (4th Cir. 1968)*

Moore v. Willis-Knighton Medical Center, *720 So. 2nd 425 (La. App. 1998)*

In re Mount Sinai Hospital and Ontario Nurses Association, *17 L.A.C.2d 242 (1978)*

Mutual Insurance of Arizona v. American Casualty Co. of Reading, PA, *189 Ariz. 22, 938 P.2d 71 (1997)*

N

Nathanson v. Kline, *186 Kan. 393, 350 P.2d 1093 (1960)*

Nelson v. Trinity Medical Center, *419 N.W.2d 886 (S. Ct. N.D. 1988)*

New York v. Class, *475 U.S. 106, 106 S. Ct. 960 (1985)*

NLRB v. Baptist Hospital, *442 U.S. 773, 99 S. Ct. 2598 (1979)*

NLRB v. Health Care & Retirement Corporation, *114 S. Ct. 1778 (1994)*

NLRB v. Health Care & Retirement Corp., *511 U.S. 571 (1994)*

NLRB v. Kentucky River Community Care, Inc., *532 U.S. 706 (2001)*

Norman v. Good Shepard Medical Center, *2001 Tex. App. LEXIS 5571, August 17, 2001. Filed.*

Norton v. Argonaut Insurance Co., *144 So. 2d 249 (La. Ct. App. 1962)*

N.Y.C. Health and Hospitals Corporation v. Sulsona, *367 N.Y.S.2d 686, 81 Misc. 2d 1002 (1975)*

N.Y. State Association for Retarded Children, Inc. v. Carey, *438 F. Supp. 440 (E.D. N.Y. 1977)*

O

O'Connor v. Donaldson, *422 U.S. 563, 95 S. Ct. 2486 (1975)*

Ohio v. Akron Center for Reproductive Health, *110 S. Ct. 2972, 111 L. Ed. 2d 405 (1990)*

Oliff v. Florida State Board of Nursing, *374 So. 2d 1054 (Fla. Dist. Ct. App. 1979)*

O'Neill v. Montefiore Hospital, *202 N.Y.S.2d 436, 11 A.D. 2d 132 (1960)*

In re **Osborne,** *294 A.2d 372 (D.C. 1972)*

P

Pedersen v. Zielski, *Adv 3785, 822 P.2d 903 (Ak. 1991)*

People v. Doe, *410 N.Y.S.2d 233, 96 Misc. 2d 975 (1978)*

People v. Kraft, *3 Cal. App. 3d 890, 84 Cal. Rptr. 280 (1970)*

Planned Parenthood of Central Missouri v. Danforth, *428 U.S. 52, 96 S. Ct. 2831 (1976)*

Planned Parenthood of Northwest Ind. v. Vines, *543 N.E.2d 654 (Ind. App. 1989)*

Planned Parenthood of S.E. Pennsylvania v. Casey, *127 L.E.2d 352, 114 S. Ct. 909 (1992)*

Pommier v. ABC Insurance Co., et al., *715 So. 2d 1270 (La. App. 3d Cir. 1998)*

Poor Sisters of St. Francis Seraph of the Perpetual Adoration, et al. v. Catron, *435 N.E.2d 305 (Ind. Ct. App. 1982)*

Pounders v. Trinity Court Nursing Home, *265 Ark. 1, 576 S.W.2d 934 (1979)*

Powell v. Columbia-Presbyterian Medical Center, *267 N.Y.S.2d 450, 49 Misc. 2d 215 (Sup. Ct. 1965)*

Prairie v. University of Chicago Hospitals, *298 Ill. App. 3d 316, 327 (1998)*

Q

In re **Quinlan,** *137 N.J. Super. 227, 348 A. 2d 801 (Ch. Div. 1975); modified, 70 N.J. 10, 355 A.2d 647 (1976)*

R

Ramos v. Lamm, *639 F.2d 559 (10th Cir. 1980)*

Richardson v. Brunelle, *119 N.H. 104, 398 A.2d 838 (1979)*

Roach v. Springfield Clinic, *Ill. App. 4 Dist., 166 Ill. Dec. 48, 585 N.E.2d 1070, 223 Ill. App.3d 597, appeal allowed 173 Ill. Dec. 13, 596 N.E.2d 637, 145 Ill. 2d*

644, aff'd in part, rev'd in part 191 Ill. Dec. 1, 623 N.E.2d 246, 157 Ill. 2d 29 (1992)

Rochin v. California, *342 U.S. 165, 72 S. Ct. 205 (1952)*

Roe v. Wade, *410 U.S. 113, 93 S. Ct. 705 (1973)*

Rogers v. Kasdan, *612 S.W.2d 133 (Ky. 1981)*

Rohde v. Lawrence General Hospital, *34 Mass. App. Ct. 584, 614 N.E.2d 686 (1993)*

Rust v. Sullivan, *59 U.S.L.W. 4451 (1991)*

S

Salgo v. Leland Stanford Jr. Univ. Board of Trustees, *154 Cal. App. 2d 560, 317 P.2d 170 (1957)*

In re **Sampson,** *328 N.Y.S.2d 686, 278 N.E.2d 918 (1972)*

Sanchez v. Bay General Hospital, *116 Ca. App. 3d 776, 172 Cal. Rptr. 342, Cal. App. 4 Dist., (1981)*

In re **SAS,** *1 LMQ 139 (1977)*

Schloendorff v. Society of New York Hospitals, *211 N.Y. 125, 105 N.E. 92 (1914)*

Schmerber v. California, *384 U.S. 757, 86 S. Ct. 1826 (1966)*

Schneckloth v. Bustamonte, *412 U.S. 218, 93 S. Ct. 2041 (1973)*

Sengstack v. Sengstack, *4 N.Y.2d 502, 176 N.Y.S.2d 337; 151 N.E.2d 887 (1958)*

Shannon v. McNulty and HealthAmerica Pennsylvania, *718 A.2d 828; 1998 Pa. Super LEXIS 2383, filed October 5, 1998*

Simonsen v. Swenson, *104 Neb. 224, 177 N.W. 831 (1920)*

Snelson v. Culton, *141 Me. 242, 42 A.2d 505 (1949)*

Stack v. Wapner, *368 A.2d 292, 244 (Pa. Super. Ct. 278, 1976)*

Stahlin v. Hilton Hotels Corp., *484 F.2d 580 (7th Cir. 1973)*

State v. Brown, *8 Ore. App. 72, 491 P.2d 1193 (1971)*

State v. Perea, *95 N.M. 777, 626 P.2d 851 (1981)*

State v. Riggins, *348 So. 2d 1209 (Fla. Dist. Ct. App. 1977)*

Stefanik v. Nursing Education Committee, *70 R.I. 136, 37 A.2d 661 (1944)*

Stevenson v. Alta Bates, *20 Cal. App. 2d 303, 66 P.2d 1265 (1937)*

Stone v. Commonwealth, *418 S.W.2d 646 (Ky. 1967); cert. denied, 390 U.S. 1010*

Story v. McCurtain Memorial Management, Inc., *634 P.2d 778 (Okla. Ct. App. 1981)*

Story v. St. Mary Parish Service District, *La. No. 77, 471C (January 17, 1987)*

St. Paul Fire and Marine Insurance Co. v. Prothro, *266 Ark. 1020, 590 S.W.2d 35 (Ark. Ct. App. 1979)*

St. Germain v. Pfeifer, *637 N.E.2d 848 (Mass. 1994)*

Sweet v. Providence Hospital, *881 P.2d 304, Alaska (1995)*

T

Tarasoff v. Regents of the University of California, *131 Cal. Rptr. 14, 551 P.2d 334 (1976)*

Thompson v. The Nason Hospital, *527 Pa. 330, 591 A.2d 703 (1991)*

Thor v. Boska, *38 Cal. App. 3d 558, 113 Cal. Rptr. 296 (1974)*

Tighe v. State Board of Nurse Examiners, *40 Pa. Cmwlth. 367, 397 A.2d 1261 (1979)*

Tuma v. Board of Nursing, *100 Idaho 74, 593 P.2d 711 (1979)*

U

Ullo v. State Board of Examiners, *41 Pa. Cmwlth. 204, 398 A.2d 764 (1979)*

United States v. Montoya de Hernandez, *473 U.S. 531, 105 S. Ct. 3304 (1985)*

United States v. Winbush, *428 F.2d 357 (6th Cir. 1970)*

Utter v. United Health Center, *160 W. Va. 703, 236 S.E.2d 213 (1977)*

V

Viletto v. Weilbaecher, *377 So. 2d 132 (La. Ct. App. 1979)*

Vinnedge v. Gibbs, *550 F.2d 926 (CA 4 VA 1977)*

WX

Warden v. Hayden, *387 U.S. 294, 87 S. Ct. 1642 (1967)*

Washington State Nurses Ass'n v. Board of Medical Examiners, *93 Wash. 2d 117, 605 P.2d 1269 (1980)*

Webster v. Reproductive Health Services, *492 U.S. 490, 109 S. Ct. 3040 (1989)*

Whalen v. Roe, *429 U.S. 589, 97 S. Ct. 869 (1977)*

Whitney v. Day, *100 Mich. App. 707, 300 N.W.2d 380 (Ct. App. 1980)*

Widman v. Paoli Memorial Hospital, *No. 85-1034 Pa 1989*

Winters v. Miller, *446 F.2d 65 (2nd Cir. 1971)*

Woodward v. Myres, Dean, and Correctional Medical Services of Illinois, *2001 WL 506863 (N.D. Ill. 2001)*

Wyatt v. Stickney, *325 F. Supp. 781 (M.D. Ala. 1971); 344 F. Supp. 387 (M.D. Ala. 1972)*

YZ

Ybarra v. Spangard, *154 2nd 687 (California, 1994)*

Younts v. St. Francis Hospital and School of Nursing, *205 Kan. 292, 469 P.2d 330 (1970)*

Young v. Board of Hospital Directors, Lee County, *#82-429 (Fl. 1984)*

Index

A

Abortifacients, 339
Abortion
  autonomy and, 340
  care following, 340
  ethics of, 338–350
  illegal, 384
  legal, 387
  for minors, 206
  resolving views about, 340
  therapeutic, 400
Abortion law, and right to privacy, 109
Abortion rights
  for minors, 110
  restrictions on, 109
Abuse, 207–214
  abuser in, 207–208, 212
  adult, 208–209
  child. *See* Child abuse.
  cycle of, 208
  documenting, 212
  drug. *See* Drug abuse.
  elder, 208, 210
  legal aspects of, 209–211
  public education and, 214
  recognizing, 212
  reporting, 211–212
  support services for, 212–214
Abuser
  assessing, 212
  help for, 213
  profile of, 207–208

Abuse of process, 371
Acquired immunodeficiency syndrome,
    331–338
  care refusal in, 334–337
  contact notification in, 337
  economic burden of, 338
  pregnancy and, 337–338
  standard precautions for, 324
Ad hoc committee, 371
Addiction, drug, 380
Administrative review, 41, 371
  Canadian, 43
Admissible evidence, 371
Adolescents. *See* Minors.
Advance directive, 94, 371. *See also*
    Living wills; Right to die.
  ethics of, 314
  malpractice law and, 144
Advance directive system, 371
Advance practice nurse, 1, 371
  nurse practice acts and, 16
Adverse reaction, 371
Advice
  free health care, 264–267
    risks of, 265
    standards for, 266–267
  neighborly, 266
Affidavit, 372
Affirmative defense, 372
Age Discrimination in Employment Act
    of 1967, 293
Age of majority, 371

---

t refers to a table.

---

t refers to a table.

t refers to a table.

t refers to a table.

t refers to a table.

t refers to a table.

t refers to a table.

J

Jehovah's Witnesses, 94, 95
   treatment of minors and, 207
Job description, 386
Joint Commission of Accreditation of
      Healthcare Organizations, 386
   patient safety goals of, 35
   standards of, 19, 30-33
Joint practice, 386
Joint responsibility, 129
Joint statement, 386
Judgments, lawsuits and, 169
Judicial bypass statutes, 386
Judicial precedent, 127
Judicial process, 402-403
Judicial review process, 43
Jury, lay, 387
Jury selection, 166
Just cause, 387

K

Kaiser Permanente, 404
Kevorkian, Jack, 318

L

Labor Management Relations Act, 284
Latex allergies, workplace safety and, 355
Law
   definition of, 387
   nursing practice and, 1-45
   versus ethics, 295-296, 297
Lawsuits
   attorney selection in, 163, 164
   challenging, 161t
   contacting insurance company in, 162
   cross-examination in, 169
   defending oneself in, 162-170
   defenses for, 158-162
   depositions in, 165, 167
   four elements of, 154-157
   hospital policies and, 174-175
   interrogatories in, 165
   judgment in, 169
   jury selection in, 166
   legal process and, 154-170
   medical examinations in, 165

Lawsuits *(continued)*
   notifying appropriate personnel in,
      162-164
   preparing defense in, 164-165
   preparing for court in, 165-166
   pretrial events in, 166-167, 168
   preventing, 172-173
   risks of, 142
   situations that trigger, 138-139
   trial process in, 167, 168
Lay jury, 387
Legal guardian, 387
Liability, 387. *See also* Malpractice.
   abuse reporting and, 211
   in agency nursing, 66
   corporate, 127-129, 378
   criminal, 133
   in home health care, 64
   hospital, 127-129, 178-179
   immunity from, 384
   living wills and, 227
   nurse, 130-133
   patient safety and, 190-191
   physician, 129-130
   professional, 395
   restraint use and, 216, 218
   for signature, 249
   in special practice situations, 131-132
   in telephone triage, 197
   treatment refusal and, 100, 101
Liability insurance, 145-153
   in alternative practice settings, 62
   choosing, 146-147
   cost containment for, 151
   cost of, 148-149
   employer's, 151-153
   multiple insurers and, 150
   policies, 43
   role of, 149-150
Liaison nurse, 387
Libel, 387
License renewal, 38, 39-39
Licensed practical nurse, 387
   code of ethics for, 304
   drug administration and, 194
   hospital policies for, 177

---

t refers to a table.

t refers to a table.

---

t refers to a table.

---

t refers to a table.

---

t refers to a table.

t refers to a table.

t refers to a table.